Kentucky and the Great War

A
THOMAS
D. CLARK
MEDALLION
BOOK

The Thomas D. Clark Medallion was established to honor the memory and contributions of Dr. Thomas Dionysius Clark (1903–2005). A beloved teacher, prolific author, resolute activist, and enthusiastic advocate of publications about Kentucky and the region, Dr. Clark helped establish the University of Kentucky Press in 1943, which was reorganized in 1969 as the University Press of Kentucky, the state-mandated scholarly publisher for the Commonwealth. The Clark Medallion is awarded annually to one University Press of Kentucky publication that achieves Dr. Clark's high standards of excellence and addresses his wide breadth of interests about the state. Winners of the Thomas D. Clark Medallion are selected by the Board of Directors of the Thomas D. Clark Foundation Inc., a private nonprofit organization established in 1994 to provide financial support for the publication of vital books about Kentucky and the region.

KENTUCKY AND THE GREAT WAR

WORLD WAR I ON THE HOME FRONT

DAVID J. BETTEZ

UNIVERSITY PRESS OF KENTUCKY

Paperback edition 2019

Scholarly publisher for the Commonwealth,
serving Bellarmine University, Berea College, Centre College of Kentucky, Eastern Kentucky University, The Filson Historical Society, Georgetown College, Kentucky Historical Society, Kentucky State University, Morehead State University, Murray State University, Northern Kentucky University, Transylvania University, University of Kentucky, University of Louisville, and Western Kentucky University.

Editorial and Sales Offices: The University Press of Kentucky
663 South Limestone Street, Lexington, Kentucky 40508-4008
www.kentuckypress.com

Library of Congress Cataloging-in-Publication Data

Names: Bettez, David J., 1952- author.
Title: Kentucky and the Great War : World War I on the home front / David J. Bettez.
Description: Lexington, Kentucky : University Press of Kentucky, 2016. | Series: Topics in Kentucky history | Includes bibliographical references and index.
Identifiers: LCCN 2016031637| ISBN 9780813168012 (hardcover : alk. paper) | ISBN 9780813168029 (pdf) | ISBN 9780813168036 (epub)
Subjects: LCSH: World War, 1914-1918—Kentucky. | Kentucky—History, Military—20th century.
Classification: LCC D570.85.K4 B48 2016 | DDC 940.3/769—dc23

ISBN 978-0-8131-7850-9 (pbk. : alk. paper)

This book is printed on acid-free paper meeting the requirements of the American National Standard for Permanence in Paper for Printed Library Materials.

Manufactured in the United States of America.

Member of the Association of University Presses

The press is grateful to the following generous sponsors:

Victor and Virginia Fox
Bill Giles
Connie Goodman
Bennie and Rosalind Ivory
Lawrence and Sherry Jelsma
Jim and Martha Johnson
Melanie Kilpatrick
Nana Lampton
Stanley MacDonald
Mark and Kate Neikirk
Alice Stevens Sparks
Myra Leigh Tobin
Orme Wilson

For my wife

Contents

Introduction

When the United States joined the Great War—World War I—in April 1917, the Commonwealth of Kentucky remained both progressive and regressive. On the one hand, Progressives led by Governor Augustus Owsley Stanley and others had passed laws regulating child labor, workers' compensation, and other socially beneficial measures. On the other hand, just ten years before war broke out in Europe, the state legislature had passed the Day Law, officially establishing segregation in schools. Kentucky state historian Jim Klotter has aptly termed this time in Kentucky's history a "Portrait in Paradox."[1]

The Great War changed Kentuckians' daily lives, especially as they came into contact with government programs at the state and national levels that reached into areas previously untrammeled by much government beyond the local level. Far more than the Civil War, which had involved Kentuckians on both sides of the fight, the Great War reached into the smallest towns, settlement camps, and hollows. Kentuckians of all ages and races, both sexes, and every political, economic, and social status were expected to "do their part" in various ways, depending on who they were.

This book focuses primarily on the domestic aspects of the Great War, a subject pioneered by historian David Kennedy in his classic book *Over Here*. It takes a broad view and therefore cannot chronicle everything that happened in Kentucky pertaining to the war. This book examines in general what Kentuckians did to support the war effort. A detailed history of Kentucky during the war would require an exhaustive study "from the ground up," starting with efforts in each of its 120 counties. One example is the work spearheaded by Jackson County Public Library director Stephen Bowling, who has been compiling a history of that county's war efforts, including the contributions of its most famous participant, Medal of Honor recipient Willie Sandlin.[2]

While researching this study, I visited about half of the state's counties, seeking a representative sampling of the war's impact at the local level. Much of the resulting information came from surviving copies of the county histories of the war, each compiled by a local resident under the direction of Fred Caldwell, the state war historian and a Louisville lawyer. I found long-forgotten volumes stowed away in county clerks' offices, historical societies, and libraries. Sometimes the search proved futile. For example, the county clerk in Carroll County, located along the Ohio River north of Louisville, surmised that the county history had been lost in the Great Flood of 1937. Some of the county histories I found contained minimal information, primarily the individual records of local military men. Others, however, contained newspaper clippings, personal letters, and additional information that better revealed the story of how Kentuckians responded to the war.

I found other sources about the Great War in Kentucky in local, state, and national libraries and archives. Kentucky newspapers from the period found online and on microfilm also proved valuable, but gaps exist there as well. For example, a new African American newspaper founded in 1917, the *Louisville Leader,* could have provided a fascinating view of the Great War from the black point of view. Unfortunately, a fire at the company's headquarters in 1937 destroyed most extant copies; a subsequent microfilming project uncovered only one issue from 1917 and none from 1918.[3]

This book might seem Louisville-centric, for three major reasons. First, the availability of the state's leading newspaper, the *Louisville Courier-Journal,* made it an invaluable resource that provided excellent day-to-day coverage of war efforts throughout the state. Second, many of the leaders of the state's war effort came from Louisville, where key federal and state officials were headquartered. Third, the paucity of other newspaper resources proved limiting, especially in rural areas, where they either did not exist or were not preserved.

Despite these drawbacks, enough resources exist online, in local communities, and in state and national libraries and archives to glean a good overview of the war's effect on the entire commonwealth. I hope this history serves as a catalyst for future studies, particularly at the county level. (Kentuckians often identify themselves as being from a certain county, rather than a particular city or region. Consequently, I usually use counties as a naming convention when identifying people and groups.)

Famous diplomat, historian, and architect of Cold War "containment" George F. Kennan deemed World War I "*the* great seminal catastrophe of this [twentieth] century." French intellectual Raymond Aron noted that the Great War ushered in a "Century of Total War."[4] This book covers the effects of that momentous event on the Commonwealth of Kentucky.

The chapters are arranged primarily by subject. The book begins with Kentuckians' response to the outbreak of war in 1914 and the US decision to enter the war in 1917. Each chapter tackles a specific subject throughout the war years, but the topics are placed in a sequence where they logically fit together. For example, the chapter on the Kentucky Council of Defense is placed early in the book because of the council's leadership of other organizations throughout the war. One chapter describes opposition to the war, while another covers the process and impact of the draft on individuals and communities in the state.

When Kentuckians marched off to war, they often went first to Camp Zachary Taylor, just south of Louisville. One chapter covers Camp Taylor and other army installations in the state. Another chapter reviews the workings of the federal Food and Fuel Administrations in the state and how they affected people. Two chapters review important constituencies in the war: women, especially under the leadership of the Woman's Committee of the Council of National Defense, and African Americans.

One chapter reviews the impact of the war on the economy, including agriculture and industry, while others review the role of religious groups and institutions of higher education. Finally, chapters describe the contributions Kentuckians made "over there," primarily on the Western Front, and examine the end and aftermath of the war, including the great influenza epidemic of late 1918 and postwar efforts to remember and memorialize the war.

In sum, *Kentucky and the Great War* gives a broad view of the commonwealth during a period of immense national importance, but also a time of great significance to the state. Despite their differences, for a brief shining moment, Kentuckians coalesced during this tumultuous period to support energetically the nation's war efforts.

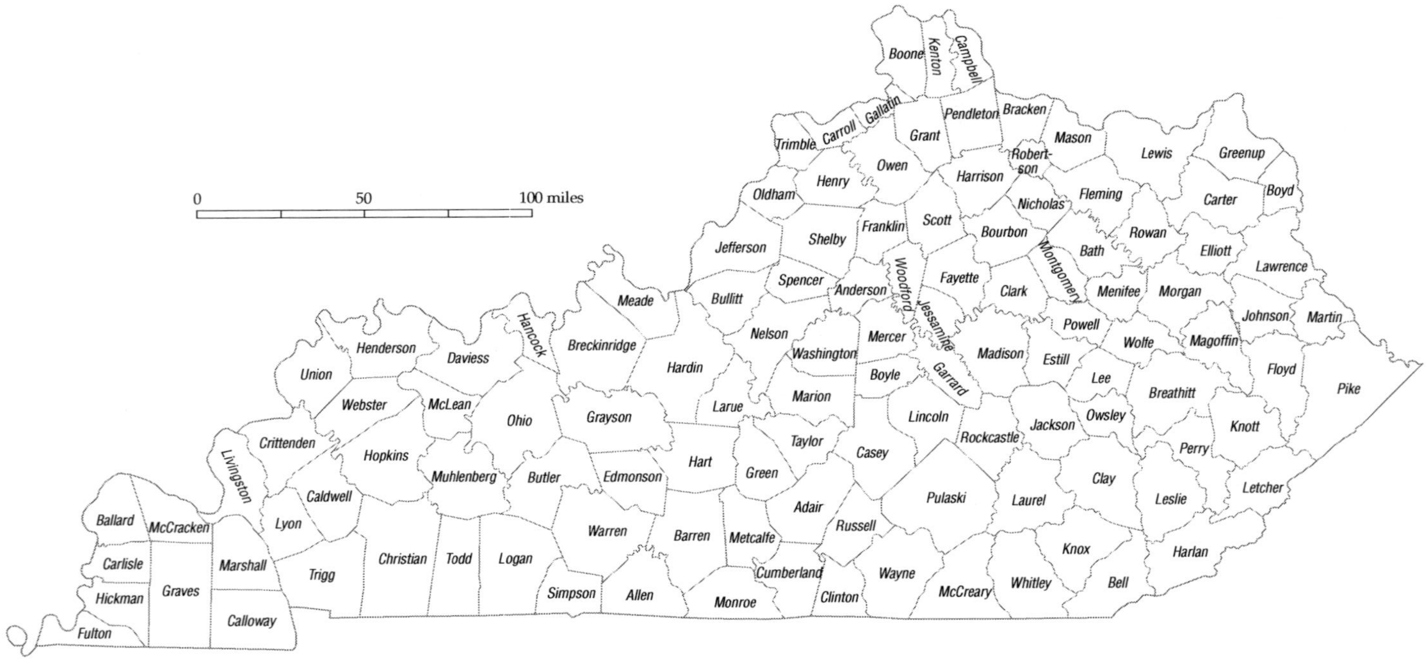
0
50
100 miles
Boone
Kenton
Campbell
Gallatin
Carroll
Trimble
Pendleton
Bracken
Grant
Mason
Lewis
Greenup
Boyd
Robert-
son
Owen
Henry
Oldham
Harrison
Nicholas
Fleming
Carter
Scott
Franklin
Shelby
Jefferson
Bourbon
Bath
Rowan
Elliott
Lawrence
Montgomery
Woodford
Fayette
Clark
Menifee
Morgan
Spencer
Anderson
Bullitt
Meade
Hancock
Jessamine
Johnson
Martin
Nelson
Mercer
Washington
Madison
Estill
Powell
Wolfe
Magoffin
Floyd
Pike
Henderson
Daviess
Breckinridge
Hardin
Boyle
Garrard
Lee
Breathitt
Union
Webster
McLean
Ohio
Grayson
Larue
Marion
Lincoln
Jackson
Owsley
Knott
Crittenden
Hopkins
Taylor
Casey
Rockcastle
Perry
Livingston
Muhlenberg
Butler
Edmonson
Hart
Green
Pulaski
Laurel
Clay
Leslie
Letcher
Caldwell
Adair
Ballard
McCracken
Lyon
Warren
Barren
Metcalfe
Russell
Knox
Harlan
Carlisle
Marshall
Trigg
Christian
Todd
Logan
Cumberland
Wayne
Whitley
Bell
Hickman
Graves
Simpson
Allen
Monroe
Clinton
McCreary
Calloway
Fulton

1

War Breaks Out!

On June 28, 1914, a young Bosnian Serb student, Gavrilo Princip, stood on a street corner in Sarajevo, Bosnia, waiting as the carriage of Austrian Archduke Franz Ferdinand approached. When it drew abreast, Princip fired a revolver and killed the archduke and his wife, Sophie. Although few foresaw it, Princip's act set off what was initially called the "Great War."

In the far-off Commonwealth of Kentucky, only some newspapers featured the assassination. Many of the smaller newspapers, published weekly in four pages, continued to focus exclusively on local news. The largest Kentucky newspaper, the *Louisville Courier-Journal,* edited by the distinguished Henry Watterson, covered the story with a major front-page article and a large picture of Archduke Franz Ferdinand and his family. Three days later, the *Courier-Journal* declared: "War Is Threatened as Result of Assassination in Austria."[1]

Under the direction of its well-known editor Desha Breckinridge, the *Lexington Herald* also featured the assassination and a family picture on the front page. However, after the funeral of the slain archduke and his wife, the *Herald* did not cover the unfolding events until the end of the July, when it became apparent that war could truly break out. Instead, the newspaper focused on issues dear to Kentuckians, such as elections, the fight for Prohibition, and the suffragist struggle for the right to vote. Its primary international coverage featured the continuing difficult relations between the United States and revolutionary Mexico, which had resulted in the landing of US Marines at Vera Cruz in April 1914. The other issue that loomed internationally was a possible civil war in Ireland.[2]

Focusing on northern Kentucky news, Covington's *Kentucky Post* started covering the events in Europe about a month after the assassination—in late July—as Europe's great powers muddled into war. For this forbearance, the *Post* cannot be blamed: most Europeans were stunned when an essentially local Austrian-Serbian conflict developed into a much larger struggle. Diplomats, newspaper reporters, and other contemporary commentators all believed the conflict would remain local and would involve weeks of negotiations and innocuous action such as those that had marked previous contretemps between the various European countries.[3]

It took a few weeks during the desultory summer months for the war to develop. By the end of July, the Austro-Hungarian Empire, backed by its ally, Germany, pressed closer to war against Serbia, which it blamed for the assassination. The Serbian government sought the aid of its supporter, Russia. In turn, the Russians counted on their fifteen-year alliance with France for help if war broke out.[4]

On July 28, 1914, Austria declared war on Serbia. Russia then fully mobilized its army, prompting Germany to declare war on Russia on August 1 and on France two days later. Great Britain joined the fray on the side of Russia and France on August 4, after the Germans had invaded neutral Belgium to attack France. The dominoes continued to fall; countries around the globe would eventually declare war.[5]

Debate over the origins of the war continues today, but what remains clear is that Princip's assassination of Franz Ferdinand set off a downward spiral that led to incredible destruction and loss of life over the next four years. More than 10 million military personnel would die in the resulting Great War. Many more would be wounded or die of disease, such as influenza. Civilian casualties proved enormous as well: more than 7 million died from the war and its aftermath.[6]

When the war broke out, Kentuckians became concerned about friends and relatives caught in the war zone. Ruth James, the wife of Kentucky's US senator Ollie James, was in Rome with two companions, an American diplomat and his wife. They had intended to leave Italy and head for the diplomat's posting in Japan by way of the trans-Siberian railroad. Instead, to escape Europe they had to travel to Berlin, then Copenhagen, and finally on to London, where many Americans gathered in anticipation of returning home. Ruth James finally arrived in Washington, DC, in late August, nearly two months after the assassination of Franz Ferdinand.[7]

The daughter of US representative from Kentucky Ben Johnson found herself in a similar situation in Venice. Nancy Johnson managed to join a group of wealthy Americans who chartered a steamer, the *Principe de Udine,* which left Genoa on August 12. Unlike Ruth James, who sailed for home with no luggage, Nancy Johnson managed to return with her twenty-six bags.[8]

Newspapers around the state reported similar experiences of Kentuckians caught in Europe. The *Lexington Herald* had sponsored a contest that sent two young women to Europe: Susan Bronston and Anna Mae McCourt. The newspaper told of their whereabouts as well as that of other stranded central Kentuckians.[9]

The *Kentucky Post* reported that nearly two dozen "prominent Northern Kentuckians" were caught in Europe, including the Right Reverend Camillus Paul Maes, a native Belgian who was the Catholic bishop of Covington, and the Reverend Henry Tappert, a Catholic pastor from Covington. Maes had been to Rome and was visiting his brother in Antwerp, Belgium, when the Germans invaded on August 4. After initial worries that Maes might be caught in the fighting, the *Post* finally reported on August 19 that Maes was safe with family. By September 2, the bishop cabled that he was in London; he returned to northern Kentucky at the end of September. Reverend Tappert had spent several months in Germany visiting relatives before the war broke out. He returned to Kentucky in early September, prophesying correctly that it would be a long war and erroneously that the Germans would win because of their excellent army.[10]

People and newspapers began to voice opinions about the countries at war. Some immigrants to Kentucky publicly took sides, and newspapers reported their comments—some enthusiastic, some skeptical. An Austrian army reservist working in Louisville, Sol Turnheim, blamed the Serbians for the war and expressed his willingness to return home to serve in the army, if needed. Frenchman Charles Mouget of Newport, who had fought the Russians in the Crimea in 1856 and proudly wore the French Legion of Honor ribbon in his lapel, said he would be proud to fight again for France (although at his advanced age, that prospect seemed dim). Ziva Mueller, a Hungarian living in Louisville, had a better idea: if the rulers could not solve their problems, he thought they should fight a duel. He preferred to remain in Louisville.[11]

The *Courier-Journal*'s famed editor, Henry Watterson, soon weighed in on the editorial page. A jingoist who favored war with Mexico, he nevertheless claimed to be an isolationist and something of a pacifist. He disliked Russia's autocracy and remained a staunch Anglophobe. After war broke out, "Marse Henry" decried the "awful spectacle of a general European war with its appalling impendencies" and counseled that "the thoughtful American will hesitate before taking sides."[12]

Watterson quickly changed his mind, however, when the Germans attacked France through Belgium on August 4. This violation of Belgian neutrality appalled the *Courier-Journal* editor, who subsequently sought the downfall of Germany's Kaiser Wilhelm in what was shaping up as a struggle between "Absolutism and Democracy." Underpinned by his antipathy toward the kaiser (but not the German people), by September 3 Watterson came down firmly on the side of the Allies, declaring in a famous editorial: "To Hell with the Hohenzollerns and Hapsburgs." A few days later, he reiterated that the newspaper was a friend of the German people. He claimed: "It is not a war of the German people. It is a War of the Kaisers waged for glory and conquest, for absolutism and arbitrary power."[13]

Watterson's hostility toward the kaiser and the German government took

Henry Watterson, editor of the *Louisville Courier-Journal*. (University of Kentucky)

on a local flavor. The German-American Alliance and the editor of the local German-language newspaper, the *Louisville Anzeiger,* protested against what they perceived as anti-German and, by extension, anti–German American sentiment spread by both the *Courier-Journal* and the *New York Times.* The *Courier-Journal*'s chief rival, the *Louisville Herald,* supported the Alliance and "declared that Marse Henry, in branding those of a different point of view as traitors, was unfair, narrow-minded, ignorant, and malicious."[14]

In Lexington, Leslie Combs Jr. was worried about his son, Brownell, who was visiting Germany when the war broke out. Combs blamed the war on the British. A former US minister to Peru under President William Howard Taft, Combs charged that "the present European war was brought about by British intrigue, for the purpose of checking Germany's commercial development." He believed the British had relied on "loans of money, promises, cajolery, and threats" to keep countries on their side. Combs asserted that the British were using the same tactics employed a hundred years previously, when they had "used the savage Indians under the British flag, commanded by British officers, to scalp, torture and butcher our Kentucky and Ohio grandfathers and their wives and children."[15]

Combs took umbrage at the *Lexington Herald*'s anti-German bias. To counter this unfairness, Combs sent a letter to the editor reproducing an Associated Press report that several American newspapermen admitted they had not seen any alleged German atrocities. The *Herald* published Combs's letter but continued to criticize the German government for its violation of Belgian neutrality.[16]

Leslie Combs Jr. was the son of War of 1812 veteran General Leslie Combs, who had been captured by Indians allied with the British during the war and forced to run a gauntlet. Combs may have sympathized with the Germans because of that family history and because of a close family connection to Germany. Ten years earlier, his daughter Annette had married a German, Herbert Schlubach. Combs and his wife had visited the couple in Hamburg in the spring of 1914. Schlubach won Germany's highest award, the Iron Cross, for gallantry in action during the fall 1914 campaign.[17]

Kentuckians not only commented about the war; they also became involved in it. They joined belligerent armies. They actively helped alleviate the suffering of Europeans threatened and damaged by the war.

War relief efforts in Louisville began immediately. The German-American Alliance sought donations to support widows and orphans of German and Austrian soldiers killed in the war, and the *Louisville Anzeiger* contributed. In August the Louisville Board of Trade created a Red Cross Committee

Desha Breckinridge, editor of the *Lexington Herald.* (University of Kentucky)

to collect money for a national campaign to send a hospital ship to Europe, equipped with surgeons, Red Cross nurses, surgical equipment, and medical supplies.[18]

Relief efforts aimed at France and Belgium garnered support. Americans were particularly outraged that the Germans had violated Belgium's neutrality and therefore favored the Belgians in relief efforts. On a national level, future US president Herbert Hoover helped organize the American Commission for Relief in Belgium to assist the beleaguered country. In Louisville the daughter of a well-known real estate developer, Lulie Henning, led Belgian relief efforts for the Belgian consular district of Ohio, Tennessee, and Kentucky. A supervisory committee included prominent Louisvillians: honorary chairman Henry Watterson; preparedness supporter William Marshall Bullitt; and George Garvin Brown, who had founded Brown-Forman liquor distillers. The Louisville Board of Trade also appointed a committee to assist Henning's efforts.[19]

The Louisville branch of the Alliance Française started raising money to send to the French ambassador for French and Belgian relief. At a meeting, the group was spurred on by Nadine Prevost, who showed pictures of the famous Rheims Cathedral, which the Germans had severely bombed.[20]

The *Courier-Journal*'s November 1 editorial page called attention to Belgian King Albert's appeal for assistance and offered to collect and send money to the appropriate authorities. A day later the paper reported that two people had already contributed, naming the donors and the amounts. As the fundraising effort continued, the newspaper received contributions from as far away as Cadiz in Trigg County, in the western part of the state.[21]

All this focus on helping people overseas caused some people to remind Kentuckians of the need at home. The general secretary of the Associated Charities of Lexington, Dorothy Embry, reminded Lexingtonians, who had raised over $2,000 for Belgian relief, that they should also attend to their own suffering. She found it ironic that poor women were knitting for Belgian relief when their own children lacked clothing.[22]

While several Kentuckians were trying to return home from Europe and some were helping war victims, others went in a different direction: toward the sound of the guns. Kentucky humorist and journalist Irvin S. Cobb went to Europe soon after the war began. Born in Paducah, Cobb had joined the staff of the *Paducah Daily News* at age seventeen. By nineteen, he had become editor. After spending a year and a half at the *Louisville Evening Post,* Cobb returned to western Kentucky and briefly managed the new *Paducah Democrat* before moving to New York to become a national journalist. He eventually ended up working for Joseph Pulitzer's *Evening Herald* and then for the *Saturday Evening Post.* Even while in New York, Cobb could not shake his roots, setting some of his voluminous writings in Kentucky (most particularly his Judge Priest stories).[23]

When the war broke out, the *Saturday Evening Post* sent Cobb abroad to report. Counting on his status as an American neutral, Cobb crisscrossed the front lines, reporting "a sequence of pictures describing some of my experiences

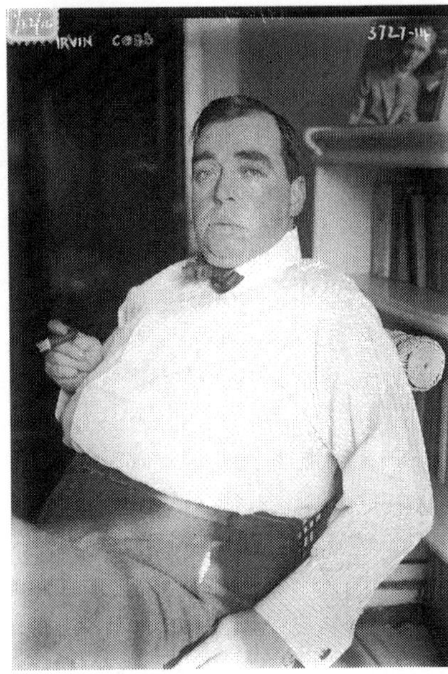

Irvin S. Cobb, a Paducah native who went to Europe to cover the Great War. (Library of Congress)

and setting forth a few of my observations" during the first three months of the war. Cobb spent time in Belgium, writing vignettes about the war's effect on people. He was in Louvain when the Germans marched through, and he spent time behind German lines. Cobb commented on the war: "I saw enough to cure any man of the delusion that war is a beautiful, glorious, inspiring thing, and to make him know it for what it is—altogether hideous and unutterably awful." Admitting that he "had been able to find in Belgium no direct proof of the mutilations, the torturings and other barbarities which were charged against the Germans by the Belgians," Cobb nevertheless concluded: "In the face of the present plight of this little country we need not look for individual atrocities. Belgium herself is the capsheaf atrocity of the war."[24]

In early 1915 Cobb produced a book of his *Saturday Evening Post* articles—*Paths of Glory*—and embarked on a speaking tour of states east of the Mississippi, including Kentucky. He joined the Vigilantes, a group of nearly 400 artists and literary figures that included author Booth Tarkington, poet Edgar Lee Masters, and illustrator James Montgomery Flagg. The Vigilantes wrote propaganda in favor of preparedness and the war, and their works appeared in newspapers throughout the country, including Kentucky. In 1917 Cobb published *Speaking of Prussians,* a virulent view of the Germans. Cobb returned to Europe after the United States entered the war, writing for the *Saturday Evening Post.* These articles were published later in book form as *The Glory of the Coming.*[25]

Kentuckians went to Europe and became involved in the war for other reasons as well. Dr. Hubbard Buckner, from Covington, was in France when the war began and remained there, serving at the American Hospital in Paris. Some Kentuckians joined foreign armies, primarily those of the Allies. Covington native Thomas Stevenson joined the British army and was killed on the Western Front in March 1915; he left behind a mother and brother in Covington. Frank Morkill from Newport joined the Canadian army and met the same deadly fate. Richmond native and former University of Kentucky student Merritt Powell joined the Canadian army, was promoted to sergeant, and traveled to the Western Front. At Ypres he was wounded in the arm, suffered through a chlorine gas attack, and afterward spent six months in a London hospital. He eventually returned home to Richmond, where he died from the effects of being gassed.[26]

The most well-publicized Kentuckian who joined Allied forces was Lexington's Alexander McClintock. In September 1915 he enlisted in the 87th Battalion, Canadian Grenadier Guards. In September 1916 on the Western Front, as part of a group of sixty men who went "over the top," McClintock was one of only seven who returned intact. His luck ran out, however, in a November nighttime attack during the Battle of the Somme. After rescuing several men during a raid, Sergeant McClintock was struck by a shell that left more than twenty pieces of shrapnel in his body. Recuperating at London's King George

Fayette County's Alexander McClintock joined the Canadian army early in the war and wrote about his experiences.

Hospital, he was one of the patients who met King George when the royal sovereign visited on Christmas Day. The king thanked McClintock for his service and gallantry, for which the Lexingtonian eventually earned the Distinguished Conduct Medal, Britain's second-highest award for bravery.[27]

After recuperating, McClintock returned to Kentucky on furlough. He wrote about his exploits in a series of six newspaper stories titled "Over There." The installments appeared in several newspapers in Kentucky, including the *Louisville Courier-Journal, Hopkinsville Kentuckian, Bourbon News,* and *Breckenridge News* in Cloverport. McClintock later collected these stories into a book titled *Best O'Luck; How a Fighting Kentuckian Won the Thanks of Britain's King.* After the United States entered the war, McClintock transferred to the US Army as a lieutenant. He attended the Plattsburg officer candidate school and was the subject of a large *New York Times* profile, which also drew from his new book. He then went to Fort Dix, New Jersey, to serve as an instructor. He anticipated going abroad again with the American doughboys.[28]

Some Kentuckians went or stayed abroad not to fight but to assist those caught in the war's destruction. One was Mary Curry Breckinridge, the sister of *Lexington Herald* editor Desha Breckinridge and of noted feminist leader and social worker Sophonisba Breckinridge. She had years of experience helping others. She had been a kindergarten teacher and had worked at a summer camp at the well-known Hindman settlement in Knott County. Then she trained as a nurse in New York City and Chicago and worked in an insane hospital in Illinois. State historian Jim Klotter has described her as "quiet, sensitive, generous, uncertain of herself, and handicapped by dyslexia."[29]

In May 1915 Curry Breckinridge departed for France to work in a British base hospital near the front lines. She then worked at the American Hospital in Paris before returning home after the United States entered the war in 1917. She toured central Kentucky giving talks about her experiences in the war. Eager to help the US war effort, she volunteered for a medical unit being raised in Lexington: Base Hospital No. 40, led by Dr. David Barrow. While the Barrow Unit awaited mobilization in late 1917, Curry Breckinridge went to Cleveland to study anesthesia. She became ill, eventually suffered a heart attack, and died in June 1918 in Chicago at the age of forty-two.[30]

The war did not end quickly, as many people had hoped and prophesied. When it carried over into 1915, Kentuckians focused more attention on it, debating whether the United States should formally get involved as the country found itself slowly but inexorably drawn into the conflict. When Germany proclaimed a submarine blockade around Great Britain on February 4, 1915, Henry Watterson warned of dire consequences. If an American ship were blown up in the

Irish Sea, he declared, "the explosion, like that of the *Maine* in Havana harbor, would reverberate from the Atlantic to the Pacific," and "war would be instantly declared by Congress." Watterson also chided German Americans for their continued support of the kaiser. His stance provoked a sharp exchange with the president of the *Courier-Journal* company, Bruce Haldeman, who was annoyed that his editor did not also criticize British interference with neutral trade. Despite this difference of opinion, and with the apparent support of the newspaper's board of directors, Watterson continued to excoriate the Germans.[31]

On May 17, 1915, a German U-boat sank the Cunard liner *Lusitania* in the waters off southern Ireland. Nearly 1,200 people died, including 124 of the 188 Americans aboard. The shock reverberated throughout America. Most Americans had watched the conflict from afar, but the *Lusitania*'s sinking made them aware that the war could affect them too. Historian Justus Doenecke notes: "Finally the nation had come face-to-face with the reality of total war, with civilians as well as armed forces now directly involved."[32]

Four days later, Watterson devoted nearly an entire page of the *Courier-Journal* to denouncing the German attack: "Nothing in the annals of piracy can in wanton and cruel ferocity equal the destruction of the 'Lusitania.'" Nevertheless, he counseled that "we must not act either in haste, or in passion." The *Courier-Journal* stopped short of calling on President Wilson to convene Congress and seek a declaration of war.[33]

President Wilson protested the *Lusitania*'s sinking, but the Germans responded by claiming the ship carried munitions and was therefore a legitimate target. At this news, Watterson called for America to break diplomatic relations or declare war. His anti-German editorials continued to agitate Louisville's German American population and drew derisory comments from the rival *Louisville Herald.*[34]

In Lexington, Leslie Combs Jr. continued to support the Germans. He sent a telegraph to President Wilson noting that the British had also violated international law and that the loss of so many passengers was due to secondary explosions from the armaments carried by the *Lusitania.* He maintained that "the loss of life, appalling as it is, is infinitesimal compared with that suffered by the Germans from the expenditure of American ammunition upon their soldiers."[35]

Other Kentucky newspapers reported the sinking of the *Lusitania,* but some questioned the need for America to act. Richmond's *Climax-Madisonian* called for a meeting of state governors to discuss the matter, noting that it was "easy to get into war but hard to get out" and that "intemperate action is what brought on the war in Europe."[36] Stanford's *Interior Journal* noted that the German government had warned Americans to stay off the ship, "but many Americans have heeded it not and have paid the penalty." The newspaper cautioned about going to war to "take a chance on losing thousands of Americans in order to obtain reparation for those hard-headed ones sent to the bottom of the sea."[37]

Debate about the US position continued nationally. Issues such as freedom of the seas and America's military preparedness generated diverse views. Early in the European war, critics such as US Representative Augustus Gardner of Massachusetts began to wonder if America's preparedness for war was at the appropriate level. A son-in-law of Henry Cabot Lodge, Gardner in October 1914 proposed a national security commission to investigate the country's military status. Gardner's cry for better military preparedness would soon be taken up by other people, primarily northeastern elites such as Lodge, former president Theodore Roosevelt, and army chief of staff Leonard Wood.[38]

In the early months of the war, the *Courier-Journal*'s Watterson questioned the need to raise the preparedness question, calling it "at best premature." He believed the Germans would be defeated before long and saw "little hurry to reorganize, and none at all to mobilize, our military establishment."[39]

Despite the views of Watterson and others, several prominent Americans decided in December 1914 to create the National Security League (NSL), the "largest and most influential of the groups that worked for preparedness." Among other things, NSL members called for compulsory military training, a stronger National Guard, and a permanent national defense council that could oversee all aspects of preparedness. US Representative J. Swagar Sherley, a Democrat from Louisville who served on the House Committee on Appropriations, expressed his belief in speeding up spending on the army and navy.[40]

The preparedness debate involved many issues: military and economic facets, the question of whether offensive or defensive measures should prevail, and which countries might be US opponents (not just Germany, but perhaps Japan or Mexico as well). In part, the debate centered on the economics of industrialized "total war," which would require extensive resources.[41]

Support for the NSL grew in Kentucky. Governor James McCreary advocated preparedness while he praised President Wilson as a proponent of peace. When the NSL held a conference in June 1915, the governor appointed three men, including Kentucky adjutant general Tandy Ellis, to attend the meeting in his stead. In Louisville, forty-nine men joined in the initial formation of an NSL chapter, including several who would play key roles in Kentucky during the war. The chapter elected Henry Watterson as honorary chairman, while former US solicitor general William Marshall Bullitt and William E. Morrow served as officers.[42]

Bullitt spent six weeks at the Plattsburg military training camp in New York, an effort to introduce businessmen to military life (a key component of the preparedness movement). Along with New York City mayor John Purroy Mitchel, Bullitt served on an eight-man national committee to organize the military training camp movement. He played a prominent role in the subsequent Military Training Camp Association, introducing a resolution at its 1916 conference supporting universal military training. Seconded by Mitchel, the resolution passed unanimously.[43]

Governor McCreary moved Kentucky toward preparedness for war. In November 1915 he appointed eighty-five women to serve on the Kentucky Committee of the Special Relief Society, a national organization of women dedicated to the preparedness movement. His action brought a scathing rejoinder from Kentucky's well-known suffragist and Progressive reformer Madeline McDowell Breckinridge. In a public letter to the governor, "Madge" Breckinridge, the wife of *Lexington Herald* editor Desha Breckinridge, criticized the notion that women should take part in a war preparedness effort if they did not have the right to vote. In an acerbic tone, she noted: "Kentucky women are not idiots—even though they are closely related to Kentucky men. You can't ignore them and treat them as if they were kindergarten children, and then when work is needed expect them to do a man's share—or a woman's, as you please to state it."[44]

Breckinridge's biographer, Melba Porter Hay, points out that the suffragist was not necessarily against war. She "also declined the invitation of the Woman's Peace Party to serve as 'Peace Chairman for Kentucky,'" admitting that she believed in "a certain amount of preparedness" and supported Allied efforts to defeat Germany.[45] Kentucky's preparedness movement ran into opposition as it intersected with one of Kentucky's primary domestic concerns: whether the state would pass a woman's suffrage bill.

President Wilson strongly supported peace, but by November 1915, he finally became convinced of the need for more preparedness. Historian Justus Doenecke acknowledges: "In undertaking a radical switch on preparedness, Wilson made his most important domestic decision of 1915." A few months later, Democratic congressman J. Campbell Cantrill of Georgetown, after a trip home, said he believed his constituents in Scott and Fayette Counties strongly agreed with Wilson's stance. Many other Americans concurred: they supported Wilson's new position that was less soft on defense. With this change of attitude, Wilson gained domestic support for himself and his Democratic Party, especially vis-à-vis the more aggressive, pro-US-involvement faction of the Republican Party.[46]

The issues of preparedness and the European war were not necessarily interrelated in the minds of some preparedness advocates, who believed the United States might also face Mexico or Japan in a future conflict. Tension with Germany, however, continued to dominate the news as the two countries disagreed over the law of the sea, particularly about whether Americans had the right to travel safely on merchant vessels armed solely for defense.

In February 1916 "Democratic representative, A. Jeff McLemore (D-Texas), introduced a resolution requesting that the president warn American citizens against traveling on armed merchant ships." Democratic senator Thomas Gore of Oklahoma pushed for a proposal that went even further: "it prohibited the State Department from issuing passports to Americans traveling on belligerent ships." In the opinion of Doenecke, "Wilson faced the gravest political challenge to date. Adopting McLemore's proposal would ruin the chief executive's standing with the Allied governments and possibly destroy potential influence over Germany's leaders, because no one would know whether it was the president or the Congress who made American policy."[47]

The Kentucky congressional delegation came to Wilson's aid. The *Courier-Journal* reported that Kentucky's Democratic senator Ollie James, in a "forceful statement" to the newspaper, "believed this nation's foreign relations should be handled by the President of the United States without interference by members of Congress, however well meant might be their intentions." As a member of the House Rules Committee, J. Campbell Cantrill would not vote to move out of committee the Gore proposal "or any similar measure designed, in the least way, to tie the hands of the nation's leader." Considered one of "Wilson's leaders in the House," Louisville congressman Swagar Sherley would not brook congressional interference in the president's conduct of American foreign relations.[48]

Both the McLemore and Gore proposals failed to garner sufficient support in Congress. "Wilson had shown himself the unquestioned leader of his party and in full control of his nation's foreign policy."[49]

Meanwhile, the Germans increased their submarine campaign against Allied and neutral shipping. After they torpedoed the passenger ship *Sussex* in March 1916, Watterson called for an immediate severing of diplomatic relations with Germany. Wilson threatened war. In response, the Germans issued the so-called Sussex pledge, modifying their rules of engagement for submarine warfare and thereby mollifying Wilson and others who preferred not to go to war or to break diplomatic relations.[50]

Throughout the rest of 1916, Americans closely monitored the forthcoming presidential election. Senator James, chairman of the Democratic National Convention, gave a lengthy convention speech in June supporting Wilson's domestic and foreign policies. James noted that Wilson had "struggled for peace" but supported preparedness so that the United States had an army "big enough to make aggressors think the second time before they strike a blow."[51]

President Wilson visited Kentucky in early September to take part in ceremonies to designate Lincoln's birthplace in Hodgenville as a national site. Nearly 20,000 people turned out to hear the president laud Lincoln as the "embodiment of true Democracy." Although the trip had an avowedly nonpolitical intent, the enthusiastic crowd greeted the president warmly, with some people shouting "to our next President."[52] The crowd was correct. Wilson went on to victory over Republican challenger and Supreme Court Justice Charles Evans Hughes in the presidential election in November. The incumbent president won all of Kentucky's electoral votes, with 51.9 percent of the state voting for him.[53]

Despite Wilson's campaign slogan that he had kept the United States out of war, 1917 proved too contentious for America to stand by as a neutral country. The Germans declared on February 1 that they would resume unrestricted submarine warfare, marking "the beginning of the end of peace with the United States."[54] On February 3 President Wilson told a joint session of Congress that he was severing US diplomatic relations with Germany, although he still hoped to keep America out of the war. Editor Watterson of the *Courier-Journal* "heartily endorsed Wilson's severance of diplomatic relations, on February 3, but did not share his [Wilson's] optimism that war might be avoided."[55]

Germany continued to bungle its relations with the United States. The discovery of the so-called Zimmermann telegram further incited Americans. Intercepted and decoded by the British, the telegram was a proposal from German foreign secretary Arthur Zimmermann to Mexico: If the United States entered the war against Germany, Mexico should enter on the side of Germany. Then, when Germany won the war, Mexico would recover its lost territories in Texas, New Mexico, and Arizona. In addition, Zimmermann recommended that Mexico make overtures to Japan about joining the war against the United States. This example of German perfidy did not surprise Watterson, who labeled it "thoroughly Prussian." The *Hopkinsville Kentuckian* trumpeted in a first-page headline: "Zimmie the Wise Old Owl Has Been Caught with Plot Goods."[56]

Throughout the spring of 1917, Congress continued to wrangle over the proper course in response to German actions. In some parts of the United States, a strong antimilitarism, antiwar sentiment existed, particularly in the South and West (although not in Kentucky). Senate leaders such as Wisconsin's Robert La Follette and North Carolina's Claude Kitchin questioned Wilson's policies and conduct. In the beginning of March, as the congressional session ended, La Follette led a filibuster to prevent voting on a bill to allow neutral ships to be armed. During the raucous proceedings, Ollie James led a swarm of Democrats accosting La Follette. La Follette supporter Harry Lane of Oregon spotted a pistol under James's coat and was prepared to stab the Kentuckian with a file if James drew his gun.[57]

After La Follette's speech, the *Lexington Herald* ran an editorial outlined by a large black border, titled "Betrayed," asserting that "Sunday, March 4, 1917, will ever stand out in American history as the day of the Nation's deepest disgrace." The newspaper condemned La Follette and other senators and representatives who had voted against the arming of neutral ships.[58]

Governor Augustus O. Stanley spoke out against La Follette's filibustering colleagues at a mass patriotic meeting attended by more than 2,000 Lexingtonians. Stanley called the filibuster a "crime against humanity." The meeting supported a resolution condemning Senate Foreign Relations Committee chairman William J. Stone of Missouri, a Kentuckian by birth, who had sided with the filibusterers. Resolutions called for Kentucky's Democratic senators Ollie James and J. C. W. Beckham to use their influence to prevent Stone from being reelected chairman of the committee because of his "obstructionism to the President's policies." At a patriotic meeting in Mt. Sterling a month later, Montgomery County citizens also condemned Stone, who, "by his conduct in using the power of his office to stifle the will of the people, has caused every true Kentuckian to regret that such a man can claim this State as his birthplace."[59] The meetings revealed a coalescing of stronger support for Wilson in the commonwealth and foreshadowed negative attitudes toward any dissent against the government's course of action during the war.

Germany continued its unrestricted submarine warfare in March 1917, sinking US-flagged merchant ships. Finally, President Wilson went to Congress on April 2 and asserted that a state of war already existed. He called for higher taxes, a stronger military, and increased financial support for the Allies. The *Courier-Journal* reported: "Kentucky Delegation as One Man behind President Wilson in Crisis." A lengthy congressional debate ensued on April 4. Many speakers favored war, including Kentucky's Senator James. According to James, "the blood-spattered monarch of Germany" had turned "the open sea, the gift of God to all mankind," into a death zone.[60]

Kentuckians rallied to support the president. Two days after Wilson's speech, at the instigation of the Kentucky legislature, a mass demonstration took place at the capitol in Frankfort. There, Governor Stanley, Lieutenant Governor James Black, and various state representatives and senators spoke in support of Wilson. Smaller patriotic meetings took place in towns such as Lancaster, where the Garrard County Agriculture Board of Control sponsored an event to "bring out the idea of patriotism from the 'man with the hoe' to the man who shoulders his gun for his country."[61] In this largely rural community, the citizens recognized that their country would need more productive agriculture to sustain its war effort. Indeed, agricultural needs were emphasized throughout the state from the war's earliest days.

Despite strong opposition from several congressmen, both houses of Congress passed a war resolution, which President Wilson signed on April 6. Kentucky's US representatives on both sides of the aisle voted for the resolution. Democrats Alben Barkley of Paducah and Ben Johnson of Nelson County, as well as Republican John Langley of Floyd County, spoke out in favor of the resolution. Called away to attend to his sick wife, Democratic representative William Fields from Carter County lamented his absence but noted that he would have voted for the measure.[62]

As noted by historian Ronald Alexander, the *Courier-Journal*'s Watterson lauded Congress's action: "With total confidence, exuberance, and relief, Marse Henry greeted the declaration of war against Germany on April 6." Watterson's editorials gained him acclaim. "Watterson's two editorials celebrating American entry into the war, which were titled 'Vae Victis' and 'War Has Its Compensations,' won him the Pulitzer Prize for best editorial writing in 1917."[63]

The stage was set for Kentuckians to participate fully in the war: overseas, by sending troops and support people, and domestically, where everyone was expected to "do their part." The rest of this book tells the story of how the Great War affected Kentucky and Kentuckians. Before that story continues, however, it is helpful to remember the situation of the commonwealth as it existed on the brink of war.

Kentucky during the years 1900 to 1950 has been called a "Portrait in Paradox" by state historian Jim Klotter. Like many Americans, Kentuckians were divided on several issues, such as woman's suffrage and the prohibition of alcohol. Questions remained about which direction the state would take.

On the positive side, in the years prior to the Great War, Kentuckians celebrated prominent writers such as John Fox Jr., James Lane Allen, and Irvin Cobb. They preceded a flowering of later Kentucky literati such as Robert Penn Warren, Jesse Stuart, and Harriette Arnow Simpson. On the negative side, racism existed in Kentucky; more than fifty African Americans were lynched in the state in the first decade of the twentieth century. Institutionally, racism was reflected in the Kentucky legislature's passage of the Day Law in 1904, which forbade "white and colored persons from attending the same school." The law was aimed at the last school to resist segregation—Berea College. In a surprising development, given that Kentucky had remained a Union state during the Civil War, many Kentuckians looked back and celebrated the "Lost Cause" of the Confederacy.[64]

At the time of the Great War, Kentucky remained primarily an agrarian society. The number of farms increased in number but declined in size during the early part of the twentieth century. Although farm values were low, the state ranked high in product value. The chief crop continued to be tobacco. Hay production increased dramatically, while hemp and wheat production declined. Livestock production was hearty, and World War I would stimulate the state's meatpacking industry.[65]

Kentucky had two major urban areas: Louisville and northern Kentucky. Both had large groups of immigrants, especially Irish and German, who flocked to the growing industrial bases in Louisville and Cincinnati. Other towns along the Ohio River, such as Owensboro, Paducah, and Ashland, were becoming more industrialized. At the turn of the century, Kentucky's industrial base ranked reasonably high, but its growth rate soon lagged precipitously compared with other states.

The state's liquor industry remained strong, despite growing agitation for Prohibition. Carriage making and hemp production were in decline, as were timber operations in eastern Kentucky's Appalachian region. To replace timber operations in Appalachia, Kentuckians turned to coal mining, which increased sixfold in the years before the Great War. Unfortunately, as Klotter has pointed out, these were primarily "colonial" operations, whereby much of the wealth derived from these industries went to out-of-state controlling entities.[66]

Other problems plagued the state, including a "virulent regionalism" and violence. Lynchings, coalfield strife, personal feuds, and political violence hampered development and offset the state's good reputation as a decent place to live. The political scene remained fractured, marred by the assassination of Governor William Goebel in 1900, a result of the political factionalism that continued to split both the Democratic and Republican Parties in Kentucky. In a state where politics was "the damnedest," factionalism thrived, as did "bossism." Political kingpins thrived: William "King Billy" Klair in Lexington, John and James Whallen in Louisville, Ben Johnson of Bardstown, and William Purcell "Percy" Dennis Haly of Frankfort, who wielded influence throughout the state.[67]

On the positive side, Progressivism had begun to take root in Kentucky. Often touted as a primarily urban phenomenon aimed at addressing the ills of a burgeoning industrialized society, Progressivism also spread into rural areas of the state, such as Nelson and Washington Counties.[68] In 1915 Kentucky elected a Progressive governor, Democrat Augustus O. Stanley, by a slim margin. Although he was a "wet" (against Prohibition) and opposed woman's suffrage, Stanley oversaw what Klotter deemed "a very progressive administration." At its biennial meeting in 1916 the legislature passed a Corrupt Practices Act, an antitrust law, and an elective workmen's compensation program, and it "established various new boards to regulate special groups." In sum, Klotter concludes, "the session had been an unusually strong one, overall."[69]

Desha and Madeline McDowell Breckinridge were key advocates for Progressivism. Madge Breckinridge supported Progressive reforms to educate children and to restrict child labor. She helped establish the Lincoln School in Lexington's poor section of Irishtown. She was a state and national leader in the woman's suffrage movement. Most of the time her husband supported her in his *Lexington Herald* editorials.

In the fight for women's rights, Madeline Breckinridge was joined by other prominent Kentuckians, including Laura Clay, the daughter of abolitionist Cassius Marcellus Clay. Like Breckinridge, Clay became a state and national leader in the suffragist movement, although they disagreed on how best to achieve this—through state or national legislation. Despite their efforts, Kentucky's male politicians continued to oppose giving women the right to vote, except in school elections (which was granted in 1912). The last effort to gain the vote before the US entry into the war resulted in yet another defeat during the Kentucky state legislature's meeting in 1916. Despite Republican support, the woman's vote issue failed to garner enough Democratic support, including that of Democratic governor Stanley.[70]

The commonwealth was also divided over Prohibition. In a state where bourbon remained a key product, Progressives teamed with church interests to prevent the sale of alcohol in 100 of Kentucky's 120 counties by the time war broke out in 1914. The issue remained controversial in the "wet" counties that allowed alcohol consumption, and Prohibitionists sought not only local but also state and national bans on the sale of alcohol. The war would provide an impetus for Prohibition efforts when thousands of men poured into the state for military training.[71]

Other issues that plagued Kentucky included illiteracy and health problems, such as a high tuberculosis (TB) rate and a lack of simple health care in large parts of the state. Cora Wilson Stewart of Morehead led state and national efforts to fight illiteracy. Her efforts received a strong boost in 1914 with the creation of a Kentucky Illiteracy Commission. She was also strongly supported by Madeline and Desha Breckinridge, who covered Stewart's efforts extensively in the *Lexington Herald*. The campaign against illiteracy would become even more important after the United States entered the war.[72]

In health care reform, Madeline Breckinridge boosted efforts to combat tuberculosis, which she suffered from herself. Kentucky ranked second highest in deaths from TB, which especially affected the state's African American community. Breckinridge helped create a state tuberculosis commission in 1912. But other health issues plagued the state, including hookworm, diarrhea, dysentery, and typhoid fever, much of this caused by insalubrious conditions and compounded by poor medical care.[73]

Despite these many problems, Kentucky benefited from the Progressive movement before the war. Several groups sought reforms in child labor, education, and health, especially the women's groups represented in the Kentucky Federation of Women's Clubs.[74]

After the United States entered the Great War in April 1917, many existing civic groups, such as the women's clubs, turned their activities to supporting the war effort. New groups sprang up to take on new tasks, such as selling savings bonds and stamps or watching for slackers, German sympathizers, and anyone who dared speak out against the war. Existing institutions took on new or changed roles; for example, colleges and universities became training grounds for soldiers.

By the time of the declaration of war in April 1917, the stage was set for the Great War to bring about even greater changes in Kentucky. Would the reform movements continue? Would Prohibition efforts be given a boost by the war? Woman's suffrage? Conditions for African Americans? Would the state emerge from the conflict in a stronger position economically, politically, and socially? Would factionalism be subsumed by the need for collectivism in carrying out war efforts? What role would the state and federal governments play in the war? What human suffering would result from the war, which had already ground up millions of soldiers and civilians in a European conflict that was turning into a world war? In short, how would Kentucky and its citizens be changed by the war?

Kentuckians would be affected by this war in ways that few foresaw in April 1917. The federal government would make some actions mandatory, such as registering for the draft. In other instances, people would be subject to what historian Christopher Capozzola calls "coercive voluntarism." They were forced to adhere to certain practices, not necessarily under pain of law, but to avoid the opprobrium of fellow citizens. For example, people would buy savings bonds to avoid being named in newspapers as "slackers."[75]

Kentuckians would observe "meatless" days, conserve fuel, raise more crops, register for military duty, and go off to war. Some people would focus their efforts where their skills or hearts already pointed: doctors would form hospital units and go abroad, farmers as well as city dwellers would grow more food, and public speakers would encourage their communities to support the war effort. In short, Kentuckians banded together in enormous efforts to support "total war."

To coordinate these activities, committees would be established all across the state, reaching into the farthest hollows and smallest communities, as well as into the large urban areas along the Ohio River. Theirs would be the task of ensuring that Kentucky and Kentuckians played a proper role in the Great War.

2

Kentucky Joins the Great War

Most newspapers across Kentucky generally supported the US entry into the war. In "Vae Victis," one of the two editorials that won him the Pulitzer for editorial writing, Henry Watterson crowed: "Surely the time has arrived—many of us think it was long since overdue—for calling the brave to the colors." In his second editorial—"War Has Its Compensations"—Watterson pointed out that "no man has more than one time to die. In bringing the realization of death nearer to us war throws a new light upon life." Noting that "a soldier is a picked man," Watterson argued that "if he falls he has paid his mortal debt with honor."[1] In short, Watterson could now support the war he had sought for so long.

Couching his editorial in Christian religious terms and elevated language, editor Desha Breckinridge of the *Lexington Herald* waited until the Sunday edition after the declaration of war to say: "Let us realize this Easter morn that we fight for the triumph of the Prince of Peace." He concluded: "In the hour when peace returns, chastened it may be, triumphant in the cause of right, as we trust, to bind up the broken hearted, to comfort the distressed, to help the helpless, to take up anew the duties of life, will be our mission. But today, that peace may triumph, we take up arms in defense of humanity."[2] Thus the nation and the commonwealth went to war, Breckinridge implied, on a holy crusade to right wrongs, to destroy the evil Prussians.

Despite its hesitancy to support the British, Louisville's *Kentucky Irish-American* averred: "Catholics pray for peace, but they are ready for war if it comes." Love of country was "enjoined by religion as a sacred duty," and "the religious man is always a patriot. Patriotism is the demand of the hour."[3]

Reflecting its agrarian surroundings, the *Mt. Vernon Signal* in Rockcastle County took a pragmatic approach, acknowledging that the United States was "at the threshold of the greatest war in all history" and that "many a war has been lost in the history of the world because of a lack of food." In short, "the great problem of the human race is food." The paper encouraged every man, woman, and child to grow more food and to conserve as much as possible. The newspaper was prescient in this regard: the US government would establish a nationwide organization, the US Food Administration, to focus efforts on food conservation nationwide.[4]

An editorial in Powell County's *Clay City Times* took a somewhat pacifist stance and tied the war to women's suffrage. It admired Congresswoman Jeannette Rankin's vote against the war. The *Times* believed that a declaration of war by any country should be decided only by a majority of votes by all its people, including women. If women voted, the newspaper asserted, "war in any country would be an impossibility." Therefore, the paper was "ten times stronger than ever for women's suffrage." It added that "if war was what Gen. Sherman said it was [hell], we need as little of it as possible."[5]

Ohio County's *Hartford Republican* took a strident and succinct stance toward the Central Powers of Germany and Austria-Hungary: "The *Courier-Journal* suggests that the battle-cry be, 'To Hell with the Habsburgs and the Hohenzollerns.' Why not shorten it and at the same time get the identical meaning by adopting the simple cry, 'Kill Them.'" The newspaper also accepted that "Kentucky has her part to play in this war against imperialism; Ohio county must help." Recognizing the larger implications of the war, the paper concluded: "Ohio county's part in this conflict does not end when her quota of men have taken the field. All hands must get busy in producing food, fuel and other necessities. We have the soil and it should be made to yield more this year than ever before."[6]

As soon as the United States declared war, groups gathered throughout the commonwealth in mass "patriotic meetings" to show their support and enthusiasm. A mass meeting in Lexington reflected the coordinated group approach that would be used throughout the war; eight representatives of participating organizations met to plan the event. The organizers established committees to deal with finances, the speakers' stand, decorations and lights, music, the reception, and the parade. More than twenty clubs and organizations pledged their support, including the Rotary Club, Knights of Columbus, Elks Club, YMCA, Fayette Equal Rights Association, Woman's Club, and Board of Commerce.[7]

Officially called by Lexington mayor James Rogers, the meeting featured Governor Stanley, who was introduced by the state's adjutant general, Tandy Ellis. More than 15,000 people heard the governor say that the United States was fighting not *against* the German people but *for* them. Borrowing from Watterson, Stanley cried out: "God bless the German people but to Hell with the Hohenzollern."[8]

While other groups planned how best to conduct the war, one group of men already stood ready: the Kentucky National Guard. In addition to the Kentuckians who were already enlisted in the US Army, Navy, and Marine Corps when the war broke out, many men had joined the state militia, the Kentucky State Guard. It was redesignated the Kentucky National Guard after a

Governor Augustus Owsley Stanley. (Library of Congress)

national military reorganization in 1912, at which time it became more intertwined with the Regular Army of the United States, with supervision from the War Department. Its men became subject to call-up for federal service.[9]

During tensions with Mexico in 1916, the Kentucky National Guard was called on to support the Mexican Punitive Expedition, in which General John "Black Jack" Pershing led US troops into Mexico to search for revolutionary leader Pancho Villa. In August 1916, mobilized by federal officials and departing from Fort Thomas in northern Kentucky, more than 2,400 Kentucky troops later patrolled a sixty-mile section of the US-Mexico border along the Rio Grande from Fort Bliss to Fort Hancock. In February 1917 the Kentucky Guard returned to Fort Thomas to muster out and return to the command of Adjutant General Ellis.[10]

A "poet, humorist, columnist, raconteur and soldier," Tandy Ellis had been born in Ghent in Carroll County. He joined the State Guard in Owensboro as a young man and served until he moved to Washington, DC, to work for then-congressman Augustus O. Stanley. After returning to Kentucky, he was appointed assistant adjutant general in 1912 and then adjutant general in 1914. He would oversee the amalgamation of the Kentucky National Guard into the federal army during the war and have overall responsibility for the selective service process in Kentucky.[11]

When the United States entered the war in April 1917, Adjutant General Ellis sent Guard units to various places across the commonwealth to protect against possible damage by German saboteurs. They served as sentries, primarily patrolling railroads, bridges, tunnels, and other vital transportation routes. Then on April 12 all Kentucky National Guard units were federalized and ordered to mobilize and meet at Camp Stanley, just outside Lexington. Married men and those with dependents were mustered out and replaced with volunteers. In August the Kentuckians began transferring to Camp Shelby, Mississippi, where the First Regiment transformed into an artillery unit, while the Second and Third Regiments remained infantry. Along with National Guard units from Indiana and West Virginia, the Kentucky Guard units became part of the Thirty-Eighth Division, which eventually went to France in spring 1918. There the men served primarily as replacement troops in other divisions.[12]

The Guard was stationed throughout Kentucky in April 1917 to protect key transportation hubs because many Kentuckians feared malevolence by people of German heritage. This apprehension was an issue in Kentucky because of its large German American population, especially in northern Kentucky, Louisville, and Lexington, but also down the Ohio River valley into Paducah and Owensboro.[13]

Immediately after the United States joined the war, finger-pointing started against Kentuckians of German heritage. Two of the most prominent Germans in Louisville, brothers Louis and Otto Seelbach, were the proprietors of the famous Seelbach Hotel. Louis had lived in America for fifty years, Otto for forty. Both had American wives. Nevertheless, "the *Louisville Herald* reported that hostelers Otto and Louis Seelbach were rumored to have made 'seditious utterances.'" The *Louisville Courier-Journal* then reported that, on behalf of his brother and himself, Otto Seelbach had written to Senator Ollie James, thanking the senator for his speech in which he had said that German Americans would be as loyal as any other Americans. The *Courier* noted, "The Seelbachs were among the very first openly to express their patriotism and undivided allegiance when war with Germany became a certainty several weeks ago."[14]

To counter possible hostility, Germans in Louisville adopted a low profile. Unlike several other German-language newspapers in the country, the *Louisville Anzeiger* continued to publish but remained discreet about the war. Although use of the German language in churches had already begun to decline in the early twentieth century, the war hastened its demise; Louisville's St. Martin of Tours Catholic Church ceased using German in its sermons and newsletters. To show its loyalty at the beginning of the war, the German Insurance Bank hung an electric American flag between its two entrances during a patriotic ceremony at which the National Guard's First Regiment band played and several officers spoke. Later, the German Insurance Bank and the German Insurance Company deleted "German" from their names and substituted "Liberty."

In 1918 the German Security Bank reverted to its original name: the Security Bank. With over 3,000 members, the German-American Alliance of Louisville, including representatives from all the German social groups in the city, considered officially suspending meetings.[15]

Northern Kentucky also contained many people of German background. The 1910 census revealed that 21 percent of Campbell County and 17 percent of Kenton County residents were of German heritage—that is, either they were born in Germany or both their parents were born there. A thriving German culture permeated the area; this was part of a larger German presence in the Greater Cincinnati area bordering the Ohio River. German newspapers from Cincinnati circulated throughout northern Kentucky, German breweries operated, and German social organizations played an important role in local life. Led by Alfred Reinhardt and Alban Wolff, the German-American State Alliance had its headquarters in Covington.[16]

After April 1917, however, reminders of things German began to disappear. "In Covington Bremen St. became Pershing Ave., and in Newport, German St. became Liberty St." The German National Bank in Covington became the Liberty National Bank; the Newport German Bank became the American National Bank. Churches also renamed themselves; for example, "German Reformed Church in Bromley was rechristened Immanuel Reformed Church." German-oriented Catholic schools stopped using the German language in catechism classes.[17]

Efforts to proscribe the use of German were not limited to schools. Finally giving in to local pressure, St. Joseph's Catholic Church in Owensboro stopped offering a sermon in German each Sunday. Because of patron complaints, the board of directors of the Louisville Old Inn cabaret considered replacing the "quaint old proverbs inscribed in German at the top of the walls" with an American flag.[18] Organizations changed their names so that their loyalties were clear. The changes were also a response to a society that would not tolerate anything but total devotion to the war effort.

Not all Kentuckians worried about people of German heritage betraying the state and the nation. In Montgomery County, where few people of foreign birth resided, the *Mt. Sterling Advocate*'s editorial cautioned on April 10: "The Government is asking all its citizens to exercise great caution in questioning the loyalty of any fellow citizen of foreign birth or whose parents were foreign born." The editorial maintained that this was good advice, noting that rumors of disloyalty about a Louisville man and "several German business men of Lexington" had proved unfounded. The newspaper chided those who would accuse people falsely.[19]

In contrast to this tolerant view, Lawrence County's *Big Sandy News* in Louisa congratulated the "brave city" of Ashland for "making life miserable for everything of a German tendency" and the Ashland school system for banning German-language classes. It also lauded the Ashland city council for not renewing the business license of the Lexington Brewing Company because it was "managed by an unworthy fellow who boasts of spelling his name 'the Hun way'—Fischer." The newspaper approved of Fischer's treatment, despite the fact that he had done business in Ashland for twenty-five years. The newspaper concluded: "'America for Americans.' Let the Huns go back to Germany, the modern Hell."[20]

Many other school systems tried to ban German-language education. So did the Kentucky state legislature. In June 1917 the Dayton public schools in northern Kentucky eliminated German classes. In fall 1917 students in other northern Kentucky schools switched their foreign-language classes to Spanish or French. Even counties not heavily populated with those of German heritage banned the language. For example, the Somerset Board of Education in Pulaski County prohibited the teaching of German in Somerset High School, replacing it with French.[21]

In Louisville the school board did not abandon plans to teach German, but far fewer students studied it in fall 1917. At Louisville's Girls High School, the number of students taking German classes decreased from 150 the previous year to 100 in fall 1917. On this topic, the city's public schools superintendent O. L. Reid was a voice of reason: he reminded people that the governments of France and England were against banning German-language studies. As Reid noted: "We are not fighting the German language. We do not hold the Latin tongue responsible for Nero."[22]

The movement to ban the teaching of German reached the Kentucky legislature. In its biennial regular session in early 1918, it considered a bill that would prohibit the teaching of German in "state public schools, the State University [University of Kentucky], and in the Normal Schools [Eastern and Western]." A "spirited debate" ensued. Republican E. L. Allen of Floyd County opposed the bill, saying that he was loyal, but "not so prejudiced that as to desire to keep the coming generations from learning the German language." Representative Ote Piper of Clinton in Hickman County, however, argued emotionally and vividly, stating, "We do not want to teach the language of soldiers who pierce babies in Belgium with their bayonets." The bill passed by wide margins in both the house and the senate and was sent to Governor Stanley for his signature.[23]

By the time the bill passed, protests against it had begun to pour into the governor's office. The state's newspapers were divided on the issue. Noting that the bill's advocates "may be patriotic in their ignorance," the *Adair County News* in Columbia editorialized that knowledge of the German language was important for US defense. It asserted: "Nothing is more essential to the defeat of Germany than that the German language shall be universally taught in America. This is as important as the making of shells, growing of wheat, and the building of ships." In contrast, the *Kentucky Post* believed the study of German was simply not necessary.[24]

Other groups chimed in. The Louisville Board of Education opposed the bill. Its chair cited several reasons, including the fact that the French had not banned the study of German, the postwar importance of the language for competitive purposes, and the fact that the US commissioner of education opposed such bills.[25]

After consulting with the US Bureau of Education and others, Governor Stanley vetoed the bill. He gave several reasons. He believed that knowing German was critical: understanding the "designs and purposes of our subtle, ingenious and powerful adversary is of incalculable value." He agreed with US Commissioner of Education P. C. Claxton, who thought it shortsighted to ban the teaching of German. The governor asserted: "We are at war with an armed despotism, not a language." He made an important distinction between Germany's leaders and military versus its culture. The United States was at war, he said, with "Germany's evil political institutions and her ruthless and domineering war lords—not her art, her literature or her marvelous scientific discoveries."[26]

Some newspapers agreed with the governor and applauded his courage. The *Hartford Republican* opined that the governor had "acted wisely" and that "no other action of the recent legislature was more ridiculously absurd and unwarranted." George Weathers, editor of the *Elkton Times* in Todd County, admitted: "Nobody had ever accused the editor of the *Times* of being unduly in love with the Governor of Kentucky, but harken onto this: The message of Owsley Stanley in vetoing the bill to prohibit the teaching of German in the public schools is one of the strongest, clearest and most scholarly papers that ever bore the signature of a state executive, and will bear favorable comparison with any ever issued from the White House."[27]

The longtime *Cincinnati Enquirer* correspondent who covered Kentucky politics, Thomas Cromwell, said his contacts believed that a majority of Kentuckians approved of the governor's veto. He pointed out that three of the English-language papers in Louisville approved of the governor's action, including the *Louisville Evening Post,* which was "never on the Stanley side in political fights," and the *Louisville Herald,* which was "Republican and anti-Stanley."[28]

Citizens in northern Kentucky, however, resented the governor's veto, and it became an issue in Stanley's senatorial campaign against Dr. Ben L. Bruner in fall 1918. President Wilson defended the governor in a letter to Kenton County Council of Defense member Polk Laffoon Jr. Wilson acknowledged that Stanley had vetoed the bill after contacting the Bureau of Education and that the governor, "in my judgment, act[ed] entirely with the view to the general educational interests, and certainly should not be considered as having in that matter been guilty of the least touch of disloyalty of any kind."[29]

Anti-German sentiment prevailed in northern Kentucky and extended beyond people's wishes to ban German in schools. It evolved into actual suppression against purported or supposed German sympathizers and other people who dared to question the war. Citizen groups such as the Citizens' Patriotic League (CPL) in northern Kentucky and the American Protective League (APL) throughout the state led these activities.

Seeking to "eliminate many aspects of German culture and language in the region," the CPL was formed in fall 1917 after a patriotic meeting in northern Kentucky. The group numbered more than 1,000 members and was led by many prominent northern Kentuckians, including Stephens Blakely, commonwealth attorney for Kenton County.[30]

The CPL sponsored so many patriotic meetings that these events became its mainstay. At a March 1918 meeting attended by more than 10,000 people, the CPL, at the instigation of Presbyterian minister I. Cochrane Hunt, unanimously passed a resolution that "Congress be petitioned by the people of Covington to interne [*sic*] every alien enemy citizen until after the war."[31]

In May 1918 the CPL sponsored a major rally at Latonia Race Track at which northern Kentucky's Democratic congressman Arthur B. Rouse of Burlington presided. Speakers that day included Governor James Cox of Ohio, Senator William King of Utah, and future Kentucky governor (and former US district attorney) Edwin Morrow. Patriotic songs and a flyover by two government planes highlighted the event, attended by an estimated 20,000 from the tristate region of Ohio, Indiana, and Kentucky. The net proceeds of the event were turned over to the Red Cross.[32]

The CPL took on many other initiatives. It lobbied Congress to pass the Sedition Act. It supported the state legislature's German-language bill and denounced Governor Stanley when he vetoed it. Reverend Hunt erroneously predicted: "He [Stanley] has made a blunder from both a political and patriotic standpoint." The CPL sought to reveal German atrocities committed during the invasion of Belgium. It tried to stop the distribution of German-language newspapers emanating from Cincinnati, and it encouraged people and businesses to fly the US flag. It wanted to "instill fear in the hearts of pro-Germans."[33]

Germans were not the CPL's only enemy. Toward the end of the war it expanded its list of enemies to anarchists and Bolsheviks, who had taken over in revolutionary Russia. It also supported stronger immigration laws to keep out those people it considered undesirable.[34]

While acting peacefully in many ways, the CPL also had a dark side. Its members severely beat a Cincinnati pacifist preacher, Reverend Bigelow, and helped spy on a group of men of German heritage, three of whom were later convicted on sedition charges and spent time in federal prison. (The Bigelow and so-called Schoberg cases, as well as other repressive CPL actions, are examined in more detail in chapter 4.)

The CPL received moral support from other parts of Kentucky. The *Louisville Courier-Journal* approved of its actions: "Theirs is the kind of work that is needed in every American city."[35]

Another group that sought out enemy aliens, pro-Germans, dissenters, and the like was a national organization with members in Kentucky: the American Patriotic League. The APL was the brainchild of Chicago businessman Albert Briggs. When it became apparent that the United States was going to war, Briggs first offered support to the Chicago office of the Department of Justice's (DOJ's) Bureau of Investigation. Then he reached out to DOJ officials in Washington and assured them that he could provide volunteers in Chicago—and across the country—to help the Bureau of Investigation root out America's enemies. The bureau sanctioned Briggs's idea of the APL and used it as a quasi-legal organization to increase its ability to track down alleged miscreants. The organization eventually established a Washington office, where two other codirectors of the APL worked in concert with federal officials. They created a "web" of informants along geographic and industry lines. A hierarchy consisting of chiefs, captains, lieutenants, and operatives existed, with the latter primarily remaining secret.[36]

Over the course of the war, the APL sought out people of German heritage, labor groups such as the Industrial Workers of the World (Wobblies), enemy spies, war dissenters, draft dodgers, and other "slackers" who failed to support the United States sufficiently. At its peak, an estimated 250,000 APL volunteers across the country spied on their fellow citizens, sometimes taking the law into their own hands despite reminders by the Bureau of Investigation that APL members were not government agents; it cautioned the APL to simply pass along information to bureau agents for action. The APL obtained leads from ordinary citizens and organizations; many requests for APL investigations came from county draft boards.

Much about the APL's activities in individual states remains unknown today because National Archives personnel decided to cull state records except for those from New York, North Carolina, Arkansas, California, and Kansas. Nevertheless, some glimpses of APL activity in Kentucky can be garnered.

The state head, or inspector, of the APL was Lexington lawyer Richard C. Stoll. Stoll was, among other things, a member of the University of Kentucky (UK) Board of Trustees and chair of the committee on public safety for the Kentucky Council of Defense (KCD). Stoll oversaw the APL's secret, quasi-military state organization, with chiefs in each county. Prominent members included KCD member Dr. S. R. Collier representing Morgan County, coal man E. O. Cox of Harlan County, KCD member William Cochran of Mason County, Frank Bataille of Fayette County, Professor George T. Ragsdale representing Louisville, and attorney J. Van Norman representing Jefferson County.[37]

The APL's official historian, Emerson Hough, wrote about the league's actions in Kentucky in his general history titled *The Web*. For example, he described APL activity in Louisville, where Professor Ragsdale led the effort. A graduate of the University of Chicago and a teacher at Louisville Male High School, Ragsdale had developed an interest in police and prison work. Instructing his network to operate "under cover," Ragsdale and his group provided the DOJ with more than 700 reports on suspected malfeasants. These included 89 cases of "disloyalty and sedition" and 308 cases of selective service violations. According to Hough, nine men went to prison as a result.[38]

In a March 1918 speech to the Louisville Advertising Club, Ragsdale asserted that, at the beginning of the war, a large group of German reservists had drilled in the basement of a Louisville building and that German agents visited the city every six weeks. However, he also "professed but little knowledge of the spy system of activities." When queried by reporters about his assertions, he declined to give more information, claiming that to do so would "defeat the purposes of the Government."[39]

When Ragsdale resigned his position at the APL, attorney J. Van Norman took over and made its existence public in August 1918. Acknowledging that Louisville had hundreds of APL members, Norman called for citizens to report "all cases of disloyalty, or violation of any of the Government laws or regulations, especially cases of slackers." He added, however, that anonymous letters would be ignored, "as all true Americans will give their names in order to aid their Government." APL historian Hough noted that, under Norman's leadership, the Louisville APL grew from 400 members to around 700 by the time of the armistice in November 1918.[40]

The APL in other parts of the state reported mixed results. In Lexington it handled 405 investigations, primarily for the local and district draft boards. Hough reported: "There were only thirty cases of disloyalty and sedition investigated, and forty cases of word-of-mouth propaganda." Since Marion County had "no foreign element," APL officials there had very little to report and merely "caution[ed] a few of our citizens as to the bad results of opposition to the United States in the war." Somerset officials reported that they "didn't stop when the Armistice was signed, but kept watching everything and giving the Government the best that was in us."[41]

The APL's day in the sun came with its famous "slacker raids," when members across the country helped round up draft dodgers. These raids originated in Minneapolis in March 1918 and picked up steam as the summer approached. Most large cities experienced them. In Kentucky, raids took place in Louisville and Lexington. Louisville's biggest slacker raid came in August, immediately after Norman announced the opening of the APL office. League members joined officials from the Bureau of Investigation and US district attorneys in rounding up thirty-five men who could not produce their draft registration cards, which were required to be carried at all times. The raid turned out to be a search for red herrings; all the detainees were later released when they produced proof that they had registered.[42]

In Lexington the slacker raid focused on the Kentucky Association Thoroughbred racetrack. There, county and city police, assisted by APL members, apprehended a dozen men. Unable to produce their draft cards, the men were taken to the courthouse and detained until they provided proof of draft registration.[43]

The culmination of the APL slacker raids occurred in New York City. On September 3 APL agents fanned across the city for three days, apprehending and detaining thousands of men in what some commentators called a gross violation of civil liberties. Despite some bad publicity because of the slacker raids, the APL could point to some national successes: unlike the Louisville raid, which was unfruitful, "by the end of the war, APL raids had netted forty thousand [draft] delinquents for the War Department."[44]

In his analysis of the group's work, Kentucky APL head Stoll observed: "There was no man or set of men anywhere who did better service during the war than the members of the American Protective League. Their work was done quietly and efficiently." Louis Flinn, the special agent in charge of the Louisville office of the Bureau of Investigation, cited the APL's great assistance to the bureau. Noting that the league's investigations section included "some of the most prominent of Kentucky's business men and professionals," Flinn asserted that the APL's "loyal, efficient and successful work was of concrete benefit to our nation in its war for freedom."[45]

The activities of the Citizens' Patriotic League and the American Protective League were apparently unopposed in Kentucky. Kentuckians were expected to "do their duty" to support the war effort, and this included being vigilant against all dissent and "slackerism." In only a few instances did Kentuckians cross the boundary between legal vigilance and extralegal vigilantism (as in the Bigelow case, discussed in a later chapter), but they came nowhere near the violence meted out in the famous case of Robert Prager, a German American miner who was lynched in Illinois.[46]

Not all groups in Kentucky came together to hunt down German "enemies," find slackers, and report people who opposed the war. Indeed, most groups were formed to help the domestic war effort in a positive way. For example, they provided support for the Red Cross and to the Savings Bond and War Stamp campaigns. Some even banded together to form distinctive military medical units.

The base hospital movement across the nation originated at universities and hospitals and included physicians, nurses, and support staff, who ranged from hospital orderlies, ambulance drivers, and stretcher bearers to cooks, bakers, and laundrymen. Hospital units supplemented previously established base hospitals. The US Army surgeon general, William Gorgas, turned to the Red Cross for assistance in forming fifty base hospital and other supplementary units.[47] Three medical units formed in Kentucky: Hospital Unit D, the Lindenberger Unit; Base Hospital No. 40, the Barrow Unit; and Base Hospital No. 59, the Abell Unit.

Unit D, the Lindenberger Unit from Louisville, was the first hospital group formed in the state. Dr. Lewis McMurtry recommended a Medical Reserve Corps officer posted at Fort Thomas, Major Irvin Lindenberger, to lead it. McMurtry's background lent weight to the nomination because he was well known and well regarded. A Louisville physician, he was a former president of the American Medical Association and member of the National Committee of the Red Cross. Lindenberger was put in charge of a hospital unit staffed primarily by professionals from the Louisville City Hospital. The Louisville chapter of the Red Cross collected supplies for the Lindenberger Unit, and the Frankfort chapter of the National League for Women's Service donated more materials. Twelve officers, twenty-one nurses, and forty-four enlisted personnel mobilized on December 19, 1917, and went to Fort McPherson, Georgia, for training.

In mid-February 1918 the Lindenberger Unit sailed for Europe and arrived in France on March 10, 1918, after a stop in England. The unit proceeded to Vichy and was attached to Base Hospital No. 1, a group from Bellevue Hospital in New York City. Major Lindenberger, the nurses, and the enlisted men worked initially in Rouen and then returned to Vichy. The unit stayed in France until April 1919; once it arrived back in the United States, the unit was mustered out at Camp Taylor in Louisville in May.[48]

In addition to the Lindenberger Unit, Louisville raised another medical group: Base Hospital No. 59, the Abell Unit. It was originally the idea of A. T. McCormack of Bowling Green, who had been transferred to the Panama Canal Zone as chief medical officer. The hospital unit was commanded by Dr. Irvin Abell, a prominent Louisville physician. It recruited more than thirty doctors and nearly a hundred nurses, most of them members of the Kentucky Medical Association. After the officers and enlisted men trained at Camp Shelby, Mississippi, the unit shipped off to France, arriving by October 1 at Rimaucourt, where it set up Base Hospital No. 59. The nurses, who had mobilized in New York City and had arrived at Rimaucourt a few days earlier, joined them there.

The Abell Unit formed part of a hospital center that eventually comprised five base hospitals that could house up to 10,000 patients in wards and tents. The unit's own complex included hospital wards, wooden barracks, and a laundry; a mess hall prepared regular, light, and special diets for the unit's members and their charges. On arrival, fifty of the unit's nurses went immediately to other base hospitals, leaving only fifty to serve in Rimaucourt, but by mid-October, Base Hospital No. 59 had created a capacity of 2,000 beds in wooden buildings and tents and had started treating victims of gas attacks, patients with the flu, and soldiers with arthritis due to exposure. The largest number of patients in the hospital at any one time was 1,660; half were victims of gas attacks, mainly mustard and phosgene gases. The official report of the base hospital noted that "Armistice Day, November 11th, was joyfully and 'uproariously' celebrated, prayerfully by some, tearfully by some, and thankfully by all." The unit lost three members—a nurse and two enlisted men—from pneumonia during the Spanish flu epidemic that struck the world in the fall of 1918.[49]

Lexington's Base Hospital No. 40 was sponsored by Good Samaritan Hospital and led by physician David Barrow, who had also been recommended by Dr. McMurtry. By October 1917, the unit consisted of 23 physicians, 66 nurses, and more than 150 enlisted men, primarily from central Kentucky. Theirs was a diverse, fascinating group. Among the first recruits was Curry Breckinridge, the sister of *Lexington Herald* editor Desha Breckinridge; she died, however, before the group left for the war. Another Barrow Unit recruit was John Marsh, a young legislative reporter and sports editor for the *Lexington Leader*, who would later marry Margaret Mitchell, the author of *Gone with the Wind*. While at Camp Taylor and in England, Marsh sent letters to a former *Leader* editor giving news of the unit.[50]

A Transylvania University graduate from Hindman in Knott County, Josiah H. Combs joined and eventually wrote a book chronicling the Barrow Unit's efforts: *The Siege of Sarisbury Court*. Combs would eventually earn a

PhD from the Sorbonne and become a noted professor and expert on folklore songs and ballads. John McClintock (a brother of Alexander McClintock, who received a medal while serving as a Canadian soldier) also joined the unit. So did Harvard graduate and millionaire horseman Louis Lee Haggin of Mt. Brilliant farm in Lexington. Although he was above the draft age, Haggin joined as a private; he was eventually commissioned a lieutenant in the Sanitary Corps and served as the unit's medical supply officer.[51]

While awaiting mobilization orders in Lexington, the Barrow Unit worked with the Red Cross to gather supplies. Then the doctors and nurses went to various camps for training; for example, on March 1, 1918, the enlisted men proceeded to Camp Taylor in Louisville. In July the unit landed in England and was posted to Sarisbury Court in the southern county of Hampshire, near the major port city of Southampton. Dominated by a large manor house, Sarisbury Court became one of the largest base hospitals in England. Because the hospital buildings were still under construction, Barrow Unit members were initially scattered throughout Britain to work in other facilities. By mid-September, the hospital was ready for patients, and the Barrow Unit eventually oversaw a thousand-bed facility that operated until March 1919. Several unit members also had temporary duty in base and evacuation hospitals in France. At the end of March the Barrow Unit returned home, where its members were feted in Lexington and demobilized at Camp Taylor in Louisville.[52]

In sum, more than 400 people in the three Kentucky medical groups provided much-needed support for US troops sent abroad.

The state's medical units demonstrated Kentuckians' willingness to share in the burden of serving "over there." Others who were unable to go abroad to serve their country could contribute while remaining at home. The organization that benefited most from people's willingness to serve at home was the American Red Cross. Officially chartered by Congress in 1900 to provide aid to wounded military, the American Red Cross grew exponentially. Chapters sprang up in many small towns across the country, and Kentucky was no exception.[53]

The first Red Cross chapter in Kentucky was formed in Lexington in March 1917. The organization grew quickly. In May 1917 the American Red Cross appointed Frank C. Greene of Carrollton as its Kentucky director. Within six months, chapters existed in nearly every county—an impressive growth rate in a state with 120 counties. A lawyer, legislator, virulent prohibitionist, and preparedness advocate, Greene oversaw the creation of a Red Cross office in Lexington.

Initially Kentucky was split into two Red Cross reporting sections, with chapters east of the Louisville & Nashville Railroad reporting to Cleveland-

Red Cross poster for Bourbon County.

based Lake Division head James R. Garfield (son of President Garfield and a former secretary of the interior), while chapters west of the railroad reported to St. Louis–based Southwestern Division head George Simmons. By December 1917, however, all Kentucky chapters reported to Garfield's Lake Division.[54]

In recognition that Lexington could lay claim to Kentucky's first Red Cross chapter, a conference of all chapters took place there in August 1917. More than 400 representatives attended. Frank Greene supervised the conference, which featured speakers such as Lieutenant Governor James Black, division heads Garfield and Simmons, and Dr. David Barrow. Black admitted he knew nothing about the Red Cross until being apprised of its work by Greene, but he believed Kentuckians would do their share to help alleviate suffering and hardship during the war, as they had during previous conflicts.[55]

National Red Cross official James G. Blaine Jr., son of a former secretary of state, addressed the predominantly female crowd, outlining the work of the Red Cross. He underscored its spectacular growth from about 22,000 members in 200 chapters nationally at the beginning of 1917 to approximately 3,000 chapters with more than 3 million members just eight months later (at the time of the conference). He explained that much of the Red Cross's work was done abroad, serving not only the American soldiers who were beginning to pour into France but also the French people. Harriett Anderson of Louisville's chapter spoke about the organization's civilian relief efforts locally, as well as efforts to help elsewhere in the state. Subsequent reports from local chapters underscored what communities were doing to support the organization.[56] The Lexington Red Cross conference revealed how quickly and effectively Kentuckians rallied to support the war.

One example of the growth of the Red Cross can be seen in Scott County, Kentucky. Within a few weeks of the US declaration of war, women in the county seat of Georgetown spurred a movement to create a Red Cross chapter. By mid-June 1917, the county had a chapter with officers, an executive committee, and a large group of more than fifty male and female trustees. Local commonwealth's attorney Victor Bradley led the chapter in this mostly rural county, and it initially raised $2,700. Some critics deemed this effort "slacker" (the ultimate home-front epithet), so the chapter planned a new campaign to raise $10,000. Group work also began immediately, focusing on making bandages at the new Red Cross headquarters above a local doctor's office. The chapter gave the bandages to the new Barrow Unit organizing in Lexington, which included a Scott County doctor and two nurses. The chapter eventually contributed hospital supplies and patient clothing to the unit, and it supplied hospital and refugee garments to the American Red Cross.[57]

In December 1917 Edwin Morrow, the Republican gubernatorial candidate who had lost the 1915 election by less than 500 votes, addressed a large crowd at the Georgetown opera house, where he spoke about "the Red Cross and the War." His appearance was intended to help increase Scott County Red Cross membership to 3,600, part of a campaign to boost nationwide membership to 10 million. A week later the *Georgetown Times* reported 350 new members in the chapter. More than 300 young people also formed a Junior Red Cross group under the directorship of Mrs. Townes R. Leigh, with the strong support of local school superintendent Mary Bradley.[58]

Although its administration was centered in the county seat of Georgetown, the work of the Scott County Red Cross chapter spread throughout many small settlements such as Stamping Ground, Great Crossing, Newtown, Sadieville, and Oxford. Its work expanded beyond medical supplies. A large number of knitters—including the nuns and students of Cardome Academy—made scarves, sweaters, and other items. The chapter created a Home Service section that assisted Scott County's military families with financial, legal, and social services. Eventually, the county raised over $44,000 for the Red Cross from donations, membership dues, and an auction.[59] It was a most impressive contribution from a primarily agricultural county with modest resources.

The Scott County Red Cross chapter typifies what happened in many Kentucky counties as the organization grew rapidly across the state. Extensive reports from several county chapters can be found in a postwar publication,

Kentucky in the World War, 1917–1919. The reports range from Boyd County in the east, to Pulaski and Knox Counties in the south, to Webster and Fulton Counties in the west.[60]

Boyd County's efforts centered in the county seat of Catlettsburg and in its main city, Ashland. The county's population was just 35,000, but more than 10,000 people joined the Red Cross. The Second National Bank of Ashland donated four rooms for Red Cross use. More than a dozen committee chairpersons coordinated their activities, which included finance, membership, sewing, surgical dressings, knitting, layettes, baby quilts, packing, and Christmas boxes. Citizens of all types contributed. Eighty-four-year-old Mrs. Vincent Calvin made "42 infant quilts from the cutting samples." Mrs. A. F. Morse of Catlettsburg "knitted 100 sweaters between her 91st and 93rd years, although partially blind." The chapter established a special committee to deal with the influenza epidemic in late 1918, and it financed a Salvation Army soup kitchen for fourteen days.[61]

One problem faced by the Red Cross was that people did not know what it was or what it did; they had to be educated. In rural Trigg County, the local chapter noted that it had "every sort of superstition, prejudice and ignorance to overcome" but believed it had done "a great work in giving the people a vision even though the amount raised in money is comparatively small." Actually, the chapter managed to sign up more than 3,000 members and raise nearly $10,000 in donations, a large sum for such a highly agricultural area.[62]

Throughout the state, stories abounded of people's efforts to contribute. These ranged from Judge Robert Worth Bingham's $25,000 contribution to the Jefferson County Red Cross to the widowed mother in Boyle County who donated for auction a handmade sofa pillow she had embroidered for her son (who had, unfortunately, died).[63]

Some of the chapters got quite creative with their fund-raising. In Fulton County in far western Kentucky, local businessman J. O. West conducted weekly auctions in Hickman to support the Red Cross chapter formed there in July 1917. He concentrated on auctioning local farm produce, livestock, and preserves donated to the chapter, but his efforts apparently went even farther. As reported later, West's "sales ranged from a bunch of green onions, contributed by a poor widow, to the local base ball park. Besides these Mr. West sold the Mississippi River, a flock of wild geese flying high overhead, and an old gentleman's whiskers." His auctions netted the chapter more than $1,200.[64]

A report by the Knox County Red Cross chapter documented the wide scope of its activities, noting that it was "indebted to almost every man and woman and child in the County, if not in a financial way, by their services in work-room and elsewhere." Apparently, this voluntary civic cooperation gave people optimism. The report concluded: "The citizens of Knox County have given liberally to all causes growing out of the War, but they have not been bled white. What has been done is only an indication of what can be done in the future." Likewise, a Pulaski County report asserted, "Material results are not the only evidence of the work of the organization; but it taught the people greater liberality, disseminated ideas of larger humanity, and its existence produced a general moral, spiritual, and patriotic uplift in Pulaski County."[65]

While the local Red Cross chapters continued to carry out their projects, the state leadership changed. After the August conference, Frank Greene's role was reduced primarily to adviser to the national officers, Garfield and Simmons, so Greene moved on in spring 1918 to work for the Bureau of War Risk Insurance in Washington. R. C. Ballard Thruston of Louisville took the helm and led Red Cross efforts in Kentucky. Part of an influential Louisville family, Thruston had graduated from Yale and worked as an engineer and geologist in eastern Kentucky for many years before retiring to engage in various business ventures. He served as the first head of the Louisville Red Cross chapter and eventually as assistant manager of the Red Cross's Lake Division. At the end of February 1918 Thruston transferred the Red Cross records from Lexington to a new headquarters in Louisville.[66]

Thruston oversaw a Red Cross drive in May 1918 designed to collect $900,000 as Kentucky's part of a national campaign to raise $100 million. The state doubled its quota, raising more than $1.8 million. Harlan County quintupled its quota of $7,500, while many other counties doubled and tripled their quotas. In all, 114 state chapters exceeded their quotas.

The campaign in Kentucky took on local color as people came up with creative ideas to raise money. With its "largest crowd ever" on hand, Shelbyville citizens witnessed a parade, participated in a benefit auction, and generally heeded a banner's advice: "Don't be a miser; throw in your change and help lick the Kaiser." Louisville's Majestic Theater donated its ticket sales for a day. Governor Stanley auctioned off two pounds of "White House wool," shorn from sheep that had grazed on the White House lawn as part of President Wilson's support of home-front activities (and as depicted in a widely circulated photograph in the newspapers).[67]

Historian Julia Irwin asserts that nearly one-third of Americans—adults and children—had joined the Red Cross by early 1919. Acknowledging that there were competing requests for time and money, she writes, "Widespread enrollment in the ARC was not inevitable." Although the Wilson administration and Red Cross leaders actively sought this positive outcome, "public interest in ARC civilian aid should be understood as a popularization of the ethos of international humanitarianism that had been emerging in U.S. culture since the nineteenth century."[68]

Kentucky's support of the Red Cross reveals an enthusiastic civic humanitarian spirit that spread into many of the state's tiniest communities. In addition, joining the Red Cross increased social activities in small towns, improved bonds among people, and seemed to boost morale. Kentuckians who could not join the military and participate directly in defeating the dreaded "Huns" could still do their part by supporting one of the major organizations involved in war work.

While the state was exceeding its Red Cross campaign quotas, other aspects of the war needed citizens to contribute as well. The United States required massive sums of money to finance the war. President Wilson appointed his son-in-law, Secretary of the Treasury William McAdoo, to oversee fund-raising efforts. Soon after the United States entered the war, McAdoo set in motion the first Liberty Loan campaign—an effort to sell $2 billion in bonds that would have a thirty-year maturity and pay 3.5 percent interest. The first campaign to sell Liberty Loan bonds opened in earnest in May 1917, offering bonds at a minimum of $50.

McAdoo intended to energize the public to buy bonds as a patriotic act. He asked prominent celebrities and famous poster artists, including Howard Chandler Christy and James Montgomery Flagg, to help. McAdoo traveled the country (including a stop in Louisville) to promote the campaigns. He relied on grassroots support; everyone in the country was expected to participate.[69] "Slackers" who did not buy bonds would be vilified. During a Liberty Loan campaign in Lexington in spring 1918, a warning appeared in the form of a slacker hanged in effigy. Dangling for several weeks in front of the courthouse, the effigy sported a sign: "Liberty Loan Slackers Beware!"[70]

To promote the bond campaigns, Kentucky was divided into districts. The eastern district, led by James W. Stoll of Lexington, president of the First National Bank, reported to the Fourth Federal Reserve District in Cleveland. The western Kentucky district reported to the Eighth Federal Reserve District, headquartered in St. Louis. Bankers played a prominent role in leading local campaigns.

Kentuckians were expected to raise $16 million in the initial Liberty Loan campaign. Despite some early organizational problems, nearly 11,000 subscribers in the eastern district raised $6.8 million. The western district had weak subscriptions in some of the more rural areas, but large contributions in Jefferson and Davies Counties helped boost the region to more than $15 million in subscriptions.[71] Kentucky met its goal in the first Liberty Loan campaign but would be asked to do even more as the war went on.

Three more Liberty Loan campaigns occurred in October 1917 and in

April and September 1918. After the war a final "Victory Loan" campaign took place in April 1919. Subscription figures for the Fourth District showed an exponential growth: the number of people giving and the amounts raised nearly doubled with each campaign. The amounts increased from $6.8 to $11.3 to $15.2 to $24.3 million, with participation peaking in the fourth campaign at 91,000 subscribers. Even the Victory Loan campaign, after the armistice was signed, raised more than $17 million. Figures in the Eighth District rose less dramatically. Sums of $22, $28, and $39 million were raised during the second, third, and fourth Liberty Loan campaigns, with participation going from 56,000 to 134,000 to the peak of 176,000. More than $26 million was raised during the Victory Loan campaign from 58,000 subscribers.[72] In sum, in the five loan campaigns, Kentuckians contributed more than $200 million to support the war effort.

Newspaper accounts reveal that the loan campaigns reached into small communities throughout the state. People of all ages helped. For example, the Boy Scouts of America played a large role in disseminating information about Liberty Bonds. Two Boy Scouts were credited with selling a $50 Liberty Bond to Secretary McAdoo when he visited Louisville. The Liberty Loan campaign was also augmented by a War Thrift Stamp program, which enabled citizens to purchase savings stamps in amounts as low as 25 cents. These were targeted at low-income families and children. All citizens were expected to help fund the war, and by buying a 25-cent stamp, they could "lick the Kaiser" (the stamps were licked and pasted into booklets). Even though it took some extra time in the more isolated counties in the state, Kentuckians for the most part met this challenge. It was their patriotic duty.[73]

While these groups worked to support the Red Cross and the Liberty Loan campaigns, others used entirely different skills to support the nation. A group of public speakers formed to disseminate information about those campaigns and other war efforts, such as food and fuel conservation, and the draft.

The Four Minute Men were the brainchild of Donald Ryerson, who began by organizing some Chicago businessmen to give patriotic speeches, initially about supporting the draft. Ryerson then convinced George Creel of the Committee on Public Information (the US government's information—or propaganda, depending on one's point of view—organization) to support a nationwide Speakers' Bureau.[74]

The Four Minute Men's speeches were commercials for the war, delivered person to person, long before radio and television broadcasts existed. The movement drew its name from the time it took to change the film reels at movie theaters, which were the Four Minute Men's primary venue. There, they could reach the large number of moviegoers, many of whom might be illiterate and thus impervious to the written word. Throughout Kentucky, Four Minute Men (and, on rare occasion, women) jumped onstage during reel changes to give short, enthusiastic talks about the war. Their talks were guided by biweekly bulletins from the Committee on Public Information (also known as the Creel Committee). These bulletins assigned the weekly topics and suggested how to approach them. They also gave general advice about effective speech making. The Four Minute Men were, in essence, government-sponsored spokespersons, volunteers in whom "uniformity was coupled with 'individuality and forcefulness of expression.'"[75]

Four Minute Men spoke in many Kentucky cities, towns, and rural communities. Richard Williams started a Louisville chapter in July 1917 and served as state director until February 1, 1918, when he resigned and was replaced by Davis Edwards. Williams and Edwards oversaw a state organization that included 76 chapters and 850 speakers.[76]

In October 1917 Williams turned over the chairmanship of the Louisville chapter to Marvin Lewis. Under Lewis, the chapter grew to 300 speakers who made more than 7,500 speeches to 3.5 million people from October 20, 1917, to January 28, 1919. The Louisville Four Minute Men made these speeches in "Theatres, Factories, Churches, Lodges, Labor Unions, School Houses, and Community Rallies." Lewis became the most well known Four Minute Man in Kentucky because of his concurrent positions as assistant director of the state Four Minute Men, head of the Louisville chapter, and member of the Speakers' Bureau of the Kentucky Council of Defense.[77]

While Four Minute Men were well organized in large cities such as Louisville, Lexington, and Covington, they also played an active role in smaller towns and counties. For example, Muhlenberg County had four movie theaters—in Greenville, Central City, Drakesboro, and Beech Creek. Four Minute Men chairman T. O. Jones, a Greenville lawyer, appointed men to coordinate speakers at theaters in the other three towns. In addition, "to keep us advised of country gatherings, where there are no picture shows," Jones created a committee of two men from South Carrollton and Millport.[78]

In Bell County, chairman John H. Chesney oversaw efforts in the town of Middlesboro and the county seat of Pineville, as well as in coal camps that had movie theaters: Logmont, Shamrock, Harrison, Gravity, and Balkan.[79] The fact that theaters existed in these small coal settlements demonstrated how popular movies were during the war years.

In Lee County, chairman E. A. Gaskell appointed speakers in eight towns and settlements. Movie theaters apparently did not exist in these small communities, because he reported a particular problem: "Our situation here in the Mountains is much different [than] in the large towns and cities," where there were opportunities to speak to gatherings in the theaters. He asserted, "In the Mountains, we will have to make our opportunities: asking the people to gather at certain district school houses, etc." Gaskell opined that the speeches needed to be longer: "In the event of asking the people to gather this way, some of them walking a distance, it appears that four minutes for the message is inadequate." Yet Gaskell acknowledged that "there is a danger in too long a talk," and he believed a fifteen-minute limit was appropriate. He also believed that such "rural gatherings" should involve two Four Minute Men. He asked, however, for further advice.[80]

Among other things, the Four Minute Men helped persuade Kentuckians to buy Liberty Bonds; register for the draft; conserve food and fuel; support the Red Cross, YMCA, and other organizations; understand US foreign policy and reasons for entering the war; and accept the new federal income tax. The speakers encouraged civic participation and feedback.

Kentucky newspapers reported on the usefulness of the Four Minute Men. The *Mt. Sterling Advocate* acknowledged that the speakers at the Tabb Theater on behalf of a Red Cross campaign "did effective work, the total membership secured in the lobby of the theatre being 150." The *Bourbon News* in Paris reminded readers that "as these speeches are delivered 'between acts' on the film dramas, it is earnestly requested that the audience remain seated and give the speaker their undivided attention. The messages they give out are directly from the Government and are fraught with great meaning in these times of war." The speaking program proved so successful that a Junior Four Minute Men organization was created in the schools in time for the third Liberty Loan campaign.[81]

After the armistice, the *Lancaster Central Record* wondered what would happen to the organization. It quipped: "Now that the war is over, what shall we do with our four-minute men? A large proportion of the laity would like to have them returned to deliver the sermons every Sunday in the churches of our land." In fact, the Methodist Church decided to use the organization's example for its own upcoming event: "Laymen of the Methodist Church will be called upon to do the same work in the coming campaign as was done in the government four-minute men drive in explaining and arousing enthusiasm in the missionary celebration to be held in Columbus June 20 to July 7, 1919."[82]

Thousands of Kentuckians throughout the state's largest cities and smallest settlements heard the message of the US government, delivered effectively, personally, and entertainingly by their own friends and neighbors. The Four Minute Men undoubtedly had a strong, positive impact on Kentuckians' views of the war and the US effort. Kentucky's success in the Liberty Loan campaigns,

Red Cross fund-raising, and other wartime ventures owed much to the Four Minute Men.[83]

Kentuckians throughout the commonwealth participated in various groups that supported the country after the United States declared war in April 1917. The above-described activities were, however, just part of Kentucky's domestic war support. Volunteers also worked on registering men for the draft and on food and fuel conservation; these topics are covered in later chapters. One small group, however, had a special place on the domestic war front: the Kentucky Council of Defense. To this group fell the task of overseeing and directing Kentuckians' efforts to support the war.

3

The Kentucky Council of Defense

To prepare the country's economy for war, President Wilson created in late 1916 a Council of National Defense (CND). Six cabinet members served, headed by Secretary of War Newton Baker; the other cabinet members were Secretary of the Navy Josephus Daniels and the secretaries of the interior, agriculture, commerce, and labor. A seven-member Advisory Commission included prominent banker Bernard Baruch, labor leader Samuel Gompers, and Sears, Roebuck & Co. president Julius Rosenwald.[1]

The CND's mandate was economic: to collect data and investigate how to produce the goods necessary for war. Under the leadership of George Porter, a Yale graduate from a wealthy Chicago family, a State Councils Section of the CND would act as a clearinghouse for information about national and state war-support programs.[2]

The council moved quickly. On April 9, 1917, Secretary of War Baker encouraged all governors to create state councils of defense. Governor Augustus O. Stanley invited about fifty prominent Kentucky men, representing Republicans and Democrats from each congressional district, to meet in Frankfort in late April to discuss the creation of this state council.[3] Governor Stanley faced a problem, however: the state legislature, which met every two years, was not scheduled to convene until January 1918. He would have to act without legislation in place and without a budget. These obstacles would hamper the council's work but not stop it. On May 4, 1917, Governor Stanley appointed a State Council of Defense by executive action, as was done in more than thirty states. This group included three men from each county and three each from the state's eleven congressional districts. About fifty of these men met in Lexington on May 18 to discuss what the governor foresaw as Kentucky's chief contribution—agriculture—as well as a Liberty Bond drive and draft registration.[4]

While Kentuckians were organizing, in early May 1917 the CND gathered state representatives at a National Defense Conference in Washington, DC. Conference attendees addressed the role of state and local authorities in supporting the national government, especially in ensuring the registration of eligible men for selective service. Governor Stanley sent prominent Louisville banker Embry Swearingen and the assistant state agricultural extension

Kentucky Council of Defense members Richard Stoll (left) and Edward Hines (middle) with University of Kentucky president Frank McVey (right) at graduation, 1919. Hines received an honorary doctorate for his work as KCD chairman. (University of Kentucky)

agent, Morgan Hughes from Bowling Green, to represent Kentucky. A few days after the conference, the CND began issuing bulletins to provide guidance and advice to state councils. For example, Bulletin No. 4 of May 15, 1917, requested that state councils cooperate in promoting the sale of Liberty Bonds.[5]

Meanwhile, Governor Stanley created a Committee on Committees to hammer out a viable council structure. The governor headed the committee, whose members included Swearingen and Hughes; Henry Hardin Cherry, president of the Western Kentucky State Normal School (currently Western Kentucky University); Lexington lawyer and University of Kentucky trustee Richard Stoll; Covington lawyer and Republican Party boss Maurice Galvin; and lawyer and Democratic Party official George B. Martin of Catlettsburg.[6]

The Committee on Committees eventually transformed into an Executive Committee and then into what became known as the Kentucky Council of Defense (KCD). Swearingen served as council chair; other members included Cherry; Stoll; Louisville attorney and president of the Brown-Forman liquor company, Owsley Brown, who served as council secretary; William Duffield Cochran, a prominent Mason County lawyer and businessman; S. R. Collier, a well-known West Liberty businessman and physician; Samuel H. Halley, a Lexington physician and tobacco man; and Robert E. Hughes, a prominent Louisville businessman. At the prodding of the state's labor leaders, the governor later added Sigmond Lee, an engine foreman for the Illinois Central Railroad at its Louisville rail yard and publisher of the *Journal of Labor*.[7]

The state council eventually met twice a month; its Executive Committee, consisting of Louisvillians Edward Hines, Robert Hughes, and Owsley Brown, met twice a week. Mimicking the national model, the KCD created a number of committees: Agriculture (chaired by Halley), Finance (Hughes), Health and Education (Cochran), Industry (Brown), Labor (Lee), Military Affairs (Collier), Public Safety (Stoll), and Publicity (Cherry).[8]

The new state council helped promote the Liberty Bond campaign, part of a national drive to raise $2 billion. Its other pressing business involved registering men between the ages of twenty-one and thirty-one for the draft on June 5, 1917. Although it was not in charge of these efforts, the new KCD helped promote them, prompting congratulations from the national council.[9]

KCD chairman Swearingen took on another task: to create county councils of defense that followed the same committee structure as the state council, and then to create smaller community councils based on school districts. In this manner, guidance from the CND would flow to the smallest communities in Kentucky. Swearingen received bulletins and advice from the CND, which he passed along to county council chairmen.

Swearingen partially succeeded. County organizations varied in size, and only a few had a full complement of nine members. Despite these limitations, county councils went to work helping to register men for the draft. Many counties held information sessions for drafted men that apprised them of their responsibilities and of the benefits and pitfalls of military service. The councils also advised men who had deserted the military, seeking to help them fulfill their duties.[10]

In mid-July Swearingen visited Washington to report on the state council's efforts. Believing the KCD to be a "thoroughly non-political body," Swearingen ascribed the council's difficulties to a lack of funding. Kentucky's government remained strained, he reported, "deeply in debt owing to an inadequate system of taxation." State "philanthropists" were "nearly exhausted" financially after the campaign to bring Camp Taylor to Louisville (covered in chapter 6). In addition, strong pro- and anti-liquor factions in the state's political parties hampered cooperation. Swearingen acknowledged that county representatives had been lax in their duties; he had sent letters to encourage activity. Dr. Cherry's tireless efforts had succeeded in organizing speakers in each county, but the

Kentucky press had not covered state council activities thoroughly. Little had been done to recruit for the army because most Kentuckians believed the draft would be a fair method of selecting men.

On the positive side, Swearingen noted that Morgan Hughes's Food Committee was "the most vigorous of all the Kentucky committees and carried on the principal work done in Kentucky." There were several reasons for this success: funding from the state agricultural department, local help from county agricultural agents, and printing facilities provided by the State Agricultural College (University of Kentucky). Good publicity had encouraged increased plantings, and the state's bankers had provided financing for farmers. No shortage of farm labor existed.[11]

When he returned to Kentucky, Swearingen tried to prompt more action in the counties. He asked county council chairmen to create local Soldiers' Business Aid Committees, consisting of at least six people, to help all servicemen "in managing the details of their private business while they are away from home, and to render them assistance in obtaining employment when they return." He recommended that these committees include a lawyer, a banker, and a "good business man" to provide free legal service, ensure that insurance policies did not lapse, and assist military dependents. Swearingen remained optimistic that the county chairmen could find "the best and most patriotic citizens" to serve on these committees. The KCD also commissioned a Louisville lawyer, William Thum, to create a *Kentucky Legal Aid Book* to guide county councilors in advising draftees and their families.[12]

KCD chairman Embry Swearingen remained concerned about the state council's relationship to other national war organizations. In July he wrote to CND official George Porter regarding the American Protective League (APL). George Ragsdale of Louisville had approached Swearingen about getting state council support for the APL, but Swearingen "judged [it] to be a 'spy' organization." Swearingen's "first impulse [was] not to have anything to do with [the APL] in any way," but Ragsdale had described the APL's connection to the Department of Justice, which gave the organization credence. Porter confirmed the existence of the APL, noting that it had over 7,000 members. He knew of the Chicago branch's work and believed it had "rendered efficient and almost indispensable service to the Government." Nevertheless, he agreed with Swearingen's view of the APL's relationship to the KCD. Given that the APL was an "independent organization sanctioned by and under the organization of the Department of Justice," he could see no reason why it should rely on state councils for support.[13]

Despite Porter's and Swearingen's reservations, the Kentucky Council of

Defense would cooperate with the APL. KCD member Richard Stoll served as the state APL director and created a network of county APL representatives. Besides spying on possible German sympathizers, the APL's main activity in Kentucky was a September 1918 hunt for "slackers"—men deemed not to be assisting the war effort.[14]

Soon after Swearingen's visit to Washington, the CND's field agent, Dr. James A. B. Sherer, completed a two-page report about the Kentucky Council of Defense. He began by noting that "Kentucky, as everybody knows, is a parlous state." Sherer believed that during his visit to Washington, Swearingen had "given us an account of local conditions which in the main is correct." Sherer had talked with KCD member Henry Hardin Cherry and concluded that the US Food Administration's view of "Governor Stanley and his associates" as "weak, undesirable, and impossible to work with" was "gravely exaggerated." Sherer believed the governor to be both able and patriotic, and although it was true that "the county committees of the [state] Council have been unfortunately constituted, it seems clear that this was not due to intention." Sherer deduced that some clerk in the governor's office had probably chosen "men of local political prominence" who had no real interest in war council work. Sherer also believed it was accidental that the "whiskey element seems to predominate in the formation of the county committees." Sherer concluded that it was "not necessary, therefore, to suspect sinister motives in the Kentucky situation." While noting that he had heard, confidentially, that Swearingen lacked "organizing capacity," Sherer seemed much more confident that the "intelligent" and "enthusiastic" Cherry would do well as head of the Publicity Committee. The Western Normal president was working on a statewide war conference to be held in August 1917, which Sherer believed would be very beneficial.[15]

Cherry in fact proved to be one of the most active members of the state council, working exhaustively on the war effort. As early as May 1917 he was busy writing to county officials to encourage more organization and activity, especially within western Kentucky's Third Congressional District in his part of the state. In one letter he noted that it was "important to impress the people with the fact that this country is at war and that it is a serious matter and one that concerns the liberty of our people." Far removed from the war, the people "failed to realize that this country is at war now and that fundamentally this country is now being attacked by German autocracy and that our liberties are at stake." Cherry also understood the two major and immediate concerns of the domestic war effort: food and financing. He believed "that possibly the most serious problem we will confront is the one that relates to subsistence. It is not only going to take bullets but bread to win the great battle that is now being waged by noble democracy and military autocracy." He believed Lib-

Henry Hardin Cherry (right), president of Western Kentucky Normal School and publicity chairman for the Kentucky Council of Defense. (University of Kentucky)

erty Bonds were a good investment but thought they should be bought out of staunch patriotism.[16]

When the United States joined the war, many citizens were unaware of its local implications. Given this lack of understanding, Cherry believed the state council's publicity efforts were essential. He spent a lot of time corresponding about the state war conference to be held in Louisville on August 17–19, 1917. After attending a conference at Chautauqua, New York, where the main theme was to "inform and to arouse" people in favor of the war, Cherry returned enthused about the Louisville conference, for which 8,000 circulars were printed and 8,000 letters written to encourage attendance. Cherry reported to the CND's Porter that the purpose of the Louisville conference was to "perfect strong organizations in every county in the Commonwealth and to launch a public speaking campaign that will reach every home in the State."[17]

Three hundred of the state's "leading citizens" attended the conference meeting held at Louisville's Seelbach Hotel, raising $750 to help defray expenses. The main result was a decision to hold a "Patriotic Week" throughout Kentucky at the end of September, during which full-day local conferences would promote enthusiasm for the war effort. The conference attendees wanted the citizens of Kentucky to realize that the country was fighting a "just and righteous" war. The state council hoped these meetings would involve a broad spectrum of interests in each county—schools, businesses, agriculture, women's organizations, and other "progressive men and women." Cherry characterized the Louisville conference as very "constructive."[18]

While the KCD remained unfunded and unrecognized by Kentucky's lawmakers, it continued to organize the state and drum up domestic support for the war. Embry Swearingen resigned in September 1917, when his son's tuberculosis prevented the chairman from spending more time on council work. In summarizing the KCD's work thus far to Porter, Swearingen asserted that about 60 percent of the state's counties were "really well organized." He reported that he had been working with the new federal food administrator, Fred Sackett, to coordinate efforts. Swearingen had also appointed Louisville lawyer Lafon Allen to chair a Law Committee to study other states' laws regarding their state councils and to craft a bill establishing the Kentucky Council of Defense. Swearingen had already consulted on this matter with Governor Stanley, who believed something could be done when the Kentucky legislature met again in January 1918.[19]

While preparations for Patriotic Week in late September continued under the leadership of Cherry, Governor Stanley appointed a prominent Louisville lawyer, Edward Hines, to replace Swearingen as head of the Kentucky Council of Defense. Born in Butler County in western Kentucky, Hines had worked as a lawyer for the Louisville & Nashville Railroad and for the federal Interstate Commerce Commission before returning to practice law in Louisville.[20]

Writing to Porter on October 3, 1917, Hines noted that his first official act had been to send letters to several county councils asking them to cooperate with their local Liberty Loan committees. He also planned to meet with Governor Stanley regarding several resignations from the county councils and lauded the state's new federal food administrator, Fred Sackett, for helping to ascertain the status of work in the counties and for "bringing about the resignations of men who have been inactive." Hines expected to visit several county councils in the coming week. He would give special attention to "organization of Soldiers Aid Committees, the introduction of courses of telegraphy in the schools, and the Food Pledge Campaign" beginning later in October under Sackett's leadership. Hines also regretted the lack of funds that kept the KCD from being more effective.[21]

While Hines was taking over KCD leadership, Governor Stanley proclaimed that the last week of September 1917 would be Patriotic Week. Cherry continued to work diligently on the project, claiming, "I am against the biggest job of my life. I will have to organize every county in the State between now and the 25th of September." Cherry believed public speeches were critical to the campaign's success because of the state's high illiteracy rate; people who could not read needed verbal communications to learn about the war. He focused on reaching rural communities, which he asserted accounted for 80 percent of the state.[22]

Cherry's efforts had a widespread impact. Throughout the commonwealth, 498 patriotic meetings took place, and 124 "leading citizens of Kentucky" spoke outside their counties. Patriotic Week activities involved 417 local volunteers and 105 patriotic celebrations that lasted all day. Attendance ranged from 75 to 5,000, and 80 percent of the meetings took place in rural counties. "Patriotic parades, flag drills, music by brass bands, quartettes, etc.," highlighted many of the programs. Cherry credited women, newspapers, ministers, Fred Mutchler (head of the state's agricultural extension service) and his district agents, farm demonstrators, county superintendents of schools, and many more. Cherry believed the week's events had produced excellent results; even counties that had not participated were planning to hold similar programs.[23]

In his first couple of months in office, new KCD chairman Hines worked with disparate interests to promote war work, ranging from the state's African American population to librarians to fraternal organizations such as the Masons. Hines also arranged for Sallie White Bruce, chair of the Kentucky Division of the Woman's Committee of the Council of National Defense, to report directly to him (Bruce's role is covered in more detail in chapter 8). Porter approved that idea: "Such a plan focuses the attention of the strongest men and women in the state on the same object and thereby strengthens the activities undertaken by either the men or the women."[24]

For the KCD's next big initiative, Hines and Cherry began planning a two-day state war conference to be held in Louisville in January 1918. Cherry had expanded the Publicity Committee and Speakers' Bureau to include key people working on war activities in the state. Among others, these included Sallie Bruce, Fred Sackett, Fred Mutchler, federal fuel administrator Wiley Bryan, chairman of the state's Four Minute Men Richard R. Williams, and state superintendent of public instruction V. O. Gilbert.[25]

Despite abysmal weather that paralyzed much of the state, the KCD held a statewide war conference in Louisville on January 15–16, 1918. Edward Hines presided; Governor Stanley addressed the audience, as did the attorney general of Great Britain, Sir Frederick Smith. Section meetings focused on war efforts stemming from national initiatives, with the Kentucky state coordinators of federal war agencies leading sessions on topics such as the Food Administration, the Fuel Administration, War Savings Stamps, and the Four Minute Men. Other sessions covered initiatives specific to Kentucky; for example, KCD chairman Hines led a session on creating county councils, and the director of the Kentucky branch of the American Red Cross, Frank C. Greene, led another session.[26]

According to both Cherry and Hines, the conference was reasonably well attended and had a positive effect. Cherry believed that although the state council had "put over a great program of action," they needed the state legislature to give the council "material support." Hines's only reservation about the conference's success was the speech by Dr. George Vincent, president of the Rockefeller Foundation and former president of the University of Minnesota. He found it to be "in too light of a vein," and it had been roundly criticized. Hines opined, "A considerable part of the address was a burlesque of the old-time 'spread-eagle' American orator reviewing the achievements of our country," an embarrassment in view of the presence of Sir Frederick Smith. (Vincent had been a last-minute substitute for Secretary of the Interior Franklin Lane.)[27]

Through early 1918, the Kentucky Council of Defense had mixed success. Relying on volunteers and donations, it had cooperated well with other war-support organizations and had sponsored two important conferences and a Patriotic Week. To become more effective, however, the KCD needed the support of the state legislature and funding.

The question of legislative support for the KCD came to a conclusion in early 1918. On January 7, 1918, secretary of war and CND chairman Newton Baker wrote to Governor Stanley, complaining that the Kentucky council had "been necessarily handicapped by want of funds and resulting lack of organization." Baker requested that the state council be put on a statutory basis. The Council of National Defense provided information and statistics about other states' council budgets, ranging from $5,000 in Oregon to $5 million in Michigan and Minnesota. Nearby Illinois funded its council at $25,000, while Indiana's budget was $50,000.[28]

To help spur the legislature, French army lieutenant Paul Perigord spoke to the assembly. Fluent in English after more than ten years of studying and teaching in the United States, Perigord had returned to his native France at the start of the war and joined the army. Twice wounded and highly decorated, he had been sent back to the United States to teach army tactics. He also proved to be an immensely popular war speaker; for example, 1,500 people showed up to hear him speak in Louisville, and another 1,000 were turned away at the door. Hines was told that Perigord spoke to the legislature "with great effect."[29]

Perigord traveled around Kentucky for a week, speaking about the war. Cherry arranged for him to speak at the large Rural Life and Rural School Conference and County Superintendents Convocation in Bowling Green. (Cherry also managed to get former president William Howard Taft to give the concluding speech.) Perigord also spoke in Lexington, Richmond, Covington, and Newport.[30]

On March 8, 1918, the Kentucky state legislature passed the bill officially creating a Kentucky Council of Defense, to be funded at $50,000 per year for two years. The legislature's financial support at a level exceeding that in most other southern states reflected the commonwealth's commitment to doing its fair share during the war. Governor Stanley quickly signed the bill, which gave the KCD a mandate to "assist the State and Federal governments during the continuance of the war." The bill gave the council wide-ranging authority to investigate anything related to the war; through its subpoena powers, the council could call witnesses and demand documents. It could also appoint special county representatives to report "treasonable acts or utterances." Other duties included coordinating all war efforts, including volunteer organization support, and providing speakers and printed material supporting the war.[31]

Describing the KCD bill as one of the "most important and serviceable acts ever passed by the Kentucky Legislature," a *Lexington Herald* editorial also pointed out that the bill gave KCD members "very great powers, powers that could, if improperly used, or used for any but the most patriotic purposes, work profound hardship and do grave injustice." The newspaper cautioned that council members would have to be wary of "citizens inflicting punishment outside the law" against pro-Germans, but they would also have the power to cooperate with local authorities to arrest those guilty of "treasonable acts or remarks indicating pro-Germanism."[32]

Judge Hines remained chairman of the new council, whose members stayed the same. He increasingly advocated stronger action at the county level. In January he had written to the county council chairmen, passing along CND advice on several matters. Among other things, he noted that county councils should not encourage people to send food to war camps, which were already well provisioned; instead, they should work with their county agricultural agents to provide mutton and wool, of which there was an appalling scarcity. Hines encouraged the county councils to publicize the extended deadline for military men to sign up for war risk insurance and noted that the CND would soon be sending 9,000 copies of a poster—"The Prussian Blot"—which Hines hoped would be properly distributed throughout the counties.[33]

County activities began to take shape. For example, Rockcastle County held a "war council" on February 25, 1918, at the county seat of Mt. Vernon. The war council divided into three sections—agriculture, livestock, and education—to tackle issues typical of rural counties.[34]

In northern Kentucky, Campbell County took a targeted approach when it sent pledge cards to carefully selected citizens and asked them to return the cards with a $1 contribution. By early March, 627 cards had been returned; the council anticipated that more than 1,000 individuals would eventually pledge. From this membership, the council selected ward and precinct captains. An executive board of nineteen men and a nearly full-time "service director," Benjamin S. Sharpless, oversaw the war-support effort, consolidating county endeavors to enroll shipbuilders, conserve food and fuel, sell Liberty Bonds, and help fraternal organizations such as the Red Cross, YMCA, and Knights of Columbus. The Campbell County council also sponsored a well-attended "patriotic meeting."[35]

County councils eventually played a major role in coordinating food and fuel production. They were also instrumental in enforcing the state's "Work or Fight" Vagrancy Act of 1918, under which all men aged sixteen to sixty (unless students) had to work at least thirty-six hours a week. This measure was aimed at solving labor shortages, particularly on farms. County councils also oversaw community efforts, which were often based on school districts. Community councils were asked to invite every man and woman in the school district to meet at the local schoolhouse to discuss local war efforts.

A glance at the Mercer County Council of Defense reveals a common pattern: scores of people were organized down to the local school district level in communities throughout the county. The all-male nine-member Mercer County Council of Defense had an advisory board that included both men—the mayor, county fuel and food administrators, farm agent, and Boys Working Reserve chair—and women—the Woman's Committee chair, school superintendent, and Red Cross chapter chair. There were separate chairmen for the twelve community council groups, each of which oversaw three or four school districts. There were more than forty county school district committees, each of which had a chairman and usually eight committee members. The five city school districts from the county seat of Harrodsburg also had a chairman assisted by eleven district members. All told, nearly 400 men served in the county council organization. The Mercer County Woman's Committee of the Council of National Defense had an equally impressive organization, replicating the men's council. Mercer County's support of the war reflected one of the most salient points about the commonwealth and the Great War: widespread civic participation permeated into even the smallest communities.[36]

Community committees had other practical goals, such as ensuring that the community's agricultural production allowed it to be self-supporting (by eliminating food waste and reducing food consumption). "Americanization" efforts also took place at the community level—teaching English to "aliens"; impressing on them "the great ideals of America, American standards, the value of American citizenship and its duties"; and helping people who wished to become naturalized citizens. Community committees collaborated with local organizations; for example, children's war efforts were coordinated through the Junior Red Cross. Communities supported fire and public safety efforts, ensured ample supplies of farm laborers, promoted Liberty Loans and War Savings Stamps, aided soldiers and their families, and coordinated the efforts of social organizations such as churches, fraternal groups, and clubs to avoid any needless duplication of effort.[37] Councils of Defense aimed to get as many people involved in the war effort as possible.

On April 24, 1918, KCD executive secretary David Morton sent a lengthy report detailing the council's efforts to the new CND State Councils Section chief, Arthur Fleming. The report described the state council's efforts to encourage county councils to support local draft boards, especially with clerical assistance. The KCD had also worked with the Associated Press (AP) office in Frankfort to send news items to local newspapers, partially at AP expense. It had also arranged for the Henry Ford and Son Company to deliver 100 tractors to Kentucky. The KCD's "Americanization" plan had been drawn up and would be put into effect immediately, and it had recently cooperated with the Four Minute Men to promote the third Liberty Loan campaign.[38]

Morton also sent the CND a copy of a news release regarding the KCD's examination of German textbooks used in the state. Stating that "in some sections of the country German Text Books contain material that is essentially Hun propaganda," Morton noted that KCD member Richard Stoll had started collecting such books for university professors to translate and for the council to review. As noted earlier, when the Kentucky legislature passed a bill banning the teaching of German in the schools, Governor Stanley vetoed it. Consequently, the Men's Auxiliary of the American Red Cross in Bellevue in northern Kentucky sent the CND a copy of its resolution condemning Stanley's veto. State Councils Section member Dorothy Pope replied that, "as there is no Federal legislation regarding the teaching of German in secondary schools, each state must regulate this matter according to its own best judgment." She sent the Bellevue resolution to the KCD, which dropped the matter.[39]

As spring came to Kentucky, the KCD turned its attention to the potential problem of labor shortages on farms growing much-needed crops. The council prodded county councils to place notices in local newspapers instructing farmers who needed labor to contact a designated county official, usually the county agricultural agent. These requests would be directed to W. D. Nicholls, a farm labor specialist at the University of Kentucky's College of Agriculture. The county farmers were also encouraged to seek the help of the Boys Working Reserve, an effort by the US Department of Labor to enroll young men aged sixteen to twenty-one in "some productive service" during school vacations.[40]

By late May 1918, the Kentucky Council of Defense had a new executive secretary, Maud Cossar, a former journalist for the *Louisville Herald.* She produced a lengthy report on the council's activities. The KCD and county councils had participated in the US War Trade Board's campaign to get people to buy domestic products instead of imports. The KCD also supported efforts to restrict unnecessary building construction, to conserve valuable labor and materials. In cooperation with civic organizations, it supervised the counseling of drafted men throughout the state on military issues, health and hygiene, war risk insurance, and other topics. To alleviate pressure on railroads, the KCD promoted motor truck hauling on short routes and, especially, the elimination of the empty haul. Through the county councils, it worked with Food Administration and Agricultural Extension Service colleagues to eliminate wastage during wheat threshing operations in the state. The KCD instructed the county councils on the new plan for the "Americanization" of aliens, which involved the teaching of English, the "inculcation of American ideals [and] customs," and the "dissemination among the aliens of correct information on the war, with special attention to America's part in the war."[41] In sum, the KCD administered and sustained a wide variety of war-support efforts under the direction of the CND, on its own initiative, and by encouraging initiatives from county councils.

The entire Kentucky Council of Defense met periodically to hear reports and to take action. At its May 28, 1918, meeting, the council decided to use its broad exploratory and subpoena powers to investigate the Reverend H. Boyce Taylor, a Baptist preacher in Murray, for alleged disloyalty (a case examined in more detail in chapter 4).

Various KCD members reported possible sedition cases. For example, chairman Hines reported to the CND that Louisville-born, Harvard-educated lawyer Herbert B. Ehrmann had been appointed a legal expert for the national Shipping Board. Hines believed that authorities in Washington should know that Ehrmann's mother and father were regarded in Louisville as "dangerously pro-German." Although the father was somewhat discreet, the mother was "quite vicious in her expressions of pro-Germanism and anti-Americanism." Hines had also informed the local Secret Service about the parents. He concluded that Ehrmann himself was "probably patriotic, but the father and mother, of course, are in a position to obtain from him information which might be used to the great damage of our country."[42]

The KCD continued to expand its presence and influence. In a move the CND found unique, the council decided to hold bimonthly meetings in various parts of the state and to invite county council chairmen from the surrounding area to attend. The first meeting took place in Lexington on June

25, with eight central Kentucky county chairmen in attendance. Subsequent regional meetings were held in Paducah, Ashland, Louisville, Danville, and Bowling Green. Nearly half the state's county councils sent representatives to these meetings.[43]

These regional meetings sparked additional county activity. For example, Livingston County in far western Kentucky finally expanded its domestic war effort with a call for mass meetings in each community school district on June 28, 1918. The Livingston council proposed many activities, including encouraging people to buy savings bonds and stamps, supporting the YMCA and Red Cross, growing crops and raising livestock while conserving food and fuel, aiding the local draft board, facilitating the enforcement of vagrancy laws and the prosecution of "slackers," and finding out who had contributed to various causes and investigating those who had "failed to do their duty."[44]

In addition to becoming more visible in different geographic regions, the KCD continued to expand its influence over target groups. At its May 28, 1918, meeting, the council addressed the issue of involving African Americans, and by July 1 it reported to county councils that a committee had been established to organize Kentucky African Americans for war work. The KCD enjoined the counties, stating, "this work should be systematically pushed and followed up, and not allowed to drag or die out, but to be an earnest, aggressive campaign for the duration of the war."[45]

On July 19, 1918, a group of African Americans met at KCD offices in Louisville to form a committee that would plan sixteen meetings throughout Kentucky to encourage African Americans to join the war effort. The committee also arranged a war conference for African Americans in Louisville on August 6 (covered in more detail in chapter 9).[46]

To help document Kentuckians' war efforts on the home front, the KCD appointed H. A. Gretter of Frankfort to be the state's war photographer. The council also worked with the University of Kentucky to publish an official biweekly newsletter.[47]

In September 1918 the KCD appointed Louisville lawyer Fred Caldwell its state war historian. His task was to compile information and assist appointed county historians in recording domestic and military contributions to the war effort. Caldwell developed a basic plan for the county histories that focused on two tasks. The first involved compiling the contributions of various organizations and efforts (e.g., fraternal organization work), Liberty Bond and War Stamp campaigns, federal agency efforts, and so forth. The second task involved completing a form for each military participant: a war record noting the service member's postings, promotions, awards, wounds, date of discharge, nearest relatives, and the like.[48]

In August 1918 the Council of National Defense reorganized, finally melding the work of the Woman's Committee into the State Councils Section and creating a new Field Division under the direction of Grosvenor Clarkson, a former reporter and publicist who had been serving as the CND's secretary. Having already spent a couple of months considering postwar reconstruction and readjustment issues, Clarkson presided over the eventual winding down of the CND's war effort. In so doing, he advised the state councils about the issues related to a demobilizing army and society's return to a prewar condition.[49]

By October 1, 1918, the possibility of an end to the war loomed. On that day, Germany's ally, Bulgaria, signed an armistice. Austria-Hungary did so on October 28, and Germany finally followed on November 11. Thousands of Kentuckians would return home, and the Kentucky Council of Defense would be asked to deal with their issues, as well as other enduring ones. The KCD continued to issue bulletins to county councils until March 1919. For example, on October 11, 1918, it called county officials' attention to the growing influenza epidemic. In early November the KCD passed along warnings from Secretary of the Interior Franklin Lane, "asking for no relaxation of efforts on account of the possibility of an early armistice." A December 2 bulletin asked for cooperation with the US Employment Service in "securing places for men released from the service."[50]

Besides creating county histories under the supervision of Caldwell, one last major act remained for the Kentucky Council of Defense: to sponsor a conference on state problems held on March 4–5, 1919, in Lexington.[51] When that conference concluded, the KCD's work was, for the most part, over, even though it continued to exist because of its original two-year mandate by the Kentucky legislature. On March 23, 1920, the Kentucky legislature gave the KCD a two-year extension "for the sole purpose of gathering, arranging and preserving the history of Kentucky's part in the World War." In 1922 similar legislative action extended the council's existence until March 1924.

Edward Hines continued as chairman until he died on January 31, 1921. He was replaced by Louisville's R. C. Ballard Thruston, who served until September 1922. Thruston was replaced by another Louisville leader, Emmet O'Neal, who served until the end of the KCD's work in March 1924, aided by remaining council members Young E. Allison of Louisville and E. H. Gaither of Harrodsburg. Along with Frances Ritchie of Louisville, the assistant state war historian, Fred Caldwell oversaw the production of 225 volumes of county histories, cataloging the 101,289 Kentucky men and women who had served in the military, including 3,315 who had died for their country.[52]

After a slow start, the KCD contributed extensively to the commonwealth's war effort. In addition to acting as a clearinghouse for information, the council took positive steps to assist other organizations. Chairman Edward Hines tried to ensure cooperation among all groups supporting the war effort. The council initiated its own activities, such as the farm tractor program and a review of nonessential construction. Given its widespread powers, the KCD acted with restraint; it led, rather than pushed, Kentuckians to support US war efforts.

4

Opposition to the War

During World War I, freedom of speech in the United States was often curtailed in the name of loyalty and patriotism. With help from the states, the federal government tried to suppress opposition to the war, which it interpreted as sedition. Government officials, however, struggled with the difference between freedom of speech and sedition.

Moving quickly after the United States entered the war, Congress on June 15 passed the Espionage Act of 1917. Under the act's terms, people were subject to fines up to $10,000 or imprisonment up to twenty years, or both, if they made "false reports or false statements" that might interfere with the success of the US military or promote the success of its enemies; attempted to cause or caused "insubordination, disloyalty, mutiny, or refusal of duty" in the military; or willfully obstructed enlistment or recruiting efforts.[1] To bolster this law, which appeared ambiguous and weak to some people, the following May the federal government passed "an even more draconian amendment," the Sedition Act of 1918, which forbade "disloyal, profane, scurrilous, or abusive language" about the US form of government, the Constitution, the military and naval forces, or the US flag.[2]

The federal government's efforts to enforce these acts involved major agencies: the Treasury Department's Secret Service, the Justice Department's Bureau of Investigation (BI), the US Army's Military Intelligence Division, and the US Navy's Office of Naval Intelligence. Eventually the Bureau of Investigation led the effort under its chief, Alexander Bruce Bielaski. He reported directly to US attorney general Thomas Watt Gregory, although the director of Gregory's War Emergency Division, John Lord O'Brian, and O'Brian's assistant, Alfred Bettman, usually handled sedition matters.

Historian William Thomas believes these three men—Bielaski, Gregory, and Bettman—were "moderate progressives." Their efforts to expand their federal agencies reflected Progressive beliefs that the government was responsible for correcting the country's problems.[3] These Department of Justice (DOJ) officials would review sedition cases brought up in federal courts in Kentucky, and their moderate Progressivism explains why some cases were prosecuted vigorously while others were not.

The Espionage and Sedition Acts were enforced. As historian Thomas points out, "between June 15, 1917, and July 1, 1919, more than 850 Americans were convicted of violating the Espionage or Sedition Acts." Americans feared these laws because, "just as significantly," they "provided the Justice Department with a tool for discreetly threatening vocal opponents of the war into silence."[4]

Kentuckians were no exception. In the words of historian Scott A. Merriman: "The Espionage and Sedition Acts in the Commonwealth were a mixture of repression, hysteria, and legal maneuvering."[5] Most Kentuckians—owing to either their own enthusiasm or "voluntary coercion"—supported the United States' war effort, but a few dissented publicly. Some were actively prosecuted, and no doubt many voices were discreetly suppressed as well. One of the more contentious sedition cases in Kentucky occurred when a Southern Baptist preacher from Murray in far western Calloway County questioned US participation in the war.

The Reverend H. Boyce Taylor was a prominent figure in the Kentucky Baptist movement. He was especially well known in the western part of the state but was also known throughout Kentucky and the southern states. The son of a Baptist preacher and a graduate of Bethel College in Russellville, he was pastor of the First Baptist Church in Murray. A strict conservative Baptist, Taylor decried Catholicism, tawdry entertainments, and the preeminence of the secular world. Strong-willed and outspoken, he wrote and published an influential newsletter, *News and Truths,* to promulgate his ideas. His convictions about and actions regarding the United States' role in the war made him a traitor to many Kentuckians but a man of conscience to others.[6]

Taylor's beliefs about the war stemmed from the biblical admonition to "render therefore unto Caesar the things which are Caesar's; and unto God the things that are God's" (Matt. 22:21). This scripture meant that allegiance to Caesar—the state, or secular government—involved obeying the law, paying "tribute and taxes," and praying for those in authority. Things that belonged to God included "every thing that pertains to conscience, soul, spirit, worship, heart life, religion and things eternal." Taylor did not believe the two duties conflicted, but he objected "when governments assume to speak for God or put the call of country above the commands of God." Because of these beliefs, he had problems with two important wartime organizations: the Red Cross, which he believed put men's bodies first before God, and the YMCA, which he believed put men's minds first.[7]

In *News and Truths,* Taylor flailed against the YMCA's prominent role in war work, especially that carried out at Camp Taylor in Louisville (a new army

H. Boyce Taylor, Southern Baptist pastor from Murray who opposed the Great War.

training camp, described in detail in a later chapter). Approved by the Federated Churches of America as one of the few government-sanctioned organizations allowed to operate at military camps across the country, the YMCA garnered a lot of attention and many followers. Taylor complained specifically that the YMCA preached little or no gospel, taught the universal brotherhood of man, and was "honeycombed with Unitarianism, especially in the North and East." Taylor labeled the YMCA "the greatest menace to spiritual religion in this country" because it provided moving picture shows, bowling alleys, soft drink stands, and Sunday entertainments, "all done in the name of religion and used by Satan as a very popular decoy to keep young men away from the worship of God's house," and all anathema to good Baptists.[8]

After the annual Kentucky State Fair in Louisville in September 1917, Taylor decried YMCA activities there. This included the sponsoring of addresses by the Louisville mayor, criticized by Taylor as "head of the Louisville Democratic whiskey machine"; a Presbyterian minister; a Jew; a former lieutenant governor who was a Catholic and a member of the Knights of Columbus; and "our Campbellite governor, fine example to soldiers if you want them to drink and cuss."[9]

Taylor disapproved of the YMCA and other groups for focusing more on soldiers' secular well-being than on their souls. Of the soldiers, Taylor wrote: "They are dying and going to hell by the thousands every day and we are wasting time and energy and money trying to make them comfortable the few hours or days or months that they live and letting them go out into eternal night and darkness and hell unprepared." Criticizing military chaplains who were "mostly men seeking soft places with good pay," Taylor called instead for Baptist missionaries to preach the gospel to soldiers "in their own tongues." This was "what Baptists should put their money in, instead of putting in it [*sic*] Red Cross and Y.M.C.A. and Liberty Bonds, etc."[10]

It was clear to Taylor that the spiritual should take precedence over the secular. It was clear to his readers that his definition of "spiritual" differed from that of the YMCA or the federal government, which gave that organization a privileged position in army camps. He even criticized a Bethel College classmate, William J. McGlothlin, for taking a leave from the Southern Baptist Theological Seminary during the war to work on food conservation issues. A future president of Furman University and president of the Southern Baptist Convention, McGlothlin was, in Taylor's opinion, stepping down from his "own higher work [of preaching] to one less important."[11]

McGlothlin had been nominated by Joshua Levering, head of the board of trustees of the Southern Baptist Theological Seminary, to represent the Southern Baptist Convention in the federal food administration work overseen by Herbert Hoover. McGlothlin found his experience valuable in influencing Southern Baptists' worldview and "attaching them afresh to the country and the world," given that they had a "sectarian, a sectional consciousness." He believed that having an "ecumenical consciousness would be an unspeakable blessing" to Southern Baptists.[12] Clearly, Taylor and McGlothlin—both prominent leaders in Baptist circles—held different views about the roles of Southern Baptists in the war and beyond.

Outspoken and influential, Taylor not only condemned individuals and institutions that supported the war effort but also decried war in general. He was a proponent of using international courts to resolve conflict. Taylor asserted: "War is anarchy against international law as truly as mob violence is anarchy against state law." He believed that "the officials of international courts are as much the ministers of God as are the officials of our own state or nation." He alleged that people were "going against the teachings of our Lord Jesus" when they supported war because Jesus had said in the Sermon on the Mount: "Blessed are the peacemakers."[13]

In November 1917 Taylor garnered more attention when he was chosen moderator, or head, of the General Association of Baptists in Kentucky during its annual meeting. There he was praised for his strong support of Baptist missionary work abroad and for his focus on strengthening Baptist Church finances. But when the association debated and unanimously passed a patriotic resolution, he absented himself.[14]

The First Baptist Church in Richmond condemned Taylor's absence during that vote and passed a resolution calling for him to resign as moderator.

A *Lexington Herald* editorial congratulated the Richmond church and called for Kentucky Baptists to "repudiate a man who dishonors them." Expressing a common sentiment throughout the country, it added: "The man who is not for the United States heart and soul, who is not ready to support every movement that promises to aid in the efficient prosecution of the war, who is not ready to make sacrifices for the honor and welfare of his country, is not in the true sense of the word an American citizen. He is in fact anti-American."[15]

The president of another Baptist organization, J. A. Burns of the Oneida Baptist Institute, suggested that Taylor be flayed. The *Adair County News* in Columbia reported on the Richmond church's action and described Taylor as the "notorious megalomaniac of Murray" who made "mendacious diatribes of personal honor and character." The newspaper averred that "such a man can be expected to be a traitor to his country, as well as a traitor to his church and his God."[16] Taylor's support base was eroding.

Although it had initially remained neutral about Taylor, the *Louisville Courier-Journal* also went on the attack, reproducing some of Taylor's own words from *News and Truths.* The newspaper denounced Taylor's writings as "un-democratic, un-Christian, un-Baptist, unscriptural, and unrighteous." It condemned Taylor as a "contemptible little bigot and silly fool who has persistently used his position in a great church to institute treason against the country that shelters him and to which he professes allegiance." The newspaper argued that the pastor should be not only under surveillance but also "under duress" by the government, as well as kicked out of the church.[17]

As criticism of his position spread throughout the state, Taylor used *News and Truths* to rebut his detractors, pointing out in January 1918 that in various editions of the newsletter he had said he was pro-American, loyal, and obedient to the law.[18] In the interest of fairness, the *Courier-Journal* printed a letter to the editor from one of Taylor's colleagues, W. M. Wood, pastor of the First Baptist Church of Mayfield, including excerpts from Taylor's self-defense in *News and Truths.*[19]

Taylor's exercise of his right to free speech seems innocuous today, but it engendered a great deal of controversy within the pastor's church and community and across the commonwealth. It also drew the attention of the federal government. In June 1917 Mr. Holland, an assistant clerk in the US House of Representatives and a Murray native, reported Taylor to the Department of Justice. Holland described the Murray preacher as "very pro-German in his sympathies and expressions" and said that on several occasions Taylor had "delivered anti-conscription addresses to his congregation." Holland asserted that Taylor had "advised all young men in the county to fight conscription," counseling them to register and then take action after they were called to service. On August 30 an anonymous "Friend of the Administration and of the Cause" from Mayfield also wrote to the US War Department, denouncing Taylor for expressing anti-American sentiments and suggesting that he be investigated and his disloyalty and unpatriotic conduct stopped.[20]

Given these two complaints, BI chief Bielaski asked agent M. S. Egan in Cairo, Illinois, to investigate Taylor's case. Bielaski wanted Egan to find out whether Taylor's remarks had been directed against the conscription law itself or whether the Murray preacher had counseled men against enlisting or obeying the requirements of the draft law.[21] The task of visiting Murray, however, fell to the bureau's Louisville agent, Robert P. Hobson.

Born in Elizabethtown, Hobson had attended Washington and Lee University as an undergraduate and law student. In 1917 he joined the Bureau of Investigation, where he would work for three years before becoming a Louisville lawyer.[22] He traveled to Paducah and Murray in mid-January 1918 to investigate the Boyce Taylor case. Hobson interviewed several community members, including the Murray postmaster, the owner of the *Murray Ledger,* the local Kentucky National Guard recruiter, the high school principal, the county medical examiner, and several businessmen. Hobson learned that Taylor had preached on "whether a Christian should go to war" at his church two days before draft registration day in June 1917. Several interviewees who had attended the church service remembered Taylor suggesting that men should register for the draft but ask to serve in a "non-fighting unit such as a hospital or cooking unit." If the men did not receive these noncombat assignments, they should refuse to fight. In addition, Taylor had encouraged his parishioners not to support the Red Cross or the Liberty Bond campaign. Hobson filed a lengthy report about the interviews and concluded by quoting several of Taylor's writings in *News and Truths.*[23]

His mid-January report was restricted to gathering facts, but in early February Hobson wrote to a friend in the bureau's Washington office, Robert Ramsey, stating that there was a good case against Taylor based on either the Selective Service Act or the Espionage Act. Hobson believed that Louisville's federal district attorney had initially been eager to prosecute the case but became less interested after seeing Hobson's report. Hobson noted that there was "a great deal of comment in the State on account of the failure of Federal authorities to act," and he urged prosecution "before the events in question have gone cold."[24]

Ramsey wrote to John Lord O'Brian, director of the DOJ's War Emergency Division, attaching Hobson's report and some newspaper clippings. Ramsey agreed with Hobson that a strong case might exist and that people in Kentucky were questioning why the federal government had not acted against Taylor. Ramsey asked whether O'Brian thought the facts warranted prosecution and whether he would advise the US attorney to proceed with an indictment.[25]

O'Brian's assistant, Alfred Bettman, apparently consulted with other DOJ lawyers because he received a departmental memo about the Taylor case in mid-February. The memo stated that there could be no prosecution under section 3 of the Espionage Act because that act had not been passed until June 15, 1917—after Taylor's sermon. Nor was there anything in the US Criminal Code that expressly covered the case. The memo reproduced several comments from Taylor's *News and Truths*. Noting Taylor's more conciliatory tone in the January 15, 1918, issue, the memo writer posited that "Taylor may have blown himself out, or he may have stopped on account of fear of prosecution. It may be advisable, therefore, under the circumstances to let the matter rest." The writer, however, believed that any number of passages from *News and Truths* could be the basis for an indictment and conviction if the DOJ chose to pursue the matter.[26]

O'Brian communicated his decision to BI chief Bielaski on March 1. Because Taylor was a preacher and had "apparently quieted down," O'Brian thought "no prosecution should be initiated." He asked, however, that Hobson keep track of the situation, so if there was "the slightest hint of Taylor resuming his activities we may initiate a prosecution." O'Brian believed there was ample basis to do so.[27]

Bielaski had continued to receive letters about Taylor from a variety of people, including Robert Y. Thomas Jr., the Democratic congressman from Logan County and, like Taylor, a graduate of Bethel College. The US War Department also wrote to the bureau chief. Responding to this inquiry, Bielaski replied that the decision not to prosecute had come from Attorney General Gregory. Bielaski also quoted from O'Brian's memorandum about Taylor being a preacher and becoming less vocal. Bielaski sent the same message to agent Hobson, adding O'Brian's admonition to keep a close eye on the Murray preacher so that if he resumed his activities, a prosecution might be started.[28]

The Taylor case would not go away. After receiving a complaint in early April 1918 from A. J. Campbell in Paducah, Bielaski again asked the Louisville office to investigate Taylor. Hobson went back to Murray and Paducah to interview people, including Campbell and V. A. Johnson at the Old Kentucky Manufacturing Company, the person who had initially brought up Taylor's behavior. The agent discovered that Johnson's complaint, which had been passed along by Campbell, was year-old news. Johnson was referring to the original problem: Taylor's sermon in June 1917. Hobson also met with another letter writer, E. J. Beale, proprietor of the Ford Automobile Works in Murray, whom he described as "one of the bitterest men in Murray against Rev. Mr.

Taylor." Beale admitted that Taylor had become quiet, probably owing to the advice of patriotic elements in the church.

Charles Wheeler, a prominent Paducah attorney and former US congressman, told Hobson he thought that not prosecuting Taylor was harmful and encouraged pro-German elements. Furthermore, Wheeler told the agent that someone in western Kentucky was spreading false information: several people had asked Wheeler whether the federal government was going to commandeer farmers' wheat supplies and pay them half in cash, half in Liberty Bonds. Wheeler believed this sort of rumor was pro-German propaganda that arose from Taylor's sentiments and remarks. Although he had advised Hobson against prosecuting Taylor when interviewed back in November, Wheeler had changed his mind, observing that people all over western Kentucky were in favor of legal action against the Murray preacher. Hobson noted in his report that several Paducah citizens thought that prosecuting Taylor would have a "wholesome effect."[29]

By late spring 1918, the newly reconstituted Kentucky Council of Defense (KCD) became embroiled in the Reverend Boyce Taylor case. The council had been given far-reaching powers in March 1918 by the Kentucky legislature, including the power to investigate war-related activities; it could subpoena witnesses and compel people to produce materials relevant to investigations. If an individual refused to comply with its subpoena, the KCD could take the case to the local circuit court. Accused persons who failed to appear at a hearing could be held in contempt of court.[30]

Responding to the complaints "received from many quarters" about Taylor, the KCD decided to conduct a public investigation. It called Reverend Taylor to appear at a hearing on June 13 conducted by KCD chairman Edward Hines and Lexington lawyer Richard Stoll, head of the council's Committee of Public Safety. Meeting at the circuit court in Murray, the hearing focused on Taylor's June 3, 1917, church speech. Judge W. A. Berry of Paducah interrogated five witnesses and then read into the record several editorials from *News and Truths.*

Believing that Taylor should be prosecuted for disloyalty, the KCD sent copies of the hearing transcript to the Louisville US attorney, Perry Miller. Miller replied that Taylor's June 1917 comments had been made ten days before passage of the Espionage Act. He asked Hines to give him any information about Taylor's disloyal utterances since passage of the Sedition Act on May 16, 1918.[31]

Miller's decision not to prosecute ended the sedition case against the Reverend H. Boyce Taylor. The Murray preacher remained quiet for most of 1918, but when a flu epidemic swept through Kentucky toward the end of the war, he once again defied civil authorities. To combat the spread of the flu, the state Board of Health had decreed that no public meetings should take place, including church services. Taylor opposed this decree and was eventually tried and twice fined $100. He refused to pay and spent a couple of weeks in jail until helpful parishioners paid his fines.[32]

The KCD also encouraged its county councils of defense to be on the lookout for disloyalty. Judge W. L. Prince of the Marshall County Council of Defense initiated such a complaint, charging the Reverend John Grady of Gilbertsville with "delivering a forged and incorrect finding to the Local Exemption Board." KCD chairman Hines went to the county seat in Benton to investigate. Grady had filed a letter with the local draft board, purportedly from Camp Taylor authorities, castigating the board for calling up Grady's son and sending him to the camp, despite the fact that he suffered from half a dozen medical ailments. Testimony revealed that the letter submitted by Grady had been typed on the same typewriter as another letter by Grady. Faced with this apparent fraud, the KCD believed a "clear case" could be made against the reverend and passed the transcript of the proceeding on to US attorney Miller. Miller found there was no basis to prosecute Grady under federal law.[33]

The KCD investigated various people but reported to the Council of National Defense that none had been prosecuted. Nevertheless, the report concluded: "In some cases where the facts are not strong enough to warrant prosecution such investigations have a wholesome effect. In many cases our County Councils have called before them men who had refused to support any of the war activities of the Government or to contribute to any war charities, and have succeeded in changing their attitude, and have also succeeded in that way in silencing some men who have been guilty of disloyal utterances."[34] Such was the dampening effect that existed domestically during the Great War.

While Boyce Taylor's sedition case and others investigated by the KCD ended with no legal convictions, a northern Kentucky case ended very differently. On July 4, 1918, seven men from northern Kentucky were arrested, brought before a state court, and charged with "treason, felony and misdemeanors." The case involved spying on the shoe shop of Charles Schoberg in Covington.

Believing that people were uttering pro-German sentiments in Schoberg's shop, the Citizens' Patriotic League hired a private detective firm in March 1918 to place a dictograph—a recording device—in a grandfather clock in Schoberg's establishment. The detectives took notes based on the recordings; their notes served as the main basis for prosecution when the case shifted to the federal court system.

In August a federal grand jury indicted Schoberg on thirty-two counts;

J. Henry Kruse and Henry Feltman, the other two defendants in this case, were indicted on fifteen and twenty-four charges, respectively. These charges included "favoring" the cause of Germany and Austria-Hungary, opposing the United States, and interfering with the military. Another four men were arrested and indicted on fewer counts; they were not tried and soon faded out of the picture.[35]

Schoberg, who had immigrated from Germany in 1857, had been a model community leader, serving as a police officer, police judge, and magistrate, among other posts. For years, Kruse had been the secretary and treasurer of the Bavarian Brewing Company and had served as an assistant county clerk for nearly two decades. Feltman was a very successful tobacco merchant and a prominent member of the Trinity Methodist Church in Latonia. Like Schoberg and many other people in northern Kentucky, Kruse and Feltman were of German heritage.[36]

Federal judge Andrew McConnell January Cochran presided over the trials of the three men. The brother of KCD member William Cochran, A. M. J. Cochran had been born in Maysville and educated at Centre College and Harvard Law School. He served in the US District Court for the Eastern District of Kentucky from 1901 until his death in 1934. US district attorney Thomas D. Slattery, another Mason County native and former county attorney, prosecuted the case. The three accused men hired prominent attorneys: Sherman T. McPherson, Stanley Bowdle, and O. M. Rogers. McPherson had been the US attorney for the Southern District of Ohio for seventeen years before resigning to take up private law practice in 1915. Bowdle had recently been the US congressman for southern Ohio.[37]

Schoberg was tried first. Based on his alleged statements, the prosecution sought to show that Schoberg "intended to aid Germany and oppose the United States." The detectives who had monitored the listening device in Schoberg's shop repeated several pro-German statements he had made and claimed that he sang German songs—"Lorelie" and "Vaterland." Schoberg took the stand in his own defense, describing how he had supported the war effort by buying Liberty Bonds and contributing to the Red Cross. Claiming to be Dutch, he stated he had never heard of the two German songs he had allegedly sung. Schoberg's two indicted colleagues, Feltman and Kruse, served as defense witnesses, which enabled prosecutor Slattery to focus on their alleged seditious actions as well. Feltman pointed out that he had spent over $45,000 supporting the war effort and added that his wife and daughter were Red Cross workers. He admitted that he opposed the war but denied any allegiance to Germany. Kruse denied making pro-German statements, although he admitted that Germany had some great generals.[38]

The jury took twenty-five minutes to deliberate before returning a guilty verdict against Schoberg. Next up was Henry Feltman's trial. Feltman had allegedly said that the worst outcome Germany could expect was for the war to end in a draw, supposedly proving that he was unenthusiastic about supporting US efforts. He was also accused of saying that poor people were being asked to do too much financially to support the war. His defense counsel argued that these comments were protected by his right to free speech. Schoberg and Kruse testified on Feltman's behalf, denying that their colleague opposed the war, but to no avail. Feltman's jury also took only twenty-five minutes to return a guilty verdict. The third accused man, Henry Kruse, fared no better. His jury required only twenty minutes to find him guilty.[39]

The three men were released on bond pending their sentencing, which came on September 13, 1918. Schoberg got twenty years; Feltman got seven years and a $40,000 fine; Kruse got five years. Their sentences were to be served in a federal penitentiary in West Virginia. The three men remained free on bond while their cases were appealed to the federal Sixth Circuit Court of Appeals in Cincinnati on the grounds that their First Amendment rights of free speech had been abridged.

The Sixth Circuit affirmed the convictions in March 1920, citing a Supreme Court standard set in 1919 in *Schenck v. United States.* In this famous case involving the Espionage Act of 1917, Justice Oliver Wendell Holmes had written that if the words uttered presented a "clear and present danger" that could bring about evil, Congress had a right to constrict such speech. Therefore, the court of appeals ruled that the defendants' First Amendment rights had not been violated.[40]

While the defendants awaited consideration of their appeal by the US Supreme Court, the Department of Justice reviewed their cases. Alfred Bettman, who had been a lawyer in Cincinnati, recommended the dismissal of all three cases. Because he was from the region and knew the reputation of the detective agency involved, Bettman looked askance at anything that agency did. His recommendation was not followed, and after the Supreme Court turned down their appeal, the men reported in December 1920 to Moundsville Prison in West Virginia.[41]

Analyzing this case, historian Scott Merriman notes that the defendants argued that their conversations had been private. Merriman points out that "the [court of appeals] decision seems unusual in allowing private conversations to be criminalized," but "privacy was not yet a right enshrined by the Constitution." (This privacy right did not gain favor until the 1960s.) Merriman also believes it was obvious the defendants did not manifest a "clear and present danger."[42]

In January 1921 Slattery, Cochran, and attorney general A. Mitchell Palmer all recommended clemency for the three men. President Wilson turned down the request. It was not until June 1921 that the new president, Warren G. Harding, commuted their sentences. In sum, in the words of Merriman, "All in all, three men were sentenced to twenty-two years in jail, after a total of seventy minutes of deliberation, on forty-four counts, all for private comments made in conversations whose only fault was being too close to a grandfather clock."[43]

The Taylor and Schoberg cases show the different paths alleged sedition cases could take in Kentucky. The handling of the cases seems inconsistent. In the Taylor case, the federal government demurred, letting state authorities in the Kentucky Council of Defense take the lead. In the Schoberg cases, the federal government took a more aggressive stance against the defendants, who, unlike Taylor, had not made public statements. In their private conversations, Schoberg and his colleagues had not even come close to the level of dissent expressed by Taylor in the pulpit and in his writings.

Taylor may have received favorable treatment because he was a preacher and because he had apparently curbed his public opposition to the war. He also had the advantage of speaking shortly after the United States entered the war and before passage of the Espionage Act of 1917. The statements by Schoberg, Feltman, and Kruse had come after a year of gearing up for war, when the strong movement toward absolute control and support for the war effort involved suppressing dissent, whether legally or through vigilantism. Furthermore, Taylor's case had been reviewed by the highest ranks at the Justice Department—John Lord O'Brian and his assistant Alfred Bettman, who would "later demonstrate a genuine commitment to civil liberties." The case of Schoberg and his colleagues went directly from state authorities to federal authorities in Covington, who began the prosecution. Despite Bettman's recommendation that the Covington cases be dismissed, they were not. Because of the timing of Taylor's remarks, his position as an influential minister, and the men who reviewed his case, Taylor was luckier than the Schoberg defendants.[44]

The Taylor and Schoberg cases were the most prominent sedition cases in Kentucky during the Great War. Historian Merriman discovered additional cases, including fifty-six federal indictments in the Eastern District of Kentucky and eleven in the Western District.[45] These numbers demonstrate that federal, state, and local officials worked together to quell dissent against the war.

Historian William Thomas has written that churchmen "played a vital role in shaping public attitudes and consequently were subjected to particular scrutiny" by the DOJ. This proved to be the case in eastern Kentucky, where seven Holiness Church preachers were indicted. An offshoot of the Methodist

Church, the Holiness Church, whose adherents were often termed "Holy Rollers," had a long tradition of pacifism.[46]

Clark Dixon, a Holiness Church preacher from Catlettsburg, was indicted for stating (among other things): "Whoever contributes to the War Chest of the United States was just as sure of hell as if they were already there." At his federal trial, Dixon was offered the opportunity to reconsider his comments. Judge A. M. J. Cochran twice asked Dixon to promise not to repeat his offenses, but the preacher refused to do so and kept quoting scripture. Exasperated, Cochran sentenced Dixon to a year and a day in jail. Dixon's subsequent attempt to obtain a pardon failed because authorities believed his position as a preacher made him influential and thus more dangerous.[47]

In April 1918 BI agent Linzy O. Thompson in Lexington received a report from the local draft board in Morgan County, which had received a letter of complaint from Yocum, Kentucky. The letter alleged that two "Holy Rollers preachers," Oliver Wilson and Kellie Dyer, had spoken "in contempt of the Government." Wilson had allegedly said he would not go to war, and neither should others. Dyer, too, had said he would not go to war and that he would just as soon kill an American as a German. In addition, Dyer claimed he had seen women in West Liberty wearing the "mark of the beast," representing the ten horns of the Devil (which actually turned out to be a Red Cross emblem). Agent Thompson wrote to the informant, requesting more information, and he asked the postmaster in Yocum for assistance. In July 1918 the American Protective League chief in Morgan County and KCD member Dr. S. R. Collier also complained about Wilson and Dyer. Thompson dispatched former Transylvania College German professor and BI agent R. E. Monroe to Morgan County to investigate.[48]

Dyer's case eventually went to federal court, where he was found guilty. Three people, including the master commissioner of the Morgan Circuit Court, wrote to Judge Cochran on Dyer's behalf (as did Dyer himself). With a wife and two children and another on the way, Dyer may have tugged at Cochran's heartstrings, or perhaps the judge was simply lenient in his interpretation of the seriousness of the offenses. He reduced Dyer's sentence from two months to twelve days, an action consistent with what he had done for others tried in his court for opposing the war.[49]

In their efforts against sedition, federal, state, and local authorities went to great lengths to track down alleged miscreants. Acting on complaints about another Holiness Church preacher, W. R. "Will" Hamlin, BI agent Monroe traveled to McCreary County to investigate. After arriving by train in Stearns, Monroe was met by McCreary County sheriff Frank Spencer. The two men traveled by automobile for five miles, then set off on foot for another five miles before obtaining two mules for the final ten-mile jaunt to Creekmore, deep in the mountains near the Kentucky-Tennessee border. There, Monroe obtained affidavits from several people who had complained about Hamlin.

The complainants accused Hamlin of trying to persuade men not to register for the draft and to desert the army. In addition, Hamlin had allegedly suggested that Germans were as good as Americans, that the kaiser was as good as President Wilson, and that government and army leaders were hell-bound. His accusers claimed that Hamlin encouraged people to defy food regulations by not following wheatless or meatless days and that he had called the Red Cross a "Blood Thirsty Band." The Holiness preacher had also advised against buying Liberty Bonds, as the war was "just a money war," and stated that people should give to the poor instead. Agent Monroe concluded this was an "aggravated case," beginning long ago and getting worse. He did not believe the complainants had any personal motives for their allegations.[50]

BI special agent Thompson in Lexington forwarded Monroe's report to the federal district attorney's office in Covington, which issued a warrant for Hamlin's arrest. After a trial in Frankfort, Hamlin received a six-month jail sentence, commuted to two months by Judge Cochran at the request of US district attorney Slattery.[51]

Two other Holiness Church preachers were tried and convicted at trials in London, Kentucky, presided over by Cochran. He sentenced Silas Saylor of Letcher County and L. H. Sturm of Pineville to serve three years in a federal prison in Atlanta for violating section 3 of the Espionage Act. Saylor had advised young men that they should throw down their arms and refuse to fight. Sturm had told young men about others who had refused to fight. After his conviction, Saylor persuaded former governor and current senator J. C. W. Beckham to ask the attorney general's office for a pardon; instead, his sentence was commuted to a year and a day. Sturm's sentence was also commuted to one year.[52]

Preachers of other denominations also garnered attention with statements they made during the war. A highly prominent Louisville clergyman and a strong proponent of socialism, the Reverend Dr. John G. Stilli of St. John Evangelical Church spoke against the war even before the United States entered the fray. He asserted that American rights were not threatened. He believed that businessmen who supported the war did so for their own profits, but workingmen would bear the brunt of the actual fighting. His attitude brought a rebuke from the *Louisville Courier-Journal,* which opined: "Dr. Stilli may be more ignoramus than Kaiserist, or more Kaiserist than ignoramus. It makes little difference which he is, his frothings will not capture the fancy of a sane American. 'Let business go to hell,' says silly Stilli. Business is not going to hell. Its chances are better than those of a parson who preaches cowardice and disloyalty."[53]

After the United States entered the war, Stilli preached against buying Liberty Bonds. He advised young men to register for the draft but to declare their status as conscientious objectors. One of Stilli's followers, John Breitenstein, tried to do so; he sought exemption from service on the grounds of "conscientious scruples against the war" and noted that the Sixth Commandment forbade killing.[54]

After a schism in his congregation, Stilli left St. John's and started a new church, the People's Church of Louisville. Then he changed his opposition to the war and claimed he had been a patriot all along. He avoided prosecution, but during the "Red Scare" that followed the war, the American Legion helped pressure Stilli to close the People's Church in October 1919.[55]

While Holiness Church and other preachers had religious beliefs that underpinned their opposition to the war, other people charged with sedition were convicted for simply expressing a bad attitude toward the war. Examples abound. In one case analyzed by Bettman of the DOJ, C. M. Nelson was tried for simply mentioning to two women that "France and England were beaten and that the war was caused by the money powers and should be brought to an end." Nelson was found guilty and sentenced to prison, but Bettman recommended (successfully this time) that his sentence be reduced to a year and a day.[56]

Elizabeth Watkins of Covington was a "foul-mouthed woman" who made pro-German statements and threatened that if anyone came to her house to enforce food regulations, she would meet them with a .45 pistol. After she was convicted of violating the Espionage Act, US district attorney Slattery and Bettman opposed a pardon. Deeming her "mannish" and belligerent, these federal officials believed Watkins was a threat to public morale and perhaps should have received a longer sentence. Historian William Thomas contrasts Watkins's case with that of other women who made similar utterances but whose more refined, feminine, demure appearance and actions may have spared them from conviction.[57]

Eastern Kentucky miner Walter Ward of Lawrence County "tossed several revolver cartridges in his hand" and allegedly said: "I would, if I could, put five of these in Woodrow Wilson's heart and about five or six of them in five or six others down there [Washington] and stop the damn war." Ward was convicted of threatening the president and sentenced to two years in the Atlanta federal penitentiary.[58]

Ester Vincent, an employee of the Mengel Box Company plant in Hickman in Fulton County, allegedly interfered with the sale of Liberty Bonds, suggesting there was graft between the box company and the US government in the sale of such bonds. In addition, he "made ugly remarks [about the] Red

Cross ladies of Hickman." These remarks stirred up the townspeople, and Vincent was transferred to Paducah for safekeeping. Federal judge Walter Evans sentenced Vincent to a year and a day in the Atlanta federal penitentiary for espionage. The charge against him stated: "when the United States is at war, [he] unlawfully then and there willfully, feloniously and falsely made and conveyed false reports and false statements with intent to interfere with the operations and success of the military and naval forces of the United States and to promote the success of its enemies etc."[59]

Other examples of sedition in Kentucky included the following: telling a man who worked in a munitions factory to blow it up; suggesting that Germany would defeat the United States; cursing America, President Wilson, and the troops and suggesting that the latter were "fresh meat"; and circulating scurrilous flyers against the war.[60] In some cases, authorities backed off prosecution. When agent Monroe visited Minerva Hill, another outspoken woman against the war, she called her family out to the porch and "began a tirade against President Wilson and the Government." She claimed the recent imposition of daylight saving time was evidence of Wilson's demonic nature, as "the Bible says the beast will seek to change the time." Despite her speech, Hill apparently avoided prosecution.[61]

In another case, a young woman at Transylvania College complained to federal authorities in Lexington that a German-language professor, Ernest Miller, had uttered disloyal statements in a class she was taking. Miller had apparently noted that German troops were nearing Paris, France, a statement that Mary Henry Thomas found disloyal. Agent Monroe, a former colleague of Miller's, believed this charge was "probably without ground." The agent knew the Transylvania professor well and believed Miller had "shown himself very loyal in war activities."[62]

BI agent Thompson received complaints about Lexington barber Barney Fotch, a naturalized German who had allegedly made pro-German comments. The case was made a bit more complicated when W. W. Fyvie also complained about Fotch—to Kentucky congressman John Langley—but when questioned by Thompson, Fyvie could not pin anything solid on Fotch. When he investigated further, Thompson could find no one who had heard Fotch make any direct comments in support of Germany. Thompson called the barber to his office, where Fotch proclaimed his loyalty and promised to make that clear in any future comments. Given this promise and the absence of any clear evidence of Fotch's pro-German sentiments, Thompson declined to pursue the case.[63]

The Fotch case provides a good example of the subtle ways federal and state authorities quelled dissent during World War I. According to historian

Thomas, the Justice Department's files "reveal that prosecutions were only the visible tip of a massive iceberg of federal suppression of dissent. Only a small proportion of the Justice Department's investigations ever resulted in an indictment or trial."[64] Admonishing people to be more patriotic or more discreet often quelled dissent.

After analyzing sedition cases in Kentucky that were tried in federal court, historian Merriman concludes that the individuals prosecuted were not usually anarchists, radicals, socialists, Germans, or members of the Non-Partisan League, as suggested by historians generalizing about opposition to the war throughout the country. The objectors were not always convicted. On the contrary, several were acquitted, and of those who were convicted, many served short sentences (less than a year). The defendants represented several social classes and included prominent members of Kentucky society. They managed to post bond and obtain competent legal counsel. Seemingly benign comments, however, had been criminalized—an assault on the First Amendment right of free speech.

While the official judicial system dealt with allegedly seditious behavior throughout the United States, there was nonjudicial activity as well. Vigilantes took action. If federal and state authorities could not quell dissent, then private citizens believed they had a right and a duty to take action, often to the extreme. This resulted in two well-known cases in which mobs killed dissenters. Miners in Illinois believed that a German American drifter, Robert Prager, was a spy. They dragged him from a house, stripped him, made him kiss the American flag, and eventually hanged him. In Montana miners also hanged Frank Little, a member of the Industrial Workers of the World (Wobblies) who had made antiwar statements.[65]

Vigilantism in Kentucky did not reach these extremes, but one nationally famous incident involved the Reverend Herbert Bigelow, a socialist and the well-known pastor of the People's Church in Cincinnati. A National Civil Liberties Bureau brochure portrayed Bigelow as a man who "combined his church activities with extensive public service in radical democratic movements," "fought privilege at every turn," was a reformer, and was an "advocate of popular control of government."[66]

Across the river from Cincinnati, a northern Kentucky group took a different view of Reverend Bigelow. Formed to root out dissent (especially among northern Kentucky's numerous German Americans, Catholics, and socialists), the Citizens' Patriotic League believed Bigelow was a traitor.[67]

In October 1917 Reverend Bigelow crossed the Ohio River and traveled to Newport, Kentucky, where he was scheduled to address a socialist meeting. Before he could enter the auditorium to speak, Bigelow was seized, handcuffed, gagged, hooded, and driven into the countryside, where he faced a crowd of about forty men. Wearing white masks and clothing, Bigelow's captors appeared to be a Ku Klux Klan group. The reverend was tied to a tree and approached by a man with a whip. He heard his captors say: "In the name of the women and children of Belgium and France lay on." Bigelow received about a dozen lashes with the whip. Then someone poured oil over his head and warned him to get out of Cincinnati. Left alone, Bigelow managed to make his way back into town, where a kindly doctor tended to his wounds. Bigelow was eventually admitted to a Cincinnati hospital to recuperate from his ordeal.[68]

The whipping of Reverend Bigelow made the national news. The *New York Times* reported: "Pacifist Whipped in Kuklux [*sic*] Style." The National Civil Liberties Bureau, the forerunner of the American Civil Liberties Union (ACLU), publicized the case. County, state, and federal authorities all declined to investigate, and no one was arrested. Bigelow remained perplexed by the episode. He did not believe he had made any unpatriotic statements and attributed the attack to businesspeople who opposed his quest for reforms of public utilities in Cincinnati. While Bigelow's ordeal did not end as tragically as the cases of Robert Prager and Frank Little, it revealed a dark side of Kentucky, especially with its connotations of Ku Klux Klan involvement.[69]

The Citizens' Patriotic League (CPL) continued its vigilante efforts. In June 1918 more than 200 of the league's 1,500 members gathered, led by "some of the most prominent residents of Kenton county," including commonwealth attorney Stevens L. Blakely and Harvey Myers Jr., a noted Covington attorney and former speaker of the Kentucky House of Representatives.[70] The CPL members formed an auto caravan and visited suspicious businesses and residences, putting up placards warning that Kenton County must be purged of pro-German elements. They visited seven residents of Erlanger and Covington, including a clergyman; accused them of being pro-German; and warned them to be loyal and avoid sedition. When the CPL crowd confronted the Reverend Anton Goebel of St. John's Catholic Church in Covington, he offered them money. He was slapped across the face. When the vigilantes asked another man, John Foltz, to explain why he gave so little to the Red Cross, he hurriedly wrote out a check for $100.[71]

Despite occasional cries of "Hang him," no serious violence ensued in these confrontations. Most people tried to appease the mob by promising more support to the Red Cross and the Liberty Bond campaigns. CPL representatives asserted that they were not looking for trouble; they merely wanted to "Americanize everything that should be American."[72]

Another CPL cavalcade two weeks later did involve violence, when nearly

350 men in automobiles visited two farmers south of Covington. They accosted wealthy farmer Paul Flynn and demanded to know why he had not bought more War Savings Stamps and had given so little to the Red Cross. When Flynn refused to sign a pledge card, CPL members took him into a field and switched his bare legs. He finally signed the pledge card. The crowd then moved down the road to confront John Schneider and his son, John Jr. The Schneiders were more resistant, and a fight broke out. The CPL men stripped young Schneider and switched him; his father then signed a pledge card.[73] Some Kentucky newspapers editorialized that the CPL's actions had "made a first class American city" of Covington, where "only 100 percent Americanism is tolerated," and noted that this "should be the rule everywhere."[74]

Vigilantism was not confined to northern Kentucky, with its heavy concentration of German Americans. A "Citizens Loyal Committee" in Paducah went on a nighttime car ride, putting up posters warning against disloyalty and noting that "traitors are shot in time of war." Other examples of officials and mobs conspiring against individuals with nonconforming views took place throughout the state. Victims included a pacifist in the northeastern Kentucky town of Staffordsburg, a labor organizer in Jefferson County, several brewers in northern Kentucky, and farmers in northern and eastern Kentucky.[75]

The threat of mob action caused some people to flee. The superintendent of the Maysville Water Company, August Shaeffer, had been openly supportive of Germany and critical of the United States and President Wilson before US entry into the war. Then he toned down his criticism but allegedly noted that he could poison all of Maysville if he wished; he also told a factory worker that the nation was getting rich off the war, but laborers were not. After these seemingly seditious remarks, several people talked about putting together a "patriotic league" in Maysville to pay Schaeffer a visit. Instead, authorities visited the president of the water company and suggested that Schaeffer resign and leave the city as soon as possible. He did so.[76]

Opposition to the Great War in Kentucky resulted in legal and extralegal actions to curb dissent. Much of this action took place in northern Kentucky, where the large German American population engendered suspicion and even hatred. Opposition to the war was quashed throughout the state, regardless of whether it was based on political, religious, ethnic, or other grounds. Federal, state, and local authorities participated in quelling dissent, as did groups of citizens. Violence in the commonwealth did not reach the level seen in other states: the Bigelow case was the only one acknowledged in Kentucky by a 1919 National Civil Liberties Bureau study, which found 164 cases of mob violence throughout the United States. Nevertheless, the Bigelow case was a major national event and is still cited today by many historians writing about the suppression of dissent.[77]

Stories about Kentuckians' opposition to the Great War reveal the dynamic tension between First Amendment free speech and what was perceived as seditious talk during the war years. This seditious talk did not have any material effect on the war effort, especially militarily. Thousands of Kentuckians would soon be called to join the military and would serve with little or no opposition to the selective service system.

5

The Draft

As the United States observed the war's unfolding in Europe after August 1914, debate increased about the nation's economic and military preparedness. Some people favored increasing the military capacity, while others did not. President Wilson resisted the idea, preferring to work for peace. But as the war progressed, he finally agreed that the country should be more prepared. The question then became: in what fashion should the country proceed to increase its military might? Debates arose over issues such as universal military training and service, the role of the Regular Army and the National Guard, volunteerism, and conscription.[1]

Before the United States entered the war, the country's military situation changed. A Reserve Officers' Training Corps (ROTC) on university campuses and summer military training camps for students and businessmen were launched. In spring 1917, as the nation was inexorably drawn into the European war, another issue took shape: the draft. Should any future US war effort be based strictly on volunteers, or would it be desirable, or necessary, to introduce conscription? Efforts at conscription during the Civil War had proved problematic. In the end, President Wilson and his military advisers decided on a selective wartime draft.[2]

The selective wartime draft afforded some advantages over a voluntary army. With a selective service system, the nation could balance the manpower needs of the military and industry. This system would help ensure that "slackers" would not place the entire burden on volunteers. The selective draft provided an equitable, democratic system to supply the necessary manpower. Only a few groups would be exempted wholesale from the draft, including federal and state officials and railroad workers. Otherwise, all strata of society would be subject to this process. In addition, a draft would ensure the increasingly obvious need for a massive army on the scale the European belligerents fielded. To support the Allies effectively, the United States needed to supply a large number of fighters and supplies as soon as possible. A selective draft could help rationally achieve this goal.[3]

Wilson preferred a selective draft, but he needed Congress to pass a law establishing a selective service system. This proved to be a contentious debate.

The day after Congress voted for war, Secretary of War Newton Baker submitted a bill to increase dramatically the Regular Army and the National Guard and to federalize the latter. He also sought a selective national draft to conscript 500,000 men between the ages of nineteen and twenty-five.

Representatives and senators primarily from agrarian areas in the South and Midwest opposed the draft for a variety of reasons. Their concerns included racial fears about drafting too many African Americans or too few; the specter of "European" militarism (large standing armies); abandoning the US tradition of voluntary, patriotic militias; centralizing power in the federal government; and protecting farm laborers from bearing the brunt of conscription and fighting.[4]

During the congressional debates about entering the war, Kentucky's eleven representatives and two senators generally supported President Wilson. On the question of the draft, however, they split. Four Democrats and two Republicans opposed the draft and supported a volunteer army: Democrats Robert Y. Thomas Jr. from Logan County, William Jason Fields from Carter County, Ben Johnson from Nelson County, and Harvey Helm from Boyle County and Republicans John W. Langley from Floyd County and Caleb Powers from Whitley County. Declaring the draft bill unconstitutional, Thomas decried: "Any nation whose citizens will not come to its defense in time of dire necessity and come voluntarily does not deserve to exist as a nation."[5]

On June 1 the *Congressional Record* printed a speech by Powers that the *Stanford Interior Journal* deemed "a vicious attack" on the president. In it, the representative "took great credit for himself for voting against the declaration of war." The *Interior Journal* concluded that Powers was a "great discredit" to both his Eleventh District and the state.[6] Subsequent comments by Powers resulted in a complaint against him to the Bureau of Investigation. O. E. Fox of Harlan, chief of the American Protective League in the county, wrote to national APL director Charles Frey about alleged "disloyal utterances" by Congressman Powers and enclosed an article from the *Harlan Enterprise* to support his contention. Frey sent the letter and article to bureau chief Bruce Bielaski, who promised to investigate Powers.[7]

After the Kentucky-born Speaker of the House, James Beauchamp "Champ" Clark (D-MO), made a two-hour speech in favor of volunteerism, Democrat Swagar Sherley from Louisville spoke in favor of the selective service draft. During an impassioned speech, Sherley quoted a letter from *Courier-Journal* editor Henry Watterson arguing that the volunteer system was "like the stagecoach . . . unequal in the expanding needs of modern time." Sherley repeated many arguments in favor of the selective draft, concluding that the country needed a system based on command, not volition, to create an army that would "bring this war to a short and glorious end."[8]

Eventually Congress approved the selective draft, changed the eligibility age (to twenty-one- to thirty-year-olds), increased soldier pay, added War Risk Insurance, and prohibited liquor and brothels near military camps (an issue that would be significant in Kentucky). President Wilson chose US Army Judge Advocate General Enoch Crowder to be provost marshal general and head of the selective service system. Crowder established a process by which the federal government supervised the draft but relied on state and local officials to carry out the major work. Civilians would be heavily involved, especially at the county and voting precinct levels. Local draft boards would form the foundation of the draft system. Nominated by the governor and appointed by the president, local draft boards would generally include a medical representative, local officials, and prominent citizens.

As first established, the selective service system involved three steps. First, eligible men registered. Second, local boards examined the registered men to determine whether they would be given exemptions. Third, nonexempted men were conscripted as necessary for the war effort, with a national lottery system determining the order in which men were drafted. A supervisory district board in each congressional district would hear appeals of local draft board decisions. To begin the process, General Crowder secretly shipped to sheriffs and county clerks around the country thousands of registration forms, in anticipation of registration day on June 5, 1917.[9]

Depending on the needs of the Army General Staff, each state received a draft quota that took into account the number of men who had already volunteered for the military. More than 600,000 men were needed by September 1, 1917, when it was estimated that sixteen new cantonments, including one in Louisville, would be ready to accept the new "selectives," as the drafted men were called.[10]

Before the draft process could start, the states had to build an organization. In May 1917 Governor A. O. Stanley named Adjutant General Tandy Ellis as the state agent and disbursing officer, in charge of paying all bills for the registration and the draft. This made Ellis the first point of contact for the selective service system in Kentucky and the liaison to General Crowder's office in Washington. He authorized the federal payment of expenses incurred by local boards, which often hired clerks to assist.[11]

Ellis relied on Henry Rhodes, who was eventually designated chief of the Selective Service Division, Kentucky. As such, he guided the day-to-day operations of the system. From Fleming County, Rhodes had worked in a bank before joining the Quartermaster Corps and being stationed as a sergeant in Ellis's office. In December 1917 he was commissioned as an infantry major in the Regular Army and put in charge of all draft work in Kentucky. (A postwar

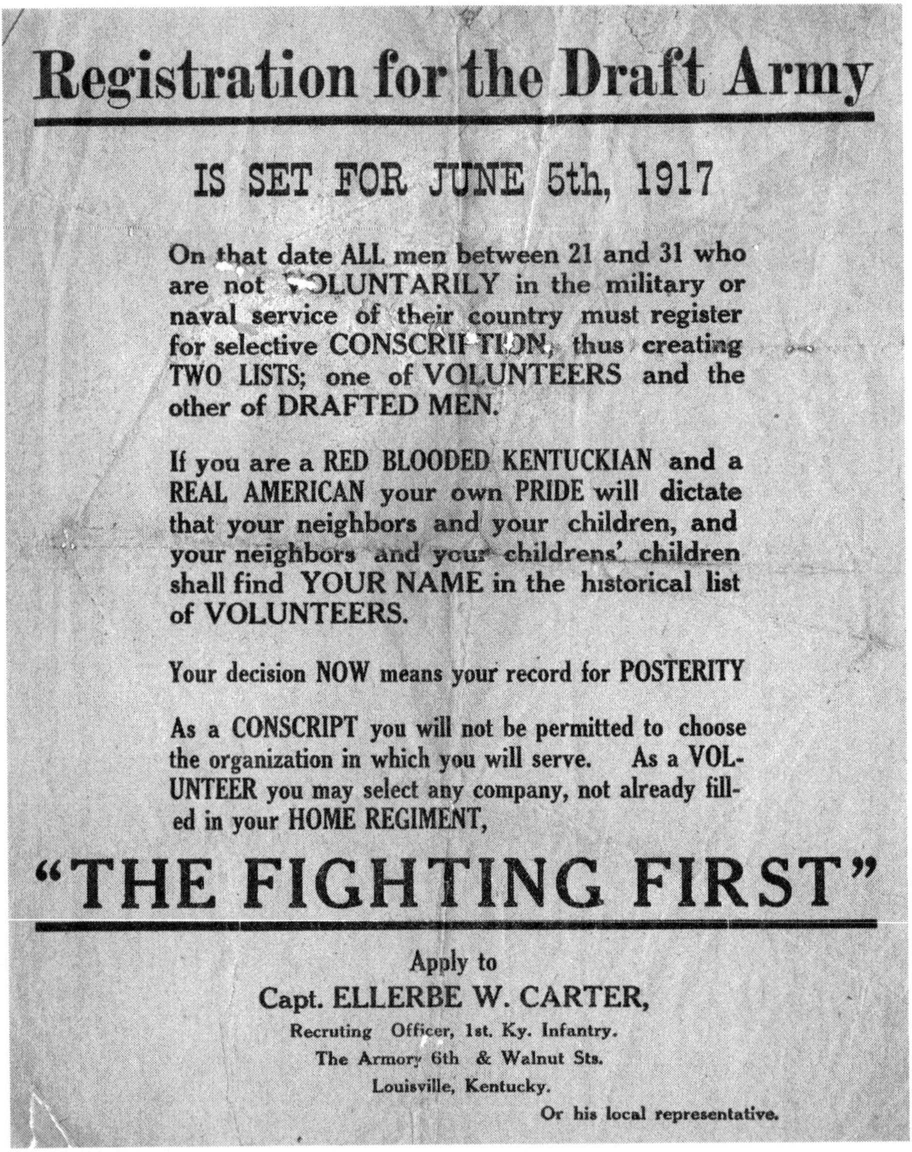

Kentucky National Guard recruiting poster urging men to volunteer before draft registration day on June 5, 1917. (University of Louisville)

report on the Kentucky selective service system noted that there had been "considerable friction" between Rhodes and Adjutant General Ellis in fall 1917. The enmity had not interfered with execution of the Selective Service Law, however, because Ellis had relinquished all direction of the work, and Rhodes reported directly to Governor Stanley.) Major Rhodes would prove to be an efficient, tireless worker who guided the selective service system in Kentucky to success.[12]

The Kentucky Selective Service Division oversaw the local and district draft boards and had a variety of other duties. These included interpreting regulations, investigating charges against boards or members thereof, preparing reports, distributing bulletins, cooperating with other agencies such as the Kentucky Council of Defense, and maintaining "a sound morale throughout the system."[13] Rhodes eventually put together a staff of twelve people to accomplish the division's duties, including his wife, who worked without pay.

To establish the selective service system in Kentucky's counties, Governor Stanley in May 1917 nominated registration boards usually consisting of the county clerk, the county sheriff, and a physician. Volunteer registrars in various wards assisted the county registration boards. In a letter to the local newspaper explaining the system, Knox County sheriff S. L. Lewis and county clerk Read P. Black correctly noted, "This registration is not conscription or draft."[14] It was merely the first step that could lead to conscription (or not). These boards would simply oversee registration; they would not examine or conscript men.

Newspapers throughout Kentucky published articles explaining the selective service system. The *Crittenden Record-Press* in Marion warned that failure to register could result in a year in prison. The *Hopkinsville Kentuckian* in Christian County asserted: "No character of an excuse will be accepted by those who fail or refuse to register. It does not matter if you are married or single, blind, deaf, dumb, legless and armless; if you are in jail or a minister of the gospel; if you are white, brown, black or yellow; if you have conscientious scruples against war, or if you are a citizen of Germany, or any other country, you must register, if between the ages of 21 and 31."[15]

The Lawrence County Council of Defense in Louisa called for women to play a special role in achieving a successful registration day. The council noted: "Let our mothers emulate the example of the Spartan Mothers, let sisters go with their brothers to register, let the dear girl sweetheart go with these brave boys to these registering places." Cities intended to make registration day a "patriotic holiday." In Lexington, Boy Scouts planned to visit houses, reminding people that registration day had arrived. As registration opened at 7:00 a.m., city church and fire bells rang and factory whistles blew to mark this auspicious occasion.[16]

On June 5, 1917, thousands of Kentucky men registered for the draft. Probably reflecting the typical experience in Kentucky counties, the *Bourbon News* in Paris reported: "There was no attempt anywhere in the city or county to influence young men against obeying the registration or the drafting law. On the contrary, many a mother, sacrificing the maternal instinct, exhorted their sons to offer their services to their country." Parents often accompanied their sons to register and stood by "proudly but perhaps tearfully"; they "gave no outward manifestation or sign of fear at the thought that the organization of any army of democracy might bring bereavement to them."[17]

In Lancaster, the festive day began with the firing of a cannon when registration opened. As "the day was made the occasion for quite a display of patriotism," a drum and trumpet corps played, bells clanged, and Boy Scouts paraded. The newspaper noted, however, that despite the noisy celebration, "the entire county seemed to have sensed the significance and solemnity of the occasion." In contrast, in Morgan County's seat of West Liberty, a solemn atmosphere prevailed. The newspaper reported: "The day passed off quietly and without excitement, but one could sense a deep feeling of patriotism in the quiet, unhesitating way the boys marched up and registered for Uncle Sam, and there were comparatively few who claimed exemptions."[18]

As it did in most of the rest of the nation, registration in Kentucky proceeded reasonably well, although the state was among the last to report results to the Provost Marshal General's Office. A few weeks later, the *Louisville Courier-Journal* reported those results: Kentucky had 165,351 "white" registrants and—reflecting the era of segregation—22,222 "coloreds." This total of 187,573 was short of the estimate of 204,998 eligible men. In total, nearly 10 million men registered across the country.[19]

Additional registration days would be necessary before the war's end. Sign-ups in 1918 occurred on June 5 and August 24, targeting all men who had reached age twenty-one since the first registration day. They recorded another 21,948 Kentuckians. A final registration day on September 12, 1918, extended the age limit downward to eighteen and upward to forty-five years; it produced another 270,803 Kentucky registrants. Nearly half a million Kentuckians registered for the draft during the Great War.[20]

After the first registration day on June 5, 1917, Governor Stanley appointed county and city draft boards. Four cities with more than 30,000 inhabitants received their own draft boards: Louisville, Newport, Covington, and Lexington. Local draft boards evaluated and conscripted eligible men. Stanley also created medical and legal advisory councils and three district boards to review appeals from local boards. Each of the district boards usually included a manufacturer, "labor man," lawyer, and physician.[21]

After the first registration day, the board physician and other assisting doctors gave the men physical examinations. Those who were found physically eligible for service could seek exemption on various grounds. This process proved cumbersome and wasted doctors' time, so in late 1917 the procedure changed. Boards sent questionnaires to registrants, who could then claim exemptions.

Those men who were liable to be called were then physically examined. This second plan established four classes of men who could be called in order of need, as well as a fifth classification for exempt men. There were three other draft categories worth noting: slackers, delinquents, and deserters (considered in more detail later).[22]

Local draft boards had the task of considering exemptions and classifications. Unfortunately, the constitution of the boards, along with their classifications and exemptions, sometimes proved controversial. Governor Stanley appointed more than 300 men to local boards (often called exemption boards), but many men resisted the appointment. The most common reason for not serving was that the nominee was running for public office. Others simply did not want to decide who would have to join the military. Governor Stanley argued that draft board service would not put people in the position of discriminating against their fellow citizens because the selective service rules and regulations did not offer much discretion.[23] This hesitation to serve on draft boards drew attention from federal officials. Provost Marshal General Crowder sent the governor a telegram underlining the seriousness of refusing to serve and stating the consequences of doing so. The nominees had, in essence, been "drafted" and could not decline to serve without imperative reasons. Failure to serve could result in one year in prison.[24]

Despite the federal government's position, more than two-thirds of the governor's nominees declined or resigned from draft board service for a variety of reasons. Some nominees joined the military; some sheriffs claimed they were too busy to do two jobs. One man declined because he was a traveling salesman and could not remain in the county and serve. Sometimes geography prompted resignations: one "mountain doctor" resigned because he rode horseback around the county and could not easily travel to the county seat to serve. Other men cited transportation problems or the fact that they had moved and were ineligible to serve in the county nominated. Health problems, old age, and death also factored into declinations.[25]

As usual in Kentucky at the time, politics played a role in the composition of boards. When a "mentally unbalanced" Republican member of the Adair County board resigned, a replacement candidate's name was submitted who was acceptable to other board members and "the Democrats [in the county]." In Pendleton County, two Democratic board members refused to add another physician after one resigned, noting that "two factions in this county have been endeavoring to bring on a political fight between the members of the Local Board." The two Democrats, however, agreed on the recommendation of a Republican county judge, an "intelligent and reputable citizen of the county" who was a farmer and patriotic, despite being "a member of the opposite political faith."[26]

One Kentuckian's appointment to a local board proved especially controversial. A. A. Bablitz of Lexington was one of the few labor representatives on Kentucky boards; among other things, he was president of Coopers Local No. 210. Some suspected the governor had appointed Bablitz to the board to "help secure the labor vote." Born in Germany, Bablitz had immigrated with his father to Chicago. An attorney, labor organizer, and president of the Bluegrass Federation of Labor, Bablitz was also disparagingly called a pro-German, a socialist, and an anarchist because he had recently helped mediate strikes by transit workers and coal miners.[27]

Bablitz had made his views about Germany clear. In a November 1914 letter to the editor of the *Lexington Herald,* he asserted that the Germans were fighting "not for the Kaiser and militarism, as The Herald would have us believe, but for the preservation of the German nation, for German culture and German ideals." Bablitz called for the United States to observe strict neutrality in the war. Nevertheless, after April 1917, Bablitz became an ardent supporter of the US war effort. He served as a Four Minute Man and volunteered to work on a farm for a week supporting wartime agriculture.[28]

The DOJ's Bureau of Investigation began delving into Bablitz's activities when a Transylvania College German-language professor and member of the American Protective League, Robert E. Monroe, complained about him. Monroe reported that he had overheard on the street a conversation in German between Bablitz and another man in which the former had happily observed "that the draft was a failure in Lexington because so many were claiming deferred classification." It appeared to Monroe that Bablitz either wanted the draft to fail or was claiming that Americans were cowards. Monroe believed that "the public was generally dissatisfied with Bablitz" and that he was duty-bound to report the man because, after the current semester, Monroe would be joining either the Department of Justice or the Intelligence Department of the Navy. (He actually became a BI agent in Lexington.)[29]

Lexington BI agent Linzy Otto Thompson conducted an investigation, interviewing the Fayette County judge, the county clerk, the president of a large bank, and others. They did not know much about Bablitz personally. Edward Bassett, president of Fayette National Bank, claimed, however, that "the public" did not like Bablitz as a board member because he was a German and stated that he was "beyond doubt a labor agitator and socialist."[30]

According to his former law partner, A. M. Baker, Bablitz had "always shown a tendency and desire to pervert the law in favor of labor, without any consideration for capital." He also said that although Bablitz had "excellent qualities," "externally he was an extremely disagreeable man." Bablitz was "socialistic in his views, but not to the extent of believing in the destruction of capital." Although Bablitz had been pro-German before the United States entered the war, Baker believed his former partner was "sincere in his loyalty to the United States, for he made efforts to get into the officers training camp." Bablitz had never made any disloyal remarks in Baker's presence. When reporting this interview, agent Thompson noted that Baker was trying to be fair to his former partner, even though he did not like him.[31]

When questioned by Thompson, local draft board chairman Frank B. Jones admitted that he and another member, Dr. E. B. Bradley, had kept a close watch on the work of Bablitz, who was the board secretary. Both thought they could get along better without Bablitz, who was an inefficient "bungler" who "gets things all tangled up." Jones had to admit, however, that "in passing upon claims, etc., [Bablitz] is fair in rendering decisions."[32]

Apparently tipped off by Baker that he was being investigated, Bablitz sought an appointment with agent Thompson. He told Thompson that his father had been naturalized before Bablitz himself had turned twenty-one (therefore Bablitz need not be naturalized). Bablitz had lived in Lexington for about sixteen years, had worked as a cooper, and had graduated from the law department at the state university (University of Kentucky) in 1912, after which he had practiced law. Bablitz professed loyalty to the United States and showed letters proving he had tried to get into an officers' training camp but had been rejected because of his age (he was forty-one) and his bad hearing. He asserted he was neither a socialist nor an anarchist. He had never heard any complaints about his loyalty while serving on the local board. Later that evening, after his interview, Bablitz returned to Thompson's office with proof of his father's naturalization.[33]

Soon after Bablitz left Thompson's office, a German-speaking BI agent from Cincinnati, Carl Jansen, arrived to carry out an undercover operation to ascertain German sentiment in the area. Jansen approached several men of German heritage in Lexington. All of them referred him to Bablitz as someone who could help a German in trouble. Jansen met Bablitz, but their conversation proved inconclusive.[34]

In agent Thompson's final report, he concluded that "it would appear that the subject is not really disloyal" but could not refrain from expressing "innate" sympathy for Germany. Thompson believed that Bablitz was loyal to the United States, even though some of his remarks made people think otherwise. Because he had expressed such strong pro-German sentiments before the war, it was hard for people to believe that Bablitz's attitude had changed. In the words of one interviewee: "It is impossible for a leopard to change its spots." Owing to his strong support of labor, Bablitz had "caused the public to dub him a socialist with anarchistic tendencies." On the positive side, since the investigation began, Bablitz had not been heard uttering any more pro-German sentiments. Thompson ended by noting that he would pass along the results of the investigation to the federal district attorney in Covington.[35]

BI chief Bielaski sent Thompson's summary report to Provost Marshal General Crowder, who in turn asked Major Rhodes to ascertain Governor Stanley's thoughts. After consulting with the governor, Bablitz resigned his position on the local board. Stanley accepted the resignation and appointed a new member.[36]

The case of A. A. Bablitz reveals the prevailing attitudes of many Kentuckians toward German Americans: they were disliked and accused of treason and sedition, of not being patriotic, or simply of not being "American." Bablitz compounded the matter by being a "socialist," which was anathema to many Americans. The Department of Justice would investigate and prosecute many avowed socialists during the war, including the famous case of Socialist Party presidential candidate Eugene Debs, who was convicted for violating the Espionage Act of 1917. His conviction was upheld by the US Supreme Court, and Debs served time in federal prison, where he languished while garnering over a million votes in the 1920 presidential election. Bablitz may have been fortunate simply to be hounded off the local draft board.[37]

Throughout the commonwealth, Kentuckians did not hesitate to complain about their local draft board members, seeking to oust those they believed guilty of chicanery. In Martin County, local board member J. P. Clark was accused of "promising exemption to registrants in return for their votes." Clark was running for county attorney and had allegedly told a group of draft-age men: "Boys, I am up here to get you down to vote for me. Come down and vote for me and I won't let you go to war." Determined to root out any scent of unfairness in the selective service process, Crowder's office requested an investigation. Based on depositions provided to him, BI agent Thompson concluded that they "failed to prove that Clark ever made any definite promise to exempt any man in order to get him to vote for him."[38]

Another local board member, Logan County sheriff James S. Taylor, was removed after federal authorities charged him with violating two acts: section 6 of the Selective Service Act, by aiding and assisting others to evade military service, and section 3 of the Espionage Act, by obstructing the enlistment and recruitment for the military. Like Clark in Martin County, Taylor was accused of promising exemptions if people voted for him. When apprised of his removal, Taylor telegraphed General Crowder and claimed to be innocent of the charges. The clerk of the local board also telegraphed Crowder to inform him that the board was in good working order, that disruption would delay fulfilling the draft quota, and that the clerk and a physician member, "holding balance of power, can see that justice is done to the public." Taylor contacted Congressman R. Y. Thomas Jr. and Senator J. C. W. Beckham for support. Thomas marched over to the Provost Marshal General's Office and spoke with Crowder's assistant, Lieutenant Colonel Hugh Johnson, arguing that Taylor's removal had been unfair. When Crowder asked Governor Stanley to explain Taylor's removal, the governor replied that Taylor's case was a federal matter, pursued by the assistant US district attorney and approved by Attorney General Gregory. Stanley protested that he had "taken no part in the case except to recommend his [Taylor's] successor." Taylor was replaced on the board and arraigned before a federal grand jury in Owensboro.[39]

In his history of the draft, historian John Whiteclay Chambers II writes, "Politically, the most important challenges to the draft were not assertions from a minority that it [the draft] was unconstitutional, but rather criticism about unfairness or illegality in the operation of conscription."[40] Cases in Kentucky support Chambers's assertion. For example, General Crowder's office received an anonymous letter from Madisonville charging impropriety by the Hopkins County draft board. Its chairman, Judge W. H. Yost, held draft board meetings at his office. Yost was a stalwart of the community, a law partner of future governor Ruby Lafoon, chairman of the district appeals board in western Kentucky, and a staunch Democrat. Yost's law partner, Charles Franklin, occupied the room next to where the local board meetings were held and had represented several men seeking exemptions. Franklin had "charged a large sum" for getting these exemptions, which were rarely turned down, "unless it was too raw even for his partner and his relative [who also served on the board]." The letter writer charged that Yost got half the money from Franklin's fees and that this situation was "making the draft law unpopular and is making the people dissatisfied with the draft law and the war." The anonymous correspondent also claimed that the son of another board member, E. H. Holeman, had improperly been placed in Class IV, despite the fact that the son's wife had plenty of money and was not dependent on him. The writer did not sign his letter because he was in business in Madisonville and believed "if these people should find it out they would ruin me." Given these grave allegations, General Crowder's office asked the Kentucky adjutant general's office to investigate, but apparently nothing ever transpired from the allegations against Yost, who was well known and admired throughout western Kentucky.[41]

One of the most contentious problems involved the secretary of the Wayne County draft board, lawyer O. B. Bertram, who was accused of improperly arranging for deferments. After several complaints about Bertram reached the

Department of Justice, BI agent Thompson made a trip to the county seat of Monticello, where he interviewed county attorney J. M. Kennedy. Kennedy acknowledged that he had heard rumors about Bertram's alleged malfeasance. In Kennedy's opinion, though, the worst that Bertram had done was to charge fees for preparing exemption claims, which he would then rule on as a member of the local board.

Thompson also spoke with board member Richard Shearer, who did not see anything wrong with Bertram preparing exemption claims for a fee, but he thought it "morally wrong" for Bertram to prepare papers that he would later consider. Shearer did not think the lawyer was unfair or crooked; he simply wanted to be paid for his services. After questioning several other people, Thompson finally interviewed Bertram himself. The Wayne County lawyer believed he was doing nothing wrong by charging such fees, and no action was taken for a year.[42]

Complaints about Bertram continued to accumulate, however, until the Wayne County Council of Defense finally intervened in September 1918. It passed a resolution asking the Department of Justice to reinvestigate charges of malfeasance against Bertram. The council provided the names of more than a dozen men who had allegedly paid Bertram to get them reclassified. This time, US district attorney Thomas Slattery asked Lexington BI agent R. E. Monroe to investigate.

In Monticello, Monroe first interviewed county attorney Kennedy but discovered that "it was quite evident that Kennedy did not intend to tell what he knew." Frustrated by this stonewalling, Monroe interviewed other people who gave specific information about men and amounts paid for reclassification. He spoke to Judge W. R. Cress, who said that Bertram had been very pro-German before the United States entered the war and that court records showed that Bertram had owed $2,500 at the beginning of the war. Despite Bertram's much diminished law practice while serving on the draft board, Cress noticed that the board secretary had recently remodeled his home and bought a car. Agent Monroe realized, however, that Cress and Bertram were political enemies, so he thought the judge's statements could be discounted 50 percent because of "personal prejudice and political feelings."[43]

The next day, agent Monroe interviewed Bertram "under cover." Pretending to be a mining company agent, Monroe suggested that his registration card from the Lexington board be transferred to Wayne County but somehow be "lost" for a while. The federal agent told Bertram that he would "make it worth his while to pigeon hole my papers for three or four months." Unsurprisingly, in a small county where news traveled fast, Bertram failed to take the bait.

The BI agent then went to the bank to check on Bertram's financial records (apparently without a subpoena). There he discovered two things: despite the decline in his law practice due to time spent on board work, Bertram had "greatly increased his income," and this increase coincided with draft calls, "from which Bertram is alleged to have drawn financial benefit." There were records of receipts from people from whom Bertram had allegedly received bribes. After interviewing some of the alleged bribers (who claimed they had paid only small sums to Bertram for legal work), Monroe returned to county attorney Kennedy. When confronted with "the facts," Kennedy was more forthcoming with information. He acknowledged signing a promissory note for one man who still owed $80 to Bertram after a $20 down payment. Despite the perception that he was Bertram's friend, Kennedy had declined to serve on the local board with Bertram and board chairman Dr. Young, who had opposed the war. Local Liberty Bond chairman George Barnes had confirmed to Kennedy that Bertram and Young were not "entirely patriotic in their attitude." Young had refused to make a speech in favor of Liberty Bonds and had never bought any, and he "had never given a cent to the Red Cross."

Monroe then went back to speak to Bertram, revealing his real status as a federal agent. Bertram acknowledged that he had promised agent Thompson he would stop charging for the preparation of exemption claims but said he was the only lawyer in town who knew how to do them. Bertram admitted receiving only small sums from men, not the larger amounts up to $200 that had been reported and were documented in his bank records.

From this investigation, agent Monroe concluded: "Summarizing the whole case I should say that the trouble is 50 per cent to political trouble and inland jealousy, and 50 per cent to facts in the case, but the situation is 100 per cent bad." He believed that Bertram and Young were in collusion. The agent asserted that matters were so bad that it would take someone from outside the county to take charge of the board and handle all the reclassifications.[44] By the time all the reports had been done and a recommendation made to the governor that he replace Bertram, the war had ended.

The draft board in Logan County in southwestern Kentucky also underwent scrutiny. Among other complaints, people reported that the local board had granted a number of deferments to wealthy men. After investigating the situation, military intelligence agent E. P. McSherry from Nashville believed there was collusion between the local board in Russellville and the regional board in Madisonville, which amounted to "a public scandal."[45] When he eventually received McSherry's report, Crowder suggested that Rhodes send an inspector to Logan County. Rhodes sent John M. Scott from Louisville to investigate.

Scott reported that many young men had left the county, drawn by higher wages to the munitions plant in Nashville, to the cantonment (Camp Taylor) in Louisville, and to mines. As a result, farm labor had become scarce. He noted that the dichotomy between poorer farms in northern Logan County and richer farms in the southern portion could give the impression that exemptions had been based on income. Inspector Scott, however, did "not find that the Board had been influenced in any degree by politics." Although the local board had misclassified some men, he believed the charges of unfair exemptions being given to the sons of prominent farmers were "unfounded." The inspector also noted that two bitter political factions were battling in the county, which may have led people to misuse the complaint process to stir up trouble for their opponents.

At Scott's suggestion, the local board had called for the reexamination of several men who had been classified as physically unfit. Scott concluded "that all charges of crookedness and favoritism filed against the Board are unfounded; that the members of the Board are honest, patriotic and are sincerely endeavoring to carry out the Selective Service Regulations." He also found that the board members were "opinionated and head strong" and that they had made errors, but these were errors of judgment and not intentional evasions of the regulations.[46] Crowder found Scott's report "a very complete one" that "showed a great deal of preparation." Perhaps thinking of other complaints about Kentucky boards, Crowder wrote to Rhodes: "This system of investigation and inspection, if pursued throughout the state, would doubtless have beneficial results."[47]

Some draft board "irregularities" involved medical officers charged with being too lenient in giving physical exemptions. At the instigation of the Medical Advisory Board in Covington, the Bureau of Investigation studied medical exemptions given by Dr. Edward J. Buten of Newport. An eye, ear, nose, and throat doctor, Buten conducted that part of the physical examinations for all registrants in Newport. The Medical Advisory Board believed Dr. Buten was "not making fair reports of the physical condition of registrants" and therefore should not be allowed to continue to perform examinations.[48]

Special Agent John Menefee of the BI's Cincinnati office met with several members of the Medical Advisory Board to discuss four specific cases that had been brought to the board's attention. Board doctors had examined the four men, and in no case did the registrants have the ear or eye problems reported by Dr. Buten. Those doctors had no information to suggest that Buten was taking bribes, but they believed he should not be allowed to conduct any more examinations. After conferring with his agent in charge in Cincinnati, Menefee met with the Newport board members and expressed the DOJ's wish that Dr. Buten perform no more examinations and that the registrants be reexamined.[49]

General Crowder asked Major Rhodes to take up the matter of Dr. Buten's appointment with Governor Stanley, given that the BI reports indicated, "if not a malfeasant in office," Buten "is careless and incompetent." Rhodes replied that the Newport board had been ordered to fire Dr. Buten and recall all registrants for reexamination. Eventually, about half of the men reexamined were reclassified as fit for duty.[50]

In Pulaski County in southern Kentucky, the local board was charged not with malfeasance but with insensitivity and overreaching its responsibilities. Board chairman Dr. A. J. Wahle notified nearly 1,800 registrants to appear at the Somerset opera house at a designated time, where they would be "required to enlist in some service for the Government, which will only require one day of your time. Failure to report may cause you to lose valuable rights." This cryptic message caused men to travel long distances, sometimes with their families, and shut down a local mill providing poplar wood for the aircraft industry. It turned out that Wahle had summoned the men to attend a campaign to sell War Savings Stamps and Liberty Bonds. When apprised of this unauthorized and inappropriate action, General Crowder demanded that Major Rhodes investigate and ensure that no other board did the same. Boards were restricted to dealing with selective service matters. In reply, Rhodes assured Crowder that such an event would not occur again. Crowder then described the Pulaski board's action (without naming the state) in a letter to all state draft directors, saying that "the splendid spirit which actuates the Local Boards might be exaggerated into causing suffering," and there should be caution to "prevent the recurrence of like instances."[51]

Most local boards performed their duties well, despite real difficulties. Classifications and exemptions proved contentious. People from all strata of Kentucky wrestled with local and district board decisions about classifications. Various authorities received petitions for reclassification. Some of the petitions described a perceived need to balance military and civilian needs. For example, the Pullman Railroad Company asked General Crowder to reconsider the case of Harold George Jones of Louisville because he was needed to help regulate the efficient movement of troops by railroad across the country. Jones's district board had initially classified him Class IV, but in May 1918 it had reclassified him Class I, believing his work with Pullman did not warrant a deferred classification. A memo by one of Crowder's lieutenants pointed out that Jones's case had been raised by the company and not the registrant, and he concluded that the appeal had merit. Major Roscoe Conkling, the chief of Crowder's reclassification division, suggested to Rhodes that the local board reconsider Jones's case.[52]

In another case, a district board asked the local board to reclassify a banker on the grounds that banking was a necessary industry; unless the banker was given a deferred classification, the bank might have to shut down. The local board refused, so the Kentucky selective service chief consulted with Crowder's office. Banks across the state were struggling because so many employees were being drafted, Rhodes explained, and he asked that the reclassification be granted on "industrial grounds." Major Conkling replied that the Provost Marshal General's Office had often ruled that bank employees were not entitled to deferred classifications.[53]

Sometimes the draftees themselves did not request reclassification; their unhappy wives did it for them. Some wives alleged that their husbands were not supporting them. If a registrant was not properly supporting his wife, he could be classified I-B, which put him at higher risk of being called into the military. In addition, the War Risk Insurance law compelled a soldier to give half his pay to his wife or child—quite an incentive for women who were struggling in poverty.

Probably with this support payment in mind, an "anonymous source"—most likely the wife of Estal Garry of Drakesboro in Muhlenberg County—wrote a plaintive letter to the Treasury Department's Bureau of War Risk Insurance. It stated: "Please send Estal Garry a card calling him to Camp Taylor by the 30 of this month he is in this draft and if he gets a notice he gets some one to destroy it or through it away he says that if anyone ant sharp enough to catch him he is as mean to his wife and children as he can be." The letter writer went on to explain that Garry would not give his family any attention and worked only when he wanted. Eventually this case made its way through General Crowder's office to Major Rhodes, who sent a letter to Estal Garry, along with a self-addressed, stamped envelope for Garry's reply indicating where he was registered. After Garry responded that he was registered in Boyd County, Rhodes asked the local board to investigate. The local board followed up, found that Garry did not properly support his wife, reclassified him as I-B, and called him for service.[54]

Neither Crowder nor Rhodes could help one poor wife in Warren County. Bessie Stovall wrote that she had a husband "who dont do anything for me or our child 4 years old. He is a trained soldier. He is an excellent nurse and a good cook. I think he would be a good man for the army his name is Elbridge A. Stovall he deserted us 1914." When Rhodes asked the local board to investigate, the board replied that Stovall was not a draft registrant. Rhodes pressed the board to investigate further, so the members talked to Stovall's brother and ascertained that Elbridge A. Stovall was forty-one years old and therefore not subject to the draft at that time.[55] The federal and state governments could not help Bessie Stovall.

When J. G. McBee of Stanford failed to register, his wife reported him from afar. She happened to be the clerk in the provost marshal general's office in Washington, DC, and wrote directly to General Crowder, asking: "Is there no law to either punish a slacker or force him into service?" Noting that her husband had deserted her and her son, Dolly McBee claimed he had also "failed to register for army service in June 1917," a fact she had just learned. She alleged that he had threatened her life if she reported him, but felt it was her "patriotic duty." Dolly McBee also wondered if she might ever get a raise! When apprised of this case by Crowder's office, Rhodes inquired and learned that the miscreant, J. G. McBee, had been indicted in US court, where he had pled guilty.[56]

One Kentucky "slacker" case drew national attention when it was covered in the *New York Times*. The newspaper reported that John Allen of Ammie, "a hamlet of 100 inhabitants in Clay County, Ky.," had traveled all the way to New York City to appear in the court of federal judge Julius Mayer (who was presiding over the famous trial of anarchists Emma Goldman and Alexander Berkman). The Kentuckian's son, John Calhoun Allen, had been charged with refusing to register for the draft. Thinking that the boy must be demented for not registering, Judge Mayer had sent him to Bellevue Hospital for evaluation, which indicated the boy suffered from "dementia praecox." The concerned judge then wrote a letter to the elder Allen, prompting the father's long train ride to New York.

When the imposing six-foot-two-inch mountaineer appeared in court, the *Times* described him as follows: "He wore the boots and the corduroy trousers of the Kentucky hills. His shirt was blue and collarless and was home made. His coat was old-fashioned, and in his hand he carried the big black sombrero." The Kentuckian told the judge he had come to see what was the matter with his boy; he already had two sons in the army, and his two younger boys would serve when they were old enough. He told the judge he was angry and asked him to return his "back slider" son home, where he would ensure that young Allen joined the service. He declared: "There ain't going to be no quitters in the Allen family." Judge Mayer released the boy into his father's custody. The old man rebuked his son, saying he "didn't come from no such stock as these slacker and quitters, or whatever else you call such cattle." The father promised his son that if he did not do right, he would take him home to the public square and shoot him. Thoroughly chastised, the son promised he would register and fight. On the way out of the federal building, the elder Allen inquired about Goldman and Berkman. When apprised that they were anarchists, Allen said: "Those are the kind'er folks who are responsible for boys like this one of mine gettin' in trouble. We don't have folks like that out our way." Recalling the incident, Judge Mayer asserted: "That old fellow is one of the kind that makes the country great. He is a real American."[57]

Other people reported family members who seemed unpatriotic. Mary Snelling reported that her sons Tinsley, James, and Sydney of Salt Lick were "slackers." All were of draft age but had apparently filed "false affidavits."[58]

Other problems occurred, sometimes bizarre ones. Occasionally men registered by mistake, believing it was their duty. This proved a problem for Mack Stringer, who registered on June 5, 1917, despite being younger than twenty-one and therefore not required to do so. He was selected and inducted into military service. The following November, his father, J. W. Stringer of Crab Orchard, approached Governor Stanley and described his son's situation. Adjutant General Ellis explained the problem to the Provost Marshal General's Office, which replied that it was too late to help. Stringer did not give up: he wrote to US Senator Ollie James asking for help. The Provost Marshal General's Office was still unsympathetic, noting that "if a man not of military age has been so remiss as to register and thereafter keep silent about his age until after induction into the service, he is not entitled to consideration in the matter of obtaining a cancellation of his registration." Once a man was inducted, jurisdiction over him passed from the selective service system to the army. In Mack Stringer's case, it was too late for the selective service system to help. He would have to take up the matter with his commanding officer.[59]

Sometimes men complained about the draft after they were in the army. Private Allen Grady Wallis protested to General Crowder's office about the Trigg County local board. He claimed he had been sent to training camp too early: he had been the 144th man accepted by the Trigg County board for service, but he was the 77th man sent to training camp. He named four men whom he believed had received preferential treatment over him. Major Rhodes sent an appeal agent, John T. King, to investigate. King's report explained away the four other men's cases. Noting that although Wallis had indeed been the 144th man accepted for service, King found that there were legitimate reasons for his being called to camp before the others. About thirty-five men who had not been called up were African Americans (who were not being sent to the camps at that time). Other men had appealed their cases to the district board, so they could not be called up while their cases were pending. King cleared the local board of any wrongdoing and concluded: "I fail to find any where that there has been done any wrong by said Board, and feel that the letter was written by young Wallis while he was in a bad humor or blue, and amounts to nothing more than the imagination of an inexperienced boy."[60]

When people filed complaints against local and district draft boards, Crowder's office counseled the Kentucky Adjutant General's Office not to reveal the source of the complaint to the board. This would avoid board members taking complaints personally, rather than seeing them as an opportunity to improve the process.[61] In effect, this was a whistle-blower's protection.

Politics also played a role in reclassification attempts. When Senator J. C. W. Beckham raised the issue of reclassification for a Grayson County man, General Crowder wrote a lengthy reply, explaining the policy and philosophy of the selective service system. Local board members made the decisions, he explained. Therefore, men were chosen for service by their neighbors, who could make the "most sympathetic and just determination" of claims based on local knowledge. Men who wished to appeal could do so to the district boards and ultimately to the president. Because his office was far removed from the facts of these local cases, Crowder explained, it could not address individual situations. "If such a thing were attempted the inevitable result would be to undermine the confidence of the country in the system and eventually to disintegrate it." Requests to local boards directly from Crowder's office would "inevitably carry a certain suggestion of authority," which was a course "neither just nor proper."[62]

When constituents asked for help, most of Kentucky's congressional representatives simply forwarded these requests to General Crowder's office to investigate and report back. In the case of Walter Coy Cann of Hart County, however, considerable pressure was exerted on Crowder, who usually acted as the buffer between Kentucky politicians in Washington and Major Rhodes in Frankfort. Cann had been inducted into the army by his local board in September 1917, sent to Camp Taylor, and discharged in March 1918 when he claimed his wife was dependent on him. The local board then determined that Cann's wife was not dependent and reclassified him as I-A; the district board agreed. A member of the neighboring Hardin County board, W. A. Barry, wrote to US Representative Ben Johnson on Cann's behalf. When Johnson asked Crowder about the case, Crowder initially thought the local board should reclassify Cann in accordance with the reason for his discharge from the army. Earlier that year, Crowder's advice about a similar case had been different. Representative John Langley had asked Crowder about a man who was already in the military on the first registration day and was subsequently discharged on account of his mother's dependence. Langley asked whether that man "could be forced back in service under the draft act." Crowder had simply replied, "yes."[63] Representative Johnson, however, was not as easily satisfied as Langley. Neither was Barry, who wrote again to Johnson about Cann's plight. Johnson wrote to Major Rhodes, saying it was clear that Cann should be classified IV-A. Unsatisfied with Rhodes's response—that both the local and district boards had agreed on the reclassification decision—Johnson wrote again to Crowder. Crowder replied that once the reason for Cann's discharge from the army ceased to exist, the local board had the right to reclassify. While all this letter writing was taking place, Cann was inducted back into the army. Crowder ended the controversy by informing Johnson that since Cann was now in the army, he was no longer under the jurisdiction of the selective service system.[64]

Amidst these controversies about classification, other problems arose for men who failed to comply with the selective service regulations. The selective service system classified these men three ways: slackers, delinquents, or deserters. Men who failed to register, either on purpose or inadvertently, were classified as slackers. Delinquents were men who registered but failed to appear for a physical examination or failed to turn in a questionnaire. Men who were called up but failed to obey the order to report for military induction were considered deserters, just as if they had been in a military camp and walked away unauthorized. In other words, delinquents had not complied with regulations that might (or might not) lead to their being called up for military service; deserters were those who had already been called up but did not appear to ship off to camp.

One problem arose when officials at Camp Taylor in Louisville discovered that an inordinate number of deserters (who had not reported for induction) came from Perry County. Authorities at the camp wired the army adjutant general in Washington that the Perry County sheriff had reported 15 deserters in one day and claimed that another 108 would follow. This was a disproportionately large number for any local board's district, and it amounted to a lot of bounty money; authorities who turned in deserters received $50 for each one delivered. (The amount was subsequently taken out of the deserter's army pay.) Camp Taylor commander Brigadier General Fred T. Austin surmised that the Perry County draft board was "certifying all delinquents as deserters."[65]

The War Department apprised General Crowder of this seeming anomaly. He telegraphed Major Rhodes, stating that his office had "no desire to interfere with the laudable efforts of local police officials to apprehend draft deserters." He noted that the figures quoted by Austin "would indicate a possible departure" from the selective service regulations. He cautioned that local boards should seek only "willful deserters." Rhodes replied that the case had been investigated and that "the Sheriff is rounding up a class of registrants who have absolutely disregarded all notices from Local Board. This county is in a m[in]ing section where we are having most trouble with delinquents and deserters."[66] Apparently, the Perry County sheriff was allowed to keep his bounty money.

This sort of problem persisted at Camp Taylor. A couple of weeks later, Sergeant Major C. A. Falvey in the Brigade Personnel Section reported a problem with Letcher County to the camp's judge advocate. Several men had voluntarily checked in with the local draft board, which had then called the sheriff to arrest them for desertion. The men protested they had never heard from the draft board, and one man showed a signed receipt for a letter he had sent inquiring about his status. Sergeant Falvey believed these charges of desertion had been "erroneously made."[67]

Camp Taylor's judge advocate, Captain Murray Jones, then wrote to General Crowder about the number of cases he was seeing and the expense involved. The camp was paying out $10,000 per month to apprehending officers who were bringing in "technical deserters." Captain Jones believed that 95 percent of the men brought to the camp were not "willful deserters," although the apprehending authorities were being paid bounties for them. Camp officers did not file desertion charges in these cases. The men were simply put on duty, and the $50 was not taken out of their paychecks. Citing the Letcher County situation, Captain Jones asserted, "It reasonably appears that local boards and peace officers are acting in collusion." He also pointed out that Camp Jackson in South Carolina was running into the same problem, also spending about $10,000 a month in apprehension fees. Jones alleged that "a certain sheriff in Kentucky" averaged about $1,000 a week, another sheriff had 100 men in custody, and yet another said the $1,000 he had received for delivering 20 men was "the easiest money he ever picked up."[68]

General Crowder apprised Major Rhodes of the situation and reassured him that the $10,000 per month was "not a cause for concern, but is rather a testimony to the efforts of the police officers of Kentucky, if the men apprehended and so delivered are *wilful* deserters." The general thought the money was well spent. He reminded Rhodes of the selective service regulations, which gave local boards the responsibility of deciding whether deserters were willful. If not willful, they were simply delinquents who should be physically examined and sent to military camp. Crowder advised Rhodes that the distinction should be "taken up vigorously" with the local boards, "particularly those in the eastern and southeastern counties, who seem to be the worst offenders."[69]

Sheriffs in southern and southeastern Kentucky may have had more opportunities to earn bounty money than officials elsewhere in the state. According to Major Rhodes, if any parts of the state could be called less than supportive of the war, they were probably located in eastern and southern Kentucky. He referred in a memo to the "mountain counties where there has never been a strong pro-war feeling." Rhodes believed this attitude had been very noticeable in recent state elections in the mountain counties. There, "much criticism was made and a hard fight based on the hard fact that men had been drafted for the service."[70]

Major Rhodes continued to have problems with the Letcher County draft board. It had sent a letter to a technical deserter stating that it had no jurisdiction in his case and advising him to take it up with the US Army adjutant general. Rhodes castigated the board, reminding it that "it is the duty of the Local Board to use every means to apprehend a deserter or delinquent." Reminding the board members that he had previously challenged their handling of cases, he charged that they were "making no effort whatever to have those men inducted into the service when they were apprehended by you." Rhodes believed that if the board cooperated with him, the number of deserters and delinquents would be greatly reduced. He asserted that "eighteen percent of the deserters and delinquents of this state are under the jurisdiction of your board," and he warned that if the board did not do better, "the men will be allowed to scatter to the ends of the earth without being apprehended."[71]

People in the eastern Kentucky mountains may have opposed the war, but antiwar sentiment in Kentucky paled in comparison with that in other states (primarily in the South and Midwest). There, individuals and sometimes armed bands of deserters resisted apprehension by shooting back at local officials and posses. In four southern states—Tennessee, Georgia, Mississippi, and Arkansas—National Guard and federal troops were sent into primarily backwoods areas to roust men who were trying to escape the draft.[72] Troops were not called out in Kentucky to apprehend deserters, but armed resistance occasionally occurred.

For example, in Fleming County in January 1918, a constable went to the Morrison home to arrest a son, Arthur, for desertion. The *Lexington Herald* reported, "The whole Morrison family took up arms in defense of Arthur and drove the constable off." A posse of six men led by the county sheriff returned the next day to arrest the father and another son for obstruction of justice. Arthur had escaped, but a few days later he surrendered and was taken to Fort Thomas. Apparently he disliked army life, so he left. After evading authorities in the Flemingsburg area for two months, he was captured in September by a deputy sheriff and taken to Camp Taylor.[73]

Sometimes firefights broke out when lawmen tried to track down deserters. William Henkle of Marion County deserted and escaped to the hills of Johnson County, where he joined fellow deserter Leonard Perry. A posse led by deputy sheriff S. M. Wells went after the two men. A gunfight ensued in which thirty shots were exchanged, and Henkle was severely wounded. Johnson County sheriff John Stambaugh brought Henkle back to Camp Taylor on a cot and turned his prisoner over to the camp's provost marshal. Perry escaped and remained on the lam.[74]

Other deserters were not so lucky as to be merely wounded during apprehension. In Menifee County, a man known only as Pitts, a deserter from Camp Taylor, died in an encounter with the law. When deputy sheriff Brock Lewis approached the deserter, Pitts pointed a rifle at him. Lewis pulled out his revolver and fatally shot Pitts. A similar situation occurred in Jackson County, where deputy sheriff Louis V. Morris and constable John D. Robinson went after deserter John Sizemore. Sizemore resisted, and the two law officers fatally shot him. Sizemore's mother sued the two officers in Jackson Circuit Court. Claiming that they were acting on behalf of the local exemption board and, therefore, federal authorities, the officers succeeded in having the case moved to federal court in Richmond, where Judge A. M. J. Cochran presided. US district attorney Thomas Slattery defended the two officers; a jury returned a not guilty verdict.[75]

Although draft-related violence did occur in Kentucky, it never approached the high level of armed resistance that occurred in the South or in neighboring states. (For example, in Mingo County, West Virginia, bordering Kentucky's Martin and Pike Counties, a pitched battle between a band of deserters hiding in the mountains and law officials resulted in two deputy sheriffs being killed.)[76]

Despite problems with a few local draft boards, Kentucky officials performed well in dealing with deserters. In October 1918 Major Rhodes forwarded to General Crowder lists of deserters from fifty-six boards and noted, "from every Local Board the number of deserters has materially decreased." Local boards had become better at distinguishing between delinquents and willful deserters. Rhodes promised to complete the lists from the remaining sixty-four counties and send copies to all law enforcement officials in the state. He estimated there would be no more than 1,800 net deserters for the entire state. He also said the trend was changing: for the June 5 and August 24, 1918, registrations, there would be fewer than 100 delinquents. Crowder congratulated him: "The draft officials of Kentucky are to be commended upon the excellent form in which these net desertion records have been presented." He liked the idea of disseminating a master list to law officials and suggested that the list also be shared with the state and local councils of defense.[77]

There is little doubt that the draft process in 1917 was an overall success, despite the difficulty of classifying men and identifying deserters. That year served as a learning experience as draft officials throughout the state became more knowledgeable about their roles and the selective service regulations.

By May 1918, Major Rhodes reported to General Crowder that Kentucky was much better prepared to process the forthcoming second registration. He questioned, however, how Kentucky compared with other states in terms of the "exceedingly low" percentage of men being classified in Class I. He thought "regulations for married men have been abused." Men who would be earning 50 percent more in the army, thus making them more capable of supporting families, were nevertheless being given deferments. Rhodes found this trend especially true in the mountain regions. He also thought the state's delinquent rate was low: "Many counties in the state had no delinquents at all and practically the only counties where we are bothered with delinquents are in the counties where last winter, in several coal strikes, the men scattered to all parts of the country." By that time, he believed local boards had done "exceptionally well in locating their delinquents."[78]

General Crowder got feedback about the Kentucky selective service system from other sources as well. After receiving Major H. W. Adams's report about his inspection trip through the Midwest, Crowder wrote to Governor Stanley in July 1918 and commended Major Rhodes. Adams had noted Rhodes's "enthusiasm and efficiency" in running the state's selective service system. The inspector also acknowledged Rhodes's "highly laudable efforts" to "maintain his organization at the lowest possible cost," but suggested that the Kentuckian should hire more people if the strain became too great. Crowder suggested that Rhodes hire an inspector to deal particularly with eastern and southeastern counties, which seemed to "temporize" in their correspondence. Crowder thought the "general high standard of administration and loyal cooperation which has been set in Kentucky should not be lowered by the inefficiency of a few Boards."[79]

Crowder also hired some national inspectors to provide him with impartial reports about the draft system. He sent Virginian Richard Farr to make a thorough investigation of the Kentucky system. In his report, Farr described Major Rhodes as "actively in charge of the State Headquarters" of the selective service system and noted that Governor Stanley lent his active support. The Kentucky office was the most economical Farr had seen during his inspections. He commented on Rhodes's mastery of details and hard work, noting that the major often toiled into the late hours of the night. The Kentucky Council of Defense had been very cooperative and helpful. State and local authorities, with the exception of those in Jackson County, had been cooperative as well. Farr believed the medical and advisory boards were doing good work, as were government appeal agents, with the exception of those in Johnson, Daviess, and Laurel Counties. Farr concluded that the twenty-two-year-old Rhodes was "anxious to make a record" and that he "had the confidence of the people."[80] In sum, Farr produced a very favorable report on the Kentucky selective service system.

Finally, Crowder received direct feedback about the selective service system from local boards via questionnaires. Sent by the Provost Marshal General's Office in Washington, the questionnaires covered thirteen topics, including local board staffs, physical examinations, exemption and discharge, discharge for dependency, and administrative matters. The returned questionnaires show that Kentucky's local board members were generally satisfied with the selective service process. The topics of physical examinations and discharges for dependency drew the most comment and controversy. Registrants feigning bad hearing and eyesight plagued some boards. Other boards had trouble sorting out dependency claims. Many boards acknowledged difficulty in finding nonexempt men for the first call-up. They were surprised at the high number of men seeking exemptions. Most acknowledged that they had called up single men first, and some boards did so exclusively. One board even suggested lowering the draft age because, "in the country districts boys marry young and in order to get unmarried men the age limit would have to be reduced to 19."[81]

Some boards complained about how the system worked. The local board of District 2 in Covington acknowledged that it had little difficulty obtaining men for its quota but cited one or two men who had claimed exemption on the grounds of "being Socialists and opposed to war." In a particularly galling case, one such man whose claim for exemption had been rejected "pretended insanity" after being sent to a military camp. After a few days in the guardhouse, he had been sent home, where he was currently working. The board opined: "If this man was too crazy to remain in the army, we think he should be sent to the State Asylum and not be allowed abroad (or, presumably, back home to work)."[82]

The strongest language from boards regarded exemptions for conscientious and religious objectors. Nearly all the boards believed those men should be drafted; some adamantly believed so. One county summed up its position by stating: "we can't see why any man that receives all the benefits derived from living under our Government could have any scruples against defending it in a live [*sic*] and death struggle."[83]

Working without pay, the men who served on local and district draft boards faced difficult decisions and had to deal with opprobrium, threats, and guilt trips because of their work. In a *Louisville Courier-Journal* article, Western District Board secretary Syd Dodds said that mothers and wives sent letters to the board accusing it of murder.[84]

Nevertheless, the selective service system seemingly worked well in Kentucky. Its success rested on the small team of administrators led by the indefatigable Major Henry Rhodes, but also on the efforts of the many men who served as local, district, medical, and legal board members. As a result of these efforts, proportionately few men resisted the system and were classified as delinquents or deserters. According to the provost marshal's second report, issued late in 1918, Kentucky had one of the lowest desertion rates in the country.

By the time of the Great War's end, some 67,899 Kentuckians had been called up through the selective service system. Of these, 60,617 were inducted and 57,177 were accepted for service; the others were rejected on various grounds.[85] Many of those men would begin their training at Camp Taylor in Louisville.

6

Army Camps

Shortly after the United States entered the war, two army installations existed in Kentucky: Camp Stanley in Lexington, and Fort Thomas in northern Kentucky. By the end of 1917, a massive new undertaking would produce a third facility in southern Louisville: Camp Zachary Taylor. This new camp—or cantonment, as it was often called—became the focal point for army training in the state and region. Toward the end of the war, the US War Department created another camp south of Louisville: Camp Knox. These military facilities proved essential not only in amassing and training soldiers but also in providing a boom to local economies.

Lexington had historically been home to military camps. Because of its central location, the city had served as the site of several small army camps during the Spanish-American War. There, members of the Kentucky State Guard gathered and trained while awaiting deployment. In the years after the Mexican Revolution began in 1910, relations between the United States and Mexico grew antagonistic and threatened war. By April 1914, anticipating a conflict with Mexico or in Europe, the Lexington Board of Commerce foresaw the benefits of housing another army camp. Subsequently, a group of Lexington businessmen formed the Lexington Development Company to seek "a mobilization center in Lexington for the state troops." The company's board of directors included *Lexington Herald* editor Desha Breckinridge and banker John G. Stoll (brother of Kentucky Council of Defense member Richard C. Stoll). The board members thought the federalized Kentucky National Guard might be concentrated in one location in Lexington or Fayette County. Federal military officials and Kentucky National Guard adjutant general Tandy Ellis agreed and considered placing a new camp on farm property just outside Lexington.

The Lexington Development Company purchased the Lansing farm on Versailles Road to use as the camp.[1] By April 21, 1917, Kentucky National Guard troops arrived at the site. Construction began with the installation of new water mains and electricity; eventually, wooden barracks replaced tents. The campsite grew when the Lexington Development Company leased adjacent acreage from Simon Weil, on whose land a camp had been established during the Spanish-American War.[2]

In mid-June Kentucky National Guard commander General Roger Williams officially christened the new camp "Camp Stanley," in honor of Governor Augustus O. Stanley. The camp had barracks, firing ranges, a YMCA tent, and a branch of the Lexington Public Library. The Women's Christian Temperance Union (WCTU) made "comfort kits" for the incoming men. At one point, nearly 4,000 men mobilized at the camp.[3]

The Guardsmen's training started immediately. They woke at 5:30 a.m. and drilled for hours in a difficult-to-maneuver plowed field. In their leisure time, the soldiers of the Second and Third Kentucky Regiments could play baseball, go to the canteen, and attend various "amusements," such as boxing.[4] Other forms of amusement, however, were forbidden.

Before the establishment of Camp Stanley, city officials had sought reforms to curb the use of liquor and prostitution. By 1915, a large vice district existed with many so-called parlor houses of prostitution, including the famous establishment run by "Belle" Brezing (aka Breezing). Lexington mayor J. Ernest Cassidy appointed a commission on social hygiene that transformed into a vice commission. A subsequent commission report revealed the extent of the vice problem in Lexington, and in December 1915 city officials passed an ordinance aimed at curbing prostitution and the sale of liquor. By the time the city sought a military mobilization camp, it claimed it had reduced the number of saloons from 140 to 105 and promised that prostitution would be "combated." Nevertheless, historian James Duane Bolin points out: "Despite the rash of promises made by city officials to secure the camp, and although Belle Breezing's establishment as well as several other less-publicized houses were shut down, Lexington's police officers continued to ignore the problem of prostitution in the city."[5]

National authorities were not ignoring the problems of prostitution and liquor. These were regarded as the key vices that appealed to young soldiers and would remain the army's concern throughout the war. To help combat these problems, in April 1917 the War Department created the Commission on Training Camp Activities (CTCA) under Raymond Fosdick. The CTCA focused on keeping soldiers busy in their free time with healthy and moral activities. Historian Nancy Bristow notes, however: "Though members of the CTCA maintained that the constructive programs of supervised recreation and social hygiene education for soldiers and civilians were the heart and soul of the CTCA design, the reformers had always accepted the complementary need for a coercive program."[6]

To combat vice around military camps, Congress included such measures in the Selective Service Act of 1917. Sections 12 and 13 provided the justification for coercive measures to curb vice. In section 12 Congress granted the president permission to establish regulations prohibiting liquor in or near army camps. That section made it a misdemeanor to sell alcohol to any military person in uniform, a crime punishable by a fine of up to $1,000 and up to a year in prison. Section 13 gave the secretary of war virtual carte blanche to establish prostitution-free zones around military facilities.[7] Consequently, the army set up "moral zones" around camps.

The *Lexington Herald* reported that federal officials sent Lexington police a message "urging the strict enforcement of all laws to keep prohibition and moral conditions in force at the mobilization camp and in Lexington while the soldiers were camped here." Camp Stanley's officials banned troops from entering Lexington's red-light district and pressured Belle Brezing and others to shut down their "bawdy houses." In addition, women found hanging around the camp itself were arrested for vagrancy in a further attempt to curb vice.[8]

Curbing soldiers' thirst for liquor proved even more problematic, despite attempts at strict discipline. Saloons provided liquor, as did bootleggers. After one payday, the "Thirsty Third" Regiment incarcerated more than forty men in the guardhouse. Lexington vice commission chairman George Hunt blamed police judge John J. Riley for refusing to enforce vice ordinances.[9]

Federal authorities joined regimental officers in trying to curtail liquor sales and consumption. Bureau of Investigation special agent Thompson learned that the US commissioner (a court officer) had sent to a federal grand jury the cases of twenty-six people who had illegally sold liquor to soldiers. Thompson also investigated liquor-related cases uncovered by Camp Stanley's provost marshal, such as a Lexington man accused of buying liquor on behalf of soldiers. Thompson traveled outside the city to investigate sales; for example, he went to Tyrone in nearby Anderson County to look into possible bootlegging.[10]

Despite efforts to curb vice, it continued. The federal government paid more than $100,000 in both June and July to the more than 2,500 soldiers stationed at Camp Stanley, so it proved a boon to the local economy. Mayor James Rogers's report that he knew of no houses of prostitution in the city caught the eye of CTCA chairman Raymond Fosdick, who sent an investigator to Lexington. The investigation determined that twenty-six houses of prostitution, "commercialized and organized," still existed. In addition, numerous saloons "were paying no attention to the federal law prohibiting the sale of liquor to soldiers." The investigator concluded: "To sum up: Prostitution and liquor are running riot."[11] Fosdick forwarded the report to BI chief Bruce Bielaski, who asked agent Thompson to proceed with prosecutions under the Selective Service Act.[12]

Besides somewhat curtailing vice in Lexington, the war resulted in other changes for the city's inhabitants. Members of the upper crust had previously vacationed during July, but in 1917, plans to leave the city were set aside in favor of "sewing for soldiers and sailors, conducting first aid classes, gathering funds for charities and entertaining the soldiers in Camp Stanley." Would-be Lexington vacationers had reportedly "resigned themselves to wartime economy" and had to "content themselves with an occasional barge party on the Kentucky River or a dip in the new Country Club swimming pool."[13]

Camp Stanley was keeping Lexington citizens busy in the summer of 1917. But the city's leaders were busy lobbying federal authorities in Washington to expand the camp beyond its designation as a mobilization site for state troops. They hoped Camp Stanley would become a regional training center for Kentucky, Indiana, and Ohio, one of sixteen new cantonments the war required.

When the United States entered the Great War, it was readily apparent that the nation would have to increase its military capabilities quickly. A large modern army would be required, and this meant that staging areas and training camps would have to be built. The army considered establishing cantonments in thirty-two locations, but eventually it settled on sixteen new camps. Cities around the country quickly grasped the potential economic benefit of having camps nearby. In Kentucky and Indiana, several cities tried to influence Washington for consideration, including Lexington, Danville, Bowling Green, Terre Haute, and Evansville.

Kentuckians began to lobby for a new cantonment in their state. The city editor of the *Louisville Courier-Journal,* Brainard Platt, recognized the desirability of a camp and talked about the possibility with Haden Moise, president of the Retail Merchants' Association. Moise took the idea to the Louisville Board of Trade, which responded with a strong, concerted effort to get a camp. The board quickly put together a committee headed by its president, Fred Sackett; members included Mayor John Buschemeyer, *Courier-Journal* managing editor Arthur Krock, and other prominent Louisville leaders. The committee raised funds to buy land just south of Louisville as a potential campsite, and an army Board of Inspection visited the site, which was envisioned as housing an army division of 30,000 men plus support units. The committee recognized that the infrastructure, such as water and transportation, would have to be improved. It called on Congressman Swagar Sherley from Louisville to talk to Washington officials about the benefits of locating a camp near the city.[14]

Meanwhile, the army board also visited Lexington, where officials made a pitch for the camp to be located at existing Camp Stanley. *Lexington Herald* editor Desha Breckinridge led a group that made a presentation to the board.[15]

The army did not take long to make a decision about where to put the cantonment. On June 11, 1917, Louisvillians learned that their city had been chosen as the location of Camp Zachary Taylor. (The twelfth president of the

United States, Taylor had spent most of his childhood and adolescence on the family farm outside of Louisville before entering the US Army.) The *Louisville Courier-Journal* proudly proclaimed that the city had won the camp "on merit."[16]

Lexingtonians immediately protested. The outcry was not unexpected, given that the US government had recently expanded Camp Stanley, and the city hoped (or expected) the government to continue that development. City and county officials sent a telegram to Secretary of War Baker warning against sending "men from mountains and uplands to mosquito-infested, fog-covered land."

An editorial by Desha Breckinridge in the *Lexington Herald* implied foul play, focusing on Fred Sackett's and the *Louisville Courier-Journal*'s praise of Congressman Sherley's assistance. Noting Sherley's position as the ranking member on the Committee of Appropriations and the chairman of the Committee on Fortifications, Breckinridge raised the specter of inappropriate influence by Sherley. The editorial dramatically concluded: "No man in or out of the army familiar with the location, the geology, the soil, the climate at the Falls of the Ohio and in the Blue Grass, would select Louisville in preference to the Blue Grass were the health and the lives and the comfort of the soldiers the sole consideration."[17]

A Lexington delegation traveled to Washington to appeal to Secretary of War Baker, enlisting the help of Senator Ollie James and Congressman J. Campbell Cantrill from Georgetown. Former mayor John Skain, Desha Breckinridge, and state senator Thomas Combs argued that Lexington offered superior health conditions and met all the other selection criteria. They asked that Lexington at least be considered as a subcantonment, perhaps hosting the Indiana and Kentucky National Guards, instead of sending them south to Mississippi to train.[18]

In a news report he filed about his trip, Breckinridge lamented: "The fact that he [Sherley] used his position and power to secure the location of a training camp for his home city, instead of having the selection made upon the recommendation of army officers, has caused, in my judgment, very keen disappointment among those who expected him to take the higher rank. It has put him in a class with those who make some other object than the best interests of the soldiers and of the army the determining motive in their actions."[19]

The *Courier-Journal* in turn scoffed at the Lexington delegation: "The funny little Tooley-streeters who have trotted off to Washington to throw mud at Louisville are not representative of Lexington."[20]

Breckinridge could not let the issue go, opining in a long editorial: "Louisville counted on political influence and won." Accusing the city's newspaper of covering up facts, especially about vice in Louisville, he alleged, "We know in all America of no newspaper that has for so long persistently pursued the policy of the prostitution of its columns as has *The Louisville Courier-Journal*." A few days later, after a controversy arose over which newspaper had the right to publish the war memoirs of Lexington's Alexander McClintock, Breckinridge asserted: "For years it has been known not only in Louisville, but throughout the State, that *The Courier-Journal* suppressed, distorted or fabricated news to accomplish its purposes."[21]

Subsequent *Herald* editorials continued to question the choice of Louisville and the process used. The Sunday, June 24, 1917, edition included a large section devoted to documents filed with federal authorities on behalf of each city's claim for a cantonment, plus an engineer's report strongly criticizing the selected site. To all this, the *Courier-Journal* replied in a headline: "Lexingtonians Licked, but Will Not Admit It."[22]

Lexington not only failed to get the new cantonment; it also lost Camp Stanley when the Kentucky National Guard was amalgamated into the US Army. Starting in late August, the Guardsmen started moving to Camp Shelby, Mississippi, for further training before being sent to Europe. Governor Stanley visited Lexington for a final parade by the Second and Third Regiments, attended by more than 20,000 spectators. The Guard finished moving south during September. Camp Stanley was shut down soon thereafter and sold to Simon Weil. Lexington Development Company secretary Denny B. Goode acknowledged that although the camp had not been used for as long as initially expected, "it had been a successful investment for Lexington business, in that it had brought thousands of soldiers [to Lexington] for many months."[23]

No doubt Congressman Sherley's influence played a role in the decision to locate the cantonment in Louisville, but other factors certainly helped. The city was much larger and had more amenities than its Kentucky rivals. (Louisville's estimated population in 1916 was over 238,000, while Lexington's was 41,000.) Its central location relative to Indiana, Ohio, Illinois, and Kentucky, combined with good railroad connections north to Indianapolis and Chicago and south to Nashville, made the city a good prospect. In addition, there was plenty of reasonably priced land south of Louisville to construct a very large camp with extensive infrastructure needs. Finally, the Board of Trade garnered strong support from private and public interests and put together a strong campaign to obtain the camp.[24]

Despite the outcry from Lexington, plans continued for a cantonment six miles south of Louisville. A central Kentucky firm, Mason and Hanger, was chosen as the site contractor. Work began before the end of June, when the Southern Railway built five spurs totaling six miles of track into the campsite. An estimated 1,500 railroad cars of material arrived over three weeks in July, much of it lumber. The cantonment construction project was a massive effort—in essence, creating a city within a city. A month after the start of construction, more than 3,500 men ranged over the site each day; eventually, their number swelled to more than 7,500. They laid out streets and provided infrastructure such as electrical lines, sewers, and water pipelines. The sudden influx of men strained housing and other resources. Mason and Hanger constructed a hostelry to house and feed government officials and construction workers. Eventually, carpenters put up more than 2,000 buildings on the site, including barracks, a hospital, headquarters buildings, theaters, stables, hay sheds, a rifle range, and buildings for organizations such as the YMCA and Knights of Columbus. The Kentucky National Guard's First Regiment encamped at the construction site, living in tents and guarding the area.[25]

Camp Taylor was planned to house more than 40,000 men, but by the summer of 1918, the camp's population swelled to nearly 60,000; the extra men were housed in an additional tent camp. The training and care of these men depended on a complex support system of people and materials. For example, the army's quartermaster general anticipated that the camp would need 240 cooks, which Louisville hotelier Otto Seelbach's committee eventually supplied. The army also foresaw that nearly fifteen tons of garbage would be created each day, requiring large disposal contracts. Bids were let out to buy 17,000 tons of coal and 500 cords of wood in anticipation of heating needs.[26] Thus the new cantonment began generating money for the Louisville economy, just as city leaders had hoped. By the third week in August, the *Lexington Herald* reported: "Within less than three months there has grown up, on the southern outskirts of Louisville, a mushroom city now nearly completed, capable of housing more than 40,000 men."[27]

The construction team worked to meet a September 1 deadline, when selectees who had registered in the June draft were expected to be called to service. Some of the new selectees were inducted at Fort Thomas in northern Kentucky before proceeding to Camp Taylor. Constructed beginning in 1889, the fort stood atop a hill overlooking the Ohio River and was named for General George H. Thomas, the Union army's "Rock of Chickamauga." The fort served as a mobilization point during the Spanish-American War; afterward, it temporarily hosted army units going to the Philippines. Because of declining activity at the fort, Congress in 1912 considered transferring it to the Marine Corps. In response, the War Department boosted activity at Fort Thomas, stationing the Ninth Infantry there after it returned from the Philippines. In 1914 the Ninth Infantry moved to the Mexican border, and the fort became the mobilization center for the Kentucky National Guard before it left for Texas during

Postcard showing the size of Camp Zachary Taylor.

the Mexican Punitive Expedition. In February 1917 the Kentucky National Guard returned to Fort Thomas from Texas and awaited demobilization.[28]

With the US entry into the Great War, the post became a major induction center. Recruits and drafted men from Indiana, Ohio, Kentucky, and West Virginia went to Fort Thomas to await shipment to training camps. Twenty temporary buildings housed them. To make the new soldiers feel more at home, the YMCA and Knights of Columbus set up facilities in camp huts. More than 70,000 men spent two days to three weeks at the fort before moving on, often to Camp Taylor.[29]

Camp Taylor became the basic training site for men from Kentucky, Indiana, and Illinois. The division they would form, the Eighty-Fourth, was appropriately nicknamed the "Lincoln Division." In addition to the Eighty-Fourth, several other units would train at the camp at various times, including those for chaplains, artillery officers, and hospital personnel. Brigadier General Wilber E. Wilder briefly served as the camp's first commander. Awarded the Medal of Honor for bravery—for rescuing a wounded comrade while fighting on the western frontier—Wilder had recently served in Pershing's Punitive Expedition to Mexico. Wilder reverted to brigade commander when Major General Harry Hale arrived in October to take over as commanding officer of Camp Taylor and the Eighty-Fourth Division.

Born in Illinois and a West Point graduate, Hale had served for many years on the US western frontier and in the Philippines. Upon his arrival in Louisville, he immediately began a round of public appearances, leading a "grand march" to a "War Fete Ball," speaking to the Transportation Club, and meeting with the Louisville Board of Trade, which had been instrumental in bringing the camp to Kentucky.[30]

The first draft selectees actually reported to Camp Taylor on September 5, lining up in chutes labeled by state to begin processing. Lester C. Monk, a

John Herbert of Louisville was the first man to line up in the Kentucky chute at the opening of Camp Taylor.

twenty-two-year-old Illinois farmer, passed through first, followed by Ward McCormick from Indiana and then John Lee Herbert from Louisville. A fireman, Herbert would remain at the camp and serve on its firefighting team for the duration of the war.[31]

Approximately 400 men showed up at Camp Taylor on the first day. At noon they received a substantial meal: "sirloin steak, mashed potatoes, stewed tomatoes, peach roll, iced tea, and bread and butter." Officers showed the new men their quarters; each inductee received two blankets, a mattress, and a cot.[32]

Draft selectees arriving from the tristate area underwent medical evaluations, received vaccinations, and began their military training. After reveille at 0545, assembly at 0600, and breakfast at 0630, the new soldiers spent all day training, ending with taps at 2230. They learned to salute and march; they trained with wooden bayonets and learned about hand grenades and machine guns. Some of the latter training was supervised by French officers, veterans of the trench fighting that dominated warfare on the Western Front.[33]

Some of the men who trained at Camp Taylor were not Americans. As historian Nancy Gentile Ford points out, "During the First World War, the U.S. government drafted into military service nearly half a million immigrants of forty-six different nationalities, creating an army with over 18 percent of its soldiers born in foreign countries." Several noncitizens ended up in the Seventh Provisional Training Battalion, where one trainer, Sergeant Murphy, had trouble with the names of some of his recruits. Instead of calling out the roll, which included some seemingly unpronounceable names such Stojakovich and Guzrencik, Murphy devised an alternative: he simply assigned Irish names to these men, who would "grin good naturedly and answer quickly to their adopted names."[34]

Sergeant Murphy's humorous solution underscored the democratic makeup of the Camp Taylor troops. It also highlights an issue the military faced: how best to manage men for war. By schooling them to become Americans, they might feel a stronger responsibility to the nation during the war. The Kentucky Council of Defense sponsored an Americanization campaign throughout the state, and this effort extended to Camp Taylor. Officials there held classes that enabled selectees to become citizens. Naturalization ceremonies took place under what was known as the "naturalization elm," a huge tree situated behind the camp laundry. There, men who wanted to become citizens could be sworn in while facing a flagpole. On one occasion, 951 soldiers marched to the tree and swore their allegiance to the United States. On another occasion, federal judge Walter Evans presided at naturalization ceremonies under the elm, creating new citizens of more than 400 men from seventeen nationalities.[35]

After they settled into the routine of camp life, soldiers participated in activities sponsored by organizations with an official presence at the cantonment. These activities fell under the general supervision of Raymond Fosdick's CTCA (which had investigated vice in Lexington). The CTCA's purpose was to "supply the normalities of life to nearly a million and a half young men in training camps, and to keep the environs of those camps clean and wholesome."[36] It led efforts to "keep men moral," addressing the issues of alcohol and prostitution around cantonments. It relied on key organizations to help: the so-called Seven Sisters included the Young Men's Christian Association (YMCA), Young Women's Christian Association (YWCA), Salvation Army, Jewish Welfare Board, Knights of Columbus, War Camp Community Service, and American Library Association.

The largest organization at Camp Taylor was the YMCA. It began its work there immediately, even before its auditorium could be built. When the auditorium was dedicated in September 1918, more than 4,000 soldiers heard a varied, ecumenical group of speakers, including Governor A. O. Stanley, Louisville mayor John Buschemeyer, Camp Taylor commander General Wilder, camp YMCA director Philo Dix, Southern Baptist Theological Seminary president Edgar Young Mullins, former lieutenant governor and prominent Catholic E. J. McDermott, Jewish leader Benjamin Washer, and Methodist pastor A. P. Lyon.[37]

The Camp Taylor YMCA had three departments that provided nonmilitary activities and services: religious, educational, and physical. (Social and business departments were added later.) Dix directed its efforts; he had been named the YMCA's Kentucky state secretary in 1908. Mullins led the religious department on a part-time basis while juggling his duties as president of the seminary. A former Kentucky superintendent of public instruction and secretary of state, Harry Vernon McChesney headed the education department, while a succession of men led the physical department.[38]

Mullins's religious department served a very important role in the camp.

It represented Protestant denominations and worked harmoniously with the Catholic Knights of Columbus and the Young Men's Hebrew Association (YMHA). The department held regular Sunday services, often with guest clergy; conducted weekly Bible services; gave out New Testaments; and sought to renew soldiers' dedication to Christianity.

McChesney's education department not only taught reading to illiterates but also offered French classes, general educational and military lectures, and special classes in mathematics. Soldiers could attend classes and lectures on the background of the war, health, sanitation, travel, and scientific subjects. Expert lecturers came from outside the camp, but they were supplemented by soldiers who had previously been college professors. Camp and YMCA authorities placed special emphasis on military lectures, which sought to explain to the soldiers why the United States needed to participate in and win the war. In February 1918 more than 4,000 soldiers heard former president William Howard Taft praise the YMCA and the Red Cross and warn against seeking a premature peace.[39]

The YMCA's physical education department complemented military training by sponsoring team activities such as baseball, football, and basketball, as well as individual sports such as boxing and wrestling. The department also encouraged other games, such as tug-of-war, relay races, and even sedentary activities such as chess. McChesney believed that "no other one thing done for the men, either by the military authorities or the 'Y' did more to contribute to the health, happiness and morale of the men than this play life made possible by the Physical Work Department."[40]

When the YMCA's social department came into being, it arranged "entertainments" such as "musicales, socials, receptions, humorous lectures, plays, vaudeville, readings, moving pictures, etc." to "promote the happiness and contentment of the men." The department used national, local, and camp talent in these offerings. A camp music director played an important role in boosting morale. One of the Y's secretaries, Joseph Severance, offered a very popular lecture entitled "Four Years behind the Bars," a humorous account of his years as chaplain at the Frankfort Penitentiary! The business department offered valuable services such as distributing the mail and providing money orders, stamps, postcards, and other sundry items to the troops.[41]

The YMCA did much more for the men at Camp Taylor. It sponsored "state" days for Kentucky, Indiana, and Illinois troops, with special receptions and speeches from officials such as Kentucky's lieutenant governor James Black. One man from the Y edited and published the local edition of *Trench and Camp,* a general newspaper that contained four pages of national boilerplate news and four pages of local news from the military and the various camp welfare organizations. The Y also organized "Britain Day," "French Day," and "Mother's Day" celebrations.[42]

These YMCA activities addressed the physical and moral aspects of preparing men to be soldiers. Camp Taylor's General Hale valued the YMCA's efforts; he believed that "when you make a man moral, you make him a better soldier." The services and activities provided by the YMCA boosted the morale of the trainees. Indianapolis native Private James B. Malone wrote to Mt. Sterling resident Sidney Johnson to thank him for contributing magazines to the camp's YMCA. He wanted the Kentuckian to know that "such reading material does come into the hands of the boys and is very much appreciated." He continued by noting that the YMCA helped ensure that "camp life is a clean, pure and good life to live."[43]

The Camp Taylor YMCA under the leadership of Dix, Mullins, and McChesney continued after the armistice, until the men were released from service on September 1, 1919. The organization had a tremendous impact on the soldiers who passed through the camp, and thousands of men participated in YMCA activities.

One of the YMCA's natural allies in its quest to educate the men at Camp Taylor was the American Library Association (ALA). As noted by archivist Caroline Daniels: "The American Library Association responded to the Great War with 'pep,' in the parlance of the day. At its 1917 annual meeting, held in Louisville in June, the association approved the Library Mobilization Committee's recommendation that the ALA be instrumental in providing the troops with access to books. It then established the War Service Committee to oversee library service in the training camps."[44]

The YMCA had provided books to soldiers on the Mexican border during the Punitive Expedition, and the Louisville Free Public Library (LFPL) had provided books to the Kentucky National Guard after it returned from its border duties. With the support of the ALA, the Louisville Free Public Library took the lead in providing a library at Camp Taylor. The LFPL's director, George Settle, simultaneously served as camp library director. Two women from the library—head of cataloging May Wood Wigginton and Jefferson branch director Minnie Dearing Miller—also played an important role in the camp's library operations. Wigginton made sure that materials were quickly cataloged and made available to the men; Miller directed the camp's hospital library. "Between September 1917 and July 1918 more than 30,000 books were processed for the camp library."[45] Even though the camp library had male leadership, Daniels concludes:

> Clearly, in the brief period in which Camp Taylor was in operation, women provided consistent support and a fair measure of leadership,

> even though they were rarely recognized via official appointments. While Minnie Dearing Miller and May Wood Wigginton were the only women who were given individual recognition on official lists of assistants and other staff members, female library workers played an important and broader role in the Camp Taylor library. The women who came from the LFPL to do their part for the war effort cataloged, labeled, and pocketed books and helped with circulation and reference; they assisted with and even led the most essential functions of the library; and they were a social presence in the camp.[46]

Under Settle's direction, the Louisville Board of Trade supported a campaign to raise $30,000 for the Camp Taylor library. Settle also led a citizens' group that organized committees throughout Kentucky to raise money for the library. As a result of the successful fund-raising campaign, a large central library building was built, complete with a reading room and a quiet room for writing. Sublibraries in officers' quarters and in the other camp welfare buildings, such as YMCA huts, gave the soldiers more access to books.[47]

In addition, a book donation campaign asked people to contribute "idle books" for the soldiers. The Kentucky Library Association and various women's clubs supported the effort to provide books for soldiers. The well-known author of *Mrs. Wiggs of the Cabbage Patch,* Louisvillian Alice Hegan Rice, appealed for books to be distributed to soldiers in camps and abroad; in particular, she focused her efforts on supplying books for the Camp Taylor hospital library. "A three-foot bookshelf was built in each of the hospital's fifty-eight wards," and "a food cart, borrowed from the officers' mess, was used for the distribution of the books." Rice attested that the soldiers received books with "eagerness." Throughout Kentucky, the various appeals produced generous contributions: more than 67,000 volumes were donated.[48]

Many Camp Taylor trainees appreciated the library. Unfortunately, not all could do so; illiteracy was a problem for some. A leader in the campaign against illiteracy in Kentucky and the nation, Cora Wilson Stewart worked to combat illiteracy among soldiers, potential draftees, and the general population. A native of Rowan County, Stewart had served as a teacher, county school superintendent, first female president of the Kentucky Educational Association, and president of the Kentucky Illiteracy Commission. In 1911 she had developed the concept of "Moonlight Schools," where adults could attend literacy classes in the evenings. Biographer Yvonne Baldwin notes: "Stewart envisioned instruction that would enable adults to function in a modernizing society and economy, provide the ability to read and write basic sentences, conduct simple business transactions, and read a few verses of the

Bible. In effect, students who completed the Moonlight curriculum acquired functional literacy."[49]

With US entry into the war, the illiteracy problem became more acute. Stewart estimated that in Kentucky alone, 25,000 to 30,000 potential draftees might be illiterate. Baldwin described the resulting difficulties: "They could not sign their name, read orders, read a manual of arms, or read their Bibles, and just as important in a rural society that valued family closeness, they could not read letters or write home. They could not understand the signals or follow the signal corps in battle, and presumably could not understand the cause for which they were fighting or the principles for which their government stood."[50]

Cora Wilson Stewart rose to the challenge. When it became apparent that state funding was inadequate, she started a grassroots campaign to raise $30,000 in funding, sending letters to school superintendents and women and encouraging them to "fill little banks for us with fifty dimes," which would "enable five men to learn to read and write." In addition, several hundred people volunteered to teach soldiers and potential draftees.[51]

To reach potential draftees, "Stewart created a 'Course of Study' for 1917 Moonlight Schools that focused on war-related issues and encouraged patriotism. Included were lessons with a clear message urging all Americans to get behind the war effort." On behalf of the YMCA, Stewart wrote "a primer for illiterate draftees" called *Soldier's First Book.* In addition to focusing on patriotism, her lesson materials had a social message: "Stewart's lessons for soldiers taught not just reading and writing but right thinking and proper behavior as well." This included keeping fit and eschewing debilitating products such as soft drinks and tobacco.[52]

In recognition of her efforts against illiteracy, the National War Work Council of the YMCA not only promoted her primer for draftees but also purchased 60,000 copies of her *Country Life Reader* to use in cantonments. This book was actually "a series of primers for adult pupils that focused almost exclusively on rural life, emphasizing its peculiarities, problems, and special beauties." In addition, Stewart became head of the National Committee on Illiteracy, which addressed the problem among men of military age across the country. Secretary of the Interior Franklin Lane estimated there were 5.5 million illiterates in the country, which included more than 700,000 men of draft age.[53]

The illiteracy campaign carried over to Camp Taylor, which received the first thousand copies of Stewart's *Soldier's First Book.* At one point, more than 2,000 illiterate trainees spent four nights a week learning to read under compulsory attendance rules mandated by General Hale. The YMCA education department led this effort, which involved volunteer YMCA personnel and fellow soldiers and used mess halls as classrooms. Many of the soldier volunteers had previously been schoolteachers. After weeks of instruction, men who passed a basic reading and writing test received a certificate.

According to McChesney, during the life of Camp Taylor, more than 14,000 illiterates passed through it, of whom 2,000 were foreigners. The YMCA held separate classes for draftees who did not speak English, using the "Peter Roberts system of teaching English." This system, devised by the immigration secretary of the YMCA's International Committee, was designed specifically for immigrants living on the East Coast.[54] As noted by Baldwin:

> Although soldiers took priority in the 1917 sessions, Stewart also wanted the public to recognize that illiteracy left civilians equally handicapped in their ability to serve the nation in its time of need. Unable to sign food pledge cards, understand bulletins, or read instructions given through the daily press, they could not read the propaganda, could not help their country by signing applications for liberty loan bonds or thrift cards, and presumably could not understand the government's purposes and principles and therefore could not give "intelligent support" to the war cause. Moreover, they could not provide "encouragement and comfort to their boys in service by writing letters from home."[55]

The literacy campaign at Camp Taylor reflected a progressive public policy designed to improve the life of the nation's citizen-soldiers.

Other social welfare organizations existed at Camp Taylor to assist the new soldiers. Two focused on specific religious constituencies: the Knights of Columbus and the Young Men's Hebrew Association. Secretary of War Baker had decreed that only the YMCA and Knights of Columbus would be allowed to erect buildings at cantonments: the YMCA to represent Protestant denominations, and the Knights to represent Catholics. This arrangement bothered some Protestant groups that wished to have their own denominations directly represented at the camps. Baker held firm in his decision, citing the history of the two organizations in assisting army troops during the Mexican Punitive Expedition. The YMHA affiliated itself with the YMCA, thereby gaining access to the camps.[56]

Under the leadership of Louisvillian Benjamin Washer, the YMHA worked with the national Jewish Welfare Board, and especially its Women's Auxiliary, to support Jewish soldiers at Camp Taylor. Washer had been city and managing editor of the *Louisville Herald* before becoming a prominent attorney. He helped the YMHA ensure that religious services took place at the camp on Friday evenings. Washer also led a campaign to raise $10,000 to provide a soldiers' club at Camp Taylor where men could relax and enjoy social and recreational activities such as dances and suppers. The soldiers' club provided other activities related to "the more serious side of military life and instruction to soldiers." In this vein, Mullins, the camp's YMCA religious department head, spoke to the YMHA soldiers on "Why America Fights."[57]

Aided by other Louisville Jewish organizations, the YMHA and Jewish Welfare Board helped families who were visiting the soldiers. They also placed soldiers in Jewish homes over the holidays, visited Jewish soldiers in the hospital, and ensured ties between the local Jewish community and the soldiers.[58]

Through the work at Camp Taylor and other cantonments, as well as other war-support efforts, the nation's Jewish leaders helped foster a recognition of American religious pluralism. In the analysis of historian Jessica Cooperman, during the war, "Judaism was recognized by the state, along with Protestantism and Catholicism, as a 'fundamentally American' religion." The Jewish community's efforts at Camp Taylor allowed the soldiers to maintain their sectarianism while helping them fit into the larger picture of "Americanism" in support of democratic ideals.[59]

When the plans for Camp Taylor were announced, the Knights of Columbus also sought funds and eventually erected five buildings. Catholic officials estimated that perhaps one-third of the camp's soldiers would be Catholic, requiring large amounts of support. Even before the initial building was finished, Catholics celebrated the first Mass at the camp in September 1917. Louisville priests conducted the services. On one October Sunday, more than 4,000 men reportedly attended Mass. Like the Jewish organizations, the Knights publicized that their activities were open to everyone, welcoming soldiers with signs over building doorways stating, "Everyone Welcome." Like the YMHA, the Knights offered many recreational activities and sponsored many events, including boxing matches.[60]

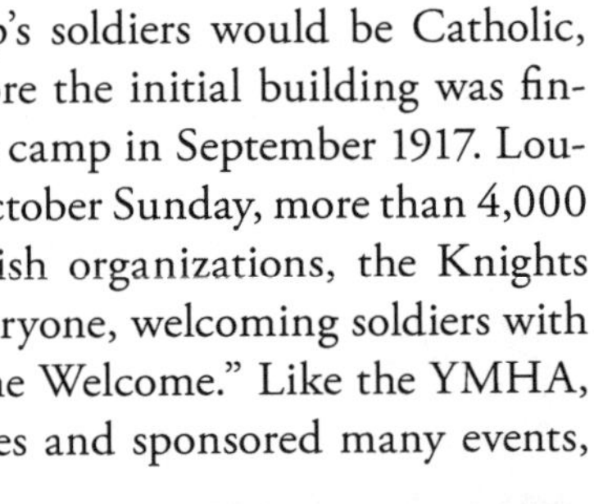

African American baseball team sponsored by the Knights of Columbus at Camp Taylor in Louisville. (Knights of Columbus)

Other organizations chipped in to help soldiers' families. The Young Women's Christian Association constructed a "Hostess House" at the camp. As described by historian Nancy Bristow, Hostess Houses were "buildings inside the camp intended to provide a safe meeting place for soldiers and civilian women. Providing what the Commission on Training Camp Activities (CTCA) understood as a feminine refuge within the male environment of the training camp, the houses offered the comforts and casualness of home, provided meals by the thousands to soldiers and their friends, housed women in emergencies, and in a pinch sometimes served as the scene for weddings."[61]

The YWCA's Hostess House at Camp Taylor provided a safe haven for female visitors. (University of Louisville)

Kentucky newspapers lauded the building of the Hostess House at Camp Taylor. The *Mt. Sterling Advocate* stated: "As most of our boys are sent to this camp, the Hostess House will be peculiarly dear to our hearts." Noting that its local fund-raising goal for the house was only $40, the *Breckenridge News* called this a "comparatively small amount" and observed, "there should be no trouble raising it"; it concluded: "We feel sure Cloverport will do its best." The Camp Taylor Hostess House opened on January 2, 1918, with the national director of the YWCA's Hostess Houses, Edna Sandlin, attending.[62]

The YWCA and military officials hoped the Hostess Houses would help combat some of the scourges associated throughout history with military camps. Alcoholism, prostitution, and venereal disease worried both military and civilian authorities. Even as the camp was being erected, the *Courier-Journal* reported: "Bootleggers Doing Big Business at Cantonment." As was the case in Lexington, vice existed in clearly established areas in Louisville. When the War Department issued an order barring vice within five miles of a military camp, people in the Portland area of Louisville became concerned. Because the neighborhood was just outside the exclusion zone, it might attract "disorderly houses and undesirable characters." Faced with the benefits of bringing a cantonment to the city, Louisville authorities finally agreed to close its vice district on September 1, 1917, despite reservations by some officials. Mayor Buschemeyer was one who questioned whether closure of the district would lead to the dissemination of vice throughout the city, as the Portland residents feared.[63]

Some people believed stronger measures against vice were needed. Jefferson County judge Samuel Greene assured people that a volunteer force would deal with the situation by picking up girls under age eighteen who were "found alone or in bad company at night and send[ing] them home to their mothers, or to the Detention Home for the second offense and to the Juvenile Court for the third."[64]

In addition to seeking out and punishing vice, the CTCA sought to divert soldiers with constructive activities at the YMCA, Knights of Columbus, and other groups. It also sponsored programs to enlighten and provide wholesome entertainment. Social hygiene programs pointed out the dangers of venereal disease. A series of athletics programs such as baseball games kept the men busy with healthy pursuits and provided a break from serious training. On the cultural side, a Liberty Theater opened at Camp Taylor in January 1918 with a performance by the Cincinnati Orchestra. Subsequent events included plays, concerts, boxing matches, and "singing carnivals." The CTCA encouraged men to sing at many events to facilitate group unity and boost morale.[65]

Efforts to provide positive entertainment were not limited to activities at the camp itself. Sponsored by the Louisville Board of Trade, a War Recreation Board helped soldiers experience some kind of normal life in Louisville. The board offered opportunities in Louisville "which they [the soldiers] have been accustomed to having in their home communities. These include a square deal in the business houses of the city, an opportunity to meet the citizens of Louisville in a friendly way, an opportunity to meet young women of Louisville in a social way, an opportunity to see something of the inside of home life in the city, an opportunity to attend parties and dances and social affairs, an opportunity for decent and entertaining theatrical performances and other commercial recreation."[66]

By the end of October 1917, the Board of Trade established a Soldiers' Club in downtown Louisville where enlisted men from Camp Taylor could eat in the canteen, go bowling, play billiards and other games, relax, and even sleep in the dormitory on weekends. The board also sponsored dances, teas, movies, and other entertainments. In addition, it lobbied on behalf of visitors, especially women, who came to Louisville to see friends and relatives at Camp Taylor. The board condemned landlords who made exorbitant profits off visitors, and it asked churches to ameliorate temporary housing shortages.[67]

Other Louisville groups provided entertainment and comfort to the servicemen. The CTCA called on the Playground and Recreation Association of America to create a War Camp Community Service (WCCS), led by a committee of prominent Kentuckians such as Samuel Thruston Ballard, Desha Breckinridge, Marshall Bullitt, Polk Laffoon, R. C. Ballard Thruston, and Edward Hines. In Louisville the WCCS sponsored dances, arranged free tickets to movies, and eventually took over the running of the Soldiers' Club.[68]

In a similar venture, the Louisville branch of the National League for Women's Service sponsored a Khaki Club in downtown Louisville. Championed by Adeline Strater, the club was established on October 10, 1917, and provided comfortable armchairs and writing tables with stationery to make soldiers feel welcome and at home. After the soldiers kept asking, "Where can we get a little food at a reasonable price with a real taste of home?" the club's sponsors established a modest canteen with a "ten foot counter of rough boards, covered with an oil cloth." This arrangement soon evolved into a more elaborate affair, where soldiers could purchase sandwiches, pies, ice cream, drinks, and other items. Proceeds from the canteen helped pay for the club's expenses and generated enough money to give soldiers treats at Thanksgiving and Christmas. The Khaki Club also gave the soldiers opportunities to interact with the women sponsors, who often served as surrogate mothers to the lonely men.[69]

The officers and men of Camp Taylor could count on various divertissements outside their training hours. Louisvillians and other Kentuckians chipped in and donated money, goods, and services in large quantities. Thousands of men took advantage of these offerings while they underwent initial training and rotated through Camp Taylor on their way to other training camps and postings abroad.

Most of the initial contingent of men reporting to Camp Taylor became part of the Eighty-Fourth, or Lincoln, Division. The majority of the enlisted men were selectees summoned by draft boards in Kentucky, Indiana, and Illinois. Many of the officers had trained together at Fort Benjamin Harrison in Indianapolis.

The division consisted of two infantry brigades, an artillery brigade, signal and machine gun battalions, and support units such as engineers. The division established various specialty training schools for engineers, cooks, artillerymen, supply clerks, and even specialists to take care of the more than 7,000 horses on the post (many of them used to haul artillery). Assisted by French advisers, the field artillery school taught men how to maintain the equipment, sight for accuracy, and handle the horses.[70]

It took a while to equip the Eighty-Fourth Division properly because of the weak state of the country's military preparation. Division strength fluctuated as men were siphoned off to serve in other units and sent for training at other camps. After reaching a low point of around 10,000 in April 1918, the division began to receive new allotments, bringing the strength back up to around 13,000 men. General Hale left the camp in November 1917 to travel to France to reconnoiter the situation, returning in February 1918.

By March 1918, a new artillery range had been created at West Point, Kentucky, about thirty miles south of Louisville, where the field artillery could actually fire weapons. With more and more US troops—"Sammies"—being sent to France monthly, the Eighty-Fourth Division anticipated a move. This occurred in June, when the division transferred to Camp Sherman in Chillicothe, Ohio, for advanced training before going abroad. The division finally left in September for France, where its men served primarily as replacement troops for other units.[71]

Despite the departure of the Eighty-Fourth Division, Camp Taylor continued to serve as a depot base, providing basic training for selectees. The 159th Depot Brigade was established in the fall of 1917, and Brigadier General Guy Carleton was assigned to command it. Men were transferred from this brigade to other units across the country in need of replacements. Some went into the Eighty-Fourth Division; many asked to be transferred to the new artillery units being formed at the camp.[72]

During the summer of 1918, Camp Taylor took on an important new national focus, transforming itself from an infantry training camp to an artillery camp. This was best exemplified by the creation of the Field Artillery Central Officers Training School (FACOTS).[73]

Before February 1918, training for field artillery had rested with individual divisions. The War Department then determined that this system resulted in ineffectual, inconsistent, or even nonexistent training. Consequently, Brigadier General William Snow was appointed to the new position of chief of field artillery and given the task of creating a new training system for field artillery units. This training system became FACOTS at Camp Taylor in June 1918. As Snow later said, the basic idea of the school was "to teach only the absolute essentials. The whole idea was to equip a graduate [so] that he could perform his duties as a commissioned officer fairly efficiently immediately upon graduation, and to lay a military foundation upon which he could build."[74]

Supervised by Regular Army officers, the new centralized artillery officer training system helped trainees in many ways. It enabled better instruction, ensured uniformity of training, and provided economy of scale in instructors and equipment. Under the command of Colonel Arthur Carter, FACOTS trained over 20,000 men and graduated more than 8,700 before the war ended. It had more than 14,000 men at its peak in November 1918. Hoping to be commissioned as second lieutenants, FACOTS trainees came from the enlisted ranks, Student Army Training Corps (SATC) units at colleges, and civilian life. Given their prior presence at Camp Taylor, many Kentuckians were accepted into the school. A two-week preparatory course in artillery observation batteries helped weed out unfit and unsuitable candidates. After showing proficiency in mathematics and a grasp of army artillery fundamentals, candidates next moved into training batteries, which involved more technical education.[75]

The men chosen for FACOTS advanced training spent forty-three hours a week in instruction and studied under supervisors in the evenings. It was an intensive course in the fundamentals of light and heavy artillery. Training included communications, range of fire, fire discipline, gun squad drill, and many other technical subjects, including the care and handling of the horses that pulled artillery. The twelfth and final week of camp involved a trip to the

Field Artillery Brigade Firing Center at West Point, Kentucky. Under field conditions, candidates carried out all duties, including firing battery drill, driving drill, and other artillery maneuvers. This was hands-on training in preparation for what might take place "over there" during actual fighting.[76]

FACOTS proved to be a great success, satisfying the army's measures of quantity and quality. Top members of the classes went on for specialized training at the School of Fire at Fort Sill, Oklahoma, where they performed well, especially given their relatively short period of instruction at Camp Taylor. The school also provided a large economic boost to Louisville and the surrounding area.

Indeed, Camp Taylor grew so large in the summer of 1918 that tents had to be erected to house nearly 17,000 men (the camp's usual population of 40,000 men had swelled to nearly 60,000). After Major General Hale left, Colonel Fred T. Austin received a promotion to temporary brigadier general and took charge of the camp, where he oversaw other schools and units established there. One such school was the School for Chaplains.

To minister to the religious needs of a massive military force, the army created a School for Chaplains in February 1918. It opened in March at Fort Monroe, Virginia. Commanded by Major Aldred Prudon, a Virginian and an Episcopal minister, the school transferred to Camp Taylor in April. Candidates had to be recommended by various denominational boards. Approximately 250 clergymen attended the school during each five-week session. Instruction included chaplains' duties, sanitation and first aid, military and international law, and horsemanship. Seasoned chaplains injected a note of realism into the training. Some of them had served on the Western Front and drew on their experiences of tending to the needs of fighting soldiers. Chaplains at the school entered as privates; after successfully completing the course, they were commissioned as first lieutenants.[77]

The chaplains' school was also a big success. The *Louisville Courier-Journal* reported, "There has never been the slightest friction because of differences in doctrine. The spirit of fraternalism prevalent in the school is exemplified by the fact that the first class graduated at Camp Zachary Taylor unanimously chose a Roman Catholic priest for the honor of making the class address."[78]

Many of the men sent to Camp Taylor reported positive experiences. Clyde Smithson from Christian County wrote to his father, C. W. Smithson, "Everything in the camp is so arranged that it makes an ideal home for us boys. We have everything for amusements that could be thought of. The drilling is very hard but we are making good time of it." Smithson especially appreciated the religious services at the camp.[79]

The Reverend C. S. Knight from Berea volunteered at the camp's YMCA for a month. He reported to his local newspaper that he was struck by how quickly the men adapted. Referring to the democratizing effect of uniforms, he asserted: "the millionaire's son and the plowboy are reduced to an exact equality." He observed that the food was first rate and that most men gained weight—something Smithson had mentioned to his father as well. Knight was especially proud of the YMCA's efforts to preach the gospel and exclaimed, "How the boys do listen."[80]

Paul Chandler from Adair County thought the situation at Camp Taylor was better than reported by those "who came here expecting to find things as they are at home and who dislike to conform to the regulations of discipline." Chandler was grateful for the heavy overcoat and wool uniforms, which were "very likely warmer than any of [the soldiers] had worn before, and surely much warmer than that worn by the average civilian." The food served one day included "beef with gravy, vegetable soup, Irish potatoes, coffee, light rolls and rice pudding." Referring to his mixed company of Adair County and Louisville colleagues, Chandler noted that the city boys learned to drill and caught on to regulations quicker, but "when it came to handling horses and shooting the rifle, the country men surpassed."[81]

Even during the worst January weather in years, the men at Camp Taylor seemed to prosper. After Paul Chandler left Louisville for Officers' Candidate School, his successor in writing to the *Adair County News,* Edwin Moore, noted that although factories had closed because of the fuel shortage, the soldiers at camp were "perfectly comfortable," with "plenty of fuel, food, clothing and bedding." Daily, weekly, and monthly inspections helped the soldiers keep "their quarters and person in perfect condition." Moore was also impressed by

Camp Taylor chaplains' school attendees lined up for mess call. (Library of Congress)

the morale: "It is remarkable how the men get along with each other. There is no quarrelling or scrapping."[82]

The spring 1918 intake into Camp Taylor included another Adair County man, J. L. Hatfield. He commented on the variegated meals, consisting of "bread, peas, beans, cabbage, steak, pork, coffee, soup, corn, lemonade, onions and raisins." He also had good words for the YMCA: "Camp Taylor is no place for a man to get home sick, for the Y.M.C.A. will sure make a fellow feel at home. They give us two shows a week, free, and the best of speaking and singing and boxing contests. We play baseball, football, box, and do a little bit of everything, but gamble. In fact, there is nothing goes on that is a discredit to a young man's character. It builds him up mentally, morally and physically."[83]

Contrary to the rosy picture painted by the Adair County men, not all the selectees at Camp Taylor behaved themselves or adapted well to being there. Soon after his arrival at the camp, General Hale visited the guardhouse, where he found prisoners "grinning contentedly while consuming huge portions of mince pies." He ordered desserts cut out for the miscreants, who would henceforth eat standing up. An officer explained: "prisoners will appreciate sitting down to a good meal so much after serving a term in the guardhouse that they will be exceedingly careful about getting into trouble."[84]

Some men did not want to be at Camp Taylor or in the army. Citing that they were conscientious objectors, several men refused to obey orders and were subsequently court-martialed. At their trials, they often cited Bible passages to underscore their refusal. Some men agreed to serve only in noncombat units; they were transferred to the Quartermaster Corps or to the base hospital. More than forty objectors agreed to work on farms, some of them owned by Mennonites, who traditionally opposed war. The *Clay City Times* in Powell County opined that accommodating these religious beliefs "speaks much for our Government."[85]

Other men refused to serve even in the base hospital. Some conscientious objectors were found guilty of disobeying orders, sentenced to ten to fifteen years in prison, and given dishonorable discharges. An Indiana Mennonite, Goshen College professor Jesse Brenneman, received a fifteen-year sentence when he and a group of objectors refused to rake grass seed at the camp. He was sent to the Fort Leavenworth Disciplinary Barracks in Kansas to serve his term but was released less than a year later, in January 1919. Brenneman later reported: "At neither place did I suffer physical injuries except to a small extent, those which came through insufficient food at Camp Taylor guard-house, and poorly prepared food at Ft. L.D.B. There were other trials, however, of psychological nature that tested deeply the foundations of our faith, especially while at Camp Taylor, just before being placed into the guard-house and even more so after we were on the inside." Brenneman acknowledged that, on arriving at the camp, he had refused a uniform and then his pay, which prompted a half-hour "grilling" and "several round cussings" from a lieutenant, who accused him of being pro-German.[86]

Although some of the conscientious objectors were imprisoned, the majority were not. They were gathered into a "conscientious objectors detachment" that reported directly to the commander of the 159th Depot Brigade. Then they were put to work, a notion to which Ohio County's *Hartford Herald* could not "conscientiously object."[87]

People who were famous or would become so spent time at Camp Taylor. Author F. Scott Fitzgerald trained there; his main character in *The Great Gatsby* passes through the camp and is smitten by a Louisville belle. Future army general Anthony McAuliffe served at the camp; he would become famous in World War II for his one-word reply to a German ultimatum to surrender his surrounded troops at Bastogne: "Nuts." A famous French painter, Albert Fleury, taught language lessons at the camp.

Famous sportsmen also went through the camp. Professional boxer Packey McFarland taught boxing to selectees and wrote a series of sports articles—"Packey McFarland's Sporting Periscope"—for the *Louisville Courier-Journal.* A teammate of Knute Rockne and Gus Dorais at Notre Dame, Al Feeny, played on the camp's football team; after the war he served as mayor of Indianapolis.

Others would make their mark as teachers and men of letters. John Peale Bishop became a well-known poet and was the inspiration for a character in fellow Princetonian F. Scott Fitzgerald's first novel. Carl Weber, a Rhodes scholar, went through the camp and became a field artillery officer; he later became a professor at Colby College in Maine and an expert on English writer Thomas Hardy.[88]

In sum, Camp Zachary Taylor proved to be one of the most significant of the new cantonments erected by the US Army after the nation's entry into the war in 1917. More than 200,000 men passed through the camp, and more than 150,000 underwent some sort of training there. The camp brought national attention to the state and served as an economic engine for Louisville and areas south of the city. Artillery training was eventually shifted to a new camp thirty miles south of the city, and Camp Taylor was scrapped by the army in 1920. The building lumber was sold and used in homes in a new suburb of Louisville: the Camp Taylor neighborhood.

When they shifted Camp Taylor's focus to artillery training and created a firing range at West Point, federal authorities decided there was a need to build a field artillery brigade firing center. Rather than building it at the firing range at West Point, which was southwest of Louisville near the Ohio River, army officials chose higher ground farther south, near Stithton, Kentucky. Officials envisioned placing six artillery brigades at the new camp, involving 45,000 men. It was named Camp Henry Knox, after George Washington's chief of artillery. This prompted the wags at the *Hopkinsville Daily Kentuckian* to declare: "The boys from there will give the Kaiser some hard knocks." Major William H. Radcliffe oversaw the camp's construction, which soon encountered difficulties.[89]

The state director of the US Employment Service, W. Pratt Dale, estimated that some 15,000 men would be needed to construct the camp. By mid-September 1918, the 6,000 men employed there were struggling to meet a December 1 completion deadline. In addition to barracks, a 2,500-bed hospital and an aviation field needed to be built. Under pressure from the federal government to either get the job done or forfeit the camp, Dale pleaded for more workmen, as did the Kentucky Council of Defense (KCD). To avoid siphoning off construction resources and labor, the US War Industries Board pressured the KCD to reject the construction of a school in Muhlenberg County (all new construction projects in the state had to be approved by the KCD). As construction at Camp Knox lagged, rumors grew that the delays were caused by a host of problems, including influenza, bad housing and sanitation, poor food, and inadequate train service to the camp. Dale, KCD chairman Ed Hines, and other officials visited the work site to investigate. They were convinced that the problems had been addressed, and work continued apace.[90]

Requests for construction workers continued. A *Louisville Courier-Journal* editorial appealed to patriotism to get this important war work done, and it noted that carpenters and other craftsmen were making good wages. A *Breckenridge News* editorial suggested that if farmers did not have livestock to care for after harvesting their crops and sowing winter wheat, they could join the carpenters at the camp. It also suggested that white-collar workers could chip in, leaving their work in the hands of women.[91]

In various newspapers across the state, full-page advertisements signed by Dale, Hines, and Frank McVey, president of the University of Kentucky and head of the state's US Public Service Reserve, appealed for men. Under the headline "Don't Wait to Be Drafted!" the advertisement called for "Volunteers as Patriots for Government Work" and noted the good wages and free housing. The ad admonished: "The credit and good name of the Commonwealth must be upheld." It noted that the federal government was willing to invest $15 million to $20 million in the camp. The ad also appealed to women to encourage their men to "volunteer" for service at the camp: "it is the duty of every loyal Kentucky woman to report them [nonvolunteers] to the nearest United States Employment Service, just as they would a Hun Spy or an army slacker." The ad's signatories expressed faith in their fellow citizens: "It is a man-sized job, all right, even for Kentuckians, but it can be done, as Kentuckians never fail in what they undertake."[92]

To help publicize the need for men, Governor Stanley scheduled a visit to the camp to coincide with the arrival of 1,000 new men and a meeting of the Public Service Reserve's county directors, who were taking the lead in trying to find laborers. As it turned out, the governor did not attend the meeting, but men did show up to work. Acknowledging that the camp would be completed whether peace came in a week or a year, the *Public Ledger* reported that a large number of men from Maysville and neighboring Flemingsburg, "genuine American patriots," were expected to leave for Camp Knox to assist.[93]

The war was ending, however. The Meuse-Argonne offensive begun at the end of September had steadily driven the Germans back, and many people anticipated an Allied victory. Construction continued at Camp Knox, but the sense of urgency slackened. After the armistice, troops moved from their tents at the West Point firing range to the wooden barracks that had been completed at Camp Knox. A labor dispute and strike prompted Major Radcliffe to get permission for soldiers to complete the camp's construction. The army redesignated the camp as a fort in 1932. Fort Knox remains a thriving army post today.[94]

The army camps in Kentucky during the Great War processed thousands of men into the military. Many Kentuckians remained in the state during their initial training at Camp Taylor. The camps provided a boon to the local economies. They also introduced men from neighboring states to the commonwealth. Louisville in particular became well known throughout the country. Kentucky's army camps united local citizens around common causes as they tried to boost the soldiers' morale and make them feel at home. The construction of Camps Taylor and Knox proved that the state could undertake large projects successfully. The camps were a source of pride and a testament to Kentuckians who did their patriotic duty. They showed what people could accomplish when they pulled together for the country. More such effort would be needed to manage food and fuel resources in the nation.

7

Food and Fuel Administration

Soon after the United States declared war, the federal government began many programs to manage resources the war would require. President Wilson and other officials realized that the "total war" would affect Americans' everyday lives. In particular, food and fuel supplies would be crucial to the country's success.

During the early years of the European war, the United States dramatically increased its food exports to the Allies as the war devastated the landscape and consumed manpower. Poor wheat harvests in 1916, however, hampered supply, and as the United States moved closer to war in spring 1917, many people recognized that managing food resources would become critical. Food would be needed to feed not only a burgeoning US military but also America's allies. The war required both increased production and decreased consumption, better means of transportation, and possibly even control of food resources and prices.

The potential for a food shortage was apparent. Processed or manufactured food did not permeate American culture in those days; many people grew what they ate or bought food locally. In March 1917 the president of the First National Bank in Knox County, J. M. Robsion, noted the need to grow more food if the United States joined the European war—a move that seemed to be forthcoming. He patriotically offered the bank's services to "lend money to farmers of Knox County who needed it to buy stock, tools, feed or fertilizer in order to put out a good big crop."[1]

The US Department of Agriculture's chief extension agent at the University of Kentucky, Fred Mutchler, immediately recognized the potential problems for agriculture. At his instigation, the Louisville Board of Trade held a statewide meeting of farmers at the beginning of April. There, they discussed food issues such as crop production, backyard gardens, farm labor, food preservation, and potential alternatives. At the meeting, the state commissioner of agriculture, Mat Cohen, asked farmers to consider reducing their tobacco acreage to grow crops that were more necessary to the war effort, such as soybeans. Fields of tobacco dominated the Kentucky landscape; most farmers depended on it for their livelihood. Even small farms grew it because tobacco was so profitable and thrived in the Kentucky soil. Nevertheless, Cohen appealed to farmers' civic pride, arguing, "Kentucky cannot stand the shame of being fed by Ohio, Illinois, Indiana, Missouri and other States while devoting her soil alone to the cultivation of tobacco as a money crop. Kentucky must feed herself and help feed others."[2]

After the Louisville meeting, Mutchler and Cohen traveled throughout the state addressing farmers and others about agriculture and the war. In Hopkinsville, Mutchler encouraged farmers to redouble their efforts to grow staple crops such as corn and wheat. He encouraged people to plant home gardens. In Maysville, the agricultural extension chief laid out an eight-point plan for city folks to grow gardens on vacant lots and for farmers to raise more livestock and poultry. Commissioner Cohen asked that people "eat less, drink less, buy less and grow more."[3]

In April, Governor Stanley created a state food committee headed by Morgan Hughes, a Bowling Green agricultural agent, to make recommendations about food conservation and greater agricultural production. Stanley believed the committee should direct food production, conservation, and distribution.[4] In a proclamation issued soon thereafter, the governor revealed the committee's recommendations, which ranged from producing a large corn crop and as much livestock as possible to calling on mayors and county judges to enforce vagrancy laws to ensure enough labor for farmers. The governor also met with two-thirds of the state's bankers to encourage them to expand credit to farmers seeking funds to increase crop production.[5]

Governor Stanley and others in Kentucky began to plan, but President Wilson acted quickly. After the United States entered the war, Wilson asked Herbert Hoover to oversee the nation's food efforts. Hoover had successfully headed the Commission for the Relief of Belgium and had "expert knowledge in dealing with the war-time food problems."[6]

Hoover would become a highly recognized public figure as head of the US Food Administration, but other federal officials also helped underscore the federal government's emphasis on food. Assistant Secretary of Agriculture Carl Vrooman traveled to Kentucky and spoke in Louisville at the Board of Trade, in Frankfort before the Kentucky legislature, and in Lexington about food conservation and increased production. Avowing that "the fight is in the furrows," Vrooman believed "the boy out here plowing corn and planting potatoes is doing as much for his country as the soldier in uniform."[7]

Vrooman and other government officials knew the country was facing the three issues outlined by Stanley: production, conservation, and distribution. The Department of Agriculture focused on increasing rural food production by doubling its county agricultural extension agents. Vrooman encouraged not only Kentucky's farmers but also "city folk" to grow more food. He was a strong proponent of a national grow-your-own movement that included school gardens and urban and suburban "war gardens."

Three major national groups focused on gardens: the Woman's Land Army of America, the United States School Garden Army, and the National War Garden Commission. These three organizations reflected the duplication found in much of the war-support effort, but each group had its own niche in the "food war."[8]

The Woman's Land Army of America concentrated on teaching urban women to work on farms. This program proved popular in large urban areas across the United States. In Kentucky, however, the other two programs had a much larger impact.

The "school garden" movement had been immensely popular nationwide during the Progressive Era. Progressives believed that gardening promoted "republican self-sufficiency, mutuality and civic contribution." More than 75,000 school gardens had been planted all over the country by 1906.[9] Building on this movement, the Bureau of Education within the Department of the Interior had created an Office of School and Home Gardening in 1914. Once US entry into the war seemed imminent, the bureau created the United States School Garden Army (USSGA).

While the US Department of Agriculture focused on increasing rural farm production, the USSGA focused on urban and suburban efforts. In the words of Rose Hayden-Smith: "The USSGA represented an unprecedented governmental effort to make agricultural education a formal (and informal) part of the public school curriculum—and home life of students—throughout the United States."[10]

US School Garden Army poster. (Library of Congress)

Federal education commissioner Philander P. Claxton served on the National War Garden Commission (NWGC) and had been a strong proponent of the prewar school garden movement. He hired former Los Angeles superintendent of schools John H. Francis to oversee the USSGA. At the state level, University of Kentucky (UK) horticulture professor Clarence Wentworth Mathews served as an assistant regional director, overseeing the USSGA's efforts in Kentucky and Tennessee.[11]

The school garden movement in Kentucky

had antecedents dating back to the early 1900s. Professor Mathews had spurred the creation of Lexington's first school garden in 1904. The gardens were so popular in Lexington that in early 1917 the local board of education hired four UK seniors to supervise some 6,000 pupils involved with school gardens.[12]

In 1918 the Lexington school garden movement became associated with the national USSGA war effort. To kick off the new collaboration, the city sponsored two elaborate parades on April 2—one in the morning for African Americans (typical in a segregated Kentucky), and one in the afternoon for white children. The mayor and city commissioners, board of education representatives, and various Fayette County luminaries attended. A USSGA official from Washington, Dr. Clarence Wood, spoke to both groups at the end of each parade, praising "the loyal cooperation of principals and teachers and the eager willingness of the boys and girls of [the] city to do their part in a strenuous effort to win the war." The 5,000 schoolchildren who participated also sang the "Garden Song," composed by Lexington schoolboy Joe Lee Davis, to the tune of the popular wartime song "Over There": "Johnnie get your hoe, get your hoe, get your hoe, Mary dig your row, dig your row, dig your row." They also carried placards with exhortations such as "Swat the Kaiser with the Hoe," "Kentucky Agriculture Kills German Kulture," and "Can the Kaiser."[13]

The USSGA proved so successful in Lexington that officials continued it into the postwar era. In April 1919 the Lexington division of the USSGA brought 4,000 schoolchildren from throughout Kentucky to the campus of Transylvania University to celebrate USSGA efforts in a pageant. They paraded through the town to Woodland Park, where they heard a speech by J. H. Francis, national director of the USSGA. School superintendent M. A. Cassidy pointed out that the Lexington division had cultivated 350 acres in 1918 and that even more was expected to be planted in 1919. By July 1, 1919, the Bureau of Education noted that 25,000 schoolchildren in the state were participating in the school garden movement.[14]

To underscore the importance of Louisville's school garden program, in April 1917 the Louisville Board of Education hired its summer employee, Emily Yunker, to be the full-time director of school gardens. Yunker had an abiding interest in school gardens. In 1911 she had written her master's thesis at the University of Louisville and titled it "The School Garden from an Educational Point of View." In it she wrote: "School gardens are not intended to create gardeners or farmers but to afford the growing boy or girl an opportunity for many aided developments." The Board of Education solicited contributions to buy seeds and fertilizer, and Yunker supervised 100 acres of gardens throughout the city. At the end of the growing season, she also demonstrated how to can the surplus produce.[15]

Louisville war garden activist Emily Yunker. (University of Louisville)

During the winter of 1917–1918, Yunker spent two months at Cornell University, where she took special courses on school gardening in anticipation of a much larger effort in 1918. Her planning proved useful when approximately 300 Louisville lots were made available for school gardens. Nearly 12,000 Louisville pupils participated in planting gardens on more than 500 acres. USSGA official Clarence Weed visited Louisville and pronounced the school garden movement a success, singling out the Albert Brandeis School as having the "ideal school garden." The *Courier-Journal* War Garden Committee handed out USSGA flags to eleven exemplary schools with high percentages of participation.[16]

Louisville's school gardens became nationally known. At a May 1919 USSGA meeting in Chicago, Helen Fitz-Randolph, a Louisvillian and the USSGA's assistant director in charge of publicity, credited Yunker with leading one of the country's top school garden efforts.[17]

The school garden movement in Kentucky was one of two successful garden movements during World War I. The war garden movement, which grew out of the school garden experience, also thrived. In March 1917 Charles Lathrop Pack created the National War Garden Commission. Its members included several prominent Americans, such as former president of Harvard University Charles Elliott and famed agriculturalist Luther Burbank. In his 1919 book about the NWGC, Pack described its aims: "put all idle land to work," teach people how to grow food, and teach them how to "conserve by canning and drying all food they could not use while fresh."[18]

Pack's NWGC made sense to Kentuckians, and they embraced it. At the end of March 1917, a headline in Covington's *Kentucky Post* proclaimed: "Boy Farmers Tugging at Leash in Garden Plans." Three days after the official declaration of war, the Covington City Commission endorsed garden plans and then appointed contractor Homer Northcutt as the first volunteer city garden supervisor. Covington residents could contribute land to be used for gardens, and Northcutt would assign the lots to citizens wishing to grow gardens.[19]

In September 1917 the Kentucky State Fair provided an opportunity to highlight Kentucky's food efforts. An early major proponent of war gardens, Helen Fitz-Randolph reported that state fair exhibits of conserved fruits and vegetables from Lexington, Frankfort, Bowling Green, Elizabethtown, and Owensboro would be available. Fair officials applied for the NWGC prize for the "best canned vegetables grown in war gardens." (Fitz-Randolph later served on the *Louisville Courier-Journal*'s War Garden Committee. The newspaper became a major proponent of war gardens, printing more than fifty NWGC "War Garden Lessons" in 1918.)[20]

The national war garden movement was a good start toward producing more food. At the beginning of 1918, the *Hopkinsville Kentuckian* reported that according to the NWGC, nearly 3 million gardens on 1.15 million acres were under cultivation, valued at approximately $350 million (retail).[21] This was good, but not good enough.

In March 1918 Herbert Hoover asked federal food administrators in the states to promote food gardens. In Kentucky, this resulted in Louisvillian Charles G. Strater being named chairman of the War Garden Division of the state Food Administration. Strater believed an even greater effort had to be made and admitted that in 1917, "by reason of the overwhelming work that devolved upon the Food Administration, the War Garden work was not thoroughly organized, nor was the need for it given sufficiently wide publicity. But, notwithstanding these serious handicaps, Mr. Hoover feels that the War Garden Movement of 1917 played an important part in saving the country from positive shortage."[22]

Local newspapers loaned their voices in 1918, calling for stronger efforts to produce war gardens. Having already appointed a War Garden Committee and a war garden editor, the *Louisville Courier-Journal* looked forward to working with Strater to promote war gardens. The *Bourbon News* underscored the role that boys and girls could play in growing war gardens. The gardens would provide money for the purchase of War Saving Stamps, as well as provide food for the country and its allies. Boys in rural areas could do even more: they could plant a War Saving Acre, while also raising a War Saving Pig. Girls could keep a War Saving Flock of Hens and participate in a War Saving Canning Club.

Teachers could encourage their students, and businesses could help by providing money.[23]

Efforts to promote war gardens in Kentucky seemed to work. The *Breckenridge News* reported, "War gardens are springing up like hops in Cloverport. Vacant lots that heretofore have been a bed of weeds are fast becoming potato patches."[24]

War garden programs targeting adults and children in urban and rural areas did more than just increase food production in the United States. By building on the Progressive garden movement, they helped bridge the gap between urban and rural society, gave people ways to prove their loyalty and patriotism, informed childhood education, and even served as a means of "Americanization" by encouraging urban immigrants to participate in an all-American effort.

Although the war garden movement generated successful national and local organizations, federal government officials realized that food issues required a more extensive, concentrated effort that went beyond increasing food production on small garden plots in urban areas.

In Washington, Herbert Hoover began to work on food issues even while Congress debated legislation that would create a Food Administration. After vigorous debate, Congress finally passed the Lever Food and Fuel Control Act, which President Wilson signed on August 10, 1917. Hoover would serve as the US food administrator and lead the new federal Food Administration, one of the first national agencies set up to coordinate war efforts. Within a couple of weeks, state food administrators were named as this federal focus flowed downward into state and local regions.[25]

Hoover faced immediate challenges, including a projected US wheat crop insufficient to meet American, much less European, needs. He believed in volunteerism to achieve food goals; he wanted to avoid using outright federal and state coercion to deal with food issues.[26]

In August 1917, at the suggestion of the Kentucky Council of Defense, Louisville lawyer Fred Sackett became federal food administrator for Kentucky. Born in Rhode Island in 1868, Sackett received his undergraduate degree from Brown University and a law degree from Harvard. He practiced law in Ohio and then moved to Louisville, where he eventually married into the prominent Speed family. He soon became involved in wife Olive's family businesses (coal and cement manufacture), served as head of Louisville utility companies, and was president of the Louisville Board of Trade in 1917. As the latter, he led the city's bid to acquire one of the US Army's new training facilities: Camp Taylor.[27]

Kentucky's federal food administrator Fred Sackett. (Library of Congress)

Sackett had much to contend with in his new role. Among other things, he oversaw publicity, assisted the national food office with licensing, helped interpret food regulations, and directed the enforcement of laws covering myriad food-related activities throughout the state. He served as the middleman between Hoover's national Food Administration and the Kentucky district and county food administrators, who oversaw efforts at the local level. For many Kentuckians, Sackett was the face of the ever-encroaching national government, which now told people what and when they could eat, what food they could produce, and how they could produce it.

Sackett put into place an organization that, like many domestic war efforts, relied extensively on volunteers. His small staff included an executive secretary, newspaperman T. R. Moss, who served in that position until being named state food director in November 1917. At that time, a wholesale sugar dealer, Paul Creel, took over as executive secretary. Volunteers chaired various committees such as conservation, war work at home, war gardens, library, and distribution of literature; they chaired divisions representing hotels, restaurants, and moving pictures. Well-known suffragist and educator Patty Semple of Louisville served as chair of the War Work at Home Committee, and Lee L. Goldberg, a well-known Louisville movie theater manager, headed the Motion Picture Division. The Conservation Committee was led by Louisvillian Marguerite Giffords; the first female dean of the UK College of Home Economics, Mary Sweeny, headed the Home Economics Section until she and her sister, Sunshine, departed for France to work near the front lines for the YMCA Canteen Service.[28]

Men and women throughout the state assisted. Eight men served as district administrators; county food administrators were appointed, and the counties were broken down into districts where people could volunteer their services to publicize conservation and encourage greater production. Volunteers received certificates of appointment after signing a pledge swearing to "support and defend the Constitution of the United States against all enemies, foreign and domestic," and to carry out faithfully their appointed duties. Sackett relied heavily on volunteers, explaining to one correspondent that he had a small office staff and "my time is absolutely locked up in the work of the county administrators and keeping them in line on interpreting to them the rules and regulations as they are issued from Washington."[29]

Sackett also appealed to the state's school superintendents and principals to help with food efforts, and he praised their school gardens. He noted that Professor Mathews at the University of Kentucky represented the Department of the Interior's "United States Garden movement." He hoped he could count on school officials' "active cooperation and participation" in the movement.[30]

Sackett knew that conserving food was just as important as producing more food. Following the lead of Hoover, who believed women would be the backbone of the food conservation movement, Sackett appealed to the presidents of various women's organizations to serve on an Executive Committee for the Food Conservation Campaign. Sackett needed their help to get women to go door-to-door to obtain food conservation pledges during the week of October 28–November 4. Among others, he approached Presbyterian, Catholic, Jewish, Methodist, and Baptist organizations; the Daughters of the American Revolution; the United Daughters of the Confederacy; the Kentucky Federation of Women's Clubs; the Kentucky Equal Rights Association; and the Women's Christian Temperance Union (WCTU).[31]

A minor controversy arose when the *Louisville Courier-Journal* reported that the president of the WCTU, Frances Beauchamp, refused to commit her organization's help until Hoover and President Wilson prohibited the raising of tobacco on wheat lands and forbade the operation of breweries, distilleries, and wineries. Sackett knew about Beauchamp's stance before it was reported in the newspapers. She had initially telegraphed Sackett stating, "as state president of the greatest food conservation organization it would be in consistent [*sic*] to decline the honor you tender," but eventually she accepted a place on the Executive Committee. Sackett telegraphed Beauchamp to request that she set the record straight, and he notified Hoover of the situation.[32]

Sackett also had to combat rumors and misgivings about the conservation campaign. County extension agents reported that fears and misunderstandings had surfaced in rural districts early in September. One rumor alleged that the federal government was going to confiscate 50 percent of all canned goods found in pantries. Another story had federal inspectors inventorying homes and taking away any surplus food. Labeling the rumors "deliberate anti-American propaganda," Sackett reassured Kentuckians that "this is America, not Germany, and those who can food will continue to eat it or sell it or give it away just as they please. Any statement to the contrary is a dangerous misrepresentation."[33]

Organizations and people throughout the state lined up to publicize the food conservation pledge from many angles. Sue Stanley, the governor's wife, issued a proclamation on September 29 asking women to take the food conservation pledge. Sackett went on a two-day speaking tour in central Kentucky to drum up support for the pledge. He also met in Louisville with some of the state's prominent newspaper editors to enlist their assistance in publicizing the campaign. Marguerite Giffords oversaw the creation of county committees led by prominent women who would publicize the campaign. A national appeal went out to libraries to disseminate information about the pledge campaign and about conservation in general. Carolyn Adelberg, secretary to the director of the Louisville Free Public Library, became "Library Publicity Director for Kentucky." Fred Mutchler, head of UK's county agricultural extension service, promised the support of the sixty extension agents throughout the state. State superintendent of education V. O. Gilbert wrote to county school superintendents, asking them to encourage their teachers to persuade their students to tell their parents that it was their patriotic duty to conserve food and sign pledge cards.[34]

The food pledge campaign reached a fever pitch at the end of October 1917. In front of a group of more than 700 women in Louisville, Sackett explained the pledge cards, while Louisville school superintendent O. L. Reid and Southern Baptist Theological Seminary president E. Y. Mullins encouraged the women to participate. A few days before the campaign's kickoff, many Kentucky newspapers published a lengthy last-minute plea by Sackett to the "Housekeepers of Kentucky." Couching the plea in noble terms, he said he hoped people would respond positively to the conservation pledge request, as "patriots determined to do their bit for the cause of civilization throughout the world and the maintenance of democracy."[35]

As the time for the pledge campaign approached, Sackett sent explicit instructions to his county coordinators. Pledge solicitors would hand out three so-called Hoover cards: a pledge card, a home card, and a window card. After obtaining the necessary signatures, the solicitors would return the pledge cards to the county chairman, who in turn would report the daily results to Sackett. The other two cards would be given to the people who had pledged: the home card was to be displayed in the kitchen, and the window card would be placed in the front window—public evidence that the household was willing to play its part to conserve food.[36]

An army of canvassers across the state (organized as precinct captains, lieutenants, and so forth) went out in inclement weather starting on October 28 to obtain pledges. Initial reports showed that 135,000 people signed the cards, a disappointing result. The fact that only about two-thirds of the counties had fully reported was discouraging.[37]

People who refused to sign the pledge cards risked being reported to the government for further investigation. In Lexington, one "German woman" with "three nephews in the ranks of the Kaiser's army" and one "highly educated" woman who had a "record of pacifist talk" refused to sign the pledge cards. Their refusals agitated Denny Goode, an assistant Fayette County food administrator, who threatened to turn them over to federal Secret Service agents. He avowed: "This campaign will smoke out the pro-Germans." Goode relented when the German woman finally signed her pledge card, and friends of the highly educated woman promised that her relatives would talk to her.[38] These cases clearly represent what historian Christopher Capozzola calls "coercive volunteerism." People either went along with wartime programs or risked public condemnation or investigation by government officials.

In sum, results of the food pledge campaign were uneven. Some counties, such as Mason and Bourbon, received more signed cards than their expected allotments; in contrast, more than a dozen other counties reported that less than 10 percent of their allotted cards had been signed. Nevertheless, Sackett seemed pleased that, in the end, more than 175,000 signed pledge cards were returned.[39]

In a further effort to conserve food, the Food Administration urged a voluntary rationing system whereby certain foodstuffs would not be eaten on certain days of the week. For example, households implemented "meatless Tuesdays" and "wheatless Wednesdays." Restaurants and hotels adopted these restrictions by November 1917. Temperance leaders questioned why there were not "drinkless" and "smokeless" days as well.[40]

Some groups were slow to get on board with conservation. Hotel and Restaurant Division leader Dennis Lindsay complained that hotels and the "traveling public" had "not shown appreciation of the situation." Efforts by hotels and restaurants slowly improved, with many agreeing to follow the guidelines for meatless Tuesdays and wheatless Wednesdays; however, Lindsay noted that many establishments were not following the pledge and served the restricted foods when patrons ordered them. To counter this failure, Food Administration officials decided to issue "slacker cards" to recalcitrant diners who had ordered the forbidden foods. A vigilante group also offered to report on hotels and restaurants that violated the guidelines.[41]

Sackett increased the ante in January 1918 by calling for an additional wheatless day on Mondays, a wheatless evening meal every day, and porkless Saturdays. Following the federal lead, however, Sackett ameliorated the proscription in March so that Kentuckians could eat fried chicken, mutton, and lamb on "meatless" Tuesdays.[42]

The effort to conserve food proved successful. The United States cut back on several commodities. After a year, the *Louisville Courier-Journal* estimated that Kentuckians had cut their flour consumption by half. Sackett emphasized

US Food Administration poster on food conservation. (Library of Congress)

the importance of conserving wheat, believing that it was both a national and an international imperative to help feed soldiers and civilians in the Allied countries, the first line of defense against the Germans.[43]

Many Kentuckians pitched in. The wags at the *Hickman Courier* opined, "Some patriots are so punctilious about observing a meatless Tuesday that they will not even order a Welsh rabbit."[44] ("Welsh rabbit" [or rarebit] is actually cheese sauce poured over bread.) Nevertheless, some people and establishments proved recalcitrant and were denounced by concerned citizens. For instance, the secretary-manager of the Chamber of Commerce in Ashland complained to Sackett that all hotels and restaurants were following meatless and wheatless days, with the exception of one restaurant run by "lawless Greeks who will not keep their word" and who "demoralize the whole situation here." Sackett sought the name of the transgressing restaurant. When apprised of miscreants, he usually sent a warning letter, noting that if establishments did not follow the rules, a licensing system might be instituted, requiring a great deal of record keeping. He warned that before long, customers "would not care to patronize hotels and restaurants that are not patriotic enough to live up to the wishes of the Government."[45] Once again, coercive volunteerism played a role in ensuring support for the government's program.

In addition to food conservation, Sackett had a host of other issues to consider as food administrator. Increased production was the other side of the coin. War gardens were part of that effort, but greater production of livestock was also necessary. For example, the US Department of Agriculture sought a 15 percent increase in hog production for Kentucky in 1918. The head of Kentucky's Live Stock Committee of the Food Administration, James Thompson, encouraged farmers to raise more hogs. They had an additional incentive to cooperate: hogs were bringing record prices. To dramatize this effort, Governor Stanley followed the lead of President Wilson, who allowed sheep to graze on the White House lawn to publicize the need to raise more livestock. Stanley chose hogs to graze on the grounds of the statehouse. This ploy garnered attention from national newspapers, including the *New York World, Baltimore American,* and *New York Evening Post.*[46]

Not all went well with efforts to conserve food and increase production. A key problem was the cost of food throughout the state. Sackett and the county food administrators had the power to set prices for certain foodstuffs, and local newspapers published the approved prices. Nevertheless, variations occurred. This proved problematic, even toward the end of the war. Sackett chided: "it is important to see to it that the ordinary margins allowed by the Food Administration on different articles of staple food are lived up to by merchants. The merchant has a tremendous opportunity to profiteer under the present condition of affairs unless his margins are rather well under control."[47]

When problems with pricing arose, Sackett had many options. He could send auditors to investigate company books, call in suspected offenders to give depositions, appoint arbitrators to determine proper pricing, or encourage "coercive volunteerism." In the case of the Merchants Wholesale Grocery Company of Louisville, Sackett found that the company had violated several regulations regarding the price of flour and sugar. He resolved the issue by asking whether the company "elects to make the voluntary contribution of $1,000 to the Red Cross, rather than suffer one week's suspension of your license." The company chose to make the donation, a classic case of coercive volunteerism.[48]

Occasionally Sackett would dismiss a case based on the further investigation by a county food administrator. In Owen County, Dr. W. R. Morgan complained that W. H. Johnson of Gratz was selling flour at too high a price. T. A. Perry, the county food administrator, discovered that the complainant was a veterinarian who had been denied a credit account by Johnson. In Perry's opinion, Morgan "had a grudge" against Johnson. Noting that the affair was "spite work," Perry asserted that as far as he knew, Johnson had been "extremely loyal, one of the first to but [*sic*] Liberty Bonds, and in every drive for our cause." Sackett promised to write to the complainant and inform him that Johnson had charged the proper price for flour.[49]

Hoarding also proved to be a problem. A *Lexington Herald* editorial summed up popular attitudes: "The hoarder is as much a slacker as is the man who flies from the battle line." Violators were often given the choice of being fined or making "voluntary contributions," usually to the local Red Cross. Local newspapers often carried warnings by county food administrators that penalties could be imposed for the inappropriate stockpiling of foodstuffs, especially sugar and flour. The food administrator in Bourbon County pointed out that the government made few demands, relying mainly on voluntary cooperation. Hoarding was, however, "the one thing that the Food Administration will not tolerate."[50]

A prominent hoarding case that made the newspapers involved a wealthy Henry County farmer and family physician, Dr. A. G. Elliston, who was accused of hoarding half a barrel of sugar, nearly 160 pounds. County food administrator S. J. Douthitt had heard rumors and notified Sackett, who asked Secret Service agent John Sturgill to investigate. Sturgill went with a Henry County deputy sheriff to search Elliston's premises, where he found the sugar hoard. Elliston was quickly brought before US commissioner Charles Wiard in Frankfort, who turned the case over to the district court; meanwhile, defendant Elliston easily paid a $3,000 bond. At his subsequent trial, Elliston tried to explain away his purchases, saying he always bought things in bulk; he also mentioned that he had bought more than $3,000 in War Savings Bonds and Stamps. A plea bargain allowed him to sign a statement admitting his guilt, which would be printed in a local paper; donate the sugar to a charitable organization; and agree to pay a "voluntary contribution" of $250 to the Red Cross.[51]

Several other "voluntary contributions" were made by people who defied the food regulations. Guilty of violating regulations about the handling of eggs, W. A. Murphy of Avenstoke in Anderson County was given the choice of having his food license suspended for a week or voluntarily donating $10 to the Red Cross. C. W. Northcutt of Grant County was accused of selling corn syrup at an excessive price. Sackett believed Northcutt's business should be closed for a week, unless this "inconvenienced the public." If so, his store would be closed for two days, and Northcutt would be allowed to make a "voluntary contribution" of $50 to the Red Cross.[52]

For the inappropriate use of sugar in its bakery, the Phoenix Hotel in Lexington paid $1,200 to the Red Cross "in lieu of further prosecution by the Food Administration for violation of rules and regulations promulgated by the Administration." A farmer in Lincoln County, G. T. Timberlake, failed to thresh his wheat, thereby denying the country of a much-needed commodity. Sackett recommended to Lincoln County food administrator J. W. Saunders that "moral suasion" be used to get Timberlake to do his duty and thresh his wheat. If he did not comply, a second option would be to take Timberlake to federal court. A third option would be for Saunders to arrange for the wheat to be threshed, pay for it out of the proceeds from the sale of the wheat, and donate $50 to the Red Cross.[53]

Kentucky's food efforts during the Great War proved successful. Food administrator Fred Sackett oversaw a complex operation to monitor food commodities and to encourage increased food production and decreased consumption. At the end of a year's work, Sackett reported that the production of commodities such as wheat had increased dramatically, while conservation measures had succeeded. State director T. R. Moss was proud of Kentucky's efforts, asserting that the state had led the way in food publicity and in military camp food savings (there had been an impressive effort to stop wasting food at Camp Taylor).[54]

Although less well known than Sackett, the state's other federal administrator, Wiley Bryan, had an important task: to oversee fuel issues throughout the commonwealth. The US Fuel Administration was created in August 1917 to regulate crucial supplies of natural resources for the war effort, especially coal and oil. President Wilson appointed Williams College president Harry Garfield as its head. Garfield created a national organization and encouraged states to develop initiatives, appointing a federal fuel administrator in each state.[55]

In Kentucky the task fell to Wiley Bryan, assistant treasurer of the Belknap Hardware and Manufacturing Company and, as such, a prominent Louisville businessman. In early November 1917 Bryan opened an office conveniently located in Louisville's Inter-Southern Building, the site of other war offices such as the Kentucky Council of Defense and the Food Administration. He also established an advisory committee and began appointing county fuel administrators.[56]

One of the first problems Bryan and the fuel administrators had to address involved coal supplies and pricing during the bitterly cold winter of 1917–1918. Fear of a "coal famine" cropped up in the early fall. At the end of November, the *Mt. Sterling Advocate* wired Bryan: "It is imperative that immediate steps be taken to relieve coal famine here. Not a bushel in the yards. Gas pressure low." The *Advocate* also decried that "hundreds of cars of coal are going to other states," while Kentuckians did without coal. It called on Governor Stanley and the legislature to take care of Kentuckians and "make it the first duty of Kentucky coal producers to supply the demand of our own state."[57]

Railroad issues caused part of the coal supply problem. For example, Hercules Coal Company in Henderson complained that it had not received any coal cars for three days and had been forced to shut down, while another company had received fourteen cars. Hercules officials questioned this seeming discrimination by the Illinois Central Railroad. After the Fuel Administration discussed the problem with Illinois Central officials, railroad cars were sent to Hercules right away.[58]

Bryan forwarded several complaints about inadequate coal supplies to Fuel Administration officials in Washington, who then contacted coal companies to ensure that coal was shipped to needy communities. The officials also proposed an alternative: communities "in wooded country" should have "no trouble in securing a good supply of wood for fuel purposes."[59]

After a month of work, Bryan reported to Fuel Administration officials that 112 counties had been organized with fuel administrators. The remaining eight counties did not need administrators because coal was neither produced nor consumed in them; instead, people relied on wood. Bryan reported that retail price margins had been established in a number of counties, but more work needed to be done. Many communities in urgent need of coal supplies had received them, but the fuel administrator remained frustrated with the "selling agents who control the output of the majority of mining operations" in the state. These out-of-state agents deferred to demands from the fuel administrators in their home states, and mines owned by out-of-state companies neglected to provide fuel to their local Kentucky communities. Bryan had therefore asked alternative suppliers to provide coal, thus affecting those companies' regular customers. He had held several meetings with coal associations and independent mine owners, seeking their cooperation in the distribution of fuel. Bryan optimistically believed these meetings would lead to better distribution and less need to contact Washington for assistance.[60]

The coal supply situation seemed odd to many Kentuckians, given that the state was blessed with abundant coal resources. Although there was plenty of coal, shipping it out of the coalfields was a real problem; the country was gearing up industrially for total war, which greatly taxed the existing railroad system. People suffered during bitter, record-breaking weather in December. At one time, snow hampered coal delivery, and people in Lexington went without heat until city and county officials intervened to ensure the delivery of the little coal available. Bryan and his team of fuel administrators had to work consistently and diligently to supply towns and residences with adequate coal.[61]

To help reduce reliance on coal and other fuel resources, the Fuel Administration also stressed conservation. Officials asked companies and people to use less electricity, much of which was generated by coal-fueled plants. Bryan publicized new rules to curtail the use of illuminated signs. The Louisville Gas and Electric Company resisted this proposed reduction and ran a newspaper advertisement stating that lighting limitation rules did not apply in Louisville because the company "does not supply power to the street railway, it mines its own coal, and it transports this coal in its own railroad cars." The company's customers did not have to feel that they were encroaching on coal supplies; instead, using electricity was "contributing to the lighting of the streets."[62] "Waving the bloody flag," Louisville Gas and Electric's vice president/general manager noted that the company had purchased $100,000 in Liberty Bonds and that his son had volunteered for service. He asserted that turning signs off would save less than half a ton of coal per day. Bryan believed that illuminated signs required more coal usage than the company indicated, and in any case, half a ton of coal a day could be used for other purposes. He also believed that shutting off display signs would set an example for others and reinforce the need to conserve coal and electric current. In the end, the Fuel Administration advised Bryan to inform Louisville Gas and Electric that the rules still applied to Louisville.[63]

In December 1917 the federal Fuel Administration decreed that there would be "lightless" days when merchants were prohibited from using lights on the outside of buildings when their shops were open and in show windows after they closed. Individuals were also encouraged to reduce lighting in their homes on these days. Bryan wrote to county fuel administrators about the new conservation measures, pointing out that the Fuel Administration's ruling would not only save coal but also "provide startling visual evidence that the United States is engaged in the conduct of the greatest of world wars."[64]

Violations of "lightless" rules persisted, causing Bryan to issue a strong ultimatum at the end of December, threatening "drastic action" if merchants did not adhere to lightless Sundays and Thursdays. In a report filed after the war, Bryan noted that although Fuel Administration directives were generally respected and obeyed throughout Kentucky, "several offenders were required to make donations to the Red Cross on account of violating the 'Lightless night order.'" He had the backing of the federal Fuel Administration, which authorized him to direct the Louisville Gas and Electric Company "to cut off entirely current from wilfull and persistent violators."[65]

Coal and railroad problems continued, in part due to congestion on certain sections of the railroads. Bryan sought strong, decisive action to get coal to Kentuckians. He suggested diverting railroad coal cars through cities other than the congested Cincinnati gateway. The Fuel Administration agreed. Bryan's postwar report noted that in December 1917, "the hardships in Kentucky resulting from a lack of fuel were so great that the Federal fuel administration for Kentucky was compelled to commandeer and divert to Kentucky consumers 485 carloads of coal, the receipt of which temporarily ameliorated the situation."[66]

In his New Year's message to Kentuckians in 1918, Bryan acknowledged the difficulty of getting mined coal distributed appropriately through the railroads. He called on citizens to focus on decreasing consumption even more and substituting wood for coal. Unfortunately, in January 1918 Kentucky experienced more record-breaking cold, and temperatures plummeted below zero degrees Fahrenheit. Serious coal shortages persisted, even in areas that were well served by railroads and rivers, such as Covington. (Northern Kentucky could normally receive coal by barge as well, but freezing on the Ohio River hampered operations.) Schools shut down. So did theaters, cinemas, bowling alleys, billiard rooms, and other divertissements.[67]

In January 1918 national fuel administrator Harry Garfield instituted "heatless and workless Mondays," ordering that businesses in twenty-eight states east of the Mississippi River shut down on Mondays for ten consecutive weeks. He also decreed a "five-day closing" for some industries in order to save fuel. Heatless and workless Mondays underscored the seriousness of the nation's fuel problems. The *Breckenridge News* opined that Garfield's decree "could not have come at a more opportune time," given that the cold weather was keeping patrons away from merchants anyway.[68]

Kentuckians adapted to these decrees in different ways. To deal with Monday closings, Stanford's *Interior Journal* simply suggested that Lincoln County folks could come to "court day" on Tuesdays, when all merchants would be open. On the first heatless Monday in Lawrenceburg, several hundred men "in all classes of life went [to] the woods and chopped fuel," some 600 cords. The *Maysville Public Ledger* noted that Red Cross rooms were allowed to be heated, and it encouraged women who were not working on Mondays to devote two hours to Red Cross work. The wags at the *Bourbon News* wondered: "Why doesn't Doc Garfield announce that heatless Mondays will be continued through July and August?"[69]

US fuel administrator Garfield soon relented. As weather and railroad traffic conditions improved, he first ceased heatless Mondays in the southern states. He predicted that the three-and-a-half-day work holiday over Lincoln's birthday weekend would also help the fuel situation. Indeed, the following Tuesday, Garfield announced the general suspension (except in New England) of the heatless Monday program, which had lasted four weeks in Kentucky.[70] State fuel administrator Bryan believed that heatless Mondays had been "splendidly observed" throughout Kentucky, because only a few recalcitrants had been reported to the Department of Justice. He believed heatless Mondays had saved 30,000 tons of coal in the state, while the initial "five-day closing" had saved another 50,000 tons.[71]

With the coming of spring, "the fuel shortage situation in Kentucky became more tranquil," according to Bryan. Nevertheless, the Fuel Administration planned for another difficult winter in 1918–1919 and promoted a "buy your coal early" movement. On February 26 Fayette County's fuel committee secretary, Henry Milward, wrote to Garfield and informed him that the committee had considered advising Fayette consumers to buy their coal in the spring and summer. Fuel Administration officials asked Bryan to travel to Washington to consult on that idea.[72]

After his discussions with federal officials, Bryan asserted that a "buy early" plan depended on ascertaining appropriate coal prices for both the retailer and the consumer. In October 1917 Garfield had established maximum retail gross margins and prices, subject to varying local conditions. The question of fair pricing for coal operators, retailers, and consumers proved vexing, and it took up much of Bryan's time. It was a complex issue that had many possible variables, including quality and quantity, availability, and local market conditions. Another issue tied to coal prices was wages. When some coal areas received price cuts, mine operators protested and claimed they would have to cut wages, which in turn would result in miners leaving their jobs and production spiraling downward.[73]

At the beginning of April 1918, Bryan sent letters to the county fuel

US Fuel Administration poster encouraging consumers to buy coal early. (Library of Congress)

administrators encouraging them to warn coal consumers that they should start laying in supplies to avoid another winter of shortages. By the end of May, however, the Kentucky fuel administrator telegraphed Washington officials: "Buying movement entirely stagnated." He blamed this on the failure to set a price, causing consumers to delay buying coal because they hoped to get a lower price in the future.[74]

A new way to conserve fuel was daylight saving time—"Wilson time"—which began on the last Sunday in March 1918. This measure enabled stores to stay open later without using lights. It also pleased war gardeners, who had long touted the benefits of daylight saving time: it gave people an extra hour after work to go home and garden. The *Bourbon News* foresaw even greater benefits: "Besides saving fuel the new order will give all of us several hours of daylight for recreation instead of dark night. This will render outdoor exercise, garden cultivating and open air recreation easier, health will be thus improved and the cool hours of the morning will replace the hot summer afternoons in our working time."[75]

Bryan continued his efforts to encourage Kentuckians to save fuel. He got Governor Stanley to issue a proclamation designating June 3–8 as "coal week" and declaring that buying coal early to help avoid another coal famine was a patriotic duty. In a letter later that month to county fuel administrators, Bryan predicted that the transportation system and factories necessary for the war would need more fuel in the coming months. He reiterated the need to save energy, even suggesting that people get their furnaces cleaned for more efficient heating.[76]

Bryan was right about the military's energy demands. A burgeoning US military effort increased the need for fuel for ships, trucks, planes, and other requirements of modern war. Consequently, in September 1918 Fuel Administration officials implemented "gasless Sundays." The *Louisville Courier-Journal* reported that "Old Dobbin and Chaise Are Popular with Sabbath 'Joy Riders,'" as Kentuckians took to the streets in horse and buggy or risked apprehension.[77]

In Scott County the sheriff stopped automobiles being driven on Sundays. County attorney Church Ford established a citizens' committee to review drivers' explanations when apprehended. The names of the unpatriotic "gas slackers" were then published in the local newspaper, along with their excuses for the violations. (Most of them were traveling to church.) The "gasless Sunday" campaign lasted only a month and a half, as it became apparent that the Allies were winning on the Western Front and the German collapse was imminent. The projected need for future resources began to diminish.[78]

State fuel administrator Bryan, however, continued to worry about the upcoming winter months. He informed Washington officials in August that because Kentucky was sending most of its coal to factories in the north, the state was susceptible to coal shortages, especially in eastern Kentucky. He concluded: "Not only my whole organization, but all the people throughout the State are alarmed and the pressure that is being brought upon me is tremendous, and adverse criticism of the Fuel Administration is growing daily, and I want you to help me be in a position to avert the impending storm."[79] In September Bryan warned again: "We are fast reaching the danger line and the demands for domestic coal for urgent necessities are increasing, whereas the available supply is apparently diminishing, due to the continued movement out of the state." A month later he pointed out that early in the season he had told his county fuel administrators that a plan to avert shortages would be worked out by November 1.[80]

Instead of improving, the coal production and distribution problem was compounded when the Spanish flu epidemic descended on the commonwealth that fall. Bryan noted that the epidemic had "materially decreased the production in this State and in some districts, mines have been forced to shut down entirely. There have also been a great many members of train crews attacked by the same epidemic, resulting in the slowing down of transportation. Altogether the outlook for production in this State is very discouraging."[81]

Even after the armistice, Bryan continued to insist that Kentuckians receive adequate coal supplies for the winter. Increasingly frustrated by what he perceived as the US Fuel Administration's inability or unwillingness to redirect the necessary coal to eastern Kentucky, he lamented in a telegram to Washington officials: "Has the signing of the armistice drawn the fangs of the FUEL ADMINISTRATION to such an extent that they are unable to compel the operators to obey their mandates?" The next day he telegraphed: "I respectfully and urgently suggest your taking over the entire distribution in Kentucky assuming full responsibility for the local situation."[82]

Despite his increasing frustration, Kentucky's fuel administrator continued to perform his duties. Bryan announced the lifting of restrictions on stockpiling coal and ended lightless nights. He also sought, however, to be relieved of his duties. The Fuel Administration asked him to continue at his post, maintaining: "We must protect the domestic consumer until winter danger is past and be prepared to relieve emergencies even after general activities have ceased." The danger did pass; in mid-December Bryan reported that "mild weather and increased coal shipments" had ameliorated the situation in Kentucky.[83]

Wiley B. Bryan remained as Kentucky's federal fuel administrator until mid-March 1919. In a summary of activities filed at the beginning of that month, Bryan estimated that coal savings over the course of the war had amounted to approximately 10 percent. He noted that retail coal dealers had refunded about $5,000 for overcharges, and they had been required to donate about $8,000 to the Red Cross and other charitable organizations.[84]

Fred Sackett and Wiley Bryan had been consummate "dollar-a-year men," the appellation given to the volunteers who received a single dollar of remuneration for their hard work on behalf of domestic war efforts. The jobs were not without stress. At one point, foreseeing that he would be classified I-A in the expanded fall 1918 draft, Bryan concluded: "after twelve months experience as a State Fuel Administrator, I am inclined to believe that it would be a relief to serve in the Army even as a 'buck private.'"[85]

Their efforts were noticed and appreciated. For his service, Sackett received a "loving cup" award from the state's district and county food administrators, and in March 1919 he received a patriotic medal at the Kentucky Council of Defense's Conference on State Problems.[86] Sackett had been the more visible of the two administrators, traveling the state and dealing with a larger scope of issues. The *Courier-Journal* noted that because there was "little of the spectacular, romantic or dramatic in the affairs of the U.S. Food Administration," Sackett's activities "were not prolific of thrills or sensations for the public." Nevertheless, the newspaper asserted that "the people are conscious of the steady, well-balanced, intelligent and able handling of the food problems," and "they will remember long the sacrifices he has made in important personal affairs to perform this big and imperative task for his neighbors and his country."[87]

In turn, the *Courier-Journal* praised Bryan for his "ability, judgment and total insensibility to personal pressure or prejudice," which enabled him to "make the best of a bad situation" in the "memorable hardships" of the winter of 1917–1918. Noting that although, "in the material sense," Bryan had received only a dollar per year, "in the spiritual sense he has earned the thanks and lifelong esteem of his State and city."[88]

After the war, Bryan and Sackett continued their efforts in Kentucky business and politics. Bryan served as the treasurer in Alben Barkley's primary campaign for governor in 1923, and he continued to be a key Louisville businessman. Sackett succeeded Augustus O. Stanley as US senator from 1925 to 1930. His service as Kentucky's federal food administrator had brought him to the attention of Herbert Hoover. When Hoover became president, he appointed Sackett to serve as US ambassador to Germany during the fateful declining years of the Weimar Republic (1930–1933), as it collapsed with the rise of Adolf Hitler.[89]

The state's federal food and fuel administrators had become the faces of an encroaching federal presence in the daily lives of Kentuckians. Sackett's and Bryan's efforts resulted in a substantial governmental intrusion, as people throughout the state were told what to eat, when to eat, what to grow, and when to turn off the lights and the heat. These two men also provided a vital link between federal authorities in Washington and the people of Kentucky, and their work to regulate food and fuel affected all Kentuckians. This was especially true during conservation efforts, when Kentuckians did their part to save on food and fuel, enabling the federal government to allocate resources to "total war" in an industrialized world.

Kentucky was ably served not only by these two leaders but also by the hundreds of other volunteers throughout the commonwealth: from the state food and fuel offices in Louisville to the most remote hollows and mining camps, people pitched in. In the final analysis, it was the state's citizenry across the board who, with few exceptions, accepted mandates from on high and contributed vigorously and patriotically to help meet the nation's food and fuel needs.

8

Women and Children

Most of the people in leadership positions in Kentucky during the Great War were white, male, and upper middle class. For example, the Kentucky Council of Defense members, federal food and fuel administrators, and other key officials were all white males, mainly lawyers and prominent businessmen. Other people, however, made significant contributions statewide. Women and African Americans led many activities on Kentucky's domestic front. Children were also expected to play their proper role in the war effort.

Even before the United States formally entered the war, women began to work in war-related activities and to consider what their roles might be. Some became involved in the preparedness movement, joining organizations such as the Women's Section of the Navy League. This group developed National Service Schools for young women, modeled somewhat on the Plattsburg military training camp movement for men. The first National Service School was established in Chevy Chase, Maryland, in May 1916, overseen by the US Marine Corps. The participants wore uniforms, rose from their tents at the call of reveille, and went to bed at the sound of taps. In between, they studied subjects such as radio telegraphy and first aid. Amelia Weitzel, the daughter of well-known Frankfort hotelier, participated, as did the wife of her brother George, who lived in Washington, DC. President Wilson addressed the school; he was accompanied by his wife, Secretary of the Navy Josephus Daniels, and Secretary of War Newton Baker.[1]

The Women's Section of the Navy League transformed into the National League for Women's Service (NLWS) and opened a headquarters in New York City on February 1, 1917, the day the United States broke diplomatic relations with Germany. The NLWS focused on training women in useful wartime skills that could free up men for fighting. It created eleven divisions to oversee this work, including health, agricultural, industrial, motor driving, and signaling.[2] The NLWS also sought to establish chapters around the country. Mary Johnston of Louisville served as the first temporary head of the NLWS in Kentucky. Women formed chapters in more than a dozen communities ranging from Lexington to Owensboro.[3]

In Louisville, where 200 women registered as members, 30 women signed up to take marksmanship classes under NLWS sponsorship, and 25 women signed up for the motor driving course. During twice-weekly training sessions held for ten weeks, they learned not only how to drive but also how to maintain cars. The women mixed social and practical activities: they sponsored a dance to fund their auto training. The course culminated in a final examination that required the Louisville candidate to drive a car out to a farm over a bad road, take the car apart, and reassemble it. Then the candidate was given an older car and instructed to drive until it broke down (apparently soon); she then had to fix the problem. Successfully passing the exam led to membership in the league's Motor Corps, which provided drivers for various war-support organizations and government agencies, such as the Red Cross and the Quartermaster Depot in Jeffersonville, Indiana, just across the Ohio River from Louisville.[4]

Many of the 1,600 students at Louisville Girl's High School showed an interest in the NLWS. Students in cooking classes and the commercial department (where they learned to be stenographers, clerks, and telephone switchboard operators) especially looked forward to participating in NLWS training.[5]

In Lexington, an NLWS detachment of University of Kentucky (UK) students and other women from the city initially performed military drills and first-aid exercises under the commander of the UK's military unit. Soon thereafter, classes in motor driving, gardening, and relief support rounded out some of the training options. UK professors Clarence Mathews and Mary Sweeny taught the gardening classes and canning, while the dean of engineering, Paul Anderson, helped supervise the motor driving class and gave lessons on wireless telegraphy. At a meeting of fifty NLWS women, George Roberts, the acting dean of agriculture, exhorted them to conserve, grow more food, and can vegetables and fruit. The *Lexington Herald* succinctly summed up: "The social life in Lexington has assumed a new aspect since war was accepted. Women are turning from the idle recreations of peace times and are devoting their energies to war work."[6]

NLWS members in other towns took on different projects. In Bowling Green and Owensboro, women distributed free seeds for gardening. In Dayton in Campbell County, they focused on sewing "907 garments, including sweaters, layettes, and socks—and 11,209 gauze dressings." League members also volunteered to copy records for draft boards.[7]

The National League for Women's Service was an early, influential organization that prepared women for war work. Other women's organizations received direction from the federal government's Council of National Defense.

Two weeks after the United States entered the war, the Council of National Defense created a Woman's Committee headed by Dr. Anna Howard Shaw.

Woman undergoing telegraphy training at the University of Kentucky. (University of Kentucky)

Trained as a Methodist preacher and a physician, Shaw had been president of the National American Woman Suffrage Association (NAWSA) from 1904 to 1915. The committee included several presidents of national women's organizations and other notables such as muckraking author Ida Tarbell and suffragist Carrie Chapman Catt.[8]

Seeking an "efficient influential non-partisan woman" to lead women's war efforts in Kentucky, Dr. Shaw telegraphed fellow suffragist Madeline McDowell Breckinridge for advice, admitting that her first pick, Lettie Robinson Adams of Louisville, had declined the position. Breckinridge suggested several names, with Sallie White Bruce at the top of the list.[9]

Born in Lexington, Virginia, Sarah "Sallie" White was the daughter of a Washington and Lee University professor. She married Louisville native and lawyer Helm Bruce, a graduate of Washington and Lee. Bruce's grandfather on his mother's side, John Helm, had been a Kentucky governor and president of the Louisville & Nashville Railroad; Bruce's father was a prominent lawyer who had served in the Confederate Congress and the Kentucky General Assembly. Helm Bruce had represented the loser in the hotly disputed Kentucky gubernatorial election of 1899, which had resulted in William Goebel eventually taking office (he was assassinated three days later). At the time of the war, Bruce practiced law with William Marshall Bullitt, another scion of a prominent Kentucky family. Thus, Sallie Bruce had entrée into Louisville society and, like the wives of several prominent men, soon developed her own fields of expertise.[10]

Sallie Bruce held leadership positions in the National and Kentucky Societies of Colonial Dames. She was a member of the Kentucky branch of the International Order of the King's Daughters, an interdenominational Christian philanthropic society, and a member of the United Daughters of the Confederacy (UDC). She was especially active in the Louisville Business Women's Club, a branch of the Women's Christian Association that, within a year of its founding in 1898, counted 800 Louisville women in its ranks. Dedicated to helping self-supporting women, the club provided self-improvement classes and opened a lunchroom, a library, and a home for women in need of lodging. Sallie Bruce initially headed the Education Department, which taught women disparate subjects such as shorthand, first aid, French, and chorus. In 1904 she won a hotly contested election for club president on a platform that allegedly favored the "secularization" of the club by promising to host dances for young women.[11]

By 1910, Sallie Bruce was involved when the Consumer's League of Kentucky sought a ten-hour workday for women in retail stores, mills, factories, and laundries. In 1913 Bruce became president of the Woman's Club of Louisville, an influential group formed under the leadership of Susan Avery in 1890. Bruce succeeded Patty Semple, who would also become well known for her war work. As president, Bruce called for Louisville to form a vice commission and a recreation board and to add women to the city's police force. She also championed legislative efforts to combat tuberculosis and to provide the vote for women. Bruce and Semple were involved in creating the Kentucky Society for Social Hygiene, a group dedicated to "improving the human race physically, mentally, and morally." Bruce also served as first vice president of the Kentucky Federation of Women's Clubs; Cora Wilson Stewart of the illiteracy campaign served as fourth vice president.[12]

By the beginning of the Great War, Sallie Bruce had become one of the preeminent female Progressive reformers in Kentucky. She was a wealthy and well-connected activist. After the war started, she became involved in many war efforts, including the Colonial Dames's support of the Red Cross and relief efforts for Belgian and French orphans. She was appointed by Governor McCreary to the Kentucky committee of the Special Relief Society, which provided relief for the "convalescent soldier abroad, and for the unemployed in the United States."[13]

Anna Howard Shaw took Breckinridge's advice and named Sallie Bruce "temporary chairman" of the Kentucky Division of the Woman's Committee of the Council of National Defense (WCCND). The appointment was temporary because a contretemps had arisen when Shaw found out that the Kentucky Council of Defense had already named the governor's wife, Sue Stanley, as head of women's war work. KCD chairman Embry Swearingen was unhappy about Shaw's taking the initiative and complained to George Porter, head of the CND's State Councils Section, about the "woman's branch in Washington ignoring completely" the KCD by appointing Bruce. To solve the controversy, Shaw suggested that Sue Stanley be made an honorary chairman, but Sallie Bruce would be the true leader of women's work.

In fact, the awkward situation was quickly resolved when Sue Stanley declined the offer (although she was always cited as an honorary chair of the committee). This paved the way for Sallie Bruce officially to lead Kentucky's women. Bruce promised close cooperation with the KCD but admitted: "This may be difficult between a committee made up of prominent and successful social workers, and a council chosen by a governor who is openly opposed to the regulation of the liquor traffic, to Equal Rights for Women and indeed to any effort on the part of women to improve existing conditions."[14]

A CND report in late July 1917 found the Kentucky women's situation "somewhat amusing." It noted, "Apparently Mrs. Stanley is a comfortable woman, well fitted to be a figure head while the other [Sallie Bruce] is rather acrimonious but [an] able executive." A supplementary report a month later concluded, "The Women's Committee situation is complicated but not hopeless." The situation had improved by April 1918, when another report stated, "The relations of the State Council are seemingly harmonious at present."[15]

Bruce moved quickly to create a state woman's committee to oversee war work. She called together representatives from more than a dozen women's organizations to form the Kentucky Division of the WCCND. Patty Semple served as first vice chairman, and Mary McDowell Lowndes of Danville, president of the Kentucky Federation of Women's Clubs, served as second vice chairman. The women planned a broad approach and created several departments, including Home Economics, Protection of Women Workers, Protection of Health and Welfare of Children, Conservation of the Moral and Spiritual Forces of the Nation, Social Service, Allied Relief, Educational Propaganda, and Publicity. Most of the department heads were from Louisville's upper class and had been involved in club work, with the exception of Mary Sweeny of Lexington, who was chair of the Home Economics Department at the University of Kentucky.[16]

Sallie Bruce encouraged women's clubs throughout Kentucky to create

Poster exhorting women to support the war effort. (Library of Congress)

local woman's committees to support the war. She encouraged them to get involved with Herbert Hoover's food conservation program. By the end of September 1917, fifty-two counties had created woman's committees; they sent representatives to Louisville in October to meet with Bruce and the Kentucky Division leadership to discuss strategies. The new director of the KCD, Edward Hines, also met with the group. At the instigation of Patty Semple, the women approved a motion asking that Hines regard Bruce as "the link between the women's work and the men's." The women decided to focus their attention on three major efforts: the Liberty Loan campaign fund, food conservation, and registering women for war work.[17]

At the end of October, Sallie Bruce presided at a "mass meeting" of women to hear from Clarinda P. Lamar, head of the WCCND Department of Organization. Lamar explained the workings of the WCCND and encouraged women to support the food conservation program, underscoring the vital role women would play in this campaign; federal food administrator Fred Sackett also appeared and encouraged the women in this vein.[18]

The Kentucky Division of the WCCND focused on the food pledge campaign led by Sackett in late 1917. The KCD had the pledge cards printed and then turned them over to the Kentucky Division to distribute throughout the state. Although men had designed the campaign, the women's groups found volunteers, exhorted their friends to assist, and helped publicize the campaign.

The women's groups enlisted people to knock on doors and ask their neighbors to sign up, collected cards, and tabulated the results.[19]

A report of activities by the various county women's committees during 1917 described some of the difficulties they encountered, but it also reflected the breadth of activities and the women's Progressive philosophy. The problems included bad weather during the winter of 1917–1918, which made getting groups together difficult in several counties. For example, Barren County reported that "no real organization of the county has been attempted on account of weather conditions," although the temporary chair and her friends had made some progress on Red Cross and food conservation efforts. The Barren County women, however, fully expected to "make a complete organization" when the weather improved.[20]

Weather was not the only problem; in rural Kentucky, geography and infrastructure prevented women from getting involved. The woman's committee in Cumberland County around Burkesville acknowledged: "Population of county loyal, but, as the county has no railroad facilities, the women of the interior are not fully informed as to war relief work." In contrast, counties with better infrastructure, such as Madison County, reported, "The county is being organized to the remotest district." In some counties women simply took the initiative to lead war work. Hickman County women were proud that they were "pioneers in getting patriotic work started." They reported that nothing was being done on the Liberty Loan campaign "until the women took up the work."[21]

While food conservation, the Red Cross, and Liberty Loan bonds remained the focus of the Kentucky Division, women tackled other issues as well. In Boyle County, the local woman's committee on child welfare concentrated on compulsory education and child labor laws. It called for better conditions in juvenile court and a curfew for young people. A series of patriotic meetings in Boyle County featured speakers explaining why the country was at war; in addition, Sallie Bruce spoke in December 1917 on the significance of the WCCND.[22]

In Clark County, the woman's committee was especially proud of its "good work along educational lines. Public school children [are] being intelligently informed on all matters pertaining to the war and patriotism." In Fayette County, the woman's committee had "taken the initiative in dealing with changing conditions in the home." It had also developed classes for "young women wanting to become typists, stenographers and bookkeepers," and it arranged for women to take civil service examinations. The Kenton County social services committee had worked with churches and the Red Cross to help soldiers' families "in sudden and desperate need."[23]

Sallie Bruce especially encouraged more nurses to join the Red Cross; they were needed both abroad and at home, especially at Camp Taylor. In May 1918 she led a Kentucky delegation to Washington for the WCCND conference. In a brief report, Bruce lamented the lack of nurses in the commonwealth, an acute situation that left some counties without public health nurses. On a more positive note, Bruce lauded the KCD's support of the Kentucky Division and praised the work of the state's women during the recent legislative session. They had successfully lobbied for an illiteracy bill, a bill for the "care of the feeble-minded, and the defeat of two bad amendments to the child labor laws of the State."[24]

The nursing situation continued to plague Kentucky and to trouble Bruce. The shortage of nurses worried national groups as well. In July 1918 the WCCND called for 25,000 young women aged eighteen to thirty-five to form a US Student Nurse Reserve; it gave Kentucky a quota of 750 recruits. Initial reports suggested that Kentucky would have no problem meeting its quota, but this optimism soon waned because many young women lacked the basic educational qualifications to enter the program. Worried that Kentucky would not meet its quota for student nurses, Bruce kept asking the national committee for more informational booklets and registration materials. She noted that mothers were opposed to the program, but girls were enthusiastic about it.[25]

Like the initial Kentucky Council of Defense, the Kentucky Division operated with no budget for 1917. The women on the committee contributed some money, but more was needed. Undeterred, the women decided to raise money, so they invited a speaker to Louisville: Sergeant Arthur Guy Empey, an American who had served in the British army. Empey had been wounded at the Battle of the Somme, written a best-selling book about his experiences, and toured the country as a propagandist for the US Army. His appearance brought in nearly $1,000 to the Kentucky Division. Proceeds from other lectures brought in another $500, and the sale of a "War Cook Book" prepared by UK's Mary Sweeny raised nearly $1,000.[26]

The women finally received state funds when the legislature created a funded Kentucky Council of Defense with a $50,000 budget in March 1918. Soon thereafter, KCD director Hines met in Louisville with representatives of various groups. Sallie Bruce represented the Kentucky Division and asked the KCD for a budget allotment of $5,000. In some states such as Minnesota and Massachusetts, woman's committee expenses were fully paid; in other states such as Indiana and Illinois, partial expenses were paid; and in some states, the woman's committee received a set amount. The Kentucky Division received the requested $5,000—a significant sum in comparison to Ohio ($1,800) and Virginia ($1,500). This enabled the division to rent an office in the Speed Building in Louisville and to hire a stenographer, greatly aiding communication and general efficiency.[27]

The Kentucky Division continued to construe "war work" in a more comprehensive fashion than the KCD, a trend that was also reflected in the national Woman's Committee. For example, at its annual meeting at Sayre College in Lexington in June 1918, the Kentucky Division sponsored a resolution calling for a vocational training school for girls, which could help address the problem of "delinquent girls" found around army camps.[28]

The women's war movement in Kentucky also spawned more calls for women's suffrage. Nationally known Kentucky suffragists such as Madeleine McDowell Breckinridge and Laura Clay had been persistently and vociferously involved in this campaign for many years. At the beginning of June 1918, noted suffragist Carrie Chapman Catt, head of the WCCND Education Department, addressed this topic in speeches in Lexington, Frankfort, and Louisville. The Kentucky Division and various women's suffrage groups, including the Louisville Woman Suffrage Association, sponsored her visit to the state. Introduced by Sallie Bruce in Louisville, Catt described the lack of free speech in Germany and blamed the German-American Alliance for the defeat of women's suffrage in six states. At the end of the meeting, the assemblage passed a unanimous resolution calling for women's suffrage. Because the federal government was "calling on women to share the burdens and responsibilities of the war," and given that allies Canada and Great Britain had already enfranchised women, the group called for Kentucky's senators—Ollie James and J. C. W. Beckham—to "help the United States keep pace with her allies by voting for the Federal suffrage amendment."[29]

Similar resolutions passed in the other cities where Catt spoke. The quest for women's suffrage appeared to be gaining ground because of their war work. As women and men developed skills and helped support the war, voting rights for women gained more acceptance. In Lexington, the head of a recent Red Cross drive announced his conversion to supporting women's right to vote because of their work for the Red Cross. Former US senator Johnson Camden and the head of the influential Central Christian Church, the Reverend I. J. Spencer, also spoke in favor of the resolution.[30]

The Kentucky Federation of Women's Clubs actively mixed patriotism and women's causes and strongly supported the activities of the Kentucky Division. At its annual convention in Lexington in June 1918, the federation focused most of its attention on how women could aid the war. Conference participants also hotly debated the best way for women to acquire the right to vote. Their national federation had passed a resolution asking local groups to support the so-called Anthony amendment (in honor of Susan B. Anthony), a campaign to pass a federal constitutional amendment granting women the right to vote. Laura Clay, president of the Fayette County Equal Rights Association and daughter of the legendary Cassius M. Clay, spoke out strongly against the resolution, arguing that suffrage was a states' rights issue. In contrast, Jennie Mengel of Louisville "urged passage of the amendment as a patriotic act" and cited the actions of Britain and Canada. Acknowledging that "we are in a war for democracy," Patty Semple argued that if each state had to grant women the right to vote, the first states to ratify would "have an unfair advantage over the more backward ones." She believed that "every woman should have the right at the same time." The group then adopted a resolution urging Kentucky's two senators to vote in favor of the Anthony amendment. It also passed a resolution strongly supporting the nation's war effort.[31]

Because many members of the Kentucky Federation of Women's Clubs were also active in the Kentucky Division, that group held its annual conference immediately following the federation's meeting. In a keynote speech, Jennie Mengel, a longtime supporter of education and libraries, called for a greater emphasis on education, such as that being undertaken for food conservation efforts. Education was also a means of countering German propaganda, she believed, which "always gets its way among the uneducated classes." Other topics of discussion that pertained to war work included the food campaign, Red Cross and Allied relief work, protection of women workers, and child welfare.[32]

Some organizational issues beleaguered the Kentucky Division. In June 1918 the national committee questioned why the division's list of local representatives included multiple representatives from each county, rather than only one. The division's corresponding secretary, Isabel Lewis, replied that twenty Kentucky counties had no railroad service, and many representatives lived fifteen to twenty miles from the nearest railroad. Given this lack of transportation, it was necessary to have multiple representatives in some counties, enabling the division to reach different parts of the county. Noting that local representatives of theses counties were "almost invariably college women, who are the head of settlement schools," Lewis asserted: "Through these women we are reaching the mountain people of Kentucky." She believed that "our mountain people are pure Anglo-Saxon blood and absolutely loyal in every respect. They need help rather than to be asked for help, but invariably . . . they respond to the request of these teachers [in the settlement schools] and are doing their best in every possible way to win the war."[33]

Despite some problems, the Kentucky Division continued to work effectively on many causes. With President Wilson's support, a national Children's Year campaign began on April 6, 1918, the first anniversary of US entry into the war. The Children's Bureau of the US Department of Labor and the WCCND cosponsored the campaign, which built on previous efforts by the bureau and the General Federation of Women's Clubs. Children's Year involved three main activities: weighing and measuring infants, improving children's recreational opportunities, and encouraging children to stay in school.[34]

The campaign to weigh and measure children under age six caught the attention of women across the state. It received impetus from the large number of draft selectees—up to one-third—who failed their physical examinations. Officials wanted children and young people to be more physically prepared if their nation had to call on them in the future. They believed there were scientific correlations between height and weight in growing children and health. Identifying children who were "below normal" in height and weight for their age could lead to changes resulting in more physically fit youth. Announcing the campaign, the *Louisville Courier-Journal* opined, "Not only will the campaign save much needless death and suffering of the little children of Kentucky but its careful observance is upheld as a patriotic duty in view of the unavoidable wastage of human life incident to war." The *Courier-Journal* surmised that Children's Year could save the lives of more than 3,000 children in the state. With children's needs appropriately identified, more specific health problems such as tuberculosis and bad eyesight and hearing, as well as nutritional needs, could be better addressed.[35]

Newspapers across the state encouraged parents to have their babies weighed. County women's committees organized the weighing, which often took place at schools. When possible, nurses and doctors assisted. Some counties achieved remarkable results. For example, in Mason County, 100 volunteers, mainly women, weighed more than 1,250 babies. The county held a follow-up clinic the next week to examine more closely those babies whose weight was lower or higher than deemed healthy. The county and city school superintendents opened their buildings so that mothers could attend classes on subjects such as proper nutrition. The campaign spawned additional conversations about the needs of children. People discussed the problem of low school attendance, which some attributed to a lack of shoes. Others believed that children needed better milk supplies.[36]

When Sarah Boggs of Blue Diamond, Kentucky, requested information about Play Week (a Children's Year recreational effort), Dr. Jessica Peixotto, head of the WCCND Child Welfare Department, forwarded her letter to Elizabeth Shaver in Louisville. Shaver was supervisor of the Babies Milk Fund Association of Louisville and chair of the Kentucky Division's Child Welfare Committee. She had set about creating a child welfare network throughout the state, which was proving difficult, given communication and transportation problems. In a letter to Peixotto, Shaver admitted: "Kentucky, as you know, presents many difficulties which prevent any prompt results in any line of work but the counties are now waking up to their responsibilities and where the weighing test has not been done, plans are under foot to put it through this Fall."[37]

In October, Peixotto attended a luncheon in her honor in Louisville and underscored the importance of the work related to children. Sallie Bruce reported that the baby-weighing campaign had been only partially successful. In the fifty counties that had public health nurses, the babies had been weighed. That left seventy counties that still lacked the appropriate information, and unfortunately, many of these counties were where such problems remained acute.[38]

The two other phases of the Children's Year campaign were the back-to-school campaign and the recreation drive. The latter sought to "promote the health and general well-being of the older boys and girls," and it had three aims: "keeping the children fit, keeping them out of mischief, and keeping them happy, a most important factor when war conditions are everywhere upsetting the normal standards of living." An official of the Playgrounds and Recreational Association of America believed the opportunity to play was a "square deal" for boys and girls, and "the winning of war depends on man power, and man power cannot be sustained without health and wholesomeness in children."[39]

The campaign geared up in July and August 1918 and ended in a recreational "Patriotic Play" celebration the first week of September. Due to the heat in Kentucky, Sallie Bruce decided to postpone the finale until the third week in October, which coincided with the start of school in many counties. Despite the postponement, Berea sponsored a Patriotic Play Day in late August when children were physically tested in events such as the sixty-yard dash, chin-ups, standing broad jump, and other measures of physical fitness. Children who surpassed certain standards received certificates. Families were encouraged to attend the celebration and bring a "simple war-time supper" so they could "eat together, sing together and play together." In addition, children sang patriotic songs and participated in a patriotic pageant.[40]

Lexington also decreed a "Patriotic Week" at playgrounds in mid-August. The playgrounds fielded teams of children in different events, such as boys' volleyball and girls' basketball. They also featured contests for individuals in events such as dashes, high jumping, and broad jumping.[41]

In Christian County, the woman's committee defined the notion of patriotic play more broadly and included folk dancing. In a report on the progress of Children's Year, the local woman's committee pointed out that soldiers had opportunities for play, which had two purposes: "keeping them physically fit and giving them healthful wholesome substitutes for idleness or commercialized exploitation of their leisure hours." The women believed that "play for children accomplishes the same purpose precisely."[42]

The third component of Children's Year involved a back-to-school drive designed to counter the effects of war, which often induced children to leave school and go to work, either because the jobs paid well or because their families desperately needed the extra income. Illiteracy among draftees underscored the need for children to stay in school. Nevertheless, the encroaching flu epidemic wreaked havoc with the schools (forcing many to close), and the back-to-school drive, along with Patriotic Play Week, suffered from a lack of emphasis.[43]

In a postwar report, the Children's Bureau admitted: "It is obviously impossible to estimate the exact results of Children's Year." Yet the bureau noted that after the war, several states, including Kentucky, had added "child-hygiene divisions" to the state government. In addition, as a result of the child-weighing campaign and the subsequent focus on birth registration, Kentucky was one of twenty-three states and the District of Columbia recognized by the Bureau of the Census as "birth-registration" areas. The data from these activities allowed the bureau to understand better such things as infant mortality rates.[44]

The Kentucky Division of the WCCND also helped publicize national Women's Year programs. In so doing, it continued the Progressive work begun by women's clubs before the war, which led to more reforms after the war.

The war was obviously winding down by October 1918. Yet the work of the woman's committee was not quite done. Even as Armistice Day approached, the Kentucky Division provided 1,500 garments for poor children in Jackson County.[45]

The Kentucky Division's Executive Committee continued to meet in the first half of 1919, but it reduced its focus to two areas: education and Americanization. Some committee work was passed over to other organizations before the division was dismantled in July. For example, the Consumer's League focused on women in industry, while the Kentucky Federation of Women's Clubs concentrated on public health nursing.[46]

The Kentucky Division focused on the Americanization of foreign miners in southeastern and southwestern Kentucky, as well as the many foreigners in Louisville and northern Kentucky. Beginning in June 1919 the *Courier-Journal* ran a series of thirty-five articles by Louisville poet and short-story writer Abby McGuire Roach titled "We Americans," to inform readers about being American. "To promote the cause of Americanization," the Kentucky Division sponsored a publication aimed at middle and high schoolers—*The*

Triumph of Humanity—by Louisville Girls' High English teacher and poet Ethel Allen Murphy.[47]

In a postwar report, WCCND official Emily Blair noted that "one who calls himself an impartial observer" had divided state woman's committees into three classes of effectiveness. He placed Kentucky in the second tier, which included New York, New Hampshire, Kansas, Colorado, and several southern states such as Tennessee, Mississippi, and Georgia. Blair cited Kentucky as an example of a state with excellent cooperation among women's groups and other organizations. She noted: "In one county in Kentucky, with a population of 38,845, 27 organizations cooperated. Another county with a population of 47,715 reported 45 organizations affiliated."[48]

In her own postwar report to the governor, Sallie Bruce asserted, "The Kentucky organization was considered at Washington one of the best." Because of the armistice, she reported, the organization never reached all the counties in the state. In the 101 counties where it did exist, however, she believed it had "reached more women than any other woman's organization has ever reached in the State, and for the first time in history brought them in touch with the government in a very real way."[49]

Although she was a member of the KCD Advisory Council, Bruce never became an official member of the KCD. Nevertheless, the Kentucky Division and the KCD cooperated well enough, and Bruce spoke at most of the KCD's major functions. Like many of its counterparts throughout the country, the Kentucky Division's focus extended beyond the traditional issues championed by the all-male KCD. Progressive themes such as child welfare, women's suffrage, and working conditions for women received attention. Not all efforts, however, proved successful. The Women in Industry Committee supported a bill to "prohibit women under age twenty-one from public messenger service" and to limit women over age twenty-one to "ten hours of labor per day, between the hours of 7:00 a.m. and 9:00 p.m." The measure passed in the Kentucky house but failed in the senate.[50]

Bruce's conclusion that the Kentucky Division of the WCCND did an excellent job seems well founded. Women's war efforts were led primarily by affluent women who had free time to devote to special causes. Nevertheless, county records reveal that large numbers of women of all social and economic strata participated in the Kentucky Division's myriad activities. These efforts were not confined to major towns and cities; they reached into the smallest hollows, mining camps, and rural communities throughout the state. Even in counties that lacked well-organized committees, women participated in conserving food, promoting Liberty Bonds, sending books to troops, attending to the needs of children, and many other activities. There were few reported instances of female slackers. The Kentucky Division of the WCCND and Kentucky women in general had a right to be proud of their strong contribution to domestic war efforts.[51]

Children and adolescents were also expected to contribute to Kentucky's war efforts. President Wilson called on all the nation's schoolchildren to join the Junior Red Cross. An editorial in the Berea newspaper acknowledged that the "conception of women taking part in war with a burning determination" was "a little new," but "the spark of the conflagration has now reached Berea." It wondered: "How many girls are ready to do National Service and will learn the lessons that are corollary to National Service—patriotism, obedience, democracy?" The newspaper suggested that girls could contribute to ambulance and field kitchen funds; supply each "Berea Boy" (local soldier) with a "three piece knitted set consisting of sleeveless sweater, muffler, and wristlets"; provide each Berea Boy with a comfort kit containing thread, needles, soap, toothpaste, and other sundry items; or take a course in making surgical dressings, first aid, home care for the sick, or dietetics.[52]

Children worked mostly in school and home gardens, as described in chapter 7. But they supported the war in other ways as well. At the Kentucky School for the Blind, children sewed and knitted items for soldiers. As part of a class project, they wrote and produced a play: "Christmas in a Red Cross Hospital." In Louisville, an exhibit of schoolwork from throughout the state featured posters about food conservation, Red Cross needs, Thrift Stamps, and other wartime themes. In Hawesville in Hancock County, boys from rival schools had a contest to see who could buy the most Thrift Stamps with their savings from chores. African American schoolchildren participated in a contest to write the best essay on thrift, a common wartime theme. In Lexington, women formed a Children's Patriotic League to "instill the spirit of love of the country and flag in the minds of the young." Children aged six to fifteen met at the public library each week to hear stories and sing patriotic songs. Girls at the junior high school, the "War Bees," met weekly to do Red Cross work.[53]

The Boy Scouts of America (BSA) was one youth organization dedicated to supporting the war. As the country drew closer to war, national BSA officials touted the organization's readiness to play a role; for example, Scouts could fill in for police doing guard duty. During the war, Boy Scouts appeared in many patriotic parades and ceremonies. Adopting the slogan "Every Scout to Feed a Soldier," the Boy Scouts participated in the war garden movement. Scouts also played a significant role in promoting the purchase of Liberty Bonds and especially War Savings Stamps and Thrift Stamps (campaigns that focused on children and less wealthy contributors). For example, Scouts in Maysville sold

Poster encouraging children to buy War Savings Stamps. (Library of Congress)

more than $14,000 worth of bonds during one campaign. The Boy Scouts also engaged in more esoteric tasks, such as when President Wilson called on them to make an inventory of black walnut trees. Wood from the trees was used to craft airplane propellers and gunstocks, making them vital for war production.[54]

The Boy Scouts of America clearly benefited from the war, but the organization also suffered in some respects. During the war, the BSA's national council sponsored a campaign to increase participation to 2 million boys. President Wilson supported the enrollment drive, acknowledging that "anything that is done or given to increase the war efficiency of the Boy Scouts of America will be a contribution to the nation, and will help us win the war." The *Maysville Public Ledger* observed, "When we turn a mere boy into a Boy Scout, we take him off the list of possible delinquents. In war time there is a special danger of boys turning to evil ways, because with fathers and big brothers absent they are under less restraint." Unfortunately, the increase in the number of Scouts required an increase in the number of troop leaders—a problem with so many men being away from home. Despite these difficulties, new Boy Scout troops developed in Kentucky and participated actively in war-support efforts.[55]

Given that Girl Scouts and Camp Fire Girls were less numerous than Boy Scouts, young girls gravitated toward the Junior Red Cross. (Although its chapters were coed, lists of members reflect an overwhelming female participation.) Begun by the Red Cross in September 1917 and endorsed by President Wilson, the Junior Red Cross in many ways emulated the work of the adult organization; members sewed and knitted vestments, assembled comfort kits, and made bandages. A special-interest group focused on sewing and knitting clothes for French orphans.[56]

Chapters also raised money for general Red Cross activities. In Lancaster, Garrard County schoolchildren eschewed exchanging Christmas presents and instead donated their money to form a Junior Red Cross group. Once they got to work, the youngsters contributed "10 layettes, 22 Comfort pillows, 4 ½ dozen Handkerchiefs, [and] 6 joke books" to the war effort. With the funds it raised, the Lawrence County Junior Red Cross chapter created 250 property bags to be used in hospitals; the bags stored patients' personal belongings and hung at the foot of hospital beds. The chapter also responded to a special campaign to collect nutshells; the fiber from the shells was used to make carbon filters for gas masks.[57]

Kentucky's children contributed their share to the war effort. They grew gardens, promoted War Savings Stamp programs, formed junior Red Cross chapters, worked in agriculture, and participated in patriotic meetings and parades.

While many women and children did their part to support the United States during the war, some Americans—male as well as female, old as well as young—faced different and difficult issues before they could wholeheartedly participate. African Americans asked why they should support the United States in making the world "safe for democracy" when they faced discrimination and marginalization at home.

9

African Americans

When the United States entered World War I in April 1917, Kentucky's African American population wrestled with a dilemma: how to support a war to "make the world safe for democracy" when blacks still lacked basic rights a half century after the Civil War.[1]

Throughout the South, most African Americans remained disenfranchised; they were subjected to Jim Crow laws imposing strict segregation and victimized by white supremacist violence. Although Kentucky African Americans retained the right to vote, segregation and violence marred the state's history. Aiming at integrated Berea College, in 1904 the Kentucky legislature had passed the Day Law, finalizing the legal segregation of all Kentucky schools. Lynchings of blacks in Shelbyville in 1911 and Paducah in 1916 underscored the existence of racial violence. Early in 1917 Governor Augustus O. Stanley traveled to Murray to stop the lynching of a black man, not so much to save the accused but to uphold the rule of law.[2]

While the war ravaged Europe, Americans debated whether the country should get involved and, if so, to what extent. Prominent leaders of the national African American community expressed mixed views about the war. Howard University dean Kelly Miller believed it was a "white man's war," while W. E. B. Du Bois, writing in the NAACP publication *The Crisis,* "sided with the Allies as the more benign imperialists."[3]

For southern whites, thoughts about the war raised racial questions. The anticipated inclusion of blacks in any war efforts, especially the military, represented a two-edged sword. On the one hand, if blacks stayed at home while whites went to war, this would threaten white supremacist control in the South. On the other hand, black participation in the military could open the floodgates for demands for equality. If African Americans fought and died for their country, surely they would deserve better treatment: the right to vote, economic and social opportunities, and protection from violence (such as lynching).

Whites also worried that the Germans would try to subvert blacks, encouraging them to oppose the war. Reports from North Middletown in Bourbon County indicated that German sympathizers were trying to induce African Americans to at least remain passive in the event of war between the United States and Germany. Previously in the county, a black preacher had allegedly told his congregation that the conflict was a "white man's war," adding, "They [whites] have 'Jim-Crowed' us and otherwise mistreated us and now when trouble comes they want us to fight for them."[4]

Summarizing African American attitudes toward the war, British historian Mark Ellis notes that several historians "have persuasively interpreted a mass of evidence showing that with regard to the declared purposes of the United States in entering the war, many African Americans—perhaps most—were ignorant, or indifferent, or skeptical, or antagonistic, and they were either unimpressed or repelled by the home-front propaganda that accompanied mobilization."[5]

When the United States joined the war in April 1917, however, many African Americans did rally to the cause, with a variety of justifications and a range of enthusiasm. For example, Du Bois called for African Americans to support the president and the war effort, "despite Woodrow Wilson's lack of concern for black people."[6]

In Kentucky, several black leaders quickly supported the US entry into the war. Within a week after the declaration of war, more than 500 African Americans attended a meeting in Louisville and passed a resolution strongly supporting the war and repudiating alleged disloyalty. A Union army veteran, the Reverend J. Ward, reminded the crowd of Kentucky blacks' contribution to the Union cause.[7]

A committee at the Asbury Chapel African Methodist Episcopal Church in Louisville wrote to former president Theodore Roosevelt, believing that he would be leading a regiment on the Western Front. Praising Roosevelt's "noble vision for International Righteousness, Justice, and Freedom," the committee asked him to "hold uncompromisingly to your announced purpose to have your Expeditionary Army made up of all the race stocks which compose our body politic." The church's pastor, Arthur G. C. Randall, also wrote to Roosevelt, offering to raise black troops to fight in France. Randall had served as a noncommissioned officer in the Third Infantry Regiment of Alabama Volunteers in the Spanish-American War, and then with the Tenth US Cavalry Regiment of "Buffalo Soldiers" in Cuba. Offering his services and those of other African Americans, the Louisville pastor noted that "visionful Negroes wish to place 25,000 Americans of their race, both as officers and enlisted men, in you[r] Expeditionary Force in Fifty days. GIVE US THE WORD AND WE WILL DO IT."[8] Their offers to serve with Roosevelt went nowhere, as the former president did not lead troops to France. African Americans would have an opportunity to serve militarily, but in very limited ways.

The foremost African American in Kentucky to support the war initially was Louisville resident Roscoe Conkling Simmons, a relative of noted black leader Booker T. Washington. Simmons was a prominent journalist, orator, and Republican Party adherent. When the United States appeared poised to join the war in March 1917, Simmons had spoken to a large assembly of African Americans in Louisville. Originally called to discuss black participation in civic and social improvements in the city, the meeting transformed into a "patriotic demonstration" under the influence of Simmons's oratory. The group denounced pacifism and pledged to support President Wilson. Simmons asserted, "There is for me and my people but one country and one flag, the flag that set me free." He admitted: "Injustice to me there is, bad laws for me there are upon the statute books, but in this hour of need I forget—and you must forget—all thoughts of self or race or creed or color. That, boys, is loyalty." Recognizing the inequalities plaguing African Americans, Simmons nevertheless put his faith in the Constitution. He derided pacifism that "disenfranchised" and "jim-crowed" blacks. He touted previous African American service to the country and put his faith in God, who represented "eternal justice" and "who in time shall right all wrongs and dry all tears."[9]

With this speech, Simmons set forth the optimistic view that if African Americans did their loyal duty, time would work in their favor to correct injustices such as lack of education, disenfranchisement, poverty, and violence. He quickly received the approbation of *Louisville Courier-Journal* editor Henry Watterson, who lauded Simmons's speech as a "rebuke to the traitors and Americans not worthy of the name." This included war opponents such as Senators Robert La Follette of Wisconsin and James Vardaman of Mississippi and "others of their ilk," who "instead of being tarred and feathered black, should be forced to read these words of a black man."[10]

With regard to participation in the war, African Americans immediately faced two major challenges: the notion that German provocateurs were successfully persuading blacks to oppose the war effort, and the question of whether blacks should be subject to the draft.[11] Simmons and other black leaders addressed these concerns.

Within a few days after the United States entered the war, Simmons met with President Wilson, Secretary of War Newton Baker, and Attorney General Thomas Gregory to discuss "German intrigue" among the African American population. Based on information he had gathered and interviews he had conducted with black leaders on a ten-day speaking tour (which included Indianapolis and Memphis), he asserted that German efforts to foster disloyalty and sedition had failed and that blacks remained "ready to shed the last drop of blood for liberty and liberty's flag." Noting that Regular Army black regiments were up to war strength and that blacks were not permitted in most National Guard units, Simmons called for legislation to raise volunteer black regiments that would be led by both white and black officers.[12]

Displays of black support for the war occurred in other Kentucky towns. At the instigation of renowned suffragist Madeline Breckinridge and Mrs. R. G. Stoner of Mt. Sterling, Simmons appeared in central Kentucky on a speaking tour in support of the war. Before a mixed crowd of whites and blacks in Mt. Sterling, Simmons gave what the *Mt. Sterling Advocate* deemed "one of the most eloquent, witty and magnetic speeches ever given in Montgomery county." In Winchester in Clark County, African Americans pledged their support for President Wilson and the war and passed a resolution stating: "That we as a race forget all our former oppression in this country and boldly and cheerfully rally to the flag and do our part in helping to bring about universal peace, and hasten the day when the nations of the world shall 'beat their swords into plowshares, nor lift up sword against nation, neither shall they learn of war.'"[13]

In Lexington, Simmons spoke before several thousand people, including "several hundred representatives of the white race who listened to the orator with intense interest." In the crowd were city and county judges and other notables. He argued in favor of allowing blacks to join Kentucky National Guard regiments (which were all white) and derided "hyphenism," arguing that blacks are not "Afro-American" or "Negro-American" but "American, down and seeking to rise, in the dark and groping for the light." Simmons recognized the problems blacks faced, acknowledging, "I rode to Lexington to declare the loyalty of my people in a Jim Crow car," but he put his faith in "the great heart of the American white man and in God's promises."[14]

Simmons caught the attention of Walter Howard Loving, a black agent in the relatively new Military Intelligence Bureau (MIB), headed by the Harvard-educated Major Ralph Van Deman. An army veteran, Loving was Van Deman's expert on what the MIB termed "Negro subversion." When he encountered Simmons giving a speech in Richmond, Virginia, Loving persuaded him to work for the MIB.

Simmons gave his first MIB-sponsored speech on January 1, 1918, in Marshall, Texas. He subsequently gave pro-war speeches throughout the South, which Loving touted to Van Deman as great successes. Simmons then expanded his speaking engagements westward, all the way to California, with many stops in between. While Loving continued to heap praise on Simmons, historian Ellis believes that unanswered questions about "the sincerity of the country's commitment to democracy" and "the daily realities of insults and potential physical danger weighed more heavily" on African Americans "than Simmons's easy sermonizing."[15]

Early efforts by state and federal authorities to garner African American support centered on the US Food Administration headed by Herbert Hoover. Historian Jennifer Keene points out, "In sharp contrast to the rather limited efforts of most government agencies to reach out to African Americans, the Food Administration undertook a substantial campaign to ensure that its propaganda reached black farmers and consumers. Food Administration propaganda contained a message of sacrifice wrapped in imagery and words that explicitly recognized the key economic role that black citizens played."[16] To carry out this propaganda, the administration relied on key black administrators.

The Food Administration also created a black press section in its education department, and section head A. U. Craig worked with African American newspapers and movie theaters to spread the idea of conservation. The press section sought to create a network of "messengers" to disseminate government propaganda regarding food issues. Craig sent Kentucky's federal food administrator, Fred Sackett, the names of a dozen black Kentucky pastors and heads of fraternal organization who had agreed to support the food effort, as well as a list of all cities and towns with black populations greater than 1,000 and counties with black populations exceeding 10 percent. He suggested that Sackett appoint a black assistant and recommended Green Pinckney Russell, president of the Kentucky Normal and Industrial Institute for Colored Persons (now known as Kentucky State University).[17]

Craig's recommendations were premature. Food Administration official J. W. Hallowell had advised Sackett to consult first with former Tuskegee business agent and football coach Ernest T. Attwell, who was appointed to promote efforts among blacks nationwide, especially in the South.[18] Sackett decided to wait before naming an assistant.

Patty Semple, a member of the Kentucky Division of the Woman's Committee of the Council of National Defense, was already busy working with black women as Sackett's representative in charge of "war work at home." Believing in the winter of 1917 that African Americans were not on board with the Food Administration's efforts and needed "fuller information," Semple arranged a series of meetings with black women's clubs, church groups, libraries, and schools. She believed these meetings led to a "revolution" in attitude and action among black women. After successful meetings in Louisville, in April and May 1918 Semple traveled throughout central and western Kentucky, talking to both white and black women about food conservation. She also pressed for a statewide meeting to coordinate efforts, where Attwell would be invited to speak.[19]

In early June 1918 Sackett appointed Phil H. Brown of Hopkinsville as his assistant to head African American food conservation efforts. Publisher of the black newspaper *Saturday News* and a stalwart Republican, Brown had taken an early interest in the war; he had tried to enroll in the black officers' training

Phil Brown, a Hopkinsville newspaper publisher, was instrumental in war-support efforts among Kentucky African Americans. (University of Louisville)

program and had served on a Liberty Bond campaign committee in Christian County. Brown's hometown white-owned newspaper reported: "Recognizing that negroes do the better part of cooking in Kentucky, the food administration will make special efforts to get them, especially the women, interested in the patriotic work of food conservation."[20]

The African American conference on food issues took place at Phoenix Hill in Louisville on June 17, 1918. Attended by more than 4,000 people, the conference resulted in a resolution pledging black support for a wheatless week at the end of June. Sackett reported to Hoover that Attwell's conference speech had been "well received," that the black organization for food conservation had received "great impetus," and that Brown's efforts had met with "enthusiasm over the state."[21]

Brown also ameliorated a controversy between Ernest Attwell and Patty Semple. Attwell took umbrage when Semple left his name out of an article and took credit for the Phoenix Hill meeting. He asked Phil Brown to "personally make note of the peculiar attitude held by some white people toward Negro effort; whenever it develops into anything good, the inclination is to absorb it for their own credit." In reply, Brown counseled: "I would advise strongly against any controversial situation with Mrs. Semple for obvious reasons. She is a very excellent lady, sincerely devoted to the work, especially as it refers to the negro's activity and benefit, and nothing would be gained, nor no good purpose served by your assuming a hostile attitude." Brown admitted to being a bit chagrined by Semple's claiming credit, but Fred Sackett and his assistant Paul Creel had persuaded him to "pursue the line of least resistance," doing what he could to "attract her good will, and [I] have encountered absolutely no trouble be [*sic*] this course." Brown concluded by suggesting in the "friendliest spirit" that Attwell "drop the matter."[22]

In mid-July Sackett forwarded to Washington a report by Brown, and officials there concluded that Kentucky was leading most states in black food administration. A subsequent report in mid-August noted that fifty-four of the fifty-eight counties with black populations over 1,000 had created organizations and were sending weekly reports. "Intelligent and patriotic" directors had been approved by the county food administrators. Brown had insisted that the directors give him the names of all the people assisting them, so that he could check up and have direct publicity communication with them, given that there were only nine black newspapers in Kentucky (all weeklies). Twenty-four directors sent in 894 names.

Brown reported that meetings had been held in twenty cities and that he had spoken in seven of them, where he had seen "great enthusiasm and the utmost willingness to aid." Directors had procured venues and covered incidental expenses through volunteer contributions. He also noted that a newly formed black committee of the Kentucky Council of Defense was planning to hold sixteen statewide general meetings; he had offered to send representatives to those meetings, which the council had "readily accepted." However, given the lack of follow-up information, Brown planned to continue conducting his own meetings to augment KCD efforts. Furthermore, twenty-four of his representatives had attended a KCD conference for blacks on August 6 to discuss their overall contributions to the war effort (Brown had also spoken at that meeting). To communicate better with Kentucky's black population, which he admitted was not highly educated, Brown asked for a "simple pamphlet" outlining the work needed. He also proposed to organize the counties with less than 1,000 blacks and promised to continue his constant communication with directors. Finally, Brown praised the efforts of Louisville black women who had created a war kitchen. He also reported that black women in Princeton had passed a resolution promising to serve three wheatless breads three times a day: "cornbread, crust and crumbs."[23]

Brown's report reflected substantial administrative progress and enthusiasm among Kentucky blacks. The national Food Administration deemed it "the best we have received from any state." Federal officials liked Brown's suggestion of the simple pamphlet and suggested that he write a draft of it. This

Brown did, titling it "Don't Cut the Rope." Using the analogy of a dastardly mountain climber who allowed his climbing companions to fall while saving his own life, Brown suggested that not conserving food, or eating more than one's fair share, was like "cutting the rope with your teeth." He posited that Americans were overfed and wasteful; blacks were no exception. The exodus from southern farms to northern cities (the "Great Migration") had shifted labor from food-producing to food-consuming areas, having a great effect on the country. Brown asserted that a person who failed to comply with food restrictions was a "traitor, lending aid to the enemy, adding to the length of the war and to the danger of our boys at the front. In fact, he is *cutting* the *rope.*" He reminded readers of their obligation to soldiers abroad, including blacks.[24]

Even as the war ended, Phil Brown continued to work diligently to support US Food Administration initiatives. He wrote to his directors and encouraged their full support for Hoover's Conservation Week in December, designed to address continuing food needs in Europe. Before they were "mustered out," he asked directors to remind their committee members that "their country needs them as essentially in peace as it did in war." Brown concluded: "The fact that we have done our share in this great movement is known to the highest authorities. Now, let's have a little more vim, a little more enthusiasm for our last stand in the great cause. We have whipped the Hun; now let's whip hunger and we shall enjoy a two-fold victory."[25]

Despite his time-consuming volunteer work on food issues, Brown had no illusions about his position as an African American. He planned to attend a meeting of female county food representatives in Louisville and assured Sackett: "I shall see you in Louisville Friday. Don't worry about me causing any embarrassment in reference to the social feature of the meeting. I know that I am a Negro, and while I am not the least bit ashamed of it, I know where I should go and where I should not." At the meeting, Brown talked about the contributions of the state's African Americans, noting that it was his patriotic duty to attend the meeting and to "add a little color to the occasion."[26]

After the war, Brown would be rewarded for his food conservation efforts and his loyalty to the Republican Party. When the Republicans swept to power under President Warren Harding in 1921, Brown moved to Washington, DC, where he became the commissioner of conciliation at the Department of Labor. He died unexpectedly of a heart attack in December 1923.[27]

While Phil Brown led Kentucky's African Americans in a food conservation program, another group of influential blacks assisted the Kentucky Council of Defense. The KCD was composed of prominent white men whom the governor had appointed to coordinate all of Kentucky's war efforts. The KCD took its lead from the Council of National Defense, which belatedly addressed the role of blacks in the nation's war-support effort.[28]

To guide the all-white southern state councils of defense, CND officials sent out General Letter No. 44 on February 23, 1918. After an analysis based on limited feedback from southern states, CND officials had concluded that black councils would be most effective at county and community levels rather than at the state level. Those local councils could be overseen by traveling agents such as Ernest Attwell. The CND believed that these separate, local black councils should be composed of both men and women, who would work with black fraternal and religious organizations. General Letter No. 44 suggested that white state councils convene conferences of prominent African American women and men and appoint black committees that would report to the state councils. Black councils could then be established in the counties under the direction of the white county councils.

General Letter No. 44 suggested activities for the black county councils, including convening mass patriotic meetings of blacks, addressed by both black and white speakers; urging teachers and ministers to promote patriotism; encouraging black southern farmers to stay at their jobs in the fields and to help conserve food; fostering thrift and savings through bonds and Thrift Stamps; and supporting the Red Cross. General Letter No. 44 concluded by reminding white state and county councils to "give the Negro every assistance."[29]

Other than the Food Administration efforts led by Phil Brown, black organization in the commonwealth had languished. With the revitalization of the KCD in March 1918, the president of the Kentucky Negro Educational Association, Professor Harvey C. Russell Sr., wrote to Louisville businessman Carl C. Ousley, offering to organize blacks and "educate them as to the spirit and aims" of the KCD and the white county councils already formed. Ousley passed along the offer to KCD chairman Edward Hines. The KCD, however, had already received an overture from the state supervisor of Negro Rural Schools, Frank C. Button, to organize the black community. Button had suggested holding patriotic meetings, and he offered to put together a list of the "best and most conservative colored speakers in the State." He also offered to get support from white men who had influence with blacks, such as prominent Louisville citizens William Speed and the Reverend John Little, superintendent of the Presbyterian Colored Missions.[30]

In the end, Button, Speed, and Little all ended up on the KCD-formed Committee on the Organization of Colored People for War Work, headed by a white Louisvillian, Captain Charles Huhlein. Other members included Lexington superintendent of schools M. A. Cassidy, Louisville insurance man John J. Barret, and Hopkinsville tobacco man Robert E. Cooper. Huhlein received copies of the CND's General Letter No. 44 and set to work following most of its suggestions. His committee met almost weekly and invited prominent blacks to join its efforts.[31]

Working with KCD member H. H. Cherry, Huhlein's committee planned sixteen patriotic meetings to be held at the end of July for blacks throughout the state. At a meeting of Huhlein's committee on July 19 at the KCD office in Louisville, Phil Brown was named head of a committee to sponsor a statewide conference to create a larger black organization to help the war effort.[32]

A separate meeting of African Americans in Louisville resulted in forty-five individuals, including several ministers and three women, volunteering to act as Four Minute Men to speak in favor of the war at churches and other venues open to blacks. A subsequent meeting of the Four Minute Men, Colored Division, heard state director Marvin Lewis talk about the mobilization of American industry. The group would later hear from Pratt Dale, the new head of the US Employment Service, which sought labor for industries and other projects such as the building of Camp Knox south of Louisville.[33]

The daylong statewide conference chaired by Huhlein took place on August 6, 1918. Appointed by Governor Stanley, more than sixty African American representatives from around the state met with KCD members at the Louisville Board of Trade building. In the morning, George Haynes, director of Negro economics at the US Department of Labor, addressed the group, as did Governor Stanley and state agriculture commissioner Mat Cohen. A last-minute speaker, British Captain E. Lucas Guest, described how the Germans had mistreated blacks in Africa.[34]

In the afternoon, a couple of committees reported on a constitution to govern the black organization and on plans to divide the state into thirty districts. The constitution proposed a committee of thirty to oversee black war efforts, including at least six women. In keeping with the multiplier effect of most war work in the state, the constitution also called for county and community committees to be established. After the committee reports, KCD chairman Edward Hines spoke about his organization, and Phil Brown spoke about black food conservation efforts. After several other participants gave short five-minute speeches, the conference adjourned with the singing of "America."[35]

The conference was followed at night by a mass patriotic meeting in Phoenix Hill, attended by more than 3,000 African Americans. Captain Huhlein and George Haynes spoke, but the majority of the program was provided by black army bands.[36]

The activities of Scott County African Americans in central Kentucky mirrored those in other communities to support the war. They rallied to the Red Cross drive in December 1917, and in the spring of 1918 the black women's

Sunshine Club began sewing and knitting for soldiers. Black men formed a Patriotic League to take care of selectees before they headed off to training camp, and they sponsored a celebratory parade when the men returned from the war. At the segregated black school, the Junior Red Cross Society made comfort bags and sponsored a parade in May 1918. Schoolchildren gave money to the Red Cross and the Jewish Relief Fund and purchased War Stamps. A lengthy article in the local Georgetown newspaper in September 1919 summed up these efforts: "The colored people of Scott county responded readily and nobly to every call made to them during the 'Great World War.'"[37]

In the summer of 1918, Scott County launched a black committee for war work under the chairmanship of G. B. Gillispie. He led Scott County black men in the United War Work Campaign, while Mrs. E. B. Davis did the same for the women; in fact, the women raised more money than their male counterparts. The white leader of the Liberty and Victory loans, George Hambrick, avowed that the Scott County African American community bought more than $20,000 in war bonds. In total, they contributed more than $35,000 to the war effort, acknowledged by the local newspaper as "a staggering amount when one considers that it comes from very poor people." The Scott County black community did more than contribute money: 170 men went off to war. Four died of disease; one—Henry Black—was killed in action. The local newspaper writer found the deceased's name rather fitting.[38]

Despite African American assurances of loyalty, federal government officials feared otherwise. Six federal agencies "maintained a constant watch on the activities of black civilians and soldiers and equal rights organizations and publications." Officials feared that German agitators and pacifists might be successful in fomenting African American opposition to the war, which could seriously hamper the United States' war efforts. Under its chief Bruce Bielaski, the Department of Justice's Bureau of Investigation took the lead in investigating allegations of espionage and disloyalty. Ralph Van Deman's Military Intelligence Bureau also investigated not only black soldiers but civilians as well.[39]

Several cases of alleged African American subversion prompted investigations in Kentucky. In July 1917 Lexington BI agent Linzy O. Thompson received two unexpected visitors: Mr. and Mrs. J. V. Shipp of Midway. Shipp told Thompson about Robert and Eliza Withers, a black couple who worked for him but had relatives in the African American community of Logan Town, near Lancaster. Robert Withers had allegedly told Mrs. Shipp that he would fight for Germany and so would the blacks in Logan Town if they could ever get to Germany. Germans in a settlement near Lancaster had supposedly spoken to the blacks, trying to incite them against the government. In his report on the matter, Thompson admitted he had no additional information and could not say whether there had been any German influence in the area. He had invited the Shipps to report back from time to time.[40]

In a case later that year, Judge Lyman Chalkley, a University of Kentucky law professor, visited Thompson to report on pro-German sentiment infecting Lexington's black population. Chalkley, a prominent Lexingtonian, was married to Eleanor Breckinridge, the daughter of former Kentucky congressman W. C. P. Breckinridge. At the behest of Episcopal bishop Lewis W. Burton, Chalkley had served as a substitute pastor at a "certain colored church," where he "could see there was an under current in favor of Germany." A black churchgoer, Alfred Titus, had received a letter from his son at college, questioning whether the American flag really protected him. Given this lead, agent Thompson asked the local head of the American Protective League, Frank Bataille, to inquire about Titus's son.[41]

Chalkley followed up with a telephone call to agent Thompson, providing the son's name—John Kenneth Titus—and the information that he was attending "Iowa Wesslyn [*sic*] University, Ames, Iowa." Thompson surmised that this was "a colored school, or at least there are possibly a number of colored students in it." If the son had written to his father questioning the flag, Thompson believed that "some kind of German propaganda is being promulgated at that institution." If so, and if it was successful among the students, it could have the same effect on parents and relatives back home, "because the average colored man who has a son at a *university* feels that such a son is very wise and that his advice should be followed." The BI agent suggested an investigation at the university and possibly an interview with John Titus, either "under a suitable pretext or openly." Even if Titus was interviewed and nothing useful were obtained, "it will serve to let him know he is under surveillance, and have its effect on the negroes here [in Lexington]."[42]

An APL investigator in Lexington followed up and reported to Thompson. The head of the Episcopal Church Diocese of Lexington, Bishop Burton, had vouched for the Lexington church, St. Andrew's; he believed its officers were "loyal to America." Burton took responsibility for a delay in dedicating a flag in the church, primarily because of cold weather. The APL investigator interviewed the father, Alfred Titus, who said his son attended the University of Iowa. Thompson noted, "The operative of the League reports that he felt Titus and wife out on the question of the war and found their views satisfactory." The BI agent concluded, "Unless other facts warrant, this matter is closed."[43]

The matter was not completely closed, however. In May 1918 Alfred Titus rushed to Thompson's office after allegedly uttering a suspicious statement about Germany gaining territory during the war. Titus disavowed any disloyal intent. In turn, Thompson obtained a letter from Titus's son at the post office, without a warrant. Although the letter was not seditious, Alfred Titus promised to keep Thompson apprised of any pro-German talk among blacks.[44]

In another case, US district attorney Thomas Slattery asked agent Thompson to investigate possible subversion by a black Richmond barber, Walter Delaney. Thompson subsequently interviewed Madison County attorney O. P. Jackson, who had been in the barbershop when Delaney had said, "This is a white man's war and the negro ought not to have anything to do with it." Jackson had also heard Delaney refer to it as "Wilson's war." When the county attorney confronted Delaney as a German sympathizer, Delaney replied that about a third of black people were. Jackson believed such talk by the barber was "dangerous among the negroes since he appears to be their leader and advisor." Other witnesses corroborated Jackson's statements. They had heard Delaney say that if blacks went to war, they would "be used as breast works." The Richmond barber had also been heard praising Wisconsin senator Robert La Follette, who strongly opposed the war and whose patriotism people still questioned. Thompson believed that prejudice played no role in these accusations, since the white witnesses patronized the barbershop. He concluded that because Delaney was a black leader and was spreading propaganda, "he is a very dangerous man at this time, and his line of speech should be suppressed." Richmond's chief of police asserted that if federal law officials did not deal with Delaney, "anything is likely to happen to him."[45]

The threat of black subversion instigated by Germans remained the subject of collaborative investigations throughout the war by the Bureau of Investigation and the Military Intelligence Bureau. In his extensive study of the subject, historian Theodore Kornweibel concludes, however, "There is almost no evidence that Germans or other enemies attempted to subvert the loyalty of African Americans during World War I, and no evidence at all that any such attempts succeeded. But a deep current of apathy and disaffection ran throughout Black America."[46] Blacks continued to question their role in the war to make the world safe for democracy. Nevertheless, after a great deal of deliberation, blacks were expected to contribute militarily to the war effort under the Selective Service Act.

On June 6, 1917, millions of American men reported to their local draft boards to register. The drafting of African Americans prompted objections from southern politicians, who feared that a valuable agricultural labor source would be diminished. Then, when it became clear that blacks would be included in the selective service system, southerners objected to stationing blacks in the region and, supported by military leaders, rejected the idea of integrated units. Blacks were assigned to all-black regiments, most of which served as labor battalions, not fighting units. These units were led by white officers. The army established a separate training camp for black officers at Fort Des Moines, Iowa.[47]

After the first draft registration in June, the initial call-up for those conscripted into the army proved disproportionate: although they constituted only 10 percent of the population, 14 percent of the men ordered to report for duty were African American. Some were sent to Houston, Texas, for training. In late August, after two of their colleagues were beaten by police, black soldiers rebelled and stormed the town. People were killed, arrests followed, and, after cursory courts-martial, thirteen black soldiers were executed.[48]

Kentucky newspapers reported the Houston riot. The *Louisville Courier-Journal*'s extensive coverage prompted a woman from Corsicana, Texas—Mamie Downard Peck—to write a scathing letter to the editor, noting that "the recent murderous action of the negro regiment sent to Houston, Tex., is but another sad reminder that the South is no place for the negro soldier." She asserted, "The negro has known so little power as a race that, clothed with authority and a uniform, he is a supercilious, overbearing savage." When northern newspapers criticized the South after the incident, a *Courier-Journal* editorial reminded critics about the racial and labor riots in the summer of 1917 in the "northern" city of East St. Louis, Illinois.[49] The *Adair County News* blamed the Houston killings on "northern" blacks who had an "exalted idea of [their] importance," while southern blacks knew how to behave. Hence it was "almost a crime to send a northern Negro soldier to the South for encampment."[50]

As a result of the Houston riot, Secretary of War Baker appointed Emmett J. Scott as his special assistant to deal with the issue of African Americans in the military. Scott had been Booker T. Washington's private secretary and secretary-treasurer at the Tuskegee Institute. Baker also decided to delay the calling up of African Americans. When drafted, they would be kept in segregated units, but they would be sent to training cantonments, such as Louisville's Camp Taylor, along with white selectees.[51]

At Camp Taylor, officials made plans to host black selectees, some of whom would be formed into a labor battalion. Army authorities asked for white volunteers to serve as noncommissioned officers. The *Louisville Courier-Journal* reported, "At first very few men took kindly to the idea of serving among negro troops, but after officers explained that their service would be in an executive capacity a large number of men stepped forward. The intimation that they would get to France many months before the 84th Division [Camp Taylor's training depot unit] was an alluring proposition to many men."[52]

In Kentucky, the conscription and training of African American soldiers proceeded reasonably well. Toward the end of the war, Provost Marshal Gen-

African American draftees at the Lexington courthouse. (National Archives and Records Administration)

eral Enoch Crowder gathered statistical information regarding various aspects of the draft. In a telegram to the governor passed on to Major Henry Rhodes, director of the selective service system in Kentucky, Crowder noted that 39 percent of Kentucky's deserters were African American.[53] (Desertion was defined not only as leaving the army after induction but also as failure to report for induction.)

Rhodes countered with a lengthy explanation. He first noted that African Americans had the greatest illiteracy, which would explain why they did not respond to draft notices. Second, most incidences of desertion among all men, including blacks, occurred in the eastern mountains, exacerbated by a coal strike in the fall of 1917. Many blacks had come from Georgia and Alabama to work in the mines, attracted by the high wages, and because they were illiterate, they had to rely on "general conversation" about the war. Blacks could easily be unaware that they had been drafted. Rhodes argued: "The percent of actual desertion or slackening has been very low. This is especially true of the negro population. The percentage of negroes that have been placed in class one in this state is far in excess of the percentage of white men, taking them in proportion to the number that are registered. It cannot be said that the negroes in this state have in any way endeavored to evade the service unless it might be in the mountain counties where there has never been a very strong pro-war feeling." Rhodes noted that when blacks did receive their notices to report, they often went to his office in Frankfort rather than their local draft boards, "using every means possible" to get there. Because they did not have any money, many of them rode the freight trains. Rhodes explained that blacks often roamed from one job to another, and they lacked "sufficient education as to be aware of the extreme importance of their keeping in touch with the local board."[54]

Slowly but surely, draft boards began calling blacks into service in the spring of 1918. The pace picked up in the summer, when more than 3,000 Kentucky African Americans were called. More than 900 were expected from Jefferson County, and more than 200 each from Fayette, Hopkins, and Christian Counties. In several Kentucky towns, large crowds of African Americans turned out to wish their selectees well as they boarded trains that took them primarily to Camp Taylor. Georgetown bid farewell to its contingent at the end of March 1918. In July more than 900 black selectees paraded through Louisville, accompanied by several bands, and then boarded forty streetcars that would take them to Camp Taylor for processing.[55] Planning to receive 3,000 to 4,000 African American troops at Camp Taylor, the War Recreation Board in Louisville established a separate Soldiers' Club in downtown Louisville and a black housing bureau at the YWCA to help friends and families of black soldiers find rooms during visits.[56]

While racial strife and riots took place in Houston and at Fort Merritt, New Jersey, Camp Taylor and the nearby Louisville community managed to avoid deadly discord. A contretemps did arise, however, soon after the camp was completed. Black Louisvillian William Glass was visiting his hometown after being newly commissioned at the black officers' training camp at Fort Des Moines. Walking down the street with his wife, he took offense when two white noncommissioned officers saluted a white officer but one of them refused to salute Glass, saying, "I don't salute a negro." Before this incident, Glass had always been saluted appropriately.[57]

To ameliorate the situation, the venerable General John Breckinridge Castleman spoke out. A former Confederate major and commander of the famous "Louisville Legion" during the Spanish-American War, Castleman asserted that army discipline had to be maintained, which required the proper saluting of officers "without regard to the color of [their] skin."[58]

As more African Americans poured into Camp Taylor, the War Department created new units for them—the 801st, 814th, and 64th Pioneer Infantry Regiments—composed of 3,000 men and 100 officers. The 814th adopted the name "Black Devils," in the hope of rivaling the famous "Blue Devils," the elite French mountain troops of the *Chasseurs Alpins*.[59] Like most black units during the war, those at Camp Taylor became labor battalions and were unlikely to see any fighting. In July 1918 the men of the 801st Pioneer Infantry received word that they would be used for railroad construction, disappointing those who had hoped to be part of a fighting organization. To counter this disappointment, military officials relented and promised that the 801st would become a "crack organization," a "shock" unit that would serve at the front lines. The 801st trained at Camp Taylor before being sent to Camp Merritt, New Jersey, for transport to France. As soldier Robert Stevens pointed out, "We marched

Quartermaster Corps band performing for African American troops at the Knights of Columbus hall, Camp Taylor, Louisville. (National Archives and Records Administration)

for a couple of weeks and practiced shooting a couple of weeks and then went (shipped out) over seas."[60]

Commanded by West Point graduate George F. Hamilton, the 801st Pioneers left the United States on September 8, 1918. Upon arriving in France, they made their way to billets near Chaumont, General Pershing's headquarters southeast of Paris. Arriving late in the war, the 801st Pioneer Infantry participated in little fighting but a lot of labor, typical for most African American units. Part of the unit received praise for their good work at Camp Pontanezen at Brest, which they helped transform "from a mudhole to the cleanest and most modern of camps."[61]

Under command of Cyrus Dolph, the 814th Pioneer Infantry "Black Devils" were black selectees from Kentucky, Indiana, Tennessee, and Alabama. After training at Camp Taylor, the 814th proceeded to Camp Dix, New Jersey, where it embarked for France in mid-October 1918. The troops were eager to fight. Sergeant John Turner from Mason County wrote home that despite "old Bill Kaiser's fake peace terms," the unit would "give him some of the Black Devil's medicine, which will do him good." Maysville native Charles Hall wrote to his parents that "the Black Devils will finish the Kaiser for we are hot after him."[62]

As African Americans appeared in France, Kentucky writer Irvin Cobb recounted their stories in the *Saturday Evening Post.* When the United States formally entered the war, Cobb revisited the Western Front. His August 1918 *Post* article about African American soldiers—"Young Black Joe"—was reprinted in the *Louisville Courier-Journal* and various black magazines. While lauding the black soldiers, Cobb also presented a stereotypical image of happy-go-lucky folks who liked to sing and dance. Cobb's best contribution described the heroic exploits of two men: Henry Lincoln Johnson and Needham Roberts. Both won the French Croix de Guerre for their bravery under fire.[63]

Several Kentucky African Americans regarded Cobb's story favorably; they overlooked the stereotyping to focus on the positive image of patriotic black soldiers fighting for America. After returning to his native Paducah, Cobb was feted by a group of prominent African Americans at the town's largest black church. In front of a packed house, Cobb spoke about blacks' military contributions since the American Revolution. Much to the delight of the crowd, Cobb finished with a reference to a black Paducah soldier, Sergeant William Kivil, who had been decorated for bravery by the French.[64]

Another Kentuckian had firsthand experience with black soldiers and recorded his thoughts in a diary. Major Austin Kinnaird of Louisville was a white officer in command of black troops. A longtime member of the "Louisville Legion," Kinnaird had been active in a businessmen's training corps in Louisville and had trained as a Regular Army officer. Eventually assigned to the 811th Pioneer Infantry, Major Kinnaird and his men shipped out in late October to quarters near Bordeaux, France. Although they had been issued rifles for fighting, Kinnaird's men worked on the docks of the American-built port of Bassans, three miles outside of Bordeaux. Kinnaird seemed to understand and sympathize with his men. On one occasion, the military police stopped a group of them in a truck, and a search revealed six bottles of liquor. All the men in the truck were thrown into the guardhouse, which the officer believed unfair. In his diary, Kinnaird maintained that the men were "hard-working, non-drinking and honest." The Louisville officer managed to get some of the innocent men released a few days later by appealing to the military police commander.[65]

According to Kinnaird, his men "were doing their bit on the docks and march to and from work like soldiers. Their marked superiority, in discipline, courtesy, appearance, and conduct, as compared with the stevedores has aroused some resentment on the part of some officers of the labor organizations in camp." The men also encountered discrimination. After an inspection in which some of them were searched by military police and nothing inappropriate was found, Kinnaird concluded: "The colored soldier is not getting a square deal, in my opinion, in this Base. Every effort seems to be exerted by the MP [military police] and Criminal Investigation Bureau to secure convictions, regardless of guilt or innocence. Also to make the men steal by plants of candy and food. Men are picked up, taken to Bordeaux and given the 'Third Degree' and evidence (?) secured. Men are made to confess and then tried with no other evidence. At the trial its [*sic*] impossible to bring out the 'Third Degree' methods as the JA [judge advocate] absolutely dominates the court, and he pretends to believe that no uncivilized methods are used."[66]

Serving on a general court-martial, Kinnaird saw more evidence of what he believed was prejudicial treatment. He observed that a defendant's counsel, "a very bright colored lieutenant," was badly insulted by the judge advocate, with no resulting admonishment by the court-martial president. Trying to underscore the inappropriateness of the "third degree," the Kentuckian ran into opposition from the court president, who noted that he himself had used these methods while working with the military police. Kinnaird concluded: "The whole court seems to be afraid of the JA or of something. The President does not run the court." The following day, Kinnaird was not surprised to discover that he had been left off the court. He lamented, "The only chance there will be for me to get the fact of the 3rd Degree being used into any record in the future will be if it is used on any of my men."[67]

The French treated black troops much better than the Americans did, much to the chagrin of whites. An acting commanding officer at Kinnaird's base declared that the French waitresses in the officers' mess "must stop playing with the negro cooks and kitchen police in kitchen at night, upon pain of dismissal." Kinnaird noted: "The girls, as a rule, apparently prefer the colored stevedores to the white officers. There is a saying that they consort with the Animites [Vietnamese] out of curiosity, with the white enlisted men for car fare, white officers for a living, and the stevedores for pleasure."[68]

Austin Kinnaird continued to look out for his men. On discovering that they were not receiving proper food at lunch on the docks and were being served spoiled food at supper, Kinnaird "showed sample to CO [commanding officer] and also raised H with the Mess Off[icer]." A day later he and the commanding officer visited the lunch mess and "found a wonderful improvement."[69]

Some Kentucky African Americans who served in the black units later recalled their experiences. Andrew Carman of Graves County in western Kentucky was drafted, trained at Camp Taylor in the 801st Regiment, and was sent to France, where he eventually served in the famous 369th Regiment—the "Harlem Hellfighters." One of two black regiments that fought under French command, the 369th garnered many French awards. Carman was wounded by shrapnel but survived the war and was discharged in 1919. During his time abroad, Carman was surprised by the lack of prejudice and segregation in France. He noted: "The French treated me like a man. They treated me better than I'd ever been treated in my own country."[70]

Hickman native Rufus Atwood distinguished himself while serving in France. A student at Fisk University in Nashville when the United States entered the war, Atwood ended up in the 92nd Division's 325th Signal Battalion. On the day before the November 11, 1918, armistice, Sergeant Atwood twice helped reconstruct a switchboard and phone lines under heavy shelling. For his coolness under fire, he was cited in the division's General Orders No. 38. After the war he became president of Kentucky State Industrial College for Colored Persons (Kentucky State University), serving from 1929 until his retirement in 1962.[71]

Before he left the army, Atwood received a letter from his father warning him not to wear his uniform home. Local police chief "Skullbuster" Wright was meeting trains at the station and forcing blacks to shed their uniforms and don their coveralls. Atwood did as his father suggested and packed his uniform in his suitcase; only later did he model it privately for his proud family.[72] Atwood's father had good reason to be worried. In December 1918 an African American soldier, Charles Lewis, was on a train passing through Fulton County, headed home to Alabama. At the train station, police officers questioned Lewis about a robbery on the train and asked to see all his belongings. Pointing to his uniform, Lewis declared that he had served honorably in the military and had never committed a crime. After Lewis left the train, the police followed the former soldier; a chase and a scuffle ensued, and a deputy sheriff was injured. Lewis was apprehended and taken to the Fulton County jail in Hickman, where a crowd gathered, seized the veteran, and took him into the country, and hanged him in his soldier's uniform. It was the first of more than a dozen lynchings of black soldiers in immediate postwar America.[73]

Members of the African American community in Kentucky responded enthusiastically to the US entry into World War I, hoping they might establish their standing and rights as full citizens and hoping to avoid being branded as "slackers." Key leaders such as Philip Brown and Roscoe Conkling Simmons supported the US war effort. Black church leaders encouraged their congregations to support the Red Cross, buy Liberty Bonds, and enroll for the draft.

A few blacks may have questioned whether the war would bring full democratic rights to the commonwealth's African American population, but most remained optimistic. Scott County's E. B. Davis wrote about black contributions to the war effort in the local newspaper's September 1919 war historical edition. He noted that Scott County's African Americans "had the utmost and explicit faith [and] confidence in their government that it should accord them in America and their soldier sons in the mud-trenches of France a square deal." Davis optimistically hoped that the "sheltering folds of the 'Red, White and Blue' would forever and securely protect and defend from prejudice, discrimination, mobs and violence, the black men and women of America that had been true to every trust and loyal to every star."[74]

The impact of the war on African American dreams of full citizenship would be limited. It would take another world war and an ensuing civil rights campaign for Kentucky's African Americans to begin to fulfill their dreams of equality before the law. But black Kentuckians could point to a proud legacy of service during the Great War.[75]

10

The Economy

The advent of the Great War in 1914 proved a boon to the US economy. America became a major exporter of food, munitions, and other commodities, primarily to the Allies. Describing the effects of the Great War on America, historian Neil Wynn asserts: "Above all else, the war brought business expansion and encouraged the optimism that was to continue, after just a brief hesitation, into the twenties." This certainly proved true in Kentucky, where key sectors of the economy such as tobacco and coal production increased dramatically because of the war.[1]

State historian Jim Klotter has pointed out that "Kentucky remained an agrarian state in the first third of the twentieth century." Leaders in the commonwealth understood its mostly rural nature and focused on agriculture and its possible contribution to the war. State agriculturalists met in Louisville in April 1917 at the suggestion of Fred Mutchler, the University of Kentucky's head of statewide federal extension agents, to discuss topics such as food production, labor, crop priorities, and funding. Mutchler and state agriculture commissioner Mat Cohen then visited various parts of Kentucky to meet farmers and exchange ideas. Cohen advised them to decrease their emphasis on tobacco and focus on raising food—not only because more food would be needed but also because labor-intensive tobacco farming might suffer due to a shortage of workers. Men who worked in the tobacco fields might be drafted and sent away.[2]

Livestock farmers met to consider the war's implications for cattle, sheep, and pig production. Horse breeders met to discuss the effects of a war that had already demanded much from them. An estimated 30,000 horses from Kentucky, and even more mules, had been sent to Europe before America entered the war. Some horse breeders suffered: Thoroughbred breeding had declined nearly 60 percent in three years.[3]

Two weeks after the United States entered the war, Governor Stanley created a food committee headed by extension agent Morgan Hughes of Bowling Green. The committee's duties included distributing seeds, monitoring farm labor needs, and advising on cultivation and crop rotation. In May 1917 Hughes accompanied state Council of Defense chair Embry Swearingen to

Washington, DC, to discuss issues with Agriculture and War Department officials. Hughes also attended a Federal Trade Commission conference, returning with the news that federal officials did not foresee imposing maximum prices on food producers.[4]

Fred Mutchler, Morgan Hughes, and other extension agents played an important role in the state's agricultural efforts. The Smith-Lever Act of 1914 had established a cooperative venture between the US Department of Agriculture and state universities to provide agricultural extension agents to counties. The Great War accelerated the creation of statewide networks of agents who were essential to the war effort. Historian David Danbom maintains, "The task of mobilizing agriculture and the rural populations fell largely on the home and farm extension agents of the United States Department of Agriculture."[5] Danbom believes that while there were "strong currents of rural opposition" to the war, "the more pervasive rural attitude seemed to be indifference." He cites an example from Fulton County extension agent Morris M. Gordon, who reported in 1917: "I longed to smash the soap box orator (in some cases one of my demonstrators) who aired his views in the country store that we were no freer than Germany." Gordon added: "And then too, when I would go back to town and eat a meal at my boarding house with bank clerks and business men their one topic of conversation was the unpatriotic farmer. And the worst of it was that most of the things they said were true."[6] Although opposition or indifference may have marked rural Kentucky initially, farmers eventually rallied to the war effort with the help of their extension agents and other federal, state, and local officials.

State officials remained concerned about the need for farm labor, with many men likely to be drafted off farms. Responding to a faculty resolution, University of Kentucky (UK) president Henry Barker announced that any students who wanted to leave school to work on farms would retain the grades they currently had. Acting dean of agriculture George Roberts, however, branded as "slackers" anyone who left school to work in a more remunerative armaments factory.[7]

Recognizing the need to balance labor needs throughout the nation, federal and state authorities cooperated through the Department of Labor's US Employment Service (USES). "In charge of recruiting and placing all labor for war industries," USES had two divisions in Kentucky. The Employment Service Division was "in charge of all branch employment bureaus and the placing of labor" and was led temporarily by Labor Department official W. G. Sprague and then by Louisville lawyer W. Pratt Dale. The Public Service Reserve Division was "in charge of recruiting and registering labor" and was directed by the new UK president Frank McVey. Dale and McVey worked through county councils of defense.[8]

In addition to increasing production, farmers were expected to support the war effort in other ways, such as by purchasing Liberty Bonds.

In addition to the two state directors, a state board had "general supervision over the recruiting and distributing of labor." They were helped by county and community volunteer boards comprising representatives from labor and management and from large and small towns. For example, in Pike County, more than two dozen voting precincts had volunteer representatives from such towns as Fish Trap, Belcher, Zebulon, and the rapidly growing coal town of McVeigh. These volunteers were usually middle-class white men; for example, in Marshall County, the county attorney served as chairman, and board members included merchants, farmers, a surveyor, a banker, and the county clerk. A fundamental principle of the boards' work was to ensure that "farms were not deprived of their essential labor."[9]

Through its state USES efforts, the federal government tried to apportion labor, shifting men from so-called nonessential work to jobs in war industries. The program intended for employers and employees to match needs and skills through a centralized system beginning on August 1, 1918. Federal officials originally believed that Kentucky could supply more than 4,100 unskilled laborers for war industries, but the total was later increased to 8,100 men.[10]

The USES focused first on finding skilled tradesmen for the shipbuilding industry, then for stevedore units to serve overseas and for mechanics and skilled railroad men. Men who were interested in these skilled jobs filled out registration cards indicating their availability. Then the Public Service Reserve expanded the registration to men deemed to be working in nonessential occupations such as the entertainment business. Farmers and miners need not apply. McVey cautioned his county representatives: "In enrolling unskilled laborers, it must be understood that farming interests must not be disturbed and the same is true of mining interests."[11]

One of McVey's letters to county representatives expressed his Progressive belief that the federal government would make fair and correct decisions. He wrote: "Private enterprises of all kinds must yield to the Government necessity. Every employer and every workman must trust the Government to make a proper distribution of the labor of the country."[12]

Sometimes men wrote individually to McVey requesting work; the UK president forwarded these requests to Dale at the USES because that organization did not want men switching jobs on their own initiative. Dale's Employment Service placed full-page advertisements in newspapers with the headline: "Don't Change Jobs without Consulting Uncle Sam." The ad counseled: "Let your Government assist you in determining the work in which you will be most valuable in helping to win the war." The Public Service Reserve advertised jobs nearby and far away. For example, in Lawrence County in eastern Kentucky, it advertised for men to fill positions in local industries such as Ashland Steel and for out-of-town work at Camp Knox, 200 miles away.[13]

The farm labor situation commanded attention throughout 1918. UK president McVey was in a good position to work on farm issues. UK had already collaborated with the US Department of Agriculture to place agricultural extension agents in about two-thirds of Kentucky's 120 counties, so there was already an easy way to reach small communities. McVey called on the new dean of the College of Agriculture and director of the Agricultural Extension Service, Thomas Poe Cooper, for help; Cooper suggested Professor W. D. Nicholls of the Farm Management Department to serve as the state farm labor specialist.[14]

Nicholls worked with the agricultural extension agents and other authorities to help meet farm labor needs. He developed a farm labor program that forced vagrants to work on farms, enlisted the help of the Boys Working Reserve, and used businessmen and students on farms. Dean Cooper helped by writing to city and county attorneys throughout the state, encouraging them to enforce the state's new vagrancy law and thereby force slackers to work on farms. President McVey wrote to state college and university presidents, asking them to encourage their students to work on farms during the summer break. A couple of colleges reported that their students were doing so, primarily on their own family farms.[15]

Maintaining that many businessmen came from rural backgrounds, Nicholls encouraged them to work on farms. He outlined a plan for merchants to allow their "clerks" to devote part of their vacations to farmwork. To organize this program, he envisioned an "Army of Defense," with quasi-military ranks, public rallies, and service badges. Nicholls believed that "the clerks would be benefited by the healthy outdoor occupation and would come back more greatly refreshed than if they had idled away their hours and spent their money during their vacation period." To support Nicholls, McVey also asked his county representatives to speak to businessmen about working on farms. He noted, "If lack of farm labor results in a short crop in any community the town in that community will suffer a loss of business next fall. Self-interest as well as patriotism should therefore prompt business men to put forth every exertion to see that a full crop is harvested."[16]

Many Kentuckians heeded the call. Teachers, firemen, police, salesmen, barbers, ministers, county and town administrators, and other people volunteered to help with the harvests. Daviess County agent J. W. Whitehouse maintained that at least 100 "city men" helped in his county, some for only a couple of days, but others for as much as twenty days. He believed that "no farmer had any loss from the lack of labor in harvesting or threshing the wheat, or harvesting the hay." Recognizing potential health or safety issues among people who were unaccustomed to hard physical labor, Whitehouse reported, "During the extremely hot weather, we sent out men who were accustomed to doing some sort of manual work." He noted that a local sand and gravel company had closed down for one day and sent its eight men to work on a farm; in addition, the city street cleaning and repair department had sent several men to work on farms. The city high school reported that some seventy-five boys had been placed on farms, some through the local YMCA. Whitehouse believed the farmers had been satisfied with the city men's work, and each now had a better understanding of the other.[17]

At the end of June 1918 McVey reported to the Emergency Farm Labor Section of the US Public Service Reserve that the grain-cutting period was over and had been "handled fairly well." He admitted that the farm labor shortage in Kentucky that spring had not been as acute as in other states.[18]

The need for farm labor clashed with the need to educate young people and to abide by child labor laws, which had recently been strengthened as part of the Progressive movement.[19] Some officials believed that boys between the ages of sixteen and eighteen should volunteer their services as part of their patri-

Boys Working Reserve members in a cornfield. (University of Kentucky)

otic duty. To this end, in April 1917 the US Department of Labor established a Boys Working Reserve with national, district, and state directors. It placed boys in some industries, such as canning, but mainly it put boys to work on farms. The program expanded to include boys aged sixteen to twenty-one and began in earnest in Kentucky in early 1918, under the direction of Philo Dix of Louisville (who also served as YMCA director at Camp Taylor). A large state advisory council included the state superintendent of education, V. O. Gilbert; the state commissioner of agriculture, Mat Cohen; KCD chair Edward Hines; and UK professor W. D. Nicholls of the state Agricultural Extension Service. By September 1918, 98 of Kentucky's 120 counties had been organized, and teams of volunteers were set to enroll boys, who had to pass a physical examination and have their parents' permission to enroll in the program. They could receive awards for working a specified amount of time. Many Kentucky boys entered the program, provided much-needed agricultural labor, and gained satisfaction from participating in the war effort. Under Dix's successor, George Stephens, the Boys Working Reserve continued into 1919, after which the program ended.[20]

These national programs undoubtedly helped farmers, especially at peak times. But throughout the war, farmers sought labor wherever they could find it. In Scott County, the raid of an illegal crap game produced twenty-two men willing to do farm labor to pay off their court fines. Women volunteered to work in farm fields. The UK College of Agriculture helped organize groups of city men to volunteer on farms. Thirty farmers in Fayette County availed themselves of labor from barbers, salesmen, lawyers, ministers, and county and city officials. Jefferson County established a farm emergency workers' office to bring together farmers and laborers. Given the high prices they received for their products, farmers were willing to pay laborers and did not have to rely on volunteers. Nevertheless, the shortage of farm labor continued through the end of the war, prompting calls after the armistice for farmers to be released first from military duty.[21]

Although their need for labor was acute at times, Kentucky's farmers prospered during and immediately after the Great War. For example, the value of cattle, hogs, and sheep from 1913 through 1917 averaged $52 million, increasing to $87 million in 1918 and $102 million in 1919. The value of horses and mules rose less dramatically, averaging $68 million from 1913 to 1917, $72 million in 1918, and $75 million in 1919. All told, in 1918 Kentucky placed eighteenth in the country in total value of cattle, hogs, sheep, horses, and mules.[22]

In his close examination of Washington and Nelson Counties during the war, historian J. Larry Hood writes that a "wave of prosperity" washed over these counties, as "farmers found they could ask for and get record prices for their crops and animals." Noting that "the value of farm land skyrocketed between 1916 and 1918," Hood also points out the problems arising from this boom: "People speculated madly, buying and selling both land and livestock in hope of realizing huge profits in a short time." The rising prices paid off, and the farmers saved some of their money. Savings deposits in banks rose dramatically in both counties: in Nelson County, from $1.7 million in 1917 to $2.5 million in 1918, and in Washington County, from $738,000 to $1.01 million.[23]

Kentucky tobacco farmers also prospered. Even before the United States entered the war, tobacco prices started to skyrocket, doubling for some grades and types of burley. The reasons for the increase included less European production, high soldier demand, and excellent quality crops. A few days before the United States entered the war, state agriculture commissioner Mat Cohen appealed to farmers' patriotism and encouraged them to grow more food and less tobacco. Other questions arose about tobacco's future; for example, whether the expanding world war would disrupt the sale and distribution of tobacco. Farmers also realized that an impending military buildup might decrease the number of men available to raise and harvest tobacco, a notoriously labor-intensive process. A proposal to increase tobacco taxes dramatically to help pay for the war also worried tobacco growers. Progressive reformers linked tobacco with alcohol, calling for a ban on both.[24]

Despite all the factors militating against the crop, Kentucky's tobacco farmers prospered. Soldier and author Arthur Guy Empey wrote an article for the *Louisville Courier-Journal* extolling the virtues of sending cigarettes to soldiers and supporting the newspaper's participation in the national campaign: "Our Boys in France Tobacco Fund." The newspaper solicited donations of $1 to $5 for the fund, noting that "every dollar puts four packages of tobacco, each with a retail value of 45 cents, into the hands of American soldiers in France." The *New York Times* came out in favor of cigarettes that would "lighten the inevitable hardships of war." General Pershing touted: "You ask me what could win the war. I answer tobacco, as much as bullets."[25]

Author Allan M. Brandt has explained how changing attitudes toward tobacco contributed to the tremendous growth of cigarette production during the war: "In the face of war's bloodshed, the traditional notions that a prohibition on tobacco protected the troops from moral harm and health risks seemed frivolous. Ideas like deferred gratification and self-discipline were eviscerated by the violence of combat." Even the YMCA had a dramatic about-face; having once strongly opposed cigarette smoking, the organization happily sold smokes to troops during the war.[26]

Smoking's popularity benefited Kentucky tobacco growers: in 1917 and 1918 tobacco yields and prices continued to climb. New demand from Europe at the beginning of 1919 helped extend the gains realized from the 1918 crop. During the war, many tobacco farmers enjoyed the largesse brought about by the high prices they got for their crops, and they would later view the war years as the apogee of tobacco farming. After the war, overproduction finally began to outstrip demand, and prices tumbled.

Hemp production also increased in Kentucky during the Great War. The state had been a major producer of hemp for more than 100 years, but the industry had been in decline since the Civil War. Iron ties and jute bagging supplanted hemp as baling material. With the turn of the new century, the three central Kentucky counties of Woodford, Fayette, and Jessamine accounted for half the hemp grown in the entire nation, but the state's production continued to fall to around 3,000 tons. When the war broke out in Europe, however, supply from abroad decreased, and domestic needs increased. Prices rose, and farmers grew more hemp. During the war, hemp fibers were used for many things, including "thread for army shoes, twine for the grain harvest, caulking for our ships." Unfortunately, rather than taking advantage of the machinery available to handle hemp, Kentucky farmers continued to use "inefficient hand labor." In Kentucky, hemp production grew from 6,500 acres in 1915 to

13,000 acres in 1916 and to 18,000 acres in 1917 (more than 40 percent of the hemp acreage nationally). The greater acreage resulted in more than 7,000 tons of hemp being harvested in Kentucky in 1917.[27]

Temporarily booming because of wartime needs, hemp production declined again after the war. Historian James Hopkins sums up the plight of Kentucky's hemp growers: "When the war ended the industry again declined. Many farmers turned to other crops less difficult to handle, for which high prices were being paid. The acute shortage of farm labor forced a decrease in acreage, especially in Kentucky where the fiber was broken and hackled by hand, and another limiting factor was the scarcity of good seed for planting in 1918 and 1919."[28] Unfortunately, the hemp industry in Kentucky turned out to be the story of an economic bubble.

Another boom occurred in the coalfields, but it was not without difficulties. Coal mining had been increasing dramatically in Kentucky since 1910, supplanting lumber cultivation as a major industry. "In 1918 Kentucky coal production was more than double its 1910 level, two-thirds coming from the mountains and one third from the Western Coal Field." In four years—from 1914 to 1918—coal production increased 50 percent, from 20 million tons to 31 million tons; production would grow to 38 million tons in 1920. Appalachian counties in eastern Kentucky changed dramatically as many new coal companies moved in. Immigrant coal miners helped diversify the population. As part of the Great Migration during the war, African Americans from the

Kentucky coal mine. (Library of Congress)

South moved into the coalfields. In 1916 Consolidated Coal Company hired more than 2,000 African Americans to work in the eastern Kentucky coalfields. Blacks worked alongside white immigrants from all over Europe, but they stayed socially segregated, each group in its own part of the coal towns.[29]

Kentuckians and out-of-state investors created new coal mining corporations to take advantage of the increasing demand and the improved railroad system that made coal easier to distribute. Existing towns grew and were improved. For example, in McRoberts in Letcher County, the Consolidated Coal Company created new streets and built fifty miners' houses. Founded only two years before the war broke out in Europe, the town employed more than 2,500 men during the war. McRoberts became a model coal town with a post office, churches, company stores, and social and sports facilities. McRoberts also became the terminus for the Lexington & Eastern Railroad line into the mountains.[30]

New coal towns sprouted, especially in the eastern mountains. The most prominent was Lynch, which was named after the president of the US Coal and Coke Company, a subsidiary of US Steel. The company began clearing land in Harlan County for a town and mining operations in mid-1917 and moved rapidly. The first permanent dwelling was occupied in November. On November 1 the company sent coal from Lynch to US Steel facilities near Chicago. By the end of that year, a thousand men were working in Lynch to build houses, mining structures, and what was planned to be the world's largest coal tipple, designed to handle the output of ten large mines. Coal production from the new mine increased exponentially, from around 12,000 tons in the latter part of 1917 to more than 500,000 tons in 1918 and 1.2 million tons in 1919. This phenomenal growth prompted the coal company to build sawmills, stores, a bank, company kitchens, schools, and eventually a hospital. Many African Americans settled and worked in Lynch, which at its wartime peak numbered nearly 10,000 inhabitants.[31]

Not all was well, however, in the eastern and western Kentucky coalfields. Workers demanded higher wages as they saw production boom and prices rise. By mid-1917, trouble was brewing in the western Kentucky coalfields. In May the United Mine Workers of America (UMWA) and the Western Kentucky Coal Operators' Association agreed to increase wages from 41.03 cents per ton of coal mined to 51.03 cents. UMWA organizers tried to expand the union's membership, especially in Webster, Hopkins, Union, Henderson, and Christian Counties. Tempers rose between pro-union miners and mine owners. A gunfight between miners and mine guards took place at Clay in Webster County. More fights followed.[32]

Tension came to a head in July, when the UMWA called for a strike primarily against the St. Bernard Coal Company's mines in Hopkins County. The strike was only partially successful. Miners shut down smaller mines, but St. Bernard claimed the strike had little overall effect, and its mines produced record amounts of coal. Efforts to bring in African American miners to replace the strikers caused more tension. As violence escalated, Governor Stanley ordered a Signal Corps unit of the Kentucky National Guard to go to Providence in Webster County and restore order.[33]

Kentucky National Guard general Roger Williams visited Providence to investigate and report on conditions. At the beginning of August, following a firefight between mine guards and striking miners, Guardsmen arrested three strikers. Then disaster struck: more than 200 men at a West Kentucky Coal Company mine in Clay were entombed after a gas explosion. Guardsmen joined with mine officials and miners to try to rescue the men, but sixty-two died, and others were maimed and burned. One family, the Browns, lost three brothers: William, Edward, and Dewey. Union officials called off the strike the same day. They denied that the disaster had prompted their action; instead, they claimed that because only 20 percent of the miners were on strike, it seemed senseless to continue. More National Guardsmen arrived and, under the command of Lieutenant Colonel E. B. Bassett of Hopkinsville, established what amounted to martial law with a 9:30 p.m. curfew. The tense situation finally calmed down.[34]

Hard on the heels of conflict in the western coalfields, miners in eastern Kentucky also sought a wage increase, union recognition, an eight-hour workday, and better working conditions. Coal operators threatened to shut down their mines rather than recognize the UMWA. Negotiations failed, and by mid-August, an estimated 15,000 miners in southeastern Kentucky were on strike in Bell, Harlan, Knox, and Whitley Counties. Each side accused the other of the unpatriotic act of stifling production. Violence broke out. Reports of shooting occurred in Wilton in Knox County. Fearing the effects of the strike on coal prices and supplies for the forthcoming winter, Lexington mayor James Rogers (on behalf of the Fayette County Council of Defense) sent telegrams to President Wilson, Governor Stanley, and several other national and state officials urging them to settle the dispute. A federal strike conciliator from Lexington, Hywell Davies, headed into the region to negotiate. National fuel administrator Harry Garfield met with representatives from both sides and strongly urged them to find a solution. The strike was finally settled at the beginning of October; the miners got a wage increase but accepted restrictions on further strikes. The settlement agreement also created a national arbitration board comprising two operators, two miners' representatives, and a representative from the US Fuel Administration.[35]

The eastern and western Kentucky coal strikes ended in time to partially alleviate the coal shortage that occurred during the bitterly cold winter of 1917–1918. With few exceptions, Kentucky miners remained on the job for the rest of the war, boosting production to unprecedented levels. They worked hard and prospered, while providing the country with the coal necessary to fuel industrial output and heat homes in America.

Coal companies' success was directly related to the ability to move coal from the mining areas, mostly by railroad. Railroads expanded during the war, moving closer to the coalfields.[36] The predominant railroad in the state remained the Louisville & Nashville (L&N), which was first chartered by the commonwealth of Kentucky in 1850. Some railroads at the outset of the war in Europe had suffered a decline in foreign investment and domestic passenger count, but the L&N's conservative management kept it well positioned to prosper. Before the United States entered the war, business began to boom for the "Old Reliable," as the L&N was nicknamed, and the company hired thousands of new employees.

Five days after the war began, railroad officials from across the nation met in Washington and created a Railroad War Board, which would set wartime policies and procedures for effective railway traffic. With war, the L&N's business immediately became more complicated. Many employees were drafted or volunteered for the military. To replace these men, the railroad hired hundreds of women for clerical jobs, such as agents. Traffic increased because of freight moving from south to north, and more raw and finished goods were being shipped. People began to fill passenger cars; in Kentucky, many of these passengers were troops traveling to the new cantonment at Louisville, which could be reached by the new track laid south of the city.[37] In one year alone, the L&N's gross revenue grew more than 18 percent; in 1917 it increased to $76.9 million from the previous year's $64.9 million. L&N passenger levels rose from 12.5 million in 1916 to 14.1 million in 1917 to 17 million in 1918.

The war's demands sometimes overwhelmed the railroads, so in December 1917 the federal government took control. At the end of the month President Wilson appointed his son-in-law, Secretary of the Treasury William McAdoo, as director general of railroads. L&N president Milton Smith wrote to the railroad's employees encouraging them to be loyal and to cooperate with the government. An employees' committee agreed with him. To this end, the employees formed a chapter of the Liberty League of America that promised to keep an eye on all pro-Germans. The chapter also held a series of patriotic meetings designed to raise money for the Red Cross. Governor Stanley addressed a crowd of more than a thousand Liberty League members, emphasizing the civilian's role in the "total war" effort: "The man with the hammer, the man with the hoe, the man with the hand on the throttle and on the switch, is engaged in a fight with the Kaiser and the forces of autocracy, just as certain and just as truly as those that carry a gun."[38]

Under federal control, the L&N (and other railroad lines) underwent change. It consolidated services such as terminal facilities and ticket offices. By a general order issued in May 1918, the government forced the railroad to pay its employees more and to institute an eight-hour workday. Despite these new benefits, nearly 4,000 L&N shop employees formed a union that represented diverse crafts, such as machinists, blacksmiths, and sheet metal workers. The men agreed not to strike.[39]

Railroads faced challenges throughout the war in terms of balancing demands from politicians and from the military and industry (e.g., moving railcars to get coal from eastern Kentucky coalfields to people during the bitter winter of 1917–1918); keeping their workforce intact when men were called away; and adhering to government restrictions. Railroad rolling stock had to be reserved to move troops and supplies. With the onset of food restrictions, even the railroad's dining cars changed their ways, taking into account meatless and wheatless days.

The Southern Railway also had important interests in Kentucky. With the announcement that Camp Taylor would be built south of Louisville, the railroad laid several tracks into the camp, provided access for materials to build and maintain the camp, and developed passenger service for arriving draftees and visitors. Like the L&N, the Southern also had to change operations, consolidate offices, and hire women.[40]

Other portions of Kentucky's economy fared well during the Great War. Long a mainstay of the state's economy in terms of people employed and output, the lumber industry had been declining as coal mining increased, especially in eastern Kentucky. However, some segments related to the lumber industry enjoyed a boom during the war. Louisville contained more than sixty wood-related factories that produced items such as furniture, whiskey barrels, veneer, baseball bats, golf sticks, and wooden wheels. The city was also the nation's center for wooden and paper box manufacturing; wood was used to make tobacco and cigar boxes. During the war, these wood product factories made ammunition shell boxes and wooden gunstocks. They also began to employ women because so many men went to war or were needed to do heavier work.[41]

After being stagnant and hindered by overproduction in the prewar years, the oil industry grew rapidly during the war. The nation and its allies needed more oil for the military. For example, naval ships began using oil rather than coal for fuel. Military vehicles used more and more oil products. Energy expert

C. C. Mengel and Bros. in Louisville was one of Kentucky's wood products companies that contributed to the war effort. (Library of Congress)

Daniel Yergin points out that during the Great War, "Oil and the internal combustion engine quickly transformed the battlefield. The British Expeditionary Force that landed in France in August 1914 had a mere 827 motorcars and just 15 motorcycles. By war's end in 1918, British military vehicles included some 56,000 trucks, 23,000 motorcars and 34,000 motorcycles and motor bicycles. When the U.S. entered the war in 1917, it brought another 50,000 vehicles to the European front." In addition, relatively new inventions such as tanks and airplanes increased the demand for oil production.[42]

A *Louisville Courier-Journal* article in March 1917 foresaw a growing need not only for coal but also for Kentucky oil, which in 1915 had amounted to only 500,000 barrels. This output increased dramatically during the war; the state produced nearly 3 million barrels in 1916 and 4 million in 1917. Many of the state's new wells appeared in eastern Kentucky, where Estill County led the way. In western Kentucky, Allen County proved especially productive. Companies drilled for oil in nearly a fourth of Kentucky's counties. Problems arose, however. Companies could not acquire adequate drilling materials; they needed more pipelines to transport the oil and more storage facilities.[43]

Oil production continued to increase in 1918. That year, Lexington and Louisville investors incorporated a new venture—the Swiss Oil Company. Swiss Oil would create Ashland Refining in 1924; the two operations would merge in 1936 to create Ashland Oil and Refining, one of Kentucky's largest corporations.[44] Thus, one of Kentucky's most significant companies arose from the Great War's needs.

Many more companies formed to prospect for oil, especially in the large Big Sinking Area in Estill, Lee, Powell, and Wolfe Counties in eastern Kentucky. The *Lexington Herald* in April 1918 reported that thirty-four new wells opened in one week in those counties. As production increased, the need for refineries became apparent. Two were built: one in Pryse in Estill County, and another in Rodemer in Allen County (built by the Pioneer Refining Company).[45] The oil industry in Kentucky grew exponentially during the Great War and was a great boon to the state's economy.

Kentucky's sporting industry faced perplexing questions during the war. The United States joined the war just as the baseball and horse-racing seasons began. There appeared to be little choice when it came to discontinuing some sporting events. For example, because of the influx of students into the military or their return to family farms, the University of Kentucky canceled athletic activities in the spring of 1917. UK and most other colleges resumed athletic contests when the new school year began in the fall, encouraged to do so by Secretary of War Newton Baker. He believed that participating in competitive sports was helpful to young men before they underwent military training.[46]

There was talk of canceling the remaining 1917 professional baseball season, but President Wilson, an avid fan, encouraged the games to continue. Controversy arose about baseball players who did not join the military, and many people considered them "slackers." In May 1918 Secretary Baker insisted that his "work or fight" order applied to baseball players, who should either join the military or work in a defense-related industry.

The Louisville Colonels, an American Association minor league baseball team, experienced the tensions between sport and war but found a way to adapt. In the spring of 1918 several teams threatened to suspend operations for the duration of the war because they were losing money, but Colonels owner Otto Wathen protested vigorously. His team played a shortened season in 1918 and, to increase support for baseball, played against soldiers from Camp Taylor. The Colonels and baseball were saved by the armistice; baseball would regain its popularity after the war, becoming strongly associated with the "Americanism" movement of the 1920s.[47]

Even more important for Kentucky, the horse industry and horse racing faced similar issues. As noted earlier, more than 30,000 horses had been shipped to Europe. Combined with decreased breeding rates, this deficit caused concern about the future of the horse industry. The parlous state of the industry became evident in May 1917 when Omar Khayyam became the first imported horse to win the Kentucky Derby.[48]

After the United States entered the war, officials in Washington quickly called for 250,000 horses to be supplied to the military; they anticipated that more than 2 million horses would eventually be needed for the cavalry and to transport supplies, haul artillery, and so forth. This would strain the horse breeding industry, which could not produce enough foals to sustain such high demand. National officials therefore made plans to increase car and truck production, but that took time, too. Military officials declared that the horse remained indispensable and a national asset.[49]

Horses were needed domestically as well. UK Animal Husbandry Department professor J. J. Harper argued, "Next to the farmer nothing is more important in the production of food than horses and mules." Government officials called on horse breeders to increase their efforts and offered to buy horses directly from farmers and breeders, in addition to procuring them from large-scale horse suppliers. Thoroughbred and trotter breeders called for a government commission to oversee breeding, which they argued was necessary to maintain breeding standards.[50]

To help counter criticism that horse racing was unnecessary and inappropriate in wartime, Kentucky Thoroughbred horse owners pledged $300,000 to the Red Cross. Prominent central Kentucky horsemen such as Hal Price Headley, John Madden, and Arthur Hancock led the fund-raising effort. The Kentucky Racing Commission supported the Red Cross pledge. To help raise the money, Hancock also proposed a voluntary tax on racetracks for the duration of the war. Various racing associations running at Kentucky tracks contributed a portion of the stakes and solicited employee contributions for the Red Cross campaign. The Kentucky Association racetrack in Lexington invited the Red Cross into the clubhouse, where members could sell coffee, tea, and sandwiches to raise funds.[51]

Horse racing continued in 1918, but it remained a contentious issue. In May, Exterminator won the Kentucky Derby in the middle of a decidedly wartime atmosphere. US and British military officials attended, including Camp Taylor commander Major General Harry Hale and British military attaché Major General J. D. McLachlan, but criticism continued. Louisville's anticorruption mayor George Weissinger Smith reminded people that the English had canceled horse racing for the winter season and alleged that it was a "sport whose existence depends upon betting and leaves the trail of crime and despair wherever it thrives." In turn, the Louisville Board of Trade wrote to President Wilson and asked him to decide whether horse racing should continue. This letter raised the ire of Mayor Smith, who adamantly decried the board's efforts and maintained that the local populace was strongly against racing during the war.[52]

In addition, prominent Democrat and horseman General W. B. Haldeman "dropped a Krupp [bomb] shell into the ranks of the horsemen by announcing at a meeting of the Racing Commission that he was unalterably opposed to the continuance of racing in this State for the duration of the war." Commission chairman and former US senator Johnson Camden strongly opposed Haldeman, as did most of the other commission members.[53] Horsemen replied that racing helped both the US treasury and the Red Cross. For instance, at the conclusion of its summer meet, Latonia racetrack in northern Kentucky reported that it had paid more than $25,000 in taxes and raised nearly $100,000 for the Red Cross. By the end of September, the horse industry had raised $240,000 for the Red Cross, with one meet still in progress at Churchill Downs and the fall Latonia meet not yet under way.[54] Finally, the armistice put an end to the controversy over wartime horse racing.

During the war, Kentucky's Progressive reformers sought to eradicate three major "vices"—tobacco, gambling, and liquor—but the Great War hurt only Kentucky's alcohol producers. For years, the state had been in the throes of a fierce debate between "wets" and "drys," those who favored the sale of alcohol and those who opposed it. Governor Stanley favored local option laws, and many Kentucky counties had banned alcohol before the start of the war.[55]

As the United States' entry into the war became more probable, both sides of the alcohol argument saw reason for hope. Kentucky alcohol distillers perceived an opportunity to do their patriotic duty (and stay in business) by producing alcohol for war purposes. The head of the Kentucky Distillers and Wholesale Liquor Dealers' Association, J. B. Wathen Jr., wrote to Secretary of War Newton Baker and suggested that Kentucky's more than 200 registered distillers could produce the alcohol required for military purposes, such as that used in the manufacture of ammunition.[56]

Alcohol opponents also realized that the war might help their cause. Pastors, Women's Christian Temperance Union members, and other staunch Prohibitionists pushed for a national "bone-dry" ban of the manufacture, sale, and consumption of alcohol. They used several arguments: "booze" was nonessential, the country needed to conserve grain for food, alcohol would have a deleterious effect on soldiers, and German Americans owned many breweries.

Federal legislators passed an emergency wartime measure in August 1917—the Lever Food and Fuel Act—that addressed the alcohol issue. The act created the Food and Fuel Administrations and also banned the production of alcohol from products that could be used for food. Most Kentucky distillers shut down; only eight stayed in business, switching to the production of industrial alcohol. The price was high: an estimated 6,000 to 7,000 people lost their jobs at distilleries and related industries, such as cooperages.[57]

Following on the heels of the Lever Act, later in 1917 Congress proposed the Eighteenth Amendment, which would prohibit the sale and distribution of alcoholic beverages. The Kentucky legislature became the third state to ratify the amendment in January 1918, much to the consternation of "wets," who had hoped the legislature would put the Prohibition issue on the ballot for a statewide vote in November. The Kentucky house passed the measure easily—sixty-six to ten—while the state senate passed it with twenty-seven votes in favor of Prohibition versus five votes against.[58]

Even though the state legislature approved the Eighteenth Amendment, Kentucky Prohibitionists continued to press for quicker action. They believed it might take a few years for enough states to ratify the national amendment, thus delaying its effect. They pressed the state legislature to put the issue on the ballot in November 1919, with a target date of Prohibition by June 30, 1920. Despite opposition in Louisville, Lexington, and northern Kentucky, the "drys" easily beat the "wets." This legislation ultimately proved unnecessary. States ratified the Eighteenth Amendment more quickly than anticipated, and national Prohibition began in January 1920.[59]

The wartime combination of the Lever Act and the Eighteenth Amendment shut down Kentucky's alcohol distilleries for nearly fifteen years and made Prohibition the law of the land—something that many people in the state had long desired.

One of the major economic issues during the war involved labor. The war required more labor in war industries and on farms, and it required good management-labor relations. So many people were needed to support the war that everyone was expected to help. Therefore, one early issue involved "slackers." Soon after the United States entered the war, the agricultural committee of the Kentucky Council of Defense called on judges and mayors to enforce vagrancy laws and "put the idle people of the towns to work on the farms." Some communities enforced vagrancy laws vigorously. The mayor of Mt. Sterling threatened that men who were not employed would be forced to work for the city without pay. Several newspapers reproduced sections of the Kentucky law on vagrancy. Judge C. H. Bush of Hopkinsville told a grand jury that "it was no time for idlers and vagrants, that it was the business of man to be employed, and in harmony with both human and divine law, that the grand jury should stand for this great principle by helping to enforce the law against vagrancy."[60]

The Kentucky legislature passed a new vagrancy law in early 1918. Subtitled "Prevention of Idleness during Present War," the law declared that all males between the ages of sixteen and sixty had to "habitually and regularily [*sic*] engage in some lawful, useful and recognized business, profession, occupation or employment, whereby he may produce or earn sufficient to support himself and those dependent upon him." Students were exempted from the law during the school term; other men had to work at least thirty-six hours per week. The law would become effective in June 1918 and last until six months after the end of the war. The initial version of the act included women, but an amendment changed it to pertain only to males. The *Mt. Sterling Advocate* applauded the new law in an editorial titled "Work or Workhouse."[61]

Anticipating the vagrancy law's effective date, Ohio County authorities arrested two men, and the local newspaper praised the arrests: "the halcyon days of the loafer are over, at least for the period of the war." A group of Hopkinsville businessmen and farmers created a Christian County Anti-Loafers League in April 1918. The purpose of the organization was to "aid city and county officials in enforcing the new vagrancy law, with no distinction as to color or station in life." To help these malefactors avoid arrest and prosecution, the league planned an employment bureau to match unemployed men with potential employers. It also persuaded Christian County authorities to impose a $500 license tax on labor agents who tried to entice men to leave the county for better-paying jobs. The league's farmers, who desperately needed labor, pushed the measure forward.[62]

In Lexington, police swept up a dozen men on vagrancy charges. Ten of them were released after claiming they had jobs and were on "vacation." The other two men—both African Americans—received thirty days in the workhouse by order of police court judge Riley.[63]

Despite officials' claims of nondiscrimination, African Americans were often arrested. In Paris, "in a personally-conducted raid on the colored poolrooms and other abiding places of colored loafers in Paris," the chief of police arrested thirty-two African Americans for vagrancy. The local newspaper opined that there was "no good excuse for men to be loafing around the streets of Paris. . . . Farmers are almost begging for farm hands, and yet the demand is greater than the supply." The *Elizabethtown News* alleged, "There are a lot of loafers around Elizabethtown. You can hardly go to the L. & N. station here that you do not see standing around six to a dozen men who do nothing but loaf. Many of this class are worthless negroes who bootleg whiskey, shoot craps and won't work." The newspaper suggested it was time to put these people to work or "force them to skip the town."[64]

The federal government also took measures to cut down on the number of "slackers" who would not work. American Federation of Labor leader Samuel Gompers insisted there was no labor shortage but simply maldistribution. Despite Gompers's objections, in May 1918 selective service head Enoch Crowder promulgated a "work or fight" regulation aimed at men of draft age. The regulation fell short of forcing national service or labor conscription but stipulated, "Any deferred registrant found by the nearest draft board to be an idler or engaged in nonproduction occupation would be liable to immediate loss of his deferment and induction into the army."[65]

Hotel owners in Kentucky worried about replacing men such as bellhops and elevator operators, which were classified as nonproductive occupations. Some made plans to employ women to do that kind of work. Sportsmen in the state, particularly those involved in baseball and horse racing, also worried about the definition of "nonproductive" occupations. Racing officials wondered if jockeys might be so classified. Otto Wathen, owner of the Louisville Colonels baseball team, admitted that his infield would be "vitally injured" if baseball players were declared nonproductive. President Wilson refused to allow deferments for baseball players but agreed to postpone their inductions until after the baseball season ended (which was soon followed by the armistice).[66]

Crowder's "work or fight" regulation went into effect in July 1918. Various Kentucky newspapers reported and commented on the order. The *Maysville Public Ledger* editorialized that the provost general's order did not go far enough. It left loopholes, allowing men in high-paying jobs (such as coal mining) to shirk their duty by not working full time. The newspaper called for all men to work six days a week, concluding: "If there is anything that will make a lazy man work it is the fear of being put in the army, where it is sometimes necessary to work twenty-four hours a day." The *Berea Citizen* took a more positive approach in supporting "work or fight," declaring, "Everybody is better for work. The individual is happier, healthier, and more prosperous. The community prospers as well. Homes are put in better shape, good order prevails, and an air of thrift appears." The wits at the *Licking Valley Courier* in West Liberty surmised that, "judging from the increased number of marriages in this county we fear that many of our men have the wrong conception of the 'work or fight' order."[67]

The Fulton County Council of Defense reminded newspaper readers that "Uncle Sam says you must work or fight." It noted the new Kentucky law prohibiting loafing and informed people that the city of Hickman had passed an ordinance "carrying a heavy penalty for idleness." County residents had to carry an "employment card" obtained free from the council or be subject to arrest and fines. In sum, the council concluded that "Hickman is a 100 per cent American city and we have no room for slackers."[68]

The commonwealth of Kentucky passed and enforced vagrancy laws supporting "work or fight" ideas. These actions reflected its citizens' strong work ethic and patriotism. Few Kentuckians would speak out against these restrictive (but civil rights–denying) efforts.

Given that Kentucky had a limited factory industrial base primarily in Louisville, northern Kentucky, and Paducah, labor relations remained reasonable during the war, but they were not without conflict. When the United States joined the war, Kentucky's United Trades and Labor Assembly criticized Governor Stanley for not acceding to its call for labor representatives to be appointed to all state war organizations (such as draft boards and county councils of defense). The Kentucky State Federation of Labor went farther. It drafted a bill for the 1918 legislative session that would compel the governor to appoint a labor representative to the Kentucky Council of Defense. Stanley relented, and when the legislature approved and funded a new KCD in the spring of 1918, the governor appointed a leader of Louisville's Brotherhood of Trainmen and editor of the *Journal of Labor*, Sigmond Lee, as a council member.[69]

As head of the KCD Committee on Labor, Lee worked with fellow council member Owsley Brown, who headed the Committee on Industry. Together they sought to ensure that management and labor cooperated. At an early council meeting, Lee pledged that "organized labor would encourage no strikes during the war," and he hoped the "manufacturers should be encouraged to meet labor half way." Lee had support from the state's labor organizations. In Lexington, the 600 members of the Bluegrass Federation of Labor pledged to oppose any strikes during the war. In Louisville, a local chapter of the National Alliance for Labor and Democracy voted to show support for the US role in the war. At the end of 1918, the annual KCD report noted that because of the Brown-Lee cooperation, Kentucky had averted strikes in essential factories.[70] This did not mean, however, that all relationships were perfect in all facets of industry.

Faced with dynamic tension between labor and manufacturers throughout the country, the Wilson administration created a War Labor Policies Board to "unify the labor policies of the Federal Government" by preparing "various contract clauses which affect industrial relations." Chaired by future Supreme Court justice Felix Frankfurter, the board aimed to reconcile, or balance, the need for more production with workers' desire to retain Progressive reforms such as an eight-hour workday and restrictions on women's and children's labor. The board called for each state governor to name a representative to cooperate with federal authorities. Governor Stanley appointed the secretary of agriculture, labor, and statistics, Mat Cohen; he passed those responsibilities on to Ethel Musgrove, who served as the woman's state labor inspector.[71]

Kentucky already had reasonably progressive child and woman labor laws; its first child labor law had been passed in 1902. Musgrove proved to be an especially strong enforcer of these laws. Believing that during wartime everyone had a patriotic duty to comply with the law, she focused on working with Kentucky education officials, whom she regarded as the first line of defense against child labor. Musgrove aggressively tracked down scofflaws; she issued a warrant to the New Albany Box and Basket Company in Louisville, which was fined for employing underage youths. In September 1918 Musgrove attended a War Labor Policies Board conference in Washington, DC, that discussed topics such as adherence to child labor standards set by Congress's Keating-Owen Child Labor Act of 1916.[72]

Musgrove then compiled an alphabetical list of jobs forbidden to children under age sixteen, a help to both parents and employers. She continued to be vigilant even after the armistice was signed. In late November 1918 Bleckner Preserving Company and Center Restaurant were fined for violating child and woman labor laws. Musgrove asserted that the federal government was "strenuously urging the preservation of all established labor standards and the vigilant safeguarding of women and children during the industrial readjustments which will follow peace." Ethel Musgrove continued as the woman's labor inspector until she was replaced in 1920 following a Republican sweep led by Governor William Morrow.[73]

When labor disputes could not be resolved amicably between employers and their employees, the National War Labor Board (NWLB) intervened. Whereas the War Labor Policies Board served an administrative function (focusing on policies such as the eight-hour workday), the NWLB served more as a judicial body, a so-called Supreme Court of labor relations. The board eventually investigated half a dozen cases in Kentucky involving tobacco workers, streetcar employees, meatpackers, gas company employees, and machinists.[74]

One of the NWLB's major cases involved tobacco workers at the American Tobacco Company plant in Louisville. In March 1918 a group of about 100 men walked out, demanding higher wages and a ten-hour workday. The plant replaced them with women. In June 1918 hostilities broke out after workers tried to unionize; police were called to keep the peace. Conflicting rumors circulated about an alleged strike by workers who wanted a wage increase and union recognition. Labor organizers denied that a strike was taking place; they said one man had simply picketed the plant to protest workers being fired for joining a union. American Tobacco had the picket, local union president J. M. Greenwell, arrested on vagrancy charges. The company instituted a lockout, prompting US Department of Labor commissioner of conciliation Fred Feick to investigate. Feick met with representatives of the company and the union, then with workers. He worked out a settlement whereby the company reinstated all but a dozen union men.[75]

Feick left Louisville believing that everyone was satisfied, but the agreement proved unsatisfactory to union representatives. Tobacco Workers' International Union president Anthony McAndrews wrote to Secretary of Labor William Wilson, reminding him that the federal government had approved the workers' right to organize. He pointed out that the men who had organized were machinists, on whom the plant's 1,000 employees relied to keep it in working order. A machinists' strike would therefore shut down the plant. McAndrews warned that the local union was threatening such a strike.[76]

The NWLB notified the company and union representatives that a hearing would take place in early September. The hearing never occurred. Local union president Greenwell notified NWLB authorities in late August that the union members "have been scattered, some have left the city, and others have taken employment in other vocations, and have lost interest in the matter." Greenwell concluded: "Knowing your board to be very busy we thought it would be best to drop the case." National leaders of the Tobacco Workers' International Union concurred with the decision, and the NWLB dropped the case. The strike never happened; the plant continued to operate.[77]

Another NWLB case that reached into Kentucky involved one of Chicago's largest meatpacking companies, Armour. The meatpacking industry had been the bane of labor organizers for years, but in early 1918, NWLB member Frank Walsh successfully argued a case that "gave meatpackers throughout the Midwest wage increases and an eight hour day." During the proceedings, Walsh "raked packer J. Ogden Armour over the coals, presenting figures that suggested that the meat baron could have doubled his employees' wages and still made a profit." Walsh asked, "Why should industry be made safe for autocracy when soldiers are dying on a thousand battlefields to make the world in general safe for democracy?"[78]

Armour also had a plant in Louisville, and it was plagued by industrial strife. Workers raised several demands: the right to join a union, higher wages, better working conditions, fewer hours, and equal pay for women. In April 1918 the company dismissed five chauffeurs for belonging to the Meat Cutters and Butcher Workers Union. This prompted another investigation and a hearing presided over by a Department of Labor conciliator, General Robert M. McWade, which led to the chauffeurs' reinstatement.[79]

The meat cutters continued to press for their overall demands, and their representative, Patrick Gorman, asked the NWLB to review the case. Noting the previous settlement with Armour in which meatpackers throughout the Midwest had received higher pay and an eight-hour workday, and claiming that workers at other Louisville meat plants received similar benefits, the Louisville union asked for the same. The meatpackers' union asserted, "The workers in Armours Plant are considered not as much as the Product that is killed in the plant, and the day has come when workers must be considered above common cattle." They also claimed they had patriotically refrained from striking and that the meatpacking industry in Louisville was vital to supplying the 60,000 soldiers at nearby Camp Taylor.[80]

Union officials believed that the Armour plant's general manager, Augustus Thomas, had promised General McWade that the company would let the NWLB arbitrate the case. Thomas played it coy when questioned about this alleged agreement, saying that although he believed the company would acquiesce to arbitration, he did not have full authority to speak on the matter. McWade believed that Thomas had been ordered by Armour's Chicago headquarters to thwart any reconciliation with the Louisville meatpackers.[81] A waiting game ensued. Armour officials equivocated, stalling in the hope that the union would give up its demands.

Eventually the NWLB sent examiners to hold a hearing in Louisville on February 19, 1919. Armour representatives failed to show up, but more than a dozen employees gave testimony. The examiners' report concluded, "Conditions at this plant are bad, both from the standpoint of inadequate wages and from the spread of hours required to be worked." The report acknowledged that some men worked eleven to thirteen hours a day, and women were working more than the maximum ten hours a day mandated by state law. It also noted, "Other independent packers in Louisville had established reasonable working hours, conditions and scales of wages, but Armour and Company has consistently refused to meet competition; in fact have refused to deal individually or collectively with their employees, or with the Department of Labor. The Company evidently holds itself above outside interference." The examiners recommended that "every means possible be taken by the [NWLB] to bring about an amelioration of present conditions at the plant."[82]

With the end of war and the gradual dismantling of Camp Taylor, the case of the Armour workers faded. The company continued to be controversial and had financial difficulties in the 1920s. The Louisville labor dispute revealed that although the federal government could intervene in Kentucky affairs, it could not necessarily make a difference when up against a recalcitrant employer.

McWade was more successful mediating disputes between other employers and employees. In September 1918 he visited the James Clark Jr. Electric Company, which had war contracts from the US Navy but was experiencing industrial unrest. On behalf of machinists, electrical workers, and other employees, McWade negotiated an eight-hour workday, a salary increase, time-and-a-half and double-time provisions, and holiday schedules. In return, the workers agreed to an innovation: a workers' Loyalty Committee consisting of five men who would help "maintain 100 per cent efficient production through loyal devotion to our country." The Loyalty Committee would help managers maintain discipline by ferreting out men who drank, were habitually late, were "malingerers," or otherwise hampered production. With the settlement of this dispute, McWade pointed out that with one notable exception, the metal manufacturers and machine works in Louisville were providing reasonable pay and appropriate hours, "the result being a happy, contented, and industrious city—full of loyal, hard-fisted American mechanics, a great and appreciable number who are paying for their own little homes on the installment . . . or other rental plan." The exception was the Vogt Brothers Manufacturing Company, which was doing government work. There, McWade dreaded the "ugly possibility of industrial trouble, caused wholly by the curt refusal to be just and generous with its work people."[83]

The Henry Vogt Machine Company in Louisville was a preeminent business, founded in 1893 by brothers Henry and Adam Vogt. When Adam retired in 1916, Henry continued to run the company. Three of Adam's sons who worked at the company joined the military when the United States entered the war. The company had military contracts for boilers for navy ships, and it had reportedly instituted a nine-hour workday in 1916. Various unions organizing at the company complained, and the Department of Labor sent conciliator Fred Feick to Louisville. Feick hammered out an agreement with Henry Vogt that included a nine-hour day and a wage increase, believing he had secured concessions of great value. He predicted that if the unions did not press Vogt, future concessions would be forthcoming. If labor agitation continued, however, a very serious situation would arise that could "cause the government a great deal of inconvenience."[84]

Union representatives were not satisfied, alleging they had had no real input into the agreement. Consequently, the Department of Labor sent McWade to sort out the problem. McWade contacted Vogt officials, suggesting a wage increase and noting that "the basic eight hour day is recognized and in full force and effect in Government workshops, and in almost all establishments." In turn, Vogt officials argued that their employees' wages had been rising incrementally and were in line with those paid at similar shops in Cincinnati and Hamilton, Ohio. Tension increased as a Vogt general manager D. T. Gray allegedly called the union men "slackers" and threatened to have them all shipped off to Camp Taylor. McWade denounced Gray and Adam Vogt (who, though retired, was apparently still involved in company affairs) for "willfully and deliberately provoking trouble."[85]

Adam Vogt visited the office of Bureau of Investigation agent L. H. Flinn to complain about McWade. Flinn informed Vogt that if the situation was simply a labor dispute, the Department of Justice probably would not investigate, but if it involved outside influences "attempting to retard production of government work" or "I.W.W. [Industrial Workers of the World] or radical socialistic propaganda," then it would look into the matter. Flinn defended McWade, believing the conciliator to be a man of high character and trustworthy who had the confidence of the Labor Department. Eventually the Department of Labor appealed to the War Department for assistance, and Ordnance Department officials hammered out an arrangement whereby Vogt agreed to higher wages, an eight-hour workday, and overtime provisions. The NWLB declared the case settled.[86]

The NWLB cases in Louisville reflected the federal government's increasing intrusion into Kentucky as a result of the Great War. Although the government ameliorated many disputes between labor and management, difficult labor relations, especially in the coal industry, remained a problem after the war. With the major exception of the alcohol industry, most sectors of Kentucky's economy prospered during the war. Unfortunately, when the war ended, that prosperity proved to be a bubble, and it burst during the 1920s.

11

Religion

Religious organizations and their leaders played key roles in Kentucky during the Great War. The war had varying effects on each group. Some of these organizations changed little; for them, it was "business as usual." Others were significantly altered by the war, at least for its duration, if not longer.

The war presented people of all religions with ethical and moral questions. The US Constitution is based on a separation of church and state. But prevailing sentiment in the country and passage of the Espionage and Sedition Acts caused people of all religions to think about loyalty.

Historian Philip Jenkins asserts, "The First World War was a thoroughly religious event, in the sense that overwhelmingly Christian nations fought each other in what many viewed as a holy war, a spiritual conflict." Jenkins believes that "religion is essential to understanding the war, to understanding why people went to war, what they hoped to achieve through war, and why they stayed at war." Each country fighting the war believed that God was on its side. This resulted in, "not just incidentally, but repeatedly and centrally, official statements and propaganda [that] declare that the war is being fought for God's cause, or for his glory, and such claims pervade the media and organs of popular culture."[1]

Jenkins points out that despite many Americans having "strong vested interests in avoiding war," a "holy war ideology became social orthodoxy to an extent that is amazing if we think of the nation's composition at the time." Americans of Irish and German ancestry opposed a traditional enemy: England. Eastern Europeans, especially Poles and Jews, opposed Russia. Several American churches had a pacifist tradition and initially opposed US entry into the war. Because of these different backgrounds and beliefs, the likelihood of these groups agreeing about the war may have seemed remote. But Jenkins asserts, "By the time the United States actually did enter the war in April 1917, . . . not only were religious calls for holy warfare clearly in the ascendant but the nation's rhetoric sounded very much like that of England or Germany three years before, and some of the most militant voices were penitent former pacifists."[2] Thus, the majority of religious denominations and churches in the nation supported the US war effort, sometimes vigorously. The notion of a holy and just war pervaded the rhetoric of churchgoers of most denominations in Kentucky, and most Kentucky churches supported the war as well.

In 1916 Southern Baptists made up the largest portion of Kentucky churchgoers, representing 26.1 percent of the population. Following were Catholics at 16.6 percent; Disciples of Christ at 13.4 percent; Methodist Episcopal Church, South, at 11.9 percent; and Baptists of the National Convention at 10.1 percent.[3] Regardless of their denomination, believers had to balance the ideas of peace and nonviolence against the notion of a "just war," a centuries-long debate.

Religious historian John F. Piper points out that many people, especially Protestants, took one of three positions about the war. Some denominations "claimed the pacifist position, which repudiated all participation in war, and rejected the war as evil."[4] Some Kentucky religious groups and individuals took this position. For example, many Holiness Church preachers opposed all wars, as did influential Southern Baptist pastor Boyce Taylor from Murray.

Piper described the second position as "militant." It "celebrated war as a weapon of righteousness, and accepted the war as a holy crusade." This idea emerged quickly in Kentucky. Within days after the United States joined the war, the Reverend D. W. Scott of Louisville's Parkland Christian Church told a crowd that Americans would be fighting for flag and country but also "for God's principles of justice and humanity" in a truly "holy war."[5]

Some militant preachers believed the war foreshadowed the Apocalypse, particularly after three years of savage and seemingly meaningless fighting on the Western Front. With the onslaught of the Russian Revolution and the taking of Jerusalem by the British in December 1917, the Great War appeared to be culminating in an apocalyptic vision, which Jenkins describes as "a story of increasing chaos, marked by war, plague, famine, and disaster, culminating in a divine act of judgment that ends the existing world order and begins a wholly new creation."[6]

Preaching a few days before Christmas 1917, the pastor of Lexington's First Baptist Church, John William Porter, asserted that the world was on the threshold of Armageddon. He cited two key events that indicated Armageddon was at hand: the spreading of the Bible throughout the world, and Jews returning to Jerusalem after its fall to the British. These events, and a possible fight between the "forces of good and evil" in the Mediterranean, would lead to the "banishment of Satan and a thousand years of righteousness, preparing the world for the second coming of Christ."[7]

After the United States joined the war, many people thought of the Germans as "Huns," the destroyers of civilization. Notable former baseball player–turned–evangelist Billy Sunday denounced the Germans and their leader, Kaiser Wilhelm, comparing "Germany against America as hell against heaven."

The bombastic, controversial, but popular Sunday (whose original family name was the German "Sonntag") represented the "militant position" of religious preachers who "celebrated war as a weapon of righteousness, and accepted the war as a holy crusade."[8] Sunday, the most well known of the militant religious figures, was frequently quoted, and his exhortations against the Germans were reported in Kentucky newspapers.

The third position identified by Piper was a middle-of-the-road stance that "focused on ministry and sought to develop a wartime ministry without damaging either war or the enemy." Several religious leaders in Kentucky belonged to this group, ministering to soldiers at Camp Taylor and supporting war fundraising efforts.[9]

Catholic sentiment, reflected in the comments of the Catholic hierarchy and its publications, favored three themes: peace, neutrality, and patriotism.[10] Kentucky had a large population of Catholics; they were centered primarily in Louisville and northern Kentucky, but large pockets of communicants existed in Lexington, Paducah, Owensboro, and Bardstown (considered the cradle of Kentucky Catholicism).[11] For a large number of Catholics of German and Irish heritage in Kentucky, the war posed a dilemma. Irish Catholics opposed British rule in Ireland, where a possible civil war loomed. After the brutal putdown of the Irish Nationalist Easter uprising in 1916 and the subsequent execution of Irish rebels, Irish Catholic immigrants opposed Britain more vehemently than ever. Many German Catholics initially favored their homeland, but the German government made this hard to do after it violated neutral Catholic Belgium and sacked the Catholic University of Louvain at the start of the war. The Catholic bishop of Covington, Camillus P. Maes, had been caught in his homeland of Belgium at the beginning of the war, and several of his family members were involved in the hostilities. He observed that the "war party at Berlin has forced this war on Europe and will end in restoring various kingdoms in Germany." He believed the war would "put an end to tyrannous militarism, which is not confined to the German people. The German people, the great mass of them do not, in their hearts, want this war." Maes, however, did not live to see his prophecy about militarism proved wrong; he died in May 1915.[12]

Catholics faced a particular problem: given that many of them were recent immigrants, people questioned their loyalty. Within a couple of weeks after the United States entered the war, Catholic archbishops attending their annual meeting sent a letter to President Wilson affirming their support. Addressing schoolchildren at St. Patrick's parochial school in Louisville, the Reverend James P. Cronin echoed the archbishops, proclaiming, "To be a 'slacker' is a sin for Catholics." Next to duty to God, patriotism was the greatest duty.

Cronin exhorted the children to show "love of the flag, devotion to the republic." The students responded by singing "The Star-Spangled Banner" and reciting the Pledge of Allegiance.[13] Catholics made a special point of showing their loyalty early on.

After Camp Taylor came to Louisville, Catholics focused on providing for the soldiers. Patrick Henry Callahan, president of the Louisville Varnish Company, a devout Catholic, and a staunch Prohibitionist, played a prominent role in local and national war-support efforts. Representing the Knights of Columbus War Work Committee, Callahan joined Protestant ministers to ask Louisville mayor John Buschemeyer to ban vice in Jefferson County so the soldiers at Camp Taylor would not be tempted. During the war, Callahan also initiated a crusade against religious intolerance, served on the Education Committee of the Commission on Training Camp Activities, and led national efforts to raise $1 million to build Knights of Columbus facilities at the nation's sixteen military cantonments, including Camp Taylor.[14]

Louisville's Bishop Denis O'Donaghue wrote a letter to all diocesan priests to be read from their pulpits, encouraging parishioners to contribute to this fund to build Knights of Columbus facilities. The Louisville Catholic Conservation Council asked for $15,000 in contributions—a reachable goal, given the three dozen Catholic parishes in the Louisville area. Officials estimated that Catholics would make up one-third of the US military; therefore, more than 12,000 Catholics might pass through Camp Taylor. After more than $16,000 had been raised, the goal was increased to $36,000 as part of the new national goal of $3 million. While money was still being sought, construction of the facilities began. A not-quite-completed Knights of Columbus building hosted the first Catholic Mass at Camp Taylor in September, which was attended by more than 4,000 men.[15]

The National Catholic War Council (NCWC), formed in September 1917 by leading Catholic clergy and laymen, wanted to expand Catholic efforts beyond the Knights of Columbus's recreational focus. For example, it tried to increase the number of Catholic chaplains in the army and to develop diocesan war-support councils. In Louisville, where Catholics were already well organized, this meant that the Catholic Conservation Council simply changed its name to the Catholic War Council. The Louisville council continued to focus on supporting the Knights of Columbus at Camp Taylor and the Red Cross, especially through the extensive Catholic school system in the area. Catholic schools and parishes dedicated service flags to its soldier parishioners and collected entertainment items, such as books and magazines, for Camp Taylor. The council also found housing for relatives of Camp Taylor soldiers and helped soldiers' wives get jobs.[16]

The NCWC campaign to increase Catholic chaplaincy in the military ran into some opposition in Kentucky. The NCWC had difficulty finding enough chaplains not only to serve in the military but also to work in civilian organizations such as the Knights of Columbus and the Red Cross. The first call for volunteers went to religious orders, such as the Jesuits, to provide chaplains. Then the council appealed to diocesan bishops to provide more clergy. Seeking to minister to their own constituents, some bishops balked. The late Bishop Maes's successor, Bavarian-born Ferdinand Brossart, encouraged Catholics in the Diocese of Covington (comprising the eastern half of the state) to pray for peace and to support the Red Cross, but he drew the line at giving up priests who were so desperately needed in the diocese.[17] Brossart served on the local Council of Defense and "gave special attention to the needs of Catholic boys stationed in Army Camps in the Diocese," which included Camp Stanley in Lexington and Camp Thomas in northern Kentucky. On Easter Sunday 1918, he issued a pastoral letter to diocese clergy and laity reminding them of their patriotic duties as citizens and their obligations to support "helpful war activities."[18]

Catholics did not focus only on their own people. Bishop O'Donaghue and Colonel Callahan served on a Red Cross fund-raising committee, and Catholics eventually formed Red Cross units. By the end of 1917, Callahan took great pride in Catholics' war efforts: "One cannot but admire the patriotism manifested among our citizens in these war times." He underscored the good work being carried out at Camp Taylor, noting that there were no efforts to proselytize; signs outside Knights of Columbus facilities stated "Everyone Welcome," a promise carried out in practice as well as principle.[19]

Not all Catholics supported the war effort wholeheartedly. The "patriotic ire of Covington Catholics" was "stirred to its depths" when the Reverend Anton Goebel initially refused to allow the American flag to be brought into his church during a parishioner's funeral, claiming there was a Catholic Church rule against it. After a lengthy delay in the proceedings, Goebel relented and allowed the flag to be brought into the back of the church. The Knights of St. George, to which the dead parishioner had belonged, protested vigorously. Bishop Brossart's vicar-general and his secretary asserted there was no rule against displaying the American flag in churches, noting that several churches did so and that the flag was used to cover caskets in some funerals.[20]

Despite some opposition, Kentucky Catholics were cooperative and patriotic during the war. Their war work helped bring Catholics into the mainstream of American society, although some suspicion remained concerning a church whose members ostensibly followed a foreign leader—the pope. (Anti-Catholicism would be a mainstay of a revived Ku Klux Klan during the 1920s.)

Protestant denominations also worked to support US war efforts. Soon after the United States entered the war, the annual Southern Baptist Convention met in New Orleans. The editor of the influential Kentucky Southern Baptist publication *Western Recorder* and a key Baptist fundamentalist, the Reverend John William Porter of Lexington, submitted a resolution supporting the war effort; it passed unanimously. Kentucky Baptists in general strongly supported the war, even though one of their leaders, Boyce Taylor of Murray, spoke out against the war and was investigated for sedition.[21]

The General Association of Kentucky Baptists, representing more than 250,000 Southern Baptists, met in Paducah in November 1917. Despite Boyce Taylor's election as moderator (the head of the association), members unanimously passed a resolution pledging support to President Wilson and the government and promising to contribute to the physical comfort and spiritual well-being of the soldiers. Members also passed a resolution put forward by Professor W. O. Carver of the Southern Baptist Theological Seminary in Louisville. It authorized the association's Executive Board to spend money wisely to minister to Baptist soldiers at Camp Taylor.[22]

Individual Baptist pastors and churches strongly supported the war. In Louisville, the Reverend Henry Tiffany of Deer Park Baptist Church preached a series of six sermons on "Christian Patriotism." Tiffany became more strident about America's enemies as the war went on. Referring to the Turkish massacre of Armenians in 1915, he asserted, "The blackest page in history is the treatment of the Armenians by the Turks, with the consent if not the encouragement of the Germans." He claimed, "The Kaiser is responsible for the Armenian atrocities: the Kaiser who commanded his soldiers to make themselves more frightening than the Huns under Attila." America would see the "curse of the Hohenzollerns removed from the earth." At one point, Tiffany told of alleged German atrocities: men buried alive in front of their wives, a soldier driving a bayonet into a two-year-old baby. Tiffany asserted that the German war record was "black as hell" and that America had entered the war "to free the world from the most immoral, iniquitous and debasing menace to Christian civilization."[23]

During a February 1918 business meeting, Hopkinsville's First Baptist Church adopted a resolution that condemned the imperial German government. The resolution called the German government "one of the most ambitious, brutal and ruthless despotisms the world has ever known," and it pledged "sympathies and prayers, our loyal support, our fortunes, our lives, our sacred honor, our all, for the vigorous and successful prosecution of this war in behalf of Democracy and humanity."[24] The church's vociferous statement acted as a counterpoint to the Reverend Boyce Taylor, whose opposition to the war had recently reached a peak. A *Louisville Courier-Journal* editorial applauded the church's resolution as "true Americanism" but opined that it was not necessary, since no one questioned its patriotism. The resolution stood in contrast to the "course of a Kentucky Baptist minister [Taylor], prominent in the organization of the church, a course which has been so odious to loyal Americans that his fellow churchmen feel thus called on to repudiate it."[25]

A few days later, the Hopkinsville church unveiled a flag at its Sunday morning patriotic service that displayed a star for each church member serving in the military. One parishioner read the Honor Roll, a list of the sixty-six congregation members serving their country, including one who had already given his life. Guest speaker George Green, who supervised Baptist Church work at military training camps in the South, reminded parishioners that the Southern Baptist Convention in New Orleans had pledged its support to President Wilson soon after the war began. Green considered the war "a crisis in which the character of every man, woman and child is being tested." He declared that the role of the church in the conflict was to make the soldiers "just as good morally as possible." Green returned to the church that evening to give a strong patriotic address, and the congregation pressed him to tell more about his work with the soldiers in the camps.[26]

Baptist ministers and churches supported specific government programs. The Reverend John C. Greene of Louisville's J. M. Weaver Memorial Baptist Church asserted that "Christ came to make men free and the United States is fighting to make men free." Hence Greene supported the Liberty Bond campaign: "An investment in Liberty bonds is as truly an investment in the cause of freedom as is a gift to foreign missions," which sent "the Gospel of Christ and its freedom to all the world." Fellow Louisville pastor Hardy Winburn of Walnut Street Baptist Church encouraged food conservation on Patriotic Sunday, July 1, 1917. He also warned against the enticements of liquor and vice confronting soldiers at Camp Taylor. He urged cooperation between city and national officials to curb these temptations, which were "a greater foe than bullets." A resolution by the Glasgow Baptist Church declared its "hearty sympathy and our cheerful cooperation" with the YMCA, Red Cross, and other "organized efforts to care for the spiritual and physical welfare of our brave boys in national service."[27]

A popular faculty member at Southern Baptist Theological Seminary (SBTS) in Louisville, William J. McGlothlin became one of the state's most active Baptist war supporters, despite being denounced by his Bethel College classmate Boyce Taylor. McGlothlin had been in Europe when the war broke out in 1914, and as country after country mobilized and went to war, he noted in his diary, "Germany has simply become insufferable, and the world has risen up to humble her." He predicted the war would be a "frightful struggle, bloody and enormously expensive, whatever the outcome." He prayed: "May the God of the nations reign and somehow bring good out of this huge evil."[28]

McGlothlin paid close attention to the war, recording in his diary significant events such as the Russian Revolution and the Zimmermann telegram, whereby Germany tried to convince Mexico to go to war against the United States. He also continued to teach, preach, and give speeches regionally and nationally, including a key address at the Southern Baptist Convention meeting in May 1917 on "What America Means to the World." In that speech, which "stirred the patriotism of the entire South," he said he regretted the war but believed that America had entered "for humanity's sake."[29] McGlothlin was poised to play a key role in representing Southern Baptists in the war effort.

McGlothlin had the strong support of Baltimore businessman and SBTS board chairman Joshua Levering. Levering had been a Prohibition Party candidate for president in 1896 and Southern Baptist Convention president in 1908, 1909, and 1910. During the war, Levering served as head of the Southern Baptist Convention's Food Conservation Commission; he subsequently nominated McGlothlin to assist with federal food conservation efforts.[30] McGlothlin therefore spent most of the late summer and fall of 1917 in Washington, DC, working with Herbert Hoover's Food Administration to "arouse Southern Baptists to do their full duty in the conservation of food-stuffs." At the end of his stay in Washington, McGlothlin hoped he had helped Southern Baptists not only to conserve food but also to "attach . . . them afresh to the country and the world." McGlothlin had a broad worldview and Christian view. He believed that Southern Baptists had a "sectarian, a sectional consciousness," and "to recover from this and develop an ecumenical consciousness would be an unspeakable blessing to me. I hope I have done something in that direction."[31]

On returning home, McGlothlin resumed his teaching duties and continued to preach and speak. He spoke on "Washington and War Times" at Camp Taylor and at a Kentucky Baptist Historical Association meeting on "Contemporary War Activities of American Baptists." He appeared at the dedication of a YWCA branch for African American girls and at a flag raising at a children's war garden. In January 1918 the Food Administration asked him to go on a speaking tour in the Midwest to encourage food conservation. Consequently, he visited several small towns in Kentucky, Indiana, Ohio, and Illinois to deliver the conservation message. He continued to monitor the war, hoping in September 1918 that it would be over by Christmas 1919. A month later he acknowledged that the war's end was near, but he feared that the Germans were "sparring for truce. My chief fear is that Allies will let them off too easily."[32]

William McGlothlin went beyond working on behalf of the Southern Baptist Convention. He served his school, denomination, state, and country. After the war he served as president of Furman University and president of the Southern Baptist Convention.[33]

Catholics and Baptists were not the only Kentucky religious groups that supported the war. The Christian Church had a strong influence in Kentucky dating back to the early 1830s, when Barton Stone and Alexander Campbell led a unification movement that produced the Disciples of Christ, or Christian Church. By the early 1900s, another group had evolved from that union: the Churches of Christ.[34]

The third largest Protestant denomination in the South, the Churches of Christ were pacifist before the United States entered the war. In the nineteenth century, David Lipscomb, noted Church of Christ leader and editor of Nashville's influential *Gospel Advocate,* had decried civil government and its resulting wars. The church's position changed radically with the coming of the Great War. Author Michael Casey points out that "the otherworldly pacifist position of the Churches of Christ was sorely tested during the super-patriotism of World War I, and it began to crumble under the severe societal pressures of the pro-war forces."[35]

While some Churches of Christ publications began to accept the notion of war, the *Gospel Advocate* did not change its pacifist stance until August 1917, when a US district attorney summoned its editor and warned him about publishing seditious material, a crime punishable under the Espionage Act. The Churches of Christ subsequently adopted a "civil religion of the war as a righteous cause and America as a Christian nation." This civil religion "was structured around three intertwining concepts: God had chosen and blessed America and made her an instrument of his purposes; patriotism was now a 'true and pure religion'; and American civilization was a Christian civilization, meaning that American soldiers were dying for both God and country."[36] The Church of Christ found a way to rationalize its beliefs with the prevailing mores brought about by US participation in a total war.

In Mercer County, Franklin Bradley was one of ten men who claimed conscientious objector status as a result of his membership in the Church of Christ. When several young men in nearby Garrard County tried to claim the same exemption, the local Christian Church minister, J. R. Moorman, wrote to Lancaster's *Central Record* to describe his church's stance. Moorman explained,

"It is a well-known fact that said Church of Christ is a part of the well known communion commonly known as the Disciples of Christ or Christian Church, and are identical in their fundamental doctrines, differing only in some matters of minor importance, such as the use of instrumental music in worship." He believed that, like the Disciples of Christ or the Christian Church, the Church of Christ's creed did not prohibit military service.[37]

Before the United States entered the war, the Reverend Edward Lindsay Powell of Louisville's First Christian Church strongly supported President Wilson and his efforts to ensure peace "with honor." After US entry, Powell declared that pastors and churches should wholeheartedly support the war. He alleged, "You cannot preach the Gospel of the Cross unless you speak the Gospel of patriotism." In his opinion, anyone who was silent in the pulpit would be "as veritable a traitor as Judas Iscariot." Powell favored conscription, believed that church resources should be put to good use to support the war, and stressed that there could be "no religious tolerance of disloyalty on the part of Jew, of Gentile or Catholic or Protestant." The Louisville pastor concluded: "God help me comfort broken hearts, but God help me to prick consciences and to rouse them to madness and fury until these consciences are honored by obedience to duty and by loyalty and devotion to country."[38] Many Kentucky ministers quickly correlated devotion to God and devotion to country.

Powell spoke of America's debt to French general Lafayette, who had assisted George Washington in the American Revolution, and he vigorously protested against the Reverend J. G. Stilli, the pastor of Louisville's St. John's Evangelical Church who opposed the war. He lauded the work of the Red Cross, supported the War Savings Stamp campaign, and sought to unify Louisville's Disciples of Christ churches to fund a "war pastor" at Camp Taylor.[39]

Powell's church invited several war speakers, including Colonel S. S. McClure, publisher of the national magazine *McClure's,* and Arthur Guy Empey, the noted American who had served with British forces and authored a best-selling book, *Over the Top.* The church also hosted a speech arranged by the Kentucky Council of Defense and featuring Paul Perigord, a Catholic priest who had been a professor in the United States before returning home to serve in the French army. Church parishioners and the invited general public heard from aid workers, soldiers, a war correspondent, a movie star, and a treasurer of the United States. Powell's First Christian Church actively supported the war throughout 1918, and it hosted an Italian soldier who spoke on the evening of Armistice Day.[40]

Kentucky's Presbyterians also answered the call to arms. The Reverend Peyton Hoge, pastor of the Presbyterian church in Peewee Valley in Oldham County, relied on scripture to justify support of the war. Before moving to

Kentucky, Hoge had been pastor of First Presbyterian Church in Wilmington, North Carolina, where his predecessor had been Woodrow Wilson's father. Hoge believed America's participation in the war was not only right but also imperative. He harkened back to Martin Luther, whose stand had "marked the birth of modern liberty" and the "death of old tyrannies." The Peewee Valley pastor believed that Germany represented a new tyranny that had to be stopped, but he carefully distinguished between Germany's despots and the German people themselves.[41]

The Reverend T. M. Hawes of Highlands Presbyterian Church in Louisville found something positive about the war: he believed it would lead to liberty and more abiding peace. Hawes believed, as did many people, that the Great War was a war to end all wars and therefore, paradoxically, a war for peace. The Reverend Charles Welch of Louisville's Fourth Avenue Presbyterian Church called for a "preparedness evangelistic campaign" that would "take advantage of the existing psychological situation to propagate the principles of religion and spirituality" while supporting the war. The campaign would involve Louisville churches pairing congregation members with men who joined the military. Giving up his summer vacation so he could help work for preparedness, Welch believed that "a spiritual revival should make clear to all men and women that their supreme duty is to assist in mobilizing every possible resource and energy." This mobilization involved support for the Red Cross and "other local organizations with patriotic motives."[42]

In the tense domestic atmosphere during the Great War, even innocuous comments could be construed as "slackerism" or even sedition or treason. The Reverend T. N. Wilson of Emanuel Presbyterian Church in Louisville was accused of making "utterances against the President of the United States" and "other unpatriotic remarks." Specifically, he had reportedly said he would not adhere to the new daylight saving time instituted during the war. But this allegedly "pacifistic" pastor backed off when faced with the prospect of being fired. His congregation published an apologia, defending the pastor's patriotism by saying that he was against militarism and therefore against Germany. Any views "were actuated by his high conception of the Christian principles as set forth in the Bible, and by them only."[43] Wilson's less-than-fervent support of the war illustrates a dilemma many religious figures faced: how to support a war that seemed antithetical to biblical teachings.

Methodists across the state became involved in the war effort. A few days after US entry, Louisville area Methodists met and affirmed their support of President Wilson. They also used this platform to call for nationwide Prohibition. Noting Wilson's forbearance in trying to avoid war, the Reverend Frank Thomas of the Fourth Avenue Methodist Church maintained that it was inevitable: militarism and democracy must clash. Thomas hoped that German militarism would be crushed so that men could "breathe the air of freedom and peace in every land."[44]

The issue of Prohibition continued to animate Methodists during the war. At a statewide conference of the Methodist Episcopal Church, South, in Lexington in September 1917, Lieutenant Governor James Black predicted that the war would lead to prohibition of the manufacture and sale of whiskey. The *Lexington Herald* later reported that Methodist bishop William Quayle of Chicago had written to Herbert Hoover about conserving wheat by prohibiting beer manufacturing. Quayle had even equated beer drinking with being sympathetic to the Germans, asserting:

> Beer consumption is a very significant form of pro-German friendship. The unthinkable barbarism of the German armies in this present war is, in all reasonableness, to be accounted for largely by their centuries of beer-drinking, which has deadened their moral sense and coarsened their moral fiber until barbaric tragedies have become a delight and brutalities have been reduced to a code, when the rape of women, the herding of girls like sheep to be driven away to lives of enforced slavery, the slavery of millions and the starvation of millions, the poisoning of wells, are thought of as trifling accidents.[45]

The two major Methodist organizations in Kentucky, the Louisville Conference and the Kentucky Conference, enthusiastically supported the war effort. They strongly backed the war with "sermons, encouragement of government programs such as the sale of Liberty Bonds, the observance of wheatless days, and meatless days, the displaying of service flags, and providing programs for service men in local churches near military camps." In 1918 both conferences appointed War Work Commissions, with a chaplain and YMCA secretaries. More than a dozen Kentucky Conference pastors became military chaplains; four were from the Louisville Conference, including the Reverend Lesley Baker of Cloverport in Breckinridge County, who had attended the chaplains' school at Camp Taylor.[46]

Mason County Methodists at a Ruggles Campground meeting heard from Dr. Ernest Bysshe, superintendent of Methodist missions in France. After Bysshe spoke about the impact of the war, attendees collected $100 for French war orphans. Maysville's Methodist pastor S. K. Hunt took a temporary leave of absence from his church to become a YMCA official at Camp Johnson near Jacksonville, Florida. Focusing on the war, the Methodist church in Hopkinsville held a "Watch Night" meeting attended by 300 people. They listened to short talks on subjects such as German history, "Kultur," "The Horrors of German Ruthlessness," and the church's mission in the war. The Reverend A. D. Litchfield of Hartford in Ohio County helped lead Red Cross and Liberty Bond sales. He also "went to the fields and helped the farmers harvest their wheat."[47]

Black Methodist churchmen also supported the war, hoping it would better the plight of African Americans. As noted earlier, leaders of Louisville's oldest black Methodist church, the Asbury Chapel African Methodist Episcopal (AME) Church, had written to Theodore Roosevelt in May 1917 fully supporting the righteousness of the war. The church's pastor, the Reverend A. G. C. Randall, resigned to take up YMCA work at Camp Taylor. Bishops of the nation's AME churches who met in Louisville in early 1918 pledged the support of a quarter million parishioners. They also called on the federal government to grant leniency to the African American soldiers jailed because of the Houston riots, and they predicted better conditions for the "new negro" after the war.[48] Neither the leniency nor the better conditions transpired.

At the national level, the Federal Council of the Churches of Christ in America took the lead in Protestant war work. The council represented about 75 percent of the nation's Protestant ministers and church members; Southern Baptists were the major exception. The council formed a General War-Time Commission "to fulfil its wartime ministry." Despite Southern Baptists' official absence from the council, SBTS president Edgar Young Mullins served on the commission, which formed various committees to work on "definite needs or proposed programs," such as a Committee on National Prohibition as a War Measure and a Committee on Industrial Conditions. According to Piper, "The General War-Time Commission had a useful and fruitful life" and served as a "genuine vehicle for cooperative Protestant wartime ministry."[49]

A cooperative Protestant effort took place in Louisville. At the start of 1918, Reverend Thomas of the Fourth Avenue Methodist Church joined other Protestant pastors in the Churchmen's Federation, an ecumenical effort to deal not only with war issues but with general social issues as well. Affiliated with the Federal Council of the Churches of Christ, the organization included representatives from Christian, Presbyterian, Methodist, and other Protestant denominations.[50]

The Churchmen's Federation worked with the YMCA to ensure that Bible classes were taught at Camp Taylor. It considered President Wilson's proposal for a League of Nations, but federation officials were careful to deny that they supported pacifism. In May 1918 the federation reached beyond Protestant denominations when it sponsored a patriotic meeting that included not only prominent Protestant pastors, such as the Reverends Thomas and Powell, but also Catholic Bishop O'Donaghue and Rabbi Joseph Rauch of Temple Adath Israel. Secular leaders also attended, including KCD chairman Edward Hines, local Red Cross leader R. C. Ballard Thruston, and Louisville city attorney Huston Quin.[51]

The Churchmen's Federation addressed social issues confronting soldiers at Camp Taylor. To this end, it employed three undercover men to "pose in the guise of 'sports' and 'good fellows'" to gather evidence against women allegedly "engage[d] in immoral traffic." Sixty-five warrants resulted, and the Louisville vice squad arrested fifty-three women. US Public Health authorities examined the women for "social diseases" but disclaimed any official sanction of the federation's vice campaign. The campaign backfired, however, when the out-of-town investigators were themselves charged with "false swearing and fornication." The women involved were either lightly fined or dismissed. One of the investigators was also charged with not having a draft card in his possession.[52]

Despite this setback, the Churchmen's Federation continued its campaign to close the Galt House and St. Nicholas Hotel, sites of alleged vice. The federation issued a strong statement justifying its methods in "its battle against the immoral forces" in Louisville. In turn, a *Louisville Courier-Journal* editorial decried the federation's "crazy immoral crusade," arguing that "a line must be drawn between the rights of the people and the jurisdiction of the State." The newspaper warned: "Assumptions of power by unauthorized groups, claiming religious inspiration, are apt to grow tyrannical if left unchecked. The Church is not the State."[53] In the end, a judge warned the Galt House and St. Nicholas Hotel to "clean house" but decided against closing down the establishments.[54]

The Churchmen's Federation campaign demonstrates how Progressive reformers aligned themselves with churches to use the war to bring about social change. Piper asserts, "The Roman Catholics stressed the national character of their ministry and the Protestants the ecumenical nature of theirs, but on occasion the two groups worked together to create a fuller ecumenism."[55]

The Churchmen's Federation meeting in May 1918 began this cooperation, and it continued in Kentucky during the United War Work Campaign. The campaign's goal was to raise funds for seven organizations that helped soldiers at home and abroad: Knights of Columbus, YMCA, YWCA, YMHA, Salvation Army, American Library Association, and War Camp Community Service. President Wilson believed that one comprehensive effort would raise more money than seven separate campaigns. In addition, a united campaign would be more ecumenical because Protestant, Catholic, and Jewish interests would be represented.[56]

Serving as one of the state vice chairmen of the campaign, Catholic leader Patrick Henry Callahan praised the "broad spirit" that was evident in soldiers' camps at home and abroad, where "Americanism" was displayed. To Callahan, the campaign presented "an unparalleled opportunity to the American people once and for all time to abolish any religious animosity, jealousy or ill will that may heretofore have existed" by focusing on the needs of the soldiers and "upholding the common weal."[57]

Planning for the United War Work Campaign began in September, but its official kickoff happened to coincide with Armistice Day. Despite this timing, Americans recognized that need still existed, and they responded enthusiastically. Bishop O'Donaghue wrote a letter to be read from all Louisville diocese pulpits, asking that the "signs and rumors of peace" not diminish contributions; he encouraged parishioners to "subscribe generously." Pastor Welch of the Fourth Avenue Presbyterian Church believed that religion and patriotism were being put to a decisive test by the campaign.[58]

In Lexington, campaign chairman Joseph Porter noted that African Americans would conduct their own campaign under the leadership of William H. Fouse, head of Russell High School. Fouse selected a team of African Americans, and the *Lexington Herald* reported: "No negro is expected to make a contribution to any white solicitor. In a word, the negroes of Kentucky want to know and to show what they can do by themselves in this big work."[59]

The deadly Spanish flu raged through the state as the campaign began. Despite the attention focused on the epidemic, Kentuckians rallied to the cause. County after county exceeded their goals. In total, the state raised more than $2 million for the campaign, $400,000 more than the initial goal. The *Louisville Courier-Journal* reported a "spirit of harmony" when "Protestant ministers spoke from the pulpits of Catholic churches and Catholic priests addressed audiences in Protestant churches. Jewish rabbis interchanged with ministers and priests in presenting the cause of the seven organizations."[60]

Author Lerond Curry acknowledges that "the causes of Protestant-Catholic tensions in America by World War I were deep and complicated." Faced with the growing number of Catholics in America (from 2 million in the mid-nineteenth century to more than 10 million by 1917), some Protestants worried about the Catholic influence, particularly in urban areas, where new Catholic immigrants competed for jobs. Tension resulted from economic as well as doctrinal differences, but during the Great War, Catholics and Protestants cooperated at least temporarily, sharing "an active concern for the well-being of those directly affected in adverse ways by the war effort."[61]

Religious organizations in Kentucky played a large role in supporting America's war effort. Pastors from most denominations justified the war, and religious organizations supported efforts to help soldiers by providing both spiritual guidance and more temporal niceties. Religious organizations also used the war to achieve societal reforms, including Prohibition and an attack on social vices. Ecumenical efforts showed that Kentuckians of various religious beliefs could put aside their differences in pursuit of national security.

12

Higher Education

Colleges and universities in Kentucky stayed relatively aloof from the Great War until the United States entered it. Then they were strongly affected by it. In his comprehensive history of education in the commonwealth, William Ellis notes that the war had an immediate and far-reaching impact on educational institutions because male teachers and students joined the military. The colleges and universities, and their leaders, adapted and made important contributions to the domestic war effort.[1] At least three Kentucky college presidents played large roles beyond their schools: Henry Hardin Cherry of Western Kentucky State Normal School, Frank McVey of the University of Kentucky, and Edgar Young Mullins of the Southern Baptist Theological Seminary.

Henry Hardin Cherry was one of the first people involved in Kentucky's war effort. A native of Warren County, Cherry had previously headed Southern Normal School and Bowling Green Business College. In 1906, when the state created two normal schools for teacher education—Eastern Kentucky State Normal School (now Eastern Kentucky University) in Richmond, and Western Kentucky State Normal School (now Western Kentucky University) in Bowling Green—Cherry was appointed president of the latter.[2]

When the United States entered the war, Cherry became head of the Publicity and Speakers' Bureau Committee of the first KCD. He threw himself into his work. First, he helped organize a meeting of county defense council representatives in his congressional district in May 1917. Cherry realized how important publicity would be to rural areas: "Owing to the fact that the people are far removed from the actual seat of the war, they have failed to realize that this country is at war now and that fundamentally this country is now being attacked by German autocracy and that our liberties are at stake." Cherry believed a strong publicity campaign was imperative for programs such as food conservation and the Liberty Loan campaign to make progress.[3]

In July Cherry promoted a conference about food conservation and canning at Western Normal. In August he helped arrange a conference in Louisville that brought together members of the KCD, local council chairmen, and about 300 of the state's prominent citizens. The meeting was designed to develop a strategy and a campaign to "inform and arouse" people in the commonwealth about domestic war needs. Cherry also spoke at the state fair on "Fraternalism Day" in September, where he said he was already looking forward to the end of the war with "greatest optimism" and believed that when the war was over, "we shall know each other better and love each other more in the universal peace that it will bring."[4]

The culmination of Cherry's early war efforts came with "Patriotic Week," proclaimed by Governor Stanley to start on September 25. Kentuckians throughout the commonwealth celebrated with patriotic events. In Adair County, schools closed down for a day, and patriotic meetings were held in several small communities and rural school districts; a countywide meeting took place in Columbia. In Muhlenberg County, every school held a patriotic meeting, and every citizen was encouraged to attend. In the small coal town of Hellier in Pike County, "an immense throng of school children" filed into a new theater to hear a speaker from Pikeville College. The teachers gave their earnest support to the war awareness theme: "Wake Up Kentucky."[5]

Cherry quite proudly reported to Council of National Defense official George Porter that "four hundred ninety-eight different patriotic meetings were held in Kentucky" during Patriotic Week, and 124 "leading citizens" had given their time to speak outside their communities at their own expense; their work was augmented by 417 local speakers. Seventy-five counties participated. Meeting attendance ranged from 75 to 5,000 people. More counties were slated to hold meetings, including three during the week of Cherry's report. There were 105 all-day meetings, with sessions in the morning and afternoon followed by dinner. Cherry was especially happy that 80 percent of the meetings took place in rural communities, a target of the campaign. Women, ministers, and schoolteachers supported these patriotic efforts, and special recognition went to the University of Kentucky's Fred Mutchler, whose network of extension agents were "influential, active and effective in their support" of the week. Cherry saw to it that 30,000 copies of the special "war number" of the Western Kentucky Normal newspaper, *Normal Heights,* were distributed throughout the state. He concluded: "There cannot be any doubt about the success of the week."[6]

After attending a meeting of state council of defense publicity chairmen in Chicago in December, Cherry turned his attention to supporting the KCD War Conference in Louisville in January 1918. He then helped organize and publicize eighty-seven daylong war conferences in Kentucky communities, arranged speakers for Fourth of July celebrations, and brought in national and international figures to speak throughout the state. For example, Cherry helped put together a Rural Life Conference in Bowling Green featuring former president William Howard Taft and French clergyman-turned-soldier Paul Perigord as speakers. Perigord appeared at various venues in Kentucky, including a combined session of the Kentucky General Assembly.[7]

Cherry himself traveled across the state and spoke at many places. For example, in January 1918 he went to far eastern Lawrence County and appeared at the inaugural Eastern Kentucky Mountain Life Conference, billed as a "Big Progressive Movement." There, Cherry spoke about "Community Patriotism." In May he returned to eastern Kentucky and spoke at a patriotic meeting in West Liberty in Morgan County.[8]

Cherry received plaudits for his indefatigable war work. When the *Adair County News* in Columbia reported on the publication and dissemination of the *Normal Heights* war issue, it praised Cherry as "easily the biggest of Kentucky's school teachers." The paper added: "As a teacher, statesman and leader we think of him as the golden mean between Horace Mann and Woodrow Wilson. The country needs and will soon appreciate the wisdom and vision of such men, and the modesty and dignity of such patriots."[9]

Cherry kept up a heavy speaking schedule in the summer of 1918, but his efforts began to take a toll on him. That summer Cherry wrote to various people that he was swamped and worn out by his war-support activities, and he was worried about losing his focus on Western Normal. Prior to the war, Cherry had been a vigorous president, bringing in outstanding professors, fostering a rapidly growing student population, and building a burgeoning physical plant. From its start in 1907–1908 with 1,024 students, enrollment had peaked in 1915–1916 at 1,821, only to decline to 1,241 in 1917–1918. To stem the tide of declining enrollment, Cherry successfully lobbied for a military training detachment at Western Normal.[10]

Possibly because of his background as a university president, President Wilson understood higher education's challenges and sought to maintain enrollment. He believed the nation needed well-trained and well-educated citizens. The War Department created a new Student Army Training Corps (SATC) program in the fall of 1918, encouraging youths to "enlist and go to college." The SATC program sought to train potential officers for the army and navy quickly and efficiently. Students accepted into the program would be enlisted in the military and placed on inactive service until they graduated. They would attend summer camp for training. The program's purpose was "to mobilize and develop the brain power of the young men of the country for those services that require special training," such as "officers, engineers, chemists, doctors, administrators."[11] Cherry managed to get an SATC detachment approved for Western Normal. It involved about 150 men and spawned two barracks, a mess hall, and offices. The program terminated quickly after the armistice, but the barracks came in handy as dormitories when enrollment increased again after the war.

In October 1918 Cherry resigned as chair of the KCD Publicity Committee to concentrate on Western Kentucky Normal affairs. He cited several reasons for the decision, including his work to obtain an SATC unit, the influenza outbreak, and the notion that the Publicity Committee's work might be more efficiently handled out of the KCD office in Louisville. Summing up the committee's work under his direction, he noted with characteristic optimism that "all of Kentucky is aroused upon the issues of the war. The people are making noble spiritual and material contributions."[12]

Cherry had been an unsuccessful candidate for the Democratic gubernatorial nomination in 1915. He used his wartime popularity to make another attempt in 1919 but withdrew owing to poor health.[13] Cherry continued as president of Western Normal until his death in 1937. He had worked indefatigably on Kentucky's domestic war efforts, garnering well-deserved praise for his contributions.

Edgar Young Mullins was another Kentucky leader who served the state and nation well during the war. Born in Mississippi, Mullins graduated from the Southern Baptist Theological Seminary in Louisville and eventually returned there as president and professor of theology in 1899. A prolific writer and preacher, Mullins quickly embraced the war effort. In April 1917 he wrote to Secretary of War Newton Baker about the war's possible effects on his students and inquired how they could best render service to the military: as chaplains, as officers, or as YMCA workers? Addressing the SBTS student body, he decried slackers and "peace at any price" advocates and encouraged his students to enlist as military chaplains. He supported Wilson's selective conscription and justified US participation in the war as a "righteous cause." He believed that a "righteous war" was consistent with Christian beliefs if it were conducted "to protect the weak, protect liberty, and to prevent the destruction of the fruits of civilization."[14]

Mullins became a popular patriotic speaker, appearing at churches and civic organizations. He spoke to Louisville's Conversation Club about German culture, which he believed unified "in a governmental and social system all those factors of civilization which oppose freedom and self-determination." At the Southern Baptist Convention in New Orleans in May 1918, he delivered a keynote speech about how preachers could interpret the war in favor of the United States and the Allies and help win it.[15]

He was not content, however, to simply speak about a war that he believed was the "will of Christ." With the encouragement of SBTS board chairman Joshua Levering, Mullins served as the YMCA camp secretary for religious work at Camp Taylor. As such, he preached and conducted some of the Bible classes that were a key component of the YMCA's work there. He also over-

Edgar Young Mullins, president of the Southern Baptist Theological Seminary, Louisville. (Baptist Historical Society)

saw administrative duties such as the dissemination of religious materials. In an informative *Louisville Courier-Journal* article on YMCA activities at Camp Taylor, Mullins asserted in an ecumenical spirit that "religion is being taught and exemplified in a large way, with nothing of narrow sectarian appeal."[16]

Historian William Ellis notes that Mullins's "greatest challenge" occurred during the Spanish flu crisis in the fall of 1918: "Disregarding his own poor health he made daily trips to the camp [Taylor] to minister to the sick and dying."[17]

Mullins did not restrict himself to religious endeavors; he addressed overall war efforts as well. For example, he preached in support of food conservation and recruited Baptists to grow war gardens. He supported his colleague William McGlothlin when the SBTS professor took a leave of absence to work for Hoover's Food Administration.[18]

Although he worked locally, Mullins's view of the war extended beyond Louisville. He had a broad understanding of the war's implications. In a prescient analysis published in the *Courier-Journal,* he focused on the future of the Turkish Ottoman Empire, observing, "This part of Asia is going to be brought into the political and economic life of the world." Noting that "the Eastern theater of war is scarcely less important for the cause of freedom than the Western," Mullins believed Great Britain would guide the former Ottoman Empire and bring it "liberty, justice, and peace," in contrast to the Turkish sultan's rule of "injustice and bondage."[19]

Because of his YMCA war work, Mullins had to fend off attacks by Southern Baptist pastors such as Murray's Boyce Taylor and Lexington's J. W. Porter, who decried the YMCA as subversive and discriminatory against Baptists. Mullins faced other difficulties as well. The number of SBTS students declined from 322 at the start of 1916 to 239 in 1918. In addition, he had continuing problems with faculty, some of whom resented the fact that they were not well paid, while Mullins collected $2,000 for his YMCA war work.[20]

Despite some tribulations, Edgar Young Mullins served his school and his country well. He represented an emerging Southern Baptist national consciousness, supporting the country as well as his church. He continued as president of Southern Baptist Theological Seminary until his death in 1928 and was considered "the most important moderate Baptist leader in the country."[21]

The third university president to play a prominent role arrived in the commonwealth half a year after the United States entered the war. With a PhD in economics from Yale and seven years' experience as president of the University of North Dakota, Frank McVey became president of the newly renamed University of Kentucky (UK) in late 1917. Before his arrival, the university had been mired in problems. Former president Henry Barker had to contend with the continued influence of president emeritus James Patterson, compounding a number of problems. When Barker tried to combine three colleges of engineering into one, an outcry prompted a review by the Board of Trustees. A highly

University of Kentucky president Frank McVey overseeing military exercises. (University of Kentucky)

critical report suggested reforms and the hiring of a new president. Barker resigned, and KCD member and UK Board of Trustees vice chairman Richard Stoll headed the presidential search committee that hired McVey.[22]

McVey had been active in North Dakota's war effort. He also served on the Education Committee of the Council of National Defense. In January 1918 KCD chair Edward Hines nominated McVey to be state director of the US Public Service Reserve (USPSR). In addition, McVey became a member of the KCD Advisory Board after the council was reorganized and received state funding in March 1918.[23]

After settling in Lexington, the new UK president gave speeches and participated in war conferences in 1918. He and federal food administrator Fred Sackett spoke to a farmers' conference in late January. In February McVey spoke at the Lexington YMCA about the duties of citizens during the war. Later in the month he appeared at Cherry's Rural Life Conference in Bowling Green, along with former president William Howard Taft; there, McVey decried "slacker" citizenship.[24]

As the newly appointed USPSR state director, McVey set about creating a network of helpers. He and Hines convinced the KCD's county labor committee chairmen to serve as USPSR recruiters. Like other state support efforts, this network reached many of the smallest settlements in Kentucky.[25]

One of McVey's first tasks was to encourage Kentuckians to work in shipyards, a national priority. McVey and US Employment Service director Pratt Dale also recruited workers for the new Camp Knox being constructed south of Louisville. McVey corresponded extensively with Dale, national officials, county enrollment agents, district organizers, and men seeking jobs. Given the university's agricultural college and extension service responsibilities, McVey also got involved in farm labor discussions. Fortunately, he could rely on professors Fred Mutchler and W. D. Nicholls to sort out most agricultural issues. Thomas Poe Cooper, the new dean of the College of Agriculture, also worked on these issues. Recruited by McVey from North Dakota in 1918, Cooper became involved with the US Boys Working Reserve to supply temporary farm labor.[26]

In addition to his work for the USPSR, McVey spent a great deal of time seeking opportunities for the university from the military. It already had a Military Department under the command of US Army captain Herbert N. Royden, who had arrived in October 1917. A West Point graduate in the class of 1891, Royden had retired from the army in 1903 but had been recalled to duty in February 1916. With Royden's arrival, a formal Reserve Officers' Training Corps (ROTC) program was begun.[27]

To increase military activities on campus, Royden and McVey worked with

Captain Herbert N. Royden, who headed the University of Kentucky's military contingent. (University of Kentucky)

the War Department to institute a Signal Corps training course at UK. The course began in January 1918 and was aimed at men eligible for the draft. Enrollees took classes in electrical engineering, telegraphy, telephony, radio instruments and apparatus, and military French. Although participation in the course did not change a student's draft status, a certificate of completion could help the army place him in the appropriate unit after arriving at training camp.[28]

At the end of March 1918, McVey telegraphed the War Department's Committee on Education and Special Training and offered to provide training to drafted men. Within a couple of weeks the committee accepted the offer. McVey declined to delegate someone else to work with the committee, and he remained the chief contact. The university then secured a government contract in May 1918 to create a training facility, Camp Buell, on land owned by the Kentucky Trotting Horse Breeders' Association not far from the university. The program taught enlisted men useful technical skills such as carpentry, blacksmithing, auto mechanics, electrical work, radio telegraphy, truck driving, and other vocational skills. Army captain Justin Harding oversaw their military training, and UK's dean of engineering F. Paul Anderson supervised their technical training.[29]

The first contingent of the UK training detachments consisted of 400 drafted men from Tennessee, who reported to the university on May 7. In total, three contingents of approximately 400 men each trained at UK in two-month increments before the end of the war. The men attended technical classes for seven hours a day and then received military training after 1630 hours. The training program even had an official photographer, professor of engineering drawing Louis E. Nollau, who made hundreds of glass plate photographs depicting all aspects of the program, including housing, social events, athletic competitions, and drill activities.[30]

McVey's efforts to improve draftees' technical skills no doubt benefited the men and, particularly, the armed forces. Despite these programs, male enrollment at UK declined. At the end of June 1918, the number of men enrolled at the university was approximately 40 percent lower than the previous year. When the ROTC had been inspected earlier in the year, 260 students were enrolled; by the end of June 1918, only 85 men remained in training. By then, 502 students and 305 alumni had joined the military.[31]

With an ROTC unit and a technical training program already on campus, McVey next sought an SATC unit. After receiving confirmation that the university had been selected to participate in the program, in late August 1918 McVey traveled to Fort Sheridan in Chicago to discuss SATC issues and problems.[32]

Plans proceeded for the new SATC unit, and construction began on four new barracks. Lieutenant E. T. Campbell, a former UK student, inspected the housing, facilities, and equipment and in September "expressed himself as highly gratified at the excellent progress made" in a short time. Officers from Fort Sheridan, Illinois, were ordered to the university to oversee the training.[33]

Professor Louis E. Nollau, University of Kentucky photographer. (University of Kentucky)

Congressman J. Campbell Cantrill from Georgetown visited the campus on October 1 to inaugurate the new SATC program. Established under the command of Captain Royden, the SATC incorporated the already functioning vocational training classes and added a training section for potential officers. More than 1,200 men participated in the training units. The Lexington draft board inducted more than 100 new SATC men into the army. Two men, a Scot and a Frenchman, became naturalized citizens in a ceremony presided over by federal judge A. M. J. Cochran.[34]

Just as the SATC effort was gearing up, the Spanish flu epidemic struck the university. More than 170 men were hospitalized. The Lexington chapter of the Red Cross and other women took care of the sick students. Men who were not sick were furloughed home because the university had ceased most activity. Despite precautions and treatment, five SATC members died in October before the epidemic abated. Captain Royden nevertheless prepared to resume activities and arranged for his students to use a local YMCA rifle range. An army inspector visited the range and the hospitals treating the sick SATC students and declared them "highly satisfactory."[35]

As the flu epidemic subsided, furloughed SATC men returned to the university at the beginning of November, and UK students returned to classes on Armistice Day. Military officials asserted that the SATC would continue, but the nation quickly demobilized after the armistice; the UK's SATC detachment mustered out in December.[36]

UK's military training and contributions to the armed forces proved successful. President McVey played a strong role, working with students, professors, and national authorities to develop and implement important training programs.[37] In addition to the effort to train male students for the military, many other parts of the campus and the university community did their part to support the war. In spring 1918 McVey established a committee to lead war-related activities on campus. Dr. Joseph Pryor, professor of anatomy and physiology, led the committee. Members included Captain Royden, Dean Anderson, registrar Ezra Gillis, home economics professor Mary Sweeny, agronomy professor George Roberts, Board of Trustees secretary and extension director Wellington Patrick, and four student representatives. The committee established five campus subcommittees on war education, patriotic exercises, war service organizations, war service records, and publicity. Among other activities, the committee arranged for war films to be shown and raised money for the National Surgical Dressings Committee.[38]

As the war progressed, the UK community wholeheartedly supported it. Two campus Red Cross chapters focused on sewing hospital shirts and pajamas, knitting socks, and making surgical dressings. Members of the university's Women's Club joined Liberty Loan campaigns, supported the Red Cross, participated in activities of the women's branch of the Fayette County Council of Defense, supplied food to students at Camp Buell, and helped weigh babies.

University registrar Ezra Gillis kept Washington authorities apprised of alumni who had special skills the government might need. President McVey and other officials such as law professor Lyman Chalkley made speeches in support of the war.[39]

UK students and professors put their energy into war projects, and the UK administration quickly developed policies so that those who joined the military would not lose ground academically or professionally. In April 1917 the university's Executive Board voted to allow seniors to receive their degrees without taking final exams, if they had joined the military. Other undergraduates entering the military could matriculate to the next year as if they had successfully completed their exams. Faculty members were allowed to take leaves of absence to join the military. Over the course of the war, nearly 1,200 UK students and alumni joined the military (exclusive of the training programs), as did 26 faculty members. Twenty students and one faculty member died in the service of their country.[40]

The University of Kentucky, under the leadership of its president, was also very involved in supporting the home front during the war, and as a result, the university garnered attention and support. With their reach into the commonwealth through extension agents, university officials such as Fred Mutchler, Mary Sweeny, and Thomas Poe Cooper ensured that people all over the state cooperated with UK's war efforts. Kentuckians helped UK achieve its goals by working locally on many of its initiatives.

Summing up McVey's contribution during the war, biographer Eric Moyen concludes: "McVey's progressive leadership during the war demonstrated his ability to identify needs at both the state and national levels and to determine ways in which higher education could help meet them. In so doing, he managed to place the university on firm footing despite the tumultuous times."[41]

The University of Kentucky was not the only university poised to support the domestic war effort. Other colleges and universities did their part. For example, several formed SATC units, including the University of Louisville, Western and Eastern Kentucky State Normal Schools, and Transylvania, Georgetown, Berea, Centre, Kentucky Wesleyan (Winchester), Bethel (Russellville), and Ogden (Bowling Green) Colleges. These units helped address a major concern as the war took its toll on male attendance at most colleges.

The University of Louisville's academic dean, John Patterson, apparently believed (as did many people in early 1917) that the war might last several years. He therefore passed along the government's encouragement for medical students to remain in school to guarantee a future supply of doctors. Despite Patterson's exhortations, the university's well-regarded medical school suffered grave financial losses as students left to join the military. Several of its graduates joined Hospital Unit D, the Lindenberger Unit. In addition, an estimated half of all male students in the College of Arts and Sciences had enlisted or been drafted by the fall of 1917. In the fall of 1918, however, more than 200 students joined the SATC unit. Headquartered on the campus of the Presbyterian Seminary, the SATC unit experienced a setback when the influenza epidemic caused academic classes to be postponed.[42]

Dean Patterson led war efforts both on and off campus, serving as a vice president of the national Permanent Blind Relief War Fund and head of its Louisville chapter. In March 1918 the University of Louisville Players raised more than $1,000 for the fund by staging performances of Sir James M. Barrie's *Admirable Crichton*. Barrie himself donated his royalties to the fund. Faculty members also supported the war effort; eighteen of twenty-five College of Arts and Sciences professors reportedly contributed to the Liberty Loan program, and seven served as patriotic speakers. One unfortunate outcome of the war was the resignation of a professor of history, Eckart von Walther, presumably because of his German origins.[43]

In Richmond, Eastern Kentucky State Normal School had a relatively new president, Thomas Jackson Coates from Pikeville. Appointed in 1916, Coates had been educated at H. H. Cherry's Southern Normal School in Bowling Green and had served as supervisor of the state's rural schools. Like other colleges and universities, Eastern Normal's enrollment declined during the war, so school officials decided to accept students who were not intending to become teachers. The school supported the war in many ways; for example, professors made speeches and even joined students in army training camps. Coates himself "made a special trip to Washington to get a Student Army Training Corps (SATC) unit assigned to Eastern." But because of the influenza epidemic and the armistice, the SATC unit remained quite small.[44]

At Centre College in Danville, 175 men joined the SATC unit. The quick settling of the war on November 11 brought mixed sentiments. SATC members were disappointed they would not be able to take part in the war, but they were happy "knowing that friends and relatives over there were no longer exposed to common danger." In December the Centre SATC unit demobilized.[45]

A few days after the United States entered the war, the faculty at Georgetown College passed a resolution affirming allegiance to the "noble and Christian principles and wise policies" presented by President Wilson to Congress. The school's newspaper, the *Georgetonian* (edited by college president Maldon Browning Adams's son), encouraged students to consider carefully their motives and skills before volunteering for the military. In an editorial titled "Enlist or Wait," the newspaper advised:

> If you have not particular aim in life, or have ambitions to be a great soldier—enlist. If you think that your country calls for you to lay down your life for her—lay it down, and you will be honored as the hero that you are. But if you are joining the army or navy now with the idea that you will get into a safe place before they are all filled up, beware that you do not come within the definition of a slacker. If you have high ideals in life, and feel that with your training you are equipped to perform a greater service to the nation than killing men, wait for the call of your country to the place for which you are best fitted.

The editorial concluded: "The best way to stand by your President and your country is to continue to train yourself so that selective conscription will be able to find a place for you, for which you are best fitted."[46]

The *Georgetonian* editorial raised the wrath of the *Lexington Herald*'s Desha Breckinridge, who wrote an editorial lambasting its position. Although Breckinridge did not name the *Georgetonian,* he reproduced its motto and castigated both the newspaper and the college president as being hostile to army service. Such students would never be leaders, he opined: "If they are saving themselves and scorning those who offer their bodies and their lives in defense for their country, they are unfit for the high calling to which they profess to aspire." The *Herald* also criticized the college for continuing classes as normal: "No effort is there to induce students at that college to join the army; no effort is there to induce those students to give their labor on the farm or in the factory."[47]

Georgetown's president Adams defended the newspaper and pointed out that the *Herald* had gotten its facts wrong: the college faculty had agreed to grant credits to students who left for officer training camps and would give early exams to those who were going home to farm. Adams was simply heeding the notice from Washington that higher education was important to the nation; therefore, classes at the college continued.[48]

Two popular Georgetown College professors took up war work with the YMCA: biology professor and football coach Robert Hinton, and D. E. Fogle, head of modern languages. Georgetown chemistry professor Townes Leigh made national news when he published an article deriding alleged German scientific innovations. Leigh argued that the Germans were not innovators but "perfectors" of science. Leigh also worked on a smoke-creating machine used to hide Allied ships from German submarines.[49]

Georgetown students helped the war effort by raising funds, hosting speakers, participating in summer military training, and enrolling in the SATC. A Baptist college, Georgetown invited SBTS president Mullins to address the

200 SATC members on "What Is America Fighting For?" Curry Breckinridge, Desha's sister, also appeared at the college to talk about her experience as a nurse in France; she was introduced by president Adams himself. Despite the war, Georgetown College opened the fall 1918 academic year with record enrollments, bolstered by its largest-ever intake of women and a surprisingly large number of men, given the circumstances. In an expression of solidarity with France, the college enrolled a French soldier, Sergeant Paul Ranchier. During his four years in the army, twenty-two-year-old Ranchier had won medals and been wounded. In addition to studying, he gave talks about his war experiences. During the war, Georgetown College provided more than 280 men to the military, 3 of whom died.[50]

Historian John D. Wright Jr. asserts that at Transylvania College, "the fight for prohibition was apparently as significant an issue as the war" before April 1917, but "once war was declared, all fell before it." In March 1917 Transylvania's president Richard Crossfield foresaw US entry and called for the formation of a Transylvania military unit to start drilling. Within a couple of months, 100 Transylvania students had signed up for the unit, most of them hoping to move on to officer training at Fort Benjamin Harrison near Indianapolis. The *Lexington Herald* praised Transylvania's patriotism, reminding readers, "In Transylvania lives an old tradition that her men respond to their country's need on the first call. In every national crisis since her founding, Transylvania has given freely of her best blood."[51]

Transylvania president Crossfield "urged that soldiers should enter this conflict with idealism, not hatred." In a speech at Louisville's First Christian Church, he asserted that the war would "result in a reign of democracy" and "the reign of temperance," where "John Barleycorn" would be "deposed." He prophesied that "the great war will result in the humiliation of the nations." By "humiliation," Crossfield meant that nations would be much poorer financially. He concluded that the war would also help spread Christianity: "Democracy, temperance and humility point to the way of the Cross." Unlike many people, Crossfield did not separate the German people from the German government.[52]

Despite sending many students to the military, Transylvania managed to maintain nearly 85 percent of its normal enrollment during the war. Record numbers of women entered the school in the fall of 1917. Eventually, nearly 350 Transylvanians served in the military during the war, including Major General George Duncan, son of a Lexington mayor and an army division commander. At least a dozen Transylvanians died in the war.[53]

According to Wright, "Transylvania's experience during World War I was probably typical of most colleges. The themes of neutrality, pacifism and detachment heard on campuses before the U.S. entry into the war were suddenly and effectively muted. Loyalty, patriotism and war fever swept over all. Church-related colleges, even those with seminaries on the campus, acted no differently."[54]

This was certainly true in Kentucky, where colleges and universities willingly supported the war. As post–Civil War institutions, the largest schools—UK, Western Normal, and Eastern Normal—faced their first real national crisis. Kentucky universities and colleges supported domestic war efforts such as promoting Liberty Bonds, encouraging food conservation, and educating the public about citizens' responsibilities in a total war. All the schools provided alumni, students, and faculty who either served in the military or contributed as civilians; others, such as men in the SATC, were prepared to go if called on. Kentucky's universities and its leaders adapted quickly and effectively to tackle the challenges they and the nation faced during the war.

13

"Over There"

The Great War affected people throughout Kentucky, from its largest cities to its smallest coal camps. Many people contributed locally by purchasing Liberty Bonds and War Savings Stamps and by participating in other domestic campaigns. Some Kentuckians served in the military in the United States, at sea, and abroad; others served in civilian organizations such as the YMCA and the Red Cross. Approximately 100,000 Kentucky men served in the military sometime during the war. Some were already enrolled in the US Army, Navy, or Marine Corps, and some had National Guard experience, but most were selectees. Many went abroad, most of them for the first time, and their lives were forever altered by their experiences.

Kentucky military men, from newly conscripted privates to generals with years of experience, garnered many decorations for their bravery and service. Two Kentuckians received the nation's highest award for military valor: the Medal of Honor. One was a born Kentuckian, and the other was an "adopted son" who lived in the state for many years: Willy Sandlin and Samuel Woodfill.

According to his Medal of Honor citation, Willy Sandlin was born in Jackson in Breathitt County. (Other counties also claim him, including Perry, Leslie, and Owsley. His citation notes he joined the army from Hyden in Leslie County.) Sandlin was an eastern Kentucky mountaineer who became the commonwealth's version of Alvin York, although he was slightly less famous and less decorated than his Tennessee counterpart. Sandlin joined the US Army before the Great War and served on the Mexican border. Sent to France in 1917, he was wounded on July 4, 1918, but recuperated and rejoined the fighting in late September at the beginning of the Meuse-Argonne offensive. As a sergeant in the Thirty-Third Infantry Division—the "Prairie Division," made up mostly of Illinois National Guardsmen—Sandlin displayed exceptional gallantry near the Bois (Forest) of Forges in northeastern France. Encountering a machine gun nest manned by eight German soldiers, Sandlin charged forward alone. Using grenades, a pistol, and a bayonet, he wiped out the nest. That same day, he destroyed two more German machine gun nests in much the same manner. For these actions "above and beyond the call of duty," Sandlin received the Medal of Honor and the French Croix de Guerre.[1]

Medal of Honor recipients Willie Sandlin and Samuel Woodfill with President Calvin Coolidge in 1924. (Library of Congress)

Although he was gassed in October, Sandlin fought until Armistice Day. Soon after he returned to Kentucky in 1919, Sandlin helped Cora Wilson Stewart in her literacy campaign. He traveled throughout the state describing how his illiteracy had been an impediment to obtaining an officer's commission. He emphasized the value of education and encouraged people to support and attend Stewart's Moonlight Schools. At the behest of Secretary of War Baker, he returned to France in 1920 to escort the remains of deceased soldiers being repatriated. But Sandlin soon expressed regret about this role. He opposed the plan and called it impracticable. He believed the bodies of dead soldiers "who made the supreme sacrifice should lie where they died." Sandlin settled down near Hyden in Leslie County but continued to have health problems as a result of being gassed. He died in 1949. Buried first in Hyden, Sandlin was reinterred in 1990 in Zachary Taylor National Cemetery in Louisville.[2]

Samuel Woodfill was born in Indiana, but before and after the war he lived in northern Kentucky, where an elementary school in Fort Thomas is named after him. Woodfill joined the army in Louisville in 1901; he served in the Philippines and on the Mexican border just prior to the war. He was posted at Fort Thomas in Campbell County for several years and married a Kentuckian, Lorena Wiltshire.

Sent to France when the United States entered the war, Lieutenant Woodfill commanded a company in the Fifth Division near Cunel during the Meuse-Argonne campaign in the war's latter stages. A few days after Willie Sandlin's exploits, Woodfill's company became pinned down by German machine guns. Woodfill charged ahead, captured several machine guns, and killed many Germans in hand-to-hand combat using a pistol and a pickax. For his actions he was promoted temporarily to captain and awarded the Medal of Honor and Croix de Guerre. Like Sandlin, he was hit by shrapnel and gassed during the war.[3]

Reverting to his prewar rank of sergeant, Woodfill returned to his wife in Fort Thomas after the war. Along with Alvin York and "Lost Battalion" leader Charles Whittlesey, he was commended by General John Pershing, who called him one of the war's greatest heroes. Woodfill was selected to be a pallbearer at the 1923 ceremony of the burial of the Unknown Soldier in Arlington National Cemetery. A tall, straight-backed military figure, he became a Kentucky celebrity and a popular speaker. When Woodfill ran into financial difficulties (like York), Kentucky senator Richard Ernst tried to get a bill passed so that Woodfill could retire as a captain. The bill failed, and Woodfill eked out a living. When World War II broke out, he rejoined the army (as did York). His wife died during the war, and afterward, Woodfill retired to a farm in Indiana, where he died in 1951. Initially buried in the Hoosier State, he was reinterred in Arlington National Cemetery in 1955.[4]

Several Kentuckians were prominent military leaders during the Great War. At least six major generals and nine brigadier generals with Kentucky ties served during the war or were promoted to that rank soon thereafter because of their wartime exploits. Three Kentuckians served as rear admirals.[5]

Kentucky's general officers demonstrated strong leadership skills during the war; three of them commanded army divisions. Major General Henry T. Allen, a native of Sharpsburg in Bath County, graduated from the US Military Academy at West Point in 1882 and was commissioned as a cavalry officer. He served on the western frontier and in Cuba, the Philippines, and Mexico.

During the Great War, Allen commanded the Ninetieth Infantry Division in France from the St. Mihiel campaign through the Meuse-Argonne offensive that led to the armistice. He then commanded all American troops in the postwar occupation of the German Rhineland. Born in Winchester in Clark County, Major General Frank Long Winn graduated from West Point in 1886 and won Silver Stars in Cuba and the Philippines. He commanded the Eighty-Ninth Division through the St. Mihiel and Meuse-Argonne campaigns during the Great War. The son of Lexington mayor Henry Duncan, Major General George B. Duncan also graduated from West Point in 1886 and had a distinguished career in Cuba and the Philippines. Appointed to command the famous Seventy-Seventh "Rainbow" Division at the outset of the war, Duncan moved on to command the Eighty-Second Division during the Meuse-Argonne campaign.[6]

Besides commanding divisions in France, Kentucky's major generals played other key roles. Major General Hugh Scott from Danville in Boyle County served at the beginning of the war in Washington, DC, as the army's chief of staff. He was then statutorily retired for age but still commanded a division in training at Camp Dix, New Jersey. Major General William Sibert, another "adopted Kentuckian" who later retired to Bowling Green in Warren County, had played a key role in building the Panama Canal. After serving briefly as commander of the First Division in the war, he became head of the army's new Chemical Warfare Service. As such, he "was responsible for all research, development, procurement, and supply of all chemicals to the Army, as well as offensive and defensive gas war training." Major General J. Franklin Bell from Shelby County graduated from West Point in 1876 and served in the Philippines, where he earned a Medal of Honor. Approaching retirement, he commanded the newly formed Seventy-Seventh "Rainbow" Division while it trained in the United States and then went to France on an observation mission.[7]

Kentucky's brigadier generals also had distinguished military careers. A lieutenant colonel when the war began, Lexingtonian Preston Brown was promoted in 1918 to colonel and then became a brigadier general when given command of the Third Division for the Meuse-Argonne campaign. Born in Midway in Woodford County, Adrian Fleming graduated from West Point in 1895 and received a Silver Star for his actions in the Philippine insurrection; he commanded the 158th Field Artillery Brigade during the war. Brigadier General John S. Winn from Winchester served as an inspector general in the Services of Supply and then commanded army brigades in France.[8]

Not all the state's high-ranking military officers were in the army; some Kentuckians served in the navy as admirals. Frankfort native Hugh Rodman graduated from the US Naval Academy at Annapolis in 1880. Through the years, he served on shore commands, such as at Cavite naval base in the Philippines, and on various ships, such as the battleship USS *Connecticut.* In 1917 he was promoted to rear admiral and commanded a battleship division serving first with the US Atlantic Fleet and then with a British fleet in the North Sea. For his service, the British made him a Knight Commander of the Order of Bath. A Pineville native and 1888 Naval Academy graduate, Rear Admiral Carlo Brittain commanded a battleship division in the Atlantic Fleet during the war and received a Navy Cross. Described as an indefatigable worker, Brittain served after the war as chief of staff to the commander of the Atlantic Fleet, but poor health hampered his efforts. After being hospitalized and then released, Brittain committed suicide in 1920.[9]

Two Christian County Marine Corps officers served with distinction and became brigadier generals: Cyrus Radford and Logan Feland. After graduating from Annapolis, Radford served on several ships and in Cuba and the Philippines. During the war he worked as a quartermaster at the Marine Corps Depot of Supplies in Philadelphia, helping to ensure that Marines were properly equipped for war. Like many officers, he received a temporary promotion to brigadier general during the war but reverted to his old rank of colonel immediately afterward. Nevertheless, he eventually served as Marine Corps quartermaster general and retired as a brigadier general.[10]

Hopkinsville native Logan Feland was a graduate of the Massachusetts Institute of Technology. He had been a practicing architect in Owensboro and had commanded a company of Kentucky State Guards during the occupation of Cuba after the Spanish-American War. He joined the Marine Corps in 1899 and saw duty on various ships and on expeditions to the Philippines, Cuba, and Mexico. Just prior to the war, he commanded the Marine Corps' version of a Plattsburgh training camp in Philadelphia, part of the preparedness movement to give students and businessmen rudimentary military training. He was one of two Marine Corps officers assigned to join General John Pershing's initial contingent that sailed to France on the SS *Baltic* in late May 1917.

In France Feland became second in command of the Fifth Marine Regiment and won the nation's second highest military valor award, the Distinguished Service Cross, at the iconic Marine Corps Battle of Belleau Wood. As a colonel he commanded the Fifth Regiment through the rest of the war, including the final Meuse-Argonne campaign. One of the Marine Corps' most highly decorated officers of the Great War, Feland was promoted to brigadier general while leading the Fifth Regiment during the Rhineland occupation.

During the 1920s he served as assistant to the Marine Corps commandant. He was the guest of honor during Louisville's Armistice Day celebration in 1922, and his photograph appeared on the front page of the *Louisville Courier-Journal.* Later that decade, he served under Commandant John Lejeune and led Marines in Nicaragua from 1927 to 1929. There he ensured a successful Nicaraguan national election in November 1928 and guided Marine efforts against insurgent Augusto Sandino. He was considered a candidate for the Marine Corps commandant position in 1930. He retired from the Marine Corps in 1933, died in 1936, and was buried in Arlington National Cemetery. In 1942 the navy commissioned a ship named after him.[11]

Several Kentuckians received the nation's second highest medal for bravery: the Distinguished Service Cross (DSC). Like Feland, Marine Corps private Morris Fleitz of Louisville received his award for gallantry at Belleau Wood in June 1918. On one day at Belleau Wood—June 6—the Marine Corps lost more men than it had in its entire history. Fleitz was cited for making several trips under fire to bring much-needed ammunition and supplies to his comrades in the horrendous battle. In October's bloody Blanc Mont attack, one of Feland's Fifth Marines, Sergeant James Courtney of Falmouth in Pendleton County, made numerous trips under machine gun and rifle fire to rescue wounded comrades. He received a DSC for those heroic actions. Another Fifth Regiment Marine, Theodore Keller of Lexington, had joined the Leathernecks before the war and served in Santo Domingo before shipping to France. Wounded during the Battle of Belleau Wood, he continued to fight in subsequent battles at St. Mihiel and during the final Meuse-Argonne campaign. At the beginning of November, Sergeant Keller managed to keep his Marines in contact with flanking forces during three German counterattacks, thus ensuring they would not be outflanked and overwhelmed. Keller received both the DSC and the French Croix de Guerre for his bravery. Just a few days later, on the last night of the war, a Fifth Regiment Kentuckian from Driprock in Jackson County, Sergeant Samuel Clarkston, distinguished himself by leading a machine gun crew across the Meuse River to establish a stronghold on the other side.[12]

Three Kentuckians received the DSC for their collective action: Lewis County natives Russell Adair (from Tollesboro) and Thomas Gassoway (from Vanceburg), and Clarence Awbry (from Taylorsville in Spencer County). While serving in the army's Company B, Sixth Infantry, on November 7, the three men and a Tennessee soldier, Roland Lynch, "volunteered and went out under heavy machine-gun fire and artillery to rescue a wounded comrade." Failing in their first attempt, the four tried again and brought the wounded man back to shelter.[13]

Known as a "mountain man" and a member of the feuding McCoys, Private Pete McCoy from Thomas in Floyd County "unexpectedly encounter[ed] seven of the enemy" and single-handedly "killed them all with his bayonet and a hand-grenade. As a result of this feat, he captured 4 hostile machine-gun emplacements and took 17 prisoners out of a nearby dugout." McCoy continued to move forward, found a wounded American officer, and had him sent back to safety. McCoy described the encounter more prosaically and in more detail in a 1919 interview in the local Prestonsburg newspaper. Admitting to being "a little scared," McCoy described being pinned down by machine gun fire and throwing a grenade. He recalled, "I went in after them with my bayonet. It wasn't nerve that done it; it was ignorance." He admitted, "I was feeling sick and bloody all over." He concluded, "When it was all over I had killed seven and captured seventeen. I goes on fighting and we kept driving up until the 18th of October, when they got me. I went through them all up to that time, and then I had to be taken to the hospital. I went over the top nine times."[14]

For his bravery, McCoy received not only the DSC but also the Croix de Guerre. The *Washington Post* picked up his story, noting that "Private Pete wears a fighting name and comes from a fighting State, and it will be conceded that upon this eventful September day in France he lived up to his family name." The *Post* opined, "There is no doubt this was one of the greatest individual records made in the American army," and it concluded: "May he wear his medal proudly, and may his descendents cherish it, for Private Pete McCoy is a typical fightin' Yank from Old Kaintuck."[15]

Several other Kentucky DSC recipients were wounded in action. Fifth Marine corporal Edward Melcher from Louisville was wounded in the head and thigh at Belleau Wood but "nevertheless continued valiantly to lead his group through machine-gun and rifle fire to their objective." The head wound required the insertion of a "silver plate." Melcher remained in France until he was gassed, after which he was sent home to recuperate. An Ohio County native from Fordsville, army captain Clarence Mitchell received shrapnel wounds in the leg on November 1, 1918. Aided by a cane and with help from his company runners, he continued to lead his men forward nearly two miles against the enemy. His DSC citation concluded: "His conspicuous courage and fortitude inspired his men to a successful assault against a strongly entrenched position desperately defended by the enemy."[16]

Not all Kentuckians lived to receive their Distinguished Service Crosses. After all the officers and noncommissioned officers in his unit had been killed or wounded, Corporal Steve Combs from Tellega in Lee County took command of his patrol and "pushed forward, capturing a machine gun and his crew. Although mortally wounded a short time afterwards, he constantly called to his companions to continue to advance until he lost consciousness." Private

Carter Koon of Fredonia in Caldwell County made two trips under heavy shell fire to bring wounded comrades to safety; he was killed on his third trip out. Fielding Meek of Smithfield in Henry County died similarly, making his way to help a wounded soldier.[17]

According to his DSC citation, Private Ambers Sapp from Nepton in Fleming County "displayed great coolness and courage under a heavy barrage when he unhesitatingly went forward to destroy enemy wire entanglements and continued this extremely hazardous duty until killed." In July 1918 at Soissons, Sergeant John Simpson from Ready in Grayson County was severely wounded but pressed on, leading a group of men to outflank and take out a machine gun nest; he was killed in the process. A Lincoln County native from Hustonville, Captain John Taylor was wounded five times at Soissons. Nevertheless, when his battalion major was killed, Taylor assumed command and led his men forward in a successful attack. He died of his multiple injuries a month later.[18]

The Great War did not spare famous Kentuckians. A native of Bourbon County, Reuben Hutchcraft Jr. was a talented young man with a bright future. Born in 1886, he was a valedictorian at Transylvania College, an associate editor of the *Harvard Law Review,* and a UK law professor. Elected as a Democrat to the Kentucky House of Representatives for two terms, Paris lawyer Hutchcraft seemed to be on the cusp of a brilliant career when the war broke out. He joined the army in May 1917 and trained to be an officer at Fort Benjamin Harrison in Indianapolis. With a premonition that he might never return, he went to France in late 1917 to fight in the Great War. Writing back home, Lieutenant Hutchcraft at one point assured his mother that he was "very pleasantly located in a place as safe as Fort Benjamin Harrison was." He wrote long letters home describing French country life and what the Yanks did during their seemingly idyllic time behind the lines.[19]

The easy times ended for Hutchcraft and his Rainbow Division comrades with the coming of 1918. As American troops became better trained, they moved into the front lines. Newly promoted Captain Hutchcraft and his men fought in all the major campaigns of the summer. By mid-October, the Americans were helping to roll back the Germans in the final campaign of the war: the Meuse-Argonne offensive. At one point during the battle, Hutchcraft's company captured 200 German prisoners, twenty-seven machine guns, four cannon, and three towns. On November 6, five days before the armistice, Hutchcraft and his men stopped to rest in a bombed-out church. Early the next morning, armed with his Colt .45 pistol, Hutchcraft led a reconnaissance patrol looking for German machine gun posts. When his patrol was pinned down by heavy fire, Hutchcraft crawled ahead to check out the situation and was shot dead.[20]

Reuben Hutchcraft, former state legislator and University of Kentucky law faculty member who died late in the war. (University of Kentucky)

Hutchcraft received the DSC for his actions that evening, and his body was buried in France. His hometown of Paris, Kentucky, held a memorial service for him in February 1919. At the January 1920 opening of the Kentucky General Assembly, Governor Edwin Morrow, senators, representatives, and other state officials held another memorial service. Huchcraft's body was repatriated in 1921, and another service was held. A crowd of 6,000 people came to pay final respects to one of Bourbon County's finest, a hero of the Great War.[21]

Foreseeing US entry into the war, John T. Sullivan Jr. of Newport joined the navy in March 1917 but became dissatisfied by the lack of action. He walked away from his ship in October 1917 and joined the army as John Shannon. Assigned to a machine gun battalion, in July 1918 Shannon "heroically worked alone, exposed to heavy enemy fire, in helping wounded to shelter. He carried water to wounded exposed to sniper fire. When he himself was severely wounded he refused attention, directing that other wounded be removed."

Shannon died when a high-explosive shell shattered his legs; he received the DSC for his bravery under fire. The mystery of his identity was cleared up after the war. Although the navy had listed him as a deserter, Secretary of the Navy Josephus Daniels had a notation about the DSC added to his official record. John T. Sullivan Jr., aka John Shannon, died with honor.[22]

During the war, at least seventy-seven Kentuckians received the Distinguished Service Cross for valor. Nearly all received the award for ground fighting, but two men received theirs for exploits in the air: flying aces Jesse Orin Creech from Harlan and Victor Strahm from Bowling Green.[23]

Jesse Creech joined the Royal Flying Corps in 1917 and trained in Canada. After the United States entered the war, Creech transferred to the US Air Service and served with the 148th Aero Squadron. Creech was credited with shooting down two German airplanes in August 1918. On September 2, 1918, Creech and the other squadron pilots encountered fifteen German Fokker airplanes. In the ensuing dogfight, Creech and four comrades were shot down, but Creech managed to land safely behind Allied lines. He went back up a few days later and was eventually credited with shooting down four more enemy aircraft in September. His seventh victory came toward the end of the war, on October 28, 1918. His DSC citation summed up his actions: "In all of these encounters Lieutenant Creech displayed high courage, great valor, and utter disregard of danger. He constantly went to the assistance of members of his flight and exposed himself with great fearlessness, and yet with all displayed keen judgment and tireless energy. He proved himself a leader of unusual ability, and was a constant inspiration to the members of his command." The British also awarded him the Distinguished Flying Cross.[24]

Captain Victor Strahm was the son of Franz Strahm, a German immigrant and popular music professor at Western Kentucky State Normal School. Strahm graduated from Western in 1915, joined the Army Air Service in 1917, and was posted to France with the Ninety-First Aero Squadron. Strahm had many close encounters during the war. He was one of six American aces who

American flying ace Victor Strahm from Bowling Green. (Western Kentucky University)

flew the French Salmson 2 reconnaissance biplane. While flying low over enemy territory, Strahm shot down five enemy planes. On one occasion, three German triplanes attacked his plane, but he and his rear-seat observer drove them off and outdistanced them. One mission in particular earned Strahm the Distinguished Service Cross. Flying less than 300 feet above the ground and subject to intense antiaircraft fire, Strahm was attacked by several German planes near Metz, France. He managed to shoot down one of them and complete his mission, thereby "displaying remarkable courage and skill." For his actions he also received the Croix de Guerre.[25]

Several Kentuckians received the French Croix de Guerre, often in addition to other medals. Sergeant Gordon Hambrick of Georgetown received both the Croix de Guerre and the French Medaille Militaire, as well as the DSC, for his actions. As noted earlier, then-colonel Logan Feland of Hopkinsville received the DSC and a total of six Croix de Guerres for his action at Belleau Wood and subsequent leadership of the Fifth Marine Regiment.[26]

The French awarded the Croix de Guerre for a variety of actions they deemed heroic (not necessarily for gallantry under exceptional circumstances). For example, an honoree could receive the medal for being mentioned in a citation, even though his actions might not merit a Medal of Honor or a Distinguished Service Cross. A chaplain and Dominican priest from Louisville, the Reverend Edmund Baxter, was twice cited for meritorious conduct. He ministered to the wounded and dying while under continuous shell fire, thus earning the French decoration.[27]

John Shishmanian received the Croix de Guerre for his service in the French Foreign Legion. Born in Lexington to an Armenian father, the Reverend George Shishmanian, John graduated from Transylvania College, attended the University of Virginia Law School, and served in the Kentucky National Guard. At the onset of war he went to France as part of the American Ambulance Field Service, which transferred wounded French soldiers from the battlefields to hospitals in Paris. He then joined the French Foreign Legion, rising from private to captain. He was twice wounded and appeared nine times in citations.[28]

Kentucky African Americans faced discrimination from US officials but were given awards by the French government for their services. Gus Nurse of Earlington in Hopkins County received the Croix de Guerre for rescuing his sergeant from the battlefield. Lon Adams from Mayfield and Leslie Burnham from Mt. Sterling also received the award.[29]

Women also received the Croix de Guerre. Having been a nurse for a dozen years, Mary Willie Arvin of Henderson joined Base Hospital No. 5—the "Harvard Unit"—in July 1917 and served for twenty-two months as a Red Cross nurse in France. The hospital where she worked was bombed twice. Writing home to her sister, she described one attack in which German planes dropped five bombs, killing the unit adjutant and five patients and wounding sixteen others: "The explosion threw me to the floor. A wounded man yelled at me to lie on the floor." Eschewing this advice, Arvin ran to assist another nurse caring for her patients. For her actions, Arvin received a citation from General John Pershing, in which he noted that her "presence of mind and courage in quieting our patients was, under the circumstances, deserving of the highest praise." Pershing concluded: "I am proud to have in the American Expeditionary forces a nurse whose devotion to duty is of such a high character as yours." In addition to receiving the Croix de Guerre, Arvin was presented the British Royal Red Cross medal by Edward, Prince of Wales, in a ceremony in Washington, DC, in November 1919.[30]

Possibly the most unpublicized and intriguing war work by a Kentuckian was that of Louisvillian Louis Hite Jr. As a result, he was awarded France's highest honor, the Legion of Honor, established by Napoleon Bonaparte in 1802. Hite received the Legion of Honor's first rank—Chevalier (Knight)—for his intelligence work during the war while attached to the French army and for his postwar efforts with Herbert Hoover's American Relief Commission in the Near East and the Balkans. A *Louisville Times* article noted that although Hite's intelligence exploits could not be revealed, they "were thrilling enough to form the chapters of a Phillips Oppenheim novel." (A forerunner of Ian Fleming of James Bond fame, E. Phillips Oppenheim was a prolific and popular British writer of spy novels.) Hite also received the French Order of the Black Star. His war service led him to range far from Kentucky, visiting more than twenty countries during his time abroad.[31]

At least one Kentuckian received an award from France's neighbor, Belgium. Lexington jeweler Victor Bogaert had been visiting his family in Belgium when the war broke out in August 1914. Caught by the Germans behind the rapidly moving forward lines, Bogaert faced the possibility of being executed by firing squad for being a French spy. He proved he was an American citizen and returned home safely. From Kentucky, Bogaert indefatigably championed the Belgian cause, raising money for Belgian relief. For his wartime services, Bogaert received the Belgian Leopold Cross, as well as a Belgian knighthood.[32]

Kentuckians also received awards for actions far from the Western Front or for activities that occurred after Armistice Day on November 11, 1918, but before the final treaty with Turkey was signed in 1923.

Several men fought in Russia. Charles Bell of Louisville ended up going to Archangel in northern Russia to fight in the aftermath of the Russian Revolution. He was part of the so-called Polar Bear Expedition, the American North Russia Expeditionary Force that fought alongside British and French forces against the Bolshevik Red Army. During an attack on his blockhouse by the Bolsheviks, Bell received a head wound that blinded him in one eye. Despite the injury, he continued to man his machine gun until relieved. For his bravery under fire he received a British Military Medal, the second highest award given to enlisted men (after the Victoria Cross). Sergeant Harry Keating of Louisville received a British Meritorious Service Medal for capturing a machine gun from the Bolsheviks. A former sergeant in the Kentucky National Guard, Lieutenant Creswell Carson from Richmond in Madison County ended up in the 310th Engineers and received the Russian Order of St. Stanislaus for his participation in the Polar Bear Expedition. Lieutenant Milton Rogers of Lebanon in Marion County received a French Croix de Guerre for his action against the Bolsheviks near Murmansk.[33]

The twin brother of future Kentucky governor Edwin Morrow, Somerset native Colonel Charles Morrow, also served in Russia, but he was stationed in the Far East, in the Baikal sector of Siberia. There he led the Twenty-First Regiment—the "Wolfhounds"—in the Siberian intervention during the Russian Civil War that followed the Revolution. Morrow and his men faced both Bolsheviks and their Cossack opponents while trying to keep the trans-Siberian railway open. The Kentuckian stubbornly faced down notorious Cossack leader Grigorii Semenov, who had a reputation for committing atrocities. For his leadership, Morrow received the Army Distinguished Service Medal, the French Croix de Guerre, and perhaps the most esoteric war decoration earned by any Kentuckian: he was conferred the Third Class of the Japanese Imperial Order of Meiji and invested with the insignia of the Order of the Sacred Treasure.[34]

Kentuckians received awards from Serbia for their medical work during and after the war. Having spent four years in the Sanitary Service in Panama, Frankfort native Clement Chinn served in Serbia in 1915 on an American Red Cross mission to combat a typhus epidemic. When the United States entered the war, he was commissioned in the US Army at Camp Taylor and then served on a sanitary squad with the American Expeditionary Force. On his return to Camp Taylor, newly promoted Captain Chinn worked for the Health Service Department. For his work with the Red Cross in Serbia, Chinn received the Serbian Order of St. Sava. Dr. Dallis Cornwell joined Louisville's Unit D, the Lindenberger Unit; he worked in a Red Cross hospital in Paris and then volunteered for relief work in northern Serbia after the war. He received a Serbian Red Cross medal.[35]

Kentucky newspapers reported that the most decorated Kentuckian was Lieutenant Colonel Edgar Erskine Hume from Frankfort. A graduate of Centre College, Hume studied at Johns Hopkins University to become a physician and then pursued further studies in Germany and Italy. He joined the US Army Medical Corps in 1916, serving on the Mexican border and in the surgeon general's office in Washington, DC. In 1918 Hume went to Italy to command a base hospital and then served in France. In 1919 he became Red Cross commissioner to Serbia. He traveled to the Balkans to oversee medical relief efforts and, in particular, an anti-typhus campaign. For his work in Italy and the Balkans, Hume received nearly two dozen awards from a variety of countries, including Italy, Serbia, Montenegro, Poland, Greece, Romania, Britain, and France.[36]

Many Kentuckians were decorated and cited for their service during and after the war, but thousands of Kentuckians joined the military or civilian agencies and served at home or abroad without decorations or fanfare. Sometimes their experiences were revealed in letters sent home that were reprinted in their hometown newspapers. Due to military censorship rules, wartime letters lacked significant details, such as where the soldiers were fighting. After the armistice, a spate of letters filled in those details.

The Kentuckians who served abroad were exposed to danger, and receiving citations and decorations was irrelevant to how their experiences changed them. Soldiers' letters give us a good idea of what it meant for Kentuckians to serve "over there." They describe training, motivation, battlefield conditions, and leisure activities, and they make observations about foreign countries' customs, people, and landscape.

Although the vast majority of Kentuckians in the military were drafted, they were often strongly motivated to serve a righteous cause. Thomas Hammond of Louisa in Lawrence County wrote that he was "proud to be a Kentucky boy of an organization formed to defend the principles of Democracy and human liberty, and dedicated to the task of keeping unsullied and spotless that great emblem of liberty, truth and unselfishness, the glorious red, white and blue."[37]

John Franklin McDermott of Adair County wrote home from "somewhere in France" in June 1918: "We are drilling pretty hard now, we have got British Instructions, we practice putting on our gass [*sic*] mask most every day, and we have a lot of bayonet practice also." Training to be a sniper, McDermott proudly noted that at the rifle range he had scored bull's-eyes on three out of five shots, and "the others were fairly close." He confided: "If I learn to be a scout it will be hard luck for Germans I see first ha ha." The Adair County boy concluded that he was glad to be in France: "This is a nice looking country. Over here, wheat is almost ripe, pastures are nice and green and they have some nice horse and cattle over here."[38]

Writing on Bastille Day, July 14, Corporal J. B. Bowen of Butler County observed: "France is a beautiful country. It resembles the good old U.S.A. in several ways, but it is old-fashioned, and the scythe is used to cut hay and grain, and the oxen and cart are part of every-day life. The people are a thrifty class, and deserve much credit. The country is in good condition, although it has felt the pressure of an angry War Lord." Bowen explained to his family that he could not tell them exactly where he was in France, since that would be "blue-penciled" by the army censors.[39]

In a letter Lieutenant John Polin wrote to the *Springfield Sun* from "somewhere in France," he marveled: "In this town there is a magnificent Cathedral, the tower of which is some 200 feet high. This morning several of us were up on the top of it, and could see the country for miles; down in the long valley below were numerous old castles and small villages—a prettier sight I have never seen, save the Bluegrass of Kentucky." Polin echoed a theme found in many letters: France was beautiful and fascinating, but it still ranked second behind Kentucky.[40]

Lieutenant David Kahn wrote home about a unique experience: Rosh Hashanah in France. The son of a prominent Jewish grocer in Lexington, Kahn received his officer's commission in October 1917, spent a month at Camp Taylor, and then moved on to serve as payroll officer for the Thirty-Sixth Division at Camp Bowie in Fort Worth, Texas. Sent with his division to France, Kahn made a good connection with Hyman G. Enelow, who had been a rabbi in Paducah and Louisville. Enelow served as overseas commander and general field secretary of the Jewish Welfare Board. Enelow suggested that Paris synagogues would welcome Jewish soldiers, so Kahn and about 2,000 others received permission to visit the French capital for a Sabbath service. Kahn wrote about his experience: "Never in my life have I seen a more beautiful service, more impressive, or more sincere, and never have I been so glad that I was a Jew." The service was conducted in Hebrew, but the sermon was in French. The head of Jewish temples in France, Baron Edmond Rothschild, presented the visiting multinational officers with prayer shawls and prayer books with a French translation. Kahn also witnessed the reading of the Kaddish, the Prayer for the Dead, and was struck by the large number of widows wearing black at the temple.[41]

After the armistice, the soldiers had time to write letters under less restricted circumstances, and their readers were able to experience the war from firsthand sources. Corporal Robert Sheehan from Washington County participated in the Marine Corps' attack on Belleau Wood in June 1918 and later described the battle: "Father such experiences thru which we passed are bound to be filled with a certain amount of confusion. Sometimes they consisted of running, crawling and charging thru a terrific hail of machine-gun bullets, another it would be holding our gains thru rocking barrages of big exploding shells."[42]

In a long letter to his parents, Corporal Ivor Roberts of Springfield wrote about his experiences in a signal battalion during the St. Mihiel offensive. After moving up to the front and digging a foxhole, Roberts settled in under a six-hour artillery barrage. He reported: "We had no longer fixed ourselves in the hole, when the guns began. They seemed to spring up all around us. The whole sky was light as day. The battle was on." He continued: "This barrage lasted for six hours. It was the longest six hours of my life. Each second seemed like the last one. It was folly to even hope of being missed." Roberts admitted: "Anyone who can say he was not scared when he sees shells bursting all around him is either a fool or not in his right mind. I was scared, not of death, because that was certain, but of the gruesome sounds and the awful suspense." A prolific letter writer, Roberts also participated in the final Meuse-Argonne campaign. As the Americans pushed back the Germans, they encountered displaced French refugees. Roberts observed: "They are pitiful to see. They have no homes, are cold, hungry and thinly clad. But even with that they can smile and say 'Bon Americans.'"[43]

Marine Roscoe Nally of Springfield in Washington County wrote to his dad about his battle experience: "I have had three bullets thru my coat, one knocked off my helmet and a big piece of shrapnel tore off a large piece of my coat. I almost gave up hope twice, but I trusted in God and came thru on top."[44]

Having participated in two drives—St. Mihiel and Meuse-Argonne—George Johnston of Russellville in Logan County felt fortunate to have survived "without a scratch," but he admitted, "There were times when it looked as tho' Mrs. Johnston was to become a widow." Johnston lived through two gas attacks and concluded: "My personal opinion is that its horrors have been grossly exaggerated as, with our mask, properly adjusted, one is perfectly safe, and has nothing to fear if, in the case of mustard gas, he changes his clothes and bathes within a few hours after exposure." Johnston recognized, however, that the gas attacks were usually accompanied by heavy shelling, and for wounded men who could not adjust their masks, this meant death.[45]

Serving in the 120th Infantry Division, Private Owen Watson of Adair County wrote about the Meuse-Argonne offensive: "We started on the 29th of Sept. to break the Hindenburg line and we have been after them ever since, but I think we are out for awhile now. And mother I went through some awful dangerous places. I don't see how I got through. I am sure the Lord was with me and he will always be with me now, and I am not afraid now, and I think I will get through alright. So don't worry about me." He continued: "We run the Dutch [Germans] back the other day and captured some French people the Germans had captured the first of the war. They sure were glad to see us Americans and to be free again." Noting that folks back home had asked about France, he wrote: "It is the prettiest place I ever saw but is badly torn up. The towns are tore to pieces."[46]

Bryan Royce of Adair County told his wife about a "big battle" where he had "lost several of my good friends." He was "thankful to God though that it was as well as it was." Reflecting his religious beliefs, Royce wrote that before the battle, "I was praying to God, and asking him to guide us through the battle that we were to take part in. I was not excited hardly at all." Obviously taking his strength from the Bible, Royce suggested to his wife, "If you have not read the 11th chapter of St. Mark, read from the 22nd verse on down, anyway." He concluded: "I feel that if God is with us we can do whatever we undertake to do." Royce was wounded on October 11, 1918, and died the next day. He left behind a wife and a young son that he never saw.[47]

After the war, Fred Ragland of Butler County admitted he had "seen some tough times over here, and been over the top three times. It was burning hell, but I made it through, though some of my comrades got wounded and killed. I am in Germany doing guard duty, guarding tunnels and bridges." He added: "I was on the front the day the guns ceased firing. Our company was the first to cross over the river into the town of Stenay. We did not holler, as we were afraid it was not so. The Dutch [Germans] treated us fine, and you would not think they were our enemies. When I am mustered out of the army I am coming home as straight as the train can bring me."[48]

After being shot and then captured near the end of the war, Sergeant Homer Beliles of Butler County wrote home: "We were making a little drive on the 1st of November, and had completed our drive with great success. And after we got our line the Germans gave us a counter attack and I got shot in the leg just below the hip joint. I reckon I am getting along all right now. I was shot through the bone. But the worst of all, I will tell you now." Beliles had faced about a dozen attacking Germans, and he shot twelve times. Then, he told his mother, "I don't like to say what I did to them [the Germans]. So you can guess as I am a good shot with my rifle." Beliles was being taken to the aid station when he was captured by Germans, who took him to Metz, France. The armistice came soon thereafter, but Beliles complained: "The Americans have neglected us. They pass through daily but don't give us any assistance. The French are all that help, and they are very good to us."[49]

Some letters recounted experiences at sea. Sailing across the Atlantic on the British troopship HMS *Kashmir,* Seaman Bernard Smith from Springfield witnessed one of the worst naval tragedies of the war. Writing after the war, Smith described standing on the hurricane deck during a fearful storm, with waves "rolling up a hundred feet high" and "tossing [the ship] around side to side like a piece of paper in a whirlwind." Holding on to a post, Smith watched with horror as the troopship HMS *Otranto* cut across the *Kashmir*'s bow. Smith described the collision: "Our ship tried to stop, but too late. It came up on the crest of a big wave and bang, it went down on the side of *Otranto* and tore an awful hole in the side of the ship and almost upset it." A half dozen Kentuckians died on the *Otranto,* but more than a dozen survived. Overall, 470 Americans perished.[50]

Noting that he had been away from home for eighteen months, with six of them spent in France, Private S. H. Parks hoped he would not have to spend another six months abroad. He wanted to return home to Butler County. But perhaps like most Kentuckians who went abroad, he concluded: "I sure am glad I came over here for I have seen lots otherwise I would'nt."[51]

As recounted in an earlier chapter, Kentuckians created medical units to serve abroad. A Woodford County native from Versailles, Alpha Barnes Nash graduated from Lexington's Good Samaritan Hospital School of Nursing in 1910. Through the Red Cross, she joined the Barrow Unit, Base Hospital No. 40, in the summer of 1917. In March 1918 she received an appointment as a reserve nurse in the Army Nurse Corps before shipping out to England in July. There she served in a hospital in Liverpool, putting in long hours caring for convalescing soldiers. During her limited leisure time, she managed to travel a bit in England. Based on his examination of Nash's diary, Clark County author Jerry Cecil believes she acted in a "motherly way" toward her patients and was "motivated by the drive to both comfort the men professionally and emotionally."[52]

Nash cared for soldiers during the flu epidemic in the fall of 1918, and although she did not contract the flu, she did become ill. Nevertheless, she continued to assist other sick nurses as well as her patients. Her work became more enjoyable after the armistice in November, when the hospital became an embarkation facility for soldiers returning home. At the beginning of 1919 she traveled not only in England but also in Scotland, Ireland, and Wales. She returned home in April 1919 and was discharged from the Army Nurse Corps in May. Cecil believes that by serving in England, Nash had a broader experience than if she had served at the front: "She did not escape the 'vulgarity of the battlefield,' but instead became a participant and observer in the larger effort to nurture and care for everyone, not just the shattered bodies and souls of those who went 'over the top.'"[53]

Sometimes several members of a Kentucky family served their country simultaneously. The *Louisville Evening Post* ran a periodic column, "War Families," dedicated to families with three or more members in the military. The Hertzmans of Louisville had six sons ranging in age from eighteen to twenty-six who had joined the army. The third oldest made it to France, while the others remained in the United States; the two youngest were enrolled in the SATC. Mr. and Mrs. Gottlieb Wittwer from Oldham County had a blended family of six sons. Three ended up going abroad, and three served in the United States. Fortunately, all six came through the war without a scratch. The Minnichs from Oil Springs in Johnson County had two daughters, Elizabeth and Margaret, who graduated from Berea College with nursing degrees and went to England with the Barrow Unit. Elizabeth served at Sarisbury Court, the unit headquarters near Winchester in the south, while Margaret was detached to a Red Cross hospital at Paignton in Devonshire in southwestern England. After the armistice both women went to France, where they served until they sailed home in July 1918 and were discharged a month later. Their brother John, also a Berea graduate, served domestically with the new Chemical Warfare Service until being discharged in December 1918.[54]

Not all Kentuckians who went abroad served in the military. Many were affiliated with civilian organizations, primarily the Red Cross and YMCA. Nearly two dozen Kentuckians served overseas with the Red Cross, including William Marshall Bullitt and William Belknap of Louisville. A Princeton graduate and former US solicitor general, Bullitt served as deputy commissioner of the Red Cross in Europe. Yale graduate Belknap served as a captain in command of a Red Cross district in Romsey, in southern England, and then in Plymouth, in southwestern England.

Sisters Mary and Sunshine Sweeny from Lexington joined the YMCA and went to France to be canteen workers. Mary had been chair of the Department of Home Economics at the University of Kentucky, and Sunshine had revitalized the family farm. When Mary decided to go to France with the YMCA, Sunshine followed. Attached to the Eighty-Second Division, the "All-Americans," the sisters worked in YMCA units near the front lines under shell fire, serving food and drink to soldiers. They were subsequently cited by the division for gallantry and "exceptional meritorious service."[55]

More than seventy Kentuckians spent time as German prisoners of war, and some recounted horrific experiences. Louisvillian Leslie Pedigo was aboard the British steamer *Esmeraldas* when it was captured by the Germans in March 1917. Pedigo later reported that he had been housed in Lubeck on Germany's northern coast, where he was forced to unload pig iron from ships for fourteen hours a day. Sleeping in ship bunks in a warehouse, Pedigo and his fellow prisoners subsisted on "snail soup, and boiled, and sometimes raw turnips." Pedigo tried to escape four times, for which he suffered: "The treatment which we got when we were recaptured, I can't describe. It was too terrible." Another Kentuckian from the *Esmeraldas,* Charles Perkins of Lott in Whitley County, was a German prisoner at the same time as Pedigo.[56]

Charles Porter of Louisville enlisted with the Canadians in 1914, was wounded three times, and was captured by the Germans and spent four months in a German hospital. Sent to a farm in Westphalia, Porter claimed he was "beaten with iron rods and starved." He later worked as a prisoner of war in coal mines and steel mills. (A question later arose, however, about whether he had truly been a prisoner. His wife Pearl sought and received a divorce, claiming Porter had remarried while in Germany.)[57]

The Germans captured Lee Whitehead of Jeffrey in Monroe County in July 1918. He recalled meeting some of the 250 British prisoners (out of 1,500) the Germans had recently captured; the other 1,250 had died of starvation. Whitehead believed that had it not been for the Red Cross, he and others also would have died of starvation. Ray Boyd of Hopkinsville was captured just a few days before the armistice. "Bringing down" two Germans in a fight, he was wounded, hospitalized, and eventually repatriated to the United States in spring 1919.[58]

At least one Kentuckian was captured by the Bolsheviks after fighting in Russia: John Triplett of Lackey in Floyd County. He was released by way of Sweden, allegedly as part of a plot by his Russian captors to convert prisoners to Bolshevism and send them home to agitate in favor of communism.[59]

Kentuckians went "over there" in great numbers. Some went "over the top," fighting in fierce battles on the Western Front and in northern Russia, Siberia, and the Middle East. Other Kentuckians served in support units, often close to the front lines and danger. Many had never before traveled out of their counties, much less the state or the nation. They had transformative experiences, meeting new people, seeing new sights, and encountering new customs.

Some Kentuckians received decorations; most simply served to the best of their ability, without official recognition. Instead, they were welcomed home by their communities, feted with parades, and commemorated in memorials. For most Kentuckians, their service abroad had been relatively short term, usually less than a year. That time abroad, however, could make an impression that lasted a lifetime.

14

End of the War and Aftermath

American troops began pouring into France in large numbers in 1918, and by summer they were heavily engaged in the fighting. Kentuckians found themselves in the thick of the battle abroad while war support at home increased. The newly funded Kentucky Council of Defense continued to coordinate state war efforts, working with various organizations and county councils of defense. In the meantime, American troops in France began pushing back the Germans as Allied forces went on the offensive in the late summer. After nearly four years of stalemate on the Western Front, the war started to change rapidly. At the beginning of October, Germany made overtures seeking a possible end to the war.

In Kentucky, as well as in the rest of the United States, another crisis began in late summer 1918: the onset of the "Spanish lady"—the influenza epidemic. Historian Nancy Disher Baird notes: "For several months the disease ravaged Kentucky. It restricted social, cultural, economic, and political life, killed 15,000 and weakened 300,000 of the Commonwealth's residents."[1]

The large concentration of troops at Camp Taylor offered ripe ground for the flu to spread: the first cases at the camp were reported in September. Despite efforts to contain it, the epidemic soon overwhelmed camp facilities as more and more men became ill. Fifteen barracks became hospital wards; doctors and nurses from the Red Cross and civilian ranks were pressed into service, as were hundreds of volunteers. People sent food and drink, and loved ones visited sick soldiers. Despite this help, the epidemic worsened and devastated the camp. Baird points out that "one-sixth of the camp's 60,000 men were hospitalized and 1,500 died." Governor Stanley visited Camp Taylor in mid-October to quell rumors that the soldiers were not receiving proper care. By that time, the epidemic at the camp had reached its peak; although people continued to die, the outbreak of new cases slowed down.[2]

In the far western part of the commonwealth known as the Jackson Purchase, many people "were led to believe that the epidemic was caused by the spreading of 'flu germs' by German agents." At the beginning of October, all public gatherings were banned, resulting in the curtailment of war-related and holiday activities. "Halloween, one of the most traditional of all American holidays, was severely affected by the epidemic." In addition, "the epidemic . . . played a significant role in Kentucky politics . . . because 1918 was an election year." The Purchase's Democratic congressman, Alben Barkley, "was unable to visit his hometown of Paducah due to the impact of the flu." Voters reelected Barkley, but voter turnout was low. After officials lifted the ban on public assemblies in early November, people throughout the region celebrated the end of the war. A second wave of influenza struck, but it was less severe than the first outbreak. Nevertheless, more than 800 people died from the Spanish flu in the eight-county Jackson Purchase region.[3]

Other Kentucky communities suffered from the flu epidemic as well. Baird notes, "By mid-October the disease was ravaging nearly every town, village, and hamlet across the Commonwealth." Cases in large towns numbered in the thousands, while up to 90 percent of the residents of smaller communities suffered. The disease reached into the Governor's mansion, where Stanley's wife and children became ill. In eastern Kentucky, "coal mines closed and oil rigs stood still," resulting in economic hardship because people were not paid when they did not work.[4]

Trying to isolate the disease, the state Board of Health restricted public meetings. Patriotic meetings and campaigns were postponed; churches and schools closed, and other public gatherings were canceled. Universities canceled classes and SATC training. Communities transformed buildings into makeshift hospital wards.

Doctors, nurses, and hospitals were overwhelmed, so other people helped where they could. Traditionally focused on teaching and nursing, various orders of nuns in Kentucky volunteered to help deal with the flu, and stories of their experiences underscore the severity of the epidemic. A Catholic chaplain at Camp Taylor, the Reverend Regis Barrett, issued a call for help, and more than ninety nuns answered. Eleven Sisters of Loretto from Marion County traveled to Camp Taylor, arriving on October 11 to care for patients. One of the youngest nuns, Sister Mary Jean, contracted the flu and died on October 28. Her funeral services, which included a flag-draped casket and a Knights of Columbus honor guard, were attended by military and civilian dignitaries. Sister Mary Jean's body was taken back to her order's Mother House at Loretto and buried.[5]

Other orders of nuns that volunteered at Camp Taylor included the Sisters of St. Francis at Louisville's St. Anthony's Hospital, the Sisters of Mercy at the Sacred Heart Home for elderly women, and the Ursuline Sisters from St. Angela's Home. Several Sisters of St. Dominic traveled up from St. Catherine of Sienna Academy in Springfield to help. A number of other nuns became ill, but survived.

Captain Royden and the medical staff who attended to ill cadets during the flu epidemic. (University of Kentucky)

One of the Sisters of Mercy left an account of her experiences. Assigned to a ward of 120 men, she wrote about her soldier patients: "Many were on the verge of pneumonia. The racking cough, the hemorrhage, fever and delirium, and extreme weakness prostrated these strong men and rendered them utterly helpless." Medical supplies were limited, and the conditions were unsanitary. Working twelve-hour shifts through the night, the Catholic nun admitted: "For the first two weeks at least, the nights spent in the wards were hours of incessant toil and watch." The nuns also cared for patients with other medical problems, including "measles, chicken-pox, diphtheria, and worst of all, meningitis."[6]

A large contingent of Sisters of Mercy from Cincinnati traveled to Lexington at the beginning of November and dispersed into eastern Kentucky, where the lack of medical resources was especially critical. Four pairs of nuns went to West Liberty (Morgan County), Hazard (Perry County), Blackey (Letcher County), and Grahn (Carter County). Another eight sisters went to Van Lear in Johnson County, where Sister Mary Raphael O'Conner contracted the flu and eventually returned to the Mother House in Cincinnati to die. The Sisters of Mercy reported heart-rending scenes from eastern Kentucky; in one family, seven children were sick in one bed.[7]

As the epidemic finally began to abate, schools reopened on November 10, and people across the state gradually resumed the natural rhythms of life. Flu cases continued into 1919, but not at the epidemic level. Flu deaths in Kentucky numbered 545 in 1917, rose dramatically to 8,699 in 1918, and numbered 4,943 in 1919. Historian Baird sums up: "Kentucky suffered severely from the Spanish influenza—more severely than she had suffered from the war in Europe. The impact of the disease on the state was immeasurable. During the crucial final months of the war the illness hampered war production, almost brought military training to a standstill, temporarily curtailed the education of the state's youth and caused untold hardships because of financial losses. Six times as many of the state's citizens died of Spanish influenza as gave their lives while serving their country."[8]

In early October 1918 Kentucky newspapers reported a German overture toward armistice. In early November the premature news of an armistice was reported in several communities. On November 8 the *Big Sandy News* in Louisa proclaimed: "War Is Over." The newspaper stated that the armistice had been signed and fighting would cease nine hours later. The false stories were the result of an erroneous United Press report that was reproduced in many newspapers across the country. The premature news produced a "pandemonic celebration in Wickliffe" in western Kentucky, as the town "went wild with enthusiasm, and every bell, pistol, shotgun, anvil, automobile and flag available were employed by men and women."[9]

When the real armistice was signed, signaling the end of hostilities at the eleventh hour of the eleventh day of the eleventh month, massive celebrations erupted throughout Kentucky. People poured into the streets; Kentuckians fired pistols into the air; businesses suspended work. The armistice proved to be a boon for fund-raising for the United War Work Campaign in Elkton, which raised $1,200 of its $1,800 quota in less than an hour.[10]

With more than 4 million Americans under arms, demobilization of the military required a huge effort. Two million men remained overseas at war's end, and they needed transportation home and out-processing. When the troops arrived home, many of them passed through Camp Taylor. It was one of the largest demobilization centers in the United States, with an anticipated half a million men scheduled to rotate through on their way home. The Field Artillery Central Officers Training School (FACOTS) was one of the first programs to disband, as its 7,000 men wished to return home immediately.

Men had to be physically examined before being discharged, equipment had to be accounted for, and various forms had to be signed. Administrative

Armistice Day celebration in Louisville. (University of Louisville)

problems cropped up, ranging from a lack of sufficient forms to poor coordination of trains to transport men from Louisville to their homes. A *Louisville Courier-Journal* editorial cautioned, "As the peace-loving people of the world learned to their sorrow that a million men didn't and couldn't 'spring to arms overnight' to check the aggressions of militant autocracy, now we are learning to our vexation that the army omelette can't be unscrambled quite as quickly as some expected in the hope of having the soldier boy home by Thanksgiving."[11]

After the soldiers serving at Camp Taylor were demobilized, the camp began to receive troops returning from abroad. The arrival of three units caused special celebrations: the 138th Field Artillery, composed largely of Kentuckians from the old First Kentucky Regiment, the "Louisville Legion"; the 84th Division, the "Lincoln Division," comprising men from Kentucky, Indiana, and Illinois; and the 814th Pioneer Regiment, the "Black Devils," composed of African Americans from Kentucky, Tennessee, and Alabama.[12]

The demobilization process took time. For example, the hospital group from Lexington, the Barrow Unit, did not return home from England until April 1919. Some Kentuckians served in military units occupying parts of Germany during the negotiations in Paris leading to the Treaty of Versailles. The peace treaty was finally signed on June 28, 1919, five years after the assassination of Austrian duke Franz Ferdinand.

By April 1, 1919, army chief of staff General Peyton March estimated that about 40 percent of the troops had been demobilized. The *Louisville Courier-Journal* editorialized that demobilization had in fact been rapid, but it cautioned that people were equating armistice with peace. The newspaper pointed to unrest in Germany and Russia as it chided critics for demanding more rapid demobilization.[13]

Kentuckians in the military were in a hurry to return home. This was especially true of farmers from rural areas, where corn and tobacco crops still needed tending and next year's spring planting had to be planned. The state's selective service head, Major Henry Rhodes, asked General Crowder to release agricultural workers first. Rhodes cited the need to keep the farms producing food for Europe's starving populations. Crowder passed along the request to the army adjutant general.[14]

Businessmen also wanted to get home quickly to take care of their affairs, and some Kentuckians asked their political contacts for help. Governor Stanley telegraphed General Crowder asking that W. B. Wickliffe be released from his service at Camp Taylor, where he had languished for fourteen months in the camp's Quartermaster Department. Wickliffe's father, W. A. Wickliffe, was a lawyer, judge, coal company owner, and chairman of the Green County Democratic Committee. Stanley argued that young Wickliffe was needed to help run his father's coal company in Greenville and thus maintain its maximum output of badly needed coal. Crowder replied that he did not have jurisdiction over this matter but would take it up with the army's adjutant general.[15]

Various organizations tried to assist the men who were returning home. The US Employment Service, Red Cross, and YMCA placed men in jobs. The Kentucky Council of Defense urged city, county, and state officials to renew public improvement projects and thus provide employment for returning veterans. The KCD also encouraged counties to establish soldier employment bureaus.[16]

Another idea to help soldiers was a settlement program in rural areas, in keeping with the American tradition of rewarding veterans with land. The most prominent proposal came from Secretary of the Interior Franklin K. Lane. This plan envisioned soldiers moving into agricultural communities that were "large enough to insure social and economic advantages to the colonists with adequate governmental supervision and guidance to assure successful settlement." These colonies would be the result of federal-state cooperation: the states would provide reclaimable land, and the federal government would provide the economic resources necessary for reclamation projects as a prelude to the soldiers becoming farm owners.[17]

In early 1918 the Kentucky General Assembly passed a resolution encouraging the federal government to use soldiers to reclaim land. The Louisville Board of Trade (BOT) established a committee headed by Charles Huhlein to investigate the possibility of reclaiming 225,000 acres of western Kentucky land, enough to provide 80 acres for 2,500 soldiers. Agricultural Extension Service director Fred Mutchler, extension agents Morgan Hughes and D. D. Slade, and BOT secretary William E. Morrow assisted Huhlein. Interior Department official H. P. Griffith of the Reclamation Service visited Louisville to discuss the project.[18]

The dean of UK's College of Agriculture, Thomas Poe Cooper, considered this idea "a most important one" and suggested to UK president Frank McVey that the university play a large role in this project. McVey agreed; he believed the project was "a matter of considerable importance." He suggested to Interior Department official Elwood Mead that the College of Agriculture manage the project.[19]

Another Interior Department official, George Wheeler, visited Louisville in mid-February 1919 to discuss the state's participation in the soldier land settlement program. He estimated that Kentucky could contribute 100,000 to 150,000 acres for reclamation. Wheeler emphasized that the communities the soldiers built should include churches, schools, entertainment venues, and the like. Noting that Kentucky's soil produced excellent crops, Wheeler believed it was a shame that so many acres of land remained unused.[20]

Governor A. O. Stanley appointed a Soldiers' Land Settlement Committee headed by McVey; members included Owsley Brown from the KCD, as well as prominent farmers and businessmen Harvey Chenault of Richmond, W. A. Wickless of Greenville, and W. F. Bradshaw of Paducah. McVey envisioned that the committee would have land surveyed to determine what could be used for the project. Federal authorities looked forward to Kentucky's participation in the Interior Department's proposed program, and department officials noted that they continued to receive many inquiries from Kentucky soldiers about the plan.[21]

Opposition to the soldier land settlement plan began to build, however. At the national level, House of Representatives majority leader Frank Mondell (R-WY) introduced a bill to fund the soldier settlement act but encountered problems within his own party. Representative William Boies (R-IA) thought the plan was a swindle backed by men trying to sell swampland or desert. He favored giving direct payments to veterans. A *Louisville Courier-Journal* editorial noted that respected Representative "Uncle Joe" Cannon (R-IL) had decried the plan as a land-grab scheme by development companies. The *Courier-Journal* questioned the alleged demand for farms by veterans, noting a popular musical comedy song about the "unwillingness of soldiers to return to the farm 'after having seen Broadway.'"[22]

In Kentucky, John Humphrey, head of the Department of Markets at UK's College of Agriculture, wrote to Dean Cooper criticizing Mondell's bill, especially the proposed $500 million expenditure. Humphrey found the bill too restrictive with regard to the soldiers' ability to resell the land, and he believed the country had "not yet reached the point where the dearth of agricultural lands should compel the Government to enter into a paternalistic proposition of this kind." He also questioned whether soldiers and sailors were really clamoring for farms, especially under the conditions laid down in the bill. As a result, Cooper had a change of heart, and in a letter to McVey, he concurred with Humphrey and concluded that the act "from an agricultural standpoint is not advisable." He questioned whether land had to be reclaimed to supply farms to soldiers, observing that funds would be better used to enable soldiers to buy property in their respective communities.[23]

Despite the backing of the newly formed and quickly powerful American Legion, the farm settlement program never received the necessary support from Congress. Commercial farmers opposed the plan, and it became branded as a "reclamation scheme and speculator's plot." Secretary Lane's plan lacked true support, and given the political opposition, "the Interior plan could not attract sufficient backing to carry it into effect."[24]

The issue of soldier land settlement also came up at a major postwar conference sponsored by the KCD and led by McVey. Consistent with the Progressive nature of some of the state's domestic war efforts, a State Conference on Kentucky Problems took place at the University of Kentucky on March 4–5, 1919. The 120 attendees represented individual and organizational interests. For example, Frances Beauchamp represented the WCTU, and Mat Cohen the Kentucky Department of Agriculture. Other attendees included Dean Cooper and his wife; KCD member Sam Halley and his wife, representing the Woman's Club; and future governor Edwin Morrow (1919–1923).[25]

Speakers included leaders of Kentucky's domestic war efforts, such as Sallie Bruce and Charles Huhlein, and experts from outside the state. KCD chairman Edward Hines called the meeting to order and gave a short speech in which he noted, "The Great War has shown us many things in our American life which need to be changed if our democracy is to endure." He praised the wartime spirit of community organization and cooperation and said he believed it should be applied to peacetime. He asked attendees to keep alive the spirit of public service. For this reason, a large segment of the conference was devoted to community organizations. Hines particularly stressed the role of quality education in creating the good citizens who were vital for democracy to thrive.[26]

UK president McVey gave a lengthy talk about the general problems facing the commonwealth in the areas of education, public health, industry, efficient government, and community organization. He too believed the key to solving these problems was education. He suggested that the state quadruple the number of seniors graduating from high school, put more emphasis on science, and apply the arts to practical things. He decried the state's high illiteracy rate—nearly 11 percent—and called for its elimination.

McVey addressed other areas of concern. For instance, the draft had shown that many people suffered from poor health, and the influenza epidemic had revealed the nation's inadequate health care and sanitation systems. McVey hailed the growth of "new agriculture," with better production as a basis for the state's "industry." Mining, lumbering, and oil industries needed legislative help, along with better transportation provided by good roads and reasonable railway tariffs. Capital and labor interests needed to be balanced. Reflecting the Progressive philosophy, McVey argued that efficient local, state, and national government had to operate "free from graft" and must be supported by an adequate taxation system.

The UK president lauded the patriotic wartime spirit but lamented, "When the ordinary routine of peace comes, this spirit of patriotism drops back and the consequences are that the community continues to move along in the old rut." In concluding his speech, McVey asserted that the Great War had been a turning point in history and that the Commonwealth of Kentucky should "grasp some idea of the great awakening that has taken place." Its citizens should "take steps to carry out some of the things hoped for" and undertake the responsibilities of the "new type of citizenship" engendered by the war.[27]

McVey's speech was filled with Progressive rhetoric, emphasizing the role of education, appropriate government assistance, and the good works of a community that attacked problems through scientific means and the cooperation of its citizenry. Other speakers built on these themes. Arthur Macmahon of the Council of National Defense acknowledged that the country was entering into a difficult period of readjustment that he called "reconstruction." He emphasized the national government's role in solving problems, citing, for example, the US Department of Agriculture's work with state land-grant universities such as the University of Kentucky. During the war the CND had promulgated general principles and encouraged their specific application at the local level, and the council hoped postwar community councils would continue this work.[28]

Speakers at subsequent conference sessions dealt specifically with Kentucky problems. Superintendent of schools V. O. Gilbert presided over an afternoon session on education that included presentations about rural education, care of the mentally ill, education bills before Congress, and illiteracy. Cora Wilson Stewart had been invited to address the group, but she pleaded illness; future governor Edwin Morrow took her place. Presentations about community organization made up the bulk of the conference, with Lieutenant Governor James Black, state agriculture secretary Mat Cohen, and McVey leading sessions. State commissioner of highways Rodman Wiley spoke about the need for good roads, and state health director Dr. Arthur McCormack talked about health issues. Formerly the chief health officer in the Panama Canal Zone, McCormack asserted that Kentucky wasted $127 million a year because of death and illness due to preventable diseases.

The president of the Kentucky Federation of Women's Clubs, Mrs. Lafon Riker, spoke about the role of women's clubs, and Charles Huhlein spoke about commercial organizations such as the Louisville Board of Trade. Speaking primarily about women's work during the war, Sallie Bruce suggested a new goal for the postwar period—a state movie censorship board—on the premise that "the devil has recreation in his hands." On a lighter note, the sessions included community singing, a carryover of a wartime project to help boost morale.[29]

A highlight of the conference came when Huhlein presented three "patriotic medals" to key figures in Kentucky's wartime activities: KCD chairman Edward Hines, food administrator Fred Sackett, and KCD member William D. Cochran (posthumously, as Cochran had died unexpectedly in early February 1919). Chair of the KCD committee on health and education, Cochran was cited for visiting all of Kentucky's counties in support of the war effort. Huhlein presented the medals on behalf of the Kentucky Committee of the National Institute of Social Sciences.[30]

The State Conference on Kentucky Problems proved to be the climax of the Kentucky Council of Defense's efforts. Although he served officially as KCD head until 1920, Hines became the dean of the University of Louisville School of Law in 1919. KCD executive secretary Pendleton Beckley resigned in January 1919 and moved to Paris, France, in 1920 to practice as an attorney and European trust officer for the American Trust Company.[31]

The KCD's work, however, was not quite done. It requested from the state legislature extra time and money to complete a major postwar project: the compilation of county histories of the war effort. This project was overseen by Louisville lawyer Fred Caldwell, who had been appointed state war historian in September 1918. The General Assembly obliged in 1920 by voting funds for the project and extending the council's official life, which eventually ended in

March 1924. Caldwell asked county councils of defense to appoint a network of historians to create histories of county efforts during the war. He provided a template for the historians to use, with sections ranging from the composition of the county council and activities of the various war organizations to clippings, war poems, and pictures. Some county historians made great efforts to include supplementary materials, primarily local newspaper clippings about county organizations and individuals involved in the war. The major part of these volumes consisted of individual records of the county's servicemen and -women. Reflecting the times, the service records were usually segregated. The compilations were sent to Frankfort, bound in brown buckram, and deposited in the respective county clerk's office. Caldwell himself put together a twenty-volume compilation about Kentucky and the Great War, covering more than 100 subjects.[32]

Even while the war raged, Americans formed organizations to memorialize the war and to help both military and civilians with war-related needs. One of the first organizations to crop up was the American War Mothers (AWM); a state chapter was organized in Indiana in 1917, led by Alice French of Indianapolis. French's initial war efforts had focused on food conservation, but she envisioned an expanded role for the mothers of soldiers, believing they had special rights and responsibilities. Thus, she formed this new women's organization "to promote wartime mobilization, to hold the government accountable for their sons' welfare, and to 'sympathize with one another.'"[33]

After French's son Donald went to Camp Taylor for training, she wrote to C. C. Owsley, head of the Camp Taylor Christmas Cheer Club, in November 1917 about sending Christmas presents to motherless boys. At the end of the letter, she added: "We are the first State to organize the mothers of our boys for war service, approved by the Government at Washington."[34]

Alice French had broader ambitions: to expand the group and create a national AWM organization. Membership was restricted to mothers (not stepmothers) whose sons or daughters had served in the military. French wrote to Governor Stanley and asked him to appoint a war mother for Kentucky. Stanley responded by naming Reuben Hutchcraft's mother, Dorcas Ashbrook Hutchcraft, to represent the commonwealth.[35]

The Kentucky war mothers organized an AWM chapter in Lexington on September 26, 1918; a Louisville chapter was also formed that month.[36] The state AWM continued to grow, particularly in central Kentucky. Fayette County war mothers organized a chapter in December 1918 and in two years numbered more than 370 members. After New Year's 1919, war mothers organized in Montgomery, Madison, Bourbon, and Clark Counties. In April 1919 an organizational AWM meeting reaffirmed Dorcas Hutchcraft as its head, and in October the first annual meeting of the Kentucky chapter of the American War Mothers took place in Lexington. In a little more than a year, thirteen chapters had been formed and more than a thousand Kentucky women had joined the AWM. Hutchcraft also served on the national AWM Board of Directors.[37]

At the first annual meeting in October, the Kentucky chapter outlined its goals: support a state memorial building to be built at the University of Kentucky; work with the Kentucky Federation of Women's Clubs to promote conservation; oppose all forms of Bolshevism; cooperate with the American Legion. A key project focused on designating a bridge in Frankfort as the American War Mothers Memorial Bridge (which finally occurred when a new bridge across the Kentucky River was completed in 1938). Other concerns included supporting Americanization processes and helping soldiers rehabilitate.[38]

In September 1920 the national AWM convention met in Louisville. At the first meeting of its Executive Committee, the AWM supported the creation of the League of Nations, a position that was becoming increasingly unpopular throughout the United States. The organization also considered a pilgrimage for mothers to visit the tombs of their sons buried overseas.[39]

The national AWM organization continued to grow; it had around 23,000 members by the time it was chartered by Congress in 1924. In Kentucky, the AWM solidified its support of the American Legion. The Kentucky state commander of the American Legion, Emmett O'Neal of Louisville, served as the keynote speaker at the AWM's state meeting in Frankfort in October 1921.[40]

The American Legion had originated from a meeting of American Expeditionary Force members in Paris, France, in March 1919. Initiated by Lieutenant Colonel Theodore Roosevelt Jr. and other officers, the legion's purpose was "the fostering of the spirit of bon-camaraderie developed among the officers and men during the war, a love for the flag and the perpetuation of peace." The 4 million men who had served in the army or navy from April 6, 1917, to November 11, 1918 (and not dishonorably discharged), would be eligible to join.[41]

Judge Henry Moorman from Hardinsburg in Breckinridge County served as the temporary state commander of the Kentucky legionnaires; he had been an artillery corporal during the war. American Legion posts soon sprang up in towns across the commonwealth. By August 1919, sixteen local American Legion posts had been chartered, with another sixteen waiting approval.[42]

The first state convention of the American Legion took place in Louisville in October. Twenty-six Kentuckians from around the state attended as delegates. There, they endorsed pending congressional legislation for more pay for veterans, declined to condemn the League of Nations, condemned the Ford

Motor Company and Standard Oil of Kentucky for failing to keep promises to employees, and suggested to national headquarters a union of the American Legion and US Secret Service "for the purpose of ferreting out secret, intriguing, un-American individuals and societies operating to undermine the Government."[43]

A caucus in St. Louis drafted a constitution in May, and in September the American Legion received a charter from Congress. At the first annual meeting in Minneapolis in November, the legion adopted the constitution, established that its headquarters would be located in Indianapolis, and passed a resolution supporting the Boy Scouts of America. The American Legion quickly became one of the largest and most powerful proponents of veterans' rights, as well as an opponent of Bolshevism and a supporter of youth programs designed to promote "Americanism."[44]

One of the most visible accomplishments of the American Legion was its memorial activities. Author Steven Trout asserts that the American Legion was "*the* driving force in American First World War commemoration." He notes that "between 1919 and 1941, no remembrance organization in the United States expended more energy, raised more money, or enjoyed more success when working to maintain the Great War (especially the memory of its fallen) as a living presence in American culture."[45] The legion's efforts can be found throughout Kentucky, as part of a larger state effort to remember its veterans and, in particular, its war dead.

Kentucky already had a history of memorializing its war participants. Historian Ann Marshall points out that post–Civil War memorials to the Confederacy helped create a "Confederate Kentucky" in the latter part of the nineteenth century.[46] The idea of commemorating the Great War through memorialization developed quickly after the armistice in November 1918.

Kentuckians sought to honor and memorialize their fallen soldiers in several ways. In a letter to Governor Stanley, Secretary of Agriculture David Houston suggested planting trees on Arbor Day to commemorate Kentucky's fallen military. Lexingtonians followed through on this suggestion in April 1919 when a thousand spectators, including many soldiers and sailors in uniform, gathered on the University of Kentucky campus to plant fifty-two trees dedicated to the men from Fayette County who had died in the war. Congressman J. Campbell Cantrill eulogized the fallen men. The gathering also dedicated a fifty-third tree to the memory of recently deceased former president Theodore Roosevelt.[47]

By mid-1919, a fifty-person committee led by KCD chairman Hines considered building a statewide war memorial on the University of Kentucky campus. The committee included politicians such as former US senator Johnson

Camden from Versailles, KCD officials such as Richard Stoll, war organization leaders such as R. C. Ballard Thruston, state officials such as highway commissioner Rodman Wiley, Women's Club leader Mrs. Lafon Riker, and other state notables such as Patrick Henry Callahan. They envisioned a multipurpose student building with a large auditorium, "in the abiding hope that it shall be a source of inspiration and helpfulness to the generations of young Kentuckians who shall, from year to year, seek education and leadership at the University." A subscription campaign to raise the estimated $300,000 in building costs started in earnest at the UK commencement in June 1919, when students pledged $3,500 and faculty pledged $4,500 for the project. Mrs. Riker's Kentucky Federation of Women's Clubs endorsed the project, as did the Kentucky Educational Association and various civic organizations.[48]

Fund-raising for the project languished, however, in the face of other needs. Nevertheless, UK's Memorial Hall, topped by a now-iconic clock tower and featuring a Corinthian-columned porch, was finally dedicated in 1929. Inside the building, tablets commemorate the names of Kentucky's soldiers who died during the Great War.[49]

Similarly, an attempt by Louisvillians to create a war memorial initially ran into difficulty. Early in 1919 the construction of a memorial civic center was proposed, an outgrowth of a prewar proposal to build a municipal auditorium. This project merged into a combined auditorium and war memorial costing $1 million. The state legislature authorized the project in 1920, stipulating that half the sum be funded by donations and the other half by a bond issue approved by voters. The project garnered support from several groups, including the Louisville Board of Trade and Jefferson County Democrats, as well as prominent citizens such as the new owner of *Louisville Courier-Journal* and *Louisville Times:* Robert Bingham. Despite an optimistic prediction of success, the bond issue failed to garner the necessary two-thirds majority in the November 1920 election.[50]

Supporters of the Louisville war memorial auditorium were unbowed by their defeat. They had to wait, however, until another bond issue was authorized by the 1922 state legislature, which met only in even-numbered years. Another memorial commission, again headed by Bingham and including Fred Sackett, Henry Vogt, and Patrick Henry Callahan, drummed up support for the new bond issue totaling $750,000, and an intensive publicity campaign led to its passage. After a few years of building delays, the Louisville Memorial Auditorium was finally dedicated on Memorial Day, May 30, 1929.[51]

Communities throughout the commonwealth erected their own memorials, primarily to honor the local men who had died in the war. Some of these memorials came from the shop of Indiana native, sculptor, and entrepreneur

Memorial Hall at the University of Kentucky, commemorating the service of Kentuckians during the Great War. (University of Kentucky)

Ernest Moore Viquesney. After the war, Viquesney sculpted a statue, "Spirit of the American Doughboy," that became the basis of his cottage industry. He fashioned life-size renderings for memorials, as well as miniatures and table-lamp versions. Eight of the full-sized sculptures attributed to Viquesney serve as memorials in Kentucky—in Harlan, Liberty, Monticello, Morehead, Pikeville, Winchester, Grayson, and Jamestown. American Legion posts helped sponsor some of these Viquesney doughboys, including those dedicated in Monticello (1923), Harlan (1930), Liberty (1935), Jamestown (1937), and Grayson (1941). In Morehead, the Rowan County Women's Club sponsored the construction of a pedestal commemorating the county's war dead; it was dedicated on the first anniversary of Armistice Day, November 11, 1919. A decade later, Morehead American Legion Post No. 126 sponsored the addition of Viquesney's doughboy, also dedicated on the anniversary of Armistice Day.[52]

Other cities erected unique memorials. Initially identified erroneously as a Viquesney creation, the impressive World War I memorial in Springfield (Washington County) features statues of both a soldier and a sailor. The inscription pays homage to the "noble sons of Washington County" who "served that liberty shall not perish from the earth." On Armistice Day 1922 a crowd estimated at 10,000 people attended the dedication of the memorial, touted as "the first public stone tribute in Kentucky to be erected by popular subscription." Washington County native George Colvin, then the state superintendent of schools, spoke at the ceremony, as did Colonel Charles Morrow, a much-decorated veteran and Governor Edwin Morrow's brother. Colvin spoke wistfully of his former pupils who had died in the war, while Morrow stressed the need for the nation to remain prepared to counter aggression.[53]

On Armistice Day in 1924, Lexingtonians gathered to dedicate a war memorial, a stone tablet listing the names of Fayette County men who "gave their lives in service during the world war." A project of local American Legion Post No. 8, the tablet includes the name of Lieutenant Alex McClintock. As noted in chapter 1, McClintock had served with British forces on the Western Front before transferring to the US Army. But before he could return to the fighting after the United States committed troops abroad, McClintock committed suicide in a New York City hotel. Acknowledging his traumatic wartime experience and its aftermath, Lexingtonians included his name on the memorial as another Kentucky victim of the Great War.[54]

While memorials were being erected in Kentucky's cities and towns, the US government was building memorials overseas to honor America's fallen. Congress created the American Battle Monuments Commission (ABMC) in 1923 to establish and oversee burial grounds and monuments on foreign soil. General John J. Pershing served as the ABMC's first chairman. More than 30,000 American war dead were buried in eight cemeteries in France, Belgium, and the United Kingdom, with memorials commemorating those listed as missing in action or lost or buried at sea. The largest cemeteries carry the names of major US military actions, such as the St. Mihiel and Meuse-Argonne

World War I memorial, Springfield, Kentucky.

cemeteries. (After World War I, families had a choice: they could have their loved ones' bodies repatriated to the United States for burial, or they could have them buried in these cemeteries.)[55]

Most families could not afford the trip to Europe to visit their loved ones' grave sites, so in the late 1920s the American Gold Star Mothers lobbied Congress for funds to send the mothers of deceased military members to visit their overseas grave sites and memorials. Named after the gold stars worn on armbands or included on service flags to denote the loss of a family member in the Great War, the Gold Star Mothers persuaded Congress in 1929 to authorize funding to send mothers and widows on pilgrimages to European cemeteries. These pilgrimages began in 1930 and concluded in 1933. More than 6,000 women made the voyage, including a few from Kentucky.[56]

Nola Miller Kinne Fogg made the trip in 1933. She was the mother of Howard Kinne of Stearns in McCreary County. Kinne had been an engineering student at the University of Kentucky and a star member of the football and track teams before he joined the army in 1917 at the end of his junior year. After officer and aviation training, he served in France as an aerial observer, taking photographs and operating a machine gun in a two-seat aircraft in the

Ninety-Ninth Aero Squadron. He and his pilot were shot down and reported missing in action behind German lines in late September 1919. Officials later confirmed that the two men had been killed.[57]

On May 15, 1933, Nola Fogg left Kentucky on a train bound for New York City via Washington, DC. In New York she joined more than 120 mothers and widows, including Kate Mike, an "octogenarian Winnebago Indian" who garnered a lot of attention throughout the trip. After being feted in New York City, the party boarded the SS *President Harding* for the six-day voyage to France. Along the way, the Gold Star pilgrimage participants were fed lavishly and entertained, and they watched a ceremony in which a wreath was dropped into the ocean to commemorate all those who had died at sea.[58]

After arriving in France, the women visited tourist sites in Paris for a few days and then moved to Verdun to begin their visits to the battlefields and cemeteries. Nola Fogg was taken to the Meuse-Argonne cemetery, where her son was buried. As she moved toward his grave, she "saw this beautiful wreath and began feeling sad that I had not tried to purchase such a beautiful tribute for my own boy—but as soon as the guide reached it he told me it was for me, and I discovered later that each and *every* one was given just such a wreath." Because the following day was Decoration Day, the more than 14,000 graves were all decorated with French and US flags. Fogg commented in her diary: "It was indeed a beautiful spot and wonderfully kept, but only the wives and mothers could know the agony with the thought of our own being there, so silent." She appreciated the US officers who served as guides, and the doctors and nurses who "often find it necessary to care for pilgrims who are overcome." Fogg could "think of nothing that would be harder to bear than this visit to my dear boy's grave—thinking of our hopes and plans for his future, the wonderful man that he would have been and our great loss as well as his chance to live and I know he wanted to live for he told me."

Each pilgrim was photographed with the cross marking the deceased's grave. Afterward the women proceeded to where the Montfaucon American Monument was being constructed. Along the way, Nola Fogg spotted a pillbox containing machine gun emplacements. Realizing that this was near where her son Howard had been shot down, she wondered if those machine guns had been responsible. Admiring the beautiful countryside, she also noted: "Oh, it was so sad to notice the shell-holes and to wonder if this one or that one might have been the very place where his [her son's] body was found. We will never know, but I do know that he had a part in a great victory and I know that he was brave as well as good and true. It is hard to bear but there is no alternative."[59]

At the St. Mihiel cemetery, Fogg encountered a young officer, Lieutenant

John Hunter, who had served as an aerial observer in the Ninety-Ninth Aero Squadron and had known Howard Kinne and his pilot, "Mack" McElroy. Two days later, after a last visit to the Meuse-Argonne cemetery, the women made their way back to Paris and eventually home, carrying the memories of what would probably be their only visit to their loved ones' graves.[60]

By the time of the Gold Star Mothers pilgrimages in 1933, the world had changed dramatically, especially because of the Great Depression. The Japanese invasion of Manchuria in 1931 and the rise to power of Adolf Hitler in January 1933 portended future conflict. As the 1930s progressed, more and more consideration would be given to future war, rather than the past world war. Some people suggested that the Great War simply sowed the seeds for the follow-up conflict of World War II that began in September 1939.

The Great War had a strong impact on the Commonwealth of Kentucky. Before the United States entered the war, individual Kentuckians who were caught abroad or had relatives in Europe experienced the shock of the war. After the war settled into a deadlock on the Western Front in late 1914, Kentuckians generally turned their attention back to their everyday domestic concerns. Signs of an economic upsurge began to appear, especially in the state's coal and oil industries. In general, however, Kentuckians had little reason to be concerned about the European war; war coverage in most local newspapers was nearly nonexistent. Front pages were dominated by local events, except for momentous occasions such as the sinking of the *Lusitania* in May 1915.

Given its large German and Irish immigrant population, especially in towns along the Ohio River, Kentucky could have been a hotbed of agitation for or against the Allied or Central powers. It was not. Immigrants usually maintained their neutrality, in keeping with President Woodrow Wilson's appeal to the nation. After the Germans resumed unrestricted submarine warfare and US involvement became likely in early 1917, people of the state became more aware of the possibility of war. Unlike neighboring states to the south, where opposition to the war proved somewhat formidable, Kentuckians and their national political leaders fell in line with Wilson's policies. Congressman Swagar Sherley of Louisville was a mainstay of Wilsonian policy regarding US entry into the war, but Kentucky's other congressional delegates also supported the president. Unlike in Mississippi, where James Vardaman emerged as a leader of the opposition, no such figure stepped forward in Kentucky.

After the United States declared war on Germany in April 1917, many Kentuckians enthusiastically supported the war effort. Governor Stanley created the Kentucky Council of Defense, and after a rough, unfunded start, it brought together disparate elements involved in supporting the war. The KCD served its purpose well, coordinating and publicizing efforts when and where necessary and initiating programs as needed. The commonwealth's war support proved most impressive, however, at the county level. Although some counties remained somewhat unorganized and less supportive, these cases were anomalies.[61]

Through the county, state, and national councils of defense, Kentuckians became more directly affected by and tied to the government; during the war they were subject to far more governmental directives and guidance than ever before. The federal and state governments worked hand in hand to decide, to some extent, what people could eat, and when. The government determined what people should believe through a massive propaganda system controlled by George Creel's Committee on Public Information. Together, state and federal governmental entities tracked down and stifled what little dissent cropped up in the commonwealth.

As a result of the war, Kentuckians became more aware that they were part of a larger community. No longer could they relate only narrowly to their own localities—their coal camps, settlements, towns, or cities—or even to their counties. Through such wartime phenomena as the draft, Liberty Bond drives, and Red Cross campaigns, they realized they were part of a larger national consciousness that played a role in international events. This new awareness manifested itself in the many patriotic meetings that took place throughout the commonwealth. American flags, service flags, Gold Star Mother banners, food pledge cards in the window—all these things reflected an increased pride in country and illustrated the contributions made during a time of perceived crisis. The total war spawned by the Great War required that every man, woman, and child do their part, and Kentuckians largely accepted this civic duty.

World War I was a foretaste of greater government intervention during the Great Depression and World War II. But this government supervision in pursuit of a total war effort exacted a price. While government officials quelled dissent, individuals strongly supported these efforts. There were several cases, however of "concerned citizens" who were much too eager to accuse their neighbors of being "slackers." The idea of rugged individualism, a legacy of the commonwealth's earlier settlers, suffered. People either joined in the collective pursuit of war victory or remained outside the pale, ostracized as unpatriotic.

In some cases, such as the first and second Liberty Loan campaigns, support for the war started slowly. Once Kentuckians were drafted, sent abroad to fight, and sometimes killed, the war became more personal and urgent. When the Kentucky Council of Defense and federal food and fuel administrators became more organized, war-support efforts increased and became more efficient. By the spring of 1918, Kentuckians in general were fully invested in the war, supporting a variety of programs. Civic consciousness grew exponentially, as more people participated in these programs. The tremendous growth of the Red Cross in the state best reflected these efforts, as thousands of Kentuckians gathered together to do their part to "help lick the Kaiser."

A striking feature of Kentucky during the Great War was the overall willingness of most people in even the smallest communities to contribute. Kentuckians oversubscribed to Liberty Loan, Red Cross, and other fund-raising campaigns in the latter part of the war. Only a small number of men resisted the draft or deserted. African Americans supported the war despite their legitimate right to question why they should make the world safe for democracy when they lacked political, social, and economic equality at home. Despite rallying to the flag, the commonwealth's African Americans did not forget that they still lived in a segregated and sometimes violent society.

The war had a positive effect on the commonwealth's economy, primarily in its coal- and oil-producing regions. Louisville's economy grew with the construction of Camp Taylor. *Lexington Herald* editor Desha Breckinridge was right when he recognized that a cantonment could be a catalyst for strong economic change. After providing a boost to the Louisville economy during the war, Camp Taylor's postwar dismantling and sale and the subsequent construction of new homes in the neighborhood helped expand Louisville's infrastructure. The camp brought national attention to the city as an example of Henry Watterson's New South, an economic modernization based on urbanization and industrialization. The city's population grew by 5 percent from 1910 to 1920, but from 1920 to 1930 it would boom, increasing by more than 30 percent.

The war accelerated the growing divide between urban and rural Kentuckians. Yet it also helped modernize the latter. The need for increased agricultural production provided an incentive for farmers to become more efficient. The agricultural extension agent system, which received great impetus during the war, and the KCD's reasonably priced tractor program provided scientific, modern approaches to meet increasing demands.

The Great War also had an important social and cultural effect on the commonwealth. Although the war was not solely responsible for Prohibition and women's suffrage, it certainly accelerated the call for both. The state's Prohibitionists reveled in wartime measures such as banning liquor from the vicinity of soldier camps and prohibiting the manufacture of alcohol. Women's sturdy support for the war effort signaled their readiness to participate more fully in civic democracy. In the face of their contributions, Kentucky's male political leadership could no longer reasonably thwart women's quest to vote.

During the war, Progressive reform activities were subsumed to the concentrated war-support effort. Nevertheless, Kentuckians continued to seek Progressive reforms. Eight-hour workdays, campaigns for increased literacy and better health, and an effort to keep children in school all marked an ongoing commitment to making the commonwealth a better place to live. The Kentucky Council of Defense's spring 1919 conference on the state's problems demonstrated an awareness that much more needed to be done. Reform efforts waned, however, in the 1920s during the nation's "return to normalcy."[62]

Kentuckians—both military and civilian—went abroad in great numbers to serve at sea and on land from England to Siberia. Their neighbors enthusiastically supported their actions. At the end of the war the commonwealth proudly touted the contributions and sacrifices of Kentuckians who had served their country. Communities commemorated them with statues, buildings, and bridges.

For a period of nearly two years during the Great War, Kentuckians sublimated their differences to pursue a larger goal: supporting America's war effort. Their differences did not disappear, and issues such as Prohibition and women's voting rights still engendered disagreement. During the Great War, however, Kentuckians of both genders; of all races, religions, political affiliations, and social backgrounds; and from all locales banded together to support the war. They personified the first part of the commonwealth's motto: United We Stand, Divided We Fall.[63]

Acknowledgments

This book has been a pleasure to research because it took me to portions of the commonwealth of Kentucky I have never visited or had not seen in many years. I thank the many librarians, archivists, and historical society members across the state who provided advice and assistance. County clerks graciously allowed me to snoop through their records rooms in search of invaluable county histories regarding the Great War. Kentucky Historical Society director Kent Whitworth and librarian Jennifer Howard went above the call of duty by tracking down materials buried deep in boxes, displaced by the refurbishment of the Kentucky Military Museum. The associate dean in charge of the University of Kentucky Special Collections Research Center, Deidre Scaggs, went the extra mile in uncovering editions of the Kentucky Council of Defense newspaper published by the university. Archivist Brandon Slone at the Kentucky Department of Military Affairs was particularly enthusiastic about helping me with this project.

I am also grateful for the support of friends. Many of them I mentioned in the preface to my previous book, *Kentucky Marine.* Special thanks for their support this time go to the "So Far, So Good" sailing friends: Paul and Susan Harbour and Bill and Billie Strunk. While providing good companionship on canal boat trips in France and sailing trips along the Maine coast, they were truly supportive of my writing endeavors. Billie was especially interested in this one; we had many good conversations about her father, John William Stewart of Trigg County, one of the many Kentuckians who left the commonwealth to serve in France.

Thanks also to Joni and Dale Stowe, Karen and Wayne Yeager, and Rick and Sally Showalter for their interest and support.

At our weekly lunches and golf games, Mark Pittman once again patiently listened to me drone on about Kentucky and the Great War. He always asks good questions and provides enthusiastic support. Thanks, Marine.

The folks at the University Press of Kentucky were once again supportive. Acquisitions editor Ashley Runyon was always positive, helpful, and enthusiastic about this project. I appreciate what Fred "Mack" McCormick, Cameron Ludwick, Jackie Wilson, and Ila McEntire have done for me and look forward to future collaborations. I once again thank copyeditor Linda Lotz for her excellent work on this book.

I give special thanks to my wife, Roi-Ann Bettez, to whom this book is dedicated. She traveled with me to disparate parts of the commonwealth for research, read and discussed the manuscript, and has been the ultimate loving, supporting wife.

I finish with the usual disclaimer: any mistakes in this book are mine alone. I hope that this book encourages other people to study Kentucky history at the local level. I believe they will find it as fascinating and rewarding as I have.

Notes

Abbreviations

KHS	Kentucky Historical Society
KSC	Kentucky State Council
NARA-ATL	National Archives and Records Administration, Atlanta, GA
NARA-CP	National Archives and Records Administration, College Park, MD
OG	Old German
RG	Record Group
SBTS	Southern Baptist Theological Seminary, Louisville, KY
UK	University of Kentucky, Lexington
USPSR	US Public Service Reserve
WKU	Western Kentucky University, Bowling Green, KY

Introduction

1. James Klotter, *Kentucky: A Portrait in Paradox, 1900–1950* (Frankfort: Kentucky Historical Society, 1996).

2. See David Kennedy, *Over Here: The First World War and American Society* (New York: Oxford University Press, 1980). Other books focusing on domestic war efforts include Christopher Capozzola, *Uncle Sam Wants You: World War I and the Making of the Modern American Citizen* (New York: Oxford University Press, 2010); Robert Zieger, *America's Great War: World War I and the American Experience* (New York: Rowman and Littlefield, 2000); and Neil Wynn, *From Progressivism to Prosperity: World War I and American Society* (New York: Holmes and Meier, 1986). Modern studies of state efforts in the Great War remain scarce and focus on only one aspect of the war effort, such as state councils of defense. Exceptions are Michael D. Polston and Guy Lancaster, eds., *To Can the Kaiser: Arkansas and the Great War* (Little Rock, AR: Butler Center Books, 2015); Preston Jones, *The Fires of Patriotism: Alaskans in the Days of the First World War 1910–1920* (Fairbanks: University of Alaska Press, 2013); Martin T. Oliff, *The Great War in the Heart of Dixie: Alabama during World War I* (Tuscaloosa: University of Alabama Press, 2008); and Carl H. Chrislock, *Watchdog of Loyalty: The Minnesota Commission of Public Safety during World War I* (St. Paul: Minnesota Historical Society Press, 1991). For a closer look at two Kentucky counties during the war, placed in the larger context of the early-twentieth-century Progressive movement, see J. Larry Hood, *Visions of Zion: Christianity, Modernization and the American Pursuit of Liberty: Progressivism in Rural Nelson and Washington Counties Kentucky* (Lanham, MD: University Press of America, 2005).

3. A list of county histories and their whereabouts is included in the bibliography. Issues of the *Louisville Leader* can be found online at the University of Louisville Archives and Records Center website: digital.library.louisville.edu/cdm/landingpage/collection/leader/.

4. George Kennan, *The Decline of Bismarck's European Order: Franco-Russian Relations 1875–1890* (Princeton, NJ: Princeton University Press, 1981), 3; Raymond Aron, *The Century of Total War* (Garden City, NY: Doubleday, 1954).

1. War Breaks Out!

1. *Louisville Courier-Journal,* June 29 and July 2, 1914.

2. For coverage of the assassination and its immediate aftermath, see *Lexington Herald,* June 29 and 30, July 3 and 4, 1914.

3. For more on European reactions to the crisis brought about by the assassination of Archduke Franz Ferdinand, see Michael Neiberg, *Dance of the Furies: Europe and the Outbreak of World War I* (Cambridge, MA: Belknap Press of Harvard University Press, 2011), 10–120. Neiberg notes that the European powers had dealt with the Agadir crisis (1911) and two prior Balkan wars (1912 and 1913) that had not led to a major conflict, and "as late as July 28 the Balkan crisis seemed to be far less significant than those previous crises" (86).

4. For more on the Austro-Hungarian versus Serbian aspects of the war, see Geoffrey Wawro, *A Mad Catastrophe: The Outbreak of World War I and the Collapse of the Habsburg Empire* (New York: Basic Books, 2014). See also Sean McMeekin, *The Russian Origins of the First World War* (Cambridge, MA: Belknap Press of Harvard University Press, 2013), for a unique analysis of the origins of the war.

5. There is a vast array of history books on the war. One of the most ambitious recent efforts is Jay Winter, ed., *The Cambridge History of the First World War,* 3 vols. (New York: Cambridge University Press, 2014). Classics include Hew Strachan, *The First World War* (New York: Viking, 2004), and John Keegan, *The First World War* (New York: Knopf, 1999).

6. Ever since the war, historians have debated its causes, some blaming Austrian or Russian aggression, Germany's support of its ally with a "blank check," and the unwillingness of other countries such as France and Britain to take the necessary steps to prevent a localized "third Balkan conflict" from becoming a major European, and eventually world, war. Other historians look for more general causes, including nationalism, militarism, and entangling alliances. The debate continues to fascinate historians. For some of the most recent accounts, see Thomas Otte, *July Crisis: The World's Descent into War, Summer 1914* (New York: Cambridge University Press, 2014); Max Hastings, *Catastrophe 1914: Europe Goes to War* (New York: Knopf, 2013); Christopher Clark, *The Sleepwalkers: How Europe Went to War in 1914* (New York: Harper, 2013); Sean McMeekin, *July 1914: Countdown to War* (New York: Basic Books, 2013); Margaret McMillan, *The War that Ended Peace: The Road to 1914* (New York: Random House, 1913).

7. For news of Ruth James, see *Louisville Courier-Journal,* August 8, 20, and 31, 1914.

8. The story of Nancy Johnson's European trip and escape from the war is found in Mary W. Schaller, *Deliver Us from Evil: A Southern Belle in Europe at the Outbreak of World War I* (Columbia: University of South Carolina Press, 2011).

9. See *Lexington Herald,* July 29, 1914, for a report on Bronston and McCourt, who were in Rome, anticipating a trip to Heidelberg. On August 4, 1914, the *Herald* reported that, according to Thomas Cook and Co., the noted British travel agency, Bronston and McCourt were safe. Another group of central Kentuckians was reported safe in London. See also *Herald,* August 15, 1914.

10. For Bishop Maes and other northern Kentuckians in Europe, see *Kentucky Post,* August 3, 1914. Follow-up stories on Maes are found in *Kentucky Post,* August 19, September 2, 21, 22, and 26, 1914. See *Kentucky Post,* September 9, 1914, for Tappert's comments.

11. See *Louisville Courier-Journal,* July 30, 1914, for articles quoting Turnheim and Mueller; see *Cincinnati Enquirer,* July 28, 1914, for Mouget's willingness to fight for France, despite his advanced age.

12. *Louisville Courier-Journal,* August 4, 1914.

13. *Louisville Courier-Journal,* August 7, September 3 and 9, 1914. See Ronald R. Alexander, "Henry Watterson and World War I," *Journal of the West Virginia Historical Association* 1, 1 (Spring 1977): 15–25, for Watterson's developing views regarding the war. For a biography of Watterson, see Daniel S. Margolies, *Henry Watterson and the New South: The Politics of Empire, Free Trade, and Globalization* (Lexington: University Press of Kentucky, 2006).

14. For the *Louisville Herald*'s stance, see Alexander, "Henry Watterson and World War I," 18. On September 7 and October 1, 1914, the *Louisville Courier-Journal* reported on the German-American Alliance's charge of "discrimination" against Germany by the American press. The editor of the local German newspaper, the *Louisville Anzeiger,* "said it was plain that editorials in the Courier-Journal were dictated by a sense of animosity which he was unable to understand, since the writer [Watterson], for years, had on numerous occasions expressed his friendship and admiration for Germany and German-Americans."

15. *Lexington Herald,* August 30, 1914. Leslie Combs Jr. had been appointed minister to Guatemala and Honduras in 1902 and the first ambassador to Peru in 1906, resigning in 1911; see *New York Times,* January 6, 1911. See *Lexington Herald,* August 14, September 10 and 12, 1914, for reports about Brownell Combs, who, as the newspaper pointed out, "was not near the actual fighting and suffered little inconvenience because of the state of affairs in Europe."

16. See *Lexington Herald,* September 10, 1914, for Combs's letter to the editor. See also the September 12, 1914, editorial acknowledging Combs's letter but noting the "destruction of Louvain, dropping of bombs on Antwerp and Paris, [and] mining of the North Sea" as evidence of German misdeeds.

17. Schlubach's award was reported in *Lexington Herald,* October 13, 1914. Leslie Combs Jr. helped raise his grandson, Leslie Combs II, who would found one of the most successful Thoroughbred farms in central Kentucky: Spendthrift. See Mary Marshall, *Great Breeders and Their Methods: Leslie Combs II and Spendthrift Farm* (Neenah, WI: Russell Meerdink, 2008), 9–11.

18. See *Louisville Courier-Journal,* August 27, 30, and September 2, 1914, for German-American Alliance relief efforts. The *Louisville Anzeiger*'s donation was reported on September 3, 1914. The *Courier-Journal* reported on September 14, 1914, that a Red Cross ship had sailed for Europe with 30 surgeons and 125 nurses, who would be distributed in countries on both sides of the conflict.

19. See *Louisville Courier-Journal,* November 14, 1914, for Lulie Henning as head of the district Belgian Relief Fund; November 15, 1914, for the creation of the supervisory committee; November 28, 1914, for the Louisville Board of Trade support. For a brief review of Hoover's efforts, see George H. Nash, "'An American Epic': Herbert Hoover and Belgian Relief in World War I," *Prologue: Quarterly of the National Archives and Records Administration* 21, 1 (Spring 1989), www.archives.gov/publications/prologue/1989/spring/hoover-belgium.html.

20. See *Louisville Courier-Journal,* October 29, 1914, for the Alliance Française effort.

21. See *Louisville Courier-Journal,* November 2, 3, and 4, 1914, for the favorable editorial on Belgian relief and for the donors' names and sums.

22. See *Lexington Herald,* December 6, 1914, for Embry's remarks. A December 10, 1914, *Herald* editorial agreed with Embry, asserting that relief for Europe should be "in addition to, not instead of contributions made for local relief." Money given for Belgium should come from "superabundance, or from self-denial." See also *Louisville Courier-Journal,* December 7, 1914.

23. For a short biography of Cobb, see the entry by Anita Lawson in John Kleber, ed., *The Kentucky Encyclopedia* (Lexington: University Press of Kentucky, 1992), available online at www.kyenc.org/entry/c/COBBI01.html. For a full-length biography, see Anita Lawson, *Irvin S. Cobb* (Bowling Green, OH: Bowling Green University Popular Press, 1984).

24. Irvin S. Cobb, *Paths of Glory: Impressions of War Written at and Near the Front* (New York: George H. Doran, 1915), 112, 375.

25. Irvin S. Cobb, *Speaking of Prussians* (New York: George H. Doran, 1917); Irvin S. Cobb, *The Glory of the Coming: What Mine Eyes Have Seen of Americans in Action in This Year of Grace and Allied Endeavor* (London: Hodder and Stoughton, 1919). The Vigilantes organization is explained in *Bulletin of the Author's League* 6, 2 (May 1918): 5–6; *Outlook* 119, 2 (May 8, 1918): 67–69; and *Crittenden Record-Press* (Marion, KY), June 21, 1917. Examples of war poetry by the Vigilantes' most prolific writers, Amelia Josephine Burr and Theodosia Garrison, can be found in *Central Record* (Lancaster, KY), July 5, 1917, and *Breckenridge News* (Cloverport, KY), July 25, 1917, respectively. An analysis of their poetry is found in Mark W. van Wienen, *Partisans and Poets: The Political Work of American Poetry in the Great War* (New York: Cambridge University Press, 1997), 142–68.

26. Stevenson's death was reported in *Kentucky Post,* January 31, 1916, and Morkill's death was reported on September 22, 1916. For more on Powell, see *Lexington Herald,* December 17, 1915, July 14, 1917, and August 22, 1918.

27. *Hopkinsville Kentuckian,* December 18, 1915; *Louisville Courier-Journal,* April 20, May 17, and August 16, 1917, which notes McClintock's receipt of the Distinguished Conduct Medal. See also *New York Times,* August 16, 1917.

28. Alexander McClintock, *Best O'Luck; How a Fighting Kentuckian Won the Thanks of Britain's King* (New York: George H. Doran, 1917). The Canadian version of the book substituted "Canadian" for "Kentuckian." The "Over There" newspaper series generally appeared from mid-June to mid-July 1917. See also *New York Times,* September 11, 1917, for McClintock as an instructor at Plattsburg, and December 23, 1917, for his profile.

29. James Klotter, *The Breckinridges of Kentucky, 1760–1981* (Lexington: University Press of Kentucky, 1986), 183.

30. See *Woman Citizen* 3, 8 (July 20, 1918): 152; *Trained Nurse and Hospital Review* 61, 3 (September 1918): 179–80. Breckinridge's talks on behalf of Red Cross fund-raising were reported in *Bourbon News* (Paris, KY), October 2, 1917, and *Mt. Sterling Advocate,* October 9, 1917. For more on Mary Curry Breckinridge, see *Lexington Herald,* June 25, 1918.

31. *Louisville Courier-Journal,* February 22, 1915. For more on the exchange between Haldeman and Watterson, see Alexander, "Henry Watterson and World War I," 19. The US entry into the war is covered in Justus Doenecke, *Nothing Less than War: A New History of America's Entry into World War I* (Lexington: University Press of Kentucky, 2011).

32. Doenecke, *Nothing Less than War,* 70.

33. *Louisville Courier-Journal,* May 5 and 9, 1918.

34. Alexander, "Henry Watterson and World War I," 20.

35. *Lexington Herald,* May 12, 1915.

36. *Climax-Madisonian* (Richmond, KY), May 19, 1915.

37. *Interior Journal* (Stanford, KY), May 11, 1915.

38. See *Louisville Courier-Journal,* October 16 and 17, 1914, for Gardner's position. For the debate on US preparedness for war, see John Patrick Finnegan, *Against the Specter of a Dragon: The Campaign for American Military Preparedness, 1914–1917* (Westport, CT: Greenwood Press, 1974).

39. *Louisville Courier-Journal,* October 17, 1914.

40. Robert D. Ward, "The Origin and Activities of the National Security League, 1914–1919," *Mississippi Valley Historical Review* 47, 1 (June 1960): 51. See also *Louisville Courier-Journal,* June 15, July 14, and October 23, 1915, for coverage of the NSL. For Sherley's comments to the NSL and subsequent efforts to create a chapter in Louisville, see *Courier-Journal,* May 27, October 20, and November 5, 1915.

41. For more on the preparedness debate, see Finnegan, *Against the Specter of a Dragon.*

42. On McCreary's stance, see *Louisville Courier-Journal,* October 28, 1915. See *Lexington Herald,* May 27, 1915, for the governor's appointments to the NSL conference.

43. See *Louisville Courier-Journal,* September 4, 11, 22, and October 29, 1915, for Bullitt at Plattsburg and subsequent support of the training camp movement. He hoped to see such a camp in Louisville, but it never transpired. For more on the Plattsburg movement, see J. Garry Clifford, *The Citizen Soldiers: The Plattsburg Training Camp Movement, 1913–1920* (Lexington: University of Kentucky Press, 1972). For Bullitt's successful resolution supporting universal military training, see ibid., 209.

44. The *Louisville Courier-Journal,* November 12, 1915, announced the formation of the Kentucky Committee of the Special Relief Society and gave the names of the women invited to join. See *Public Ledger* (Maysville, KY), November 17, 1915, for Breckinridge's open letter to McCreary.

45. Melba Porter Hay, *Madeline McDowell Breckinridge and the Battle for a New South* (Lexington: University Press of Kentucky, 2009), 184.

46. Doenecke, *Nothing Less than War,* 147; *Louisville Courier-Journal,* February 10, 1916.

47. Doenecke, *Nothing Less than War,* 159, 160, 161.

48. *Louisville Courier-Journal,* February 26, 1916.

49. Doenecke, *Nothing Less than War,* 166.

50. *Louisville Courier-Journal,* April 19, 1916. See also Doenecke, *Nothing Less than War,* 167–73.

51. James's Democratic National Convention speech was reproduced in *Lexington Herald,* June 16, 1916, and *Louisville Courier-Journal,* September 3, 1916. State historian Jim Klotter calls it "his greatest speech" and notes that it "marked him as a potential presidential candidate in 1920." See Klotter, *Kentucky: Portrait in Paradox,* 230.

52. Wilson's visit to Hodgenville was covered in *Louisville Courier-Journal,* September 5, 1916.

53. Klotter, *Kentucky: Portrait in Paradox,* 230.

54. Doenecke, *Nothing Less than War,* 249.

55. Alexander, "Henry Watterson and World War I," 22.

56. See Thomas Boghardt, *The Zimmermann Telegram: Intelligence, Diplomacy, and America's Entry into World War I* (Annapolis, MD: Naval Institute Press, 2012), for more on the telegram and its role in propelling America into the war. See also *Louisville Courier-Journal,* March 3, 1917, and *Hopkinsville Kentuckian,* March 3, 1917.

57. David Thelen, *Robert M. La Follette and the Insurgent Spirit* (Madison: University of Wisconsin Press, 1976). Earlier in his career, La Follette had published a laudatory article about Ollie James in his magazine; see *La Follette's Weekly Magazine* 3, 17 (April 29, 1911): 4–6.

58. See *Lexington Herald,* March 5, 1917, for "Betrayed" editorial.

59. *Louisville Courier-Journal,* March 12, 1917. The *Mt. Sterling Advocate,* April 10, 1917, printed the complete text of the resolutions passed in Montgomery County, including the condemnation of Stone.

60. See *Louisville Courier-Journal,* April 3, 1917, for a report on the Kentucky delegation's support for Wilson. James is quoted in Doenecke, *Nothing Less than War,* 291.

61. See *Louisville Courier-Journal,* April 4 and 5, 1917; *Central Record* (Lancaster, KY), May 3, 1917.

62. See *Louisville Courier-Journal,* April 6, 1917, for the texts of the Barkley, Johnson, and Langley speeches, as well as Fields's statement regarding the vote.

63. Alexander, "Henry Watterson and World War I," 22.

64. Material for the overview of Kentucky prior to the outbreak of the Great War is primarily from Klotter, *Kentucky: Portrait in Paradox.* Racial lynchings are covered on pages 65–70, while the Day law is covered on pages 152–54. For more on Ken-

tucky's remembrance of the Confederacy's "Lost Cause," see Anne Marshall, *Creating a Confederate Kentucky: The Lost Cause and Civil War Memory in a Border State* (Chapel Hill: University of North Carolina Press, 2010).

65. Klotter, *Kentucky: Portrait in Paradox,* 126–30.

66. Ibid., 134.

67. Ibid., 190–94. For a dedicated study of Billy Klair, see James Duane Bolin, *Bossism and Reform in a Southern City: Lexington, Kentucky 1880–1940* (Lexington: University Press of Kentucky, 2000).

68. For more on rural Progressivism, see J. Larry Hood, "The Collapse of Zion: Rural Progressivism in Nelson and Washington Counties, Kentucky" (PhD diss., University of Kentucky, 1980); J. Larry Hood, *Visions of Zion: Christianity, Modernization and the American Pursuit of Liberty: Progressivism in Rural Nelson and Washington Counties Kentucky* (Lanham, MD: University Press of America, 2005).

69. Klotter, *Kentucky: Portrait in Paradox,* 228–29.

70. For more on the woman's suffrage movement in Kentucky, see the biographies of its two major proponents: Hay, *Madeline McDowell Breckinridge,* and Paul Fuller, *Laura Clay and the Woman's Rights Movement* (Lexington: University Press of Kentucky, 1975). See also Claudia Knott, "The Woman Suffrage Movement in Kentucky, 1879–1920" (PhD diss., University of Kentucky, 1989).

71. For the temperance movement and subsequent quest for Prohibition in Kentucky, see Thomas H. Appleton Jr., "'Moral Suasion Has Had Its Day': From Temperance to Prohibition in Antebellum Kentucky," in *A Mythic Land Apart: Reassessing Southerners and Their History,* ed. John David Smith and Thomas H. Appleton Jr. (Westport, CT: Greenwood Press, 1997), 19–42; Thomas H. Appleton Jr., "'Like Banquo's Ghost': The Emergence of the Prohibition Issue in Kentucky Politics" (PhD diss., University of Kentucky, 1981); Thomas H. Appleton Jr., "Prohibition and Politics in Kentucky: The Gubernatorial Campaign and Election of 1915," *Register of the Kentucky Historical Society* 75, 1 (January 1977): 28–54.

72. For Stewart's campaign against illiteracy, see Yvonne Baldwin, *Cora Wilson Stewart and Kentucky's Moonlight Schools: Fighting for Literacy in America* (Lexington: University Press of Kentucky, 2006).

73. Klotter, *Kentucky: Portrait in Paradox,* 41–46.

74. See Nancy K. Forderhase, "'The Clear Call of Thoroughbred Women': The Kentucky Federation of Women's Clubs and the Crusade for Educational Reform, 1903–1909," *Register of the Kentucky Historical Society* 83, 1 (Winter 1985): 19–35, for one aspect of how women's clubs addressed reform before the Great War.

75. See Capozzola, *Uncle Sam Wants You,* 8, where the author introduces the term "coercive voluntarism." He devotes all of chapter 3 to this notion: "The Obligation to Volunteer: Women and Coercive Voluntarism."

2. Kentucky Joins the Great War

1. *Louisville Courier-Journal,* April 7 and 10, 1917. See also Alexander, "Henry Watterson and World War I," 22.

2. *Lexington Herald,* April 10, 1917.

3. *Kentucky Irish-American* (Louisville), April 7, 1917.

4. *Mt. Vernon Signal,* April 13 and 20, 1917. See chapter 7 for more on the US Food Administration and Kentucky's role in food conservation and production.

5. *Clay City Times,* April 12, 1917.

6. *Hartford Republican,* April 13, 1917.

7. *Lexington Herald,* April 6 and 8, 1917.

8. *Lexington Herald,* April 15, 1917.

9. For more on the Kentucky State Guard and National Guard, see G. Lee McClain, *Military History of Kentucky* (Frankfort, KY: State Journal, 1939), especially 168–82 for the development of the Guard from 1900 to 1914. McClain was the adjutant general and, as such, was the sponsor of the book project, which was written by members of the Kentucky Division of the Federal Writers' Project of the Works Progress Administration.

10. For the Kentucky National Guard's history during the Mexican Punitive Expedition, see the Guard's website: kynghistory.ky.gov/history/3qtr/mexexp.htm.

11. For a profile of Adjutant General James Tandy Ellis, see kynghistory.ky.gov/history/3qtr/addinfo/jtellisbio.htm.

12. McClain, *Military History of Kentucky,* 182–88.

13. John D. Stevens, "Suppression of Expression in Wisconsin during World War I" (PhD diss., University of Wisconsin, 1967), 8, maintains that Kentucky had a slightly larger population of German Americans (48.2 percent) than did Wisconsin (45.5 percent), based on his analysis of the 1910 census. The influence of German Americans along the Ohio River valley west of Louisville is covered in Darrel E. Bigham, *Towns & Villages of the Lower Ohio* (Lexington: University Press of Kentucky, 1998).

14. *Louisville Courier-Journal,* April 8, 1917. For the *Louisville Herald*'s coverage of the Seelbachs, see Eric George, "Hostility on the Home Front," *Louisville Magazine* 44, 10 (October 1993): 34. Otto Seelbach later headed a committee of hotel men to oversee a cadre of civilian cooks who helped create the proper mess arrangements at the new cantonment in Louisville, Camp Taylor. *Louisville Courier-Journal,* July 29, 1917.

15. For Germans in Louisville during World War I, see John Kleber, ed., *The Encyclopedia of Louisville* (Lexington: University Press of Kentucky, 2001), 953–54. The *Louisville Anzeiger* is mentioned in George, "Hostility on the Home Front." For the German Insurance Bank flag ceremony, see *Louisville Courier-Journal,* May 13, 1917. The German-American Alliance's suspension of meetings was reported in *Louisville Courier-Journal,* November 16, 1917. Recognizing the growing anti-German agitation as the United States drew nearer to war, the Alliance had already reduced its profile.

16. See Lisa Stamm, "The German-American Population of Northern Kentucky during the First World War: The Victimization of an Ethnic Group and Its Culture" (senior honors thesis, Northern Kentucky University, 1989), 1; a copy of this work is available in the Covington branch of the Kenton County Public Library. It was also published in *Perspectives in History* 4, 2 (Spring 1989): 3–20. Stamm notes that the census figures were not comprehensive with regard to German heritage; for example, no accounting was made of people with only one German parent.

17. For more on the war's effect on northern Kentucky's German population, see the "Anti-German Hysteria, 1917–1920," "German Americans," and "World War I," in *The Encyclopedia of Northern Kentucky,* ed. Paul A. Tenkotte and James C. Claypool (Lexington: University Press of Kentucky, 2009), 30, 394–95, 975–76. See also *Kentucky Post,* December 5, 1917, for bank name changes, and February 28, 1918, for street name changes.

18. See *Louisville Courier-Journal,* April 8, 1918, for the Owensboro church action, and April 19, 1918, for the Louisville Old Inn case.

19. *Mt. Sterling Advocate,* April 10, 1917.

20. *Big Sandy News* (Louisa, KY), April 19, 1918.

21. For Dayton's elimination of German-language teaching, see *Kentucky Times Star,* June 6, 1917. The switch to other languages in northern Kentucky was reported in *Kentucky Post,* September 11, 1917. See *Louisville Courier-Journal,* February 28, 1918, for the Somerset board's action.

22. Louisville's decline in foreign-language study was reported in *Louisville Courier-Journal,* September 17 and November 27, 1917.

23. For more on the debate, see *Public Ledger* (Maysville, KY), March 9, 1918. See also *Louisville Courier-Journal,* March 8 and 30, 1918.

24. *Adair County News* (Columbia, KY), March 13, 1918; *Kentucky Post,* January 19, 1918.

25. *Louisville Courier-Journal,* March 2, 1918.

26. *Louisville Courier-Journal,* March 31, 1918.

27. *Hartford Republican,* April 5, 1918; *Elkton Times* editorial reported in *Cincinnati Enquirer,* April 14, 1918.

28. *Cincinnati Enquirer,* April 7, 1918.

29. Woodrow Wilson to Polk Lafoon, October 10, 1918, folder 9, box 4, Augustus O. Stanley Papers, UK Special Collections and Archives. Laffoon's name was often misspelled, even in northern Kentucky newspapers. The son of a former Confederate general and US congressman, he was a successful business executive, horse breeder, and racing enthusiast. Bruner made an issue of Stanley's veto when he opened his campaign in September 1918; see *Louisville Courier-Journal,* September 17, 1918. Stanley retorted in a lengthy speech, once again outlining his reasons; see *Courier-Journal,* September 22, 1918. For a comparative view of how the German language was treated in Minnesota, see La Vern J. Rippley, "Conflict in the Classroom: Anti-Germanism in Minnesota Schools, 1917–19," *Minnesota History* 47, 5 (Spring 1981): 170–83. For more on Minnesota and the war, see Chrislock, *Watchdog of Loyalty.*

30. See *Kentucky Post,* October 3, 10, 18, and 23, 1917, for the formation of the Citizens' Patriotic League and its initial mass meeting.

31. *Hartford Republican,* March 22, 1918. See also *Kentucky Post,* February 7, March 13 and 28, 1918.

32. *Cincinnati Enquirer,* May 19 and 22, 1918. See also *Kentucky Post,* April 23, May 14 and 15, 1918.

33. Hunt quoted in *Cincinnati Enquirer,* May 31, 1918. See also *Kentucky Post,* July 2 and 10, September 25, 1918. Hunt had earlier been involved in a mass meeting at which a resolution was passed denouncing Stanley's veto. Federal judge A. M. J.

Cochran presided over that meeting; he would also preside over several sedition trials in his judicial district. See *Public Ledger* (Maysville, KY), April 5, 1918. Political correspondent Thomas Cromwell of the *Cincinnati Enquirer* believed Hunt's denunciation of Stanley was a reflection of animosity by disgruntled Kenton and Campbell County Democrats over Stanley's failure to appoint a county judge candidate they favored. *Cincinnati Enquirer,* April 7, 1918.

34. *Kentucky Times Star,* November 20, 1918; *Kentucky Post,* November 20,1918.

35. *Louisville Courier-Journal,* July 6, 1918. For more on vigilantism in the United States during World War I, see Christopher Capozzola, "The Only Badge Needed Is Your Patriotic Fervor: Vigilance, Coercion, and the Law in World War I America," *Journal of American History* 88, 4 (March 2002): 1354–82.

36. This introduction to the American Protective League is condensed from the standard work on the group: Joan Jensen, *The Price of Vigilance* (New York: Rand McNally, 1968). The APL's official historian, Emerson Hough, also wrote about the volunteer spy organization in *The Web: A Revelation of Patriotism* (Chicago: Reilly and Lee, 1919). Like Irvin Cobb, he was a member of the Vigilantes, propagandists for the war.

37. Stoll's list of the APL's county chiefs is found in Lyman Chalkley, *History of Fayette County, Ky., in the World War, 1917–1919,* vol. 1 (Frankfort: Kentucky Council of Defense, n.d.). Stoll sent the list to state war historian Fred Caldwell of the Kentucky Council of Defense in a letter dated March 16, 1923.

38. See Hough, *The Web,* 430, for statistics on the Louisville APL under Ragsdale. After the war Ragsdale taught at the new Louisville Police School.

39. Ragsdale's comments about German activities were reported in *Louisville Courier-Journal,* March 2, 1918. For more about Ragsdale's career and involvement with police and prisons, see *Louisville Courier-Journal,* July 20, 1919.

40. See *Louisville Courier-Journal,* August 3, 1918, for Norman's appointment. See also Hough, *The Web,* 430.

41. Hough, *The Web,* 431.

42. *Louisville Courier-Journal,* August 5, 1918.

43. *Citizen* (Berea, KY), September 19, 1918; *Bourbon News* (Paris, KY), September 17, 1917.

44. Jensen, *Price of Vigilance,* 217. For the larger national context, see Jensen's chapter on "Slacker Raiding," 188–218. Although some members wished to continue the organization, the Department of Justice officially disbanded the APL as of February 1, 1919.

45. *Louisville Courier-Journal,* February 4, 1919.

46. Capozzola, "Only Badge Needed," notes, "The line between vigilance and vigilantism was contested throughout the war and post-war years." This produced a conundrum: "Government officials who denounced lawless vigilantism also praised vigilance organizations' policing. They insisted that only uncontrolled physical violence was politically illegitimate—precisely because it subverted the spirit of a nation of laws." With a long history of "vigilance as a form of collective self-defense," the United States witnessed four main categories during the war: citizen policing, antilabor vigilance, moral vigilance, and racial vigilance. According to Capozzola, the war

changed the relationship between citizen vigilance and the state: "vigilance societies that had done the work of the state outside its boundaries now saw those actions folded within it" (1356–57).

47. For the genesis of the base hospital movement, see Margaret Clark, "Base Hospital 43: The Emory Unit," *MedGenMed* 9, 3 (2007): 10, www.ncbi.nlm.nih.gov/pmc/articles/PMC2100082/#R8.

48. *Louisville Courier-Journal,* July 24, August 1, 3, and 6, 1917, March 23, 1919. See also the section on Unit D in Fred P. Caldwell, *Kentucky in the World War, 1917–1919,* 20 vols. (Frankfort: Kentucky Council of Defense, n.d.), vol. 4, held in the Military Records and Research Branch, Kentucky Department of Military Affairs, Frankfort, KY. Caldwell was the state war historian of the Kentucky Council of Defense and, as such, supervised the creation of 120 county histories of the war effort, as well as the above-cited twenty-volume collection.

49. Quote from "History of Base Hospital No. 59," collections.nlm.nih.gov/bookviewer?PID=nlm:nlmuid-101260871-bk. See *Louisville Courier-Journal,* February 17 and 19, 1918, May 2, 1919, for news of the hospital's work. See also the annual report of the surgeon general in United States War Department, *Annual Reports, 1919* (Washington, DC: Government Printing Office, 1920), vol. 1, pt. 3, 3684–86. For details of the hospital center, see Lt. Col. Irvin Abell, Base Hospital 59, A.E.F., to Major Charles Lucas, Camp MacArthur, Waco, Texas, October 13, 1918, and Abell to "Muddie" (his wife Carrie), October 17, 1918, folder 7: October 1918, Irvin Abell Papers, Filson Historical Society, Louisville, KY. This extensive collection includes letters to his wife and two sons dating from Abell's arrival at the Rockefeller Institute in New York City for training in February 1918, through his posting at Camp Shelby in Hattiesburg, Mississippi, to his service in France during and after the war.

50. For McMurtry's recommendation, see Lewis McMurtry to Surgeon General W. C. Gorgas, May 16, 1917, Barrow Unit microfilm, UK Special Collections and Archives. For more on Curry Breckinridge, see *Lexington Herald,* June 25, 1918. John Marsh's letters were sometimes reproduced in the *Lexington Leader,* such as one on March 8 that detailed events at Camp Taylor. An example of a letter from Marsh to the *Leader*'s editor, sent from Sarisbury Court, Hants. [Hampshire], England, and dated September 27, 1918, can be found on the Barrow Unit microfilm; see also the newspaper clipping labeled October 16, 1917. For more on Marsh and Mitchell, see Marianne Walker, *Margaret Mitchell and John Marsh: The Love Story behind* Gone with the Wind (Atlanta: Peachtree Publishers, 1993).

51. See Josiah H. Combs, *The Siege of Sarisbury Court which Chronicles the Feat of Base Hospital 40 in Winning the World War* (Lexington, KY: Hurst and Byers, 1923). The Josiah H. Combs Papers are found in Special Collections and Archives, Hutchins Library, Berea College, Berea, KY. Lists of Barrow Unit members can be found on the Barrow Unit microfilm. Haggin's enlistment in the Barrow Unit was reported in several central Kentucky newspapers, including the *Stanford Interior Journal,* March 22, 1918. For more on Haggin's commissioning, see John Marsh, "Barrow Hospital Unit Busy in England," *Lexington Leader,* November [24], 1918, Barrow Unit microfilm.

52. See *Lexington Herald,* February 26 and March 2, 1918, for the mobilization and send-off of Barrow Unit enlisted members to Camp Taylor. The *Lexington Leader*

reported on March 11, 1918, that the unit's nurses would be sent to various cantonments for training. For more on the work of the Barrow Unit, see Dr. David Barrow's speech to the Kentucky State Medical Association in September 1919, reproduced in the December 1919 issue of the *Kentucky Medical Journal,* and an article by G. Y. Marsden, "A Visit to Sarisbury Court," *American Red Cross Bulletin, London* 7 (September 18, 1918), Barrow Unit microfilm. Marsden's article was also reproduced in *Lexington Leader,* November 3, 1918.

53. For a contemporary history, see Henry Davison, *The American Red Cross in the Great War* (New York: Macmillan, 1919). Davison was chairman of the War Council of the American Red Cross (officially chartered as the American National Red Cross).

54. For the Red Cross divisions, their heads, and the decision to combine all of Kentucky into the Lake Division, see *Red Cross Bulletin, American Red Cross* 1, 9 (August 17, 1917): 2, and 1, 31 (December 3, 1917): 3.

55. The Lexington Red Cross conference was reported in *Lexington Herald,* August 22, 23, and 24, 1917.

56. For a comprehensive view of the conference, see *First Kentucky State Convention (And First in the United States) of the American National Red Cross Held at Lexington, August 22–23, 1917* (Frankfort, KY: State Journal Co., [1917]). The 140-page publication reproduces the speeches and chapter reports.

57. See *Georgetown Times,* May 30, June 6, 13, and 27, and August 1, 1917, for Red Cross chapter developments and Barrow Unit members from Scott County.

58. *Georgetown Times,* December 12 and 19, 1917, January 16 and March 13, 1918. See also the clippings on local Red Cross and Junior Red Cross efforts contained in Mrs. William H. Coffman, *History of Scott County, Ky., in the World War, 1917–1919,* 3 vols. (Frankfort: Kentucky Council of Defense, [1919]), taken from the *Georgetown Times* "Historical Edition," September 17, 1919. This volume is part of the statewide effort to produce a history of each county's activity during the war, overseen by the Kentucky Council of Defense and state war historian Fred P. Caldwell. (This historical effort is covered in more detail in the last chapter.)

59. See Red Cross report and newspaper clippings in Coffman, *History of Scott County,* vol. 1.

60. See Caldwell, *Kentucky in the World War,* vol. 2.

61. See "History of the Boyd County, Kentucky Chapter of the American Red Cross," ibid.

62. See the Trigg County report in ibid. The Webster County report also acknowledged that a majority of the populace originally had no idea about the work of the Red Cross.

63. See Boyle County reports in Caldwell, *Kentucky in the World War,* vol. 2, and *Louisville Courier-Journal,* May 19, 1918, noting Bingham's contribution. Having controversially inherited $5 million from his deceased wife, Bingham bought the *Louisville Courier-Journal* and *Times* in 1918. For his support of Franklin D. Roosevelt, Bingham became US ambassador to Great Britain in 1933; he was succeeded by Joseph P. Kennedy in 1937.

64. See "Hickman Chapter, American Red Cross, Hickman, Fulton County, Kentucky," in Caldwell, *Kentucky in the World War,* vol. 2.

65. See the reports of Knox and Pulaski Counties in ibid.

66. For Greene's appointment in the Bureau of War Risk Insurance, see *National Underwriter,* April 11, 1918, 10. For more on R. C. Ballard Thruston, see *Long Rifle* 2, 4 (July 2011): 9–12, www.louthrustonsar.org/July%20NewsletterOrig3.pdf. His appointment as assistant manager of the Red Cross's Lake Division and the transfer of records to Louisville are mentioned in *Louisville Courier-Journal,* February 17 and 27, 1918. Thruston was a prolific photographer who donated thousands of pictures taken in eastern Kentucky and other places around the world to the Filson Historical Society. He also served as Filson's president and as chairman of the Kentucky Council of Defense after the war.

67. For more on the Red Cross fund drive, see *Louisville Courier-Journal,* May 19, 23, 25, and 28, 1918. Stanley's efforts to auction wool were reported on May 21, 1918. On its website, the White House Historical Association explains why President Wilson kept a flock of sheep on the White House lawn: "The sight of sheep grazing on the south lawn of the White House may seem unusual, but during World War I, it was a highly visible symbol of home front support of the troops overseas. The flock, which numbered 48 at its peak, saved manpower by cutting the grass and earned $52,823 for the Red Cross through an auction of their wool." See www.whitehousehistory.org/history/white-house-facts-trivia/facts-wilson-sheep-world-war-one.html.

68. Julia Irwin, *Making the World Safe: The American Red Cross and a Nation's Humanitarian Awakening* (New York: Oxford University Press, 2013), 68.

69. For more on McAdoo and the Liberty Loan campaigns, see Kennedy, *Over Here,* 98–113. See also *Louisville Courier-Journal,* June 12, 1917, for the treasury secretary's visit to Louisville.

70. See *Lexington Herald,* May 1, 1918, for reports of the effigy and warning sign; the May 16, 1918, edition reported that the effigy had finally been taken down.

71. District and county chairs, as well as contribution figures for the Kentucky counties in the Fourth and Eighth Federal Reserve Districts, can be found in Caldwell, *Kentucky in the World War,* vol. 1. For the Kentucky quota, see *Louisville Courier-Journal,* May 23, 1917. For more on Liberty Loans, see Sung Won Kang and Hugh Rockoff, "Capitalizing Patriotism: The Liberty Loans of World War I," National Bureau of Economic Research Working Paper 11919, January 2006, www.nber.org/papers/w11919.

72. All figures (which are rounded off) are taken from reports found in Caldwell, *Kentucky in the World War,* vol. 1.

73. Income tax statistics compiled by the Internal Revenue Service for 1917 revealed an average Kentucky income of $550, in comparison to $671 for Ohio, $626 for Illinois, $553 for Tennessee, and $478 for Indiana. These figures paled in comparison to states like Pennsylvania ($733) and New York ($985). See United States Treasury Department, Internal Revenue, *Statistics of Income Compiled from the Returns for 1917 under the Direction of the Commissioner of Internal Revenue* (Washington, DC: Government Printing Office, 1919), 42–43.

74. For the organization's origins, see the standard work on the Four Minute Men: Alfred Cornebise, *War as Advertised: The Four Minute Men and America's Crusade, 1917–1918* (Philadelphia: American Philosophical Society, 1984), ix–17. See also

Lisa Mastrangelo, "World War I, Public Intellectuals, and the Four Minute Men: Convergent Ideals of Public Speaking and Civic Participation," *Rhetoric & Public Affairs* 12, 4 (Winter 2009): 607–34. The creation of the national organization was reported in *Public Ledger* (Maysville, KY), July 2, 1917, and *Bourbon News* (Paris, KY), July 6, 1917.

75. Cornebise, *War as Advertised,* 11. An extensive collection of Four Minute Men bulletins can be found in Caldwell, *Kentucky in the World War,* vol. 2.

76. A copy of Davis Edwards's appointment document from national director William McCormick Blair, dated February 1, 1918, is in Caldwell, *Kentucky in the World War,* vol. 2.

77. See Caldwell, *Kentucky in the World War,* 1:309–11, for a report on the Kentucky Four Minute Men. See ibid., 305, for the Louisville chapter's speech and audience numbers and venues, contained in a resolution commending Marvin Lewis.

78. See undated letter from T. O. Jones, Greenville, Ky., to Division of Four Minute Men, Washington, DC, ibid., 341.

79. See Jno. H. Chesney, Middlesborough [*sic*], Ky., to Davis Edwards, State Director, Four Minute Men, April 8, 1918, ibid., 339.

80. See E. A. Gaskell to Davis Edwards, July 6, 1918, ibid., 343.

81. *Mt. Sterling Advocate,* January 1, 1918; *Bourbon News* (Paris, KY), March 29, 1918. See *Bourbon News,* December 6, 1918, and *Central Record* (Lancaster, KY), December 12, 1918, for a Junior Four Minute Men contest to promote the Red Cross Christmas Roll Call campaign.

82. *Central Record* (Lancaster, KY), November 21, 1918; *Public Ledger* (Maysville, KY), December 11, 1918.

83. An example of how the Four Minute Men helped the Red Cross throughout the country can be found in Krystina Benson, "The Four Minute Men and the Red Cross: 1917–1918," www.inter-disciplinary.net/probing-the-boundaries/wp-content/uploads/2012/10/KBenson9thWCCSCPCFinalDraftPaper.pdf.

3. The Kentucky Council of Defense

1. William J. Breen, *Uncle Sam at Home: Civilian Mobilization, Wartime Federalism, and the Council of National Defense, 1917–1919* (Westport, CT: Greenwood Press, 1984), 4; "President Names Defense Advisers," *New York Times,* October 12, 1916.

2. Breen, *Uncle Sam at Home,* 9–19.

3. See *Louisville Courier-Journal,* April 21, 1917, for a list of meeting attendees.

4. For more on the KCD, see Kentucky Council of Defense, *Annual Report of the Kentucky Council of Defense, December 31, 1918* (Frankfort, KY: State Journal Co., [1919]), and *Report of the Activities of the Kentucky Council of Defense to January 1, 1920* (Frankfort, KY: State Journal Co., 1920). For state councils established by executive action, see United States Council of National Defense, Section on Cooperation with States, *Report on Organization and Activities of State Councils of Defense, June 18, 1917* (Washington, DC, 1917), 7. In its early stages, the council was variously known as the State Council of Defense or sometimes the Kentucky Council of National Defense. Here, it will simply be referred to as the Kentucky Council of Defense (KCD). This

chapter focuses on a broad overview of the KCD and its work. More extensive details of its efforts are woven into subsequent chapters, such as its work with the Kentucky Division of the Woman's Committee of the Council of National Defense, which is covered in chapter 8.

5. See telegram from A. O. Stanley to George Porter, Chief, State Cooperation Section, Council of National Defense, April 25, 1917, National Defense Conference folder, box 763, entry 347, RG 62 (Council of National Defense), NARA-CP. Swearingen and Hughes's trip to Washington was reported in *Louisville Courier-Journal,* May 10, 1917. For more on Swearingen, see William Elsey Connelley and Ellis Merton Coulter, *History of Kentucky,* 5 vols. (Chicago: American Historical Society, 1922), 4:322. Swearingen was a Democrat and attended the University of Virginia. For more on Hughes, see J. Allan Smith, *The College of Agriculture of the University of Kentucky: Early and Middle Years, 1865–1961* (Lexington: Kentucky Agricultural Extension Service, 1981), 120. For more on the National Defense Conference, see "Advises Governors How to Aid in War," *New York Times,* May 20, 1917. See US Council of National Defense, *Report on Organization and Activities,* 2–3, for topics of bulletins.

6. See *Lexington Herald,* May 5, 1917, for the names of the newly appointed State Council of Defense members, and May 18 and 19, 1917, for reports on the first council meeting. The Committee on Committees was listed in *Louisville Courier-Journal,* May 19, 1917.

7. For more on Owsley Brown, see Kleber, *Encyclopedia of Louisville,* 135. Brown at one time served as Jefferson County Democratic Party chairman. Swearingen's wife, Lalla Robinson Owsley, was Brown's half sister and a great-granddaughter of former Kentucky governor William Owsley (1844–1848). Lalla's mother was Amelia Owsley Robinson; after Amelia's husband Lawrence Robinson died, she married George Brown, and they had a son: Owsley Brown. For more on Richard Stoll, see his biographical entry in Connelley and Coulter, *History of Kentucky,* 5:571. For more on William Cochran, see *Public Ledger* (Maysville, KY), February 8, 1919. He was the brother of federal judge A. M. J. Cochran, who would be involved in trying sedition cases throughout eastern Kentucky. Robert Hughes had served as president of Kentucky Electric Company and then as business manager for the *Louisville Courier-Journal.* See *Courier-Journal,* June 12, 1921. For more on Sigmond Lee, see "Employe [*sic*]-Editor Finds Time to Be Loyal to Company and Country," *Illinois Central Magazine,* July 1921. The *Louisville Courier-Journal,* June 13, 1917, reported that the United Trades and Labor Assembly had adopted a resolution criticizing the governor for not including labor representatives on war councils.

8. KCD, *Annual Report, December 31, 1918,* 4–5.

9. Director [George F. Porter, chief of the State Councils Section] to Swearingen, June 13, 1917, folder 208 KSC June [1917], box 661 (Kansas to Louisiana), entry 338, RG 62, NARA-CP.

10. See KCD, *Annual Report, December 31, 1918,* 6–10, for county council activities.

11. "Report of Mr. Embry L. Swearingen, Chairman of the Kentucky Council of Defense," July 20, 1917, folder 208 KSC July [1917], box 661 (Kansas to Louisiana), entry 338, RG 62, NARA-CP. This report was apparently prepared by a CND

staff member, possibly George Porter, the chief of the section on cooperation with the states, after Swearingen's visit to the council office in Washington, DC. A few days later, Porter passed along the good news of the success of Kentucky's Food Committee to the head of US food production efforts, future president Herbert Hoover, with whom Swearingen had unsuccessfully sought a meeting. See Porter to Hoover, July 23, 1917, ibid. (While the letters are sent from "Chief of Section of Cooperation with States," i.e., Porter, it appears that they were really written by one of his assistants, Elliot Dunlap Smith, a young Harvard-trained lawyer from Chicago.) Morgan Hughes served as head of a large statewide Food Committee (also known as the Conservation Committee) established by Governor Stanley in April 1917. See *Lexington Herald,* April 18, 1917.

12. See letter from Swearingen to county council chairman regarding the Soldiers' Business Aid Committees, contained in a report sent to George Porter, July 26, 1917, folder 208 KSC June [1917], box 661 (Kansas to Louisiana), entry 338, RG 62, NARA-CP. Swearingen based this letter on a similar plan adopted by the North Carolina Council of Defense and forwarded to Swearingen by the CND in its key role as a clearinghouse for the sharing of information among state councils. See W. W. Thum, *Kentucky Legal Aid Book for the Use of Legal Aid Committees and County Councils of Defense* (Frankfort, KY: State Journal Co., n.d.).

13. Swearingen to Porter, July 21, 1917, and Porter to Swearingen, July 24, 1917, folder 208 KSC July [1917], box 661 (Kansas to Louisiana), entry 338, RG 62, NARA-CP.

14. See *Citizen* (Berea, KY), September 19, 1918; *Bourbon News* (Paris, KY), September 17, 1917. The KCD had recommended Stoll to head the APL in Kentucky. See "Minutes of the Meeting of the Kentucky Council of Defense Held Tuesday, May 28, 1918," folder 208 KSC May [1918], box 714, entry 339, RG 62, NARA-CP.

15. "Dr. Sherer's Report on Kentucky, Second Itinerary," box 783, entry 364, RG 62, NARA-CP. Sherer served as president of what is today the California Institute of Technology in Pasadena.

16. H. H. Cherry to James Utterback, Paducah, KY, May 29, 1917, file 114, box 2, H. H. Cherry Papers, WKU Special Collections.

17. H. H. Cherry to George Porter, August 1, 1917, folder 208 KSC August [1917], box 660, entry 338, RG 62, NARA-CP.

18. "Report of H. H. Cherry, Chairman Publicity and Speakers' Bureau Committee, Kentucky Council of Defense," November 20, 1918, Report to Kentucky Council of Defense folder, box 73, Cherry Papers, WKU. See also H. H. Cherry to George Porter, August 22, 1917, folder 208 KSC August [1917], box 660, entry 338, RG 62, NARA-CP, for Cherry's assessment of the conference.

19. See Swearingen to George Porter, September 11, 1917, noting that Swearingen had tendered his resignation to Governor Stanley; George Porter to Embry Swearingen, September 13, 1917, acknowledging Swearingen's resignation and expressing sympathy; and Swearingen to Porter, September 15, 1917, reporting on the KCD's progress, folder 208 KSC September [1917], box 660, entry 338, RG 62, NARA-CP.

20. Edward Hines file, University of Louisville Archives and Special Collections, Louisville, KY.

21. Hines to Porter, October 3, 1917, folder 208 KSC October [1917], box 660, entry 338, RG 62, NARA-CP. See also Swearingen to Porter, September 29, 1917, folder 208 KSC September [1917], ibid., noting the appointment of Hines.

22. See Cherry to G. Wesley Turner, Mayfield, KY, September 1, 1917, folder 38, box 3, and Cherry to Ralph Quinn, Henderson, KY, August 8, 1917, file 114—Kentucky Council of Defense, box 2, Cherry Papers, WKU.

23. For the report on Patriotic Week, see Cherry to Porter, October 27, 1917, file 114—Kentucky Council of Defense, box 2, Cherry Papers, WKU. A typical example of county participation in Patriotic Week is reflected in a full-page announcement in the *Adair County News,* September 16, 1917. Noting that the event had the approval of Governor Stanley, the announcement pointed out that there would be speeches in the south-central county's seat of Columbia, as well as in the small communities of Sparksville, Cane Valley, Glenville, and Knifley. The newspaper admonished: "Everyone interested in the welfare of our young men who must fight the battles and win the Victory should cease from work on the day appointed in their district and participate in the meeting and the organization of the community." In the announcement, spaced around the seal of the Commonwealth of Kentucky, were the words: "We Are Together in This Struggle. Down with Kaiserism."

24. See Hines to Porter, November 19, 1917, questioning CND policy and practices with regard to working with "fraternal organizations" such as the Masons, and Porter to Hines, November 23, 1917, encouraging cooperation with state fraternal organizations and noting that the War Department allowed many such organizations, such as the YMCA and Knights of Columbus, to establish a presence at training camp sites. (Camp Taylor in Louisville served as a good example, with a strong YMCA presence.) For librarians' work, see Chief of Section to Hines, November 22, 1917, and Hines to Porter, November 26, 1917, in which Hines agrees to Porter's suggestion that he work with Carolyn Adelberg of the Louisville Free Public Library; she would coordinate state library efforts to post information from the federal Food Administration regarding food issues. In Hines to Porter, October 3, 1917, the KCD director asks for advice and information about working with African Americans, having received an offer from an African American teacher to work on the war effort. In Porter to Hines, October 5, 1917, Porter forwards to Hines an abstract regarding how other states dealt with this issue. For women's work, see Porter to Hines, October 30, 1917, congratulating Hines on working out an arrangement with Sallie Bruce. All this correspondence is in folder 208 KSC November [1917] and October [1917], box 660, entry 338, RG 62, NARA-CP.

25. See Cherry to Porter, November 22, 1917, ibid., announcing the state council's plans. Cherry promised Governor Stanley's "active support."

26. See Kentucky Council of Defense, *Kentucky War Council Held under the Auspices of the Council of National Defense and the Kentucky Council of Defense, January 15th–16th, 1918* (n.p., n.d.), 2–7, for a list of meetings and their leaders.

27. For brief reports on the conference, see Cherry to Porter, January 17, 1918, and Hines to Porter, January 26, 1918, folder 208 KSC January 16–31 [1918], box 715, entry 339, RG 62, NARA-CP.

28. Baker's letter is in folder 208 KSC January 1–16 [1918], ibid. For CND guid-

ance, see Chief of Section to Hines, January 23, 1918, folder 208 KSC January 16–31 [1918], ibid.

29. See Hines to Porter, February 23, 1918, folder 208 KSC February [1918], ibid., mentioning Perigord's speeches in Louisville and Frankfort. After the war, Perigord gave many speeches supporting the League of Nations. He became an American citizen and taught in the California university system.

30. See Cherry to Porter, February 1, 1918 (including a letter from Cherry to Byron Shimp, February 1, 1918, outlining Perigord's speaking tour in Kentucky), ibid. See *Lexington Herald,* February 22, 1918, for a report on Perigord's speech in Lexington.

31. See Hines to Porter, March 8, 1918, folder 208 KSC March [1918], box 715, entry 339, RG 62, NARA-CP. Hines noted that the Kentucky bill closely followed an outline provided by the CND, with the exception that the governor retained the power to appoint the nine state council members. The legislation establishing the Kentucky Council of Defense is found in Kentucky Court of Appeals, *The Kentucky Statutes,* 5th ed., *1918 Supplement* (Louisville, KY: Baldwin Law Book Co., 1918), 245–49. Breen, *Uncle Sam at Home,* points out: "Reflecting the general poverty of the South, the money made available to state councils was very limited by comparison with other regions" (98). For example, the Virginia legislature appropriated $5,000, and Georgia set aside $2,500 for their respective state councils. State councils in Alabama and South Carolina had to raise money through private subscriptions. This contrasted strongly with midwestern states, which "responded quickly and generously to the call of the federal government to establish state councils of defense." The Michigan legislature appropriated $5 million, while Illinois and other states approved large budgets in excess of $100,000, derived from public and private funding (ibid., 71–72).

32. *Lexington Herald,* April 21, 1918. In this edition, the *Herald* also reproduced the complete legislative act establishing the KCD. KCD executive secretary David Morton sent a copy of the editorial to Arthur Fleming, the new State Councils Section chief. See Morton to Arthur Fleming, April 23, 1918, folder 208 KSC April [1918], box 715, entry 339, RG 62, NARA-CP.

33. See Hines to Porter, March 6, 1918, which includes letters sent to county councils on January 24 and February 28, 1918, offering advice and mentioning "The Prussian Blot" poster. Used across the country, the poster features a map of Europe with Belgium, Germany, Austria-Hungary, the Balkans, and the Ottoman Empire in red—that is, the blot. The poster reads: "The World Cannot Live Half Slave, Half Free. 100,000,000 people already enslaved by Germany. President Wilson says of the Germans: 'Their plan was to throw a broad belt of German military power and political control across the very center of Europe and beyond the Mediterranean Sea into the heart of Asia. They have actually carried the greater part of this amazing plan into execution.' The Kaiser proclaims: 'Woe and death unto those who oppose my will. Death to the infidel who denies my mission. Let all the enemies of the German nation perish. God demands their destruction.' While Germany Dreams of Dominating the World by Force There Can Be No Peace."

34. See Hines to Porter, March 6, 1918, folder 208 KSC March [1918], box 715, entry 339, RG 62, NARA-CP, which includes a Rockcastle flyer—"Vital Facts for

Everybody"—announcing the war council and disseminating other war effort news. Hines also included a copy of the prize-winning essay on food conservation written by a Mt. Vernon High School student, noting that there had been more than 200 entries in the contest. Hines had heard that the war council was a "great success" and added, "Altho Rockcastle County is not one of our more prosperous counties, no county has done better war work." CND staffer LHG thanked Hines for sending the material and encouraged him to pass along more information about how Rockcastle County had organized the war council. LHG observed, "It is just such local enthusiasm that will carry this war through successfully." LHG to Hines, March 9, 1918, ibid.

35. See Hines to Porter, March 11, 1918, transmitting a copy of Benj. S. Sharpless, Service Director, to Hines, March 8, 1918, ibid. Sharpless had been a member of the Kentucky House of Representatives at the beginning of the century and remained prominent in northern Kentucky municipal activism. He also sent Hines a copy of the rather detailed constitution of the Campbell County Council of Defense. See also Hines to Porter, March 14, 1918, ibid., enclosing a newspaper clipping about the patriotic meeting in Alexandria. Reflecting the CND's ongoing encouragement of the state councils, Frederick Lewis Allen wrote to Hines on March 19, 1918, ibid., asking him to pass along congratulations.

36. See H. C. Wood, *History of Mercer County, Ky., in the World War, 1917–1919* (Frankfort: Kentucky Council of Defense, n.d.), including clippings from the *Harrodsburg Herald,* June 21, 1918, listing members of all the local community councils.

37. Community duties are outlined in a pamphlet produced by the Kentucky Council of Defense, "Organize for Victory," a copy of which can be found in Caldwell, *Kentucky in the World War,* vol. 6.

38. David Morton to Arthur Fleming, April 24, 1918, folder 208 KSC April [1918], box 715, entry 339, RG 62, NARA-CP, enclosing "Report of Executive Secretary of the Kentucky Council of Defense, for Period April 9 to April 22." For Morton's report, see also World War I Journal, Smith Library, KHS. This collection contains copies of Morton's reports, as well as copies of executive committee meetings, Hines's letters to the county councils, announcements distributed to newspaper editors, and other supplementary materials. An article from the May 4, 1918, *Louisville Courier-Journal* regarding the tractor distribution is found in Morton to Fleming, May 6, 1918, folder 208 KSC May [1918], box 714, entry 339, RG 62, NARA-CP. "Under the direction of the Kentucky Council of Defense," the tractors were distributed primarily in Jefferson County and in central and western Kentucky.

39. See Morton to Arthur Fleming, April 26, 1918, folder 208 KSC April [1918], box 715, entry 339, RG 62, NARA-CP, containing a copy of the news release sent to state editors about the council's actions regarding German textbooks. The Bellevue Red Cross Auxiliary resolution of April 4 and Dorothy Pope's reply to C. A. DeVane, April 13, 1918, are in ibid.

40. See Hines and Morton to Chairmen of County Councils, May 16, 1918, folder 208 KSC May [1918], box 714, entry 339, RG 62, NARA-CP. The purpose of the Boys Working Reserve was outlined in *Mt. Vernon Signal,* March 22, 1918. *Breckenridge News* (Cloverport, KY), March 27, 1918, noted that Kentucky authorities sought to enroll 5,000 boys to work on farms. For more on the Boys Working Reserve, see chapter 10.

41. See Maud Cossar to Arthur Fleming, May 28, 1918, folder 208 KSC May [1918], box 714, entry 339, RG 62, NARA-CP, forwarding "Report of Executive Secretary of the Kentucky Council of Defense for Period April 22 to May 28." For more on Cossar, see Kleber, *Encyclopedia of Louisville,* 223–24. The *Encyclopedia* and other sources often refer to her as "Maude," although she signed her KCD documents as "Maud. "After the war she became one of the first women elected to the Louisville government, serving as city treasurer under Mayor Houston Quin.

42. Hines to Fleming, June 24, 1918, folder 208 KSC May [1918], box 714, entry 339, RG 62, NARA-CP.

43. See KCD, *Report of Activities to January 1, 1920,* 23–24, for the regional meetings. *Lexington Herald,* June 22, 1918, announced that the next council meeting would be in Lexington on June 25, followed by a meeting in Paducah on July 9. See Frederick Lewis Allen to Kentucky Council of Defense, June 29, 1918, folder 208 KSC June [1918], box 714, entry 339, RG 62, NARA-CP, noting that the "idea of holding the semi-monthly Council meetings in various towns throughout the state is, as far as we know, something entirely new and it looks to us like a most valuable innovation."

44. A clipping from the *Paducah Evening Sun,* July 10, 1918, folder 208 KSC July [1918], box 714, entry 339, RG 62, NARA-CP, notes that Colonel John L. Smith, the Livingstone County chairman and editor of the *Livingstone County Enterprise,* reported record crop harvests; in addition, "three investigations of suspected disloyalty and punishment resulted in a quick suppression of further pro-German talk." See also "The Livingstone County Council of National Defense Proclaims Its Purpose," ibid., a flyer in which the council proposes its many tasks. Pendleton Beckley to Fleming, July 12, 1918, ibid., notes that "one of the most complete County organizations in Kentucky is that of Mercer County, which contains one thousand active members." Beckley, a former Louisville city government lawyer, was the new KCD executive secretary.

45. See "Minutes of the Meeting of the Kentucky Council of Defense Held on May 28, 1918," folder 208 KSC June [1918], ibid. See also letter to the County Councils of Defense, July 1, 1918, folder 208 KSC July [1918], ibid., announcing an African American committee and encouraging county work.

46. See Pendleton Buckley to Fleming, July 30, 1918, folder 208 KSC July [1918], box 714, entry 339, RG 62, NARA-CP, for the committee's creation and war conference plans. See also Hines to Fleming, August 15, 1918, folder 208 KSC August [1918], ibid., containing the minutes of the August 6 meeting.

47. Gretter's appointment was noted in Kentucky Council of Defense, *Report of the Activities of the Kentucky Council of Defense to January 1, 1919* (Frankfort, KY: State Journal Co., 1919), 8. The Kentucky Historical Society houses a large collection of Gretter's photographs. Copies of several *University of Kentucky Press Bulletins,* serving as the official KCD newsletter, can be found in UK Special Collections and Archives.

48. Caldwell's efforts as state historian of the war effort are outlined in KCD, *Report of Activities to January 1, 1920,* 43–49. This pamphlet also includes the names of all the county historians.

49. See Breen, *Uncle Sam at Home,* 177–79, for the creation of the Field Division. See also E. Jay Howenstine Jr., "Federal Planning for Demobilization during World War I," *American Journal of Economics and Sociology* 3, 4 (July 1944): 631–45, for more

on Clarkson and CND efforts. In December 1918 Clarkson would become the CND's director, succeeding its original director, Walter S. Gifford. *New York Times,* December 22, 1918.

50. The list of bulletins sent by the KCD to county councils is contained in KCD, *Report of Activities to January 1, 1920,* 66–70.

51. The conference is covered in more detail in chapter 14.

52. See Kentucky Council of Defense, *Final Report of the War Historical Work of the Kentucky Council of Defense* (n.p., n.d.). For a comparison of the KCD with other state councils, see William J. Breen, "The North Carolina Council of Defense during World War I, 1917–1918," *North Carolina Historical Review* 50, 1 (Winter 1973): 1–31; Lawrence O. Christiansen, "Missouri's Response to World War I: The Missouri Council of Defense," *Midwest Review,* 3rd ser., 12 (1990): 34–44; Gerald Senn, "'Molders of Thought, Directors of Action': The Arkansas Council of Defense, 1917–1918," *Arkansas Historical Quarterly* 36, 3 (Autumn 1977): 280–90.

4. Opposition to the War

1. See William H. Thomas, *Unsafe for Democracy: World War I and the U.S. Justice Department's Covert Campaign to Suppress Dissent* (Madison: University of Wisconsin Press, 2008), 30.

2. Ibid. For a good brief summary of the antecedents to the Espionage and Sedition Acts, see Scott A. Merriman, "'An Intensive School of Disloyalty': The C. B. Schoberg Case under the Espionage and Sedition Acts in Kentucky during World War I," *Register of the Kentucky Historical Society* 98, 2 (Spring 2000): 179–82.

3. Thomas, *Unsafe for Democracy,* 27.

4. Ibid., 30.

5. Scott A. Merriman, "Ordinary People in Extraordinary Times? Defendants, Attorneys, and the Federal Government's Policy under the Espionage and Sedition Acts during World War I in the Sixth Circuit Court of Appeals District," (PhD diss., University of Kentucky, 2003), 251.

6. For more about Boyce Taylor and his pastorate at the First Baptist Church in Murray, Calloway County, see Ira V. Birdwhistell, *A Heart for Missions: A History of First Baptist Church, Murray, Kentucky, 1846–1996* (Franklin, TN: Providence House, 1996); see especially chapter 3, "A Time of Growth, 1897–1918," for biographical information and Taylor's pastorate through the end of the Great War. Many thanks to Dr. Greg Earwood, a successor to Taylor at First Baptist and current president of the Baptist Seminary of Kentucky, for providing me with this resource.

7. *News and Truths* 12, 49 (December 5, 1917): 769, 772–74. Microfilm copies of *News and Truths* can be found in Murray State University Special Collections.

8. *News and Truths* 12, 35 (August 29, 1917): 553.

9. *News and Truths* 12, 39 (September 26, 1917): 614.

10. *News and Truths* 12, 35 (August 29, 1917): 545, 548.

11. *News and Truths* 12, 39 (September 26, 1917): 609, 612.

12. William J. McGlothlin diary, November 16, 1917, Archives and Special Collections, James P. Boyce Centennial Library, SBTS. McGlothlin was not the only one

at the seminary who supported the war effort. SBTS president Edgar Young Mullins agreed to serve as head of the Religious Department of the YMCA at Camp Taylor. See John R. Mott to E. Y. Mullins, August 23, 1917, folder 53, box 22 (November 1916–October 1917), E. Y. Mullins Papers, SBTS Archives, congratulating Mullins on his appointment. Mott received the Nobel Peace Prize in 1946 for his YMCA work. McGlothlin and Mullins are covered in greater detail in later chapters on military camps and on religion in Kentucky during the war.

13. *News and Truths* 12, 39 (September 26, 1917): 611, 616–17. In this matter of nations engaging in mob violence, Taylor was most assuredly reminded of a famous situation earlier in 1917 when a Murray mob had threatened grievous harm against a local judge in a case involving an African American accused of killing a policeman. The tension in the city prompted a visit by Governor Augustus O. Stanley, who called for the rule of law to be maintained and subsequently dispatched the Kentucky militia to keep order.

14. *Hopkinsville Kentuckian,* November 17 and 24, 1917. See also *Louisville Courier-Journal,* November 16, 1917, for Taylor's absence during the resolution, which called for support of President Wilson and the US government, and *Lexington Herald,* November 16, 1917, which reported that Taylor's excuse for being absent was that he had to attend a budget committee meeting.

15. Editorial, *Lexington Herald,* January 16, 1918. See also the letter to the editor from O. Olin Green, pastor of Richmond's First Baptist Church, noting that church deacon and Richmond mayor L. P. Evans had written to Taylor asking for clarification of his views; the Murray pastor sent Evans the December 5, 1917, edition of *News and Truths,* which "made comments derogatory to the work of the Red Cross and Y.M.C.A. work." The church consequently passed its resolution. *Louisville Courier-Journal,* January 16, 1918, reported on the Richmond church's condemnation.

16. See *Lexington Herald,* January 30, 1918, for the letter from Burns suggesting that Taylor be flayed. See also *Adair County News,* January 23, 1918.

17. *Louisville Courier-Journal,* January 19 and 20, 1918. The *Adair County News* reproduced the *Courier-Journal*'s January 20 editorial condemning Taylor in its January 30 edition.

18. *News and Truths* 13, 3 (January 16, 1918): 40.

19. *Louisville Courier-Journal,* January 21, 1918.

20. See Report of W. W. Grimes, Washington, DC, June 15, 1917, in re: Boyce Taylor, Minister, Murray, Ky., Anti-Conscription Matter, and "Friend of the Administration and of the Cause" to the War Department, August 30, 1917, OG file 24788, RG 65 (Federal Bureau of Investigation), NARA-CP. The DOJ's Bureau of Investigation underwent a name change in 1935 and became the Federal Bureau of Investigation (FBI).

21. Chief [Bielaski] to M. S. Egan, September 27, 1917, OG file 24788, RG 65, NARA-CP.

22. *American Bar Association Journal* 51, 4 (April 1965): 348.

23. Report of R. P. Hobson, Louisville, Ky., January 22, 1918, re: Rev. H. Boyce Taylor, Alleged Violations Selective Service and Espionage Acts, OG file 24788, RG 65, NARA-CP.

24. Hobson to R. D. Ramsey, February 9, 1918, ibid.

25. Memorandum for Mr. O'Brian, February 12, 1918, ibid.

26. Memorandum for Mr. Bettman, February 13, 1918, ibid.

27. Memorandum for Mr. Bielaski, March 1, 1918, ibid.

28. See R. Y. Thomas Jr. to Attorney General T. W. Gregory, January 16, 1918, and Chief [Bielaski] to Hon. R. Y. Thomas, January 23, 1918; Colonel R. H. Van Deman, General Staff, War Department, to Bruce Bielaski, February 26, 1918, and Bielaski to Van Deman, March 2, 1918; Chief [Bielaski] to Robert Hobson, March 2, 1918, ibid. Thomas served as a US representative from 1909 to his death in 1925. Van Deman was chief of military intelligence.

29. Bielaski to T. R. Cartmell, April 5, 1917, and Hobson report, Louisville, Ky., April 17, 1918, in re Rev. H. Boyce Taylor, Pro German Matter, ibid.

30. See *Journal of the Regular Session of the Senate,* vol. 1 (Frankfort, KY: State Journal Company, 1918).

31. See news story prepared by KCD news director Maud W. Cossar dated June 20, 1918, and "Report of Executive Secretary (Read at Meeting of Kentucky Council of Defense, June 15, 1918)," "Meeting of the Executive Committee August 31, 1918," and letter from Perry Miller to Edward Hines, August 14, 1918, contained in Kentucky Council of Defense, *World War I Journal,* Schmidt Library, KHS. The news story was sent to local newspapers and to the Associated Press. See also KCD, *Report of the Activities to January 1, 1920,* 34–35; *Louisville Courier-Journal,* June 21, 1918; *Daily Kentuckian* (Hopkinsville, KY), July 4, 1918.

32. For more on Taylor's refusal to comply with the health quarantine and his subsequent trials, fines, and jailing, see *Richmond Daily Register,* January 28, 29, and 30, 1919; *Louisville Courier-Journal,* January 30 and February 1, 1919; *Maysville Public Ledger,* January 30, 1919; *Richmond Daily Ledger,* February 24, 1919; *Hartford Herald,* February 26, 1919; *Richmond Daily Register,* April 11, 1919; *Adair County News,* April 16, 1919; and *Hopkinsville Kentuckian,* April 23, 1919. For more on Taylor's lengthy career, see "Calloway County Churches—First Baptist—Boyce Taylor," Vertical File, Special Collections and Archives, Pogue Library, Murray State University, Murray, KY. The file contains a lengthy eight-part retrospective on Taylor's life published by the *Murray Ledger and Times* beginning in June 1939.

33. See "Report of the Executive Secretary from August 14 to August 28, 1918," and "Report of the Executive Secretary from August 28, 1918, to September 25, 1918," in KCD, *World War I Journal.* See also *Louisville Courier-Journal,* August 25, 1918.

34. "Some of the Things the Kentucky Council of Defense Has Done," July 1918, in KCD, *World War I Journal.*

35. Merriman, "'Intensive School of Disloyalty,'" 185–87.

36. For more on the three indicted men, see Lisa Gillham with Bethany Richter Pollitt, "J. H. Kruse, War & the Terrible Threateners: Anti-German Hysteria in World War I Covington," *Northern Kentucky Heritage* 15, 1 (Fall–Winter 2007): 3–38.

37. Merriman, "'Intensive School of Disloyalty,'" 187–88. For more on Cochran, see his entry in Biographical Directory of Federal Judges, Federal Judicial Center, www.fjc.gov/servlet/nGetInfo?jid=463&cid=999&ctype=na&instate=na. A Democrat, Slattery served as US district attorney until 1921, when he was asked

to resign by President Harding after the regime change. Slattery did not go quietly, maintaining that his appointment was for a term set by law. When forced out, he returned home to practice law in Maysville. See *New York Times,* October 7, 1921. For more on McPherson, see his obituary and tribute in Vinton Shephard, ed., *Ohio Law Reporter,* vol. 18 (Cincinnati: Ohio Law Reporter Co., 1921), 229–30, 235–36. For more on Bowdle, see his entry in Biographical Dictionary of the United States Congress, bioguide.congress.gov/scripts/biodisplay.pl?index=B000679. Rogers served as a Kentucky state legislator and highway commissioner.

38. Merriman, "'Intensive School of Disloyalty,'" 186–91.

39. Ibid., 192–95.

40. Ibid., 196–97.

41. Ibid., 200–202.

42. Ibid., 198–200.

43. Ibid., 202–4.

44. Thomas, *Unsafe for Democracy,* 75.

45. Merriman, "Ordinary People in Extraordinary Times?" 251.

46. Thomas, *Unsafe for Democracy,* 4. For more on the Holiness Church and pacifism, see Jay Beaman and Brian K. Pipkin, eds., *Pentecostal and Holiness Statements on War and Peace* (Eugene, OR: Wipf and Stock, 2013).

47. Merriman, "Ordinary People in Extraordinary Times?" 276, 280.

48. Reports of L. O. Thompson, Lexington, Ky., April 30 and July 16, 1918, OG file 192171. Dyer's name is spelled "Dyre" in these reports. It remains unclear whether Dyer was really a member of the Holiness Church.

49. Merriman, "Ordinary People in Extraordinary Times?" 277.

50. Report of R. E. Monroe, June 18, 1918, in re: W. R. Hamlin—Alleged Disloyal Propaganda in Connection with the Draft, OG file 209033.

51. Merriman, "Ordinary People in Extraordinary Times?" 275. See also "'Holy Roller' Who Said 'Dead Soldiers Go to Hell' Imprisoned," *Louisville Courier-Journal,* September 26, 1918.

52. *Louisville Courier-Journal,* May 17, 1918; Merriman, "Ordinary People in Extraordinary Times?" 283, 297.

53. *Louisville Courier-Journal,* March 21, 1917.

54. See *Louisville Courier-Journal,* March 19, June 4, September 7, 1917, January 24 and 31, February 2 and 5, 1918, for articles on Stilli and Breitenstein.

55. See Jacob Lee, "American Legion, Jefferson Post #15, Records 1919–1988," *Filson Newmagazine* 6, 1 (n.d.), www.filsonhistorical.org/archive/news_N6n1_legion.html, and *Hopkinsville Kentuckian,* November 1, 1919, for the demise of the People's Church.

56. Merriman, "Ordinary People in Extraordinary Times?" 282.

57. Ibid., 283–86. Merriman believes that "some of Bettman's decisions were at least partially based on his ideologies of class and gender" (ibid., 286). See Thomas, *Unsafe for Democracy,* 56, in which the author argues that "prevailing class and gender expectations played a role in how the [Justice] department evaluated women. Upper-class women who expressed their dissent in a genteel fashion seemed to pose less of a threat than those from a lower social and economic class." See also *Kentucky Post,* June 13, 1918.

58. See *Big Sandy News* (Louisa, KY), March 15, 1918, for Ward's alleged quote about Wilson. Ward's conviction and sentencing were reported in *Louisville Courier-Journal,* June 13, 1918, and *Big Sandy News,* June 21, 1918. See also Case File 8537, Walter Ward, Atlanta Penitentiary Files, RG 129 (Bureau of Prisons), NARA-ATL.

59. See *Louisville Courier-Journal,* May 18, 1918, for complaints against Vincent and his transfer to Paducah. *Lexington Herald,* June 9, 1918, reported on his sentencing. The charge against him is quoted from a sentencing document in Case File 8467, Ester Vincent, Atlanta Penitentiary Files, RG 129, NARA-ATL.

60. Merriman, "Ordinary People in Extraordinary Times?" 293–94.

61. Thomas, *Unsafe for Democracy,* 55–56.

62. Report of R. E. Monroe, December 13, 1918, in re: Ernest Miller—Alleged Disloyalty, OG file 334432. Although this report was dated 1918, it must have been filed in 1917, given that Professor Miller alluded to the Germans being very near Paris, which was definitely not the case in December 1918.

63. See Report of L. O. Thompson, April 17, 1918, in re: Barney Fotch—Alleged to Be Pro-German, and Thompson to Bielaski, May 16, 1918, OG file 178556.

64. Thomas, *Unsafe for Democracy,* 31.

65. For vigilantism in America during the Great War, see Capozzola, "Only Badge Needed," 1354–82, and the chapter on "Vigilantism" in Thomas, *Unsafe for Democracy,* 146–71.

66. National Civil Liberties Bureau, *The Outrage on Rev. Herbert S. Bigelow of Cincinnati, Ohio* (New York: National Civil Liberties Bureau, 1918), 3.

67. For more on the Citizens' Patriotic League, see Tenkotte and Claypool, *Encyclopedia of Northern Kentucky,* 475–76.

68. National Civil Liberties Union, *Outrage on Bigelow,* 8–12. See also *Lexington Herald,* October 30, 1917. A *Herald* editorial on November 2, 1917, chided the "pacifist" secretary of war Newton Baker, calling him a friend of Bigelow and "a prominent member of the People's Peace Party, a notorious pro-German outfit."

69. *New York Times,* October 30, 1917, and January 14, 1918; *Louisville Courier-Journal,* October 30, 1917. See also Robert Kirschenbaum, "Klan and Commonwealth: The Ku Klux Klan and Politics in Kentucky, 1921–1928" (MA thesis, University of Kentucky, 2005), 26–27, which cites the Bigelow case as an example of vigilante justice condoned by local elites.

70. *Louisville Courier-Journal,* June 9, 1918. The *Courier-Journal* misidentified Blakely as "Stephen D. Blakely." Noting that Blakely was "present and actively involved in these outbursts of mob violence," Kirschenbaum concludes: "Given free reign by both state and federal officials, Blakely is typical of the Kentucky local elites who held both their official position and served informally as leaders of vigilante groups." In explaining the weakness of the Klan in Kentucky in the 1920s, Kirschenbaum notes: "Thus the Klan could not effectively demand a role in driving out subversives without undermining the role of local elites. This was quite simply something local elites were unwilling to accept." Kirschenbaum, "Klan and Commonwealth," 30, 34. For more on Blakely, see Tenkotte and Claypool, *Encyclopedia of Northern Kentucky,* 92–93. For more on Harvey Myers Jr., see E. Polk Johnson, *A History of Kentucky and Kentuck-*

ians: The Leaders and Representative Men in Commerce, Industry and Modern Activities (Chicago: Lewis Publishing Co., 1912), 2:993–94.

71. *Cincinnati Enquirer,* June 6, 1918. A copy of the CPL placard was printed in *Kentucky Post,* June 6, 1918. See also *Louisville Courier-Journal,* June 9, 1918.

72. *Cincinnati Enquirer,* June 7, 1918.

73. *Cincinnati Enquirer,* June 15, 1918.

74. Identical pieces supporting the CPL can be found in *Interior Journal* (Stanford, KY), August 6, 1918, and *Bourbon News* (Paris, KY), August 9, 1918.

75. See *Louisville Courier-Journal,* April 30, 1918, for the Paducah Citizens Loyal Committee. The other instances of mob violence are noted in Kirschenbaum, "Klan and Commonwealth," 33, based on a review of ACLU archives.

76. *Public Ledger* (Maysville, KY), July 6, 1918.

77. National Civil Liberties Bureau, *War-Time Prosecutions and Mob Violence, Involving the Rights of Free Speech, Free Press and Peaceful Assemblage* (New York: National Civil Liberties Bureau, 1919), 164. The Bigelow case is mentioned in Capozzolla, *Uncle Sam Wants You,* 163; Thomas, *Unsafe for Democracy,* 151; Kennedy, *Over Here,* 73.

5. The Draft

1. The debate on preparedness is covered in Clifford, *Citizen Soldiers.*

2. See John Whiteclay Chambers II, *To Raise an Army: The Draft Comes to Modern America* (New York: Free Press, 1987), 1–124, for the antecedents to the Great War draft, the preparedness discussion, and the form that military reorganization would take.

3. See ibid., 125–51.

4. For the congressional debate, see ibid., 153–77. For the opposition to the war and the draft in the southern states, see Jeanette Keith, *Rich Man's War, Poor Man's Fight: Race, Class, and Power in the Rural South during the First World War* (Chapel Hill: University of North Carolina Press, 2004), 13–56. Keith describes strong opposition from southern agrarian politicians such as Democrats Claude Kitchens of North Carolina and James Vardaman of Mississippi, as well as populist leader Tom Watson of Georgia.

5. *Louisville Courier-Journal,* May 4, 1917.

6. *Interior Journal* (Stanford, KY), June 15, 1917.

7. See O. E. Fox to Charles Frey, January 14, 1917; Charles Frey to Bruce Bielaski, January 14, 1917; Bielaski to Frey, January 15, 1918, A1, Correspondence on Investigations 1918–1919, folder E. 15, box 1, entries 14, 15, 16, RG 65, NARA-CP. In failing health and having lost the endorsements of several newspapers in his district, Powers eventually withdrew from his 1918 reelection campaign against fellow Republican John Robsion, a Barbourville lawyer. See *Mt. Vernon Signal,* November 16, 1917, reprinting an editorial from the *Barbourville Mountain Advocate* noting its switch from Powers to Robsion, and November 23, 1917, reprinting an editorial from the *Whitley Republican* suggesting that Powers not seek reelection.

8. *Louisville Courier-Journal,* April 26, 1917; *New York Times,* April 16, 1917. In

its April 27, 1917, editorial, the *Courier-Journal* lauded Sherley as a "striking example of patriotic service" whose speech "deserves position among the historic documents touching crucial periods of American history."

9. Chambers, *To Raise an Army,* 172–86. See *Louisville Courier-Journal,* May 24, 1917, for a listing of physicians named to local boards by Governor Stanley.

10. Chambers, *To Raise an Army,* 186–204.

11. See telegram from Governor A. O. Stanley to Secretary of War, May 7, 1917, recommending Ellis as disbursing officer, and Tandy Ellis to Provost Marshal General, May 22, 1917, accepting the appointment, folder 1, box 141, entry 2 States Files, RG 163 (Selective Service), NARA-CP.

12. See *Louisville Courier-Journal,* July 23, 1917, for Rhodes as sergeant in the Adjutant General's Office, and December 6, 1917, for his appointment as head of the state selective service system. Stanley's nomination of Rhodes is in Stanley to Crowder, November 15, 1917. See also O.P.M.G. to General James Tandy Ellis, January 4, 1918, noting that Rhodes was the disbursing officer effective December 25, 1917, file KY 65 (1–20), box 144, entry 2 States Files, RG 163, NARA-CP. The postwar report is in memorandum for General Crowder by Captain Jesse I. Miller, January 6, 1919, file KY 22 (1–20), box 143, entry 2 States Files, RG 163, NARA-CP.

13. See United States War Department, Provost Marshal General's Bureau, *Second Report of the Provost Marshal General to the Secretary of War on the Operations of the Selective Service System to December 20, 1918* (Washington, DC: Government Printing Office, 1919), 266.

14. *Mountain Advocate* (Barbourville, KY), May 25, 1917. For an example of volunteer registrars, see *Public Ledger* (Maysville, KY), May 25, 1917. Governor Stanley's appointment of physicians for the boards was reported in *Louisville Courier-Journal,* May 24, 1917.

15. *Crittenden Record-Press,* May 31, 1917; *Hopkinsville Kentuckian,* June 5, 1917. For examples of selective service explanations, see *Mt. Sterling Advocate,* May 7, 1917; *Hickman Courier,* May 10, 1917.

16. See *Lexington Herald,* May 26, 1917; *Big Sandy News* (Louisa, KY), June 1, 1917.

17. *Bourbon News* (Paris, KY), June 8, 1917.

18. *Central Record* (Lancaster, KY), June 7, 1917; *Licking Valley Courier* (West Liberty, KY), June 7, 1917.

19. *Louisville Courier-Journal,* June 22, 1917. These figures are contained in a telegram from Governor A. O. Stanley to General E. H. Crowder, June 18, 1918, file KY 13 (21–40), box 141, entry 2 States Files, RG 163, NARA-CP. According to a postwar provost marshal general's report, the Kentucky total registered on June 5, 1917, was 193,988 out of the nation's 9,780,535. See *Second Report of the Provost Marshal General,* 396. Chambers asserts in *To Raise an Army,* 211: "Registration was universally hailed as an enormous success." See also telegram from Governor A. O. Stanley to Provost Marshal General, June 5, 1917, file 4, box 141, entry 2 States Files, RG 163, NARA-CP, in which the governor states: "No interference reported with registration at this time am receiving good reports from all over the state."

20. United States War Department, Provost Marshal General's Bureau, *Final*

Report of the Provost Marshal General to the Secretary of War on the Operations of the Selective Service System to July 15, 1919 (Washington, DC: Government Printing Office, 1920), 19, puts the number of Kentucky registrants at 486,739, which was 2.05 percent of the total national registration of over 23 million men.

21. See transmittal letter from Stanley to P.M.G., June 6, 1917, and lists of medical and legal boards in file KY 21 (1–20), box 142, entry 2 States Files, RG 163, NARA-CP. The district boards are set out in Stanley to Crowder, July 10, 1917, file KY 23 (1–20), box 143, entry 2 States Files, RG 163, NARA-CP. See also *Lexington Herald,* May 23, 1917; *Louisville Courier-Journal,* May 4, 1917, for news of registration boards.

22. *Second Report of the Provost Marshal General,* 22–32, 199–201.

23. *Louisville Courier-Journal,* July 4 and August 1, 1917. The August 1 and 15, 1917, editions reported that two men in Shelby County declined to serve in the place of two men who had resigned.

24. See Crowder's warning telegram to Stanley, July 16, 1917, file KY 20, box 142, entry 2 States Files, RG 163, NARA-CP.

25. Examples of resignation correspondence are in files KY 21 (1–20), KY 21 (21–40), KY 21 (41–60), box 142, entry 2 States Files, RG 163, NARA-CP. For the "mountain doctor" case, see Rhodes to Crowder, February 13, 1918, file KY 21 (61–80), ibid.

26. For the Adair County case, see N. T. Mercer to Senator Ollie James, February 27, 1918; James to Crowder, March 2, 1918; Crowder to James, March 4, 1918; P.M.G.O. to Governor of Kentucky, March 4, 1918, file KY 21 (61–80), box 142, entry 2 States Files, RG 163, NARA-CP. For the Pendleton County case, see Local Board, Pendleton County, Kentucky, to Rhodes, September 7, 1918; Rhodes to P.M.G., September 12, 1918, file KY 21 (81–100), ibid.

27. For more on Bablitz's activities, see *Louisville Courier-Journal,* March 13, 1916, and September 21, 1917; *Cincinnati Enquirer,* July 14, 1913, and September 4, 1916; *Lexington Leader,* October 31, 1907, and December 3, 1913.

28. See *Lexington Herald,* November 15, 1914. For Bablitz's membership in the Four Minute Men, see the October 21, 1917, edition; for his work on a farm, see the June 20, 1918, edition.

29. Report of L. O. Thompson, in re: A. A. Bablitz (German)—Objected to as Member Local Board for City of Lexington, Kentucky, February 4, 1918, file KY 17 (1–20), box 141, entry 2 States Files, RG 163, NARA-CP. Monroe received his bachelor's and master's degrees from the University of Michigan and taught at Georgetown College before moving on to Transylvania. He became a Bureau of Investigation agent on June 1, 1918. He eventually became a German-language professor at Ohio State University. See *Michigan Alumnus* 15, 137 (October 1908): 32; 16, 151 (February 1910): 267; 45, 1 (October 8, 1938): 13. See also Monroe to A. Bruce Bielaski, September 20, 1918, requesting that he not be given a deferred draft classification despite having a wife and daughter, and Bruce Bielaski, memorandum for the Attorney General, October 4, 1918, in which the BI chief asserts that Monroe was "an exceptionally qualified and high grade man," OG files, Agents' Draft Classifications, RG 65, NARA-CP.

30. Report of Thompson, February 4, 1918. Thompson was the BI local officer from December 6, 1913, to June 1, 1918, when he became the special agent in charge

in Lexington. He had no grounds for a deferment, but Bielaski sought one for him because he was one of the bureau's older agents, his service had been "conscientious and satisfactory," and his "experience and training" would be a "material loss to the Bureau." A. B. Bielaski, memorandum for the Attorney General, October 4, 1918, OG files, Agents' Draft Classifications, RG 65, NARA-CP.

31. Report of L. O. Thompson, in re: A. A. Bablitz (German)—Objected to as Member Local Board for City of Lexington, Kentucky, February 13, 1918, file KY 17 (1–20), box 141, entry 2 States Files, RG 163, NARA-CP. Although he may have found Bablitz disagreeable in public, Baker himself had been involved in a fistfight and the knifing of Leving Young, a Confederate veteran and one of John Hunt Morgan's men. See *Louisville Courier-Journal,* May 12, 1909. Baker and Bablitz were partners for three years.

32. Report of L. O. Thompson, in re: A. A. Bablitz (German)—Objected to as Member Local Board for City of Lexington, Kentucky, February 9, 1918, file KY 17 (1–20), box 141, entry 2 States Files, RG 163, NARA-CP.

33. Ibid., February 19, 1918.

34. Report of Carl Jansen, in re: A. A. Bablitz (German)—Objected to as Member Local Board for City of Lexington, Kentucky, February 19, 1918, file KY 17 (1–20), box 141, entry 2 States Files, RG 163, NARA-CP.

35. Report of L. O. Thompson, in re: A. A. Bablitz (German)—Objected to as Member Local Board for City of Lexington, Kentucky, March 8, 1918, ibid.

36. Bielaski to Crowder, March 15, 1918; Crowder to Bielaski, March 18, 1918; P.M.G.O. to Major Henry F. Rhodes, March 18, 1918; Rhodes to P.M.G., April 12, 1918, ibid. Bablitz's resignation was reported in *Lexington Herald,* April 16, 1918. He continued his career as a successful labor lawyer and passed away in 1964. See his obituary in *Kentucky Alumnus* 3, 35 (Fall 1964): 30.

37. For more on Debs, see Kennedy, *Over Here,* 84–86. The Supreme Court case was *Debs v. United States,* 249 US 211 (1919). For more on "policing the Left," especially socialists, see Thomas, *Unsafe for Democracy,* 89–109.

38. Report of L. O. Thompson, in re: J. B. Clark—Member, Local Board, Martin, Ky.—Irregularities, October 20, 1917; depositions of Henry Preece, Jesse Mattox, Garfield Cassady, Andy Goble, and Jasper Stacy; A. B. Bielaski to E. H. Crowder, October 31, 1917; O.P.M.G. to A.G.K., November 16, 1917, file KY 17 (1–20), box 141, entry 2 States Files, RG 163, NARA-CP.

39. *Hartford Herald,* August 22, 1917; *Crittenden Record-Press* (Marion, KY), September 6, 1917; and *Lexington Herald,* August 21, 22, and 30, 1917, reported the charges against Taylor. See also *Louisville Courier-Journal,* August 17, 18, and 30, 1917. Telegrams from Stanley to Crowder, August 15, 17, 18, and 21, 1917; telegrams from Crowder to Stanley, August 18, 21, and 22, 1917; Gaines Cooksey Clerk to Provost Marshal, August 17, 1917; J. S. Taylor to Crowder, August 17, 1918; Representative R. Y. Thomas Jr. to J. S. Taylor, August 19, 1917; Thomas to Crowder, August 19, 1917; Bruce Bielaski, Chief, DOJ Bureau of Investigation, to Crowder, August 21, 1917; Crowder to Bielaski, August 30, 1917, file KY 21 (21–40), box 142, entry 2 States Files, RG 163, NARA-CP.

40. Chambers, *To Raise an Army,* 222.

41. Anonymous letter from Madisonville, Ky.; P.M.G.O. to A.G.K., February 5, 1918, file KY 17 (1–20), box 141, entry 2 States Files, RG 163, NARA-CP. For more on Yost, see Johnson, *History of Kentucky and Kentuckians,* 3:1409–10; *Louisville Courier-Journal,* August 25 and 27, September 16, 1917. The district appeals board that Yost headed overturned many local board exemptions given to men who were married but had no children. Charles Franklin was appointed a member of the legal advisory committee to the local board in Madisonville. *Louisville Courier-Journal,* December 3, 1917.

42. Reports of L. O. Thompson, in re: Irregularities of Draft Board of Wayne County, Ky., September 16 and 19, 1917, file KY 17 (141–60), box 142, entry 2 States Files, RG 163, NARA-CP.

43. Reports of R. E. Monroe, Irregularities of Draft Board of Wayne County, Ky. (O. B. Bertram, Secretary, Dr. Young, Chairman), October 6, 1918, ibid.

44. Ibid.

45. E. P. McSherry to Edmund Leigh, Chief, Plant Protection Section, July 30, 1918; Chief, Military Intelligence Branch to Provost Marshal General, August 6, 1918; O.P.M.G. to Rhodes, August 15, 1918, file KY 17 (21–40), box 141, entry 2 States Files, RG 163, NARA-CP.

46. M. Scott to Rhodes, October 8, 1918, ibid.

47. Crowder to Rhodes, October 28, 1918, ibid.

48. Bielaski to Crowder, April 2, 1918, ibid.

49. Ibid.; reports of Special Agent John Menefee, in re: Dr. E. J. Buten—Irregular Physical Examinations of Registrants of Local Board for Newport, Ky., March 15 and 21, 1918, file KY 17 (21–40), box 141, entry 2 States Files, RG 163, NARA-CP.

50. Crowder to Rhodes, April 5, 1918; Rhodes to Crowder, April 12, 1918; reports of agent Menefee, April 1 and 6, 1918; Bielaski to Crowder, April 23, 1918; Crowder to Bielaski, April 27, 1918, ibid.

51. See notice from Dr. A. J. Wahle, June 20, 1918; H. M. Curl, Manager, Chicago Veneer Co., Burnside, Ky., to B. W. Lord, Pres., Chicago Veneer Co., Chicago, Ill., July 1, 1918; B. W. Lord to Plywood Section, Office of the Chief Signal Officer, Washington, DC, June 26, 1918; Crowder to Rhodes, July 9, 1918; Rhodes to Crowder, July 16, 1918, file KY 22 (1–20), box 143, entry 2 States Files, RG 163, NARA-CP. See also follow-up material in B. W. Lord to Walter Clark, Bureau of Aircraft Production, Washington, DC, July 3, 1918; Marion Weddle, Ingle, Ky., to Secretary of War, July 2, 1918; Crowder to C. Blanchard, Bureau of Aircraft Production, July 10, 1918; memorandum for General Crowder, July 18, 1918; O.P.M.G. to Draft Representatives in all States, July 18, 1918, file KY (101–120), box 144, entry 2 States Files, RG 163, NARA-CP. The memorandum of July 18 noted: "It would be one of the most humorous episodes of the S. S. L. if it were not for the sacrifices it caused."

52. Office of the Provost Marshal General to Rhodes, June 1, 1918; memorandum for Major Conkling by Lieutenant W. W. Holloway, June 1, 1918, file KY 53 (1), box 144, entry 2 States Files, RG 163, NARA-CP.

53. Rhodes to District Board Division 1, Western District, Louisville, Ky., August 8, 1918; Rhodes to Provost Marshal General, August 16, 1918; War Dept., P.M.G.O. to Rhodes, August 26, 1918, ibid.

54. Letter to the Treasury Department, June 17, 1918; P.M.G.O. to Rhodes, July 9, 1918; Rhodes to Estal Garry, July 17, 1918; Rhodes to Local Board, Boyd County, Catlettsburg, Kentucky, September 7, 1918; Local Board for Boyd County to Rhodes, November 15, 1918, file KY 17 (1–20), box 141, entry 2 States Files, RG 163, NARA-CP.

55. Undated letter from Bessie Stovall; P.M.G.O. to Rhodes, July 19, 1918; Local Board Warren County, Bowling Green, Ky., to Rhodes, July 19, 1918; Rhodes to Local Board Warren County, July 19, 1918; Local Board Warren County to Charles Stovall, July 22, 1918; Local Board Warren County to Rhodes, July 29, 1918, file KY 17 (41–60), box 141, entry 2 States Files, RG 163, NARA-CP. The draft eligibility age was raised to forty-five when the Selective Service Act was amended on August 1918.

56. Dolly McBee to Provost Marshal General Crowder, August 8, 1918; P.M.G.O. to Rhodes, August 13, 1918; Local Board Lincoln County, August 27, 1918; Rhodes to P.M.G., September 2, 1918, ibid.

57. *New York Times,* July 3, 1917.

58. Crowder to Mary Snelling, Clothier, W.Va., March 7, 1918, ibid.

59. State of Ky., A.G.O., Frankfort to P.M.G., November 26, 1917; P.M.G.O. to Adjutant General, November 30, 1917; Senator Ollie James to Provost Marshal General, December 31, 1917; H. S. Johnson, P.M.G.O., to Ollie James, January 2, 1918, file KY 13 (21–40), box 141, entry 2 States Files, RG 163, NARA-CP.

60. See P.M.G.O. to A.G.K., January 31, 1918; John T. King to Major Henry Rhodes, April 3, 1918; Rhodes to P.M.G., April 5, 1918, file KY 17 (1–20), box 141, entry 2 States Files, RG 163, NARA-CP.

61. P.M.G.O. to Major Henry F. Rhodes, February 26, 1918, ibid.

62. Senator J. C. W. Beckham to P.M.G., February 16, 1918; Crowder to Senator J. C. W. Beckham, February 18, 1917, file KY 58 (1–20), box 144, entry 2 States Files, RG 163, NARA-CP.

63. Crowder to Johnson, June 11, 1918, file KY 50 (1–20), box 143, entry 2 States Files, RG 163, NARA-CP; telegram from John W. Langley M.C. to P.M.G., May 22, 1918; telegram from Crowder to Langley, May 24, 1918, file KY 59 (1–20), box 144, entry 2 States Files, RG 163, NARA-CP.

64. Johnson to Rhodes, June 14, 1918; Rhodes to Johnson, June 25, 1918; Johnson to Crowder, July 2, 1918; Crowder to Johnson, July 8, 1918; Crowder to Rhodes, July 8, 1918; W. A. Barry to Johnson, August 12, 1918; Crowder to Rhodes, August 19, 1918; Crowder to Johnson, August 19, 1918, file KY 50 (1–20), box 143, entry 2 States Files, RG 163, NARA-CP.

65. Telegram from Austin to Adjutant General, Washington, DC, July 4, 1918, file KY 17 (1–20), box 141, entry 2 States Files, RG 163, NARA-CP. For more on Brigadier General Austin, an artillery officer who took command of Camp Taylor in June 1918, see *Louisville Courier-Journal,* June 24, 1918.

66. Telegram from Crowder to Rhodes, July 6, 1918; telegram from Rhodes to Crowder, undated, file KY 17 (1–20), box 141, entry 2 States Files, RG 163, NARA-CP.

67. Memorandum for Captain Jones, Judge Advocate, July 11, 1918, file KY 17 (21–40), box 141, entry 2 States Files, RG 163, NARA-CP.

68. Camp Judge Advocate to Crowder, July 14, 1918, ibid.

69. Office of the Provost Marshal General to Rhodes, July 17, 1918, ibid. See also *Louisville Courier-Journal,* August 31, 1918, which noted that Crowder had informed Rhodes that "all cases of obstinate willful desertion are to be vigorously prosecuted."

70. Rhodes to P.M.G., November 21, 1918, file KY 17 (141–60), box 142, entry 2 States Files, RG 163, NARA-CP.

71. Rhodes to Local Board for Letcher County, Whitesburg, Ky., October 22, 1918, ibid.

72. See Keith, *Rich Man's War,* 184–93, for more on armed resistance in the South.

73. For the Morrison case, see *Lexington Herald,* January 12 and September 11, 1918; *Licking Valley Courier* (West Liberty, KY), January 24, 1918; *Public Ledger* (Maysville, KY), March 18, 1918.

74. For the Henkle case, see *Louisville Courier-Journal,* July 9 and 10, 1918.

75. For the Pitts shooting, see *Mt. Sterling Advocate,* August 20, 1918. For the Sizemore case, see *Citizen* (Berea, KY), July 11, 1918; *Louisville Courier-Journal,* July 27, 1918, and May 2, 1919.

76. For the Mingo County pitched battle, see *Cincinnati Enquirer,* August 22, 1918; *Public Ledger* (Maysville, KY), August 22, 1918; *Big Sandy News* (Louisa, KY), August 23, 1918.

77. Rhodes to Crowder, October 8, 1918; Crowder to Rhodes, October 14, 1918, file KY 17 (141–60), box 142, entry 2 States Files, RG 163, NARA-CP. Rhodes distributed a list of deserters to key officials in the state; a copy of the deserter list arranged by counties can be found in folder 20, box 1, Joseph Llewellyn Price Collection (MSS 88), Manuscripts and Folklife Archives, Department of Library Special Collections, WKU. A lawyer and county judge, Price was head of the American Protective League and the food administrator for Marshall County.

78. Rhodes to P.M.G., May 22, 1918, file KY (101–20), box 144, entry 2 States Files, RG 163, NARA-CP.

79. Crowder to Governor Stanley, July 12, 1918, ibid.

80. Richard R. Farr, National Inspector, to P.M.G., October 29, 1918, file KY 75, box 144, entry 2 States Files, RG 163, NARA-CP.

81. See questionnaire of Local Board for Washington County, Ky., box 16, entry 14 Local Board Experiences, RG 163, NARA-CP.

82. George A. Read, Chairman, Local Board #2, Covington, Kenton County, Ky., to Provost Marshal General, December 3, 1917, file KY 13 (21–40), box 141, entry 2 States Files, RG 163, NARA-CP.

83. See questionnaire of Local Board for Hart County, Ky., box 16, entry 14 Local Board Experiences, RG 163, NARA-CP.

84. *Louisville Courier-Journal,* August 13, 1917.

85. *Final Report of the Provost Marshal General,* 54.

6. Army Camps

1. See *Lexington Herald,* October 4, 1917, for the history of the development of the Lansing farm camp. For more on the camp, see the Lexington History Museum

website at lexhistory.org/wikilex/camp-stanley. This site apparently reproduces material found in William M. Ambrose, *Bluegrass Military Camps* (Lexington, KY: Limestone Press, 2012).

2. *Lexington Herald,* April 14, 18, 21, 22, and 24, 1917.

3. The naming of Camp Stanley was reported in *Lexington Herald,* June 18, 1917. Mobilization at Camp Stanley was reported in *Louisville Courier-Journal,* June 20, 1917. WCTU efforts were reported in the *Courier-Journal* on June 23, 1917. See also lexhistory.org/wikilex/camp-stanley.

4. See *Louisville Courier-Journal,* July 1, 1917, for the Camp Stanley training program.

5. See Bolin, *Bossism and Reform in a Southern City,* 64–69, for efforts to analyze the problems and "clean up" Lexington so the city could host a mobilization camp. For more on Belle Brezing, see Maryjean Wall, *Madam Belle: Sex, Money, and Influence in a Southern Brothel* (Lexington: University Press of Kentucky, 2015). Brezing was supposedly the model for Belle Watling in Margaret Mitchell's *Gone with the Wind* (Mitchell's husband, John Marsh, was the Lexington newspaperman who had joined the Barrow Unit, and he knew Brezing's reputation).

6. Nancy K. Bristow, *Making Men Moral: Social Engineering during the Great War* (New York: New York University Press, 1996), 98.

7. John G. Buchanan, "War Legislation against Alcoholic Liquor and Prostitution," *Journal of Criminal Law and Criminology* 9, 4 (1919): 520–21.

8. See *Lexington Herald,* June 12, 1917. The arrest of a woman found inside the camp was reported in *Louisville Courier-Journal,* July 10, 1918.

9. See "Pay Day Proves Too Much for the Men of the 'Thirsty Third,'" *Louisville Courier-Journal,* July 29, 1917. For the complaint against Riley, see *Lexington Herald,* October 13, 1917. Riley had previously been condemned in a resolution by Lexington physicians, including Dr. David Barrow, for failing to punish violations of the local health code; see Arthur T. McCormack, MD, ed., *Kentucky Medical Journal* 14 (January 1, 1916): 53.

10. See L. O. Thompson, in re: Al Overstreet—Selling Liquor to Soldiers in Uniform, Alleged Violation Section 12 [*sic*] Conscription Act, August 4 and 9, September 19, 1917; L. O. Thompson, in re: Violation Section 12 [*sic*] Conscription Act (Selling Liquor to Soldiers in Uniform), July 26, 1917; Bielaski to Thompson, July 30, 1917; L. O. Thompson, in re: Selling Liquor to Soldiers in Uniform (Tyrone, Ky.), Alleged Violations Section 12 [*sic*] Conscription Act, August 6 and 11, 1917, OG file 29369.

11. See lexhistory.org/wikilex/camp-stanley for payroll figures. The *Louisville Courier-Journal,* July 24, 1917, reported $10,000 in payroll distributed, but at the new army standard of $30 per month, a force of over 2,500 men would have received much nearer the $100,000 mark. This was the figure reported in *Lexington Herald,* July 23, 1917. See Raymond Fosdick to Bruce Bielaski, September 29, 1917, and accompanying reports of September 23, 24, and 25, OG file 29369. See also *Lexington Herald,* October 13, 1917.

12. Bielaski to Thompson, October 10 and 15, 1917, OG file 29369.

13. *Louisville Courier-Journal,* July 15, 1917.

14. *Louisville Courier-Journal,* June 12, 1917.

15. *Lexington Herald,* May 21 and 24, 1917.

16. The announcement of Louisville's selection was in *Louisville Courier-Journal,* June 12, 1917, and *Lexington Herald,* June 12, 1917.

17. *Lexington Herald,* June 14, 1917.

18. See *Lexington Herald,* June 14, 15, and 17, 1917, for the Lexington delegation's trip to Washington; see *Louisville Courier-Journal,* June 15, 1917, reporting that the Lexington delegation did not seek to reverse the choice of Louisville but instead asked for a subcantonment.

19. *Lexington Herald,* June 17, 1917.

20. *Louisville Courier-Journal,* June 14, 1917.

21. *Lexington Herald,* June 19 and 21, 1917.

22. See the editorials in *Lexington Herald,* June 22, 23, 24, 28, 29, and 30, 1917, and *Louisville Courier-Journal,* June 27, 1917.

23. Goode's remarks and the sale of Camp Stanley were reported in *Lexington Herald,* October 10, 1917. For more on the Guard's move to Mississippi, see *Lexington Herald,* August 22, 26, and 28, September 3, 6, 8, 9, and 11, 1917.

24. See *Louisville Courier-Journal,* January 1, 1917, for population estimates.

25. For the choice of Mason and Hanger, see *Lexington Herald,* June 29, 1917. Key sources about Camp Taylor are Maurice Dunn, *Camp Zachary Taylor Souvenir, Louisville, Kentucky* (Louisville, KY: Lambertson Service Bureau, [1918]), and the website for the Camp Zachary Taylor Historical Society: camptaylorhistorical.org. For camp construction, see a *Courier-Journal Magazine* article dated November 8, 1959, in Camp Taylor File #1, Vertical Files, Schmidt Research Library, KHS. The laying of new telegraph lines to the cantonment was reported in *Louisville Courier-Journal,* July 7, 1917, and new sewers were reported on July 9, 1917. For more details about the material needed to build the camp, see *Louisville Courier-Journal*, July 2, 15, 18, 19, 23, and 29, August 2, 1917.

26. *Louisville Courier-Journal,* July 22 and August 4, 1917.

27. *Lexington Herald,* August 22, 1917.

28. Material on the early history of Fort Thomas is from Charles Bogart, "The Military Post at Ft. Thomas, Kentucky," *Journal of America's Military Past* 25, 3 (Winter 1999): 60–70. See also the City of Fort Thomas website: www.ftthomas.org/History.html. See *Lexington Herald,* February 1 and 6, 1917, for the return of the Kentucky National Guard.

29. Bogart, "Military Post at Ft. Thomas," 70–71. See *Kentucky Post,* May 14, 1917, announcing that Fort Thomas would be a recruit depot. For more on the YMCA hut, see *Kentucky Post,* June 14 and 26, July 7, 1917; for the Knights of Columbus facility, see *Kentucky Post,* January 7, 1918. See also Tenkotte and Claypool, *Encyclopedia of Northern Kentucky,* 361–63.

30. See *Louisville Courier-Journal,* October 7, 1917, for more on Brigadier General Wilder; October 14, 1917, for more on Major General Hale and his appearance at the "War Fete Ball"; October 21, 1917, for Hale's first public speech to the Transportation Club; and October 25, 1917, for his appearance at the Board of Trade.

31. Dunn, *Camp Zachary Taylor Souvenir,* 13; Vertical Files: Camp Zachary Taylor, folder 1, Schmidt Library, KHS.

32. *Lexington Herald,* September 6, 1917. See also *Louisville Courier-Journal,* September 6, 1917.

33. Dunn, *Camp Zachary Taylor Souvenir,* 13–19; pictures of staff officers of the Eighty-Fourth Division include two French captains and two lieutenants (ibid., 22–23).

34. Nancy Gentile Ford, *Americans All: Foreign-born Soldiers in World War I* (College Station: Texas A&M University Press, 2001), 3. Sergeant Murphy's story was reported in *Louisville Courier-Journal,* December 17, 1917.

35. Launching of the Americanization campaign was announced in *Louisville Courier-Journal,* May 14, 1918. See the August 21 and October 3, 1918, editions for the large naturalization ceremonies under the elm tree.

36. United States War Department, *Commission on Training Camp Activities* (Washington, DC: n.p., n.d.), 3. For more on the CTCA's morality campaigns, see Bristow, *Making Men Moral.*

37. See *Kentucky Irish-American,* September 15, 1917, and *Louisville Courier-Journal,* September 12, 1917, for the opening ceremonies at the YMCA auditorium.

38. Harry Vernon McChesney, *History of Army Y.M.C.A. Work at Camp Zachary Taylor* (Louisville, KY: n.p., 1920), 1–2. See *Louisville Courier-Journal,* February 23, 1908, for Dix's appointment as YMCA state secretary, and November 13, 1917, for an article by Mullins about the YMCA's work at Camp Taylor. For more on Mullins, see William E. Ellis, *A Man of Books and a Man of the People: E. Y. Mullins and the Crisis of Moderate Southern Baptist Leadership* (Macon, GA: Mercer University Press, 1985). Mullins served as president of the SBTS from 1899 to his death in 1928. He was also head of the Southern Baptist Convention from 1921 to 1924. For more on McChesney, see Barksdale Hamlett, "History of Education in Kentucky," *Bulletin of Kentucky Department of Education* 7, 4 (July 1914): 177–78. At various times a teacher, newspaper editor, and lawyer, McChesney served as state school superintendent from 1899 to 1903 and as secretary of state from 1903 to 1907.

39. McChesney, *History of Y.M.C.A. Work at Camp Taylor,* 4–10. See *Louisville Courier-Journal,* February 14, 1917, and *Lexington Herald,* February 14, 1917, for details of Taft's speech.

40. McChesney, *History of Y.M.C.A. Work at Camp Taylor,* 12.

41. Ibid., 12–13.

42. Ibid., 18–19. Local issues of *Trench and Camp* can be found at the Filson Historical Society, Louisville, KY.

43. For Hale's comments, see *Louisville Courier-Journal,* March 15, 1918. Malone's letter was reported in *Mt. Sterling Advocate,* October 30, 1917.

44. Caroline Daniels, "'The Feminine Touch Has Not Been Wanting': Women Librarians at Camp Zachary Taylor, 1917–1919," *Libraries and the Cultural Record* 43, 3 (2008): 287. Reports of the ALA's annual meeting can be found in *Louisville Courier-Journal,* June 25 and 28, 1917. According to the latter, "Patriotic Service Was Keynote of Convention Sessions." For more on ALA efforts during the war, see Arthur P. Young, *Books for Sammies: The American Library Association and World War I* (Pittsburgh, PA: Beta Phi Mu, 1981).

45. Daniels, "Feminine Touch," 298.

46. Ibid., 302.

47. Library fund-raising campaign reported in *Louisville Courier-Journal,* August 30 and September 24, 1917; *Citizen* (Berea, KY), September 13, 1917; *Central Record* (Lancaster, KY), September 27, 1917.

48. See Alice Hegan Rice, "Wanted—Books for the Soldiers! Some Personal Experiences at Camp Zachary Taylor," *Red Cross Magazine* 13, 12 (December 1918): 27–32. The call for books was reported in *Louisville Courier-Journal,* July 26, 1917, March 10 and 17, April 23, 1918; the donation of 40,000 books was reported on May 7, 1918, and 67,072 books on July 18, 1918. See also Theodore Wesley Koch, *War Service of the American Library Association* (Washington, DC: ALA War Service, Library of Congress, 1918), 33; Theodore Wesley Koch, *Books in the War: The Romance of Library War Service* (Boston: Houghton Mifflin, 1919), 152–53.

49. Baldwin, *Cora Wilson Stewart,* 40.

50. Ibid., 103.

51. For Stewart's estimation of illiterate soldiers' prospects, see *Louisville Courier-Journal,* June 23, 1917. Multiple examples of Stewart's appeals to communities for funding can be found in the Cora Wilson Stewart Papers, folder 1912–1919, box 21, UK Special Collections and Archives. The campaign to raise funds and enlist volunteers to teach illiterate soldiers was reported in *Louisville Courier-Journal,* July 11, 14, 22, and August 3, 1917. The last contained a letter from Stewart appealing for funds.

52. Baldwin, *Cora Wilson Stewart,* 103–5. Stewart also kept up her efforts to support education for illiterates in the general population; with her prodding, in the spring of 1918 the Kentucky legislature appropriated $25,000 per year for three years to support the illiteracy campaign; however, it also declared that the Kentucky Illiteracy Commission would cease to exist after 1920 (ibid., 112–13). The commission had first been funded in 1914.

53. Ibid., 87. The Country Life movement was "a disparate and diffuse effort that focused on inadequate farm profits as the reason for widespread poverty in the South and attempted to teach farmers more efficient agricultural practices. Some Country Lifers thought rural education had failed and should be changed to inculcate both a love of country living and an appreciation for scientific farming methods" (ibid., 31). Stewart's appointment to the national committee was reported in *Louisville Courier-Journal,* February 27, 1918; Secretary Lane's estimate was reported on March 31, 1918.

54. See Ella Hutchinson Ellwanger, "Camp Zachary Taylor," *Register of the Kentucky Historical Society* 16, 47 (May 1918): 13; *Louisville Courier-Journal,* September 23 and October 21, 1917; McChesney, *History of Y.M.C.A. Work at Camp Taylor,* 7.

55. Baldwin, *Cora Wilson Stewart,* 103.

56. Baker's decision and the YMHA's affiliation with the YMCA were reported in *Louisville Courier-Journal,* September 23, 1917.

57. Fund-raising effort reported in *Louisville Courier-Journal,* September 30, 1917; services and new soldiers' club reported on November 19, 1917; Mullins's speech reported on November 29, 1917. In 1918 Washer also became chairman of the Board of Presidents of the National Council of the YMHA; see *Courier-Journal,* April 4, 1918.

58. For information about the work of Jewish organizations in conjunction with Camp Taylor, see the fifteen-page report by Bessie Millman, "Young Men's Hebrew

Association War-Time Activities, Conducted in Conjunction with the Jewish Welfare Board"; "Report of the Woman's Auxiliary of the Jewish Welfare Board," by Mrs. Jacob Zellner, Mrs. Leon Goodman, and Mrs. Ben S. Washer; and "Adath Israel Sisterhood," by Mrs. Isaac Trost and Mrs. Ernest J. Wiley, in Caldwell, *Kentucky in the World War,* vol. 3.

59. Jessica Cooperman, "The Jewish Welfare Board and Religious Pluralism in the American Military of World War I," *American Jewish History* 98, 4 (October 2014): 238.

60. The estimate of Catholic trainees was reported in *Kentucky Irish-American,* August 4, 1917; Secretary of War Baker had also anticipated that about 35 percent of the army would be Catholic. The estimate of attendance at Mass was reported in *Irish-American,* October 20, 1917. See also *Irish-American,* September 15, 1917, for a report on the first Catholic Mass offered at the camp. The *Kentucky Irish-American* regularly ran a column titled "Camp News." See also *Louisville Courier-Journal,* August 1, September 10, 17, and 24, 1917, for activities of the Knights of Columbus in support of Camp Taylor.

61. Bristow, *Making Men Moral,* 49. For more on Hostess Houses, see Cynthia Brandimarte, "Women on the Home Front: Hostess Houses during World War I," *Winterthur Portfolio* 42, 4 (Winter 2008): 201–22. Brandimarte concludes: "Hostess houses deserve recognition for having provided the American military with places in which it could satisfy soldiers eager to see their loved ones, control to some degree soldiers' social interactions, and offer wartime luxuries associated with home—food, comfortable surroundings, and conviviality. Hostess houses gave soldiers a place in which to mingle with friends and families and to escape, temporarily, military hardships. The houses provided their women workers with income, with an important credential for future careers, with greater travel, and with increased confidence about making their own way in the world" (222).

62. See *Mt. Sterling Advocate,* December 21, 1917; *Breckenridge News* (Cloverport, KY), January 16, 1918. For more on the Camp Taylor YWCA Hostess House, see the reproduction of a January 2, 1918, *Louisville Post* article titled "Hostess House Is Opened for Public Inspection," in Caldwell, *Kentucky in the World War,* vol. 3. See also *Louisville Courier-Journal,* January 2, 3, and 5, 1918.

63. Bootlegging at the cantonment was reported in *Louisville Courier-Journal,* July 31, 1917; Portland neighborhood fears were reported on July 18, 1917, and supported by an editorial on July 20. See also Bristow, *Making Men Moral,* 103, for a discussion of Louisville's vice district issues.

64. *Louisville Courier-Journal,* August 25, 1917.

65. See *Louisville Courier-Journal,* January 30, 1918, for the opening of the Liberty Theater, and February 5 and 17, March 29, 1918, for examples of Liberty Theater activities. See also Bristow, *Making Men Moral,* 57, for a discussion of other activities.

66. See *Louisville Courier-Journal,* November 7, 1917. For more on the War Recreation Board, see *Kentucky Irish-American,* October 27, 1917; *Courier-Journal,* December 1, 1917, and January 23, 1918.

67. See *Louisville Courier-Journal,* October 28, November 1, and December 16, 1917, September 29 and November 2, 1918.

68. For War Camp Community Service efforts, see *Louisville Courier-Journal,* July 28, August 1 and 14, 1918. More on the WCCS can be found in Caldwell, *Kentucky in the World War,* vol. 3. See also Robert Bertrand Brown, *War Camp Community Service Calls* (New York: War Camp Community Service, 1918).

69. See "Report of the Khaki Club and Its Origins" and "History of the Khaki Club Canteen," Khaki Club Papers, Filson Historical Society. Another Khaki Club history is found in Mrs. Harrison Robertson, *History of Jefferson County, Ky. in the World War, 1917–1919,* 34 vols. (Frankfort: Kentucky Council of Defense, n.d.), 1:265–70. For more on the Khaki Club, see *Louisville Courier-Journal,* November 9, 11, and 12, 1917, May 23 and November 20, 1918.

70. See *Louisville Courier-Journal,* November 7 and December 5, 1917. Makeup of the Eighty-Fourth Division is in Caldwell, *Kentucky in the World War,* vol. 5.

71. Much of the history of the Eighty-Fourth Division is from an article by Captain Warner Sayers in Caldwell, *Kentucky in the World War,* vol. 5. See also *Louisville Courier-Journal,* December 18, 1917, April 18, May 29, and June 10, 1918.

72. Carleton's appointment was reported in *Louisville Courier-Journal,* October 21, 1917; for more information on the 159th Depot Brigade, see the February 19, May 2 and 23, June 13, 17, and 27, 1918, editions.

73. The transformation of Camp Taylor was covered in *Louisville Courier-Journal,* May 30, June 10 and 11, 1918. The standard work on FACOTS is Raymond Walters, George Palmer Putnam, John Kirby, Arthur Baer, Homer Dye Jr., and Forrest B. Myers, *F.A.C.O.T.S.: The Story of the Field Artillery Central Officers Training School, Camp Zachary Taylor, Kentucky* (New York: Knickerbocker Press, 1919).

74. Walters et al., *F.A.C.O.T.S.,* 11.

75. Ibid., 26–28, 37–39, 49–51. Observation batteries are described in *Louisville Courier-Journal,* July 17, 1918, and the influx of civilians on July 31, 1918. The September 2, 1918, edition noted that nineteen men from Louisville and twenty-three from elsewhere in Kentucky were part of that week's graduating class. Lists of Kentuckians who went to the school are found in Walters et al., *F.A.C.O.T.S.,* 205–10.

76. Walters, *F.A.C.O.T.S.,* 54–60; *Louisville Courier-Journal,* September 22, 1918.

77. See Richard M. Budd, *Serving Two Masters: The Development of American Military Chaplaincy, 1860–1920* (Lincoln: University of Nebraska Press, 2002), 146–48, for the history of the chaplains' school.

78. *Louisville Courier-Journal,* July 29, 1918.

79. Smithson's letter to his father was reproduced in *Daily Kentuckian* (Hopkinsville, KY), May 22, 1918.

80. *Citizen* (Berea, KY), September 5, 1918.

81. *Adair County News* (Columbia, KY), November 14 and December 26, 1917. It was later reported that Sergeant Chandler had gained twenty-three pounds while at camp. *Adair County News,* May 1, 1918. For three years before entering the army, Chandler was the principal of Lindsey Wilson Training School, a preparatory school in Columbia, which eventually became Lindsey Wilson College. Born in Princeton, Kentucky, Chandler received his master's and doctorate degrees from Columbia after the war. He taught and coached football at Kent State University and eventually served

twenty-three years as president of what is now Clarion University in Pennsylvania. See *Clarion College Alumni Bulletin* 5, 2 (April 1960): 1.

82. *Adair County News,* January 23, 1918.

83. *Adair County News,* May 15, 1918.

84. *Louisville Courier-Journal,* November 17, 1917.

85. *Clay City Times,* April 18, 1918. See also *Louisville Courier-Journal,* May 17, 18, and 22, June 22, 1918. Forty-five objectors were released to farms, as reported on July 27, 1918. Carl Hensen of Shelby County, a German native with three sons in the army, secured the services of some of the objectors. *Louisville Courier-Journal,* July 19, 1918.

86. See *Louisville Courier-Journal,* June 29 and July 10, 1918, for the sentencing of seven men to ten to fifteen years in prison. None of them were Kentuckians; they were from Indiana and Illinois. See also Jesse L. Brenneman, "Experiences and Trials in Military Service," http://replica.palni.edu/cdm/compoundobject/collection/gopplow/id/4327/rec/3. This is part of the Goshen Plowshares Collection of the Plowshares Digital Archive for Peace Studies, a collaboration among Goshen, Earlham, and Manchester Colleges, which are affiliated with the Mennonites, Quakers, and Church of the Brethren, respectively. For more on Brenneman, see the World War I Conscientious Objection online database compiled by Swarthmore College Peace Collection archivist Anne Yoder at http://fm12.swarthmore.edu/detail.php?dbName=WWI&rid=2202. She notes that Brenneman was offered noncombatant status but did not accept it. Yoder's database includes information on more than seventy conscientious objectors at Camp Taylor; see http://fm12.swarthmore.edu/list.php?searchFor=camp+taylor&dbName=WWI&sortBy=0. Although most of these men were Quakers, Mennonites, and Church of the Brethren adherents, the objectors also included Catholic, Church of God, Church of Christ, Seventh-Day Adventist, and International Bible Students Association members.

87. *Public Ledger* (Maysville, KY), April 25, 1918; *Hartford Herald,* May 1, 1918.

88. The author is grateful to Ken Maguire, head of the Camp Taylor Historical Society and the foremost expert on the history of the camp, for providing these references. See more about the society at camptaylorhistorical.org.

89. For the choice of Stithton as the site of the new cantonment, see *Louisville Courier-Journal,* July 4, 9, and 10, 1918. Radcliffe's appointment was announced in the July 25, 1918, edition. A new town would start up as a result of the building of Camp Knox, and it was named after Radcliffe. See *Courier-Journal,* August 17, 1918, for the announcement of the camp name, and *Daily Kentuckian* (Hopkinsville, KY), August 18, 1918, for the pun.

90. See *Louisville Courier-Journal,* August 23, 1918, for Dale's pronouncement; September 14, 1918, for the deadline; September 24, 1918, for the announcement of the new hospital; October 4 and 7, 1918, for efforts by Dale and the KCD; and October 11, 1918, for the problems and investigation.

91. *Louisville Courier-Journal,* October 12, 15, and 23, 1918; *Breckenridge News* (Cloverport, KY), October 16, 1918.

92. The advertisement appeared in, for example, *Public Ledger* (Maysville, KY), October 12, 1918; *Citizen* (Berea, KY), October 17, 1918; *Hartford Herald,* October

16, 1918; *Big Sandy News* (Louisa, KY), October 18, 1918. Newspapers that did not run the advertisement often repeated much of its content in a news column.

93. Caught in the throes of a senatorial campaign, Stanley apparently went to Washington, DC, and missed the meeting at Camp Knox. He did, however, visit the base hospital at Camp Taylor and spoke at a graduating class of FACOTS. See *Hartford Herald,* October 16, 1918, reporting that Stanley went to Washington unexpectedly, and *Louisville Courier-Journal,* October 17, 1918, for Stanley's visit to the Camp Taylor hospital and his FACOTS speech. See also *Public Ledger* (Maysville, KY), October 30, 1918.

94. See *Louisville Courier-Journal,* November 23, 1918, for the movement of men into Camp Knox, and December 17 and 20, 1918, for the labor dispute and the decision to complete the camp using soldiers.

7. Food and Fuel Administration

1. See *Barboursville Mountain Advocate,* March 30, 1917. The *Mountain Advocate* advertised itself as "The Official Organ of the Republican Party in Knox County."

2. Cohen quoted in *Louisville Courier-Journal,* April 3, 1917; see also the March 31, April 2, 4, 6, and 8, 1917, editions for more on farmers' preparedness efforts. Despite the call to reduce tobacco farming, a later government campaign to provide cigarettes for troops resulted in increased demand for tobacco; see chapter 10 on Kentucky's wartime economy.

3. *Hopkinsville Kentuckian,* April 12, 1917; *Public Ledger* (Maysville, KY), April 18, 1917.

4. Creation of the food committee and appointment of Hughes reported in *Lexington Herald,* April 18, 1917; *Clay City Times,* April 19, 1917; *Big Sandy News* (Louisa, KY), April 20, 1917. The committee included a dozen men from around the state, ranging from Paintsville to Paducah.

5. See *Louisville Courier-Journal,* April 22, 1917, for committee recommendations; April 23, 1917, for Stanley's proclamation. See *Louisville Courier-Journal,* April 28, 1917, and *Public Ledger* (Maysville, KY), April 30, 1917, for Stanley's meeting with bankers.

6. See *Louisville Courier-Journal,* April 8, 1917, for news that Hoover would head a US food board. See also William Clinton Mullendore, *History of the United States Food Administration, 1917–1919* (Stanford, CA: Stanford University Press, 1941), 51. This is the "official" history of the Food Administration, and Hoover wrote the introduction to the book. See also Kennedy, *Over Here,* 116–23, for the Food Administration's role in domestic wartime efforts.

7. Vrooman's speeches reported in *Louisville Courier-Journal,* April 16, 17, 18, and 21, 1917; *Lexington Herald,* April 18, 1917; *Hartford Republican,* April 20, 1917. The *Courier-Journal* reported on April 18 that because of Vrooman's speech, the Louisville Board of Trade had decided to reduce its food ration at meetings.

8. Rose Hayden-Smith, "Sowing the Seeds of Victory: National Wartime Gardening Programs in the United States during World War I" (PhD diss., University of California–Santa Barbara, 2010), 4–10. In addition to the three major organizations, Hayden-Smith covers a fourth—a prewar program at the Pennsylvania School of Hor-

ticulture for Women at Ambler—which the author notes was "vital for the formation of the Woman's Land Army of America, and also demonstrates Progressive impulses and trends that influenced all of the wartime programs" (5).

9. Ibid., 7–8.

10. Ibid., 153.

11. Ibid., 154–55. See also C. W. Mathews to Fred Sackett, November 18, 1918, Gardens file, box 10, State and Local Food Administration, Louisville, Kentucky (hereafter, KY Records), RG 4 (US Food Administration), NARA-ATL, announcing that the professor had taken a leave of absence from the university to work for the USSGA.

12. See *Lexington Herald,* April 27, 1904, and February 7, 1905, for Professor Mathews's reports on Lexington's first school garden project. See the March 17, 1917, edition for the hiring of the four UK students.

13. *Lexington Herald,* April 2 and 3, 1918.

14. See Helen Fitz-Randolph, "Lexington's School Garden Pageant," *School Life* 2, 8 (April 16, 1919): 13–14. *School Life* was the "Official Organ of the United States Bureau of Education, U.S. Department of the Interior." See *School Life* 3, 1 (July 1, 1919): 11, for the number of Kentucky schoolchildren involved in the USSGA.

15. See *Louisville Courier-Journal,* April 22, 28, and 30, July 18, 1917, for Yunker and school garden efforts. Her master's thesis can be found online at digital.library.louisville.edu/utils/getfile/collection/etd/id/641/filename/642.pdf. Yunker was the daughter of German parents. For a report on Yunker's 1917 efforts, see also *Town Development* 20, 1 (September 1917): 24.

16. See *Louisville Courier-Journal,* March 4 and 10, April 1 and 9, May 4, July 15, 1918. See the January 12, 1919, edition for a report on 1918 projects.

17. *Louisville Courier-Journal,* March 16, 1919. Yunker died in 1940 and was buried in Cave Hill Cemetery in Louisville. Her tombstone is engraved with these words: "She Left the World More Beautiful than She Found It."

18. Charles Lathrop Pack, *The War Garden Victorious: Its War Time Need and Its Economic Value in Peace* (Philadelphia: J. B. Lippincott, 1919), 10. For more on Pack and the commission's plans to get a million "boys, girls and adults" to plant gardens, see *Lexington Herald,* March 22 and May 20, 1917. On April 18, 1917, the *Hartford Herald* reported that Secretary of War Newton Baker had written to Pack, telling him that the home garden movement was a vital component of the war effort.

19. See *Kentucky Post* (Covington, KY), March 30, April 9, 12, and 14, 1917, for war garden efforts in northern Kentucky.

20. Fitz-Randolph's comments noted in *Lexington Herald,* September 3, 1917, and *Bourbon News* (Paris, KY), September 7, 1917. War Garden Lesson No. 1 appeared in *Louisville Courier-Journal,* February 18, 1918; the lessons continued through May 1918. Fitz-Randolph became a *Courier-Journal* contributor on other issues as well.

21. *Hopkinsville Kentuckian,* January 15, 1918.

22. Strater quoted in *Bourbon News* (Paris, KY), March 19, 1918. See also Fred Sackett, Kentucky Food Administrator, to J. W. Hallowell, U.S. Food Administration, March 2, 1918, Gardens file, box 10, KY Records, RG 4, NARA-ATL, noting Strater's appointment.

23. For *Courier-Journal* support, see Arthur Krock, Managing Editor, to Sackett, March 4, 1918, Gardens file, box 10, KY Records, RG 4, NARA-ATL. See *Bourbon News* (Paris, KY), March 22, 1918, for suggestions on how youths could contribute. The *Hartford Republican,* March 22, 1918, reported that the Union National Bank of Louisville had donated $250 to a fund for those who could not afford to buy seeds. Applications for money could be directed to War Garden Committee chairman Charles Strater.

24. *Breckenridge News* (Cloverport, KY), April 3, 1918.

25. See Mullendore, *History of the US Food Administration,* 53–56, for passage of the Lever Act. For food efforts in other states, see Erika Janik, "Food Will Win the War: Food Conservation in World War I Wisconsin," *Wisconsin Magazine of History* 93, 3 (Spring 2010): 17–27; Rae Katherine Eighmey, "'Food Will Win the War': Minnesota Conservation Efforts, 1917–18," *Minnesota History* 59, 7 (Fall 2005): 272–86; Rae Katherine Eighmey, *Food Will Win the War: Minnesota Crops, Cooks, and Conservation during World War I* (St. Paul: Minnesota Historical Society Press, 2010).

26. Kennedy, *Over Here,* 118. Capozzola, *Uncle Sam Wants You,* covers Food Administration efforts in the chapter titled "The Obligation to Volunteer" (95–103). Although Hoover emphasized volunteerism, authorities would rely on what Capozzola refers to as "coercive volunteerism." For more on Hoover's "volunteerism," see Robert D. Cuff, "Herbert Hoover, the Ideology of Voluntarism and War Organization during the Great War," *Journal of American History* 64, 2 (September 1977): 358–72.

27. Sackett's appointment was reported in *Lexington Herald,* August 17 and 19, 1917. For more information about Sackett, see T. R. Moss, "History of the United States Food Administration in Kentucky," in Caldwell, *Kentucky in the Great War,* vol. 3.

28. The committee members are listed in Sackett to Edward Hines, Kentucky Council of Defense, April 18, 1918, Council of National Defense file, box 4, KY Records, RG 4, NARA-ATL. See also Moss, "History of US Food Administration in Kentucky." The *Lexington Herald,* September 12, 1917, noted the need for people to volunteer to help Sackett.

29. Sackett to Temple Bodley, February 26, 1918, Gardens file, box 10, KY Records, RG 4, NARA-ATL. The *Bourbon News* (Paris, KY) reported on September 21, 1917, that Sackett had opened an office in the Speed Building in Louisville and that "the food administration of Kentucky will be dependent in large measure upon volunteer workers, and men from every county in the State are invited to tender their services." Lists of county food administrators and of district administrators and the counties they oversaw are in Robertson, *History of Jefferson County,* 1:97–103. Examples of the volunteers' appointment certificates can be found in General Correspondence file, box 1, General Correspondence, 1917–1919, KY Records, RG 4, NARA-ATL. A list of county food administrators is also contained in Directory file, box 4, KY Records, RG 4, NARA-ATL.

30. Sackett to County School Superintendents and Principals of Schools, November 30, 1918, Gardens file, box 10, KY Records, RG 4, NARA-ATL.

31. See correspondence between Sackett and various women's organizations, as well as the proclamation signed by fifteen presidents in Executive Committee file, box 5, KY Records, RG 4, NARA-ATL.

32. An undated copy of the *Courier-Journal* article is in Enemy Propaganda file, box 20, KY Records, RG 4, NARA-ATL. The *Courier-Journal* sarcastically noted, "The lady must be placated. Her failure to sign the card will be a national calamity." For the exchange of telegrams, see Beauchamp to Sackett, October 23, 1917; Sackett to Beauchamp, November 1, 1917; Sackett to Hoover, November 1, 1917, Executive Committee file, box 5, KY Records, RG 4, NARA-ATL.

33. Sackett quoted in *Lexington Herald,* September 27, 1917; see also the September 28, 1917, edition.

34. Sue Stanley's proclamation is mentioned in Moss, "History of the US Food Administration in Kentucky"; a copy can be found in Publicity folder, box 20, KY Records, RG 4, NARA-ATL. Sackett's speeches in central Kentucky were reported in *Lexington Herald,* October 8, 10, 11, and 12, 1917; see also the September 15, 1917, edition for the establishment of a newspapermen's committee to handle food campaign publicity. For promotion efforts, see *Louisville Courier-Journal,* September 15, October 7, 9, and 11, 1917; *Adair County News* (Columbia, KY), October 3, 1917; *Citizen* (Berea, KY), October 4, 1917. For Adelberg's acceptance of the position of library publicity director, see Adelberg to Sackett, October 27, 1917, and Sackett to Adelberg, October 31, 1917, Libraries folder, box 13, KY Records, RG 4, NARA-ATL.

35. Examples of Sackett's last-minute plea are in *Lexington Herald,* October 25, 1917; *Hartford Republican,* October 26, 1917; *Big Sandy News* (Louisa, KY), October 26, 1917. See also *Louisville Courier-Journal,* October 20, 26, and 28, 1917, for last-minute preparations.

36. Sackett's instructions are in box 4, KY Records, RG 4, NARA-ATL.

37. See *Louisville Courier-Journal,* October 30, November 3, 7, 9, 10, 11, and 13, 1917, for results of the conservation pledge campaign.

38. *Lexington Herald,* October 30 and 31, 1917.

39. Results of each county, along with the names of the women leading the campaign, were published in *Louisville Courier-Journal,* December 30, 1917. Sackett's satisfaction was reported on January 1, 1918.

40. See "W.C.T.U. Notes," *Lexington Herald,* August 6, 1917, for the suggestion about drinkless and smokeless days. See the October 25, 1917, edition for the announcement that, at the request of Sackett, the venerable Phoenix Hotel would institute meatless and wheatless days in its restaurant starting November 1.

41. Lindsay's complaints are in *Louisville Courier-Journal,* October 23, November 11, and December 11, 1917. See the January 4, 1918, edition for the wording of the "slacker card," and January 8, 1918, for the vigilante effort.

42. See *Louisville Courier-Journal,* November 8, 1917, and *Breckenridge News* (Cloverport, KY), November 14, 1917, noting meatless Tuesdays and wheatless Wednesdays. See *Louisville Courier-Journal,* January 28, 1918, and, especially, *Hopkinsville Kentuckian,* February 2, 1918, which thoroughly explained the "New Food Rules" and defined "wheatless," "meatless," and "porkless." See *Louisville Courier-Journal,* March 2, 1918, and *Public Ledger* (Maysville, KY), March 4, 1918, for the restoration of chicken, mutton, and lamb to Kentuckians' diets. For more about food restrictions during the war, see Helen Veit, "Victory over Ourselves: American Food and Progressivism in the Era of the Great War" (PhD diss., Yale University, 2008), and Elizabeth

Cafer du Plessis, "Meatless Days and Sleepless Nights: Food, Agriculture, and Environment in World War I America" (PhD diss., Indiana University, 2009). See also Mullendore, *History of the US Food Administration,* 96–97.

43. See *Louisville Courier-Journal,* September 10, 1918. For his views on the importance of wheat, see Sackett to A. P. Haight, Editor, *East Kentucky Journal,* Grayson, Ky., April 8, 1918, General Correspondence folder, box 3, KY Records, RG 4, NARA-ATL.

44. *Hickman Courier,* January 2, 1919.

45. See W. C. Hollister to Sackett, January 7, 1918, about the Greek restaurateurs in Ashland; warning letter from Sackett to S. A. Webb, Proprietor, Webb Hotel, Paintsville, Ky., January 19, 1918, Complaints folder (Wheatless and Meatless Days), box 4, KY Records, RG 4, NARA-ATL.

46. See *Louisville Courier-Journal,* February 23, 1918, for the increased hog production goal. See also the circular from Sackett and Thomson, "Pigs, Patriotism, and Profits," August 10, 1918, Live Stock folder, box 15, KY Records, RG 4, NARA-ATL. James Thompson was the president of Glenmore Distilleries but devoted a lot of time to his duties as head of the Live Stock Committee. Several copies of his correspondence are contained in the previously cited Live Stock folder. For Governor Stanley's alleged hog grazing, see *Louisville Courier-Journal,* June 10, 1918, reproducing editorials from the three East Coast newspapers lauding the governor's initiative. There was a question whether Stanley's alleged horde of hogs existed, although he apparently did keep a sow and piglet behind the governor's mansion. *Courier-Journal,* June 11, 1918. Unlike the well-publicized photograph of sheep on the White House lawn, there was apparently no similar picture of Governor Stanley's project.

47. See Henry Hazlewood to Sackett, October 30, 1918, and Sackett to Hazlewood, November 4, 1918, General Correspondence folder, box 2, KY Records, RG 4, NARA-ATL. For an example of prices, see *Mt. Sterling Advocate,* February 12, 1918, which reported Montgomery County price ranges for about a dozen commodities, including sugar, flour, lard, bacon, and bread.

48. See Sackett to Merchants Wholesale Grocery Company, September 3, 1918; J. A. Doll to Sackett, September 5, 1918; Sackett to Food Administration Enforcement Division, October 29, 1918, General Correspondence Enforcement Division, J. A. Doll folder, box 1 Acme-Jones to R. O. Pace, KY Records, RG 4, NARA-ATL.

49. Perry to Sackett, August 2, 1918; Sackett to Perry, August 6, 1918, General Correspondence Enforcement Division, W. R. Morgan folder, box 1 Acme-Jones to R. O. Pace, KY Records, RG 4, NARA-ATL.

50. *Lexington Herald,* February 4, 1918. For county food administrator L. D. Mitchell's cautionary note, see *Bourbon News* (Paris, KY), April 23, 1918; county food administrator L. T. Hovermale warned against sugar and flour hoarding in *Licking Valley Courier,* July 18, 1918. See also *Louisville Courier-Journal,* March 22, 1918, in which W. H. Kaye, food administrator for the Fifth Congressional District, noted that six people accused of hoarding sugar had been reported to the Food Administration.

51. See *Louisville Courier-Journal,* September 1, 1918 (which misspelled Elliston's name as "Ellison"); *Mt. Sterling Advocate,* September 3, 1918. See also S. J. Douthitt to Sackett, August 26, 1918; Sackett to Douthitt, August 26, 1918; report of exam-

ining trial proceedings, September 3, 1918; Sackett to Douthitt, September 21, 1918 (confirming plea-bargain arrangements); Sackett to Food Administration Enforcement Division, September 26, 1918 (reporting on disposition of the case); undated newspaper clipping acknowledging violation, General Correspondence Enforcement Division, A. G. Elliston file, box 1 Acme-Jones to R. O. Pace, KY Records, RG 4, NARA-ATL.

52. Sackett to Ernest W. Ripy, September 26, 1918, General Correspondence Enforcement Division, W. A. Murphy file, box 1 Acme-Jones to R. O. Pace, KY Records, RG 4, NARA-ATL; Sackett to Grant County Food Administrator John Steers, October 5, 1918, C. W. Northcutt file, ibid.

53. Fayette Food Administrator J. H. Combs to Sackett, October 23, 1918, General Correspondence Enforcement Division, Phoenix Hotel Case file, box 2 Paducah Ice to Miscellaneous Correspondence, KY Records, RG 4, NARA-ATL; Sackett to J. W. Saunders, November 14, 1918, G. T. Timberlake file, ibid.

54. A nearly 100 percent increase in wheat output was reported in some counties; see *Louisville Courier-Journal,* January 24, 1919. See T. R. Moss's article in *Courier-Journal,* January 1, 1919, in which he credited Fred Sackett, Marguerite Giffords, and Sallie Bruce for their work on food issues.

55. For more on Harry Garfield, see Robert D. Cuff, "Harry Garfield, the Fuel Administration, and the Search for a Cooperative Order during World War I," *American Quarterly* 30, 1 (Spring 1978): 39–53.

56. Bryan accepted the position in a telegram to Garfield, October 31, 1917, file KY Fuel Admin Oct–Dec 1917, General Correspondence Administrative Division, Records of the Bureau of State Organizations (Evans Woolen, Director), 1917–1919, box 774 Kansas A–Kentucky folder 4, RG 67 (US Fuel Administration), NARA-CP. Bryan's appointment was reported on November 1, 1917, in the *Louisville Courier-Journal, Nashville Tennessean,* and *Nashville American* (Bryan was a native of Nashville). See also *Louisville Courier-Journal,* November 15 and 17, 1917, announcing county appointments, acknowledging that Bryan's powers were broad, and stating that it was "his duty to see that fuel is equitably distributed at fair prices." Bryan hoped that cooperation would obviate the need to use legal action to ensure compliance with Fuel Administration regulations. The *Lexington Herald,* November 9, 1917, reported on the advisory committee, which included Lexingtonian Sam Halley, who was also a Kentucky Council of Defense member.

57. *Mt. Sterling Advocate,* November 27 and December 11, 1917. See the early report of a coal famine in *Central Record* (Lancaster, KY), October 18, 1917; see also *Public Ledger* (Maysville, KY), October 29, 1917. The *Clay City Times,* November 15, 1917, reported that Powell County schools were without coal and had to resort to the unsatisfactory expedient of burning wood.

58. Telegram from J. C. McManham to Harry Garfield, November 23, 1917; telegram from Bryan to U.S. Fuel Administration, November 24 and 26, 1917, file KY Fuel Admin Oct–Dec 1917, box 774 Kansas A–Kentucky folder 4, RG 67, NARA-CP.

59. See the Fuel Administration's reply and suggestion in L. A. Snead, U.S. Fuel Administration, to Bryan, November 30, 1917, ibid. This file contains several other letters indicating that the Fuel Administration had contacted coal companies to ensure

deliveries to communities such as Harrodsburg, Paris, and Silver Creek. See also *Lexington Herald,* November 30, 1917, which reported the Fuel Administration's campaign to substitute wood for coal.

60. See Bryan's "Report of Progress of Organization," December 7, 1917, file KY Fuel Admin Oct–Dec 1917, box 774 Kansas A–Kentucky folder 4, RG 67, NARA-CP.

61. See *Lexington Herald,* December 19, 1917, for a report that 800 homes finally received coal after city and county officials and volunteers distributed more than 350 bushels for home heating.

62. See newspaper advertisement attached to Bryan to Federal Fuel Administration, November 17, 1917, file KY Fuel Admin Oct–Dec 1917, box 774 Kansas A–Kentucky folder 4, RG 67, NARA-CP.

63. See Donald McDonald to Bryan, November 191, 1917, and Bryan to Fuel Administrator, November 19, 1917, ibid.

64. For the new fuel conservation regulations and Bryan's letter to county fuel administrators, see *Lexington Herald,* December 21, 1917.

65. Bryan's warning on lightless nights appeared in *Louisville Courier-Journal,* December 18, 1917. See also *Mt. Sterling Advocate,* December 21, 1917. Bryan's final report of March 1, 1919, is reproduced in United States Fuel Administration, *Report of the Administrative Division, 1917–1919,* pt. 1, *Reports of the Bureau of State Organizations and of the Federal Fuel Administrators for the Various States and Districts* (Washington, DC: Government Printing Office, 1920), 121. See U.S. Fuel Administration to Bryan, January 4, 1918, authorizing action against recalcitrant companies, file KY Fuel Admin Jan–Feb 1918, box 774 Kansas A–Kentucky folder 4, RG 67, NARA-CP.

66. See telegram from Bryan to Fuel Agent Snead, U.S. Fuel Administration, December 11, 1917, asserting that "Central Kentucky towns suffering acutely" due to congestion on Chesapeake and Ohio Railroad, and telegram from Snead to Bryan, December 14, 1917, authorizing diversions, file KY Fuel Admin Oct–Dec 1917, box 774 Kansas A–Kentucky folder 4, RG 67, NARA-CP. See Bryan's final report in US Fuel Administration, *Report of the Administrative Division,* 121. The acuteness of the coal shortage in central Kentucky was reported in *Louisville Courier-Journal,* December 11, 1917, and congestion was noted on December 13, 1917.

67. See *Louisville Courier-Journal,* January 1, 1918, for Bryan's message, and January 23, 1918, for bad conditions in northern Kentucky.

68. For "heatless and workless Mondays," see *Record* (Greenville, KY), January 24, 1918; *Bourbon News* (Paris, KY), January 25, 1918; *Louisville Courier-Journal,* January 28 and February 5, 1918. See also *Breckenridge News* (Cloverport, KY), January 30, 1918.

69. *Interior Journal* (Stanford, KY), January 29, 1918; *Adair County News* (Columbia, KY), January 30, 1918; *Public Ledger* (Maysville, KY), February 4, 1918; *Bourbon News* (Paris, KY), February 8, 1918.

70. See *Public Ledger* (Maysville, KY), February 9 and 14, 1918, for the cessation of heatless Mondays.

71. Bryan's figures on coal savings are in US Fuel Administration, *Report of the Administrative Division,* 121.

72. Bryan quoted in ibid. See also Milward to Garfield, February 26, 1918; tele-

gram from U.S. Fuel Administration to Bryan, February 28, 1918, file KY Fuel Admin Jan–Feb 1918, box 774 Kansas A–Kentucky folder 4, RG 67, NARA-CP.

73. Bryan to W. E. Hope, March 18, 1918, file KY Fuel Admin Mar–Apr 1918, box 774 Kansas A–Kentucky folder 4, RG 67, NARA-CP, asking for set fuel prices. Garfield's actions are summarized in US Fuel Administration, *Report of the Administrative Division,* 11–12. See *Louisville Courier-Journal,* November 22, 1917, which reported, "Coal Dealers Protest Price." See also *Big Sandy News* (Louisa, KY), April 5, 1918, reporting that a delegation of eastern Kentucky coal operators had gone to Washington to protest price cuts and warn of dire consequences.

74. Bryan's warning reported in *Louisville Courier-Journal,* April 5, 1918. See *Bourbon News* (Paris, KY), April 16, 1918, for an example of a local fuel administrator passing on the admonition to buy coal early. For the stymied "buy early" program, see telegram from Bryan to Fuel Administration, May 24, 1918, file KY Fuel Admin May–June 1918, box 775 Kansas A–Kentucky folder 4, RG 67, NARA-CP. A full-page Fuel Administration advertisement to "Order Your Coal Now" appeared in *Breckenridge News* (Cloverport, KY), June 5, 1918.

75. For daylight saving time, see *Courier-Journal,* March 5 and 31, 1918; *Bourbon News* (Paris, KY), March 26, 1918.

76. For Stanley's proclamation, see *Louisville Courier-Journal,* June 3, 1918; *Public Ledger* (Maysville, KY), June 6, 1918. Bryan's letter to county fuel administrators was reproduced in *Public Ledger,* June 22, 1918.

77. See *Hartford Republican,* September 27, 1918, and *Louisville Courier-Journal,* September 9 and 29, 1918, for "gasless Sundays."

78. *Georgetown Times,* September 11 and 18, 1918; the latter listed the names of "gasless Sunday" slackers and their excuses. The citizens' committee believed that most excuses were legitimate.

79. Bryan to A. M. Ogle, Director, State Distribution, August 13, 1918, file KY Fuel Admin July–August 1918, box 775 Kansas A–Kentucky folder 4, RG 67, NARA-CP.

80. Bryan to Ogle, September 20 and October 16, 1918, file KY Fuel Admin September–October 1918, ibid.

81. Bryan to Evans Woolen, October 16, 1918, ibid.

82. Telegrams from Bryan to Ogle, November 21 and 22, 1918, file KY Fuel Admin November–December 1918, ibid.

83. For the lifting of restrictions, see *Louisville Courier-Journal,* November 15 and 23, 1918. For his request to be relieved and responses, see Bryan to Garfield, November 26, 1918; Garfield to Bryan, December 2, 1918; Bryan to Garfield, December 6, 1918; U.S. Fuel Administration to Bryan, December 10, 1918; Bryan to H. A. Huskey, December 10, 1918, file KY Fuel Admin November–December 1918, box 775 Kansas A–Kentucky folder 4, RG 67, NARA-CP.

84. See Bryan's summary report in US Fuel Administration, *Report of the Administrative Division,* 121. The paperwork terminating his appointment is in file KY Fuel Admin January–March 1919, box 775 Kansas A–Kentucky folder 4, RG 67, NARA-CP; see especially Garfield to Bryan, March 27, 1918, thanking the Kentucky fuel administrator for his "loyal and patriotic service."

85. Bryan to Garfield, October 3, 1918, file KY Fuel Admin September–October 1918, box 775 Kansas A–Kentucky folder 4, RG 67, NARA-CP.

86. See *Louisville Courier-Journal,* November 26, 1918, for Sackett's "loving cup" award, and March 5, 1919, for his medal awarded by the Kentucky Committee of the National Institute of Social Sciences.

87. *Louisville Courier-Journal,* October 10, 1918.

88. *Louisville Courier-Journal,* October 27, 1918.

89. For a biography of Sackett, see Bernard V. Burke, *Ambassador Frederic Sackett and the Collapse of the Weimar Republic, 1930–1933* (New York: Cambridge University Press, 1994). Bryan is mentioned as Barkley's campaign treasurer in James K. Libbey, *Dear Alben: Mr. Barkley of Kentucky* (Lexington: University Press of Kentucky, 1979), 39.

8. Women and Children

1. For more on the women's preparedness movement and the National Service Schools, see Elaine Weiss, *Fruits of Victory: The Women's Land Army of America in the Great War* (Washington, DC: Potomac Books, 2008), 13–22; see especially 15–17 for more about the schools. The *Louisville Courier-Journal,* April 30, 1916, reported news of the upcoming school, and the May 14, 1916, edition contained a lengthy article about the Chevy Chase school and mentioned Amelia Weitzel. The article was written by Daisy Fitz-Hugh Ayres, the *Courier-Journal*'s special correspondent who reported on the social activities of Kentuckians in the nation's capital.

2. For more about the NLWS, see Weiss, *Fruits of Victory,* 17–20; Bessie Rowland James, *For God, for Country, for Home, the National League for Woman's Service: A Story of the First National Organization of American Women Mobilized for War Service* (New York: G. P. Putnam's Sons, 1920). See *Lexington Herald,* March 12 and 14, April 5, 1917, for details of NLWS divisions and training.

3. See *Louisville Courier-Journal,* February 4, 1917, for creation of the NLWS; March 2, 1917, for Johnston as the first head of the state NLWS organization; and March 11, 1917, for the naming of Ellen Woodcock as the first Louisville branch head. Woodcock was the wife of the Episcopal bishop of Kentucky, Charles E. Woodcock. See the newspaper's April 17, 1917, edition for state chapter locations and the names of the women who headed them.

4. See *Louisville Courier-Journal,* April 1, 1917, for the number of NLWS registrants; April 4, 1917, for marksmanship classes (which were also noted in *Adair County News* [Columbia, KY], April 11, 1917); and December 2, 1917, for the fund-raising dance. For the description of the motor driving final exam, see James, *For God, for Country, for Home,* 66.

5. See *Louisville Courier-Journal,* April 12 and 22, 1917.

6. *Lexington Herald,* May 2, 5, 6, 8, and 22, June 5, 9, and 12, 1917. See also *Louisville Courier-Journal,* April 17, 1918.

7. James, *For God, for Country, for Home,* 83–84, 132, 145.

8. For the basic history of the Woman's Committee, see Ida Clyde Clarke, *American Women and the World War* (New York: D. Appleton, 1918), and Emily Newell

Blair, *Women's Committee, National Council of Defense: An Interpretive Report from April 21, 1917 to February 27, 1919* (Washington, DC: Government Printing Office, 1920). In 1915 Shaw turned over the presidency of NAWSA to her friend Carrie Chapman Catt, who had been president from 1900 to 1904. For her work as head of the Woman's Committee, the War Department awarded Shaw the Distinguished Service Medal, usually given to military officers. See her obituary in *New York Times,* July 3, 1919.

9. Telegram from Shaw to Breckenridge, May 16, 1917; telegram from Breckinridge to Shaw, May 16, 1917, folder 105 Kentucky Division, Mrs. D. Breckinridge, box 464, entry 256, RG 62, NARA-CP. See also telegram from Lettie Robinson Adams to Shaw, April 15, 1917, folder 103 Kentucky Division, box 465, entry 256, ibid., in which Adams regrets that she is "heavily burdened with local work cannot accept." Lettie Robinson Adams was the wife of Gilmer Speed Adams of the famous Speed family of Louisville.

10. For more on Helm Bruce, see Kleber, *Encyclopedia of Louisville,* 138.

11. See *Louisville Courier-Journal,* May 7, 1899, for more on Sallie Bruce; May 22, 1904, for Bruce's activities in the National Society of Colonial Dames; November 3, 1904, for her membership in the International Order of the King's Daughters; and May 26, 1907, for UDC activities. See the April 29, 1900, edition for the phenomenal growth of the Business Women's Club; May 14, 1904, for Bruce's election as club president; and May 15, 1905, for her presentation of the annual report.

12. See *Louisville Courier-Journal,* June 4, 1910, for Bruce in the Consumer's League; March 20, 1913, for her election as president of the Woman's Club of Louisville; April 27, 1913, for the new Kentucky Society for Social Hygiene; June 13, 1913, for her election as first vice president of the Federation of Women's Clubs; October 8, 1914, for her suggestions for social reforms in Louisville; and November 10, 1915, for her calls for legislation. The federation's reform efforts are discussed in Forderhase, "'Clear Call of Thoroughbred Women.'"

13. See *Louisville Courier-Journal,* November 12, 1915, for the governor's committee, and May 13, 1916, for activities of the Colonial Dames. A preparedness organization, the Special Relief Society intended to "render comprehensive and invaluable aid to the nation in taking care of the humanitarian needs of the soldiery" in the event of war; see *Louisville Courier-Journal,* August 8, 1915. For a list of its national officers, see *Countryside Magazine,* May 1915, 302. The Special Relief Society later changed its name to the National Special Aid Society; see *Countryside* 24, 5 (May 1917): 250–51, for more about the organization.

14. See *Louisville Courier-Journal,* June 10, 1917, for the announcement of Sallie Bruce as chair of the "Kentucky Branch of the Women's National Defense Committee." See also *Lexington Herald,* June 10, 1917. Assisting Bruce, Lettie Adams served as the first vice president of the Kentucky Division of the WCCND. See Sue Stanley to Bruce, June 14, 1917, Women's Committee Kentucky file, box 759, entry 340, RG 62, NARA-CP, for Stanley's regret that personal and professional duties would prevent her from "giving to this work the attention which it requires." See also George Porter, CND States Division, to Swearingen, July 9, 1917, and Swearingen to Porter, July 12, 1917, in which Swearingen complains about the Woman's Committee; Shaw to Bruce,

July 19, 1917, suggesting that Sue Stanley be made honorary chairman; Bruce to Shaw, July 27, 1917, Women's Committee KY through Mont. folder, box 759, entry 341, RG 62, NARA-CP.

15. Confidential Report on Kentucky, July 27, 1917, Supplementary to the Report of Mr. Swearingen, August 28, 1917, and Report on Kentucky, April 5, 1918, State Reports Kentucky folder, box 796, RG 62, NARA-CP.

16. *Louisville Courier-Journal,* June 16, 1917. See *Lexington Herald,* August 5, 1917, for an article listing all the officers and department heads, as well as a lengthy explanation of the national and Kentucky organizations and their tasks. The article was written by Maud Woodson Cossar, apparently for the *Kentucky Woman's Journal.* Cossar was head of the Kentucky Division's press committee and worked briefly for the KCD.

17. See *Louisville Courier-Journal,* July 6, 1917, for food conservation; July 7, 1917, for creation of a woman's committee in Louisville; August 26, 1917, for Owensboro's efforts to create a committee; October 7, 1917, for the number of woman's committees formed; and October 10, 1917, for the meeting of woman's committee representatives.

18. See *Louisville Courier-Journal,* October 21, 27, and 30, 1917, for Lamar's visit. Lamar was also president of the National Society of the Colonial Dames of America.

19. See telegram from Swearingen to Gifford, June 30, 1917; letter from Swearingen to Gifford, July 5, 1917, folder 103 Kentucky Division, box 464, entry 256, RG 62, NARA-CP.

20. For the reports from the county women's councils, see the undated *Bulletin of the Kentucky Division, Women's Committee, National Council of Defense,* compiled by Mrs. Marvin (Isabel) Lewis, a copy of which is held at the University of Wisconsin library.

21. Ibid.

22. See "Broad Field Being Covered by Women's Committee of Defense Council," *Louisville Courier-Journal,* November 7, 1917.

23. *Bulletin of Kentucky Division, Women's Committee, National Council of Defense.*

24. See *Louisville Courier-Journal,* November 17 and 20, 1917, for Bruce's encouragement of Red Cross enlistment at the State Graduate Nurses' Association meeting; May 28, 1918, for Bruce's report at the national conference; and April 7, 1918, for the newspaper's assessment of the new law for the feebleminded: "By this enactment Kentucky passed from the Dark Ages of provision for the feebleminded to a plan which is surpassed in no State in the Union." Among the law's more progressive aspects, it provided for a training school for children and new standards and licensing for private institutions; however, it also made it a crime to aid and abet the marriage of a feebleminded person.

25. The WCCND campaign to recruit nurses was reported in *Lexington Herald,* May 26, 1918. See Bruce to Hannah Patterson, CND Woman's Committee, August 13, 1918, folder 103 Mrs. Helm Bruce, box 502, entry 257, RG 62, NARA-CP, inquiring about the number of Kentucky applicants and noting mothers' concerns (unspecified) about the program. See also telegram from Patterson to Bruce, August 31, 1918, mentioning the end of the recruitment campaign on September 5. For more on Kentucky's quota and the national campaign to recruit student nurses, see *Citizen* (Berea, KY), July 25, 1918; *Bourbon News* (Paris, KY), July 30, 1918. The

Public Ledger (Maysville, KY), September 4, 1918, reported that the campaign was ending on September 5 and that although Mason County had achieved its quota of ten young women, some of them might fail the necessary examination. It also noted that Kentucky would probably fall short of its quota. Although final figures for Kentucky could not be found, final figures for the country indicated that 13,889 young women enrolled in the program. See Isabel M. Stewart, "Nursing Preparedness: Some Lessons from World War I," *American Journal of Nursing* 41, 7 (July 1941): 810. See also World War I Women's Scrapbook, Schmidt Research Library, KHS, for many clippings about the US Student Nurse Reserve campaign, including some that were optimistic about Kentucky's ability to meet its quota.

26. Isabel Lewis to Lamar, November 30, 1917, folder 103 Kentucky Division, box 464, entry 256, RG 62, NARA-CP. Empey's book *Over the Top* was excerpted in *Louisville Courier-Journal,* September 23, 1917, and in several other Kentucky newspapers, including *Big Sandy News* (Louisa, KY), June 7, 1918, and *Central Record* (Lancaster, KY), June 27, 1918. Empey also wrote and starred in a film by the same name; it appeared in Kentucky movie houses in 1918. See, for example, the advertisement in *Bourbon News* (Paris, KY), August 13, 1918. Regarding his appearance in Louisville, the *Courier-Journal,* November 21, 1917, reported, "Empey Thrills Big Audience." Isabel Lewis believed that about 1,800 people attended Empey's lecture.

27. See *Louisville Courier-Journal,* April 16, 1918, regarding the KCD's meeting with other organization representatives. Budget figures are from the Treasurer's Report in KCD, *Report of Activities to January 1, 1920,* 91. See Hannah Patterson, CND, to Mrs. John South, February 9, 1918, KY Organization, Local folder, box 502, entry 237, RG 62, NARA-CP, noting allotments from other states. See also Bruce to Lamar, April 8, 1918, folder 103 Mrs. Helm Bruce, box 502, entry 257, RG 62, NARA-CP, in which Bruce notes that she applied for $5,000 from the KCD. The $5,000 allotment to the Women's Division is also mentioned in the Kentucky Division report in KCD, *Report of Activities to January 1, 1920,* 81. Actually, the Kentucky Division used only $2,881.23 of its allotment (see Treasurer's Report, ibid., 91). The opening of the Kentucky Division's office in the Speed Building was reported in *Louisville Courier-Journal,* June 5, 1918.

28. *Public Ledger* (Maysville, KY), June 20, 1918. Sayre College was a private girls' school at the time.

29. See *Louisville Courier-Journal,* June 4, 1918.

30. For Catt's speeches in Lexington and Frankfort, see *Lexington Herald,* June 2 and 4, 1918.

31. Clay's position was outlined in a letter to the *Lexington Herald,* June 2, 1918. For the federation conference, see *Lexington Herald,* June 11, 12, and 13, 1918. See also *Louisville Courier-Journal,* June 13, 1918. For more on Laura Clay, see Fuller, *Laura Clay and the Woman's Rights Movement.*

32. See *Lexington Herald,* June 9, 13, and 14, 1918. See also *Louisville Courier-Journal,* June 14, 1918.

33. Ruth Wilson to Lewis, June 4, 1918; Lewis to Wilson, June 10, 1918, folder 103 Kentucky Division L to Z, box 502, entry 257, RG 62, NARA-CP.

34. For more on Children's Year, see Breen, *Uncle Sam at Home,* 127–28; Jessica B.

Peixotto, "The Children's Year and the Woman's Committee," *Annals of the American Academy of Political and Social Science* 79 (September 1918): 257–62. A professor at the University of California–Berkeley, Peixotto served as executive chairman of the Child Welfare Department, Woman's Committee, CND. The *Crittenden Record-Press* (Marion, KY), May 16, 1918, reproduced President Wilson's letter to Secretary of Labor William B. Wilson supporting Children's Year. For more on the Children's Bureau, see Jacqueline K. Parker and Edward M. Carpenter, "Julia Lathrop and the Children's Bureau: The Emergence of an Institution," *Social Service Review* 55, 1 (March 1981): 60–77.

35. *Louisville Courier-Journal,* March 31, 1918. See also *Lexington Herald,* April 17 and 28, 1918, for the kickoff of "Child Year," as the newspaper termed it.

36. See, for example, *Public Ledger* (Maysville, KY), April 4 and May 27, 1918; *Citizen* (Berea, KY), April 8, 1918; *Adair County News* (Columbia, KY), April 10, 1918; *Daily Kentuckian* (Hopkinsville, KY), April 11 and August 3, 1918. See *Daily Kentuckian,* June 19, 1918, for an article detailing how the campaign would proceed in Christian County. The results of the campaign in Mason County were covered in *Public Ledger,* June 17, 1918.

37. See Peixotto to Shaver, September 12, 1918, Kentucky Division L to Z folder, box 502, entry 257, RG 62, NARA-CP, for Boggs's request regarding Play Week. Inquiries also came in from disparate parts of the state, including Fulton, Edmonton, and Richmond. See Shaver to Peixotto, September 20, 1918, ibid., for Shaver's comments about difficulties.

38. *Louisville Courier-Journal,* October 5, 1918. For a report on Mason County's success with baby weighing, see *Public Ledger* (Maysville, KY), June 17, 1918.

39. *Louisville Courier-Journal,* July 13 and August 22, 1918. Notices about Patriotic Play Week appeared in *Central Record* (Lancaster, KY), July 25, 1918, and *Crittenden Record-Press* (Marion, KY), August 1, 1918, which quoted the official from the Playgrounds and Recreational Association of America.

40. For Berea activities, see *Citizen,* August 22, 1918.

41. *Lexington Herald,* August 18, 1918.

42. *Daily Kentuckian* (Hopkinsville, KY), August 3, 1918.

43. See *Louisville Courier-Journal,* October 27, 1918; *Bourbon News* (Paris, KY), November 1, 1918; *Lexington Herald,* October 27 and November 1, 1918, for the back-to-school campaign.

44. United States Department of Labor, Children's Bureau, *Children's Year: A Brief Summary of Work Done and Suggestions for Follow-up Work* (Washington, DC: US Department of Labor, 1920), 8, 9, 19; United States Department of Commerce, Bureau of the Census, *Birth Statistics for the Birth Registration Area of the United States, 1919* (Washington, DC: Government Printing Office, 1921), 7.

45. *Louisville Courier-Journal,* November 8, 1918.

46. *Louisville Courier-Journal,* February 20, March 23, and April 14, 1919.

47. Ethel Allen Murphy, *The Triumph of Humanity: A Pageant of Victory, Reconstruction, and Democracy* ([Louisville]: Kentucky Division, Woman's Committee, Council of National Defense, [1919]). See also *Louisville Courier-Journal,* March 10, 1919, for an announcement of the book's publication. On May 2, 1919, the *Courier-Journal* reported a meeting of nearly 100 Italians "for the purpose of forming

classes for naturalization." See also Professor G. T. Ragsdale, "Americanization in Louisville," *Courier-Journal,* October 12, 1919. Americanization continued to be a strong postwar theme as the "Red Scare" grew. Many states passed laws making English the sole language of instruction, but researchers Adriana Lleras-Muney and Allison Shertzer note that along with nine other states, Kentucky did not; see "Did the Americanization Movement Succeed? An Evaluation of the Effect of English-Only and Compulsory Schooling Laws on Immigrants," www.ewi-ssl.pitt.edu/econ/files/faculty/wp/131217_wp_ShertzerAllison_Did%20the%20Americanization%20Movement%20Succeed%20Dec%202013%20Resubmission.pdf. For the role of women in Americanization, see John F. McClymer, "Gender and the 'American Way of Life': Women in the Americanization Movement," *Journal of American Ethnic History* 10, 3 (Spring 1991): 3–20. For a view of Americanization in a nearby state, see John C. Hennen, *The Americanization of West Virginia: Creating a Modern Industrial State, 1916–1925* (Lexington: University Press of Kentucky, 1996).

48. See Blair, *Women's Committee, National Council of Defense,* 106–7, 108. Blair cautioned that any rating system had to "take into consideration and weight, as does the statistician, the necessities, population, railroads, problems, and all the social and economic conditions that affect the result. Otherwise the rating might merely mean that the first State in class A [Illinois] is richer in money, in railroads, in women, in resources. Undoubtedly many of the Southern States worked under great handicaps. What they may have accomplished in the way of results may mean more energy expended per worker, and may mean a greater gain, permanently, to the social body than that of the States in class A." To compare Kentucky's work with that of "class A" Illinois, see Virginia R. Boynton, "'Even in the Remotest Parts of the State': Downstate 'Woman's Committee' Activities on the Illinois Home Front during World War I," *Journal of the Illinois State Historical Society* 96, 4 (Winter 2003–2004): 318–46. For a southern state's activities, see William J. Breen, "Southern Women in the War: The North Carolina Woman's Committee, 1917–1919," *North Carolina Historical Review* 55, 3 (July 1978): 251–83. Noting the difficulties the North Carolina Woman's Committee had in gaining support, including the "condescending attitude of the men in the state (253), Breen concludes that its work "was among the weakest in the Union" (280).

49. KCD, *Report of Activities to January 1, 1920,* 89.

50. Ibid., 83.

51. For more on the role of American women in the war, see Kimberly Jensen, *Mobilizing Minerva: American Women in the First World War* (Urbana: University of Illinois Press, 2008). For a case study of women's wartime efforts, see Lynn Dumenil, "Women's Reform Organizations and Wartime Mobilization in World War I–Era Los Angeles," *Journal of the Gilded Age and Progressive Era* 10, 2 (April 2011): 213–45. Dumenil concludes: "Women's groups engaged so wholeheartedly in war mobilization not simply from unalloyed patriotism, although certainly nationalistic patriotism formed the backdrop of war mobilization for most Americans. They had their own agendas—of enlivening their associations, supporting reform goals, and justifying women's claim to full citizenship—but these agendas dovetailed with the national priority of keeping Americans committed to a remote and not universally popular war" (245).

52. *Citizen* (Berea, KY), July 5, 1917. Wilson's appeal to schoolchildren was reported in *Louisville Courier-Journal,* September 19, 1917.

53. See *Louisville Courier-Journal,* January 7, 1918, for Kentucky School for the Blind activities; April 26, 1918, for the Louisville exhibit; March 3, 1918, for Hawesville Thrift Stamp efforts; March 23, 1918, for African American schoolchildren's essay contest; and August 4, 1918, for Lexington's "War Bees."

54. See *Bourbon News* (Paris, KY), April 3, 1917, for BSA president Colin Livingston's remarks about the value of the organization. He acknowledged that the BSA was not military but focused on "character building and citizen making," attributes that could be useful in wartime. See *Big Sandy News* (Louisa, KY), June 8, 1917, for an example of Boy Scouts participating in a draft registration parade on June 5; *Public Ledger* (Maysville, KY), April 29, 1918, for Boy Scout fund-raising; and *Bourbon News* (Paris, KY), May 28, 1918, for President Wilson's appeal to the Scouts regarding the black walnut inventory.

55. *Public Ledger* (Maysville, KY), February 27, 1918. At the time, the Boy Scouts of America was still a new movement, having been incorporated only in 1910. For examples of new Scout troops in Kentucky, see *Adair County News* (Columbia, KY), July 4, 1917; *Big Sandy News* (Louisa, KY), August 17, 1917; *Breckenridge News* (Cloverport, KY), November 24, 1917, reporting on a new Scout troop in Big Springs at the juncture of Meade, Breckinridge, and Hardin Counties.

56. For a comparison of organization numbers, see Edward Clopper, ed., *Child Welfare in Kentucky* (New York: National Child Labor Committee, 1919), 137. According to this report, there were 4,402 Boy Scouts, 519 Girl Scouts, and 322 Camp Fire Girls. Clopper begins his introduction with a stark analysis: "Kentucky neglects her children." The *Mt. Sterling Advocate,* September 4, 1918, reported the beginning of the Junior Red Cross. President Wilson's proclamation supporting the Junior Red Cross was printed in several Kentucky newspapers; see, for example, *Lexington Herald,* September 19, 1917, and *Mt. Sterling Advocate,* September 25, 1917. Knitting for French orphans was reported in *Bourbon News* (Paris, KY), September 28, 1917.

57. For accounts of Junior Red Cross chapter formation and activity, see *Licking Valley Courier* (West Liberty, KY), October 11, 1917; *Hartford Herald,* April 10, 1918; *Breckenridge News* (Cloverport, KY), April 24, 1918; *Central Record* (Lancaster, KY), June 6, 1918. Garrard County schoolchildren's decision not to exchange Christmas gifts was reported in *Central Record,* December 27, 1917; the fruits of their labor were reported in the June 6, 1918, edition. The Lawrence County Junior Red Cross's donation of property bags was reported in *Big Sandy News,* September 20, 1918, and the collection of nutshells was reported in the October 11, 1918, edition. Several Kentucky newspapers reported the nutshell-gathering campaign; see, for example, *Mt. Vernon Signal,* September 20, 1918.

9. African Americans

1. For more on the African American experience during World War I, see Nina Mjagkij, *Loyalty in Time of Trial: The African American Experience during World War I* (New York: Rowman and Littlefield, 2011); Adriane Lentz-Smith, *Freedom Strug-*

gles: African Americans and World War I (Cambridge, MA: Harvard University Press, 2009); Mark Whalan, *The Great War and the Culture of the New Negro* (Gainesville: University Press of Florida, 2008); Emmett J. Scott, *Scott's Official History of the American Negro in the World War* (Washington, DC: War Department, [1919]). Scott was a longtime assistant to Booker T. Washington and was appointed special adviser to Secretary of War Newton Baker after the United States entered the war. See also Jennifer Keene, "The Memory of the Great War in the African American Community," in *Unknown Soldiers: The American Expeditionary Forces in Memory and Remembrance,* ed. Mark A. Snell (Kent, OH: Kent State University Press, 2008), 207–40.

2. See Klotter, "The Black Community," in *Kentucky: Portrait in Paradox,* 115–21. See George C. Wright, *Racial Violence in Kentucky, 1865–1940: Lynchings, Mob Rule, and "Legal Lynchings"* (Baton Rouge: Louisiana State University Press, 1990), 110–14, for lynchings in Shelbyville and Paducah, and 193–94, 218–20, for Governor Stanley's trip to Murray to prevent the lynching of Lube Martin, who was accused of killing a policeman. After a trial and appeals, Martin was executed in the electric chair in 1919.

3. Mark Ellis, *Race, War, and Surveillance: African Americans and the United States Government during World War I* (Bloomington: Indiana University Press, 2001), 1.

4. *Bourbon News* (Paris, KY), March 25, 1917. See also *Louisville Courier-Journal,* March 25, 1917.

5. Ellis, *Race, War, and Surveillance,* 1.

6. Ibid., 16.

7. *Louisville Courier-Journal,* April 13, 1917.

8. See Committee of the Asbury Chapel African Methodist Episcopal Church to Theodore Roosevelt, May 18, 1917, Dickenson State University's Theodore Roosevelt Center website, www.theodorerooseveltcenter.org/Research/Digital-Library/Record/ImageViewer.aspx?libID=0279550. The committee consisted of seven women and seven men, including pastor Randall. See Arthur G. C. Randall to Roosevelt, May 18, 1917, www.theodorerooseveltcenter.org/Research/Digital-Library/Record/ImageViewer.aspx?libID=0279551. A white Louisville businessman, Ira S. Barnett, also wrote to Roosevelt offering to raise a black regiment. Barnett had been instrumental in reorganizing the State Guard's First Kentucky Volunteers—the "Louisville Legion"—after the Spanish-American War. See Barnett to Roosevelt, April 7, 1917, www.theodorerooseveltcenter.org/Research/Digital-Library/Record/ImageViewer.aspx?libID=0279443. Both Randall and Barnett received a stock reply from Roosevelt's spokesman, noting that the matter of raising troops should be taken up with the War Department.

9. See *Louisville Courier-Journal,* March 5, 1917, for the text of Simmons's speech, and April 6, 1917, for an editorial supporting Simmons and reassuring readers that "German intrigue will find among the negroes of the United States a more barren field than it has found elsewhere." For more on Simmons, see Andrew Kaye, "Roscoe Conkling Simmons and the Significance of African American Oratory," *Historical Journal* 45, 1 (March 2002): 79–102, and Andrew Kaye, "Colonel Roscoe Conkling Simmons and the Mechanics of Black Leadership," *Journal of American Studies* 37, 1 (April 2003): 79–98.

10. *Louisville Courier-Journal,* March 8, 1917.

11. Ellis, *Race, War, and Surveillance,* 5.

12. See *Louisville Courier-Journal,* April 9, 1917, which reproduced the text of Simmons's report, and the follow-up editorial on April 10, which concluded that "White Americans and black Americans will be the better Americans for marching together to the defense of [the] Flag."

13. *Mt. Sterling Advocate,* April 17, 1917; *Lexington Herald,* April 16, 1917.

14. *Lexington Herald,* April 18, 1917.

15. Ellis, *Race, War, and Surveillance,* 57–64.

16. Jennifer Keene, "Images of Racial Pride: African American Propaganda Posters in the First World War," in *Picture This: World War I Posters and Visual Culture,* ed. Pearl James (Lincoln: University of Nebraska Press, 2009), 212–13. Keene notes that the black administrators "tailored a message of conservation and production that showered attention on black America's economic vitality" (213). For more on the Food Administration, see Mullendore, *History of the US Food Administration.* For Hoover as food administrator, see George H. Nash, *The Life of Herbert Hoover: Master of Emergencies, 1917–1918* (New York: W. W. Norton, 1996).

17. See Inter-Office Memorandum prepared by Negro Press Section head A. U. Craig, March 23, 1918, Subject: "'Messengers' to Deliver the Message of the United States Food Administration to the Negro"; A. U. Craig to Fred Sackett, March 23 and April 16, 1918, the latter transmitting a list of African American religious leaders and fraternal organization contacts, Negroes folder, box 17: Mill Reports to Negroes, RG 4, NARA-ATL.

18. J. W. Hallowell, Chief, States Administration Division, to Sackett, April 12, 1918, announcing Attwell's appointment and transmitting a copy of Hoover's "An Appeal to the Twelve Million Negroes of the United States"; telegram from J. W. Hallowell to Sackett, April 27, 1918; Food Administration to Sackett, April 30, 1918, ibid.

19. See Semple to Sackett, March 26, 1918, describing her efforts, and various letters dated May 15, 1918, from Sackett to pastors and county food administrators announcing that Semple would be in their counties and urging their support of her speaking engagements, ibid. For a comparison of black women's efforts in other southern states, see William J. Breen, "Black Women and the Great War: Mobilization and Reform in the South," *Journal of Southern History* 44, 3 (August 1978): 421–40. Breen concludes: "By mid-1918 the war had begun to create pressures for profound social change in domestic America. Chief among these pressures was the need for a more rational approach to the utilization of all resources, including human resources. The potential for social reform inherent in the situation was grasped by southern black women. Their quiet struggle over organization was an important aspect of this battle for social reform. It formed part of the effort to erode the southern caste system and to gain more responsibility and self-respect. Similarly, in the drives for greater food production and conservation, for improved employment opportunities, and particularly in the different aspects of the child-welfare program, southern black women like their white counterparts had an opportunity both to demonstrate their patriotism and to advance social reforms that would have long-term significance for the entire community. The war ended too soon to allow any substantial or permanent social change to take place in the South, but the direction of the change was clear."

20. *Hopkinsville Kentuckian,* June 7, 1918, reported Brown's appointment as Sackett's assistant. The June 5, 1917, edition reported Brown's attempt to join the army, noting he had served in the Spanish-American War, and the October 18, 1917, edition reported his membership on the executive committee of the Liberty Bond campaign. See also Sackett to Brown, May 25, 1918, enclosing a letter from Sackett to Attwell about Brown's willingness to form a black organization to support food efforts; Brown to Sackett, May 26, 1918, promising support and expressing a willingness to attend a conference; Semple to Sackett, n.d., expressing pleasure at Brown's consent; Attwell to Sackett, June 9, 1918, suggesting that the Kentucky food administrator use his network to garner black support for the proposed conference, Negroes folder, box 17, RG 4, NARA-ATL.

21. See telegram from Sackett to Hoover, June 18, 1918; copy of the wheatless week resolution; telegram from Hoover to Sackett, June 18, 1918, congratulating him on the success of the meeting, Negroes folder, box 17, RG 4, NARA-ATL. See also *Louisville Courier-Journal,* June 12, 14, 16, and 18, 1918, for the Phoenix Hill meeting.

22. Attwell to Brown, November 6, 1918; Brown to Attwell, November 8, 1918; Brown to Sackett, November 9, 1918, sending copies of Attwell's letter and Brown's reply, Negroes folder, box 17, RG 4, NARA-ATL.

23. See Food Administration to Sackett, July 16, 1918; Brown to Sackett, August 12, 1918, along with an accompanying report and the Princeton resolution; Sackett to Hallowell, August 20, 1918, passing along Brown's report, ibid.

24. Food Administration to Sackett, August 23, 1918; Brown to Sackett, August 31, 1918, enclosing a copy of "Don't Cut the Rope" and inviting Sackett to make changes as necessary, given that Brown was working under his orders and was "not in the slightest degree sensitive"; Sackett to Hallowell, September 9, 1918, sending Brown's pamphlet draft, as submitted, with no changes, ibid. The Food Administration had 20,000 copies of the pamphlet printed for distribution in southern states. US Government Printing Office, *Annual Report of the Public Printer for the Fiscal Year Ending June 30, 1919* (Washington, DC: Government Printing Office, 1920), 183. In his *Official History of the American Negro in the World War,* 364, Scott calls the publication notable for its admonition.

25. See Brown to Sackett, November 20, 1918, enclosing a copy of the letter to directors, Negroes folder, box 17, RG 4, NARA-ATL.

26. Ibid. For Brown's quote at the meeting, see *Louisville Courier-Journal,* November 23, 1918.

27. For Brown's death, see *Afro-American* (Baltimore), December 7, 1923.

28. See KCD, *Report on Activities to January 1, 1920,* 54–55, for the KCD's work with African Americans.

29. See copy of General Letter No. 44 and letter of W. S. Gifford, February 23, 1918, G. L. 44 Organization of the Negroes folder, box 753, entry 340, RG 62, NARA-CP.

30. Minutes of the meeting of the Kentucky Council of Defense held Tuesday, May 28, 1918, folder 208 KSC June [1918], box 714, entry 339, RG 62, NARA-CP.

31. For news of the committee appointments, see *Louisville Courier-Journal,* June 16 and July 16, 1918. See also letter from Hines and Beckley to County Councils of

Defense, July 1, 1918, World War I Journal, Martin F. Schmidt Research Library, KHS, giving the names of the committee members and encouraging an "earnest, aggressive campaign" publicizing the war effort among African Americans. The letter from the CND transmitting three copies of General Letter No. 44 to Huhlein, with a handwritten note dated June 25, 1918, is in G. L. 44 Organization of the Negroes folder, box 753, entry 340, RG 62, NARA-CP. John J. Barret was instrumental in the formation of a technical training school for blacks in Louisville. Barret's attitude toward blacks was expressed in a December 9, 1908, letter he wrote to William Frost, president of Berea College. Barret recommended that Frost's proposed school for blacks (which became the Lincoln Institute in Shelby County) include only white or only black teachers. There should not be a mixture, he wrote, "because it means that the white teachers will be, or the public will consider them to be in a position of social equality with the negro teachers. This will to my mind create a prejudice against the school." Barret continued: "This question of social equality is one that creates the greatest amount of prejudice against the negro, particularly in the minds of our ignorant classes and is a condition that a majority of our people fear, foolishly it seems to me, because I know that no one is going to be recognized as my social equal unless I permit it, but others do not look at it in this way." He concluded: "I, being one of the masses, can understand their thoughts, prejudices and feelings better than one who is living in a different atmosphere and on a more ideal plane than I am [i.e., Frost]. The fact that I am anxious to see your plan for the school succeed is the reason that prompts me to write to you." Letter available at digital.berea.edu/cdm/singleitem/collection/p272901c0115/id/1802/rec/1.

32. See "Meeting of the Committee for the Organization of the Colored People for War Work, July 19, 1918," World War I Journal, Schmidt Library, KHS.

33. Pendleton Beckley to Arthur Fleming, July 30, 1918, folder 208 KSC July [1918], box 714, entry 339, RG 62, NARA-CP. See also *Louisville Courier-Journal,* July 14, 16, 17, 19, 25, and 27, 1918, for more about the black Four Minute Men and plans for a conference.

34. *Louisville Courier-Journal,* August 7, 1918. A list of the black conference delegates appointed by Governor Stanley appeared in *Lexington Herald,* August 1, 1918. The Germans had already been accused of atrocities in the treatment of the Herero tribe in southwestern Africa from 1904 to 1907. See Isabel V. Hull, "The Military Campaign in German Southwest Africa, 1904–1907," *GHI [German Historical Institute] Bulletin* 37 (Fall 2005): 39–44, www.ghi-dc.org/publications/ghipubs/bu/037/6hull.pdf. Born in South Africa, Guest had fought in the Boer War; in World War I he served in southwestern Africa and then in France, where he was wounded. He went on a propaganda tour of the United States in late 1918. After the war he became a prominent Rhodesian politician.

35. See Beckley to Fleming, August 16, 1918; Program of State Conference, August 6, 1918; Minutes: Conference on War Work among Negroes in Kentucky Held under Auspices Kentucky Council of Defense, Louisville, Ky., August 6, 1918; Constitution for Negro War Work in Kentucky, folder 208 KSC August [1918], box 714, entry 339, RG 62, NARA-CP. See also *Louisville Courier-Journal,* August 5 and 7, 1918.

36. *Louisville Courier-Journal,* August 7, 1918.

37. See copy of newspaper clipping "Colored War Activities Outstanding Feature in Scott's War Record," in Coffman, *History of Scott County,* vol. 2. The clipping is from the *Georgetown Times,* September 17, 1919. The article writer was E. B. Davis, a Scott County educator who became president of the Kentucky Negro Educational Association.

38. Ibid.

39. Ellis, *Race, War, and Surveillance,* xvi. For more on the US government and African Americans during the war, see Theodore Kornweibel Jr., *"Investigate Everything": Federal Efforts to Compel Black Loyalty during World War I* (Bloomington: Indiana University Press, 2002).

40. Report of L. O. Thompson, in re: Possible Uprising of Negroes (Lancaster, Ky.) Alleged Acts of German Sympathizers, July 31, 1917, case file 10218-2, series 10218, folder 001360-019-0311, Military Intelligence Division, RG 165 (War Department: General and Special Staffs), NARA-CP.

41. Report of L. O. Thompson, in re: Possible Pro-German Feeling among Negroes (Lexington, Ky.), December 4, 1917, case file 10218-61, RG 165, NARA-CP. Eleanor Breckinridge Chalkley was the sister of social work pioneer Sophonisba Breckinridge, *Lexington Herald* editor Desha Breckinridge, and Curry Breckinridge, who had served as a nurse in wartime France. This was not Chalkley's first communication with the Bureau of Investigation. In July he had sent Bielaski a letter concerning the daughter of a Lexingtonian who had married a German officer and her recent letters back home. Chalkley claimed he was acting "only under a sense of obligation to communicate anything that could have any significance." See Chalkley to the Director, Bureau of Investigations, July 9, 1917, ibid. Historian Mark Ellis notes: "At its peak, in the summer of 1917, [the] torrent of letters from alarmed citizens would reach a thousand per day, of which an estimated 95 percent turned out to be of no significance." Ellis, *Race, War, and Surveillance,* xvii.

42. Report of L. O. Thompson, in re: Possible Pro-German Feeling among Negroes (Lexington, Ky.), December 12, 1917, OG file 106021, RG 65, NARA-CP.

43. Ibid., December 17, 1917. The American Protective League was a quasi-official arm of the Department of Justice; its 250,000 volunteers nationwide kept an eye out for sedition. Lexington lawyer and University of Kentucky Board of Trustees member Richard Stoll headed the APL in Kentucky.

44. Kornweibel, *"Investigate Everything,"* 60. Kornweibel notes, "This practice of warning or intimidating 'suspects' when they could not be prosecuted continued throughout the war and was often the only concrete action that Bureau agents and U.S. attorneys could take because violations of federal law had not occurred" (59). To understand how BI agent Thompson could obtain a letter from the post office without a warrant, see Peter Conolly-Smith, "'Reading between the Lines': The Bureau of Investigation, the United States Post Office, and Domestic Surveillance during World War I," *Social Justice* 36, 1 (2009): 7–24.

45. Report of L. O. Thompson, in re: Walter Delaney (Colored)—Alleged Violation Espionage Act (Richmond, Ky.), April 26, 1918, case file 10218-132, RG 165, NARA-CP.

46. Kornweibel, *"Investigate Everything,"* 77.

47. Chambers, *To Raise an Army,* 156–58.

48. For more on the Houston riot and aftermath, see Lentz-Smith, *Freedom Struggles,* 43–79.

49. See *Louisville Courier-Journal,* August 24, 25, 26, 27, and 29, November 2, 3, and 9, December 1, 12, and 23, 1917. See the September 2, 1917, edition for Mamie Peck's letter to the editor, and September 18, 1917, for the rebuttal to northern criticism. See also *Public Ledger* (Maysville, KY), August 25, 1917; *Hartford Herald,* August 30, 1917; *Citizen* (Berea, KY), August 30, 1917. For more on the riots in 1917, see Malcolm McLaughlin, "Ghetto Formation and Armed Resistance in East St. Louis, Illinois," *Journal of American Studies* 41, 2 (August 2007): 435–67. In those riots, at least thirty-nine blacks were killed. McLaughlin concludes: "The East St. Louis race riot shattered any lingering faith in the belief that the North was a promised land, and it was a tragic setback to the development of the black community" (465).

50. See *Adair County News* (Columbia, KY), September 5, 1917, which criticized the stationing of northern blacks in southern cantonments.

51. Chambers, *To Raise an Army,* 223–25.

52. *Louisville Courier-Journal,* October 23, 1917.

53. Telegram from Crowder to Governor of Kentucky, November 7, 1918, file KY 17 (141–60), box 142, entry 2: States Files, RG 163, NARA-CP.

54. Rhodes to Provost Marshal General, November 21, 1918, ibid.

55. *Georgetown Times,* March 27, 1918; *Louisville Courier-Journal,* July 20, 1918. See *Louisville Courier-Journal,* February 3, March 21 and 27, April 2, 1918, for reports on anticipated black troops, including 1,650 from Kentucky, and their arrival at Camp Taylor. See the June 30, 1918, edition for the report of 3,000 more blacks being called up, and August 11, 1918, for another 815 blacks called up. The latter reveals the number of whites and blacks in each county.

56. See *Louisville Courier-Journal,* March 12, 1918, for the establishment of a black Soldiers' Club, and August 1, 1918, for the creation of the housing bureau.

57. For the Glass incident, see *Louisville Courier-Journal,* October 17, 1917. For more on the riot at Fort Merritt, see Jennifer Keene, *Doughboys, the Great War, and the Remaking of America* (Baltimore: Johns Hopkins Press, 2001), 94–98. Keene also gives examples of how the issue of whites saluting black officers was handled in different ways—noncompliance, grudgingly, and with the hope that black officers "would not look for salutes" (88).

58. See *Louisville Courier-Journal,* October 25, 1917, for Castleman's quote, and October 27, 1917, for an editorial approving of his attitude. Castleman's stance made national news; see *New York Times,* November 12, 1917.

59. See *Louisville Courier-Journal,* August 15, September 21, and October 26, 1918, for news of the 814th and 64th Pioneer Infantry Regiments. The 814th was not the only African American unit known as the "Black Devils." This was also the name of the 370th Regiment from Illinois; see William Allison Sweeney, *History of the American Negro in the Great World War* (Chicago: G. G. Sapp, 1919), 153–79. Sweeney was a contributing editor of the *Chicago Defender,* one of the country's most influential African American newspapers. Roscoe Conkling Simmons also wrote for the *Defender.*

60. See *Louisville Courier-Journal,* July 30 and 31, 1918, and *Public Ledger* (Maysville, KY), August 3, 1918, for more about the creation of the 801st Pioneer Infantry Regiment (originally, simply the 801st Infantry). Stevens quoted in Chad Williams, *Torchbearers of Democracy: African American Soldiers in the World War I Era* (Chapel Hill: University of North Carolina Press, 2010), 114. A brief history of the 801st can be found in *Bourbon News* (Paris, KY), April 29, 1919. An African American soldier from Paris, Kentucky, Alonzo Jackson of Company C, sent home a clipping from a French newspaper written in English. The *Bourbon News* reproduced the article and added, "Jackson asks its publication 'in order that the people of Paris may know what the colored soldiers did in France during the war.'"

61. George F. Hamilton took command of the 801st Pioneers on June 27, 1918, and stayed with the unit until it was disbanded at Camp Taylor in June 1919. He was an 1894 graduate of the US Military Academy, finishing thirteenth in his class. He was the son-in-law of famous army general Adna Chaffee, who had led American relief forces during the Boxer Rebellion in 1900. Hamilton's career is summarized in George Washington Cullum and Wilt Robinson, eds., *Biographical Register of the Officers and Graduates of the U.S. Military Academy,* supplement, vol. 6-A, *1910–1920* (Saginaw, MI: Seeman and Peters, 1920), 687–88. The quote about the 801st at Camp Pontanezen is in Addie Hunton and Kathryn Johnson, *Two Colored Women with the American Expeditionary Forces* (Brooklyn, NY: Brooklyn Eagle Press, 1920), 127. Hunton and Johnson worked for the YMCA at Camp Pontanezen. The camp was in bad condition when Marine Corps colonel Smedley Darlington Butler arrived in the fall of 1918. A two-time recipient of the Medal of Honor, Butler was put in charge of the camp and sorted it out. To conquer the omnipresent mud, he spread wooden duckboards over the camp, earning him the nickname "General Duckboard." See Hans Schmidt, *Maverick Marine: General Smedley D. Butler and the Contradictions of American Military History* (Lexington: University Press of Kentucky, 1987), 96–109.

62. See *Public Ledger* (Maysville, KY), December 3 and 9, 1918, for Hall's and Turner's letters, respectively.

63. Cobb's reporting on blacks in the war was reprinted in *Louisville Courier-Journal,* August 28, 29, and 30, 1918. The original article appeared in *Saturday Evening Post,* August 24, 1918, and was included in Cobb's book *The Glory of the Coming.* For Johnson and Roberts, see Richard Slotkin, "The Battle of Henry Johnson: 'Another Way to Spell "American,"'" in *Lost Battalions: The Great War and the Crisis of American Nationality* (New York: Henry Holt, 2005), 138–51. Although other journalists reported the story, Slotkin believes that Cobb's coverage was important because he was a southerner whose view of black soldiers changed after the Johnson and Roberts episode. Johnson posthumously received the United States' second highest medal for bravery, the Distinguished Service Cross, in 2003; he finally received the highest award, the Medal of Honor, in June 2015. See *New York Times,* June 2, 2015.

64. For Cobb's visit to Paducah, see Lawson, *Irvin S. Cobb,* 165–66.

65. Austin Kinnaird diary, entry for November 19, 1918, Schmidt Library, KHS.

66. Ibid., November 23, 1918, and January 19, 1919.

67. Ibid., January 23 and 24, 1919.

68. Ibid., February 1, 1919. For more on African American soldiers' experiences in

France, see Lentz-Smith, *Freedom Struggles,* 80–136. While American blacks in France may not have encountered the rigid Jim Crowism of the United States, Lentz-Smith notes: "That ideal France invoked by black soldiers and decried by white supremacists did not actually exist. Like its American ally, France was mundane, flawed, complex." Lentz-Smith acknowledges, however, "France did serve the African American freedom movement by allowing black soldiers to conceive of a life unfettered by segregation. African American soldiers focused on the relative fluidity of their relations with white French men and women, and contrasted those relations with the rigid rituals of Jim Crow" (108).

69. Kinnaird diary, February 4 and 5, 1919. In February 1919 Kinnaird was transferred to Camp Lusitania, St. Nazaire, where two companies of the 811th Pioneers were stationed. There he ran into an acquaintance from the 814th Pioneers—Will Allen, the husband of Nellie, who had served as the Kinnaird family cook "for quite a while." He finally returned to Louisville in May 1919. Ibid., February 9 and 10, 1919.

70. Quoted in Berry Craig, *Hidden History of Kentucky Soldiers* (Charleston, SC: History Press, 2011), 74. Craig's short section on Carman is based on interviews with the veteran, who eventually received a Purple Heart; see the photograph of Carman with his medal in ibid., 72. For more on the Harlem Hellfighters, also known as the Black Rattlers, see Jeffrey T. Sammons and John H. Morrow Jr., *Harlem's Rattlers and the Great War: The Undaunted 369th Regiment & the African American Quest for Equality* (Lawrence: University Press of Kansas, 2014), and Peter N. Nelson, *The Harlem Hellfighters' Struggle for Freedom in WW I and Equality at Home* (New York: Basic Civitas Books, 2009).

71. See Gerald L. Smith, *A Black Educator in the Segregated South: Kentucky's Rufus B. Atwood* (Lexington: University Press of Kentucky, 1994), 22–25. A reproduction of Atwood's citation is found in a newspaper clipping in Caldwell, *Kentucky in the World War,* vol. 11.

72. Smith, *Black Educator in the Segregated South,* 25.

73. The Lewis lynching is covered extensively in Vincent Mikkelsen, "Coming from Battle to Face a War: The Lynching of Black Soldiers in the World War I Era" (PhD diss., Florida State University, 2007), 99–108; see also "Table 3: Black Soldiers Lynched, 1918–1920," 213. For more on lynching during the Great War, see David A. Davis, "Not Only War Is Hell: World War I and African American Lynching Narratives," *African American Review* 42, 3–4 (Fall–Winter 2008): 477–91.

74. Newspaper clipping from *Georgetown Times,* September 17, 1919, in Coffman, *History of Scott County,* vol. 2.

75. For a comparative view of African Americans in another state, see Randy Finley, "Black Arkansans and World War One," *Arkansas Historical Quarterly* 49, 3 (Autumn 1990): 249–77. Finley concludes: "Black Arkansans contributed to the war effort by enlisting in the army, by purchasing thousands of dollars of war bonds and war stamps, by fostering patriotism and nationalism, and by adhering to the myriad conservation proposals of the government. Although some left for greener pastures north, most remained in their home state. Although black elites fostered a belief among the black masses that the world after Versailles would surely undoubtedly be different, such was not the case. Lynching, discrimination, and racism remained an

integral part of life in Arkansas. World War I was not to be the catalyst which would metamorphose racial attitudes. For the time being, old times here were still not forgotten" (277).

10. The Economy

1. Wynn, *From Progressivism to Prosperity,* 79. See also Zieger, *America's Great War,* 16, for the growth of the US economy at the start of the war.

2. Klotter, *Kentucky: Portrait in Paradox,* 123. The state's reliance on agriculture is well reflected in the *Lexington Herald*'s periodic "Bluegrass Farmer" section; see, for example, the March 5, 1917, edition. See also *Louisville Courier-Journal,* April 2, 3, and 4, 1917.

3. *Louisville Courier-Journal,* April 6 and 7, 1917.

4. *Louisville Courier-Journal,* April 18, May 7 and 10, 1917. For a portrait of Hughes as a modern, scientific, progressive farmer, see Robert McMahon, ed., *How These Farmers Succeeded* (New York: Henry Holt, 1919), 93–106.

5. David B. Danbom, "The Agricultural Extension System and the First World War," *Historian* 41, 2 (February 1, 1979): 315. Danbom believes that extension agents not only helped increase farm production but also led the overall social mobilization of rural areas in support of the war. Although problems existed, both the war effort and the extension agent system benefited. Danbom concludes: "Although its most optimistic hopes were not realized, extension did emerge from the war stronger both in the Federal government and in rural America. Thus, just as the extension system was a key element in the mobilization of rural America during the First World War, so too was the war a key element in the growth of the extension system" (331).

6. Ibid., 319. Danbom is quoting from Gordon's "Report of the Work of the Fulton County Agent—1917," *Extension Service Annual Reports: Kentucky 1912–1944,* US National Archives microfilm T-862, roll 2, p. 68.

7. For an examination of farm labor during the war, see Harry Schwartz, "Agricultural Labor in the First World War," *Journal of Farm Economics* 24, 1 (February 1942): 178–87. The faculty resolution was reported in *Lexington Herald,* April 19, 1917. For Barker's and Roberts's comments, see *Louisville Courier-Journal,* April 21, 1917. Barker resigned in June 1917 after a committee appointed by the governor issued a report critical of his leadership.

8. Explanation of the US Employment Service in Kentucky is found in memorandum relating to the work of the US Employment Service, folder 1, County Organization U.S. Federal Reserve Service, box 59, Frank McVey Papers, UK Special Collections and Archives. See also telegram from W. E. Hall, National Director, Public Service Reserve, to McVey, July 24, 1918, ibid., announcing Dale as the new state director of the Federal Employment Service. See *Bourbon News* (Paris, KY), July 17, 1917, for notice of the creation of a Public Service Reserve. See also *Louisville Courier-Journal,* December 15, 1917, and January 9, 1918, announcing plans for the Federal Employment Service and noting an especially acute need for skilled workers in the shipbuilding industry. The *Breckenridge News* (Cloverport, KY), February 6, 1918, announced McVey's appointment as state director of the Public Service Reserve. For

more on McVey, see Eric A. Moyen, *Frank L. McVey and the University of Kentucky: A Progressive President and the Modernization of a Southern University* (Lexington: University Press of Kentucky, 2011).

9. Besides Dale and McVey, the four other men on the state board included a sheet metal worker and a plant supervisor. McVey also had three paid district supervisors to assist him. See folder 1, County Organization U.S. Federal Reserve Service, box 59, McVey Papers, for lists of county boards naming the chair, employer, and employee representatives. For Pike County, see letter from Tom Williamson to McVey, July 9, 1918, ibid., enclosing a list of representatives. For the Marshall County list, see E. L. Cooper to McVey, July 12, 1918, ibid. One man was listed as a banker/farmer, while another was listed as a farmer/teacher. Like many county leaders, Cooper wore many hats: government appeal agent for the draft, executive committee member for the Red Cross and War Savings program, and chair of the county Liberty Loan program.

10. *Louisville Courier-Journal,* July 23 and 31, 1918. See McVey to Dale, August 2, 1918, for Kentucky's 4,100-man quota, a figure transmitted to McVey from John B. Densmore, Director General of the USES, folder 2, Pratt Dale State Director, box 59, McVey Papers. See also *U.S. Employment Service Bulletin* 1, 28 (August 6, 1918): 1. For the revised figure of 8,100, see N. A. Smythe, Asst. Director General, U.S. Employment Service, to McVey, August 20, 1918, and McVey to County Chairmen and Agents, August 16, 1918, folder 4, County Agent Materials, USPSR, box 59, McVey Papers.

11. For shipbuilding efforts, see McVey to Chairmen of County Committees of the State Council of Defense, February 1, 1918, and for stevedore efforts, see McVey to County Enrollment Agents, May 3, 1918, folder 4, County Agent Materials, USPSR, box 59, McVey Papers. For the registration of nonessential workers, see *Louisville Courier-Journal,* July 14, 1918. The *Bourbon News* (Paris, KY), February 8, 1918, reported on the need for mechanics, while the *Hopkinsville Kentuckian,* February 12, 1918, called for "Artisans to Register." A list of nonessential industries was printed in the *Bourbon News,* August 27, 1918; it included entertainment businesses such as bowling alleys and poolrooms, florists, pawnbrokers, and any construction not focused on war needs. Caution against disturbing farming and mining interests is found in McVey to County Chairmen and Agents, August 26, 1918, folder 4, County Agent Materials, USPSR, box 59, McVey Papers.

12. McVey to County Chairmen, USPSR, October 25, 1918, folder 4, County Agent Materials, USPSR, box 59, McVey Papers. Historian Neil Wynn asserts that despite variations, "the one thing almost all [Progressives] had in common was the faith in society's ability to resolve major problems satisfactorily through political action. This belief led Progressives to look increasingly to government and resulted in the gradual spread of the movement from the state and local level up to the national level." Wynn, *From Progressivism to Prosperity,* 10.

13. Several letters from McVey to Dale forwarding requests for work are contained in folder 2, Pratt Dale State Director, box 59, McVey Papers. An example of the ad requesting that men not switch jobs without approval appeared in *Kentucky Irish-American,* September 7, 1918. The Lawrence County advertisement was in *Big Sandy News* (Louisa, KY), September 20, 1918.

14. See "Outline of the Program of the College of Agriculture for Meeting the Farm Labor Problem in Kentucky," folder 10, Farm Labor USPSR, box 59, McVey Papers.

15. Nicholls's plan is outlined in "Work of the College of Agriculture on the Farm Labor Problem for Kentucky," ibid. For an example of the letter to college presidents, see McVey to William G. Frost, President, Berea College, April 23, 1918, ibid., along with an attached list of other recipients. In a letter to McVey on June 3, 1918 (ibid.), Nicholls reported that of thirty-seven students at Georgetown College, all but five were working on their home farms; at Bethel College in Russellville, seventeen students had enrolled in the summer work program, all on their own family farms.

16. See "Plan for the Summer Husbandry of the Clerkship of Kentucky," ibid., for Nicholls's program to enlist merchants for farmwork. See also McVey to County Enrollment Agents, USPSR, May 1, 1918, ibid.

17. The multiple volunteers were reported in *Daily Kentuckian* (Hopkinsville, KY), August 14, 1918. J. W. Whitehouse to W. D. Nicholls, July 6, 1918, folder 10, Farm Labor USPSR, box 59, McVey Papers.

18. See Nicholls to McVey, June 28, 1918, and McVey to H. E. Blakeslee, June 27, 1918, reporting on the reasonable farm labor situation in Kentucky, folder 10, Farm Labor USPSR, box 59, McVey Papers.

19. For an example of the dynamic tension between the needs of farming and schooling, see the National Child Labor Committee's pamphlet *Children in Food Production* (New York: Clarence S. Nathan, 1917), 4. It warned about holding children back from school to do farmwork: "In seven counties in Kentucky in 1916, 46 per cent of the children absent from school for farmwork were retarded as compared with 13 per cent of the daily attendants." Among other things, the committee recommended that "children under 16 shall be used where there is opportunity either on home farms and gardens or in community or school gardens under supervision, but no compulsory education laws shall be relaxed to allow children to work in agriculture even at home" (7).

20. See *Louisville Courier-Journal,* November 16, 1917, urging voluntary action by boys. The *Public Ledger* (Maysville, KY), April 25, 1917, reported on the formation of the Boys Working Reserve under the directorship of William Edwin Hall, president of the Boys Club Federation. For examples of the organization in Mason and Rockcastle Counties, respectively, see *Public Ledger,* March 13, 1918, and *Mt. Vernon Signal,* March 15, 1918. The *Mt. Vernon Signal,* March 15, 1918, and *Record* (Greenville, KY), March 21, 1918, reported on the program and announced that local committees, made up of both men and women, would help enroll the boys. The Boys Working Reserve organization in Kentucky was covered in *Boy Power: Official Bulletin of the United States Boys Working Reserve* 1, 9 (September 15, 1918): 2. See also Schwartz, "Agricultural Labor in the First World War," 185.

21. See *Louisville Courier-Journal,* July 30, August 7, September 22, and November 22, 1918.

22. *Yearbook of the United States Department of Agriculture, 1918* (Washington, DC: Government Printing Office, 1919), 703.

23. Hood, *Visions of Zion,* 109.

24. *Louisville Courier-Journal,* January 1, April 3, and September 3, 1917.

25. See Empey's plea in *Louisville Courier-Journal,* September 23, 1917. The Our Boys in France Tobacco Fund was headquartered in New York City. The organization printed posters admonishing, "Send Smokes to Sammy." "Sammy" was the common name for American soldiers during the war.

26. A. M. Brandt, *The Cigarette Century: The Rise, Fall, and Deadly Persistence of the Product that Defined America* (New York: Basic Books, 2007), 51–52.

27. James F. Hopkins, *A History of the Hemp Industry in Kentucky* (Lexington: University of Kentucky Press, 1951), 207–9, 219. The *Lexington Herald,* February 22, 1917, reported that UK hemp expert E. J. Kinney believed that hemp growers were "making good money."

28. Hopkins, *History of the Hemp Industry,* 209. Hopkins notes that after the war, the lead in hemp production passed to Wisconsin, which had invested heavily in the product, especially in machinery to break down hemp into fiber.

29. Kleber, *Kentucky Encyclopedia,* 281; Klotter, *Kentucky: Portrait in Paradox,* 135; George C. Wright, *A History of Blacks in Kentucky,* vol. 2, *In Pursuit of Equality, 1890–1980* (Frankfort: Kentucky Historical Society, 1992), 25. Wright notes that the number of black miners rose from 2,206 in 1900 to 7,407 by 1920. For more on the development of coal towns in eastern Kentucky, see George D. Torok, *A Guide to the Historic Coal Towns: Of the Big Sandy River Valley* (Knoxville: University of Tennessee Press, 2004).

30. The development of McRoberts was reported in *Louisville Courier-Journal,* April 30, 1917. For more on Consolidated Coal Company, see Geoffrey L. Buckley, *Extracting Appalachia: Images of the Consolidation Coal Company, 1910/1945* (Athens: Ohio University Press, 2004). See *Louisville Courier-Journal,* June 18, 1917, for the organization of four new coal companies; new incorporations were listed periodically in the *Courier-Journal* under "Incorporation Articles Approved by J. P. Lewis" (Lewis was Kentucky's secretary of state).

31. For the establishment and growth of Lynch, see Thomas A. Kelemen, "A History of Lynch, Kentucky, 1917 to 1930" (MA thesis, University of Kentucky, 1972); Thomas A. Kelemen, "A History of Lynch, Kentucky, 1917–1930," *Filson Club History Quarterly* 48, 2 (April 1974): 156–76. See *Louisville Courier-Journal,* December 5, 1918, for the number of inhabitants and news of a new 140-room hotel, and December 16, 1917, for activity in the town; the newspaper also surmised that Harlan County led eastern Kentucky in coal production. For more on African Americans in Lynch, see Thomas E. Wagner and Phillip J. Obermiller, *African American Miners and Migrants: The Eastern Kentucky Social Club* (Urbana: University of Illinois Press, 2004), 91–99.

32. See *Hartford Republican,* June 22, 1917, for the announcement of a pending strike and miners' grievances. See *Louisville Courier-Journal,* June 24, 1917, for news of the gunfight in Clay.

33. See *Lexington Herald,* July 4, 1917, and *Hopkinsville Kentuckian,* July 5, 1917, for news of the western Kentucky coal strike and conflicting views of its effects. See *Lexington Herald,* July 11 and 14, 1917, for the National Guard's deployment to Webster County; on July 29, 1917, the newspaper reported that adjutant general Tandy Ellis believed the Signal Corps unit had done a good job ensuring peace in the area. See also *Louisville Courier-Journal,* July 3, 4, 5, 6, 11, 13, 15, and 16, 1917.

34. Arrest of the three miners reported in *Lexington Herald,* August 4, 1917; end of the strike reported in *Hartford Republican,* August 10, 1917. See also *Louisville Courier-Journal,* August 3, 4, 5, 6, 7, and 8, 1917, for coverage of the strike and the mine disaster.

35. See *Lexington Herald,* August 12, 1917, for the coal strike; August 14, 1917, for Hywell Davies being sent to eastern Kentucky; August 28, September 6 and 7, 1917, for reports of violence; and September 22, 1917, for Mayor Rogers's appeal to authorities. See also *Hartford Herald,* August 15, 1917; *Citizen* (Berea, KY), August 16, 1917; *Hopkinsville Kentuckian,* August 16 and October 6, 1917; *Big Sandy News* (Louisa, KY), September 28, 1917; *Mt. Sterling Advocate,* October 2, 1917; *Louisville Courier-Journal,* July 8, 17, 19, 20, and 21, August 6, 10, 12, 14, 22, and 23, September 21 and 28, October 5 and 10, 1917, January 20, 1918, for news of demands, failed negotiations, strikes, and settlements.

36. See, for example, the notice in *Louisville Courier-Journal,* July 2, 1917, noting that the Louisville & Nashville Railroad would build a twelve-mile branch line in Perry County, "one of the most important short line railroad extensions ever built in eastern Kentucky." A dozen coal companies would begin working along the line.

37. Most of the material on the Louisville & Nashville Railroad is taken from Kincaid Herr, *The Louisville and Nashville Railroad, 1850–1963,* rev. ed. (Lexington: University Press of Kentucky, 2000), 207–22. Herr was an L&N employee who usually worked on the company magazine, where much of the history appeared serially starting in 1939. Herr admits the history "does not pose as either an unbiased or a complete history of the L. & N." For another source, see Maury Klein, *History of the Louisville & Nashville Railroad* (Lexington: University Press of Kentucky, 2003), which emphasizes the role of Milton Smith, the railroad's iconic president for thirty years.

38. Formation of the Liberty League reported in *Louisville Courier-Journal,* April 16, 1917; employee reply to Smith's call for loyalty reproduced on April 27, 1918. Liberty League meetings, which were attended by up to 3,000 people, were reported by the *Courier-Journal* on April 20, May 25, August 5, and October 6, 1918. Governor Stanley's remarks quoted in the September 2, 1918, edition.

39. Herr, *Louisville and Nashville Railroad,* 220–21. Union creation reported in *Louisville Courier-Journal,* August 17, 1918.

40. Announcement of five new tracks and a railway station at Camp Taylor in *Louisville Courier-Journal,* July 1 and 19, 1917; expected hiring of women reported on May 12, 1917; office consolidation reported on May 15, 1917; hiring of first female Southern Railway agent in Harrodsburg reported on March 11, 1918. According to the *Courier-Journal,* the new agent, Edna Campbell, came from "a family of railroaders" and was a "prominent business woman" of the city.

41. *Louisville Courier-Journal,* November 7, 1917, and March 12, 1918. On May 10, 1917, the newspaper reported that the Mengel Box Company in Louisville had received an $800,000 contract from the navy to manufacture 355,000 naval cartridge boxes.

42. Daniel Yergin, "The First War to Run on Oil—World War I Made Gasoline Central to World Politics," *Wall Street Journal,* August 16, 2014.

43. *Louisville Courier-Journal,* March 5, 1917. The growth of the oil industry was reported repeatedly in the *Courier-Journal;* see, for example, April 16, May 7, June 4, July 9, and August 13, 1917, January 7, 1918. The *Lexington Herald,* March 25, 1917, reported, "Oil Men Rush to Kentucky"; on June 27, 1918, it reported on promising new oil discoveries in Estill and Allen Counties.

44. Formation of Swiss Oil mentioned in *Louisville Courier-Journal,* July 8, 1918. For the creation of Ashland Refining and the merger with Swiss Oil, see the Ashland website: www.ashland.com/about/history-heritage.

45. See *Lexington Herald,* April 21, 1918, for new wells in the Big Sinking Area. New refineries reported in *Louisville Courier-Journal,* November 19, 1917, and January 21, 1918. For more on eastern Kentucky oil field development, see Brandon C. Nuttall, "Historic Oil Fields of Eastern Kentucky and Big Andy Ridge," Kentucky Society of Professional Geologists website: www.kspg.org/pdf/KSPG01.pdf.

46. For UK canceling sports activities, see *Louisville Courier-Journal,* May 2, 1917. For Secretary Baker's comments to the National Athletic Association, see the August 12, 1917, edition.

47. See *Louisville Courier-Journal,* June 30, 1918, for Wathen's opposition to terminating the league. See also the July 16, 1918, edition, which noted that the public had little enthusiasm for the game, hence the declining revenue and calls to end the league, if not for good then at least until the end of the war. On July 20, 1918, an article noted the implications of Secretary Baker's "work or fight" order and surmised that major and minor league baseball would be suspended. For accounts of the Colonels versus the Camp Taylor team, see *Louisville Courier-Journal,* April 7 and 28, 1918. For more on the importance of postwar baseball, see Robin F. Bachin, "At the Nexus of Labor and Leisure: Baseball, Nativism, and the 1919 Black Sox Scandal," *Journal of Social History* 36, 4 (Summer 2003): 941–62. Bachin asserts: "The scandal became a symbol of the rising post-war tensions over labor relations, race, ethnicity, and nationalism in America. It also became a vehicle for circumscribing the meanings of Americanism" (941).

48. For the war's impact on the horse industry prior to US entry, especially in the Bluegrass region, see *Lexington Herald,* April 15, 1917. See also *Louisville Courier-Journal,* April 7 and May 13, 1917.

49. British army general G. T. M. Bridges acknowledged that the military used more motor vehicles than ever before, but he still believed horses could go where vehicles could not; see *Lexington Herald,* May 22, 1917.

50. Harper's assertion was reported in *Lexington Herald,* May 21, 1917. Harper was also head of the State Racing Commission's Breeding Bureau. See also *Louisville Courier-Journal,* June 10, 11, and 28, 1917, January 29, 1918.

51. *Lexington Herald,* April 11, 1918. See also *Louisville Courier-Journal,* December 23, 1917, January 16, April 7, June 2 and 19, 1918.

52. See *Louisville Courier-Journal,* May 12, 1918, for news of the Kentucky Derby; June 20, 1918, for Mayor Smith's criticisms; and September 12 and 13, 1918, for the Board of Trade's letter to Wilson and Smith's response.

53. *Lexington Herald,* June 15, 1918; see also the July 7, 1918, edition. Haldeman later pleaded that the political campaign season be postponed until after the conclu-

sion of a Liberty Bond campaign at the beginning of October; see *Lexington Herald,* September 8, 1918.

54. *Lexington Herald,* October 2, 1918. See also *Louisville Courier-Journal,* July 21, 1918.

55. For more on Kentucky's debate regarding alcohol and Prohibition, see Appleton, "'Like Banquo's Ghost.'"

56. *Louisville Courier-Journal,* February 6, 1917. Alcohol was one of the four substances needed to produce modern ammunition, along with cotton, sulfuric acid, and nitric acid; see *Courier-Journal,* March 18, 1917.

57. For the effects of the Lever Act shutdowns, see *Louisville Courier-Journal,* September 7 and 9, 1917.

58. *Lexington Herald,* January 15, 1918. *Louisville Courier-Journal* editorials on January 24 and 26, 1918, railed against the state legislature's perfidy in ratifying Prohibition and not sending the issue to the voters.

59. See *Big Sandy News* (Louisa, KY), January 18, 1918, for the state legislature's Eighteenth Amendment vote. The newspaper lauded this action but supported the movement for a statewide Prohibition bill. See also *Interior Journal* (Stanford, KY), January 25, 1918, regarding the statewide Prohibition bill and calling for a vote in November 1919. For results, see *Lexington Herald,* November 6, 1919; *Louisville Courier-Journal,* November 8 and 23, 1919.

60. For KCD pleas for the enforcement of vagrancy laws, see *Louisville Courier-Journal,* April 22, 1917. See also *Mt. Sterling Advocate,* May 1, 1917. Sections of the vagrancy law were reproduced in *Hopkinsville Kentuckian,* May 15, 1917, and *Central Record* (Lancaster, KY), May 24, 1917. Judge Bush's remarks were quoted in *Hopkinsville Kentuckian,* August 21, 1917.

61. *Mt. Sterling Advocate,* April 9, 1918. For the full text of the vagrancy law, see John D. Carroll, ed., *The Kentucky Statutes,* 5th ed. (Louisville, KY: Baldwin Law Book Co., 1918), 3:1002–4. The law was also published in *Bourbon News* (Paris, KY), June 18, 1918, with a warning: "Read it carefully, and if you are idle, heed, and take warning." For the initial act and amendment, see Kentucky General Assembly, *Journal of the Regular Session of the House of Representatives of the Commonwealth of Kentucky* (Frankfort, 1918), 896–900. The *Bourbon News,* May 24, 1918, erroneously reported that the law's "language was not confined to a 'man.'"

62. Ohio County actions reported in *Hartford Republican,* May 3, 1918. Formation of Anti-Loafers League reported in *Daily Kentuckian* (Hopkinsville, KY), April 12, 1918, and *Louisville Courier-Journal,* April 12, 1918, which cited the league's purpose. Employment bureau and license tax reported in *Daily Kentuckian,* April 23 and June 19, 1918, respectively.

63. *Lexington Herald,* April 26, 1917.

64. See *Bourbon News* (Paris, KY), May 11, 1917; *Central Record* (Lancaster, KY), June 28, 1917, reproducing an article from the *Elizabethtown News.* African Americans remained a target for antivagrancy efforts in Paris; in July police "surprised the residents of the negro villages of Claysville and Bucknerville" in a "simultaneous raid" to round up "loiters." *Lexington Herald,* July 10, 1917.

65. Chambers, *To Raise an Army,* 194.

66. Hotel owners' fears reported in *Louisville Courier-Journal,* June 23, 1918. For more about sports-related concerns, see *Louisville Courier-Journal,* May 24, 1918; Chambers, *To Raise an Army,* 195–96.

67. See *Public Ledger* (Maysville, KY), July 6, 1918; *Citizen* (Berea, KY), July 25, 1918; *Licking Valley Courier* (West Liberty, KY), August 25, 1918. In a scathing article attacking the "Bolsheviki administration" of Louisville mayor Smith, the *Kentucky Irish-American* wondered on July 6, 1918, if the vacationing Smith might be forced into the military for violating "work or fight."

68. *Hickman Courier,* October 10, 1918.

69. See *Louisville Courier-Journal,* June 13, 1917, for criticism of Governor Stanley; June 16, 1917, for labor representation on draft boards; August 20, 1917, for state Federation of Labor action; February 7, 1917, for Lee's purchase of the *Journal of Labor.* Lee's appointment to the KCD was noted in *Daily Kentuckian* (Hopkinsville, KY), April 17, 1918. For more on Lee, who was also an engine foreman in the Kentucky Division of the Illinois Central Railroad, see *Illinois Central Magazine* 10, 1 (July 1921): 14–16.

70. Lee quoted in KCD, *Report of Activities to January 1, 1920,* 33. See also KCD, *Report of Activities to January 1, 1919,* 12. Action by the Bluegrass Federation of Labor reported in *Lexington Herald,* October 7, 1917.

71. Quote from Felix Frankfurter to Governor Augustus O. Stanley, August 17, 1918, Correspondence with State Officials on Labor Standards, August 1918–January 1919, folder General Correspondence, box 1 (General) Ala.–N.J., entry 3, RG 1 (War Labor Policies Board), NARA-CP. Correspondence regarding the appointment of Ethel Musgrove is found in ibid., folder Kentucky. For more on the War Labor Policies Board, see William J. Breen, *Labor Market Politics and the Great War: The Department of Labor, the States, and the First U.S. Employment Service, 1907–1933* (Kent, OH: Kent State University Press, 1997), 67–88.

72. For Musgrove's views and actions, see *Louisville Courier-Journal,* June 10, 1917, and April 21, 1918; *Lexington Herald,* October 31, 1918. Musgrove sent copies of Kentucky's child labor law and the "Act to Regulate the Employment of Females in Order to Safeguard Their Health" to federal officials; see folder Kentucky, box 1 (General) Ala.–N.J., entry 3, RG 1, NARA-CP. Musgrove had been appointed by Governor Stanley as a Kentucky representative to the Thirteenth National Conference on Child Labor held in Baltimore in March 1917, along with Madeline McDowell Breckinridge and other notable Progressive Kentucky women; see *Citizen* (Berea, KY), March 1, 1917. She was married to well-known Louisville poet and *Evening Post* newspaperman Charles Hamilton Musgrove. The Keating-Owen Act relied on the Constitution's commerce clause to regulate the interstate flow of goods produced by child labor and to set maximum working hours for child labor. Earlier in 1918 the Supreme Court had struck down the law as unconstitutional. Frankfurter nevertheless insisted that federal contracts contain a clause that upheld those standards. See Hugh D. Hindman, *Child Labor: An American History* (Armonk, NY: M. E. Sharpe, 2002), 70.

73. A copy of Musgrove's compilation is found in folder Kentucky, box 1 (General) Ala.–N.J., entry 3, RG 1, NARA-CP. See also *Louisville Courier-Journal,* November 24 and 30, 1918. Musgrove's explanation of the child labor law appeared in some

Kentucky newspapers; see, for example, *Lexington Herald,* October 9, 1918; *Public Ledger* (Maysville, KY), November 25, 1918. The *Louisville Courier-Journal,* March 24, 1920, reported that Musgrove had been replaced by Republican Pansy Denunzio.

74. For more on the NWLB, see Valerie Jean Conner, *The National War Labor Board: Stability, Social Justice, and the Voluntary State in World War I* (Chapel Hill: University of North Carolina Press, 1983), vii, 33. The board comprised six representatives from labor, six from capital, and two from the public: former president William Howard Taft and Frank Walsh, a labor lawyer who had been chairman of the US Commission on Labor Relations. See *Louisville Courier-Journal,* March 31, 1918.

75. See *Louisville Courier-Journal,* March 8, 1918, for the strike at American Tobacco; June 20, 1918, for details of the alleged strike; June 23, 1918, for Feick addressing workers at American Tobacco and Vogt Machine Company, another case under investigation. Federal records pertaining to the case are in file 202, Employees vs. American Tobacco Co., Louisville, Ky., box 93, National War Labor Board Case Files, 1918–1919, RG 2 (National War Labor Board), NARA-CP. See preliminary and final reports of Feick, June 22, 1918, and supplementary report of July 24, 1918, ibid. Feick noted that the lockout directly affected 80 workers and indirectly affected 3,000 workers by threatening the plant with a closedown. On April 22, 1918, he cabled Secretary of Labor Wilson: "Satisfactory settlement American Tobacco Company vs Employes [*sic*] reached today." Union representatives meeting with Feick included Joe Lee, attorney and brother of KCD member Sigmond Lee.

76. McAndrews to Wilson, June 21, 1918, file 202, Employees vs. American Tobacco Co., Louisville, Ky., box 93, National War Labor Board Case Files, 1918–1919, RG 2, NARA-CP.

77. *Louisville Courier-Journal,* August 30, 1918, reported that the tobacco workers' complaint would be heard by the NWLB. See J. M. Greenwell, President, Tobacco Workers' International Union, No. 142, to W. Jett Lauck, Secretary, NWLB, August 24, 1918, announcing the local union's intention to drop the case, and E. Lewis Evans, Secretary-Treasurer, Tobacco Workers' International Union, to Secretary of Labor Wilson, August 23, 1918, file 324, box 124, National War Labor Board Case Files, 1918–1919, RG 2, NARA-CP.

78. Joseph A. McCartin, *Labor's Great War: The Struggle for Industrial Democracy and the Origins of Modern American Labor Relations, 1912–1921* (Chapel Hill: University of North Carolina Press, 1997), 83.

79. For the chauffeur incident, see *Louisville Courier-Journal,* August 9, 1918. Reinstatement noted in telegram from Patrick Gorman, Business Agent, Meat Cutters and Butchers Union, to Jett Lauck, Secretary, NWLB, August 22, 1918, file 324, box 124, National War Labor Board Case Files, 1918–1919, RG 2, NARA-CP.

80. The union's complaint, with figures showing wages paid by other Louisville plants and noting that several Armour employees worked more than twelve hours per day, is in "Examiner's Report, Docket 324, Employees (Amalgamated Meat Cutters and Butchers Workmen of North America, Local 227) vs. Armour and Company, Louisville, Kentucky," file 324, box 124, National War Labor Board Case Files, 1918–1919, RG 2, NARA-CP. The quote is from James Byerly, Secretary, Meat Cutters and Butcher Workmen of North America, Local 227, to Jett Lauck, October 3, 1918, ibid.

81. See telegrams from McWade to Hugh Kerwin, Assistant Secretary of Labor, August 15 and 22, 1918, ibid.

82. See James Blainey, Examiner, to Jett Lauck, February 24, 1919, ibid., for the examiners' report and transcript of hearing proceedings. See also *Louisville Courier-Journal,* February 20, 1919.

83. Quotes are from McWade to Secretary of Labor Wilson, September 18, 1918, file 924, box 207, National War Labor Board Case Files, 1918–1919, RG 2, NARA-CP; see also attached summary document, settlement agreement, and telegrams from McWade to Kerwin, September 14 and 17, 1918, ibid. In July 1919 Clark Electric reinstituted a nine-hour workday, prompting a strike; see *Louisville Courier-Journal,* July 15, 1919.

84. See *Louisville Courier-Journal,* January 12, 1916, for company history and Adam Vogt's retirement; January 31, 1919, for three Vogt brothers in the army; June 12, 1917, for reports of a nine-hour day. See also Fred Feick to Secretary Wilson, June 22, 1918, enclosing "Final Report in re: Employes vs. Henry Vogt Machine Co., Louisville, Ky.," and Feick to Wilson, July 6, 1918, noting possible inconvenience to the federal government, file 924, box 207, National War Labor Board Case Files, 1918–1919, RG 2, NARA-CP.

85. See J. F. Anderson, International Vice President, International Association of Machinists, to Secretary of Labor Wilson, July 2, 1918, ibid., for complaints about the Feick agreement; McWade to D. T. Gray, Superintendent, Vogt Brothers Mfg Co., September 13, 1918; Gray to McWade, September 18, 1918; telegrams from McWade to Kerwin, September 20 and 23, 1918, ibid.

86. See report of L. H. Flinn, in re: Vogt Brothers Manufacturing Co.—Industrial unrest, September 18, 1918; James Tole, Ordnance Dept., to Jett Lauck, November 8, 1918; Order for Docket No. 924, Machinists vs. Henry Vogt Machine Company, December 3, 1918, ibid.

11. Religion

1. Philip Jenkins, *The Great and Holy War: How World War I Became a Religious Crusade* (New York: HarperCollins, 2014), 4, 6.

2. Ibid., 92. Regarding Britain, Jenkins asserts: "Especially in its early days, it is painfully easy to find British writers reading the war in bloodthirsty religious terms." He cites, for example, the Anglican bishop of London, Arthur F. Winnington-Ingram, "who in 1915 wrote to a newspaper, declaring the church's explicit duty 'to mobilize the nation for a holy war.'" Regarding Germany, Jenkins notes: "Beginning with denunciations of German barbarism, preachers soon passed to condemning German culture as radically anti-Christian, and even demonic, making war a Christian obligation" (72–73). Jenkins writes that Germany "above all stands out for the power and consistency of religious-based militarism," noting that "German clerical statements were significantly more warlike in both degree and volume." For one German pastor, "war was a cure for individualism and selfishness; it presented the highest moral test; it gave abundant opportunities to practice Christian virtues; it taught holy zeal; it led

believers from death to life." Jenkins points out that this German holy war zeal applied to both Lutherans and Catholics (74–78).

3. United States Department of Commerce, Bureau of the Census, *Religious Bodies: 1916* (Washington, DC: Government Printing Office, 1919), 111. No other single denomination accounted for more than 3.1 percent of the population; these included smaller Presbyterian, Methodist, and Episcopal groups. The Census Bureau considered "Disciples of Christ" one category; presumably, this meant Disciples of Christ, Churches of Christ, and Christian Churches, all of which were used interchangeably. See also Alonzo Willard Fortune, *The Disciples in Kentucky* (n.p.: Convention of the Christian Churches in Kentucky, 1932).

4. John F. Piper, *The American Churches in World War I* (Athens: Ohio University Press, 1985), 11.

5. Ibid.; *Louisville Courier-Journal,* May 1, 1917.

6. Jenkins, *Great and Holy War,* ix. For more on the Great War's apocalyptic theme, see ibid., 163–88.

7. Porter's sermon reported in *Lexington Herald,* December 24, 1917.

8. For Sunday's comments, see *New York Times,* February 19, 1918. See also the December 21, 1917, edition, noting that during an Atlanta speech that included a "vigorous attack on the Germans and their allies," a pro-German carpenter, H. W. H. Beuterbaugh, accosted the evangelist, and a short but intense fight ensued. Although Sunday initially derided the war as the work of murdering fools, he came to believe that "the First World War stood as the hour of reckoning, the challenge to God's anointed to sacrifice, to serve, to achieve glory against evil, to vanquish the forces of Satan. This was a war for righteousness, liberty, morality, for the souls of men. It was America and Christ, indissolubly linked, forging ahead in a glorious struggle." Roger A. Bruns, *Preacher: Billy Sunday and Big-Time American Evangelism* (Champaign: University of Illinois Press, 1992), 248–49. Sunday was also a strong opponent of liquor, believing "the prevalence of people of German extraction in the brewing industry and distilling industries tied two of his causes neatly together." Sunday "exhorted Americans to use their booze money for war bonds." Lyle Dorsett, *Billy Sunday and the Redemption of Urban America* (Macon, GA: Mercer University Press, 2004), 113–14. For more on Billy Sunday and the Great War, see David T. Morgan, "The Revivalist as Patriot: Billy Sunday and World War," *Journal of Presbyterian History* 51, 2 (Summer 1973): 199–215. Kentuckian Irvin Cobb wrote a contemporary analysis of the evangelist in "Sunday, as Cobb Saw Him," *Literary Digest,* June 16, 1917, 1872.

9. Piper, *American Churches in World War I,* 12.

10. Edward Cuddy, "Pro-Germanism and American Catholicism, 1914–1917," *Catholic Historical Review* 54, 3 (October 1968): 454.

11. The growth of Kentucky Catholicism, stemming from early Catholic pioneers who settled around Bardstown, is chronicled in Clyde F. Crews, *An American Holy Land: A History of the Archdiocese of Louisville* (Louisville, KY: Ikonographics, 1987).

12. *Kentucky Post,* September 26, 1914; *Public Ledger* (Maysville, KY), September 30, 1914. Bishop Maes's death was reported in *Kentucky Post,* May 11, 1915.

13. *Louisville Courier-Journal,* April 15 and 20, May 2, 1917.

14. For Callahan's activities, see US War Department, *Commission on Training*

Camp Activities, 20; *Louisville Courier-Journal,* July 27, 1917. For more on Callahan, who was a "Kentucky Colonel," see Kleber, *Encyclopedia of Louisville,* 155–56; William E. Ellis, *Patrick Henry Callahan (1866–1940): Progressive Catholic Layman in the American South* (Lewiston, NY: E. Mellen Press, 1989); William E. Ellis, "Patrick Henry Callahan: A Maverick Catholic and the Prohibition Issue," *Register of the Kentucky Historical Society* 92, 2 (Spring 1994): 175–99. During his short career as a baseball player, Callahan had been advised by fellow ballplayer Billy Sunday to join a Cleveland varnish company, which led to his presidency of the Louisville Varnish Company. There, "Patrick Callahan and John A. Ryan of the Catholic University of America produced a profit sharing plan that was implemented in Callahan's plant. Callahan was very active in industry and labor during these years, organizing the Catholic Conference on Industrial Problems, participating in industry and labor conferences and speaking out against child labor. The success of the Ryan-Callahan Plan became widely known and Callahan soon implemented other labor-friendly measures such as a fund for employees to purchase homes, group insurance and so on." See Biographical Note on Callahan, American Catholic History Research Center and University Archives, Catholic University of America, archives.lib.cua.edu/findingaid/callahan.cfm.

15. See *Louisville Courier-Journal,* July 29, 1917, for Bishop O'Donaghue's call for funds; August 1, 1917, for the $15,000 goal; August 5, 1917, for a list of the Catholic parishes and details of the fund-raising campaign; August 13, 1917, for the expanded campaign; September 10, 1917, for the first Catholic Mass at Camp Taylor.

16. Name change reported in *Louisville Courier-Journal,* February 6, 1918; council activities reported on March 6, 1918; school support for the Red Cross reported on July 21, 1918. For more on the National Catholic War Council, see Piper, *American Churches in World War I,* 69–87.

17. See *Kentucky Post,* April 17, 1917, where Brossart asks clergy to pray for peace; and July 23, 1917, for Brossart's belief that priests were needed at home. For more on Brossart and the war, see *Kentucky Post,* December 15, 1917, February 8 and September 20, 1918. Archbishop Henry Moeller of Cincinnati had consecrated Brossart as bishop of Covington on January 25, 1916; see *Cincinnati Enquirer,* January 26, 1916. As an infant, Brossart had moved from Germany to Cincinnati and then to Campbell County. He was ordained in Covington in 1872 and served in several parishes in the diocese, including Newport, Cynthiana, Lexington, and Covington. He was serving as vicar-general, the principal diocesan administrator, before being named bishop. See the brief biography of Brossart at the Diocese of Covington website: www.covington-diocese.org/index.cfm/NewsItem?ID=86690&From=Home.

18. Rev. Paul Ryan, *History of the Diocese of Covington, Kentucky* (Diocese of Covington, Kentucky, 1954), 271–72.

19. *Louisville Courier-Journal,* June 16, 1917, February 21, 1918.

20. See *Cincinnati Enquirer,* January 18, 1918; *Kentucky Post,* January 18, 1918.

21. *Louisville Courier-Journal,* May 20, 1917.

22. Frank M. Masters, *A History of Baptists in Kentucky* (Louisville: Kentucky Baptist Historical Society, 1953), 471.

23. *Louisville Courier-Journal,* July 9 and December 31, 1917, February 11, 1918.

24. *Hopkinsville Kentuckian,* February 9, 1918.

25. *Louisville Courier-Journal,* February 9 and 10, 1918.

26. *Hopkinsville Kentuckian,* February 12, 1918.

27. Greene's comments are in *Louisville Courier-Journal,* June 4, 1917; Winburn's are in the July 2 and August 27, 1917, editions. The July article noted, "Insofar as could be ascertained, the President and Mr. Hoover's request [for food conservation] was honored by every pastor in Louisville, white and black, Catholic and Protestant, Jew and Gentile." Glasgow Baptist resolution reported in the February 12, 1918, edition.

28. McGlothlin diary, August 7, 1914, Archives and Special Collections, SBTS.

29. McGlothlin's speech was reported in *Louisville Courier-Journal,* May 22, 1917; the July 2, 1917, edition noted that he repeated the address at a patriotic meeting in Louisville.

30. Gregory A. Wills, *Southern Baptist Theological Seminary, 1859–2009* (New York: Oxford University Press, 2009), 283. See also *Louisville Courier-Journal,* August 10, 1917; *Interior Journal* (Stanford, KY), August 10, 1917, noting that McGlothlin had been asked to serve as Southern Baptist representative to the Food Administration. For more on Levering, see Emir Caner and Ergun Caner, *The Sacred Trust: Sketches of the Southern Baptist Convention Presidents* (Nashville, TN: Broadman and Holman, 2003), 37–39. Levering served as chairman of the SBTS board for forty years (1895–1935). A cousin of famed Baptist missionary Annie Armstrong, Levering also remained active in YMCA affairs.

31. McGlothlin diary, August 27 and November 16, 1917. See also *Louisville Courier-Journal,* August 21, 1917.

32. McGlothlin diary, December 20, 1917, January 4, February 2, and September 11, 1918; *Louisville Courier-Journal,* December 31, 1917, February 28 and June 7, 1918.

33. Wills, *Southern Baptist Theological Seminary,* 284–85. McGlothlin was elected president of the Southern Baptist Convention three times (1930–1932), and he served as Furman University president from 1919 to 1933, when he died in a car accident.

34. For an understanding of the development of the Christian Churches in Kentucky, see Kleber, *Kentucky Encyclopedia,* 185–86, 186–87, 189–90, for entries on "Christian Church," "Christian Church (Disciples of Christ)," and "Church of Christ." For more on the distinctions between the Disciples of Christ and the Churches of Christ, see Richard T. Hughes, *Reviving the Ancient Faith: The Story of Churches of Christ in America* (Grand Rapids, MI: Wm. B. Eerdmans, 1996).

35. Michael W. Casey, "From Pacifism to Patriotism: The Emergence of Civil Religion in the Churches of Christ during World War I," *Mennonite Quarterly Review* 66 (July 1992): 378.

36. Ibid., 382.

37. For Bradley's case, see *Louisville Courier-Journal,* August 30, 1917. See *Central Record* (Lancaster, KY), January 17, 1918, for Moorman's letter. The three other Protestant ministers in town—Baptist, Presbyterian, and Methodist Episcopal Church, South—joined Moorman in writing another letter and asserting, "It is our humble judgment, that the New Testament, which contains the recorded teachings of Jesus Christ and his Apostles, does not forbid participation in defensive warfare."

38. *Louisville Courier-Journal,* April 30, 1917.

39. Powell's pro-war efforts reported in *Louisville Courier-Journal,* January 29,

April 30, and December 17, 1917, January 7, February 5, March 12, May 20, June 21, and September 9, 1918. Some of his wartime sermons are reproduced in Edward Lindsay Powell, *The Prophet's Vision and the President's Dream* (St. Louis, MO: Christian Board of Publication, 1919).

40. See *Louisville Courier-Journal,* November 11, 18, and 19, 1917, February 9 and 20, March 31, April 20 and 24, November 11, 1918.

41. *Louisville Courier-Journal,* April 16, 1917.

42. *Louisville Courier-Journal,* May 2 and 5, July 19, 1917.

43. *Louisville Courier-Journal,* April 7 and 8, 1918.

44. *Louisville Courier-Journal,* May 12 and November 19, 1917. Thomas also sought a reunion between northern and southern Methodists, who had split over the slavery issue prior to the Civil War; see Roy Hunter Short, *Methodism in Kentucky* (Rutland, VT: Academy Books, 1979), 103.

45. For the Methodist conference, see *Public Ledger* (Maysville, KY), September 10, 1917; *Lexington Herald,* September 9, 1917. The *Herald* also reported that a speaker on the subject of education protested against "the developing of athletic aristocrats at the expense of the general physical building up of the whole student body." The speaker asserted that 83 percent of men were not "up to par physically"; therefore "new athletics should include every student in the University. Let there be interclass athletics at the expense of intercollegiate athletics." Bishop Quayle's remarks reported in *Lexington Herald,* October 22, 1917.

46. Short, *Methodism in Kentucky,* 52, 61. See also *Breckenridge News* (Cloverport, KY), September 25, 1918, for Baker's entry into the chaplaincy.

47. *Public Ledger* (Maysville, KY), July 27 and August 7, 1917, June 4 and August 1, 1918; *Hopkinsville Kentuckian,* January 3, 1918; *Hartford Republican,* June 21, 1918. For more on Methodists and their national war-support efforts, see "The Religious Rambler," *Lexington Herald,* September 30, 1917.

48. See letter from Asbury Chapel AME Church leaders to Theodore Roosevelt, May 15, 1917, www.theodorerooseveltcenter.org/en/Research/Digital-Library/Record/ImageViewer.aspx?libID=0279550. See also *Louisville Courier-Journal,* February 15 and 16, 1918, for the AME conference. Dr. Randall's resignation and service in the cantonments were noted in the November 4, 1917, edition.

49. Piper, *American Churches in World War I,* 47. See also Ellis, *A Man of Books and a Man of the People,* 73, noting that the SBTS president "cautiously cooperated with the Federal Council. He understood that most Southern Baptists opposed interdenominationalism because of the influence of 'Landmarkism.'" Landmarkism was a mid-nineteenth-century belief that Southern Baptists represented the only true church; they therefore eschewed cooperation with any other churches. See Stephen Stookey, "Baptists and Landmarkism and the Turn toward Provincialism: 1851," in *Turning Points in Baptist History: A Festschrift in Honor of Harry Leon McBeth,* ed. Michael E. Williams Sr. and Walter B. Shurden (Macon, GA: Mercer University Press, 2008), 178–93.

50. *Louisville Courier-Journal,* January 13 and 20, 1918.

51. *Louisville Courier-Journal,* January 13 and 20, April 7, May 31, 1918.

52. *Louisville Courier-Journal,* July 24, 25, and 27, 1918.

53. *Louisville Courier-Journal,* July 28 and 30, August 3, 11, and 21, 1918.

54. *Louisville Courier-Journal,* August 22, September 21, 1918. In its proceedings against the hotels, the Churchmen's Federation was represented by lawyer Helm Bruce, husband of Sallie Bruce, head of women's war efforts in the state.

55. Piper, *American Churches in World War I,* 3.

56. *Louisville Courier-Journal,* September 8, 1918.

57. *Louisville Courier-Journal,* November 8 and 10, 1918.

58. O'Donaghue's letter reproduced in *Louisville Courier-Journal,* November 3, 1918; Welch's comments reported in the November 11, 1918, edition.

59. *Lexington Herald,* October 30, 1918. Fouse went on to become the first principal of Lexington's Dunbar High School in 1923, serving until his retirement in 1938.

60. *Louisville Courier-Journal,* November 24, December 1, 1918. See also *Lexington Herald,* October 31, November 19, 1918. For examples of county fund-raising totals, see *Lexington Herald,* November 27, 1918, reporting that Bourbon, Harrison, Nicholas, and Fleming Counties had all exceeded their quotas; and November 25, 1918, reporting that Letcher County had trebled its goal.

61. Lerond Curry, *Protestant-Catholic Relations in America: World War I through Vatican II* (Lexington: University Press of Kentucky, 1972), 4–6. After the war, tension would increase again, reflected by the resurgence of an urban-based Ku Klux Klan and the unsuccessful campaign of Catholic candidate Al Smith in the 1928 presidential race. In Kentucky, however, Klan efforts failed, in part because primarily Catholic political bosses who controlled major urban areas such as Louisville managed to quash Klan attempts to appear in public. This contrasted with Indianapolis, Indiana, a hotbed of Klan activity during the 1920s. For more on the Klan in Kentucky, see Kirschenbaum, "Klan and Commonwealth."

12. Higher Education

1. William E. Ellis, *A History of Education in Kentucky* (Lexington: University Press of Kentucky, 2011), 176–77. For more on higher education in the early years of the twentieth century, see ibid., 221–68.

2. For Cherry's early years, see Lowell Harrison, *Western Kentucky University* (Lexington: University Press of Kentucky, 1987), 5–18.

3. See H. H. Cherry to Gen. E. H. Wood, Paigeville, Ky., May 28, 1917; Cherry to James Utterback, Paducah, Ky., May 29, 1917, file 114, box 2, H. H. Cherry Papers, Special Collections, WKU. See also "Report of H. H. Cherry, Chairman Publicity and Speakers' Bureau Committee, Kentucky Council of Defense," file Report to Kentucky Council of Defense, box 73, Cherry Papers, for a summary of Cherry's activities on behalf of the council; hereafter cited as Cherry Report.

4. Cherry to Embry Swearingen, July 2, 1917, file 114, box 2, Cherry Papers; see also *Louisville Courier-Journal,* August 5 and 14, September 15, 1917.

5. For Stanley's "Patriotic Week" proclamation, see *Louisville Courier-Journal,* September 22, 1917. For the Adair County Patriotic Week, see *Adair County News* (Columbia, KY), September 26, October 3, 1917; for Muhlenberg County, see *Record*

(Greenville, KY), September 20, 1917; for Hellier, see *Big Sandy News* (Louisa, KY), September 28, 1917.

6. Cherry to George Porter, October 27, 1917, file 114, box 2, Cherry Papers; see also Cherry Report. The latter document cites higher numbers, probably indicating that at the time of his report to Porter, Cherry did not have the final results of community activities. See also *Louisville Courier-Journal,* October 20, 1917, reporting that KCD executives considered the week "a huge success."

7. See Cherry to William Howard Taft, November 9, 1917, inviting the former president to speak at the Rural Life Conference; Cherry to Governor A. O. Stanley, January 31, 1918, regarding Perigord's speaking engagements in Kentucky; Cherry to Prof. A. W. Mell, Louisville, Ky., February 23, 1918, reporting that 3,000 people packed the hall on the last evening to hear a "masterful address" by Taft, file 114, box 2, Cherry Papers. For details of one of Perigord's speaking engagements on Washington's Birthday, see the University of Kentucky publications *Kentucky Alumnus* 9 (May 1918): 19, and *Kentucky Kernel* 10, 19 (February 28, 1918): 1. Cherry sought several times to have Perigord return to Kentucky, but the popular French officer had many other commitments. See, for example, Cherry to Arthur Bester, Speaking Division, Committee on Public Information, March 9, 1918, file Kentucky, box 9, entry 71, RG 63 (Committee on Public Information), NARA-CP.

8. See Cherry Report for Publicity and Speakers' Bureau Committee activities. For Cherry at the Eastern Kentucky Mountain Life Conference, see *Big Sandy News* (Louisa, KY), January 11 and 18, 1918. The *Licking Valley Courier* (West Liberty, KY), January 31, 1918, reported the creation of a permanent organization with the objective of promoting "agricultural pursuits, schools and good roads in the Big Sandy Valley." See also *Licking Valley Courier,* May 23, 1918, for Cherry's appearance under the auspices of the Morgan County Council of Defense. Articles on forthcoming war conferences appeared in *Central Record* (Lancaster, KY), August 1, 1918, for Garrard County and *Public Ledger,* August 20, 1918, for Mason County.

9. *Adair County News* (Columbia, KY), November 21, 1917.

10. For Cherry's leadership at Western Normal during the war years, see Harrison, *Western Kentucky University,* 32–38. For an example of the pressure he felt, see Cherry to Byron Shimp, CPI [Committee on Public Information], June 6, 1918, file Kentucky, box 9, entry 71, RG 63, NARA-CP, in which he claimed to be "literally submerged with work."

11. For Wilson's sentiments about education, see copy of Wilson to Secretary of the Interior Franklin Lane, July 31, 1918, folder 8, Military Department 1917–March 1919, box 13, Frank L. McVey Papers, UK Special Collections and Archives. For the SATC, see the flyer "Enlist and Go to College" prepared by KCD Education Committee chairman W. D. Cochran, folder 5, CND Misc General 1917–1919, box 49, McVey Papers. For more on the SATC, see *The Students Army Training Corps, Descriptive Circular,* 2nd ed., *Corrected to October 24, 1918* (Washington, DC: War Department, 1918).

12. Cherry to J. J. Pettyjohn, Committee on Public Information (CPI), October 10, 1918; Pettyjohn to Cherry, October 14, 1918, file Kentucky, box 9, entry 71, RG 63, NARA-CP. Pettyjohn was associate director of the CPI's Four Minute Men divi-

sion. In his reply to Cherry's resignation, he asserted that the work of Kentucky's division stood in the upper ranks with that of Connecticut and Indiana.

13. See *Louisville Courier-Journal,* April 30, 1915, for Cherry's withdrawal from the gubernatorial race, and April 8, 1919, for his withdrawal because of poor health. In 1915 Cherry had opposed the call for statewide Prohibition, preferring instead the local option approach.

14. See Mullins to Baker, April 30, 1917; Mullins to W. M. Bagby Jr., April 30, 1917, in E. Y. Mullins Letterbook, 7-17-16 to 9-14-17, Special Collections and Archives, SBTS. See also *Louisville Courier-Journal,* April 20, 1917.

15. See *Louisville Courier-Journal,* May 8, 1918, for Mullins's address to the Conversation Club, and May 20, 1918, for his appearance at the Southern Baptist Convention.

16. See *Louisville Courier-Journal,* September 10, 1917, for Mullins's "will of Christ" comment; September 7, 1917, for his appointment as YMCA camp secretary; and November 13, 1917, for the article about the YMCA at Camp Taylor. The prominence of Bible study was also noted in Ellwanger, "Camp Zachary Taylor," 16.

17. Ellis, *A Man of Books and a Man of the People,* 140–45.

18. See *Louisville Courier-Journal,* October 20, 1917, May 2, 1918.

19. *Louisville Courier-Journal,* October 24, 1918.

20. Porter was the editor of the Kentucky Southern Baptist publication *Western Recorder,* which represented a "fundamentalist, anti-Seminary faction" that objected to the moderate stance of SBTS professors such as Mullins and McLaughlin. Ellis, *A Man of Books and a Man of the People,* 100.

21. Ellis, *A Man of Books and a Man of the People,* 145.

22. See Carl B. Cone, *The University of Kentucky: A Pictorial History* (Lexington: University Press of Kentucky, 1989), 67–70.

23. See Moyen, *Frank L. McVey,* 58–90. See also "Minutes of the Fifth Meeting of the College and University Division of the Education Section of the Advisory Commission of the Council of National Defense," September 11, 1917, folder 5, CND and Misc General 1917–1919, box 49, McVey Papers; Hines to McVey, January 8, 1918, folder Military Department 1917–March 1919, box 13, McVey Papers, acknowledging Stoll's nomination, McVey's willingness to serve, and Hines's nomination of McVey to Washington authorities. McVey's appointment as USPSR director was reported in *Lexington Herald,* January 29, 1918.

24. See *Lexington Herald,* January 7, 28, 29, and 30, February 4, 1918. See also *Bourbon News* (Paris, KY), January 8, March 19, May 17, 1918; *Adair County News* (Columbia, KY), February 27, 1918.

25. McVey to Hines, July 9, 1918; Hines to McVey, July 10, 1918, folder 3, KY Council of Defense, box 59, McVey Papers.

26. See folders 1–10, box 59, McVey Papers, for McVey's correspondence with Pratt Dale, Edward Hines, county enrollment agents, district supervisors, and national labor officials. See also State Council of Defense folder, box 24, Thomas Poe Cooper Papers, UK Special Collections and Archives, for correspondence regarding the Boys Working Reserve. Because of their war work, KCD chairman Hines nominated McVey and Cooper to the well-regarded Conversation Club in Louisville. See Edward Hines to Cooper, January 10, 1919, ibid.

27. See *Lexington Herald,* October 6, 17, and 18, 1917, for Royden's appointment, arrival, and implementation of the ROTC program. Royden's career was summarized in *Lexington Herald,* November 24, 1918. See also Association of the Graduates of the United States Military Academy, *Fifty-Third Annual Report, June 12, 1922* (Saginaw, MI: Seemann and Peters, 1922), 129–30.

28. See memo from Office Department Signal Officer to Royden, November 22, 1917; Royden to McVey, November 23, 1917; McVey to Royden, November 26, 1917, regarding the establishment of a Signal Corps course, folder 8, Military Department 1917–March 1919, box 13, McVey Papers. This folder also contains an outline of the course, scheduled to last twenty weeks. See also *Lexington Herald,* December 4, 1917, January 3, 1918; *Hartford Republican,* December 21, 1917.

29. For more about Camp Buell, see the Lexington History Museum website: lexhistory.org/wikilex/camp-buell. Much of the material on the website is taken from the *Lexington Herald* and William M. Ambrose, *Bluegrass Military Camps* (Lexington, KY: Limestone Press, 2012). See letter from Committee Executive Secretary William Lough to McVey, March 30, 1918, acknowledging receipt of McVey's March 29 telegram offering to provide training; McVey to Committee, April 20, 1918, acknowledging that the president would supervise the training program and be the liaison; and telegram from Committee to McVey, April 22, 1918, announcing the first contingent of 400 men reporting on May 7, folder 7, SATC President's Desk, box 49, McVey Papers. See also *Lexington Herald,* May 7, 11, and 12, 1918, for more on the first detachment training program.

30. Material on the training program conducted from May to December 1918 is contained in the extensive University of Kentucky Training of the Fighting Mechanic Records, UK Special Collections and Archives. President McVey's correspondence concerning the training program is found in folder 6, School for Drafted Men, box 49, McVey Papers. For a good overview of the program, see *University of Kentucky, U.S. Army Training Detachment, Second Detachment of 1918* (Cincinnati, OH: Schultz Press, n.d.). This book explains the program and includes several pages of photographs taken by Professor Nollau and R. L. McClure, who are credited as "Official Camp Photographers." The book also notes that "Dr. Frank L. McVey, president of the University, and Dean F. Paul Anderson, of the College of Mechanical and Electrical Engineering, exercised a close, personal supervision over the technical training courses. To their capacity for organization and administration is due a large measure of the gratifying success attained by students in the shops" (14). See *Lexington Herald,* September 24, 1918, for the arrival of the third training detachment. Professor Nollau's extensive collection of photographs taken at the university from his student days in 1904 to his death in 1955 is in UK Special Collections and Archives.

31. See McVey to E. F. Baldwin, The Outlook Company, New York, NY, June 29, 1918; "Memorandum on Military Work in the University of Kentucky," folder 8, Military Department 1917–March 1919, box 13, McVey Papers.

32. See telegram from Adjutant General McCain to McVey, August 14, 1918, file 13, Telegrams, Military, SATC, 1918–1919, box 13, McVey Papers. See also *Lexington Herald,* August 27, September 3 and 11, October 17, 1918, for more on the SATC at the university.

33. *Lexington Herald,* September 22, 24, and 27, 1918.

34. Photographs of Representative Cantrill inaugurating the SATC detachment can be found online at kdl.kyvl.org/catalog/xt7wm32n6p7v_3_23? Other photos depict a parade and the reading of orders establishing the unit. See also *University of Kentucky Press Bulletin* 1, 19 (October 15, 1918); *Lexington Herald,* October 1, 2, 4, and 5, 1918.

35. *Lexington Herald,* October 13, 14, 15, 17, 22, 23, and 24, 1918.

36. *Lexington Herald,* November 3, 5, 12, 13, and 28, December 6, 19, and 20, 1918.

37. Training activities are described in the section titled "Training of Students at the University" in the document "A Brief Statement of the War Work at the University of Kentucky during the Year 1918," folder 25, War Activities 1918, box 49, McVey Papers.

38. Committee members were listed in McVey letter, March 2, 1918, folder 22, War Committee, Personnel, Minutes, etc., box 49, McVey Papers. See also *Lexington Herald,* April 27 and 28, May 3, 1918.

39. See "A Brief Statement of the War Work at the University of Kentucky during the Year 1918."

40. See Minutes of the Executive Board, University of Kentucky, April 9, 1917, exploreuk.uky.edu/catalog/xt7qbz61634d_1. The board also approved a resolution that the Registrar's Office would cooperate fully with the federal government to assist in recruiting. For numbers of UK military, see *Bulletin of the University of Kentucky* 11, 7 (July 1919): 36–37.

41. Moyen, *Frank L. McVey,* 93.

42. For an explanation of the SATC program, see United States War Department, Advisory Board, *Committee on Education and Special Training: A Review of Its Work during 1918* (Washington, DC: War Department, 1919); see ibid., 88, for a list of Kentucky institutions with SATC units. For the University of Louisville during the Great War, see Dwayne Cox and William Morison, *The University of Louisville* (Lexington: University Press of Kentucky, 2000), 63–64; *Louisville Courier-Journal,* May 1, July 24, 1917, February 7, September 1, October 16, 1918.

43. See *Louisville Courier-Journal,* December 1, 1917, March 8 and 20, 1918, for the Permanent Blind Relief War Fund; July 4, 1917, for the University of Louisville doing its part during the war. For von Walther's plight, see Cox and Morison, *University of Louisville,* 63.

44. See William E. Ellis, A *History of Eastern Kentucky University: The School of Opportunity* (Lexington: University Press of Kentucky, 2005), 39–41.

45. See "Students' Army Training Corps Centre College," in Caldwell, *Kentucky in the World War,* vol. 3.

46. The *Georgetonian* editorial was reprinted in *Lexington Herald,* May 10, 1917.

47. *Lexington Herald,* May 10, 1917.

48. Adams's response to the *Herald* criticism was in *Georgetown Times,* May 16, 1917.

49. For Hinton and Fogle leaving Georgetown for the YMCA, see *Bourbon News* (Paris, KY), May 7, 1918. Professor Leigh's argument against German scientific inven-

tiveness was reproduced in *Louisville Courier-Journal,* October 21, 1917. In 1920 Leigh moved to the University of Florida, where he was Chemistry Department chair, founding dean of the College of Pharmacy, and university vice president.

50. Robert Snyder, *A History of Georgetown College* (n.p., n.d.), 90–92. Curry Breckinridge's appearance at the Georgetown College Chapel was reported in *Georgetown Times,* October 10, 1917. Ranchier's attendance at Georgetown College and his appearances were reported in *Lexington Herald,* November 7 and 15, December 4, 1918, June 2, 1919; see also *Louisville Courier-Journal,* December 5, 1918, February 17, 1919.

51. John D. Wright Jr., *Transylvania: Tutor to the West* (Lexington, KY: Transylvania University, 1975), 333; *Lexington Herald,* May 10, 1917.

52. See *Louisville Courier-Journal,* August 6, 1917, for Crossfield's speech.

53. Wright, *Transylvania,* 332–35. See also *Lexington Herald,* August 19, September 11, 1917; *Louisville Courier-Journal,* December 21, 1918.

54. Wright, *Transylvania,* 336.

13. "Over There"

1. For more on Sandlin, see Fred Caldwell, "Above and Beyond the Call of Duty," *Register of the Kentucky Historical Society* 18, 53 (May 1920): 9–11. See also Craig, *Hidden History of Kentucky Soldiers,* 69–71. A long description of Sandlin's Medal of Honor battle can be found in *Mt. Sterling Advocate,* October 7, 1919. See also *Hopkinsville Kentuckian,* April 19, 1919; *Richmond Daily Register,* October 3, 1919; and *Pittsburgh Post-Gazette,* December 24, 1941. Sandlin's military unit is covered in *33rd Division A.E.F. from Its Arrival in France until the Armistice with Germany, November 11, 1918* (Diekirch, Luxembourg: n.p., 1919).

2. For Sandlin's work on Stewart's illiteracy campaign, see Baldwin, *Cora Wilson Stewart,* 113–14; *Lexington Herald,* September 7, October 4, 1919. See also Caldwell, *Kentucky in the World War,* vol. 10, for mostly undated, unidentified newspaper clippings about Sandlin's war exploits and his work on the illiteracy campaign. The clippings note that Sandlin joined the army in 1913 and served along the Texas border. According to a *Louisville Courier-Journal* (July 21, 1919) clipping, he was wounded by shrapnel on July 4, 1918, in the Amiens sector and was gassed on October 9, 1918. For his experience with soldier repatriation, see *Lexington Herald,* December 18, 1919, May 29, 1920; *Courier-Journal,* January 9, May 29, 1920. For his health problems, see *Richmond Daily Register,* October 19, 1921.

3. Caldwell, "Above and Beyond the Call of Duty," 11–12. See also Caldwell, *Kentucky in the World War,* vol. 10, for numerous clippings about Woodfill; Mrs. Thomas P. Carothers, *History of Campbell County, Ky., in the World War, 1917–1919* (Frankfort: Kentucky Council of Defense, n.d.), vol. 1.

4. Unlike York and Whittlesey, Woodfill remains relatively unknown, and no book has been published about his exploits. For more on York, see David Lee, *Sergeant York: An American Hero* (Lexington: University Press of Kentucky, 1985); Douglas V. Mastriano, *Alvin York: A New Biography of the Hero of the Argonne* (Lexington: University Press of Kentucky, 2014). For more on Whittlesey and the "Lost Battalion,"

see Robert Ferrell, *Five Days in October: The Lost Battalion of World War I* (Columbia: University of Missouri Press, 2005).

5. Lists of major generals, admirals, and other officers are in Caldwell, *Kentucky in the World War,* vol. 10.

6. For more on Allen, see Anne Cipriano Venzon, ed., *The United States in the First World War: An Encyclopedia* (New York: Routledge, 2012), 21, and the Arlington National Cemetery website: www.arlingtoncemetery.net/htallen.htm. For more on Winn, see projects.militarytimes.com/citations-medals-awards/recipient.php?recipientid=18377. For more on Duncan, see *Louisville Courier-Journal,* July 21, 1918. Duncan's two-volume manuscript, *Reminiscences, 1861–1950,* is held at the UK Special Collections and Archives.

7. For more on Scott, Sibert, and Bell, see these Arlington National Cemetery websites: www.arlingtoncemetery.net/hlscotthtm, www.arlingtoncemetery.net/wlsibert.htm, www.arlingtoncemetery.net/jfbell.htm. See also entries on Bell, Scott, and Sibert in Venzon, *United States in the First World War,* 73, 551, 532–34. Sibert's duties quoted from Albert J. Mauroni, *Chemical and Biological Warfare: A Reference Handbook,* 2nd ed. (Santa Barbara, CA: ABC-CLIO, 2007), 141.

8. For more on Brown, see Venzon, *United States in the First World War,* 107. After being court-martialed in the Philippines, Brown went on to have a distinguished army career. See Meredith Mason Brown, "A Killing in the Philippines, 1900: A Kentuckian Faces Insurgency and Military Justice," *Register of the Kentucky Historical Society* 104, 1 (Winter 2006): 43–76. The author sums up: "Brown was charged with murder, convicted by court-martial of manslaughter, and sentenced to dismissal from the army and five years' hard labor. President Theodore Roosevelt commuted the sentence to a loss of a few months' pay and a brief delay in promotion. Brown subsequently rose through the ranks, served with distinction in World War I, and retired in 1934 as a major general" (43). For more on Fleming, see projects.militarytimes.com/citations-medals-awards/recipient.php?recipientid=17537. For Winn, see Joseph W. A. Whitehorne, *The Inspectors General of the United States Army, 1903–1939* (Rockville, MD: Wildside Press, 2012), 179–81.

9. For more on Rodman, see his autobiography, *Yarns of a Kentucky Admiral* (Indianapolis: Bobbs-Merrill, 1928). For Brittain, see *Louisville Courier-Journal,* August 22, 1918, April 24, 1920.

10. For more on Radford, see www.arlingtoncemetery.net/csradfordsr.htm.

11. For more on Feland, see David J. Bettez, *Kentucky Marine: Major General Logan Feland and the Development of the Modern USMC* (Lexington: University Press of Kentucky, 2014); see 83–119 for Feland's service during the war. See *Louisville Courier-Journal,* November 12, 1922, for a photograph of Feland on the parade reviewing stand with Governor Edwin Morrow and Louisville mayor Huston Quin.

12. For more on Fleitz, see *Louisville Courier-Journal,* October 29, 1918. For Keller, see Chalkley, *History of Fayette County,* vol. 2. For Courtney and Clarkston, see Caldwell, *Kentucky in the World War,* vol. 10.

13. For the three Kentuckians, see Caldwell, *Kentucky in the World War,* vol. 10. The *Louisville Courier-Journal,* March 12, 1919, reproduced the four identical citations.

14. See Caldwell, *Kentucky in the World War,* vol. 10, for material on McCoy.

McCoy's story in his own words initially appeared in the *Prestonsburg Citizen* and was reproduced in the *Big Sandy News* (Louisa, KY), July 11, 1919. In its initial report of McCoy's award, the *Big Sandy News,* April 18, 1919, summed up his exploits: "That was the way Private Pete McCoy took the spirit of the boys of the Blue Ridge county into the great allied drive against the Hindenburg line."

15. For McCoy's awards, see *Louisville Courier-Journal,* August 23, September 14, 1919; *Hopkinsville Kentuckian,* September 17, 1919. See Caldwell, *Kentucky in the World War,* vol. 10, for an undated, unattributed clipping reproducing the *Washington Post* editorial. This volume also has two photographs of McCoy: the first appears to depict him as a new soldier at training camp, standing at attention and holding his rifle across his body; in the second, he is a veteran fighter wearing his Distinguished Service Cross.

16. See Caldwell, *Kentucky in the World War,* vol. 10, for Melcher's and Mitchell's citations and newspaper clippings.

17. Reproductions of the Combs, Koon, and Meek citations are in ibid.

18. See ibid. for material on Sapp, Simpson, and Taylor.

19. Quote from the Hutchcraft letter reproduced in *Louisville Courier-Journal,* February 24, 1918. Background material is from Philip Ardery, "Reuben Brent Hutchcraft, Jr.: Kentucky Hero," *Filson Club History Quarterly* 60, 4 (October 1896): 455–61. For another Hutchcraft letter, see *Lexington Herald,* March 17, 1918; this letter was reprinted in the UK student newspaper the *Kernel,* March 21, 1918.

20. News of Captain Hutchcraft's company, derived from a letter home, was reported in *Louisville Courier-Journal,* November 1, 1918. For his demise, see Ardery, "Reuben Brent Hutchraft, Jr.," 453–55. See another description in *Kentucky Alumnus* 3, 10 (1919): 9–12.

21. Ardery, "Reuben Brent Hutchcraft, Jr.," 461–62. See *Bourbon News* (Paris, KY), February 4, 1919, for the hometown memorial; March 29, 1921, for his final interment in the Paris cemetery. See *Louisville Courier-Journal,* January 15, 1920, for his memorial at the legislature; March 28, 1921, for his final burial.

22. See Caldwell, *Kentucky in the World War,* vol. 10, for more on Sullivan/Shannon.

23. *Louisville Courier-Journal,* January 20, 1920, listed the seventy-seven DSC recipients to date.

24. A list of Creech's air victories and his DSC and Distinguished Flying Cross citations can be found at theaerodrome.com/aces/usa/creech.php. For more on Creech, see Caldwell, *Kentucky in the World War,* vol. 10; Jason LeMay, John M. Trowbridge, and M. Harold Canon, *Kentucky's Flying Soldiers: A History of the Kentucky Army National Guard's Fixed Wing Aviation* (Frankfort, KY: Office of the Adjutant General, 2006), 22–23. Creech received his DSC in 1922 at a Veterans of Foreign War ceremony in Lexington; it was presented by Colonel Charles Morrow, twin brother of Governor Edwin Morrow, who attended the presentation. See *Louisville Courier-Journal,* December 30, 1922, for a report of the presentation ceremony.

25. Caldwell, *Kentucky in the World War,* vol. 10. A list of Strahm's air victories and his DSC citation can be found at www.theaerodrome.com/aces/usa/creech.php. His citation for the Croix de Guerre and a *Louisville Post* clipping appear in Caldwell,

Kentucky in the World War, vol. 11. For more on Strahm's Great War career, see the three-page typescript contained in Mrs. Max B. Nahm, *History of Warren County, Ky. in the World War, 1917–1919* (Frankfort: Kentucky Council of Defense, n.d.). See also letters to his parents reproduced in *Nashville Tennessean,* July 28 and 31, 1918, describing some of his missions. Strahm was born in Nashville, where his parents ran a music studio before his father moved to Western Normal to teach.

26. See Caldwell, *Kentucky in the World War,* vol. 11, for more on Hambrick and Feland.

27. See *Louisville Post,* March 24, 1919, in ibid.

28. See *Louisville Courier-Journal,* February 20, 1921; "The French Record in Cilicia," *New Armenia* 13, 2 (March–April 1921): 22–24. Shishmanian helped train an Armenian legion to fight the Turks and became involved in the Armenian struggle after the war.

29. See Caldwell, *Kentucky in the World War,* vol. 11, for a clipping on Nurse; see also *Hopkinsville Kentuckian,* June 18, 1919. Adams and Burnham were listed in a *Louisville Courier-Journal* article, June 16, 1919, on various Kentucky award recipients.

30. Arvin's letter to her sister was reproduced in *Hopkinsville Kentuckian,* October 18, 1917. See Caldwell, *Kentucky in the World War,* vol. 11, for a copy of Arvin's citation from Pershing. See *Louisville Courier-Journal,* November 14, 1919, for the presentation of the Royal Red Cross. For more information about Arvin, see the Mary Willie Arvin file at the Henderson County Public Library.

31. See Caldwell, *Kentucky in the World War,* vol. 12, including an article clipped from *Louisville Times,* March 17, 1920.

32. For more on Bogaert, see Caldwell, *Kentucky in the World War,* vol. 12. See *Mt. Sterling Advocate,* March 20, 1917; *Climax-Madisonian* (Richmond, KY), April 4, 1917; and *Louisville Courier-Journal,* September 15, 1918, for examples of Bogaert's fund-raising for Belgian relief.

33. Material on Bell, Keating, Carson, and Rogers is from Caldwell, *Kentucky in the World War,* vol. 12. Carson was also mentioned in *Climax-Madisonian,* March 21, 1917; *Richmond Daily Register,* July 26, 1919.

34. Morrow's citations are noted in Judge James M. Denton, *History of Pulaski County, Ky., in the World War, 1917–1919* (Frankfort: Kentucky Council of Defense, n.d.), vol. 1. See also Caldwell, *Kentucky in the World War,* vols. 11, 12, for material on Morrow. His exploits in the Siberian expedition are covered in Carl J. Richard, *When the United States Invaded Russia: Woodrow Wilson's Siberian Disaster* (New York: Rowman and Littlefield, 2013); Jamie Bisher, *White Terror: Cossack Warlords of the Trans-Siberian* (New York: Routledge, 2005).

35. For Chinn and Cornwell, see Caldwell, *Kentucky in the World War,* vol. 12; *Louisville Courier-Journal,* August 26, 1917. See also Ellwanger, "Camp Zachary Taylor," 23, for Chinn at Camp Taylor. See *Courier-Journal,* August 3, 1917, May 23, 1919, for Cornwell as part of Unit D; November 18, 1919, for his receipt of the Serbian decoration.

36. There are several articles on Hume in Caldwell, *Kentucky in the World War,* vol. 12. Hume served in the army through World War II, retiring as a major general. His lengthy career is summed up at www.arlingtoncemetery.net/eehume.htm.

37. *Big Sandy News* (Louisa, KY), August 16, 1918.

38. McDermott letter, binder 2: Veterans from WW I—C–M, Adair County Library, Columbia, KY.

39. Bowen letter quoted in Cora Guffey, *History of Butler County, Ky., in the World War, 1917–1919* (Frankfort: Kentucky Council of Defense, n.d.).

40. Clipping of Polin letter in George Colvin and Emma Noonan, *History of Washington County, Ky., in the World War, 1917–1919* (Frankfort: Kentucky Council of Defense, n.d.). Colvin and Noonan made a special effort to include several newspaper clippings of letters from Washington County soldiers to the folks back home. Colvin served on the county council of defense and in 1919 became state superintendent of instruction and eventually president of the University of Louisville.

41. *Lexington Herald,* October 27, 1918. For more on Kahn, see *Lexington Herald,* March 24, 1918. As a young boy, Kahn met Christian County native and psychic Edgar Cayce, and they formed a friendship that Kahn wrote about (with Will Oursler) in *My Life with Edgar Cayce* (Garden City, NY: Doubleday, 1970).

42. Clipping of Sheehan letter in Colvin and Noonan, *History of Washington County.*

43. Clippings of Roberts letters in ibid.

44. Clipping of Nally letter in ibid.

45. George Johnston to Cousin Amy, January 6, 1919, in Letters of George Andrew Johnston, Logan County Archives, Russellville, KY.

46. Watson letter, binder 2: Veterans from WW I—C–M, Adair County Library, Columbia, KY. American doughboys abroad often referred to the Germans as "Dutch," a corruption of the German word *Deutsch* (which means "German").

47. Royce letter and article noting his death in ibid.

48. Ragland letter in Guffey, *History of Butler County.*

49. Beliles letter to his mother in ibid.

50. Clipping of Smith letter dated January 7, 1919, in Colvin and Noonan, *History of Washington County.* For more on the *Otranto* tragedy, see R. Neill Scott, *Many Were Held by the Sea: The Tragic Sinking of HMS* Otranto (New York: Rowman and Littlefield, 2012), appendix 1 for a list of American casualties, appendix 2 for a list of American survivors.

51. Clipping of letter from Parks to his sister in Guffey, *History of Butler County.*

52. Material on Alpha Barnes Nash is based on Jerry Cecil, "Alpha Barnes Nash and the Barrow Unit of World War I: Serving as a Nurse in Good Samaritan Base Hospital Unit 40, 1918–1919" (graduate seminar paper, University of Kentucky History Department, 1998, copy deposited in US Army Military History Institute, Carlisle, PA), 9.

53. Ibid., 18. Cecil also points out that by serving in the vastly expanded nursing corps in the war, Nash was a pioneer in an effort that "confirmed the need to continue the Army Nurse Corps as a regular element of the War Department, assured the continuance of the Army School of Nursing, and validated the imperative to fully integrate nurses into the Army."

54. For some of the *Evening Post* clippings acknowledging war families and the list of the Hertzman sons and their military postings, see Caldwell, *Kentucky in the*

World War, vol. 9. For the sons of the Wittwers, see Mary C. Gainsborough, *History of Oldham County, Ky., in the World War, 1917–1919* (Frankfort: Kentucky Council of Defense, n.d.). For more on the Minnich family, see John Trowbridge, "A Patriotic Clan from Eastern Kentucky in the War to End All Wars," *Kentucky Ancestors* 43, 3 (Spring 2008): 114–23.

55. A list of Kentuckians who worked for the Red Cross overseas, a clipping on Belknap, and a clipping on the Sweeny sisters can be found in Caldwell, *Kentucky in the World War,* vol. 2. A list of Kentucky YMCA workers, including names and hometowns of those working abroad, is in Fred Caldwell, *Kentucky in the World War, 1917–1919: Civilian Records,* 144 vols. (Frankfort: Kentucky Council of Defense, n.d.), vol. 1. The Sweeny sisters are mentioned in James Cooke, *The All-Americans at War: The 82nd Division in the Great War, 1917–1918* (New York: Praeger, 1999), 92. The Eighty-Second Division was commanded by Major General George B. Duncan, a Lexingtonian and the son of a former mayor. A profile of Sunshine Sweeny, who "lived up to her name" at the front, can be found in *Louisville Courier-Journal,* December 8, 1918.

56. See *Louisville Courier-Journal,* May 30, 1917, reporting Pedigo as captured, and *Hopkinsville Kentuckian,* June 11, 1919, for his incarceration in Lubeck. The *Hopkinsville Kentuckian,* June 5, 1917, reported that both Perkins and Pedigo had been captured. The *Nashville Tennessean* and *Nashville American,* March 24, 1918, reported that Perkins had been on the *Esmeraldas.* A list of twenty-eight Kentuckians held by Germans at the end of the war was printed in *Louisville Courier-Journal,* November 16, 1918; a more comprehensive list appeared in the June 9, 1919, edition.

57. For more on Porter, see *Louisville Courier-Journal,* July 1, August 31, 1916; his divorce was reported on October 9, 1917. His war service, capture, and treatment as a prisoner were reported in *Hopkinsville Kentuckian,* June 11, 1919.

58. For Whitehead, see *Louisville Courier-Journal,* July 13, 1918. For Boyd's return to the United States, see *Hopkinsville Kentuckian,* May 10, 1919. The stories of both men were reported in *Hopkinsville Kentuckian,* June 11, 1919.

59. See *Louisville Courier-Journal,* April 21, 1919, for Triplett's release. His incarceration and release were also covered in *Hopkinsville Kentuckian,* June 11, 1919.

14. End of the War and Aftermath

1. Nancy D. Baird, "The 'Spanish Lady' in Kentucky, 1918–1919," *Filson Club History Quarterly* 50, 3 (July 1976): 290.

2. Ibid., 292. See *Louisville Courier-Journal,* October 17, 1918, for Governor Stanley's visit.

3. Gregory K. Culver, "The Impact of the 1918 Spanish Influenza Epidemic on the Jackson Purchase," *Filson Club History Quarterly* 65, 4 (October 1991): 487–504.

4. Baird, "'Spanish Lady' in Kentucky," 292–99.

5. Sister Mary Jean's death and burial services were reported in *Louisville Courier-Journal,* October 31, 1918.

6. A section of a journal kept by a Sister of Mercy at Camp Taylor is reproduced in "The Sisters of Mercy, East Broadway, Louisville, KY—Influenza, October 1918," in Caldwell, *Kentucky in the World War,* vol. 3.

7. See "Assistance Rendered the Stricken Miners of Kentucky, November 1918, by the Sisters of Mercy of Cincinnati, Ohio," in Caldwell, *Kentucky in the World War,* vol. 3. See also *Louisville Courier-Journal,* November 5, 1918, reporting the nuns' arrival in Lexington and their subsequent dispersal across eastern Kentucky.

8. Baird, "'Spanish Lady' in Kentucky," 300–301.

9. For the German armistice overture, see *Public Ledger* (Maysville, KY), October 9, 1918; *Citizen* (Berea, KY), October 10, 1918. For the false armistice report, see *Big Sandy News* (Louisa, KY), November 8, 1918; for Wickliffe, see *Louisville Courier-Journal,* November 8, 1918. The genesis and aftermath of the erroneous United Press report are covered in Dale Zacher, *The Scripps Newspapers Go to War, 1914–1918* (Urbana: University of Illinois Press, 2008), 204–15.

10. *Louisville Courier-Journal,* November 12, 1918, reported on celebrations across the commonwealth in Lexington, Henderson, Elkton, Paducah, Hopkinsville, Glasgow, Owensboro, Covington, Shelbyville, Lebanon, Guthrie, Richmond, Franklin, and Frankfort.

11. For figures on demobilization, see Jennifer Keene, "A 'Brutalizing' War: The USA after the First World War," *Journal of Contemporary History* 50, 1 (Spring 2015): 78, n. 3. Keene notes: "Over-crowded debarkation camps, the ongoing influenza epidemic, and horrendous winter weather turned the demobilization experience into a nightmare for many overseas troops. Protesting these conditions, troops in France organized demonstrations, sent petitions to officials and newspapers, and enrolled their families in the campaign to return them home quickly and safely." For Camp Taylor, see *Louisville Courier-Journal,* November 22, December 14, 1918; see also the editorial on November 28, 1918.

12. Demobilization of units with strong Kentucky ties reported in *Louisville Courier-Journal,* January 10, 25, and 31, 1919.

13. Barrow Unit demobilization reported in *Louisville Courier-Journal,* April 17, 1919. General March's estimate reported in *Hopkinsville Kentuckian,* April 9, 1919. See also *Louisville Courier-Journal,* February 17, 1919.

14. *Louisville Courier-Journal,* November 22, 1918.

15. Telegram from Governor A. O. Stanley to Gen. E. H. Crowder, November 22, 1918; Crowder to Stanley, November 25, 1918, folder KY 53 (1), box 144, entry 2 States Files, RG 163, NARA-CP.

16. KCD efforts reported in *Louisville Courier-Journal,* December 23, 1918, April 6, 1919.

17. The Interior Department plan is covered in Bill G. Reid, "Franklin K. Lane's Idea for Veterans' Colonization, 1918–1921," *Pacific Historical Review* 33, 4 (November 1964): 447–61; quote on 451. The *Louisville Courier-Journal,* December 8, 1918, carried a three-quarter-page article explaining the soldier land settlement program; see other articles on Lane's plan in the January 5 and 25, 1919, editions.

18. For the Louisville Board of Trade committee, see *Louisville Courier-Journal,* October 26, 1918; clipping from *Lexington Leader,* October 27, 1918, folder 20, Soldiers Land 1918, box 49, McVey Papers, UK Special Collections and Archives. Also in folder 20 is a copy of the committee's eight-page report, addressed to Griffith and dated October 24, 1918, sent by Fred Mutchler to McVey with an accompanying letter on November 4, 1918.

19. McVey to Cooper, October 21, 1918; Cooper to McVey, October 22, 1918; McVey to Mead, November 1, 1918, folder 20, Soldiers Land 1918, box 49, McVey Papers.

20. *Louisville Courier-Journal,* February 16, 1919.

21. Governor's appointment of Soldiers' Land Settlement Committee, with names, noted in *Public Ledger* (Maysville, KY), May 13, 1919; *Louisville Courier-Journal,* April 6, 1919. The *Courier-Journal* reported federal optimism on May 12, 1919; McVey's survey committee on May 13, 1919; Kentucky requests for land settlement information on May 19, 1919.

22. Mondell's bill reported in *Public Ledger* (Maysville, KY), June 11, 1919. See *Louisville Courier-Journal,* June 8, 1919, for Boies's objections; August 30, 1919, for the editorial opposing the project.

23. See Humphrey to Cooper, June 5, 1919; Cooper to McVey, June 10, 1919, folder 20, Soldiers Land 1918, box 49, McVey Papers.

24. Reid, "Lane's Idea for Veterans' Colonization," 460. American Legion support reported in *Louisville Courier-Journal,* November 14, 1919. For more on opposition to the program, see Bill G. Reid, "Agrarian Opposition to Franklin K. Lane's Proposal for Soldier Settlement, 1918–1921," *Agricultural History* 41, 2 (April 1967): 167–80.

25. For the conference program, see Kentucky Council of Defense, *State Conference on Kentucky Problems Held at the University of Kentucky, March 4–5, 1919: Program and Addresses* (Frankfort, KY: State Journal Co., 1919); a list of conference attendees is at the back of this pamphlet.

26. Ibid., 8–9.

27. Ibid., 9–15.

28. Ibid., 16–20. The *Louisville Courier-Journal,* March 4, 1919, referred to the meeting as a "reconstruction" conference.

29. See KCD, *State Conference on Kentucky Problems,* 20–115, for the session addresses. It quotes Sallie Bruce as saying: "Wholesome recreation is absolutely necessary. Why should we leave so much of it in the hands of the devil?" (94). See also *Louisville Courier-Journal,* March 4, 5, and 6, 1919; Bruce's comments were reported in the March 6 edition, which used the quote cited in text as a subheadline.

30. See *Louisville Courier-Journal,* March 5, 1919, for the awarding of medals. Cochran's sudden death was reported in *Public Ledger* (Maysville, KY), February 8, 1919. Cochran had just traveled to Louisville with fellow KCD member Richard Stoll of Lexington to attend a KCD meeting. The newspaper eulogized: "He died a hero as much so as any of our fine young men who fell on the European battlefields pierced by the bullets of the Huns. His name will always be written in the Honor Roll of the dead in this great war Democracy has just won over Autocracy by the people of Maysville, for there is no doubt but that the great amount of the work thrust upon him by the war and which he bore without complaint, caused his untimely death."

31. Beckley's career is summarized in *American Bar Association Journal* 36 (January 1950): 64.

32. See KCD, *Report of Activities to January 1, 1920;* Kentucky Council of Defense, *Report of the War Historical Work of the Kentucky Council of Defense from March 23, 1920 to December 31, 1921* (Frankfort, KY: State Journal Co., [1922]); KCD, *Final*

Report of the War Historical Work. Instructions to the county historians are contained in the KCD pamphlet *Statewide Movement to Make a Record of Kentucky's Part in the World War Including Military Service Records of Fighting Forces, War Work Done by Civilians, Collection and Preservation of Other Historical Matter* (Louisville: Kentucky Council of Defense, 1919); a list of county historians is included. See also "How Kentucky's War History was Written" and "Historical Drive," in Caldwell, *Kentucky in the World War,* vol. 9. This volume contains several memoranda Caldwell sent to county councils of defense about the war history effort, as well as several newspaper clippings about the project.

33. Elizabeth Cafer du Plessis, "Alice French, Indiana War Mothers, from World War I 'Kitchen Soldiers' to Postwar Immigrant Reformers," in *Feminist Frontiers: Women Who Shaped the Midwest,* ed. Yvonne Johnson (Kirksville, MO: Truman State University Press, 2010), 103.

34. *Louisville Courier-Journal,* November 30, 1917.

35. Alice French to Stanley, July 22, 1918; Stanley to French, August 7, 1918, American War Mothers Records, bound scrapbook, Filson Historical Society. In addition to the bound scrapbook, there is a file containing an unbound scrapbook. Together, they present profiles of the war mothers who followed Dorcas Hutchcraft, as well as newspaper clippings and reports from annual meetings.

36. See Dorcas Hutchcraft, "Salutation to the State War Mothers," first annual meeting of the Kentucky chapter, American War Mothers, Lexington, October 28, 1919, American War Mothers Records, bound scrapbook, Filson Historical Society. Organization of the Louisville AWM chapter was reported in *Louisville Courier-Journal,* August 9, September 7, 1918.

37. See American War Mothers, Fayette County, Kentucky Chapter, *Year Book* (Lexington, KY, [1920]). See also *Mt. Sterling Advocate,* January 28, February 11, 1919; *Richmond Daily Register,* February 7, September 17, 1919; *Bourbon News* (Paris, KY), September 19, 1919. The last also gave the names of the Kentucky chapter's executive board led by Mrs. Hutchcraft; although it was composed mainly of women from central Kentucky, there were representatives from Louisville, Bowling Green, and Covington.

38. Goals set forth in *Bourbon News* (Paris, KY), October 31, 1919. See *Mt. Sterling Advocate,* February 1, 1921, for the Montgomery County chapter's pledge to help the American Legion men furnish their meeting hall.

39. Lisa Budreau, *Bodies of War: World War I and the Politics of Commemoration in America, 1919–1933* (New York: New York University Press, 2010), 196. See also *Richmond Daily Register,* October 2, 1920; *Central Record* (Lancaster, KY), October 7, 1920, for news of the annual AWM meeting. See *Hartford Republican,* October 22, 1920, for a four-part article by American ace Captain Eddie Rickenbacker on "Why Soldiers Are against the League of Nations."

40. *Richmond Register,* September 29, 1921. In addition, the AWM's Kentucky chapter cooperated with the American Legion when it held its third annual meeting in 1921; see letter of thanks from American Legion of Kentucky Adjutant S. S. Jones to Mrs. William Oldham, President State War Mothers, September 26, 1921, American War Mothers Records, bound scrapbook, Filson Historical Society.

41. *Louisville Courier-Journal,* March 26, April 9 and 11, 1919.

42. *Louisville Courier-Journal,* May 2, 11, 12, and 19, August 23, 1919. Moorman served one term as a congressman from 1927 to 1929. An American Legion post in Cloverport in Breckinridge County is named Henry Dehaven Moorman, KY Post 1.

43. *Louisville Courier-Journal,* October 5 and 7, 1919.

44. For more on the American Legion, see William Pencak, *For God and Country: The American Legion, 1919–1941* (Boston: Northeastern University Press, 1989); Thomas Rumer, *The American Legion: An Official History, 1919–1989* (New York: M. Evans, 1990).

45. Steven Trout, *On the Battlefield of Memory: The First World War and American Remembrance, 1919–1941* (Tuscaloosa: University of Alabama Press, 2010), 47–49.

46. See chapter 4, "What Shall Be the Moral to Young Kentuckians: Civil War Memorial Activity in the Commonwealth, 1865–1895," in Marshall, *Creating a Confederate Kentucky,* 81–110.

47. See *Louisville Courier-Journal,* March 24, 1919, for Houston's letter to Stanley; April 7, 1919, for the planting of trees on the UK campus. Roosevelt had died on January 6, 1919.

48. For details of the Memorial Hall project, see "Kentucky State Memorial for the Boys Who Lost Their Lives in the Great War," *Bulletin of the University of Kentucky* 11, 7 (July 1919).

49. For more on the fund-raising, construction, and dedication of Memorial Hall, see Moyen, *Frank L. McVey,* 101, 136–67. See also Cone, *University of Kentucky,* 83. Memorial Hall's clock tower is the central motif in the UK logo.

50. *Louisville Courier-Journal,* February 23, 1919, March 22, May 5 and 11, October 18 and 21, November 2 and 3, 1920.

51. *Louisville Courier-Journal,* November 6, 1920, March 10, 1921, March 4, April 25, June 16, October 8, November 15 and 21, 1922. See also the entry for the Louisville Memorial Auditorium in Kleber, *Encyclopedia of Louisville,* 561.

52. For a discussion of Viquesney and his contributions to remembrance, see chapter 2, "Soldiers Well-Known and Unknown: Monuments to the American Doughboy, 1920–1941," in Trout, *On the Battlefield of Memory,* 107–56. See also the website produced by Les Kopel and Earl Goldsmith, "The E. M. Viquesney Doughboy Database," at doughboysearcher.weebly.com. For Viquesney in the context of other postwar memorial sculptors, see Jennifer Wingate, *Sculpting Doughboys: Memory, Gender, and Taste in America's World War I Memorials* (Burlington, VT: Ashgate, 2013).

53. See copies of newspaper articles in Colvin and Noonan, *History of Washington County,* including a clipping from *Louisville Courier-Journal,* November 12, 1922.

54. For more on Americans' remembrance of the war, see Trout, *On the Battlefield of Memory,* especially chap. 2.

55. Details about the American Battle Monuments Commission and its work can be found at its website: www.abmc.gov. The website contains the lengthy 1938 publication *American Armies and Battlefields in Europe: A History, Guide and Reference Book;* see chap. 11, "American Military Cemeteries in Europe." With more than 14,000 grave sites, the largest World War I cemetery is the Meuse-Argonne cemetery, for those who died in the last major offensive of the war. The smallest, with only 368 grave sites, is at Flanders Field in Belgium.

56. For more on the pilgrimages, see Constance Potter's two-part article, "World War I Gold Star Mothers Pilgrimages," *Prologue: Quarterly of the National Archives and Records Administration* 31, 2 and 3 (Summer and Fall 1999), available online at www.archives.gov. For the Gold Star Mothers pilgrimages in the context of postwar remembrance, see Budreau, *Bodies of War,* 185–241. See also Holly S. Fenelon, *That Knock at the Door: The History of Gold Star Mothers in America* (Bloomington, IN: iUniverse, 2012). Still in existence, American Gold Star Mothers has a website with a section on the organization's history; see www.goldstarmoms.com/About/History.htm.

57. See *Lexington Herald,* November 5, 1918, for Kinne's apparent death, and April 4, 1919, for confirmation of his death and the location of his grave. Moving to Stearns as a young child, Kinne graduated from Somerset High School. He played an instrumental role in the UK football team's defeat of the University of Louisville and Purdue University. For letters regarding Kinne's training, see folder 1, School and Training Camp Correspondence 1912–1917, and folder 2, Correspondence—99th Aero Squadron HASAEF France 1918–1919, box 1, Kinne Family Papers, UK Special Collections and Archives. Letters regarding Kinne's possible death are in folder 2; a letter confirming his death and burial in a temporary grave near Romagne, France, was sent to his mother from Captain Lyle Powell, 99th Aero Obs. Squadron, February 27, 1919, Scrapbook, box 2, Kinne Family Papers.

58. For material about the pilgrimage, see the extensive scrapbook compiled by Nola Miller Kinne Fogg, box 2, Kinne Family Papers. The scrapbook contains letters and information from the government, the official invitation, material from the ships on which she traveled, clippings, postcards depicting the sites visited, and typed explanations of what she saw. The scrapbook supplements a diary also contained in box 2.

59. Quotes in the preceding paragraphs are from Fogg's diary, file: Nola Miller Kinne Fogg travel diary France 1933 May 15–June 1, box 2, Kinne Family Papers.

60. Budreau notes that of the more than 11,000 women eligible for the pilgrimages, a little more than half participated (*Bodies of War,* 239). Given the politics surrounding Congress, the military, and some of the Gold Star leaders, she questions whether the pilgrimages truly provided closure to the grieving participants (ibid., 9). For more on the Gold Star pilgrimages, see John W. Graham, *The Gold Star Mother Pilgrimages of the 1930s: Overseas Grave Visitations by Mothers and Widows of Fallen U.S. World War I Soldiers* (Jefferson, NC: McFarland, 2005).

61. Hood notes in his study of Washington and Nelson Counties that during the initial phase of the war, support was less than enthusiastic, as reflected in the poor results of the first two Liberty Bond campaigns. Nevertheless, when country boys were drafted and the war became more personal, war support picked up. The excellent results of the third Liberty Loan campaign in May 1918, in which donations far surpassed quotas, "was an indication of deepening commitment to the war effort." Hood, *Visions of Zion,* 133.

62. See Robert Zieger, *Republicans and Labor: 1919–1929* (Lexington: University of Kentucky Press, 1969), in which the author notes, "By 1920 progressivism had both succeeded and failed." While Progressivism did not disappear in the 1920s, Zieger asserts, "Throughout the 1920s progressivism remained largely without cohesion and leadership. A number of factors weakened this once-dominant movement. The success

of past programs, the death of Theodore Roosevelt and the illness of President Wilson, the impact of the war, the debate over foreign policy, rapidly changing economic and political circumstances, and the powerful pull of traditional party loyalties helped to spawn a variety of progressive programs, but at the same time to fragment further the already divided progressive movement" (162).

63. Although the phrase "United We Stand, Divided We Fall" was not officially adopted as the state motto until 1942, it had appeared on the state seal since 1792.

Selected Bibliography

Archives, Libraries, and Historical Societies

Filson Historical Society, Louisville, KY

Irvin Abel Papers
American War Mothers Collection
Clara Gibson Papers
Khaki Club Papers
Moseley-Goode-Bannister Collection
Neblett Family Correspondence

Kentucky Historical Society, Frankfort, KY

Austin Kinnaird Diary
Vertical files
World War I
World War I Camp Zachary Taylor
World War I Flying Aces
World War I Journal (of the Kentucky Council of Defense)
World War I Soldiers
World War I Women's Scrapbook

Murray State University, Murray, KY

Calloway County Churches—First Baptist—Boyce Taylor
Calloway County WW I Heroes
Robert McCune Diary
Vertical files
World War I

National Archives, Atlanta, GA

Record Group 4: US Food Administration
Record Group 21: US District Courts
Record Group 129: Bureau of Prisons

National Archives, College Park, MD

Record Group 1: War Labor Policies Board
Record Group 2: National War Labor Board
Record Group 62: Council of National Defense

Record Group 63: Committee on Public Information
Record Group 65: Federal Bureau of Investigation
Record Group 67: US Fuel Administration
Record Group 92: Office of the Quartermaster General
Record Group 163: Selective Service
Record Group 165: War Department

Southern Baptist Theological Seminary Special Collections and Archives, Louisville, KY

Diary of William J. McGlothlin
Letterbooks of E. Y. Mullins
E. Y. Mullins Papers, Mills Collection

University of Kentucky Special Collections, Lexington, KY

Barrow Unit Collection
Madeline McDowell Breckinridge Papers
Thomas Poe Cooper Papers
Fayette Equal Rights Association Collection
Kinne Papers
Frank McVey Papers
Augustus O. Stanley Papers
Cora Wilson Stewart Papers

University of Louisville Archives and Special Collections, Louisville, KY

Edward Hines File
J. Swagar Sherley Papers

Western Kentucky University Special Collections and Archives, Bowling Green, KY

Henry Hardin Cherry Collection
Joseph Llewellyn Price Collection

State and County Histories

History of Allen County, Ky., in the World War, 1917–1919. Prepared by D. F. Riherd. Housed in the Allen County Clerk's Office, Scottsville, KY.

History of Barren County, Ky., in the World War, 1917–1919. Housed in the Barren County Clerk's Office, Glasgow, KY.

History of Boyd County, Ky., in the World War, 1917–1919. Prepared by Mrs. L. N. Davis. Housed in the Boyd County Clerk's Office, Catlettsburg, KY.

History of Boyle County, Ky., in the World War, 1917–1919. Prepared by Dr. Fayette Dunlap. Housed in the Boyle County Public Library, Danville, KY.

History of Breathitt County, Ky., in the World War, 1917–1919. Housed in the Breathitt County Public Library, Jackson, KY.

History of Butler County, Ky., in the World War, 1917–1919. Prepared by Miss Cora Guffy. Housed in the Butler County Public Library, Morgantown, KY.

History of Campbell County, Ky., in the World War, 1917–1919. Prepared by Mrs. Thomas P. Carothers. Housed in the Campbell County Historical and Genealogical Society, Alexandria, KY.

History of Christian County, Ky., in the World War, 1919–1919. Prepared by Mrs. W. T. Fowler. Housed in the Christian County Public Library, Hopkinsville, KY.

History of Clark County, Ky., in the World War, 1917–1919. Prepared by Judge J. M. Benton. Housed in the Clark County Public Library, Winchester, KY.

History of Daviess County, Ky., in the World War, 1917–1919. Prepared by Prof. J. L. Faust. Housed in the Daviess County Public Library, Owensboro, KY.

History of Fayette County, Ky., in the World War, 1917–1919. 3 vols. Prepared by Judge Lyman Chalkley. Housed in the Fayette County Public Library, Lexington, KY.

History of Franklin County, Ky., in the World War, 1917–1919. Prepared by L. F. Johnson. Housed in the Kentucky Department of Libraries and Archives, Frankfort, KY.

History of Fulton County, Ky., in the World War, 1917–1919. Prepared by Miss Bessie Thompson. Housed in the Fulton County Clerk's Office, Hickman, KY.

History of Grayson County, Ky., in the World War, 1917–1919. Prepared by Mrs. Effie Sadler Basham. Housed in the Grayson County Historical Society, Litchfield, KY.

History of Green County, Ky., in the World War, 1917–1919. Prepared by J. McV. Shreve and J. H. Woodward. Housed in the Green County Public Library, Greensburg, KY.

History of Harrison County, Ky., in the World War, 1917–1919. Housed in the Harrison County Clerk's Office, Cynthiana, KY.

History of Henderson County, Ky., in the World War, 1917–1919. 5 vols. Prepared by the Henderson Women's Club, Miss Virginia Lockett, chairman. Housed in the Henderson County Public Library, Henderson, KY.

History of Henry County, Ky., in the World War, 1917–1919. Housed in the Henry County Clerk's Office, New Castle, KY.

History of Jefferson County, Ky., in the World War, 1917–1919. 34 vols. Prepared by Mrs. Harrison Robertson. Housed in the Louisville Free Public Library.

History of Kenton County, Ky., in the World War, 1917–1919. 10 vols. Prepared by Shelley D. Rouse. Housed in the Kenton County Public Library, Covington, KY.

History of Laurel County, Ky., in the World War, 1917–1919. Prepared by J. M. Feltner. Housed in the Laurel County Clerk's Office, London, KY.

History of Letcher County, Ky., in the World War, 1917–1919. 2 vols. Prepared by Mrs. French Hawk. Housed in the Caudill Public Library, Whitesburg, KY.

History of McCracken County, Ky., in the World War, 1917–1919. Prepared by Martha Grassham Purcell. Housed in the McCracken County Library, Paducah, KY.

History of Meade County, Ky., in the World War, 1917–1919. Prepared by Ella Gregory. Housed in the Kentucky Department of Libraries and Archives, Frankfort, KY.

History of Mercer County, Ky., in the World War, 1917–1919. Prepared by H. C. Wood. Housed in the Mercer County Clerk's Office, Harrodsburg, KY.

History of Morgan County, Ky., in the World War, 1917–1919. Prepared by Bernard E. Whitt. Housed in the Morgan County Clerk's Office, West Liberty, KY.

History of Nelson County, Ky., in the World War, 1917–1919. Prepared by Ludwell McCay and Lunette Coyle. Housed in the Nelson County Clerk's Office, Bardstown, KY.

History of Oldham County, Ky., in the World War, 1917–1919. Prepared by Mary C. Gainsborough. Housed in the Oldham County Clerk's Office, LaGrange, KY.

History of Pulaski County, Ky., in the World War, 1917–1919. Prepared by Judge James M. Denton. Housed in the Pulaski County Historical Society, Somerset, KY.

History of Rowan County, Ky., in the World War, 1917–1919. Prepared by T. B. Tippett. Housed in the Morehead State University Library Special Collections, Morehead, KY.

History of Scott County, Ky., in the World War, 1917–1919. 3 vols. Prepared by Mrs. William H. Coffman. Housed in the Scott County Public Library, Georgetown, KY.

History of Simpson County, Ky., in the World War, 1917–1919. Prepared by Mrs. S. A. Whiteside. Housed in the Simpson County Archives, Franklin, KY.

History of Spencer County, Ky., in the World War, 1917–1919. Prepared by Annie Anderson. Housed in the Spencer County Clerk's Office, Taylorsville, KY.

History of Trimble County, Ky., in the World War, 1917–1919. Prepared by Henry Clay Black. Housed in the Schmidt Research Library, Kentucky Historical Society, Frankfort, KY.

History of Warren County, Ky., in the World War, 1917–1919. Prepared by Mrs. Max B. Nahm. Housed in the Western Kentucky University Library Special Collections, Bowling Green, KY.

History of Washington County, Ky., in the World War, 1917–1919. Prepared by George Colvin and Emma Noonan. Housed in the Washington County Clerk's Office, Springfield, KY.

Kentucky in the World War, 1917–1919. 20 vols. Prepared by state war historian Fred Caldwell. Housed in the Kentucky Department of Military Affairs, Frankfort, KY.

Kentucky in the World War, 1917–1919: Civilian Records. 144 vols. Prepared by state war historian Fred Caldwell. Housed in the Filson Historical Society, Louisville, KY.

Newspapers

Adair County News (Columbia, KY)
Big Sandy News (Louisa, KY)
Bourbon News (Paris, KY)
Breckenridge News (Cloverport, KY)
Central Record (Lancaster, KY)
Cincinnati Enquirer
The Citizen (Berea, KY)
Climax-Madisonian (Richmond, KY)
Crittenden Record-Press (Marion, KY)

Daily Kentuckian (Hopkinsville, KY)
Georgetown Times
Hartford Herald
Hartford Republican
Hopkinsville Kentuckian
Interior Journal (Stanford, KY)
Kentucky Irish-American (Louisville, KY)
Kentucky Post (Covington, KY)
Lexington Herald
Licking Valley Courier (West Liberty, KY)
Louisville Anzeiger
Louisville Courier-Journal
Mountain Advocate (Barbourville, KY)
Mt. Sterling Advocate
Mt. Vernon Signal
Nashville Tennessean and the Nashville American
New York Times
Public Ledger (Maysville, KY)
The Record (Greenville, KY)
Richmond Daily Register

Books, Articles, Reports, and Dissertations

Alexander, Ronald R. "Henry Watterson and World War I." *Journal of the West Virginia Historical Association* 1, 1 (Spring 1977): 15–25.

Ambrose, William M. *Bluegrass Military Camps.* Lexington, KY: Limestone Press, 2012.

Appleton, Thomas H., Jr. "'Like Banquo's Ghost': The Emergence of the Prohibition Issue in Kentucky Politics." PhD diss., University of Kentucky, 1981.

———. "'Moral Suasion Has Had Its Day': From Temperance to Prohibition in Antebellum Kentucky." In *A Mythic Land Apart: Reassessing Southerners and Their History,* ed. John David Smith and Thomas H. Appleton Jr. Westport, CT: Greenwood Press, 1997.

———. "Prohibition and Politics in Kentucky: The Gubernatorial Campaign and Election of 1915." *Register of the Kentucky Historical Society* 75, 1 (January 1977): 28–54.

Appleton, Thomas H., Jr., and Lowell H. Harrison, eds. *Kentucky's Governors.* Lexington: University Press of Kentucky, 2004.

Ardery, Philip. "Reuben Brent Hutchcraft, Jr.: Kentucky Hero." *Filson Club History Quarterly* 60, 4 (October 1896): 455–61.

Aron, Raymond. *The Century of Total War.* Garden City, NY: Doubleday, 1954.

Association of the Graduates of the United States Military Academy. *Fifty-Third Annual Report, June 12, 1922.* Saginaw, MI: Seemann and Peters, 1922.

Bachin, Robin F. "At the Nexus of Labor and Leisure: Baseball, Nativism, and the 1919 Black Sox Scandal." *Journal of Social History* 36, 4 (Summer 2003): 941–62.

Baird, Nancy D. "The 'Spanish Lady' in Kentucky, 1918–1919." *Filson Club History Quarterly* 50, 3 (July 1976): 290–301.

Baldwin, Yvonne. *Cora Wilson Stewart and Kentucky's Moonlight Schools: Fighting for Literacy in America.* Lexington: University Press of Kentucky, 2006.

Beaman, Jay, and Brian K. Pipkin, eds. *Pentecostal and Holiness Statements on War and Peace.* Eugene, OR: Wipf and Stock, 2013.

Bettez, David J. *Kentucky Marine: Major General Logan Feland and the Development of the Modern USMC.* Lexington: University Press of Kentucky, 2014.

Bigham, Darrel E. *Towns & Villages of the Lower Ohio.* Lexington: University Press of Kentucky, 1998.

Birdwhistell, Ira V. *A Heart for Missions: A History of First Baptist Church, Murray, Kentucky, 1846–1996.* Franklin, TN: Providence House, 1996.

Bisher, Jamie. *White Terror: Cossack Warlords of the Trans-Siberian.* New York: Routledge, 2005.

Blair, Emily Newell. *Women's Committee, National Council of Defense: An Interpretive Report from April 21, 1917 to February 27, 1919.* Washington, DC: Government Printing Office, 1920.

Bogart, Charles. "The Military Post at Ft. Thomas, Kentucky." *Journal of America's Military Past* 25, 3 (Winter 1999): 60–75.

Boghardt, Thomas. *The Zimmermann Telegram: Intelligence, Diplomacy, and America's Entry into World War I.* Annapolis, MD: Naval Institute Press, 2012.

Bolin, James Duane. *Bossism and Reform in a Southern City: Lexington, Kentucky 1880–1940.* Lexington: University Press of Kentucky, 2000.

Boynton, Virginia R. "'Even in the Remotest Parts of the State': Downstate 'Woman's Committee' Activities on the Illinois Home Front during World War I." *Journal of the Illinois State Historical Society* 96, 4 (Winter 2003–2004): 318–46.

Brakebill, Tina Stewart. "From 'German Days' to '100 Percent Americanism': McLean County, Illinois 1913–1918; German Americans, World War One, and One Community's Reaction." *Journal of the Illinois State Historical Society* 95, 2 (Summer 2002): 148–71.

Brandimarte, Cynthia. "Women on the Home Front: Hostess Houses during World War I." *Winterthur Portfolio* 42, 4 (Winter 2008): 201–22.

Brandt, A. M. *The Cigarette Century: The Rise, Fall, and Deadly Persistence of the Product that Defined America.* New York: Basic Books, 2007.

Breen, William J. "Black Women and the Great War: Mobilization and Reform in the South." *Journal of Southern History* 44, 3 (August 1978): 421–40.

———. *Labor Market Politics and the Great War: The Department of Labor, the States, and the First U.S. Employment Service, 1907–1933.* Kent, OH: Kent State University Press, 1997.

———. "Mobilization and Cooperative Federalism: The Connecticut State Council of Defense, 1917–1919." *Historian* 42, 1 (November 1979): 58–84.

———. "The Mobilization of Skilled Labor in World War I: 'Voluntarism,' the U.S. Public Service Reserve, and the Department of Labor, 1917–1918." *Labor History* 32, 2 (1991): 253–72.

———. "The North Carolina Council of Defense during World War I, 1917–1918." *North Carolina Historical Review* 50, 1 (Winter 1973): 1–31.

———. "Southern Women in the War: The North Carolina Woman's Committee, 1917–1919." *North Carolina Historical Review* 55, 3 (July 1978): 251–83.

———. *Uncle Sam at Home: Civilian Mobilization, Wartime Federalism, and the Council of National Defense, 1917–1919.* Westport, CT: Greenwood Press, 1984.

Bristow, Nancy K. *Making Men Moral: Social Engineering during the Great War.* New York: New York University Press, 1996.

Brown, Meredith Mason. "A Killing in the Philippines, 1900: A Kentuckian Faces Insurgency and Military Justice." *Register of the Kentucky Historical Society* 104, 1 (Winter 2006): 43–76.

Bruns, Roger A. *Preacher: Billy Sunday and Big-Time American Evangelism.* Champaign: University of Illinois Press, 1992.

Buchanan, John G. "War Legislation against Alcoholic Liquor and Prostitution." *Journal of Criminal Law and Criminology* 9, 4 (1919): 520–29.

Buckley, Geoffrey L. *Extracting Appalachia: Images of the Consolidation Coal Company, 1910/1945.* Athens: Ohio University Press, 2004.

Budd, Richard M. *Serving Two Masters: The Development of American Military Chaplaincy, 1860–1920.* Lincoln: University of Nebraska Press, 2002.

Budreau, Lisa. *Bodies of War: World War I and the Politics of Commemoration in America, 1919–1933.* New York: New York University Press, 2010.

Burckel, Nicholas C. "A. O. Stanley and Progressive Reform, 1902–1919." *Register of the Kentucky Historical Society* 79, 2 (Spring 1981): 136–61.

Burke, Bernard V. *Ambassador Frederic Sackett and the Collapse of the Weimar Republic, 1930–1933.* New York: Cambridge University Press, 1994.

Cafer du Plessis, Elizabeth. "Alice French, Indiana War Mothers, from World War I 'Kitchen Soldiers' to Postwar Immigrant Reformers." In *Feminist Frontiers: Women Who Shaped the Midwest,* ed. Yvonne Johnson. Kirksville, MO: Truman State University Press, 2010.

———. "Meatless Days and Sleepless Nights: Food, Agriculture, and Environment in World War I America." PhD diss., Indiana University, 2009.

Caldwell, Fred. "Above and Beyond the Call of Duty." *Register of the Kentucky Historical Society* 18, 53 (May 1920): 9–11.

Campbell, Anne G. "Mary Breckinridge and the American Committee for Devastated France: The Foundations of the Frontier Nursing Service." *Register of the Kentucky Historical Society* 82, 3 (Summer 1984): 257–76.

Caner, Emir, and Ergun Caner. *The Sacred Trust: Sketches of the Southern Baptist Convention Presidents.* Nashville, TN: Broadman and Holman, 2003.

Capozzola, Christopher. "The Only Badge Needed Is Your Patriotic Fervor: Vigilance, Coercion, and the Law in World War I America." *Journal of American History* 88, 4 (March 2002): 1354–82.

———. *Uncle Sam Wants You: World War I and the Making of the Modern American Citizen.* New York: Oxford University Press, 2010.

Casey, Michael W. "From Pacifism to Patriotism: The Emergence of Civil Religion in the Churches of Christ during World War I." *Mennonite Quarterly Review* 66 (July 1992): 376–90.

Cecil, Jerry. "Alpha Barnes Nash and the Barrow Unit of World War I: Serving as a Nurse in Good Samaritan Base Hospital Unit No. 40, 1918–1919." Graduate seminar paper, University of Kentucky History Department, 1998, deposited in US Army Military History Institute, Carlisle, PA.

Chafee, Zechariah. *Free Speech in the United States.* New York: Atheneum, 1969.

Chambers, John Whiteclay, II. *To Raise an Army: The Draft Comes to Modern America.* New York: Free Press, 1987.

Chrislock, Carl H. *Watchdog of Loyalty: The Minnesota Commission of Public Safety during World War I.* St. Paul: Minnesota Historical Society Press, 1991.

Christiansen, Lawrence O. "Missouri's Response to World War I: The Missouri Council of Defense." *Midwest Review,* 3rd ser., 12 (1990): 34–44.

———. "Popular Reaction to World War I in Missouri." *Missouri Historical Review* 86, 4 (July 1992): 386–95.

———. "World War I in Missouri: Part I." *Missouri Historical Review* 90, 3 (April 1996): 330–54.

———. "World War I in Missouri: Part II." *Missouri Historical Review* 90, 4 (July 1996): 410–28.

Clark, Christopher. *The Sleepwalkers: How Europe Went to War in 1914.* New York: Harper, 2013.

Clark, Margaret. "Base Hospital 43: The Emory Unit." *MedGenMed* 9, 3 (2007): 10.

Clarke, Ida Clyde. *American Women and the World War.* New York: D. Appleton, 1918.

Clifford, J. Garry. *The Citizen Soldiers: The Plattsburg Training Camp Movement, 1913–1920.* Lexington: University of Kentucky Press, 1972.

Clopper, Edward, ed. *Child Welfare in Kentucky.* New York: National Child Labor Committee, 1919.

Cobb, Irvin S. *The Glory of the Coming: What Mine Eyes Have Seen of Americans in Action in This Year of Grace and Allied Endeavor.* London: Hodder and Stoughton, 1919.

———. *Paths of Glory: Impressions of War Written at and Near the Front.* New York: George H. Doran, 1915.

———. *Speaking of Prussians.* New York: George H. Doran, 1917.

———. "Sunday, as Cobb Saw Him." *Literary Digest,* June 16, 1917.

Combs, Josiah Henry. *The Siege of Sarisbury Court which Chronicles the Feat of Base Hospital 40 in Winning the World War.* Lexington, KY: Hurst and Byers, 1923.

Cone, Carl B. *The University of Kentucky: A Pictorial History.* Lexington: University Press of Kentucky, 1989.

Connelley, William Elsey, and Ellis Merton Coulter. *History of Kentucky.* 5 vols. Chicago: American Historical Society, 1922.

Conner, Valerie Jean. *The National War Labor Board: Stability, Social Justice, and the Voluntary State in World War I.* Chapel Hill: University of North Carolina Press, 1983.

Conolly-Smith, Peter. "'Reading between the Lines': The Bureau of Investigation, the

United States Post Office, and Domestic Surveillance during World War I." *Social Justice* 36, 1 (2009): 7–24.

Cooke, James. *The All-Americans at War: The 82nd Division in the Great War, 1917–1918*. New York: Praeger, 1999.

Cooperman, Jessica. "The Jewish Welfare Board and Religious Pluralism in the American Military of World War I." *American Jewish History* 98, 4 (October 2014): 237–61.

Cornebise, Alfred. *War as Advertised: The Four Minute Men and America's Crusade, 1917–1918*. Philadelphia: American Philosophical Society, 1984.

Cox, Dwayne, and William Morison. *The University of Louisville*. Lexington: University Press of Kentucky, 2000.

Craig, Berry. *Hidden History of Kentucky Soldiers*. Charleston, SC: History Press, 2011.

Crews, Clyde F. *An American Holy Land: A History of the Archdiocese of Louisville*. Louisville, KY: Ikonographics, 1987.

Cuddy, Edward. "Pro-Germanism and American Catholicism, 1914–1917." *Catholic Historical Review* 54, 3 (October 1968): 427–54.

Cuff, Robert D. "Harry Garfield, the Fuel Administration, and the Search for a Cooperative Order during World War I." *American Quarterly* 30, 1 (Spring 1978): 39–53.

———. "Herbert Hoover, the Ideology of Voluntarism and War Organization during the Great War." *Journal of American History* 64, 2 (September 1977): 358–72.

Culver, Gregory K. "The Impact of the 1918 Spanish Influenza Epidemic on the Jackson Purchase." *Filson Club History Quarterly* 65, 4 (October 1991): 487–504.

Curry, Lerond. *Protestant-Catholic Relations in America: World War I through Vatican II*. Lexington: University Press of Kentucky, 1972.

Danbom, David B. "The Agricultural Extension System and the First World War." *Historian* 41, 2 (February 1, 1979): 315–31.

Daniels, Caroline. "'The Feminine Touch Has Not Been Wanting': Women Librarians at Camp Zachary Taylor, 1917–1919." *Libraries and the Cultural Record* 43, 3 (2008): 286–307.

Davis, David A. "Not Only War Is Hell: World War I and African American Lynching Narratives." *African American Review* 42, 3–4 (Fall–Winter 2008): 477–91.

Davison, Henry. *The American Red Cross in the Great War*. New York: Macmillan, 1919.

Doenecke, Justus. *Nothing Less than War: A New History of America's Entry into World War I*. Lexington: University Press of Kentucky, 2011.

Dorsett, Lyle. *Billy Sunday and the Redemption of Urban America*. Macon, GA: Mercer University Press, 2004.

Dumenil, Lynn. "Women's Reform Organizations and Wartime Mobilization in World War I–Era Los Angeles." *Journal of the Gilded Age and Progressive Era* 10, 2 (April 2011): 213–45.

Dunn, Maurice. *Camp Zachary Taylor Souvenir, Louisville, Kentucky*. Louisville, KY: Lambertson Service Bureau, [1918].

Eighmey, Rae Katherine. "'Food Will Win the War': Minnesota Conservation Efforts, 1917–18." *Minnesota History* 59, 7 (Fall 2005): 272–86.

———. *Food Will Win the War: Minnesota Crops, Cooks, and Conservation during World War I*. St. Paul: Minnesota Historical Society Press, 2010.

Ellis, Mark. *Race, War, and Surveillance: African Americans and the United States Government during World War I.* Bloomington: Indiana University Press, 2001.

———. "W. E. B. Du Bois and the Formation of Black Opinion in World War I: A Commentary on 'The Damnable Dilemma.'" *Journal of American History* 81, 4 (March 1995): 1584–90.

Ellis, William E. *A History of Eastern Kentucky University: The School of Opportunity.* Lexington: University Press of Kentucky, 2005.

———. *A History of Education in Kentucky.* Lexington: University Press of Kentucky, 2011.

———. *A Man of Books and a Man of the People: E. Y. Mullins and the Crisis of Moderate Southern Baptist Leadership.* Macon, GA: Mercer University Press, 1985.

———. "Patrick Henry Callahan: A Maverick Catholic and the Prohibition Issue." *Register of the Kentucky Historical Society* 92, 2 (Spring 1994): 175–99.

———. *Patrick Henry Callahan (1866–1940): Progressive Catholic Layman in the American South.* Lewiston, NY: E. Mellen Press, 1989.

Ellwanger, Ella Hutchinson. "Camp Zachary Taylor." *Register of the Kentucky Historical Society* 16, 47 (May 1918): 9–24.

Fenelon, Holly S. *That Knock at the Door: The History of Gold Star Mothers in America.* Bloomington, IN: iUniverse, 2012.

Ferrell, Robert. *Five Days in October: The Lost Battalion of World War I.* Columbia: University of Missouri Press, 2005.

Finley, Randy. "Black Arkansans and World War One." *Arkansas Historical Quarterly* 49, 3 (Autumn 1990): 249–77.

Finnegan, John Patrick. *Against the Specter of a Dragon: The Campaign for American Military Preparedness, 1914–1917.* Westport, CT: Greenwood Press, 1974.

First Kentucky State Convention (and First in the United States) of the American National Red Cross Held at Lexington, August 22–23, 1917. Frankfort, KY: State Journal Co., [1917].

Fitz-Randolph, Helen. "Lexington's School Garden Pageant." *School Life* 2, 8 (April 16, 1919): 13–14.

Ford, Nancy Gentile. *Americans All: Foreign-born Soldiers in World War I.* College Station: Texas A&M University Press, 2001.

———. *The Great War and America: Civil-Military Relations during World War I.* Westport, CT: Praeger Security International, 2008.

Forderhase, Nancy K. "'The Clear Call of Thoroughbred Women': The Kentucky Federation of Women's Clubs and the Crusade for Educational Reform, 1903–1909." *Register of the Kentucky Historical Society* 83, 1 (Winter 1985): 19–35.

Fortune, Alonzo Willard. *The Disciples in Kentucky.* N.p.: Convention of the Christian Churches in Kentucky, 1932.

"The French Record in Cilicia." *New Armenia* 13, 2 (March–April 1921): 22–24.

Fuller, Paul E. *Laura Clay and the Woman's Rights Movement.* Lexington: University Press of Kentucky, 1975.

George, Eric. "Hostility on the Home Front." *Louisville Magazine* 44, 10 (October 1993): 34.

Gillham, Lisa, with Bethany Richter Pollitt. "J. H. Kruse, War & the Terrible Threateners: Anti-German Hysteria in World War I Covington." *Northern Kentucky Heritage* 15, 1 (Fall–Winter 2007): 3–38.

Glazier, Jack. *Been Coming through Some Hard Times: Race, History, and Memory in Western Kentucky*. Knoxville: University of Tennessee Press, 2012.

Graham, John W. *The Gold Star Mother Pilgrimages of the 1930s: Overseas Grave Visitations by Mothers and Widows of Fallen U.S. World War I Soldiers*. Jefferson, NC: McFarland, 2005.

Hagan, George Dan. "Kentucky's Part in the World War." MA thesis, University of Kentucky, 1926.

Harrison, Lowell. *Western Kentucky University*. Lexington: University Press of Kentucky, 1987.

Hastings, Max. *Catastrophe 1914: Europe Goes to War*. New York: Knopf, 2013.

Hay, Melba Porter. *Madeline McDowell Breckinridge and the Battle for a New South*. Lexington: University Press of Kentucky, 2009.

Hayden-Smith, Rose. "Soldiers of the Soil: A Historical Review of the United States School Garden Army." University of California, 4-H Center for Youth Development Monograph (Winter 2006): 1–19.

———. "Sowing the Seeds of Victory: National Wartime Gardening Programs in the United States during World War I." PhD diss., University of California–Santa Barbara, 2010.

Hemmingway, Theodore. "Prelude to Change: Black Carolinians in the War Years, 1914–1920," *Journal of Negro History* 65, 3 (Summer 1980): 212–27.

Hennen, John C. *The Americanization of West Virginia: Creating a Modern Industrial State, 1916–1925*. Lexington: University Press of Kentucky, 1996.

Herr, Kincaid. *The Louisville and Nashville Railroad, 1850–1963*. Rev. ed. Lexington: University Press of Kentucky, 2000.

Hindman, Hugh D. *Child Labor: An American History*. Armonk, NY: M. E. Sharpe, 2002.

Holbrooke, Franklin F., and Livia Appel. *Minnesota in the War with Germany*. Vol. 1. St. Paul: Minnesota Historical Society, 1928.

Hood, J. Larry. "The Collapse of Zion: Rural Progressivism in Nelson and Washington Counties, Kentucky." PhD diss., University of Kentucky, 1980.

———. *Visions of Zion: Christianity, Modernization and the American Pursuit of Liberty: Progressivism in Rural Nelson and Washington Counties Kentucky*. Lanham, MD: University Press of America, 2005.

Hopkins, James F. *A History of the Hemp Industry in Kentucky*. Lexington: University of Kentucky Press, 1951.

Hough, Emerson. *The Web: A Revelation of Patriotism*. Chicago: Reilly and Lee, 1919.

Howenstine, E. Jay, Jr. "Federal Planning for Demobilization during World War I." *American Journal of Economics and Sociology* 3, 4 (July 1944): 631–45.

Hughes, Richard T. *Reviving the Ancient Faith: The Story of Churches of Christ in America*. Grand Rapids, MI: Wm. B. Eerdmans, 1996.

Hunton, Addie, and Kathryn Johnson. *Two Colored Women with the American Expeditionary Forces*. Brooklyn, NY: Brooklyn Eagle Press, 1920.

James, Bessie Rowland. *For God, for Country, for Home, the National League for Wom-*

an's Service: A Story of the First National Organization of American Women Mobilized for War Service. New York: G. P. Putnam's Sons, 1920.

James, Pearl, ed. *Picture This: World War I Posters and Visual Culture.* Lincoln: University of Nebraska Press, 2009.

Janik, Erika. "Food Will Win the War: Food Conservation in World War I Wisconsin." *Wisconsin Magazine of History* 93, 3 (Spring 2010): 16–27.

Jenkins, Philip. *The Great and Holy War: How World War I Became a Religious Crusade.* New York: HarperCollins, 2014.

Jensen, Joan. *The Price of Vigilance.* New York: Rand McNally, 1968.

Jensen, Kimberly. *Mobilizing Minerva: American Women and the First World War.* Urbana: University of Illinois Press, 2008.

Johnson, E. Polk. *A History of Kentucky and Kentuckians: The Leaders and Representative Men in Commerce, Industry and Modern Activities.* Chicago: Lewis Publishing Co., 1912.

Jones, Preston. *The Fires of Patriotism: Alaskans in the Days of the First World War 1910–1920.* Fairbanks: University of Alaska Press, 2013.

Jordan, William. "'The Damnable Dilemma': African-American Accommodation and Protest during World War I." *Journal of American History* 81, 4 (March 1995): 1562–83.

Journal of the Regular Session of the Senate. Vol. 1. Frankfort, KY: State Journal Co., 1918.

Kahn, David, with Will Oursler. *My Life with Edgar Cayce.* Garden City, NY: Doubleday, 1970.

Kaye, Andrew. "Colonel Roscoe Conkling Simmons and the Mechanics of Black Leadership." *Journal of American Studies* 37, 1 (April 2003): 79–98.

———. "Roscoe Conkling Simmons and the Significance of African American Oratory." *Historical Journal* 45, 1 (March 2002): 79–102.

Keegan, John. *The First World War.* New York: Knopf, 1999.

Keene, Jennifer. "A 'Brutalizing' War: The USA after the First World War." *Journal of Contemporary History* 50, 1 (Spring 2015): 78–99.

———. *Doughboys, the Great War, and the Remaking of America.* Baltimore: Johns Hopkins Press, 2001.

———. "The Memory of the Great War in the African American Community." In *Unknown Soldiers: The American Expeditionary Forces in Memory and Remembrance,* ed. Mark A. Snell, 207–40. Kent, OH: Kent State University Press, 2008.

Keith, Jeanette. *Rich Man's War, Poor Man's Fight: Race, Class, and Power in the Rural South during the First World War.* Chapel Hill: University of North Carolina Press, 2004.

Kelemen, Thomas A. "A History of Lynch, Kentucky, 1917 to 1930." MA thesis, University of Kentucky, 1972.

———. "A History of Lynch, Kentucky, 1917–1930." *Filson Club History Quarterly* 48, 2 (April 1974): 156–76.

Kennan, George. *The Decline of Bismarck's European Order: Franco-Russian Relations 1875–1890.* Princeton, NJ: Princeton University Press, 1981.

Kennedy, David. *Over Here: The First World War and American Society.* New York: Oxford University Press, 1980.

Kentucky Council of Defense. *Annual Report of the Kentucky Council of Defense, December 31, 1918.* Frankfort, KY: State Journal Co., [1919].

———. *Final Report of the War Historical Work of the Kentucky Council of Defense.* N.p., n.d.

———. *Kentucky War Council Held under the Auspices of the Council of National Defense and the Kentucky Council of Defense, January 15th–16th, 1918.* N.p., n.d.

———. *Report of the Activities of the Kentucky Council of Defense to January 1, 1919.* Frankfort, KY: State Journal Co., 1919.

———. *Report of the Activities of the Kentucky Council of Defense to January 1, 1920.* Frankfort, KY: State Journal Co., 1920.

———. *Report of the War Historical Work of the Kentucky Council of Defense from March 23, 1920 to December 31, 1921.* Frankfort, KY: State Journal Co., [1922].

———. *State Conference on Kentucky Problems Held at University of Kentucky, March 4–5, 1919: Program and Addresses.* Frankfort, KY: State Journal Co., 1919.

———. *Statewide Movement to Make a Record of Kentucky's Part in the World War Including Military Service Records of Fighting Forces, War Work Done by Civilians, Collection and Preservation of Other Historical Matter.* Louisville: Kentucky Council of Defense, 1919.

Kentucky Court of Appeals. *The Kentucky Statutes,* 5th ed. *1918 Supplement.* Louisville, KY: Baldwin Law Book Co., 1918.

Kentucky General Assembly. *Journal of the Regular Session of the House of Representatives of the Commonwealth of Kentucky.* Frankfort, 1918.

Kentucky State Memorial for the Boys Who Lost Their Lives in the Great War. Lexington: University of Kentucky, 1919.

Kingsbury, Celia Malone. *For Home and Country: World War I Propaganda on the Home Front.* Lincoln: University of Nebraska Press, 2010.

Kirschenbaum, Robert. "Klan and Commonwealth: The Ku Klux Klan and Politics in Kentucky, 1921–1928." MA thesis, University of Kentucky, 2005.

Kleber, John, ed. *The Encyclopedia of Louisville.* Lexington: University Press of Kentucky, 2001.

———. *The Kentucky Encyclopedia.* Lexington: University Press of Kentucky, 1992.

Klein, Maury. *History of the Louisville & Nashville Railroad.* Lexington: University Press of Kentucky, 2003.

Klotter, James. *The Breckinridges of Kentucky, 1760–1981.* Lexington: University Press of Kentucky, 1986.

———. *Kentucky: A Portrait in Paradox, 1900–1950.* Frankfort: Kentucky Historical Society, 1996.

Knott, Claudia. "The Woman Suffrage Movement in Kentucky, 1879–1920." PhD diss., University of Kentucky, 1989.

Koch, Theodore Wesley. *Books in the War: The Romance of Library War Service.* Boston: Houghton Mifflin, 1919.

———. *War Service of the American Library Association.* Washington, DC: ALA War Service, Library of Congress, 1918.

Kornweibel, Theodore, Jr. "Apathy and Dissent: Black America's Negative Responses to World War I." *South Atlantic Quarterly* 80, 3 (Summer 1981): 322–38.

———. *"Investigate Everything": Federal Efforts to Compel Black Loyalty during World War I.* Bloomington: Indiana University Press, 2002.

Lawson, Anita. *Irvin S. Cobb.* Bowling Green, OH: Bowling Green University Popular Press, 1984.

Lee, David D. *Sergeant York: An American Hero.* Lexington: University Press of Kentucky, 1985.

LeMay, Jason, John Trowbridge, and M. Harold Canon. *Kentucky's Flying Soldiers: A History of the Kentucky Army National Guard's Fixed Wing Aviation.* Frankfort, KY: Office of the Adjutant General, 2006.

Lentz-Smith, Adriane. *Freedom Struggles: African Americans and World War I.* Cambridge, MA: Harvard University Press, 2009.

Libbey, James K. *Dear Alben: Mr. Barkley of Kentucky.* Lexington: University Press of Kentucky, 1979.

Luebke, Frederick C. *Bonds of Loyalty: German-Americans and World War I.* De Kalb: Northern Illinois University Press, 1974.

Margolies, Daniel S. *Henry Watterson and the New South: The Politics of Empire, Free Trade, and Globalization.* Lexington: University Press of Kentucky, 2006.

Marshall, Anne. *Creating a Confederate Kentucky: The Lost Cause and Civil War Memory in a Border State.* Chapel Hill: University of North Carolina Press, 2010.

Marshall, Mary. *Great Breeders and Their Methods: Leslie Combs II and Spendthrift Farm.* Neenah, WI: Russell Meerdink, 2008.

Masters, Frank M. *A History of Baptists in Kentucky.* Louisville: Kentucky Baptist Historical Society, 1953.

Mastrangelo, Lisa. "World War I, Public Intellectuals, and the Four Minute Men: Convergent Ideals of Public Speaking and Civic Participation." *Rhetoric & Public Affairs* 12, 4 (Winter 2009): 607–34.

Mastriano, Douglas V. *Alvin York: A New Biography of the Hero of the Argonne.* Lexington: University Press of Kentucky, 2014.

Mauroni, Albert J. *Chemical and Biological Warfare: A Reference Handbook.* 2nd ed. Santa Barbara, CA: ABC-CLIO, 2007.

McCartin, Joseph A. *Labor's Great War: The Struggle for Industrial Democracy and the Origins of Modern American Labor Relations, 1912–1921.* Chapel Hill: University of North Carolina Press, 1997.

McChesney, Harry Vernon. *History of Army Y.M.C.A. Work at Camp Zachary Taylor.* Louisville, KY: n.p., 1920.

McClain, G. Lee. *Military History of Kentucky.* Frankfort, KY: State Journal, 1939.

McClintock, Alexander. *Best O'Luck; How a Fighting Kentuckian Won the Thanks of Britain's King.* New York: George H. Doran, 1917.

McLaughlin, Malcolm. "Ghetto Formation and Armed Resistance in East St. Louis, Illinois." *Journal of American Studies* 41, 2 (August 2007): 435–67.

McMahon, Robert, ed. *How These Farmers Succeeded.* New York: Henry Holt, 1919.

McMeekin, Sean. *July 1914: Countdown to War.* New York: Basic Books, 2013.

———. *The Russian Origins of the First World War.* Cambridge, MA: Belknap Press of Harvard University Press, 2013.

McMillan, Margaret. *The War that Ended Peace: The Road to 1914.* New York: Random House, 1913.

Merriman, Scott A. "'An Intensive School of Disloyalty': The C. B. Schoberg Case under the Espionage and Sedition Acts in Kentucky during World War I." *Register of the Kentucky Historical Society* 98, 2 (Spring 2000): 179–204.

———. "Ordinary People in Extraordinary Times? Defendants, Attorneys, and the Federal Government's Policy under the Espionage and Sedition Acts during World War I in the Sixth Circuit Court of Appeals District." PhD diss., University of Kentucky, 2003.

Mikkelsen, Vincent. "Coming from Battle to Face a War: The Lynching of Black Soldiers in the World War I Era." PhD diss., Florida State University, 2007.

Mjagkij, Nina. *Loyalty in Time of Trial: The African American Experience during World War I.* New York: Rowman and Littlefield, 2011.

Morgan, David T. "The Revivalist as Patriot: Billy Sunday and World War." *Journal of Presbyterian History* 51, 2 (Summer 1973): 199–215.

Moyen, Eric A. *Frank L. McVey and the University of Kentucky: A Progressive President and the Modernization of a Southern University.* Lexington: University Press of Kentucky, 2011.

Mullendore, William Clinton. *History of the United States Food Administration, 1917–1919.* Stanford, CA: Stanford University Press, 1941.

Murphy, Ethel Allen. *The Triumph of Humanity: A Pageant of Victory, Reconstruction, and Democracy.* [Louisville]: Kentucky Division, Woman's Committee, Council of National Defense, [1919].

Murphy, Paul L. *World War I and the Origin of Civil Liberties in the United States.* New York: W. W. Norton, 1979.

Nash, George H. "'An American Epic': Herbert Hoover and Belgian Relief in World War I." *Prologue: Quarterly of the National Archives and Records Administration* 21, 1 (Spring 1989). www.archives.gov/publications/prologue/1989/spring/hoover-belgium.html.

———. *The Life of Herbert Hoover: Master of Emergencies, 1917–1918.* New York: W. W. Norton, 1996.

National Child Labor Committee. *Children in Food Production.* New York: Clarence S. Nathan, 1917.

National Civil Liberties Bureau. *The Outrage on Rev. Herbert S. Bigelow of Cincinnati, Ohio.* New York: National Civil Liberties Bureau, 1918.

———. *War-Time Prosecutions and Mob Violence, Involving the Rights of Free Speech, Free Press and Peaceful Assemblage.* New York: National Civil Liberties Bureau, 1919.

Neiberg, Michael. *Dance of the Furies: Europe and the Outbreak of World War I.* Cambridge, MA: Belknap Press of Harvard University Press, 2011.

Oliff, Martin. *The Great War in the Heart of Dixie: Alabama during World War I.* Tuscaloosa: University of Alabama Press, 2008.

Otte, Thomas. *July Crisis: The World's Descent into War, Summer 1914.* New York: Cambridge University Press, 2014.

Pack, Charles Lathrop. *The War Garden Victorious: Its War Time Need and Its Economic Value in Peace.* Philadelphia: J. B. Lippincott, 1919.

Parker, Jacqueline K., and Edward M. Carpenter. "Julia Lathrop and the Children's Bureau: The Emergence of an Institution." *Social Service Review* 55, 1 (March 1981): 60–77.

Peixotto, Jessica B. "The Children's Year and the Woman's Committee." *Annals of the American Academy of Political and Social Science* 79 (September 1918): 257–62.

Pencak, William. *For God and Country: The American Legion, 1919–1941.* Boston: Northeastern University Press, 1989.

Peterson, H. C., and Gilbert C. Fite. *Opponents of War: 1917–1918.* Madison: University of Wisconsin Press, 1957.

Piper, John F. *The American Churches in World War I.* Athens: Ohio University Press, 1985.

Polston, Michael D., and Guy Lancaster, eds. *To Can the Kaiser: Arkansas and the Great War.* Little Rock, AR: Butler Center Books, 2015.

Potter, Constance. "World War I Gold Star Mothers Pilgrimages, Part I." *Prologue: Quarterly of the National Archives and Records Administration* 31, 2 (Summer 1999). www.archives.gov/publications/prologue/1999/summer/gold-star-mothers-1.html.

———. "World War I Gold Star Mothers Pilgrimages, Part II." *Prologue: Quarterly of the National Archives and Records Administration* 31, 3 (Fall 1999). www.archives.gov/publications/prologue/1999/fall/gold-star-mothers.html.

Powell, Edward Lindsay. *The Prophet's Vision and the President's Dream.* St. Louis, MO: Christian Board of Publication, 1919.

Ramage, Thomas. "Augustus Owsley Stanley: Early Twentieth Century Democrat." PhD diss., University of Kentucky, 1968.

Reid, Bill G. "Agrarian Opposition to Franklin K. Lane's Proposal for Soldier Settlement, 1918–1921." *Agricultural History* 41, 2 (April 1967): 167–80.

———. "Franklin K. Lane's Idea for Veterans' Colonization, 1918–1921." *Pacific Historical Review* 33, 4 (November 1964): 447–61.

Rice, Alice Hegan. "Wanted—Books for the Soldiers! Some Personal Experiences at Camp Zachary Taylor." *Red Cross Magazine* 13, 12 (December 1918): 27–32.

Richard, Carl J. *When the United States Invaded Russia: Woodrow Wilson's Siberian Disaster.* New York: Rowman and Littlefield, 2013.

Rippley, La Vern J. "Conflict in the Classroom: Anti-Germanism in Minnesota Schools, 1917–19." *Minnesota History* 47, 5 (Spring 1981): 170–83.

Rodman, Hugh. *Yarns of a Kentucky Admiral.* Indianapolis: Bobbs-Merrill, 1928.

Rumer, Thomas. *The American Legion: An Official History, 1919–1989.* New York: M. Evans, 1990.

Ryan, Rev. Paul. *History of the Diocese of Covington, Kentucky.* Diocese of Covington, Kentucky, 1954.

Schaffer, Ronald. *America in the Great War: The Rise of the War Welfare State.* New York: Oxford University Press, 1991.

Schaller, Mary W. *Deliver Us from Evil: A Southern Belle in Europe at the Outbreak of World War I.* Columbia: University of South Carolina Press, 2011.

Schwartz, Harry. "Agricultural Labor in the First World War." *Journal of Farm Economics* 24, 1 (February 1942): 178–87.

Scott, Emmett J. *Scott's Official History of the American Negro in the World War.* Washington, DC: War Department, [1919].

Scott, R. Neill. *Many Were Held by the Sea: The Tragic Sinking of HMS* Otranto. New York: Rowman and Littlefield, 2012.

Senn, Gerald. "'Molders of Thought, Directors of Action': The Arkansas Council of Defense, 1917–1918." *Arkansas Historical Quarterly* 36, 3 (Autumn 1977): 280–90.

Shenk, Gerald E. "Race, Manhood, and Manpower: Mobilizing Rural Georgia for World War I." *Georgia Historical Quarterly* 81, 3 (Fall 1997): 622–62.

———. *"Work or Fight": Race, Gender, and the Draft in World War One.* New York: Palgrave Macmillan, 2005.

Short, Roy Hunter. *Methodism in Kentucky.* Rutland, VT: Academy Books, 1979.

Slotkin, Richard. *Lost Battalions: The Great War and the Crisis of American Nationality.* New York: Henry Holt, 2005.

Smith, Gerald L. *A Black Educator in the Segregated South: Kentucky's Rufus B. Atwood.* Lexington: University Press of Kentucky, 1994.

Smith, J. Allan. *The College of Agriculture of the University of Kentucky: Early and Middle Years, 1865–1961.* Lexington: Kentucky Agricultural Extension Service, 1981.

Snyder, Robert. *A History of Georgetown College.* N.p., n.d.

Stamm, Lisa A. "The German-American Population of Northern Kentucky during World War I: The Victimization of an Ethnic Group and Its Culture." *Perspectives in History* 4, 2 (Spring 1989): 3–20.

Stevens, John D. "Suppression of Expression in Wisconsin during World War I." PhD diss., University of Wisconsin, 1967.

Stewart, Isabel M. "Nursing Preparedness: Some Lessons from World War I." *American Journal of Nursing* 41, 7 (July 1941): 804–15.

Stookey, Stephen. "Baptists and Landmarkism and the Turn toward Provincialism: 1851." In *Turning Points in Baptist History: A Festschrift in Honor of Harry Leon McBeth,* ed. Michael E. Williams Sr. and Walter B. Shurden, 178–93. Macon, GA: Mercer University Press, 2008.

Strachan, Hew. *The First World War.* New York: Viking, 2004.

The Students Army Training Corps, Descriptive Circular, 2nd ed., *Corrected to October 24, 1918.* Washington, DC: War Department, 1918.

Sweeney, William Allison. *History of the American Negro in the Great World War.* Chicago: G. G. Sapp, 1919.

Tenkotte, Paul A., and James C. Claypool, eds. *The Encyclopedia of Northern Kentucky.* Lexington: University Press of Kentucky, 2009.

Thelen, David. *Robert M. La Follette and the Insurgent Spirit.* Madison: University of Wisconsin Press, 1976.

33rd Division A.E.F. from Its Arrival in France until the Armistice with Germany, November 11, 1918. Diekirch, Luxembourg: n.p., 1919.

Thomas, William H., Jr. *Unsafe for Democracy: World War I and the U.S. Justice Department's Covert Campaign to Suppress Dissent.* Madison: University of Wisconsin Press, 2008.

Thum, W. W. *Kentucky Legal Aid Book for the Use of Legal Aid Committees and County Councils of Defense.* Frankfort, KY: State Journal Co., n.d.

Torok, George D. *A Guide to the Historic Coal Towns: Of the Big Sandy River Valley.* Knoxville: University of Tennessee Press, 2004.

Trout, Steven. *On the Battlefield of Memory: The First World War and American Remembrance, 1919–1941.* Tuscaloosa: University of Alabama Press, 2010.

Trowbridge, John. "A Patriotic Clan from Eastern Kentucky in the War to End All Wars." *Kentucky Ancestors* 43, 3 (Spring 2008): 114–23.

United States Council of National Defense, Section on Cooperation with States. *Report on Organization and Activities of State Councils of Defense, June 18, 1917.* Washington, DC, 1917.

United States Department of Commerce, Bureau of the Census. *Birth Statistics for the Birth Registration Area of the United States, 1919.* Washington, DC: Government Printing Office, 1921.

———. *Religious Bodies: 1916.* Washington, DC: Government Printing Office, 1919.

United States Department of Labor, Children's Bureau. *Children's Year: A Brief Summary of Work Done and Suggestions for Follow-up Work.* Washington, DC: US Department of Labor, 1920.

United States Fuel Administration. *Report of the Administrative Division, 1917–1919,* pt. 1, *Reports of the Bureau of State Organizations and of the Federal Fuel Administrators for the Various States and Districts.* Washington, DC: Government Printing Office, 1920.

United States Treasury Department, Internal Revenue. *Statistics of Income Compiled from the Returns for 1917 under the Direction of the Commissioner of Internal Revenue.* Washington, DC: Government Printing Office, 1919.

United States War Department. *Annual Reports, 1919.* Vol. 1, pt. 3. Washington, DC: Government Printing Office, 1920.

———. *Commission on Training Camp Activities.* Washington, DC: n.p., n.d.

United States War Department, Advisory Board. *Committee on Education and Special Training: A Review of Its Work during 1918.* Washington, DC: War Department, 1919.

United States War Department, Provost Marshal General's Bureau. *Final Report of the Provost Marshal General to the Secretary of War on the Operations of the Selective Service System to July 15, 1919.* Washington, DC: Government Printing Office, 1920.

———. *Second Report of the Provost Marshal General to the Secretary of War on the Operations of the Selective Service System to December 20, 1918.* Washington, DC: Government Printing Office, 1919.

University of Kentucky, U.S. Army Training Detachment, Second Detachment of 1918. Cincinnati, OH: Schultz Press, n.d.

Veit, Helen. "Victory over Ourselves: American Food and Progressivism in the Era of the Great War." PhD diss., Yale University, 2008.

Venzon, Anne Cipriano, ed. *The United States in the First World War: An Encyclopedia.* New York: Routledge, 2012.

Wagner, Thomas E., and Phillip J. Obermiller. *African American Miners and Migrants: The Eastern Kentucky Social Club.* Urbana: University of Illinois Press, 2004.

Walker, Marianne. *Margaret Mitchell and John Marsh: The Love Story behind* Gone with the Wind. Atlanta: Peachtree Publishers, 1993.

Wall, Maryjean. *Madam Belle: Sex, Money, and Influence in a Southern Brothel.* Lexington: University Press of Kentucky, 2015.

Walters, Raymond, George Palmer Putnam, John Kirby, Arthur Baer, Homer Dye Jr., and Forrest B. Myers. *F.A.C.O.T.S. The Story of the Field Artillery Central Officers Training School, Camp Zachary Taylor, Kentucky.* New York: Knickerbocker Press, 1919.

Ward, Robert D. "The Origin and Activities of the National Security League, 1914–1919." *Mississippi Valley Historical Review* 47, 1 (June 1960): 51–65.

Wawro, Geoffrey. *A Mad Catastrophe: The Outbreak of World War I and the Collapse of the Habsburg Empire.* New York: Basic Books, 2014.

Weiss, Elaine. *Fruits of Victory: The Women's Land Army of America in the Great War.* Washington, DC: Potomac Books, 2008.

Whalan, Mark. *The Great War and the Culture of the New Negro.* Gainesville: University Press of Florida, 2008.

Whisnant, David E. *All that Is Native and Fine: The Politics of Culture in an American Region.* Chapel Hill: University of North Carolina Press, 1983.

Whitehorne, Joseph W. A. *The Inspectors General of the United States Army, 1903–1939.* Rockville, MD: Wildside Press, 2012.

Wienen, Mark W. van. *Partisans and Poets: The Political Work of American Poetry in the Great War.* New York: Cambridge University Press, 1997.

Williams, Chad. *Torchbearers of Democracy: African American Soldiers in the World War I Era.* Chapel Hill: University of North Carolina Press, 2010.

Wills, Gregory A. *Southern Baptist Theological Seminary, 1859–2009.* New York: Oxford University Press, 2009.

Wingate, Jennifer. *Sculpting Doughboys: Memory, Gender, and Taste in America's World War I Memorials.* Burlington, VT: Ashgate, 2013.

Winter, Jay, ed. *The Cambridge History of the First World War.* 3 vols. New York: Cambridge University Press, 2014.

Wittke, Carl. *German-Americans and the World War.* Columbus: Ohio State Archaeological and Historical Society, 1936.

———. *The German-Language Press in America.* Lexington: University of Kentucky Press, 1957.

Wright, George C. *A History of Blacks in Kentucky,* vol. 2, *In Pursuit of Equality, 1890–1980.* Frankfort: Kentucky Historical Society, 1992.

———. *Racial Violence in Kentucky, 1865–1940: Lynchings, Mob Rule, and "Legal Lynchings."* Baton Rouge: Louisiana State University Press, 1990.

Wright, John D., Jr. *Transylvania: Tutor to the West.* Lexington, KY: Transylvania University, 1975.

Wynn, Neil. *From Progressivism to Prosperity: World War I and American Society.* New York: Holmes and Meier, 1986.

Yearbook of the United States Department of Agriculture, 1918. Washington, DC: Government Printing Office, 1919.

Yergin, Daniel. "The First War to Run on Oil—World War I Made Gasoline Central to World Politics." *Wall Street Journal,* August 16, 2014.

Young, Arthur P. *Books for Sammies: The American Library Association and World War I*. Pittsburgh, PA: Beta Phi Mu, 1981.

Zacher, Dale. *The Scripps Newspapers Go to War, 1914–1918*. Urbana: University of Illinois Press, 2008.

Zieger, Robert. *America's Great War: World War I and the American Experience*. New York: Rowman and Littlefield, 2000.

———. *Republicans and Labor: 1919–1929*. Lexington: University of Kentucky Press, 1969.

Index

Page numbers in *italics* refer to illustrations.

Topics in Kentucky History

James C. Klotter, Series Editor

Books in the Series

The Family Legacy of Henry Clay: In the Shadow of a Kentucky Patriarch
Lindsey Apple

Kentucky and the Great War
David J. Bettez

George Keats of Kentucky: A Life
Lawrence M. Crutcher

A History of Education in Kentucky
William E. Ellis

Madeline McDowell Breckinridge and the Battle for a New South
Melba Porter Hay

Committed to Victory: The Kentucky Home Front During World War II
Richard Holl

Alben Barkley: A Life in Politics
James K. Libbey

Henry Watterson and the New South: The Politics of Empire, Free Trade, and Globalization
Daniel S. Margolies

Murder and Madness: The Myth of the Kentucky Tragedy
Matthew G. Schoenbachler

How Kentucky Became Southern: A Tale of Outlaws, Horse Thieves, Gamblers, and Breeders
Maryjean Wall

Madam Belle: Sex, Money, and Influence in a Southern Brothel
Maryjean Wall